Pro SQL Server on Linux

Including Container-Based Deployment with Docker and Kubernetes

Bob Ward
Foreword by Slava Oks

Apress®

Pro SQL Server on Linux: Including Container-Based Deployment with Docker and Kubernetes

Bob Ward
North Richland Hills, TX, USA

ISBN-13 (pbk): 978-1-4842-4127-1
https://doi.org/10.1007/978-1-4842-4128-8

ISBN-13 (electronic): 978-1-4842-4128-8

Library of Congress Control Number: 2018962264

Managing Director, Apress Media LLC: Welmoed Spahr
Acquisitions Editor: Jonathan Gennick
Development Editor: Laura Berendson
Coordinating Editor: Jill Balzano

Cover image designed by Freepik (www.freepik.com)

Distributed to the book trade worldwide by Springer Science+Business Media New York, 233 Spring Street, 6th Floor, New York, NY 10013. Phone 1-800-SPRINGER, fax (201) 348-4505, e-mail orders-ny@springer-sbm.com, or visit www.springeronline.com. Apress Media, LLC is a California LLC and the sole member (owner) is Springer Science + Business Media Finance Inc (SSBM Finance Inc). SSBM Finance Inc is a **Delaware** corporation.

For information on translations, please e-mail rights@apress.com, or visit www.apress.com/rights-permissions.

Apress titles may be purchased in bulk for academic, corporate, or promotional use. eBook versions and licenses are also available for most titles. For more information, reference our Print and eBook Bulk Sales web page at www.apress.com/bulk-sales.

Any source code or other supplementary material referenced by the author in this book is available to readers on GitHub via the book's product page, located at www.apress.com/9781484241271. For more detailed information, please visit www.apress.com/source-code.

Printed on acid-free paper

This book is dedicated to all the people who have worked at Microsoft over the last 25 years to build, ship, support, and market the SQL Server product.

Table of Contents

About the Author

Bob Ward is a Principal Architect for the Microsoft SQL Server Data Services Group, which owns the development for all SQL Server versions. Bob has worked for Microsoft for 25 years on every version of SQL Server shipped from OS/2 1.1 to SQL Server 2017 including Linux. He has worked in customer support as a principal escalation engineer and Chief Technology Officer (CTO), interacting with some of the largest SQL Server deployments in the world. Bob is a well-known speaker on SQL Server, often presenting talks on new releases, internals, and performance at events such as SQL PASS Summit, SQLBits, SQLIntersection, Red Hat Summit, Microsoft Inspire, and Microsoft Ignite. You can find him on twitter at @bobwardms, read his blog posts at `http://aka.ms/bobsql` or `http://aka.ms/sqlblog`, or see his demos on `http://aka.ms/sqlchannel`.

About the Technical Reviewer

 **Anthony Nocentino** is the Founder and President of Centino Systems as well as a Pluralsight Author, a Microsoft Data Platform MVP, and SQL Server and Linux Expert. In his consulting practice, Anthony designs solutions, deploys the technology, and provides expertise on system performance, architecture, and security. Anthony has a Bachelors and Masters in Computer Science, with research publications in machine virtualization, high performance/low latency data access algorithms, and spatial database systems. You can find Anthony on Twitter at @nocentino and his blog at www.centinosystems.com/blog/.

Acknowledgments

There are so many I want to thank as part of my journey authoring this book. I would like to first give thanks and glory to my Lord and Savior Jesus Christ. My faith is the foundation of my life and I strongly believe God gives all of us our abilities. Next, I must call out my incredible wife, Ginger Ward, who has been so patient and encouraging throughout my authoring experience. She has listened to all of my complaints, fears, joys, and put up with all of my late nights authoring this book. She made many long drives in the car on trips we made together, letting me work on pieces of the book in the passenger seat of her Land Rover. I also want to thank my two sons, Troy and Ryan Ward, who give me inspiration every day to be a husband, father, and man of conviction, responsibility, and integrity.

There is no way I would have ever produced this book without Jonathan Gennick from Apress. Jonathan, thank you for taking a chance on this book and me when no other publisher would accept it. Speaking of people who made this book possible. I have to call out the incredible job of Anthony Nocentino, my technical reviewer. Anthony brought to the table a vast knowledge of Linux and SQL Server, and without that I'm not sure the book would be anything like the final version. Anthony also did an amazing job of turning around reviews quickly, even as we were meeting tight deadlines. What I loved the most about Anthony's style as a reviewer is that he was just as transparent calling out what he loved about the book as he did with pointed, truthful statements on what changes he thought needed to be made. Anthony, thanks for encouraging me throughout the entire journey. I also want to personally think Jill Balzano from Apress who kept me sane and organized during writing of the book, coordinating my writing with Anthony and Jonathan's reviews. Jill is not only nice but an amazing professional!

I also want to thank several people at Microsoft who helped review parts of the book and were so kind and professional to answer my questions, including Slava Oks, Robert Dorr, Scott Konersmann, Pradeep M M, Jason Roth, Travis Wright, Prasad Tammana, Mihaela Blendea, Vin Yu, Rathijit Sen, Brian Gianforcaro, Jamie Reding, Patrick Kilfoyle, Mitchell Sternke, Dylan Gray, Suresh Kandoth, Parikshit Savjani, Pedro Lopes, Sourabh Agarwal, Sunil Agarwal, Brooks Remy, Arnav Singh, Denzil Ribero, Tejas Shah, Michal Primke, and Harini Gupta.

ACKNOWLEDGMENTS

I also want to thank my leaders at Microsoft, Rohan Kumar and Asad Khan, who have given me the blessed opportunity to evangelize and promote the technical aspects of SQL Server including Linux to the world. I also want to thank members of the Microsoft Marketing team who have worked with me along the way on building the right strategy to get the message out on SQL Server. Thank you John 'JG' Chirapurath, Ramnik Gulati, Debbi Lyons, Anshul Rampal, Marko Hotti, Matthew Burrows, Frederico Pravatta Rezende, Jane Gao, and Joe Malesich.

I also want to thank some of the folks from Microsoft partner companies whom I've worked with over the last year to talk about SQL Server on Linux, including Wendy Harms and Urs Renggli from HPE and Nicholas Gerasimatos from Red Hat.

Finally, I want to thank the Project Helsinki team. Without their dedication and innovation, SQL Server on Linux would still be on a whiteboard somewhere. Instead it is one of the truly amazing software products I've seen built at Microsoft in my career.

Foreword

Bringing SQL Server to Linux has been an adventurous endeavor. It took us less than two years to ship the final product. However, during the first year many things had to go right for the project to succeed. In the past the SQL Server team had attempted to do the work a few times, but every time the team had hit the wall and backed off. Sometime in 2010, Hal Berenson even published a blog outlining why bringing SQL Server to Linux is not a good idea after all.

Nevertheless, in the late 2014 the team decided to look into porting SQL Server to Linux one more time. The initial team consisting of two program managers, Joe Idziorek and Tobias Ternstrom, focused on business opportunity. Very soon they were convinced that not only one, but multiple business opportunities existed. However, convincing others within the company turned out to be problematic. To be taken seriously, they had to figure out an engineering approach. The engineering estimate from the past was overwhelming. It estimated a team of 10 to 20 engineers dedicated to the project over a five-year span. The team knew they had neither these many engineers nor time. The needed a new engineering plan.

Right around that time I was considering new opportunities. My friends from the SQL Server team connected me to Joe and Tobias and we started the conversation. I agreed with the team that doing a direct port wasn't a good idea. I asked the team to give me few days to ponder over the approach. Incidentally, I was familiar with Drawbridge research and happened to leverage it as a platform abstraction layer, aka PAL, to run a Windows application inside of a different operating system in my previous project. So it wasn't long before I connected the dots and figured we could potentially leverage the Drawbridge technology to bring SQL Server to Linux. So I bit the bullet and joined the project.

The Drawbridge technology was the first thing that had to go right for us to succeed. Many, including researches and engineers that had been involved with Drawbridge, had been skeptical about the approach. They worried about impedance mismatch between Linux and Windows runtimes. Moreover, pretty much everyone had been skeptical about performance. Personally, I worried more about the former than the later. I didn't know if we could make Windows exception handling work fully and if we could make the stack growth semantics work. However I hadn't worried much about the performance. I knew how both SQL and Drawbridge work internally, so I had a pretty good idea how to squeeze the performance out of the two.

After having Drawbridge at our disposal, we had SQL Server running on Linux in less than a month. It turned out Andrew Baumann, an engineer from Microsoft research, had an early prototype of Drawbridge running on Linux already. He had made the port work for his research. Having Drawbridge running on Linux, even in a prototype fashion, was the next thing that had to go right for us. I joined the team on the second of February 2015 and with help from Andrew's prototype had SQL Server running on Linux at the end of the month. At the end of February 2015 we not only had both business case and engineering plan in place, but we also had SQL Server actually running on Linux.

Having SQL Server running on Linux made the project real. Joe, Tobias, and I launched what we called a "dog and pony show" campaign. We would go around the company and talk to influential execs to gather their feedback about the business case and other details. The fun part was that many execs wouldn't take the entire project seriously till the very end of our conversation when, after presenting and discussing the business, we would show SQL Server running on Linux. Jaws would drop then. One of the funniest stories was us talking to our fellow data execs: when we launched SQL Server on Linux, one of the Technical Fellows fell of his chair. Seeing SQL Server running on Linux, he and everyone else in the room were very much blown away.

To our surprise, hiring the team into the project hadn't been easy. What we found out is that many engineers happened to be purist by nature. Many folks that we tried to convince to join the project would have preferred a pure port approach to ours. It had taken a nontrivial amount of effort to convince the key engineers that the approach was sound. It had taken us about six months to assemble the core team consisting of six engineers: Eugene Birukov, George Reynya, Michael Nelson, Scott Konersmann, Brian Gianforcaro, and Robert Dorr. Hiring these engineers into the project had proved to be the crucial moment in the history of the project. If any of these core folks wouldn't have joined or left the team, we had almost zero chance of succeeding. Even now I still believe we had gotten lucky, very lucky, because all of these engineers joined at just the right time for the project.

Next, much of our luck came from engineers, execs, program managers, and others who had been implicitly or explicitly related to the project. In many cases people even hadn't realized the support they provided. Sometime at the end 2015 we had a new Corporate Vice President who had become a huge proponent of the project and helped us to expediate the approval process so that we could make a public announcement rather early at a Data Driven event in March of 2016. We had folks trying out the solution and becoming our evangelists within the company. Running the project openly had helped significantly. By the time of public announcement, we had about three hundred people throughout the company subscribed to our engineering distribution list. As one can guess, the project was under strict NDA. Needless to say we had zero leaks.

They say it is the way of traveling not the destination that counts. I think I agree. It has been a fun journey. Personally, I am a bit sad that it is over. At the same time, whenever I look back I get scared about how many things could have gone wrong. We had gotten really lucky during the journey. We also had fun on way to our destination. Now SQL Server DBAs, developers, and enthusiasts are the lucky ones. We have expanded your world. You have gotten real SQL Server on Linux that you all love. We, the engineering team, believe you will love and enjoy it as much as we have.

In this book, Bob Ward gives you an inside look into how we built SQL Server on Linux and the core features of setup, T-SQL, development, performance, security, and high availability. Bob has done something very unique. He has authored a book that will appeal to both the SQL Server user and the Linux developer looking for a new database platform. And you will also love the behind-the-scenes stories as Bob tells them that span the 25 year history of this product. This book also talks about some of the great tools we have built inside and outside SQL Server over the years and many that I have personally worked on. And I love that Bob was able to cover how to migrate to SQL Server, even from PostgreSQL, and also cover the very important topic of containers in the book. I've known Bob for almost 20 years now since I first started In SQL engineering and he was in technical support. We have spent many customer debugging sessions together, so I've seen his knowledge of SQL Server up close. I've also loved how he can take very technical topics and talk to all of us in a way anyone can understand, and you will see that in this book. I think you will find this book covers almost everything you need to know about SQL Server on Linux and Containers.

Slava Oks
Microsoft

Introduction

Have you ever seen the movie *Planes, Trains, and Automobiles*? It is a classic comedy and pretty much sums up the journey of authoring this book. Pieces of this book have been written on airplane trips across the world, subways in London, and car trips back and forth between Edmond, Oklahoma and Texas as my wife and I drove this spring to watch my son play his final year of college baseball. These pages in the book have traveled all over the United States and Europe, including Seattle, Washington D.C., Orlando, Sunnyvale, London, St. Andrews Scotland, Las Vegas, Waco, Texas, Edmond, Oklahoma, San Francisco, my office in Irving, Texas, and the confines of my home in North Richland Hills, Texas. Authoring the book while travelling made it a more enjoyable experience and added value to the book. For example, I learned a few specifics for Red Hat Enterprise Linux while attending the Red Hat Summit in May 2018 in San Francisco.

This book is intended for developers, DBAs, and IT Professionals who have an interest in learning about SQL Server on Linux. I made a big decision when drafting the outline and proposal to Apress for the book: I decided to author this book not only for the SQL Server professional who knows SQL Server on Windows, but also for the developer or IT Pro who knows Linux but does not know SQL Server. It was not an easy choice, because how does one author a single book about SQL Server when there have been other books that only write about one aspect of SQL Server? I decided to focus on the most important aspects of using, developing, and managing SQL Server based on my experiences of 25 years working with the product, while including the key differences between SQL Server on Windows and Linux.

This book also provides an opportunity for me to share some interesting stories along my own journey supporting and working on SQL Server over a 25-year period, including references to past and current Microsoft colleagues. It is ironic that I would finally choose to author a book during the 25th anniversary year of SQL Server on Windows NT but write it on SQL Server on Linux. My background before Microsoft was as a UNIX developer, so it was special for me to come around and get to know the Linux kernel and shell again.

No matter how you decide to read this book, I do recommend you start with Chapter 1. In that chapter, I write about the history of bringing SQL Server to Linux and why we made this choice at Microsoft. In Chapter 1, I also provide you some interesting insights into the architecture, which is one of the most innovative projects I've seen in my career at Microsoft. You may decide to then pick and choose what chapters you want to focus on. I will say that I did author the book with the intention that you would read each chapter in order, as I make references in some chapters to topics in previous chapters. However, it is very possible to read each chapter as its own topic. Some chapters are longer than others, as I felt some topics deserved more details (or I just couldn't help myself). While there are eleven chapters in the book, the book can be broken down into three sections:

1) Architecture, Deployment, and Fundamentals in Chapters 1 to 4

2) The heart of SQL Server with Tools (I introduced tools first, as then you would be familiar with the tools in the following chapters), Performance, Security, HADR, and Managing/Monitoring in Chapters 5-9

3) Final topics including Migration and Containers conclude the book with Chapters 10 and 11. And since our team was working on the next release of SQL Server as I authored this book, I've included a short Epilogue about the future.

I'm also a big believer in providing examples, especially scripts and screen shots. I want you to see what I saw as I executed the example scripts. All of the scripts and examples in this book can be found in a GitHub repo set up by Apress on the book's main page, which can be found at `www.apress.com/9781484241271`. Please post any issues with the examples on the site. I also encourage you to keep up with my GitHub repo at `https://github.com/Microsoft/bobsql`. I'm always posting examples including demos I use at events, and I'll also post the examples in the book there. Another GitHub repo to use is a set of self-pace labs Vin Yu and I built at `https://github.com/Microsoft/sqllinuxlabs`. My goal is to get others at Microsoft and the community to contribute to these. Other good resources to follow are the blog that Bob Dorr and I author at `http://aka.ms/bobsql`. We try to pick topics that no one else writes about for SQL Server. Finally, you might want to bookmark the new SQL Server YouTube channel at `https://www.youtube.com/c/microsoftsqlserver`. You will also see a lot of URLs and references in the book. As I researched a topic or used a specific set of documentation pages, I added that reference so you could dive into more details than what is possible to cover in the book.

This book has been a labor of love and not only represents my knowledge about SQL Server on Linux, but includes interesting insights into areas of SQL Server even those in the SQL Server community may not know about. It is my intention and hope that you will walk away after reading this book feeling empowered to use SQL Server on Linux in new and interesting ways.

Bob Ward
North Richland Hills, Texas
August 2018

CHAPTER 1

Why SQL Server on Linux?

Microsoft SQL Server 2017 became generally available on October 2nd, 2017. It marked the 12th major release of SQL Server in its history. SQL Server is now a leading data platform for the industry. It powers websites, industries, and business applications all over the world from laptops to small businesses to large enterprise servers. It is used as a data platform in private and public clouds. The database engine is the power behind Microsoft Azure SQL Database. SQL Server has for many years had a great reputation for ease of use, ease of administration, and as a leader in price/performance. But SQL Server has now become a major force in technology through breakthrough performance and scalability, trusted security, and new intelligence capabilities. Features like Columnstore indexes, Query Store, Always Encrypted, Graph Database, Always On Availability Groups, and Machine Learning Services demonstrate that SQL Server is not just a great relational database engine but truly a data platform for applications. Our proud history of running side by side with Windows Server over the years is an incredible story. Then why would we build SQL Server to also run on Linux?

I joined Microsoft in 1993 after spending seven years out of college working on UNIX development projects using C++ and databases such as Ingres and ORACLE. When I joined Microsoft, I thought my UNIX days were behind me. Sure enough, for 20+ years I became an expert on SQL Server running on Windows Server, thinking I would never see SQL Server run on anything else.

Then one day in 2015, my colleague Bob Dorr and I receive an email from Slava Oks, the lead development engineer for SQL Server, asking what we thought if we built SQL Server to run on Linux. Of course I had to read the email a few times before it sunk in what he was proposing. I didn't think about it much for a few months until I attended an internal Microsoft event in late 2015. At this event, to my amazement, Tobias

© Bob Ward 2018
B. Ward, *Pro SQL Server on Linux*, https://doi.org/10.1007/978-1-4842-4128-8_1

Ternstrom, one of the original program managers on the project, showed the audience an SQL Server deploying with apt-get on Ubuntu and connecting to run queries in a manner of minutes.

After getting back in my chair, I had all kinds of questions. How did we do this so quickly? What was the architecture behind taking one of the leading database engines and getting it up and running on Linux in such a quick timeframe. But also, I wanted to know why. The SQL Server product had been enjoying immense success in the industry with customers running on Windows Server.

And this is how we will start this book. I'll explain our motivations behind bringing SQL Server to the Linux platform, the fundamentals of how we made it happen, and its core capabilities. I've got a reputation with the existing SQL Server community for presenting on internals of SQL Server, so I won't be able to help myself in this chapter and throughout the book. You will see at times a peek "behind the scenes" of how this technology works on the Linux Platform.

Platform of Choice

In May of 2016, we released Microsoft SQL Server 2016, which was the 11th major release of SQL Server since we introduced 4.2 for Windows NT in 1993. This release was packed with major functionality and was positively received by the SQL Server community. While the great work was happening to launch this release, the engineering team was already working on SQL Server 2017, for which the key headlining feature would be SQL Server finally being supported on Linux and containers. The industry and the world already knew we were going to make this a reality, as earlier in the year Scott Guthrie, Executive Vice President of the Cloud and Enterprise Group at Microsoft, had made the announcement at a customer event and on our official Microsoft blog (see `https://blogs.microsoft.com/blog/2016/03/07/announcing-sql-server-on-linux`). In this blog, Scott calls out the true reason to bring SQL Server on Linux "...Bringing SQL Server to Linux is another way we are making our products and new innovations more accessible to a broader set of users and meeting them where they are." Our decision to bring SQL Server on Linux was not about moving away from Windows Server. It was about building a great data platform on *both* Windows and Linux. It was about providing a choice of platforms for our customers. And we didn't just come to this conclusion without data and customer evidence.

First, we knew that in the industry a trend was emerging for several years that Linux was becoming very popular. Research today shows approximately 30% of enterprise servers are now using some Linux distribution. Research by independent firms such as Gartner shows that Linux Server is the fastest growing OS segment (`www.gartner.com/doc/3731017/market-share-analysis-server-operating`).

Second, at Microsoft we saw the evidence ourselves. For Microsoft Azure Virtual Machine, the fastest growing guest operating system of choice had become Linux. We had customers who hosted "mixed" environments (Linux and Windows Server) come to us asking whether we would ever consider making SQL Server on Linux available. It was not that they were giving up on Windows Server, but rather they wanted to standardize on SQL Server in their companies but needed options for both Linux and Windows Server.

Finally, Linux partners started asking us whether we would consider moving to Linux. Companies like Red Hat and SUSE were seeing immense growth in their enterprise business and felt that offering a choice of data platforms would help customer adoption.

All these factors were on the minds of our SQL Server Engineering leadership in late 2014 and early 2015: Shawn Bice, Rohan Kumar, and Lindsey Allen. They were instrumental in convincing our executive leadership at Microsoft to allow us to build SQL Server for Linux. And they hired back none other than Slava Oks to build it and shift Tobias Ternstrom to lead the program management of the project. They would build an amazing team of people to start the project known as *Helsinki*.

We now had the motivation, the approval, and the resources to move forward. Now the question was how do we build it? And how do we deliver it quickly to the market?

How We Built It

Project Helsinki, SQL Server on Linux, is one of the most amazing software accomplishments I've encountered in my 25 years at Microsoft. In this section, I'll show you the amazing background and history of how we built SQL Server on Linux and were able to bring it to market with quality and performance. In this section, I'll talk about an important software component that allows SQL Server to run on Linux, called the SQL Platform Abstraction Layer (SQLPAL) based on a Microsoft Research project called Drawbridge. In addition, I'll discuss the process architecture and how the various components interact to make SQL Server run on Linux.

Drawbridge

In March of 2011, a team at Microsoft Research published a paper called **Rethinking the Library OS from the Top Down** (www.microsoft.com/en-us/research/wp-content/uploads/2016/02/asplos2011-drawbridge.pdf). The paper was based on a project prototype called Drawbridge and a concept called *library OS*. If you think about the year 2011, virtualization was a very hot topic and had become very popular. Virtual machines were a common mechanism to perform consolidation projects and abstract applications for the underlying hardware. They provide isolation, compatibility, and the ability to free you from relying on a specific host computer. Therefore, they are still popular and are still used today in public cloud environments such as Azure Virtual Machine and Amazon EC2. The only issue is that virtual machines are resource *heavy*. That is, you need the entire operating system to run in the guest to support your application, even if you don't need all the services that come with the guest operating system.

The Drawbridge team sought a way to create something lighter but retain the advantages of virtualization. Furthermore, they discovered through their research that many services and Application Programming Interface (API) calls required by Windows applications did not really need to be run within the Windows kernel. Rather, it is possible to run the code that powers many Windows APIs in user mode, thus reducing context switches to the kernel. Reducing context switches improves performance and results in a more efficient application and use of computer resources.

The result of this project was a concept called a *picoprocess* running on a library OS, effectively creating a Platform Abstraction Layer (PAL). Figure 1-1 shows the resulting architecture.

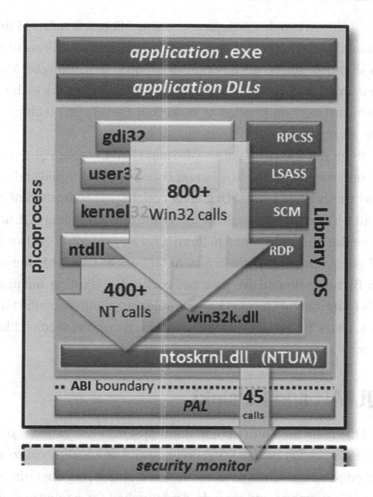

Figure 1-1. *The Drawbridge picoprocess*

In Figure 1-1, the picoprocess represents a binary that combines the application and the library OS components into a single process. The beauty of this approach is that the application and its DLLs are unchanged. No recompile or modifications are necessary. The magic that allowed Slava and the team to enable this concept and apply it to another operating system like Linux is an Application Binary Interface (ABI). Many Windows APIs (in this diagram they are represented by Win32 and NT calls) are implemented by the library OS in the process, while approximately 45 are exposed through the PAL and are mapped to the ABIs and eventually to the underlying OS.

At this time, Slava was working on a project inside Microsoft called Midori, which was another operating system project, and saw this work from the Drawbridge team. He was able to, in a short timeframe, get a Windows application running on Midori using the Drawbridge team's work. So, when Slava was asked to come back to the SQL Server Engineering Team and work on a project to make SQL Server run on Linux, his learnings from Drawbridge were of huge benefit.

If you think about the choices Slava and the team had to bring SQL Server on Linux, the most logical one was to port the SQL Server code base to compile and run natively on Linux. But as he tells it, the entire SQL Server codebase is comprised of millions of lines of code. And while taking the path of converting and compiling SQL Server to run on Linux might be the "purest" approach, there is no way we could get to market within our goal of 2017 going down this path. In fact, as far back as late 2014, one of our lead engineers, Peter Byrne, evaluated this path and concluded "Porting and productization of just the SQL NT Engine code base to Linux would be a multi-year effort requiring a large team of dev/test/PM." The Drawbridge concept, therefore, seemed like an idea to strongly consider.

SQLOS, SQLPAL, and Helsinki

Slava was part of the team that built a component of SQL Server called SQLOS (some call it SOS), which shipped as part of SQL Server 2005. The concept was to abstract the SQL Server core engine as much as possible from the underlying operating system for requests such as I/O, memory, and threads. And much of the engine was changed to use SQLOS API services (via sqldk.dll) in SQL Server 2005. SQLOS also provided built-in support for things like NUMA, resource governance, resource monitoring, and a scheduling system, much like an OS kernel. The team took this approach because the Windows operating system was not completely optimized for services like database engines. I remember asking Slava years ago why he felt the need to build SQLOS. He said "The key observation here is that DBMS and OS schedulers must cooperate. As such, OS must have built-in support for DBMS or DBMS must have a special scheduling layer."

As you read the description of SQLOS and its ability to abstract the SQL Engine developer from the underlying operating system APIs, you might be thinking, why not just take SQLOS and modify and recompile that code to use Linux Kernel APIs? There were a few problems with that approach:

- Not all of the SQL Engine uses SQLOS to use Windows APIs. For example, the engine directly makes calls to WriteFileGather() to flush data pages to disk. The evidence for this exists in the form of SQL Server wait types. There are about 88 PREEMPTIVE_OS* wait types in SQL Server, which shows how many components do not use SQLOS to use Windows APIs.

- We would still have to recompile all the SQL code with Linux compilers. This would require us to maintain two code bases.

- There are other components that can run in or outside the engine that don't use SQLOS: for example, our components that support XML in the engine and services like SQL Server Agent.

As I looked over goals for this release, it become clear to me it could be summarized as

We want to be able to run much of our executable code we built for Windows untouched on Linux. Fast and reliable, requiring no application changes.

Having SQLOS is still a great advantage. It provides a foundation for an abstraction layer that we can build on. As Slava and team tried to land on a design, they found out the Drawbridge team had built a prototype of their project to work with Linux. Now the pieces were in place. Take the work of the Drawbridge prototype, make the necessary changes to productize it, and couple that with the work and concept of SQLOS. Born from this was the SQLPAL.

Note   I make this all sound very simple, when indeed it is one of the most amazing and innovative software projects I've seen in my career at Microsoft.

As Slava tells it, within one month of landing on this design, they had a simple working version of SQL Server booting up on Linux and running queries.

Slava was smart enough to capture a photo of that first boot, as seen here in Figure 1-2.

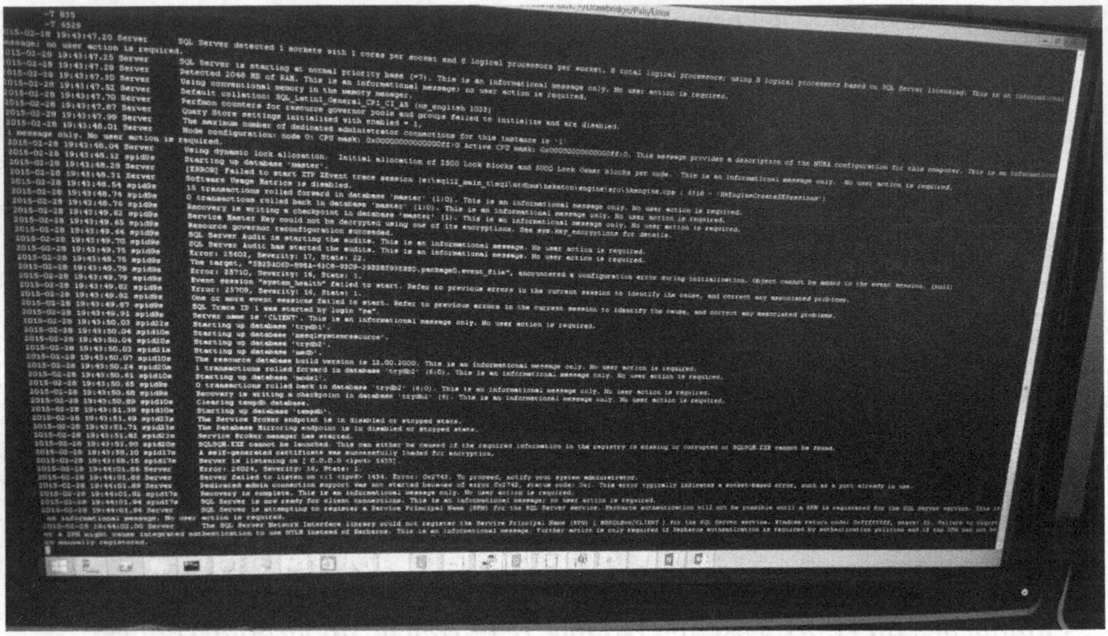

Figure 1-2. *First boot of SQL Server on Linux on Slava Oks's computer*

It was not long after this that he, Tobias Ternstrom, and the rest of the team had a project plan and a name for SQL Server on Linux. They called it *Project Helsinki* (named after the birthplace of the founder of Linux, Linus Torvalds, and where he designed and proposed the original Linux project). With an architecture in mind, the project now swung into full gear marching down a path to deliver SQL Server on Linux in 2017.

The SQL Server on Linux Architecture

As the team was blazing along making all the changes necessary to the original Drawbridge project and building out all the components for deployment, configuration, and tools, many in the industry and SQL Server community were curious how we were building this. Some demos had been done publicly about the easy deployment and basic query capabilities of SQL Server on Linux, but no one knew behind the scenes the architecture, SQLPAL, or the use of Drawbridge as a concept.

The team decided in late 2016 to go public with the architecture. The result was an excellent blog from one of the development leads on the project, Scott Konersmann, which you can read at `https://cloudblogs.microsoft.com/sqlserver/2016/12/16/sql-server-on-linux-how-introduction/`. In his blog, Scott outlined the history of Drawbridge, the main goals of the project, and the challenges of just using what the Drawbridge project provided. The key to the success of the project was SQLPAL, and he summarized what they would build:

> *As a result of the investigation, we decided on a hybrid strategy. We would merge SOS and Library OS from Drawbridge to create the SQL PAL (SQL Platform Abstraction Layer). For areas of Library OS that SQL Server does not need, we would remove them. To merge these architectures, changes were needed in all layers of the stack.*
>
> *The new architecture consists of a set of SOS direct APIs which don't go through any Win32 or NT syscalls. For code without SOS direct APIs they will either go through a hosted Windows API (like MSXML) or NTUM (NT User Mode API—this is the 1500+ Win32 and NT syscalls). All the subsystems like storage, network, or resource management will be based on SOS and will be shared between SOS direct and NTUM APIs.*

To summarize this, the final design and approach was to merge our existing SQLOS code with Library OS from Drawbridge to create the final SQLPAL concept.

Scott uses the diagram in Figure 1-3 to show the interactions with SQLPAL, SQLOS, Library OS, and something called the Host Extension.

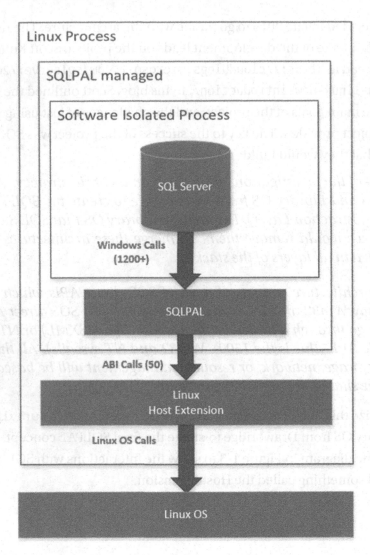

Figure 1-3. *Scott Konersmann's SQL Server on Linux architecture*

I'm a very visual person, so as I started to learn the architecture myself, I decided to revise this view to something more like the diagram in Figure 1-4. (Note: I based this on a more detailed architecture diagram built by the Helsinki team.)

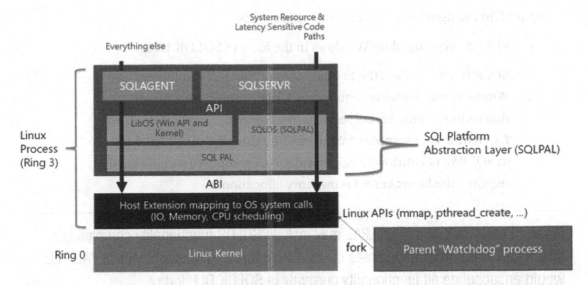

Figure 1-4. *The SQL Server on Linux architecture*

As I begin to describe the architecture, let me provide one more important comment. This is the architecture as of SQL Server 2017 at general availability. As with any internals and architecture, we reserve the right to change this and tune it. Our goal is for no user to worry about these internals, but it is interesting to understand and provides credibility to the success of our product on Linux.

I should tell you, the preceding diagram and my description don't really do justice to the amazing technology the team has built. It could take perhaps an entire book just to dive into the architecture. I see us evolving this architecture in the future to streamline and improve it, so focusing even an entire chapter on this is not practical. And our goal is that the user of SQL Server on Linux should not care about it. But so many people were interested in how we built SQL Server on Linux, I thought I should treat at least a section of a chapter to the topic.

Let's break down each component and how these interact to make up the architecture. Notice in this diagram, just like in Drawbridge, *a single Linux process* includes the application (SQLSERVR.EXE), Library OS (LibOS), and the PAL (in our case we call it SQLPAL). The name of this process on Linux is called **sqlservr**. In the gray box, SQLSERVR represents the same binary SQLSERVR.EXE from Windows and its component DLLs including sqlmin.dll, sqllang.dll, and others. LibOS in the light blue box are the DLLs and Windows services that support the Windows API. This includes DLLs such as kernel32.dll, advapi32.dll and services such as RPCSS.EXE.

11

SQLPAL in the light blue box has two components:

- *SQLOS*: as shipped on Windows in the form of SQLDK.DLL

- *SQLPAL.DLL*: This is the key component that will implement any
  Windows functionality required by LibOS or redirect any calls
  that require Linux kernel services to a component called the ***Host
  Extension***. An example of Windows functionality that is implemented
  in SQLPAL is Windows Registry calls. An example of something that
  requires the Linux kernel is memory allocation.

Note   Future versions of SQLPAL may include SQLOS functionality completely,
so we can streamline these areas of code even further. For example, SQLPAL.DLL
would encapsulate all functionality currently in SQLDK.DLL today.

The Host Extension in the black box is a set of code that is natively compiled for
Linux and understands all the necessary Linux API calls for things like memory (mmap),
threads (pthread), and I/O (aio).

The bridge for these two worlds is an Application Binary Interface (ABI). What
this means is that SQLPAL.DLL cannot directly call Host Extension code for memory,
threads, I/O, and other services like you would code for any API on Windows. This is
because Windows and Linux have different mechanisms for calling functions in code
(this is known as a *calling convention*). Since SQLPAL.DLL is compiled for Windows and
the Host Extension code is compiled for Linux, they must *talk* through a mechanism that
allows SQLPAL to translate its calling convention to Linux. This is done through a clever
series of assembly instructions and it's why it is called an Application Binary Interface. It
is very lightweight and does not require any significant overhead to make this transition.

If you have ever studied program execution on operating systems like Windows
or Linux, you know about something called the *binary format* of a program on these
systems. For Windows, it is called the Portable Execution (PE) format and for Linux it is
called the Executable and Linkable Format (ELF) format. Any program compiled and
linked for Windows uses the PE format (SQLSERVR.EXE for example) and can only be
run on Windows; likewise for an ELF binary on Linux. So, our Host Extension code is
part of the SQLSERVR Linux process compiled as an ELF binary. It has special logic to
know how to load SQLPAL.DLL directly, since it is a PE-formatted binary, and provide
it the necessary links to use the ABI interfaces in the Host Extension (in other words the

Host Extensions instructs SQLPAL how to "talk back to it on the fly"). The Host Extension also knows how to map the binaries for SQLSERVR.EXE and LibOS from specially packaged files on disk (we will discuss these more in Chapter 2) into the process address space. SQLPAL.DLL then knows how to load SQLSERVR.EXE and then let normal Windows process and DLL loading happen from there. One key point here: All of this code is compiled for Intel compatible processors and therefore, in the words of Robert Dorr, "It's all just assembly code." This is one reason our SQLSERVR.EXE code runs unchanged on Linux.

So, to summarize, SQLSERVR.EXE and its dependent DLLs are loaded and run just like they do on Windows. The same thing is true for the LibOS components. SQLPAL. DLL is compiled for Windows but has logic built in to implement Windows kernel services or, when necessary, call other functions using ABI interfaces to implement certain kernel services. But SQLPAL.DLL doesn't know these interfaces are implemented in a piece of code compiled for Linux. The Host Extension takes care of all of that.

There are two other components in the architecture diagram I haven't talked about yet:

- Notice SQLAGENT is also listed in this diagram. This is because when you install SQL Server on Linux, you load the SQLAGENT.EXE in the SQLSERVR Linux Process along with SQLSERVR.EXE. Strange I know, but it works just fine. SQLPAL enables process isolation, and these processes don't realize they are in the same Linux process.

- Notice in the bottom right-hand corner something called the *Parent Watchdog* process. You will hear more about this later in this book, but effectively this is a process called SQLSERVR natively compiled for Linux and is the program first started when SQL Server starts. We then use the Linux fork() API call to create another SQLSERVR process, which is really the SQL Server engine and all its components as you see in the diagram. It provides a handy purpose by monitoring the child SQLSERVR process via signals to perform dumps and using systemd services for restarts as necessary. You can read more about how this works in this blog post: `https://blogs.msdn.microsoft.com/bobsql/2018/07/18/sql-server-on-linux-why-do-i-have-two-sql-server-processes/`. This relationship will become more apparent in Chapter 2 as I talk about exploring what is installed for SQL Server on Linux.

I realize this looks very complicated, and it is, but it is also simple and elegant. And this is the architecture that has allowed us to move so quickly yet with great quality and performance to bring SQL Server on Linux to the market.

I included the details in this chapter not because you must know them to use SQL Server on Linux, but to clear up any confusion about how it works and to lend credibility to the design and architecture.

And here is the most important point. As you will learn in the next section, the core SQL Server database engine is the same proven, scalable SQL Server engine as we have run on thousands of customer servers over the history of the product.

SQL Server on Windows vs. Linux. Is it the Same?

I remember one conversation I had on this topic with Slava Oks, who said to me, "Bob, The Query Processor is still the same Query Processor." This quote explains why we were able to achieve comparable performance for SQL Server on Linux. It also explains why databases can be restored on different platforms and why applications can connect to SQL Server on Linux virtually unchanged if they were built to run against SQL Server on Windows Server.

SQL Server on Linux Capabilities

SQL Server 2017 has many capabilities and features focusing on performance, security, and high availability. Consider these capabilities and features that are available for SQL Server on Linux:

- A core SQLOS system for scheduling, memory management, and resource governance and management that provides built-in scalability and recognizes important server architectures such as NUMA

- The core engine components for buffer management, query processing, query execution, storage engine, and access methods

- Core management operations such as BACKUP/RESTORE, index management, and DBCC commands

- Our famous T-SQL language works unchanged except for any features or capabilities not supported in the release.

- In-Memory workload features such Columnstore Indexes and In-Memory OLTP

- New database intelligent features such as adaptive query processing (AQP) and Automatic Tuning (you will hear more about these features in Chapter 4) based on the telemetry of Query Store.

- Always On Availability Groups (I use the term Availability Groups or AGs for future references to this capability in the book) are supported with full functionality. As you will see in Chapter 8, Availability Groups are supported with major failover capabilities (with a few exceptions) using a clustering technology called *Pacemaker*. In addition, a new feature in SQL Server 2017 provides support for *clusterless* availability groups where no clustering software is required.

- Always On Failover Cluster Instance on Linux is supported using Pacemaker.

- Security features such as always encrypted, dynamic data masking, row-level security, auditing, and Transparent Data Encryption (TDE)

- SQL Server and Active Directory authentication for logins

- Encrypted connections are supported using Transport Layer Security (TLS).

- Rich programming features such as SQLCLR (SAFE assemblies only), JSON T-SQL capabilities, and the Graph database

- The SQL Server Agent scheduling service supports the T-SQL command subsystem.

- SQL Server Integration Services (SSIS) is supported for fundamental extract, transform, and load (ETL) operations.

- Tools work "as-is" against SQL Server on Linux, including SQL Server Management Studio (runs on Windows), SQL Server Data Tools (runs on Windows), and our mssql extension in Visual Studio Code (cross-platform tool).

- We support native command line tools on Linux, including sqlcmd and bcp.

- We have built new open-source, cross-platform tools that run on Windows, Linux, or MacOS and work against SQL Server on Linux or Windows: SQL Server Operations Studio and mssql-cli.

- SQL Server diagnostics such as extended events, dynamic management views, catalog views, and query plan diagnostic capabilities.

I may have missed your favorite feature, but this list makes SQL Server on Linux a very compelling story. For a complete list of features for SQL Server on Linux, check out our documentation at `https://docs.microsoft.com/sql/linux/sql-server-linux-editions-and-components-2017`.

For those reading this book who are not familiar with SQL Server editions, it is important to know that some capabilities exist only in certain editions. To get a complete list of what features are available for specific editions, see this documentation page: `https://docs.microsoft.com/sql/linux/sql-server-linux-editions-and-components-2017?view=sql-server-linux-2017#includessnoversionincludesssnoversion-mdmd-editions`.

SQL Server 2017 on Linux offers these editions:

- *Enterprise*: This is the most full-featured edition. It is designed to be used as its name denotes for Enterprise database applications. From a licensing point of view, there are two variations of Enterprise: Enterprise and Enterprise Core. Enterprise Core has full capabilities, while Enterprise has some restrictions on using a certain number of compute cores. Enterprise is only available for certain customers who have contract agreements with Microsoft.

- *Standard*: This edition is designed to provide the basic functionality of SQL Server for applications targeted for smaller departments or midsized workloads. One major change we made starting with SQL Server 2016 SP1 was to open some features to the Standard edition that were only previously available with the Enterprise edition. The rationale was to ensure that developers could build applications and not worry as much about what edition of SQL Server their application was targeting. There are restrictions on sizes of how these features work for the Standard edition, but they are now available. You can read more about this change in this blog post: `https://blogs.msdn.microsoft.com/sqlreleaseservices/sql-server-2016-service-pack-1-sp1-released/`

- *Developer*: This is a free edition that includes all features available in the Enterprise edition. However, the license for this edition restricts it from being used for production purposes. You can use this edition to build and test your application.

- *Web*: This edition is like Standard with lower limits and is specifically priced to target Web hosters.

- *Express*: This is the most basic edition but is free and could be used in production. It is limited though, enough that it shouldn't be used for any type of scalable application. But if you are just getting started with SQL Server as a developer, SQL Server Express can be useful. There is an easy upgrade path for this to the Standard and Enterprise editions. For Linux, SQL Server Express can serve a very useful purpose as a configuration-only replica server. This will be discussed in more detail in Chapter 8.

I should also mention that SQL Server offers an Evaluation edition. It contains all the features of the Enterprise edition but is not licensed for production and has a time-based expiration license. But it is a great way to test out SQL Server capabilities on an Enterprise server. In Chapter 2 I'll described how you choose which edition you want to use with SQL Server.

What Features Are Not Available

With this great lineup of features come some areas that are not available in SQL Server 2017 on Linux (as of general availability). Some features included with the SQL Server product have dependencies or require external programs that are not so straightforward to work on SQL Server on Linux.

Note   We are actively investigating many of these features to include in future versions or updates of SQL Server on Linux.

As with any release, we make tough decisions to include or not include features or enhancements that we would love to do if time were not a factor. Therefore, the following features did not make it into SQL Server 2017 on Linux for general availability:

- Transaction and Merge Replication

- Distributed Transactions (linked server queries or application distributed transactions via MSDTC)

- Stretch Database

- Polybase

- Machine Learning Services (but Native Scoring is supported)

- System extended procedures such as xp_cmdshell

I've only listed the major features that did not make it into SQL Server 2017 general availability. There are a few others, and you can read the complete list in our Release Notes at `https://docs.microsoft.com/sql/linux/sql-server-linux-release-notes#Unsupported`.

I'll add one other comment on features. The SQL Server product on Windows Server today comes with other services such as SQL Server Analysis Services (SSAS) and SQL Server Reporting Services (SSRS). These are commonly known as our *Business Intelligence (BI)* Services (this also includes Master Data Services (MDS) and Data Quality Services [DQS]). These services were not implemented for SQL Server on Linux. Note that these services have the capability to connect and query SQL Server on Linux.

Should I Use Windows or Linux?

I'll conclude this section with an answer to a common question I get: "Should I run SQL Server on Linux or Windows Server?" The answer is *Yes* (hoping for some bit of laughter at this point from my readers). The point is that we built SQL Server on Linux to give a choice, not necessarily because SQL Server runs faster or better on Windows Server vs. Linux. If the features that are not supported today for SQL Server on Linux don't affect you, make your decision on which operating system platform is best for you, your application, or your company. Some customers I talk to are creating a standard for Linux within their organization, so they will make the choice for consistency and now SQL Server gives them that opportunity. For others, they are comfortable with

Windows Server and like that platform so will stay with SQL Server on that operating system. For some, Linux is a very popular operating system for new developers, so they will enjoy building applications against SQL Server on Linux in development phases and production can then be used for SQL Server against Linux or Windows.

My great friend of many years in Microsoft Support Robert Dorr (you can find us both on our joint blog http://aka.ms/bobsql) joined the Helsinki development team in early 2016. When I was talking to him about this book he had this recollection, which sums up the experience of the team and reason behind the project.

"What I found is that I stepped onto a rocket ship. Lots of new things and lots of things to be done across the eco-system. It was best described by Scott Konersmann as we are changing out the engine of a jet plane in midflight and some days it really feels like that. We are bringing decades of tried and tuned technology and experience on Windows to the Linux platform and we don't want to remove features. Simply give the customer the choice of which 'engine' they want to run."

Containers Are the New Virtual Machine

One other major motivation for us to build SQL Server on Linux was to provide support for an emerging technology called *containers*. A later chapter in the book will cover technical details of how to use SQL Server with containers. Here I will explain a summary of SQL Server with containers and its relationship to Linux.

The emerging force in the industry for container technology is by far Docker. Rather than create a definition of containers in my own words, I absolutely love how Docker explains it (https://www.docker.com/what-container):

> *"A container image is a lightweight, stand-alone, executable package of a piece of software that includes everything needed to run it: code, runtime, system tools, system libraries, settings. Available for both Linux and Windows based apps, containerized software will always run the same, regardless of the environment. Containers isolate software from its surroundings, for example differences between development and staging environments, and help reduce conflicts between teams running different software on the same infrastructure."*

After reading this, perhaps you are wondering why didn't we just use containers instead of our architecture with SQLPAL?

There are a few major reasons for this:

- The Docker Engine on Linux only supports images that contain a Linux operating system because remember: a container interacts with the host operating system. Therefore, if we just went with containers, we would be back to square one to port all our code to Linux.

- We wanted to provide native capability directly with the Linux operating system for maximum performance.

- Even though we want to completely support SQL Server with Docker containers and the new scenarios it provides, we didn't want to rely on this to support Linux, especially if any limitations exist for containers that would not exist running natively on Linux.

I'm excited about the future of Docker containers and how SQL Server plays an important role in making containers a viable technology for new scenarios, including portability, consistency, and DevOps scenarios.

Database Containers

I remember not long ago asking my colleague Travis Wright, one of the key program managers who brought SQL Server Linux to release, about SQL Server Support for Windows Containers. His initial answer surprised me. He said: "Bob, why do you care?" His message was that wouldn't it be nice to get to a world where the focus is a *database* container including SQL Server, the database, and any dependent pieces of an application vs. worrying about the operating system in the container image. I had never thought about it that way and we may not be ready for that yet, but his idea is spot on. That is one of the promises of containers.

Platform Independence, Portability, and Consistency

"Platform" in this context is the host where containers run. Docker provides this independence because I can *compose* (you will learn what this means in the chapter on containers) a Docker image with SQL Server and run that image as a container on Windows, Linux, MacOS, or other container cloud environments such as

Azure Container Service (AKS), Amazon Elastic Container Service (ECS), Google Cloud Platform, Red Hat OpenShift, and SUSE CaaS. And since this is a container, it is the *same image* running in all these environments. Now that is portability! It provides for a reliable, *consistent* package of a known SQL Server version along with your database, scripts, or whatever dependencies you put into the image.

Continuous Integration/Continuous Deployment

Perhaps you have heard of the term *DevOps*? This concept, which has been around for several years, is all about combining roles and tasks for software development and operations. It has become popular because it provides a mechanism to shorten the development lifecycle and allow for more frequent application deployment.

Continuous integration and continuous deployment (CI/CD) are methods to enable a more efficient DevOps ecosystem. Using containers, developers can *continuously* integrate their application changes and deploy them into test and production environments. Developers have been using these techniques for some time, but database platforms like SQL Server were typically not part of the lifecycle. A typical SQL Server would be hosted on a server, and developers would struggle to maintain their containers with their applications to a decoupled SQL Server and databases (and objects like SQL Agent jobs and scripts). Now that SQL Server embraces the container world, it can now be part of a container that is included in the CI/CD pipeline.

Kubernetes

The promise of containers has a great potential for portability, consistency, and efficiency. But how do you coordinate the execution of many database containers in a CI/CD pipeline or in a large-scale production environment? A technology called Kubernetes was created to solve this problem. Kubernetes is an open-source system to help manage, deploy, and orchestrate many containers in a complete ecosystem. One of its advantages is to provide a natural high-availability solution for containers, which couples nicely with the need of many SQL Server users to provide a high-availability solution with production databases. Kubernetes has emerged as the leading solution for container management and deployment at scale, and has been adopted by almost every public cloud vendor that supports container execution and deployment.

Later in this book we will devote an entire chapter to the technical details of deploying SQL Server with Docker containers, including examples of using this in a CI/CD pipeline and implementing High Availability using Kubernetes.

Summary

Deployment is an important term to get started. This is all about installing and configuring SQL Server on Linux. And that is where our journey will begin for getting up and running with SQL Server on Linux in the next chapter.

CHAPTER 2

Install and Configuration

From the very beginning, our team wanted to make sure the installation experience for SQL Server on Linux fits well within the already well-established methods, practices, and ecosystem for Linux users. Furthermore, rather than just say that SQL Server is supported on any Linux distribution (there are hundreds out there), we wanted to ensure we provided a quality, well-tested release on popular distributions and a superior support experience for our customers.

We designed the installation experience to be fast and light. You might be surprised by seeing the number of pages devoted to the subject in this chapter. That is because installing a product is the first experience you encounter and can set the tone for your opinion of a product. If you just want to dive in and see how easy it is to install SQL Server on Linux, go straight to the "Just Install It!" section.

I wanted this chapter to cover all aspects of the installation experience, so you can know what to expect, understand how it works behind the scenes, and provide you all the options for installation and updates.

The chapter will also cover a discussion of requirements, how to verify your installation was successful, unattended install, offline install, installing other packages, installing in an Azure environment, troubleshooting installation problems, exploring what is installed, and topics on configuration. It is all based on my experiences installing the product, talking to customers, our support, and our engineering teams about our intentions to make the installation and configuration experience simple but complete.

Preparing for Install

If you want a superior experience with a product as complex as SQL Server for an enterprise-grade application, careful preparation is a key success criterion. In this section, I'm going to talk about what Linux distributions we officially support, system requirements to ensure a smooth and optimal SQL Server experience, and some

© Bob Ward 2018
B. Ward, *Pro SQL Server on Linux*, https://doi.org/10.1007/978-1-4842-4128-8_2

suggestions on how to test SQL Server capabilities as you make decisions on your target SQL Server environment. The last part of this section is only for those new to Linux, so you may want to skip the last part if you are a Linux guru. I thought it would be helpful for those making a transition from Windows to learn from some of the tips I've picked up as I made my own transition to get comfortable again with navigating Linux.

Linux Distributions

SQL Server 2017 on Linux is officially supported on the following Linux Distributions (these are minimum versions):

- Red Hat Enterprise Linux (RHEL) 7.3 and 7.4

- SUSE Linux Enterprise Server (SLES) v12SP2

- Ubuntu 16.04LTS

For future context, RHEL and SLES are considered *RPM-based* distributions although each has differences in functionality and Ubuntu is a *Debian-based* distribution (I find this resource to be very valuable when looking at various Linux distributions and their history: https://en.wikipedia.org/wiki/Linux_distribution). This distinction is significant mostly because it affects the package format we use for each distribution.

We are always looking to check on what new versions of these distributions we should support, so bookmark this page for the "latest news" on SQL Server for Linux:

https://docs.microsoft.com/sql/linux/sql-server-linux-setup.

Your choice of these distributions may be based on your preference or perhaps a standard within your company. You should know we have done basic testing on other Linux distributions such as CentOS or ORACLE Enterprise Linux (OEL) and SQL Server can run on these. However, we are not prepared to say we officially support SQL Server on Linux for distributions other than the ones I've listed here in this section.

Note   We fully support SQL Server on Docker containers, and I'll cover that topic completely in Chapter 11.

For the sake of consistency, I'm going to do all the demos and examples in this book using Red Hat Enterprise Linux. SQL Server runs very well on all three distributions and integrates the familiar experience of each. Our documentation has clear examples of how to install SQL Server on RHEL, SLES, and Ubuntu.

I recommend you consult with the documentation and installation guidance of your Linux distribution before installing SQL Server, to ensure an optimal experience. For example, since SQL Server can be an intensive I/O application, you may want to consult with your Linux guide on how to configure your disk for performance and durability. Having said that, in Chapter 6, I'll review with you the Microsoft guidance on how to configure Linux and SQL Server for maximum performance with both SQL Server and Linux Kernel tuning recommendations based on our experiences at Microsoft.

I do have a few tips on how I install and interact with Linux to use SQL Server:

- I never install the GUI. Ubuntu desktop users may prefer the GUI shell and SQL Server for developers runs just fine in that environment. I always find myself just using the command line bash shell or running GUI programs on my Windows laptop connected to my Linux Server or VM.

- If I'm going to get serious about performance, I always mount a separate drive for my database and transaction log files. To make it easier, I usually mount /var/opt on this separate drive and just use this for the default database directory (you will find out you can change this). For serious production scenarios, you likely will spread SQL Server database and log files on separate drives and even create multiple SQL Server files across drives. There is some very easy to follow documentation on how to configure Linux to use a separate disk you have added (to your VM for example), in the Azure documentation. Read the section on "Prepare Data Disks" at `https://docs.microsoft.com/azure/virtual-machines/linux/tutorial-manage-disks`.

- If you plan to connect to your Linux Server or VM on a laptop not running Linux natively, get yourself a good secured shell (**ssh**) program. For MacOS users, it comes built-in with a command line ssh client, but you can install other utilities as well. For Windows 10 users, you can install a Linux subsystem that comes with an ssh command line interface. See `https://docs.microsoft.com/windows/wsl/install-win10` for more information. For me (and I'll use this for demonstrations in the book), I use a program called MobaXterm, which you can download from `https://mobaxterm.mobatek.net/`.

Figure 2-1 shows an example of a MobaXterm ssh session for a Linux server.

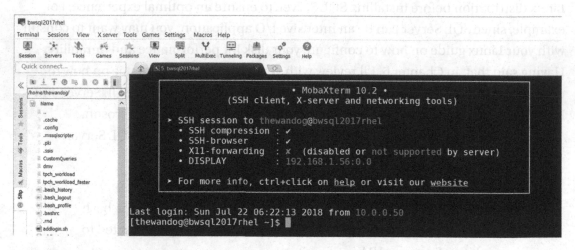

Figure 2-1. *A MobaXterm ssh session to a Linux server*

System Requirements

SQL Server runs on many different types of computer systems and virtual machine footprints. The core minimum requirements are:

- 2GB of memory (The minimum was reduced to 2GB starting with SQL Server 2017 Cumulative Update 2).

- 6GB of free disk space

- Processor speed of 2GHz

- Processor type is x64 compatible

- Two physical processor cores

While those are the minimum requirements, SQL Server can scale to the largest systems available. SQL Server can address the maximum memory possible on Linux. Currently, that is a theoretical limit of 64TB, but practically the tested limit is around 12TB. There is no limit on the number of cores SQL Server can support on Linux and the maximum database size is a whopping 524 Petabytes (PB).

SQL Server is supported on the popular native filesystems of Linux XFS and EXT4. The default filesystem type varies by distribution. It is now XFS for RHEL 7.3 and 7.4, but EXT4 for Ubuntu and SLES. In our testing at Microsoft, we have not seen a significant performance difference with one filesystem type vs. the other. However, XFS provides larger size capabilities for volume, maximum file size, and number of files than EXT4. For all my work on RHEL, I just use the default of XFS. Our testing with Ubuntu and SLES indicates the EXT4 works best with those distributions (but XFS is completely supported). There is a new filesystem type called BTRFS, which is not supported for SQL Server. You should also know that the popular remote storage system Network File System (NFS) is supported with a few restrictions, which are documented in our page on system requirements at `https://docs.microsoft.com/sql/linux/sql-server-linux-setup#system`.

Tip   For maximum performance of SQL Server, you may need to adjust certain BIOS settings for your computer. See Chapter 6 for more details on BIOS settings for your Linux system.

Testing for SQL Server

As you plan to install and explore the capabilities of SQL Server, there are some resources that can be helpful for you.

The WideWorldImporters Sample

In SQL Server 2016, we built a new sample database called WideWorldImporters along with a series of scripts and demos. I will use this sample throughout the book (along with the companion WideWorldImportersDW database). You can access a backup of this database and all the samples by starting with this documentation page: `https://docs.microsoft.com/sql/sample/world-wide-importers/wide-world-importers-documentation`. It is a very simple way for anyone to test features and basic capabilities of SQL Server without creating your own database. The sample includes a backup file of two databases (one for basic capabilities and one specifically designed for data warehouse workloads) and the original schema and data generation scripts. The backups are compatible to restore to SQL Server 2017 on both Windows and Linux.

Putting the Hammer on SQL Server

If you are looking to stress the capabilities of SQL Server on Linux for OLTP or Data Warehouse workloads, consider the popular open-source tool called HammerDB. You can download the tool from `http://www.hammerdb.com`. HammerDB supports running a derivation of the TPC benchmarks TPC-C (OLTP) and TPC-H (Data Warehouse). You should know that HammerDB requires a GUI but has some automation features. The basic interface is shown in Figure 2-2.

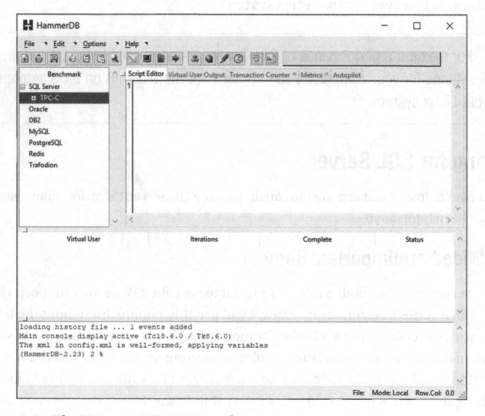

Figure 2-2. *The HammerDB 2.23 interface*

Linux Tips

If you are a Windows user and even a strong Powershell user, you may need a few tips on navigating the Linux shell and system. This section includes a few commands, scripts, and navigation tips I've learned as I've spent time installing, demonstrating, and presenting SQL Server on Linux.

Common Commands

Here is a list of the most commonly used commands I use on a regular basis from the bash shell:

ls and **ll**: List out files in a directory. ls has all type of options to list out files. I like ll because it provides a detailed list of a directory or a file(s) including size, permission, and date/time.

grep: Search for a given text string from an input stream, individual file, or set of files.

man: Short for "manual pages." Use this to find the syntax and details of any command. For example, run

```
man sqlservr
```

to see a short description of SQL Server including a list of support environment variables, where files are installed, and a pointer to the entire documentation on the Internet.

chmod: Change attributes of a file or directory. This can be read/write/execute. For example, when you create a file to execute as a script in the shell, you must change the *mode* to execute like the following:

```
chmod u+x myscript.sh
```

chown: Change ownership of a file or a directory for a group and/or user. I use this command to change the ownership of an SQL Server backup file I'm restoring to the mssql group and mssql user, so SQL Server can read the file:

```
chown mssql:mssql mybackup.bak
```

pwd: This stands for "print working directory" and allows you to see the current working directory.

ps: This stands for process status and is a simple way to get a list of processes running on the Linux server and details about them.

systemctl: This command is used to report on the status and control the execution of a systemd unit called a service on Linux. As you will see in this book, the service for SQL Server is called mssql-server. Here is a reference on how to use this command with the mssql-server service (Don't worry about sudo for now. I'll explain that in the next section):

Show if SQL Server is running

```
sudo systemctl status mssql-server
```

Stop SQL Server (SQL Server does a normal shutdown). It does nothing if SQL Server is already stopped.

```
sudo systemctl stop mssql-server
```

Start SQL Server. It does nothing if SQL Server is started.

```
sudo systemctl start mssql-server
```

Restart SQL Server. If SQL Server is running, this command will shut it down and start it again. If SQL Server is stopped, this command will start it.

```
sudo systemctl restart mssql-server
```

Tip   systemctl submits a "job" to control the service. Only the status option displays anything. When you try to start, stop, or restart the service, use the status option to see the result.

---

scp: This stands for secure file copy and can be used to copy files from one Linux server to the other.

Tip   There is a very nice free tool called **winscp**, which I use often to copy files from Windows to Linux. The Windows ssh program, MobaXterm, also includes some basic drag and drop copy capabilities.

---

df: Shows file system disk space usage for folders mounted on drives. Use the -h option to show a readable format of what directories are mounted on specific disk and their sizes. I find this helpful to see how much space the /var/opt/mssql directory has for default databases.

du: Stands for disk usage. A very handy command to show you the disk space usage by directory.

tree: You must install a package to get this one (`yum install tree`). This displays a directory and all its files and directories in a hierarchy.

In a later chapter in the book, I'll discuss the various Linux commands I use to monitor performance and system information.

sudo

When you install Linux you typically will provide a login and password to use for normal interaction with the shell and the root user password.

For security reasons, it is best not to login and run directly as the root (often called superuser). Therefore, there is a method to execute commands as the context of root (or another user) while logged in as another user.

This method is implemented by a command called **sudo** (this stands for "substitute user do" but used to be called "superuser do" because for older versions it was only for superuser commands).

For example, your default account will not have access to installation directories for SQL Server, so you would need to run this command to list out one of the directories:

```
sudo ls /var/opt/mssql
```

Note   Notice the directory navigation notation of the "/" vs. the Windows convention of "\".

Typically, in an ssh session, when you first use sudo, you are prompted for your password. By default, that authentication is cached for a period of five minutes (you can configure this value). That means, effectively, once you enter in your password, for the next five minutes all other executions of sudo will not require the password again.

As with all Linux commands, there are tons of options. Two that you might find useful are the -i and -u options. -i allows you to change context in your shell session to now run everything as superuser. For example, when you run

```
sudo -i
```

you will get prompted for your password and your shell prompt will change to indicate you are now running as root:

```
[root@bwsql2017rhel ~]#
```

The -u option allows you to run commands in the context of another user other than root.

Viewing and Editing Files and Scripts

Common tasks in any operating system for many users are viewing and editing files and building scripts. The sudo command in these examples is only required if the file requires superuser access.

The most common command to view any text file is the **cat** command. So, this command

```
sudo cat /var/opt/mssql/log/errorlog
```

dumps out the text of the SQL Server ERRORLOG (I'll explain later in this chapter the importance of this file).

The **more** command can be used to page any file.

```
sudo more /var/opt/mssql/log/errorlog
```

Tip   There is "more" to this command. When the file is displayed with more, hit the "h" key to get a list of options, which includes search capabilities.

And one of my favorite commands is the **tail** command to view the end of a file. It is very handy to see the latest entries in a file like the SQL Server ERRORLOG:

```
sudo tail /var/opt/mssql/log/errorlog
```

And if you have a file that is frequently appended to, you can "monitor" new entries to a file using tail like this:

```
sudo tail -f /var/opt/mssql/log/errorlog
```

Editing files is also another common task including writing shell scripts. I remember from my older UNIX days the famous **vi** editor. A friend of mine told me to learn vi because it is installed by default on every UNIX system in the world. And it is still there today for your use.

But now I prefer the popular **nano** editor (as suggested by Robert Dorr). nano may not be installed on your Linux server, so on RHEL I installed it with

```
sudo yum install nano
```

nano is a full screen editor and even supports cut/copy/paste. Figure 2-3 is an example nano screen of creating a shell script to install SQL Server.

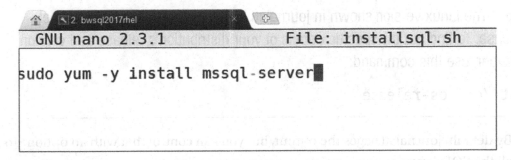

Figure 2-3. *The nano editing experience on Linux*

Just remember that when you create a shell script, you must change the "mode" to execute to run it:

```
chmod u+x installsql.sh
```

System Logging

Later in this chapter, I'll talk about a log file called ERRORLOG that SQL Server uses to provide important information about startup, errors, warnings, and other execution details. You may have the need to look at logging for other aspects of the Linux kernel or other programs. A common file from older RPM-based distributions and in current Debian systems is **/var/log/syslog**. In current versions of RPM-based systems like RHEL, there is a very nice program to view most system logging called **journalctl**. And SQL Server will write information from its ERRORLOG into this same logging facility.

By default, journalctl will only keep messages since the last boot of your Linux Server (this is configurable to make the log persisted across boots) and the default execution of journalctl is to show you all logged messages starting with the oldest since boot:

```
journalctl
```

Following is some typical output from journalctl on Linux:

```
--Logs begin at Sat 2018-02-17 09:29:49 CST, end at Tue 2018-02-20 06:43:04 CST. -
Feb 17 09:29:49 bwsql2017rhel system-journal[106]: Runtime journal is using
8.0M (max allowed 390.2M, trying to leave 545.4M f
Feb 17 09:29:49 bwsql2017rhel kernel: Initializing cgroup subsys cpuset
Feb17 09:29:49 bwsql2017rhel kernel: Initializing cgroup subsys cpu
...
```

Tip   The Linux version shown in journalctl is the version of the Linux kernel release. To find out the specific details of your distribution's release and version number, use this command:

```
cat /etc/os-release
```

By default, journalctl pages the output, but you can control that with an option. To see all the SQL Server entries, you can use a command like this:

```
journalctl | grep sqlservr
```

This only shows you logged output for sqlservr, but you may want to see the output interleaved with other kernel messages. In this case, dump out the entire journal, as each entry is marked with a timestamp. by just running journalctl.

Just Install It!

By this point in the chapter, you have seen SQL Server system requirements, discovered a few basics of testing your Linux environment and SQL Server, and if you are new to Linux received a few tips on how to work your way around the operating system and shell.

Or perhaps you just skipped here and want to dive in and install SQL Server. In this section, I will walk you through the install process and give you some behind the scenes information about it.

Deploy in 60 Seconds

Before I show you the steps to install on RHEL, here are quick pointers to install on Ubuntu (using **apt-get**) and SLES (using **zypper**). The steps are very similar but slightly different, to account for package managers on those distributions.

> *Ubuntu*: https://docs.microsoft.com/sql/linux/quickstart-install-connect-ubuntu
>
> *SLES*: https://docs.microsoft.com/sql/linux/quickstart-install-connect-suse

Installation for RHEL requires these three easy steps:

Note   These steps require your Linux server to have an Internet connection. I will discuss how to do an offline installation later in this chapter.

---

1. Download a text file called a repository (repo) configuration file to a known directory.

   ```
   sudo curl -o /etc/yum.repos.d/mssql-server.repo https://
   packages.microsoft.com/config/rhel/7/mssql-server-2017.repo
   ```

2. Run a command to do the install.

   ```
   sudo yum install -y mssql-server
   ```

Tip   This step installs the latest update of SQL Server 2017 based on a concept called Cumulative Updates (CUs). I will talk later in this chapter about how to apply specific versions. I recommend you use the latest update, as we continually improve SQL Server on Linux including fixes and minor enhancements. I also recommend that once you install SQL Server on Linux, you keep up to date monthly because this is the typical update frequency.

---

3. Run a bash shell script to *complete* the installation of SQL Server (answer a few prompts):

   ```
   sudo /opt/mssql/bin/mssql-conf setup
   ```

That's it. And if you have a decent Internet connection, it is possible that these steps can be done in about 60 seconds. I've seen and done it many times.

At this point, if you are like me, you just want to move rapidly—build database, applications, and queries. I get that, and in fact we built SQL Server on Linux so you could do that. But this is a book to cover the subject thoroughly which is why the rest of the chapter has detailed information about the complete install experience. If you plan to just start using SQL Server, I recommend you stop and scan over these resources to avoid any gotchas when you use the product:

https://docs.microsoft.com/sql/linux/sql-server-linux-release-notes and https://docs.microsoft.com/sql/linux/sql-server-linux-faq.

If you are interested in more details behind each step, read on. Otherwise, go to the next section in the chapter.

Download a Repository Config File

You only must download a repository config file once on your Linux server (unless you want to change the repository to use), even if you decide to install and uninstall several times.

```
sudo curl -o /etc/yum.repos.d/mssql-server.repo https://packages.microsoft.com/config/rhel/7/mssql-server-2017.repo
```

curl, also known as cURL (which stands for Client URL Request Library), is a command to get or send files using a URL syntax. The default is to write to stdout so the -o parameter is followed by a filename. In this case, SQL Server follows the yum repository convention by placing the file in the /etc/yum/repos.d directory.

The repo file is a simple text file that looks like this (based on mssql-server-2017.repo from the our packages.microsoft.com server):

```
[packages-microsoft-com-mssql-server-2017]
name=packages-microsoft-com-mssql-server-2017
baseurl=https://packages.microsoft.com/rhel/7/mssql-server-2017/
enabled=1
gpgcheck=1
gpgkey=https://packages.microsoft.com/keys/microsoft.asc
```

The mssql-server-2017.repo is the configuration file for the SQL Server 2017 CU repository. You may want to use a different repository (such as one for preview builds or General Distribution Release [GDR]). Refer to the section in this chapter called "Installing Other Versions" for more details. This repo file will control what package managers use to download and install packages for install and update.

The concept is to download a repo file from a location provided by the application vendor so that when you run install, the yum package manager will use the contents of the file to install the packages (as well as a key). So this URL (`https://packages.microsoft.com/rhel/7/mssql-server-2017/`) is the actual location of the RPM packages for SQL Server for RHEL. Following is an example showing how I execute the curl command on my system:

```
[thewandog@bwsql2017rhel ~]$ sudo curl - o /etc/yum.repos.d/mssql-server.
repo https://packages.microsoft.com/config/rhel/7/mssql-server-2017.repo
```

Then Figure 2-4 shows what the output looks like.

```
[thewandog@bwsql2017rhel ~]$ sudo curl -o /etc/yum.repos.d/mssql-server.repo https://packages.micros
oft.com/config/rhel/7/mssql-server-2017.repo
  % Total    % Received % Xferd  Average Speed   Time    Time     Time  Current
                                 Dload  Upload   Total   Spent    Left  Speed
100   232  100   232    0     0    694      0 --:--:-- --:--:-- --:--:--   698
[thewandog@bwsql2017rhel ~]$ █
```

Figure 2-4. *Example output of downloading the repository configuration file for RHEL*

Do the Install of the SQL Server Engine

Now that the repo file is copied, it is time to perform the installation of SQL Server on Linux on RHEL.

```
sudo yum install -y mssql-server
```

One thing I've enjoyed about getting back into Linux is the history of how various part of the operating system made its way into the distributions. Yum stands for (YellowDog Updater Modifier). Its origins trace back to a free distribution called Yellow Dog Linux and is the primary RPM-based package manager for RHEL, Fedora, and CentOS.

The installation process for the SQL Server RPM package does the following:

1. Downloads the binary RPM package file

2. Creates a Linux user and group called mssql (this will be the non-interactive login and group assigned to SQL Server non-binary files). You cannot change this.

3. Extracts out SQL Server binaries and installation files (We will explore all these files in a later section of this chapter.)

4. Registers SQL Server as a systemd service called mssql-server

The -y parameter used for yum in the example syntax stands for "assume yes" which means you are automatically asking yum to respond "yes" to any prompts. For our installation, the only prompt is whether you want to proceed with the download.

Figure 2-5 is a snapshot of the SQL Server installation process in progress when using yum on RHEL.

```
[thewandog@bwsql2017rhel ~]$ sudo yum install -y mssql-server
Loaded plugins: product-id, search-disabled-repos, subscription-manager
Resolving Dependencies
--> Running transaction check
---> Package mssql-server.x86_64 0:14.0.3022.28-2 will be installed
--> Finished Dependency Resolution

Dependencies Resolved

================================================================================
 Package          Arch        Version          Repository                   Size
================================================================================
Installing:
 mssql-server     x86_64      14.0.3022.28-2   packages-microsoft-com-mssql-server-2017   167 M

Transaction Summary
================================================================================
Install  1 Package

Total download size: 167 M
Installed size: 167 M
Downloading packages:
mssql-server-14.0.3022.28-2.x86_64.rpm                      | 167 MB  00:00:11
Running transaction check
Running transaction test
Transaction test succeeded
Running transaction
  Installing : mssql-server-14.0.3022.28-2.x86_64 [#############            ] 1/1
```

Figure 2-5. *A yum install of SQL Server on RHEL in progress*

And Figure 2-6 is an example of what a successful installation looks like.

```
 mssql-server      x86_64      14.0.3022.28-2      packages-microsoft-com-mssql-server-2017      167 M

Transaction Summary
================================================================================
Install  1 Package

Total download size: 167 M
Installed size: 167 M
Downloading packages:
mssql-server-14.0.3022.28-2.x86_64.rpm                                    | 167 MB  00:00:11
Running transaction check
Running transaction test
Transaction test succeeded
Running transaction
   Installing : mssql-server-14.0.3022.28-2.x86_64                                        1/1

+--------------------------------------------------------------+
Please run 'sudo /opt/mssql/bin/mssql-conf setup'
to complete the setup of Microsoft SQL Server
+--------------------------------------------------------------+

SQL Server needs to be restarted in order to apply this setting. Please run
'systemctl restart mssql-server.service'.
   Verifying  : mssql-server-14.0.3022.28-2.x86_64                                        1/1

Installed:
  mssql-server.x86_64 0:14.0.3022.28-2

Complete!
[thewandog@bwsql2017rhel ~]$ 
```

Figure 2-6. *A completed yum install of SQL Server on RHEL*

Complete the Setup of SQL Server

If you look carefully at this screenshot, the installation provides instructions on how to complete the setup of SQL Server:

Please run 'sudo /opt/mssql/bin/mssql-conf setup' to complete the setup of Microsoft SQL Server.

Therefore, the command to run is

```
sudo /opt/mssql/bin/mssql-conf setup
```

This step is necessary so that we can extract out the system databases from the downloaded installation files and run sqlservr to do a few post install steps. mssql-conf is a bash shell script copied as part of the installation and executes other supporting python scripts to perform various configuration tasks. This script takes several options and one of these is called **setup**. You will only use this option once after installing SQL Server, but mssql-conf supports other options, which we will cover later in this chapter.

The setup option of mssql-conf does the following:

1. Prompts you for the Edition of SQL Server

2. Asks you to accept the end user licensing agreement (EULA). You can read the agreement from /usr/share/doc/mssql-server.

3. Prompts for the password of the SQL Server system administrator account called **sa**

Tip   The SQL Server account sa is the default system administrator account. In a later chapter in the book, I will talk about how to add other login accounts to SQL Server. It is very important that you remember the password for the sa account. mssql-conf does provide an option to reset the sa password. Also note the sa password must be a "complex" password (as do all passwords for logins for SQL Server on Linux). The requirements are: at least eight characters long and contain characters from three of the following four sets: uppercase letters, lowercase letters, numbers, and symbols.

Evaluation, Developer, and Express are free editions of SQL Server. If you choose Web, Standard, Enterprise, or Enterprise Core, these are paid licenses, but choose these options if you have a paid license via a contract with Microsoft. You will not be required to enter in a product key. If you have purchased a license individually, choose option 8 and enter in your product key.

Following is an example of responding to what edition to install and accepting the License agreement:

```
[thewandog@bwsql2017rhel ~]$ sudo /opt/mssql/bin/mssql-conf setup
Choose an edition of SQL Server:
  1) Evaluation (free, no production use rights, 180-day limit)
  2) Developer (free, no production use rights)
  3) Express (free)
  4) Web (PAID)
  5) Standard (PAID)
```

6) Enterprise (PAID)

7) Enterprise Core (PAID)

8) I bought a license through a retail sales channel and have a product key to enter.

Details about editions can be found at
https://go.microsoft.com/fwlink/$LinkId=852748&clcid=0x409

Use of PAID editions of this software requires separate licensing through a
Microsoft Volume Licensing program.
By choosing a PAID edition, you are verifying that you have the appropriate
Number of licenses in place to install and run this software
Enter your edition(1-8): **2**
The license terms for this product can be found in
/usr/share/doc/mssql-server or downloaded from:
http://go.microsoft.com/fwlink/?LinkId=855862&clcid=0x409

The privacy statement can be viewed at:
https://go.microsoft.com/fwlink/?LinkId=853010&clcid=0x409

Do you accept the license terms [Yes/No]: **Yes**

Enter the SQL Server system administrator password:
Confirm the SQL Server system administrator password:
Configuring SQL Server

Setup has completed successfully. SQL Server is now starting.
[thewandog&bwsql2017rhel ~]$

In addition, mssql-conf with the setup option changes the ownership of the /var/opt/ mssql directory (and subdirectories) to user mssql and group mssql. This is the default location and ownership of this directory, and in SQL Server 2017 on Linux you cannot change this.

In the section "Unattended Install" I will show you how to use environment variables to automate these steps to avoid having to supply user input.

The Complete Installation Experience

I told you the install was easy for SQL Server. This section covers installation-related topics I believe you will find useful to provide the complete installation experience. Learn how to install other builds of SQL Server, verify your install, perform unattended and offline installations, install in the cloud, and learn troubleshooting tips.

Installing Other Versions

SQL Server 2017 has two major repositories from which to install from:

- **mssql-server-2017**: Latest released builds based on CUs for SQL Server 2017. Choose this to use the latest updates for SQL Server 2017. The steps previously shown in this chapter and in our tutorials in the official Microsoft documentation use this repository.

- **mssql-server-2017-gdr**: General Distribution Release (GDR) for SQL Server 2017. Choose this if you only want security and critical updates to SQL Server 2017. There are typically very few updates to this repository over the lifetime of a major release of SQL Server.

Future versions of SQL Server could have different repository names.

Note   There is also a preview repository called **mssql-server**. If you have used this repository, be sure to remove SQL Server and change to one of the released repositories before installing SQL Server.

On a regular basis, typically monthly, Microsoft releases an update to SQL Server 2017 called a Cumulative Update (CU). This is a collection of fixes and enhancements to the product, and they are numbered consecutively starting with CU1. By the nature of its name, each CU contains changes from the previous build. Refer to our release notes for a complete list of these builds: `https://docs.microsoft.com/sql/linux/sql-server-linux-release-notes`.

Whenever a security problem or critical issue needs to be addressed, Microsoft will publish a GDR build. This way if you want to run SQL Server based on the release to manufacturing (RTM) build AND security updates/critical fixes, you can choose the GDR repository to get the latest build.

Note   Prior to SQL Server 2017, Microsoft would publish GDR, CU, and Service Pack releases. Starting with SQL Server 2017, Microsoft will no longer publish Service Pack releases.

The instructions to copy a repository file earlier in this section use the CU repository. Once you copy a repo file, any future install or update commands with your package manager will use that repository. If you want to change what repository to use, you must delete the previous repo file and copy down the new one.

For example, if you had previously used the mssql-server-2017.repo file and wanted to uninstall and install from the GDR repository, you would need to:

1. Delete the previous repo file like this

    ```
    sudo rm etc/yum.repos.d/mssql-server.repo
    ```

2. Uninstall SQL Server

3. Copy down the new repo like this (assumes RHEL, but look at our install docs for how to do this for Ubuntu and SLES)

    ```
    sudo curl -o /etc/yum.repos.d/mssql-server.repo https://
    packages.microsoft.com/config/rhel/7/mssql-server-2017-
    gdr.repo
    ```

4. Install SQL Server

In addition, by default, install and update will use the latest build from these repositories. To install a specific package version, you can perform an offline install of a version of the package or use the following syntax with yum:

```
sudo yum install -y mssql-server:<package version>
```

To find all the package versions for SQL Server, run the following command from the bash shell:

```
sudo yum list mssql-server --showduplicates
```

At minimum, I recommend you use the latest builds from the GDR repository for any security and critical updates. Most customers use the CU repository and do not experience any major issues.

The Microsoft release notes page has a list of each update, including a reference to a Microsoft support article that describes what changes are in each update. You can read more at https://docs.microsoft.com/sql/linux/sql-server-linux-release-notes.

Verifying Install

Once you have completed the installation of SQL Server, I have recommendations to do some basic verification steps and others you can do to ensure a smoother experience after installing SQL Server. Plus, you will learn a few things about SQL Server along the way. I highly recommend you go through at least the basic recommendations to avoid problems later.

Check the mssql-server Service Is Running

Run the following command to check the mssql-server service status at any time:

```
sudo systemctl status mssql-server
```

The output of this command should look something like Figure 2-7 if SQL Server is running.

```
[thewandog@bwsql2017rhel ~]$ sudo systemctl status mssql-server
\● mssql-server.service - Microsoft SQL Server Database Engine
   Loaded: loaded (/usr/lib/systemd/system/mssql-server.service; enabled; vendor preset: disabled)
   Active: active (running) since Sun 2018-02-25 10:20:48 CST; 7min ago
     Docs: https://docs.microsoft.com/en-us/sql/linux
 Main PID: 2548 (sqlservr)
   CGroup: /system.slice/mssql-server.service
           ├─2548 /opt/mssql/bin/sqlservr
           └─2573 /opt/mssql/bin/sqlservr

Feb 25 10:20:53 bwsql2017rhel sqlservr[2548]: 2018-02-25 10:20:53.78 spid10s    Polybase feature disabled.
Feb 25 10:20:53 bwsql2017rhel sqlservr[2548]: 2018-02-25 10:20:53.78 spid10s    Clearing tempdb database.
Feb 25 10:20:54 bwsql2017rhel sqlservr[2548]: 2018-02-25 10:20:54.65 spid10s    Starting up database 'tempdb'.
Feb 25 10:20:55 bwsql2017rhel sqlservr[2548]: 2018-02-25 10:20:55.07 spid10s    The tempdb database has 1 d...(s).
Feb 25 10:20:55 bwsql2017rhel sqlservr[2548]: 2018-02-25 10:20:55.07 spid21s    The Service Broker endpoint...ate.
Feb 25 10:20:55 bwsql2017rhel sqlservr[2548]: 2018-02-25 10:20:55.08 spid21s    The Database Mirroring endp...ate.
Feb 25 10:20:55 bwsql2017rhel sqlservr[2548]: 2018-02-25 10:20:55.09 spid21s    Service Broker manager has ...ted.
Feb 25 10:20:55 bwsql2017rhel sqlservr[2548]: 2018-02-25 10:20:55.10 spid5s     Recovery is complete. This ...red.
Feb 25 10:25:57 bwsql2017rhel sqlservr[2548]: 2018-02-25 10:25:57.05 spid51     Attempting to load library ...red.
Feb 25 10:25:57 bwsql2017rhel sqlservr[2548]: 2018-02-25 10:25:57.10 spid51     Using 'xplog70.dll' version...red.
Hint: Some lines were ellipsized, use -l to show in full.
```

Figure 2-7. *A running mssql-server service*

If you look at this output, you see a Main PID (stands for process ID) and then two process IDs listed below it.

If you recall, in Chapter 1, I mentioned that a parent "watchdog" process exists when SQL Server is started. In the output you see from systemctl, the top process, 2548, is the "watchdog" process and the second process, 2573, is the actual SQLSERVR process running all the SQL Server engine code. You will always see two SQLSERVR processes on Linux, so a command like

```
ps axjf | grep sqlservr
```

yields output that looks like Figure 2-8.

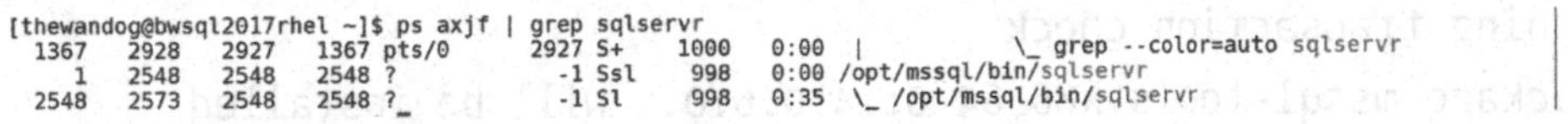

```
[thewandog@bwsql2017rhel ~]$ ps axjf | grep sqlservr
  1367  2928  2927  1367 pts/0    2927 S+   1000  0:00 |              \_ grep --color=auto sqlservr
     1  2548  2548  2548 ?          -1 Ssl   998  0:00 /opt/mssql/bin/sqlservr
  2548  2573  2548  2548 ?          -1 Sl    998  0:35  \_ /opt/mssql/bin/sqlservr
```

Figure 2-8. *Finding the processes of sqlservr*

Since I used grep, the column names of the output are not shown. The second column is the process PID and the first column is the parent PID. So, process 2548 is the "parent" watchdog SQLSERVR and 2573 is its "child" process but is the "main" SQLSERVR.

If SQL Server is not running correctly or something failed during the installation, consult the "Troubleshooting Install" section in this chapter. The most common mistake I see is skipping the step to run the mssql-conf script with the setup option.

Connect Locally and Run a Query

Follow these instructions to use the basic command line tool sqlcmd on your Linux server to demonstrate you can connect and run a query. sqlcmd is a tool that allows you to execute T-SQL commands against any installed SQL Server.

1. Install the packages for tools and ODBC for RHEL.

Note   For the full set of instructions in our documentation to install our command line tools on all distributions, visit `https://docs.microsoft.com/sql/linux/sql-server-linux-setup-tools`.

```
sudo curl -o /etc/yum.repos.d/msprod.repo https://packages.microsoft.com/
config/rhel/7/prod.repo
```

The output looks very similar to downloading the repo file for mssql-server

```
sudo yum install -y mssql-tools unixODBC-devel
```

There are two packages to install: (1) The command line tools and (2) The Linux ODBC package (sqlcmd on Linux uses ODBC). This is where yum really comes in handy, as it will automatically detect the dependency upon the msodbcsql package. For example:

```
Loaded plugins: product-id, search-disabled-repos, subscription-manager
Resolving Dependencies
--> Running transaction check
---> Package mssql-tools.x86_64 0:14.0.6.0.1 will be installed
--> Processing Dependency: msodbcsql < 13.2.0.0 for package: mssql-
      tools-14.0.6.0-1.x86_64
--> Processing Dependency: msodbcsql >= 13.1.0.0 for package: mssql-tools-
      14.0.6.0.1-x86_64
---> Package unixODBC-devel.x86_64 0:2.3.1-11.el7 will be installed
--> Running transaction check
---> Package msodbcsql.x86_64 0:13.1.9.2-1 will be installed
--> Finished Dependency Resolution
```

You will fill out a few prompts for the EULA license and the install should be very quick.

2. Put the tools in your PATH to make execution easier.

Your PATH defines directories to search for programs, so you don't have to explicitly put in the path of a program or run it from its installed directory. These commands will update the PATH for the command line tools and write them into files that will specify the PATH for any future login session.

```
echo 'export PATH="$PATH:/opt/mssql-tools/bin"' >> ~/.bash_profile
echo 'export PATH="$PATH:/opt/mssql-tools/bin"' >> ~/.bashrc
source ~/.bashrc
```

3. Connect using sqlcmd and run a query

```
sqlcmd -Usa
```

You will be prompted for the sa password you specified during installation. If you connect successfully, you will get a sqlcmd prompt that looks as follows:

```
[thewandog@bwsql2017rhel ~]$ sqlcmd -Usa
Password:
1>
```

If SQL Server was not running, and you tried to connect with sqlcmd, you would get an error the following

```
Sqlcmd: Error: Microsoft ODBC Driver 17 for SQL Server : Login timeout expired.
Sqlcmd: Error: Microsoft ODBC Driver 17 for SQL Server : TCP Provider: Error
code 0x2749.
Sqlcmd: Error: Microsoft ODBC Driver 17 for SQL Server : A network-related
or instance-specific error has occurred while establishing a connection to
SQL Server. Server is not found or not accessible. Check if instance name
is correct and if SQL Server is configured to allow remote connections. For
more information see SQL Server Books Online..
```

One mistake I've seen made by customers is to forget to run mssql-conf with the setup option after executing a yum install. The error in Figure 2-14 is the same error you will see in this scenario.

Now that you have connected, run these two "sanity check" queries:

```
1> select @@version
2> go
```

The results will depend on what version of SQL Server you install and what Linux distribution you use. The following show the results of SQL Server 2017 Cumulative Update 7 on RHEL 7.5.

```
------------------------------------------------------------------------------
------------------------------------------------------------------------------
------------------------------------------------------------------------------
------------------------------------------------------------------------------
Microsoft SQL Server 2017 (RTM-CU7) (KB4229789) - 14.0.3026.27 (X64)
        May 10 2018 12:38:11
        Copyright (C) 2017 Microsoft Corporation
        Enterprise Edition: Core-based Licensing (64-bit) on Linux (Red Hat
        Enterprise Linux)
```

```
(1 rows affected)
```

Now run this query to list out the databases installed on SQL Server:

```
1> select name, state_desc from sys.databases
2> go
```

Your results should look like the following:

```
name         state_desc
----------   ---------------------------------------------------------
Master       ONLINE
Tempdb       ONLINE
Model        ONLINE
Msdb         ONLINE
```

Type in "exit" to quit sqlcmd.

Connect Remotely

One last basic check is to remotely connect to SQL Server outside of the local Linux server. This involves these steps:

1. Open the firewall for SQL Server.

SQL Server by default listens on TCP port 1433 and it is unlikely that network traffic would be allowed to that port from other clients. Therefore, run the following commands to open this port from the firewall of the Linux server. These commands open the firewall on a RHEL server.

```
sudo firewall-cmd --zone=public --add-port=1433/tcp --permanent
sudo firewall-cmd --reload
```

2. Connect to SQL Server.

You can use any valid tool that allows a connection to SQL Server. You can get a complete list of tools of your choice from https://docs.microsoft.com/sql/tools/overview-sql-tools. Figure 2-9 shows a successful connection to SQL Server on Linux using the Windows version of sqlcmd based on its IP address. Notice the syntax includes port 1433, since I'm using the IP address directly.

```
sqlcmd –Usa -S10.0.0.0,1433
```

```
C:\WINDOWS\system32>sqlcmd -Usa -S10.0.0.100,1433
Password:
1> select @@version
2> go


--------------------------------------------------------------------------------------------------------------------------------
--------------------------------------------------------------------------------------------------------------
----------------------------------
Microsoft SQL Server 2017 (RTM-CU4) (KB4056498) - 14.0.3022.28 (x64)
        Feb  9 2018 19:39:09
        Copyright (C) 2017 Microsoft Corporation
        Enterprise Edition: Core-based Licensing (64-bit) on Linux (Red Hat Enterprise Linux)

(1 rows affected)
1>
```

Figure 2-9. *A remote connection to SQL Server on Linux*

More Ways to Verify SQL Server Functionality

There are three other tests I recommend you go through to ensure the best SQL Server experience:

- Restart the SQL Server service.

  Restart the SQL Server service using the **systemctl** command

  ```
  sudo systemctl restart mssql-server
  ```

  When this completes, there is no information provided, even when it is successful. I recommend you go through the basic verification steps earlier in this section after this restart.

- Restart the Linux Server.

  Another verification step I recommend is to restart your Linux server and perform the basic verification steps I've outlined in the previous section. This ensures all filesystems are mounted properly and SQL Server can successfully start when the Linux server starts. I've seen examples where a customer added a disk and mounted the /var/opt filesystem on that disk but did not put the entry in the /etc/fstab file. On restart, the filesystem was not mounted and therefore SQL Server did not start.

- Restore a database.

  The other step I recommend you test out is your ability to restore a database and query it. As I've mentioned earlier in this chapter, Microsoft has a sample database so you can test a restore, called WideWorldImporters.

To complete the restore, follow these steps:

1. Download the WideWorldImporters sample backup.

You can download the sample database from `https://docs.microsoft.com/sql/sample/world-wide-importers/wide-world-importers-documentation`. You can download this directly to your Linux Server if it is connected to the Internet, using the following command from the bash shell:

```
wget https://github.com/Microsoft/sql-server-samples/releases/download/
wide-world-importers-v1.0/WideWorldImporters-Full.bak
```

2. If you did not download this directly to your Linux server, copy the file to your Linux server using a program like scp or a built-in feature of your ssh client (MobaXterm provides "drag and drop" capabilities). You then need to copy the file into the /var/opt/mssql directory and change the ownership to mssql, so SQL Server can access the backup file.

```
chown mssql:mssql WideWorldImporters-Full.bak
```

3. Restore the database by executing this query using sqlcmd.

I recommend you create a file called restorewwi_linux.sql and put these T-SQL commands into the file:

```
restore database WideWorldImporters from disk = '/var/opt/mssql/
                                                  WideWorldImporters-
                                                  Full.bak' with
move 'WWI_Primary' to '/var/opt/mssql/data/WideWorldImporters.mdf',
move 'WWI_UserData' to '/var/opt/mssql/data/WideWorldImporters_UserData.ndf',
move 'WWI_Log' to '/var/opt/mssql/data/WideWorldImporters.ldf',
move 'WWI_InMemory_Data_1' to '/var/opt/mssql/data/WideWorldImporters_
    InMemory_Data_1'
go
```

Now execute the SQL script using sqlcmd (a nice tip on how to run a script with sqlcmd):

```
sqlcmd -Usa -irestorewwi_linux.sql
```

Since the WideWorldImporters backup was created with SQL Server 2016, your output will look like Figure 2-10. The restore will automatically upgrade the database to 2017).

```
[thewandog@bwsql2017rhel ~]$ sqlcmd -Usa -irestorewwi_linux.sql
Password:
Processed 1464 pages for database 'WideWorldImporters', file 'WWI_Primary' on file 1.
Processed 53096 pages for database 'WideWorldImporters', file 'WWI_UserData' on file 1.
Processed 33 pages for database 'WideWorldImporters', file 'WWI_Log' on file 1.
Processed 3862 pages for database 'WideWorldImporters', file 'WWI_InMemory_Data_1' on file 1.
Converting database 'WideWorldImporters' from version 852 to the current version 869.
Database 'WideWorldImporters' running the upgrade step from version 852 to version 853.
Database 'WideWorldImporters' running the upgrade step from version 853 to version 854.
Database 'WideWorldImporters' running the upgrade step from version 854 to version 855.
Database 'WideWorldImporters' running the upgrade step from version 855 to version 856.
Database 'WideWorldImporters' running the upgrade step from version 856 to version 857.
Database 'WideWorldImporters' running the upgrade step from version 857 to version 858.
Database 'WideWorldImporters' running the upgrade step from version 858 to version 859.
Database 'WideWorldImporters' running the upgrade step from version 859 to version 860.
Database 'WideWorldImporters' running the upgrade step from version 860 to version 861.
Database 'WideWorldImporters' running the upgrade step from version 861 to version 862.
Database 'WideWorldImporters' running the upgrade step from version 862 to version 863.
Database 'WideWorldImporters' running the upgrade step from version 863 to version 864.
Database 'WideWorldImporters' running the upgrade step from version 864 to version 865.
Database 'WideWorldImporters' running the upgrade step from version 865 to version 866.
Database 'WideWorldImporters' running the upgrade step from version 866 to version 867.
Database 'WideWorldImporters' running the upgrade step from version 867 to version 868.
Database 'WideWorldImporters' running the upgrade step from version 868 to version 869.
RESTORE DATABASE successfully processed 58455 pages in 1.002 seconds (455.763 MB/sec).
[thewandog@bwsql2017rhel ~]$
```

Figure 2-10. *A restore of the WideWorldImorters sample backup*

Now connect with sqlcmd running a query directly against the database (notice the use of the -Q option to run a query from the command line):

```
sqlcmd -Usa -Q"select count(*) from Sales.Orders" -dWideWorldImporters
```

Figure 2-11 shows the expected results of the number of rows from the Orders table in the WideWorldImporters sample database immediately after a restore.

```
[thewandog@bwsql2017rhel ~]$ sqlcmd -Usa -Q"select count(*) from Sales.Orders" -dWideWorldImporters
Password:

-----------
      73595

(1 rows affected)
[thewandog@bwsql2017rhel ~]$
```

Figure 2-11. *Getting the row count of the Orders table in WideWorldImporters*

Now that you have seen techniques to install SQL Server and verify the installation, the next sections cover other installation topics.

Unattended Install

All the package managers (e.g., yum, apt-get, zypper) offer a -y option to allow for the basic installation to complete without any user interaction. The mssql-conf setup option that I described to complete the installation also offers a method to not require user interaction.

If you execute mssql-conf like the following:

```
sudo /opt/mssql/bin/mssql-conf setup -n
```

the mssql-conf script will rely on the environment variables in Table 2-1 to automatically respond to the edition of SQL Server, accepting the EULA agreement and the sa password.

Table 2-1. *Environment Variables for the Install*

Environment Variable	Description	Possible Values
MSSQL_PID	Set the SQL Server edition or product key	Evaluation Developer Express Web Standard Enterprise <A product key>
		If specifying a product key, it must be in the form of #####-#####-#####-#####-#####, where '#' is a number or a letter
ACCEPT_EULA	Accept EULA agreement	Y
MSSQL_SA_PASSWORD	sa password in single quotes	The requirements are at least 8 characters long and contain characters from three of the following four sets: uppercase letters, lowercase letters, numbers, and symbols.

You can actually specify more options during mssql-conf setup with other environment variables, as documented at https://docs.microsoft.com/sql/linux/sql-server-linux-configure-environment-variables. For example, you could set the TCP port SQL Server will listen on other than 1433.

> **Note**   You can also use environment variables to configure SQL Server in a
> Docker container when first starting the container. See Chapter 11 for more details.

You can set these environment variables from the shell or include them all in one execution of mssql-conf like the following:

```
sudo MSSQL_PID=Developer ACCEPT_EULA=Y MSSQL_SA_PASSWORD='<YourStrong!Password>'
/opt/mssql/bin/mssql-conf -n setup
```

Figure 2-12 shows the output of an unattended execution of mssql-conf.

```
[thewandog@bwsql2017rhel ~]$ sudo MSSQL_PID=Developer ACCEPT_EULA=Y MSSQL_SA_PASSWORD='Sql2017isfast' /opt/mssql/bi
n/mssql-conf -n setup
[sudo] password for thewandog:
The license terms for this product can be found in
/usr/share/doc/mssql-server or downloaded from:
https://go.microsoft.com/fwlink/?LinkId=855862&clcid=0x409

The privacy statement can be viewed at:
https://go.microsoft.com/fwlink/?LinkId=853010&clcid=0x409

Configuring SQL Server...

Setup has completed successfully. SQL Server is now starting.
[thewandog@bwsql2017rhel ~]$
```

Figure 2-12. *Using mssql-conf for an unattended setup*

You can configure other setup tasks to be part of an entire script that installs SQL Server, installs command line tools, other packages, performs other configuration tasks, and opens the firewall for remote connectivity. For an example of a more robust unattended script, see the example for RHEL at

```
https://docs.microsoft.com/sql/linux/sample-unattended-install-redhat.
```

Our Customer Advisory Team at Microsoft have also created a GitHub repo to show a possible complete unattended installation based on their customer experiences, which you can find at `https://github.com/denzilribeiro/sqlunattended`. (Credits to Denzil Ribero from Microsoft for creating this great set of scripts).

Offline Install

There may be situations where your Linux server is not connected or often disconnected from the Internet. Therefore, you need a process to be able to install the mssql-server package when your Linux server is offline.

Tip   If you are doing demonstrations of the SQL Server install experience, I highly recommend you download a package to your Linux server as a backup should you be in a place where there is poor Internet connectivity.

The various package management systems all support this technique, provided you can download the appropriate package in a manner that you can copy to your Linux server.

Our packages for mssql-server can be found by navigating our release notes documentation page at `https://docs.microsoft.com/sql/linux/sql-server-linux-release-notes`.

Copy down the package from the desired build, copy it into your Linux server in your home directory, and use your package manager program with an option that supports a local install. For RHEL, it looks like the following:

```
sudo yum localinstall mssql-server_versionnumber.x86_64.rpm
```

The only issue with this approach is that the package manager will look for dependent packages to install but if you are not connected to the Internet, it cannot download them.

An alternate approach for RHEL and SLES (RPM-based systems) is to use the rpm command like the following:

```
rpm -ivh mssql-server_versionnumber.x86_64.rpm
```

This command will not look for dependent packages and will not try to connect to the Internet. If you get errors, because a dependent package is not available, you can use this command to find these dependencies:

```
rpm -qpR mssql-server_versionnumber.x86_64.rpm
```

Tip   The rpm package contains all the metadata to detect dependencies, so you do not need to be connected to the Internet to run this command. This command also only requires you have permission to read the .rpm file.

You could then locate the dependent packages, download, copy, and install them locally to meet the needs of the mssql-server package.

Once you complete the local installation, you would then execute

```
sudo /opt/mssql/bin/mssql-conf setup
```

just as you did for an online installation.

Installing Other Packages

One of the ways we have been able to keep the mssql-server installation light and fast is to separate other functionality into packages. The packages in Table 2-2, therefore, can be installed after mssql-server to use other features.

Table 2-2. *Optional Packages*

Package	Description	Comments
mssql-tools	Command line tools such as sqlcmd and bcp	I recommend you install these on any SQL Server Linux installation to provide basic query and data load capabilities on the Linux Server.
mssql-server-fts	Full-Text Search capabilities	Only install this if you want to use SQL Server Full-Text Search features. This book will not cover Full-Text Search. For more information, see the Microsoft documentation at https://docs.microsoft.com/sql/ relational-databases/search/full-text-search.
mssql-server-is	Integration Services (also known as SSIS)	This is a separate Linux process used for ETL operations. Install this for more complex data extract and load capabilities. This book will cover the basics of SSIS capabilities in Chapter 5.
mssql-server-ha	SQL Server Resource Agent	You are required to install this to use High Availability features with Pacemaker.

> **Note**   Prior to SQL Server 2017 CU4, SQL Server Agent was a separate package called mssql-server-agent. We made a decision that starting with SQL Server 2017 CU4, SQL Server Agent would be installed with the mssql-server package and enabled through mssql-conf. See `https://docs.microsoft.com/sql/linux/sql-server-linux-setup-sql-agent` for more information. We will cover the basics of using SQL Server Agent in Chapter 9.

The release notes contain the location for the above packages (except for mssql-tools) if you need to perform an offline installation of these: `https://docs.microsoft.com/sql/linux/sql-server-linux-release-notes`.

The mssql-tools packages for offline installation can be found at: `https://docs.microsoft.com/sql/linux/sql-server-linux-setup-tools#offline-installation`.

Installing in Azure

Azure Virtual Machine is a cloud Infrastructure as a Service (IAAS) platform for hosting Virtual Machines to run all type of applications and workloads. SQL Server is well embraced and a very popular workload in this environment.

> **Note**   SQL Server on Linux can be run in other environments such as VMWare, VirtualBox, and other Cloud Providers. For more information, see this documentation page: `https://docs.microsoft.com/sql/linux/quickstart-install-connect-clouds`.

You have two fundamental choices to install SQL Server on Linux in Azure Virtual Machine:

- Choose your favorite Linux Distribution (RHEL, SLES, or Ubuntu) from the Azure Marketplace. Then perform an installation of SQL Server like the instructions I have provided in this chapter.

- Choose a preconfigured SQL Server on Linux option from the Azure Marketplace. As part of the provisioning of the virtual machine, SQL Server will be installed and configured automatically.

Note   When you use a preconfigured SQL Server Linux VM, you will have to complete the installation once you first connect to the Linux VM with `sudo /opt/mssql/bin/mssql-conf set-sa-password` to establish the sa password.

You also have two methods to provision one of these choices with Azure Virtual Machine:

- Use the Azure Portal through a user interface (`http://portal.azure.com`).

- Use the command line Azure cli to provision a virtual machine. Read more at `https://docs.microsoft.com/cli/azure/vm?view=azure-cli-latest`.

No matter what method or choice you pick to install SQL Server on Linux in Azure Virtual Machine, there are a few unique aspects to setting up connectivity and providing access via ssh. For a walkthrough of this experience using the Azure Portal, see this documentation: `https://docs.microsoft.com/azure/virtual-machines/linux/sql/provision-sql-server-linux-virtual-machine`.

To achieve maximum performance for SQL Server on Azure Virtual Machine, consult our best practice guide at `https://docs.microsoft.com/azure/virtual-machines/windows/sql/virtual-machines-windows-sql-performance`. Some of the recommendations here are for Windows, but several of these apply to SQL Server on Linux.

In addition, our very talented documentation lead, Jason Roth, has written up this excellent FAQ on running SQL Server on Linux in Azure Virtual Machine: `https://docs.microsoft.com/azure/virtual-machines/linux/sql/sql-server-linux-faq`. Read this over carefully for a discussion about licensing and a few restrictions.

Azure Virtual Machine provides many different sizes and options for capacity including CPU, memory, and storage. The virtual machine size will be a choice you make when provisioning a virtual machine in Azure. For a complete list of current sizes, see this documentation: `https://docs.microsoft.com/azure/virtual-machines/linux/sizes`.

One of the benefits of using Azure Virtual Machine is a flexible subscription model and a "pay as you go" model. For pricing options for Linux Azure Virtual Machines, see this documentation: `https://azure.microsoft.com/pricing/details/virtual-machines/linux`.

For additional topics on Linux-based Virtual Machines in Azure, see this documentation: `https://docs.microsoft.com/azure/virtual-machines/linux`.

There are other topics that may interest you as you consider Azure Virtual Machine for SQL Server:

Security Considerations

`https://docs.microsoft.com/azure/virtual-machines/windows/sql/virtual-machines-windows-sql-security`.

Migration

`https://docs.microsoft.com/azure/virtual-machines/windows/sql/virtual-machines-windows-migrate-sql`.

High Availability and Disaster Recovery

`https://docs.microsoft.com/azure/virtual-machines/windows/sql/virtual-machines-windows-sql-high-availability-dr`.

Troubleshooting Install

To complete this section, I consulted with our expert at Microsoft in Technical Support, Pradeep M.M., on the most common issues he has seen for installation failures and how to remedy them. What I found was interesting. It turns out that because of the way we have made our installation lightweight and built into the native Linux distribution package management systems, Microsoft has seen very few problems for customers trying to install SQL Server on Linux to this point.

Having said that, the following are a few possible scenarios and how you can address them.

Poor or No Internet Connectivity

I've seen the problem of poor or no Internet connectivity myself while installing SQL Server on Linux using standard installation techniques, which requires Internet connectivity to pull down the packages.

Figure 2-13 shows an example of a failure when trying to install SQL Server on RHEL when the Linux server does not have Internet connectivity.

```
[thewandog@bwsql2017rhel ~]$ sudo yum install -y mssql-server
Loaded plugins: product-id, search-disabled-repos, subscription-manager
Resolving Dependencies
--> Running transaction check
---> Package mssql-server.x86_64 0:14.0.3022.28-2 will be installed
--> Finished Dependency Resolution

Dependencies Resolved

================================================================================================
 Package              Arch           Version            Repository                          Size
================================================================================================
Installing:
 mssql-server         x86_64         14.0.3022.28-2     packages-microsoft-com-mssql-server-2017    167 M

Transaction Summary
================================================================================================
Install  1 Package

Total download size: 167 M
Installed size: 167 M
Downloading packages:
mssql-server-14.0.3022.28-2.x8 FAILED
https://packages.microsoft.com/rhel/7/mssql-server-2017/mssql-server-14.0.3022.28-2.x86_64.rpm: [Errno 14] curl#6 -
  "Could not resolve host: packages.microsoft.com; Unknown error"
Trying other mirror.

Error downloading packages:
  mssql-server-14.0.3022.28-2.x86_64: [Errno 256] No more mirrors to try.
```

Figure 2-13. *A failed SQL Server installation due to no Internet connectivity*

It is possible to have problems like this even when your Linux server has connectivity, but the connection is so poor a consistent package cannot be downloaded.

Install Not Completed with mssql-conf

This is perhaps the most common problem support has seen, and I've seen this myself with some customers I talk to. We might have made the installation with package managers look so easy; it could be that many people don't see the message that they must run mssql-conf to complete the installation.

If you use a package manger like yum to install mssql-server but don't complete the installation with the command:

```
sudo /opt/mssql/bin/mssql-conf setup
```

and then try to connect to SQL Server with a tool like sqlcmd, you will get a failure like in Figure 2-14.

```
[thewandog@bwsql2017rhel ~]$ sqlcmd -Usa
Password:
Sqlcmd: Error: Microsoft ODBC Driver 13 for SQL Server : Login timeout expired.
Sqlcmd: Error: Microsoft ODBC Driver 13 for SQL Server : TCP Provider: Error code 0x2749.
Sqlcmd: Error: Microsoft ODBC Driver 13 for SQL Server : A network-related or instance-specific error has occurred
while establishing a connection to SQL Server. Server is not found or not accessible. Check if instance name is cor
rect and if SQL Server is configured to allow remote connections. For more information see SQL Server Books Online.
.
[thewandog@bwsql2017rhel ~]$ ▊
```

Figure 2-14. *A failed connection due to SQL Server installation not complete*

One of the clues to this problem can be seen by looking at the status of the mssql-server service with the command

```
sudo systemctl status mssql-server.
```

Figure 2-15 shows the service is enabled but not running.

```
[thewandog@bwsql2017rhel ~]$ sudo systemctl status mssql-server
● mssql-server.service - Microsoft SQL Server Database Engine
   Loaded: loaded (/usr/lib/systemd/system/mssql-server.service; enabled; vendor preset: disabled)
   Active: inactive (dead)
     Docs: https://docs.microsoft.com/en-us/sql/linux

Mar 03 03:41:22 bwsql2017rhel systemd[1]: Cannot add dependency job for unit mssql-server.service, ignoring...ound.
Hint: Some lines were ellipsized, use -l to show in full.
[thewandog@bwsql2017rhel ~]$ █
```

Figure 2-15. *The mssql-service before a completed mssql-conf setup*

The Yum Lock

Another problem you may see can happen with other package managers. Basically, we have seen an installation failure occur when more than one installation of mssql-server was attempted at the same time. We call this a "yum lock" problem. Figure 2-16 shows an example of what you will see when this occurs.

```
[thewandog@bwsql2017rhel ~]$ sudo yum install -y mssql-server
[sudo] password for thewandog:
Loaded plugins: product-id, search-disabled-repos, subscription-manager
Existing lock /var/run/yum.pid: another copy is running as pid 2023.
Another app is currently holding the yum lock; waiting for it to exit...
  The other application is: yum
    Memory : 104 M RSS (536 MB VSZ)
    Started: Thu Mar  1 20:56:41 2018 - 00:18 ago
    State  : Sleeping, pid: 2023
Another app is currently holding the yum lock; waiting for it to exit...
  The other application is: yum
    Memory : 104 M RSS (536 MB VSZ)
    Started: Thu Mar  1 20:56:41 2018 - 00:20 ago
    State  : Sleeping, pid: 2023
Another app is currently holding the yum lock; waiting for it to exit...
  The other application is: yum
    Memory : 104 M RSS (536 MB VSZ)
    Started: Thu Mar  1 20:56:41 2018 - 00:22 ago
    State  : Sleeping, pid: 2023
Another app is currently holding the yum lock; waiting for it to exit...
  The other application is: yum
    Memory : 127 M RSS (559 MB VSZ)
    Started: Thu Mar  1 20:56:41 2018 - 00:24 ago
    State  : Sleeping, pid: 2023
Another app is currently holding the yum lock; waiting for it to exit...
```

Figure 2-16. *A failed SQL Server installation when another install is in progress*

Changing Permissions or Ownership of SQL Server Directories

The SQL Server directories for /opt/mssql and /var/opt/mssql have specific permissions and ownership assigned. Do not change these or you may have issues with installation, starting SQL Server, using the product, or properly creating databases.

Debugging Installation

The various package management systems have log files and methods to provide more insights about the installation.

The following commands on RHEL can provide more information about a history of installs:

```
sudo yum history list
sudo yum history info
```

The yum package manager also provides options to dump out more details of the installation process. Here is an example command to dump out details of the mssql-server installation. Some of the details from these options may give you enough information to debug an install problem.

```
sudo yum install mssql-server --errorlevel 10 --debuglevel 10
--rpmverbosity debug --verbose
```

Exploring SQL Server on Linux

As you develop applications, use, and manage SQL Server, I think it could be useful to understand what and where everything is installed. In addition, SQL Server has several files that can aid in troubleshooting and monitoring in the LOG directory, so I will cover more details about this directory and what is contained in it.

What Is Installed

Per normal Linux guidelines as an application, SQL Server installs its binary files in the /opt directory and its "application" files including database files in the /var/opt directory. In SQL Server 2017, you cannot change the location of these directories (but you can change the default location of databases, "log" files, and backups).

/opt/mssql

The **bin** directory contains the main sqlservr binary, the mssql-conf bash script, and a series of shell scripts to support diagnostics for dump files.

The **lib** directory contains these types of files:

- **lib*.so** files, which are shared libraries used by sqlservr

- A directory called **mssql-conf** that contains python scripts called by the main mssql-conf bash shell script

- A series of files that end in a **.sfp** extension. These files are part of the magic of the architecture of SQL Server on Linux. These files are in a binary format and contain binary files loaded by the SQLPAL to run SQLSERVR.EXE, various DLLs, libOS, and other binaries. The sfp files also contain the system databases such as master, model, and msdb. We will discuss system databases in Chapter 3.

/var/opt/mssql

By default, this directory should have the following files and directories:

- The **data** directory contains system database files, user database files, and transaction log files (unless you specify a directory when creating a database or use mssql-conf to change the default directory).

- The **log** directory contains "log files" that include the ERRORLOG files and other files used for diagnostic or troubleshooting purposes.

- The **mssql.conf** file is a text file that stores the latest options when using the mssql-conf script. The mssql-conf script writes options into this file. When SQL Server starts, it reads this file to change configuration options, which is why you often must restart SQL Server for a change with mssql-conf to take effect.

Other Files

Other files installed by SQL Server include the following:

- Our EULA files (all languages) are stored in /usr/share/doc/mssql-server.

- Man pages for sqlservr and mssql-conf are stored in /usr/share/man/man1 directory.

Using Log Files

Immediately after installation, the following types of files will be available in the LOG directory (which by default is /var/opt/mssql/log):

- **errorlog***: This is a text file that has been around as long as SQL Server has been a product. It is called an "errorlog" file but has been expanded to include more than just errors. When SQL Server is started, there is rich information about the configuration and startup progress of SQL Server stored in this file. After that, while the file will contain mostly errors and warnings, it can contain other types of important information. This is one of the fundamental files to collect and analyze when you have issues with SQL Server. By default, when SQL Server is started, it copies the previous ERRORLOG file to ERRORLOG.<n> and creates a new one called ERRORLOG. SQL Server will keep six previous versions of the ERRORLOG before wrapping. I'll be talking about the ERRORLOG file from time to time in this book, but it is important up front that you know what a key file this is for SQL Server. Figure 2-17 shows a typical top of the SQL ERRORLOG file.

```
[thewandog@bwsql2017rhel ~]$ sudo cat /var/opt/mssql/log/errorlog
2018-03-03 08:51:25.09 Server      Microsoft SQL Server 2017 (RTM-CU4) (KB4056498) - 14.0.3022.28 (X64)
        Feb  9 2018 19:39:09
        Copyright (C) 2017 Microsoft Corporation
        Enterprise Edition: Core-based Licensing (64-bit) on Linux (Red Hat Enterprise Linux)
2018-03-03 08:51:25.09 Server      UTC adjustment: -6:00
2018-03-03 08:51:25.09 Server      (c) Microsoft Corporation.
2018-03-03 08:51:25.09 Server      All rights reserved.
2018-03-03 08:51:25.10 Server      Server process ID is 4120.
2018-03-03 08:51:25.10 Server      Logging SQL Server messages in file '/var/opt/mssql/log/errorlog'.
2018-03-03 08:51:25.10 Server      Registry startup parameters:
        -d /var/opt/mssql/data/master.mdf
        -l /var/opt/mssql/data/mastlog.ldf
        -e /var/opt/mssql/log/errorlog
2018-03-03 08:51:25.12 Server      SQL Server detected 1 sockets with 4 cores per socket and 4 logical processors p
er socket, 4 total logical processors; using 4 logical processors based on SQL Server licensing. This is an informa
tional message; no user action is required.
2018-03-03 08:51:25.12 Server      SQL Server is starting at normal priority base (=7). This is an informational me
ssage only. No user action is required.
2018-03-03 08:51:25.12 Server      Detected 6244 MB of RAM. This is an informational message; no user action is req
uired.
2018-03-03 08:51:25.12 Server      Using conventional memory in the memory manager.
2018-03-03 08:51:25.46 Server      Buffer pool extension is already disabled. No action is necessary.
2018-03-03 08:51:25.71 Server      InitializeExternalUserGroupSid failed. Implied authentication will be disabled.
2018-03-03 08:51:25.71 Server      Implied authentication manager initialization failed. Implied authentication wil
l be disabled.
2018-03-03 08:51:25.73 Server      Successfully initialized the TLS configuration. Allowed TLS protocol versions ar
e ['1.0 1.1 1.2']. Allowed TLS ciphers are ['ECDHE-ECDSA-AES128-GCM-SHA256:ECDHE-ECDSA-AES256-GCM-SHA384:ECDHE-RSA-
AES128-GCM-SHA256:ECDHE-RSA-AES256-GCM-SHA384:ECDHE-ECDSA-AES128-SHA256:ECDHE-ECDSA-AES256-SHA384:ECDHE-ECDSA-AES25
6-SHA:ECDHE-ECDSA-AES128-SHA:AES128-GCM-SHA256:AES256-GCM-SHA256:AES256-SHA256:AES256-SHA:AES128-SHA:
!DHE-RSA-AES256-GCM-SHA384:!DHE-RSA-AES128-GCM-SHA256:!DHE-RSA-AES256-SHA:!DHE-RSA-AES128-SHA'].
```

Figure 2-17. *The SQL Server errorlog file*

- **log*.trc**: SQL Server Trace is a legacy tracing system, and by default a trace file is collected that contains certain events such as when objects are created or deleted. I don't recommend you rely on these files, as this functionality may be completely removed in future versions of SQL Server. In fact, many users turn off the feature that generates these files. You can read more about this at `https://docs.microsoft.com//sql/database-engine/configure-windows/default-trace-enabled-server-configuration-option`.

- **system_health*.xel**: These files are called the System Health Event Session files and contain important information about the health of SQL Server. Think of this as a "black box recorder" of the state of SQL Server. These files are generated by a capability called Extended Events, which will be discussed in more length in Chapter 5. You can read more about the System Health Event Session at `https://docs.microsoft.com/sql/relational-databases/extended-events/use-the-system-health-session`.

Post-Install Configuration

Once you have installed SQL Server, there are several choices for configuration for the SQL Server instance. Many of these are related to optimize and provide maximum database performance. I will cover those topics in Chapter 6 in more detail. You will also see in that chapter that some configuration choices are at the database or even query level.

This section is intended to get your familiar with your options and methods to make configuration choices that affect the overall SQL Server instance across all databases. Some of these methods require external tools and some are built into the SQL Server engine through the T-SQL language. If you are installing SQL Server for a production enterprise-grade workload, then please review Chapter 6 to understand our recommendations to maximize performance.

Using mssql-conf

For Windows users, SQL Server provides a graphical application called the SQL Server Configuration Manager. The intent was to provide a method to make configuration choices that could not be implemented or did not make sense to implement through the T-SQL language.

For SQL Server on Linux, we provide comparable capabilities through the mssql-conf bash shell script. You have seen the use of this script to complete the setup process. The script supports other options to configure SQL Server after the initial setup.

If you look at the help for mssql-conf you can see all the arguments it supports for configuration choices.

```
sudo /opt/mssql/bin/mssql-conf --help
```

Figure 2-18 shows these options.

```
[thewandog@bwsqlrhel ~]$ sudo /opt/mssql/bin/mssql-conf --help
usage: mssql-conf [-h] [-n]  ...

positional arguments:

    setup           Initialize and setup Microsoft SQL Server
    set             Set the value of a setting
    unset           Unset the value of a setting
    list            List the supported settings
    traceflag       Enable/disable one or more traceflags
    set-sa-password
                    Set the system administrator (SA) password
    set-collation   Set the collation of system databases
    validate        Validate the configuration file
    set-edition     Set the edition of the SQL Server instance

optional arguments:
  -h, --help        show this help message and exit
  -n, --noprompt    Does not prompt the user and uses environment variables or
                    defaults.
```

Figure 2-18. *mssql-conf options*

The main arguments you will use to make configuration changes are **set**, **unset**, and **traceflag.**

> **set**: Allows you to set the value of a configuration setting. The list
> of possible settings and their values can be found by using the **list**
> argument, or look them up in our documentation at https://
> docs.microsoft.com/sql/linux/sql-server-linux-configure-
> mssql-conf. Many of these settings require a restart of the mssql-
> service. In most cases, when you set an option, you should be
> prompted to perform a restart for the setting to take effect if that is
> required.

For example, here is the method to enable the SQL Server Agent starting with SQL Server 2017 CU4.

```
sudo /opt/mssql/bin/mssql-conf set sqlagent.enabled true
```

Here are a few settings you may want to consider looking at:

filelocation.defaultdatadir: This is the default directory where database files will be stored when you create a database. The standard default is /var/opt/mssql/data. If you change the default directory, you must change the ownership to the mssql group and user.

filelocation.defaultlogdir: This is the default directory where transaction log files will be stored when you create a database. The standard default is /var/opt/mssql/data. If you change the default directory, you must change the ownership to the mssql group and user.

filelocation.errorlogfile: This is the default directory where the ERRORLOG and other "log" files will be stored. The standard default is /var/opt/mssql/log. If you change the default directory, you must change the ownership to the mssql group and user.

network.tcpport: This will become the new TCP port number for SQL Server to listen on. Port 1433 is the default and no other applications generally use this but there could be a conflict, so this gives you an option to change the default. If you change the default TCP port, you will need to specify the port when connecting to SQL Server. For example, if you change the TCP port to 1401, you would need to connect to SQL Server on the local Linux server with a tool like sqlcmd as follows:

```
sqlcmd -Usa -S localhost,1401
```

Note   As with port 1433, be sure to configure firewalld to open up the new port used for SQL Server.

---

filelocation.defaultbackupdir: This is the default directory where SQL Server backups will be stored when you use the T-SQL BACKUP command. The standard default is /var/opt/mssql. If you change the default directory for backups, you must change the ownership to the mssql group and user.

telemetry.customerfeedback: By default, SQL Server collects information about the configuration and performance of SQL Server. This helps Microsoft improve the development of current and future releases of SQL Server. No customer data is collected as part of this feedback. On paid editions of SQL Server, you can disable this information collection using this mssql-conf setting. For a complete and transparent discussion of customer feedback, please look at this documentation: `https://docs.microsoft.com/sql/linux/sql-server-linux-customer-feedback`.

I recommend you take time to review all the possible configuration settings to see if others make sense for your use of SQL Server.

unset: Allows you to revert a change you made with the set option to the default value of the setting. You could also use the set argument to set a value back to its default, but you may not remember those default settings.

For example, based on the previous example to enable the SQL Server Agent, you could use the set argument to set the sqlagent.enabled value to false or you could execute `sudo /opt/mssql/bin/mssql-conf unset sqlagent.enabled`.

Note   Many of the unset options require an mssql-server service restart to take effect, but you are not prompted to do this as of SQL Server 2017 CU4. The rule of thumb is to restart SQL Server if the equivalent set option requires a restart.

---

traceflag: Trace flags are "knobs" that affect the behavior of SQL Server at many different levels. You will learn throughout this book various trace flags that can be used in all types of scenarios. Some trace flags need to be enabled during SQL Server startup or enabled so they will be applied globally across all SQL Server sessions. Use the mssql-conf traceflag argument for these scenarios. For example, if you want to enable diagnostic information about deadlocks to be captured in the SQL Server ERRORLOG, you could turn on traceflag 1222 like this:

```
sudo /opt/mssql/bin/mssql-conf traceflag 1222 on
```

For a complete list of possible SQL Server trace flags, see this documentation: `https://docs.microsoft.com/sql/t-sql/database-console-commands/dbcc-traceon-trace-flags-transact-sql`.

Here is a brief description of the other arguments:

> **list**: Dump out the possible options that are valid to use with the set or unset arguments.

> **set-sa-password**: Use this to reset the sa password.

> **set-collation**: Use this to change the default collation of databases in SQL Server. See the full set of instructions on how to use this option in our documentation at `https://docs.microsoft.com/sql/linux/sql-server-linux-configure-mssql-conf#collation`.

> **set-edition**: Use this option to change the edition of SQL Server you specified during installation. You will be prompted just as you were to pick the edition when using the setup option of mssql-conf.

> **validate**: Whenever you make configuration changes with mssql-conf using any of these options, the values are stored in a file called /var/opt/mssql/mssql.conf. This is a text file read by SQL Server at startup to use various options other than defaults. The full format of this file is described in our documentation at `https://docs.microsoft.com/sql/linux/sql-server-linux-configure-mssql-conf?#mssql-conf-format`. You can manually change this file instead of using the mssql-conf script, although we recommend you use the script to avoid any mistakes. The validate argument of mssql-conf can be used to ensure the file has the correct format and entries.

Note   One possible use of the mssql.conf file is with Docker containers, provided you store this on a persisted volume.

SQL Server Instance Configuration

Let's spend a few moments to see what other options there are for SQL Server Instance configuration supported by the SQL Server engine. This includes the T-SQL system procedure sp_configure and the T-SQL statement ALTER SERVER CONFIGURATION. These statements are used to control configuration options that apply to the entire SQL Server instance.

sp_configure

sp_configure is a T-SQL system command called a *system stored procedure* that can be used to configure various options within the SQL Server engine. These options are persisted within the system database called master. By default, there are only about 20 or so configuration options to choose from. There are some advanced options that can only be visible if you first set the option "show advanced options" to 1.

Any user can run this to see possible values, but by default only system administrators such as the sa login in SQL Server can change options, given their possible impact to the entire server. I will discuss various configuration options for you to consider throughout the remaining chapters of this book.

All configuration changes require an execution of the T-SQL RECONFIGURE command to confirm the changes. Some of them require a restart of the SQL Server service even after executing RECONFIGURE.

To see the complete list and syntax to run this T-SQL command, see this page in our documentation `https://docs.microsoft.com/sql/relational-databases/system-stored-procedures/sp-configure-transact-sql`.

ALTER SERVER CONFIGURATION

The sp_configure procedure is good for single-value configuration options that require a simple number. Some server-wide configuration options may need more complex values or options. Therefore, the ALTER SERVER CONFIGURATION T-SQL command was created for this purpose.

An example is PROCESS AFFINITY, which can be used to control what CPUs or NUMA nodes SQL Server will schedule its threads to execute on.

For example, to schedule SQL Server threads only on NUMA node 0 on a multinode system, you would run this T-SQL command:

```
ALTER SERVER CONFIGURATION SET PROCESS AFFINITY NUMANODE=0
```

As with sp_configure options, I will discuss several of these throughout the remaining chapters of the book. Like sp_configure, most of these settings require a system administrator to make changes. For a complete list of the options, syntax, and permissions, see our documentation page https://docs.microsoft.com/sql/t-sql/statements/alter-server-configuration-transact-sql.

Windows Configuration Options on Linux

When you install SQL Server on Windows, there are a few configuration options and choices that are typically used. Following is a summary of these options and how they apply to SQL Server on Linux.

Locked Pages

Windows supports a concept where applications can avoid a working set trim of memory if they use the Address Windowing Extensions (AWE) APIs. This is enabled on SQL Server by default if you use the Enterprise or Standard edition and the SQL Server Service account has the Lock Pages in Memory privilege.

Linux does not have the concept of AWE or locked pages, so this option doesn't apply to SQL Server on Linux. Rather, Linux has concepts to page its processes or even terminate the process based on its memory consumption. SQL Server on Linux has options to prevent these types of scenarios. I will address this topic in Chapter 6.

Instant File Initialization

To speed up the initialization of a file for large sizes, Windows provides an API called SetFileValidData(). SQL Server uses this API to create or alter database files if the Perform Volume Maintenance Tasks privilege is assigned to the SQL Server service account.

Linux performs this type of initialization by default, since SQL Server in the Host Extension layer uses the fallocate() Linux API. Therefore, there is no need to configure this option for SQL Server on Linux.

Large Pages

SQL Server on Windows can use a concept called Large Pages when you enable trace flag 834. SQL Server on Linux relies on a concept called Transparent Huge Pages (THP) for memory allocation. While trace flag 834 still exists on SQL Server on Linux, we only recommend using this on high-end systems in specific scenarios. This is a trace flag whose guidance falls under the Microsoft Support article: `https://support.microsoft.com/help/920093/tuning-options-for-sql-server-when-running-in-high-performance-workloa`.

Windows Server Failover Clustering

SQL Server on Windows relies on Windows Server Failover Clustering (WSFC) for Always On Failover Cluster Instance and Always On Availability Groups for High Availability. WSFC of course does not exist on Linux and therefore SQL Server uses other software, Pacemaker, to partner together to provide high-availability options. I will discuss this further in Chapter 8. If you want to jump right into the details of how this works, start with this documentation page: `https://docs.microsoft.com/sql/linux/sql-server-linux-shared-disk-cluster-concepts`.

Updates and Uninstall

SQL Server on Linux provides simple methods to update to later versions of SQL Server, based on CUs or new GDR versions. In addition, a simple method exists to uninstall and remove SQL Server.

Updating SQL Server

Based on your configured repository for SQL Server as described previously in this chapter, using the built-in update functionality of the package manager of your distribution pulls down the latest version in that repository and applies the update to the SQL Server binaries. All database files are unaffected.

If you run the following command:

```
sudo yum update mssql-server
```

the latest updated build based on your configured repository will be downloaded and installed. If you have already installed the latest update, you will get a message that says, "No packages marked for update."

I recommend you keep up to date with Microsoft builds from the CU repository. The frequency of these updates is typically monthly (although this will become less frequent as a major release ages). Microsoft is continually improving SQL Server on Linux through fixes and updates in CUs.

Let's look at a few scenarios of how to use an update and what behavior you can expect.

If you have installed the original GA version of SQL Server 2017 at the time we released the product and then used the update process when SQL Server 2017 2017 CU4 was available, Figure 2-19 shows what you can expect.

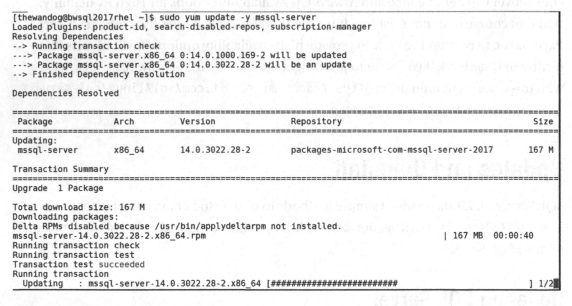

```
[thewandog@bwsql2017rhel ~]$ sudo yum update -y mssql-server
Loaded plugins: product-id, search-disabled-repos, subscription-manager
Resolving Dependencies
--> Running transaction check
---> Package mssql-server.x86_64 0:14.0.1000.169-2 will be updated
---> Package mssql-server.x86_64 0:14.0.3022.28-2 will be an update
--> Finished Dependency Resolution

Dependencies Resolved

================================================================================
 Package          Arch        Version             Repository                      Size
================================================================================
Updating:
 mssql-server     x86_64      14.0.3022.28-2      packages-microsoft-com-mssql-server-2017   167 M

Transaction Summary
================================================================================
Upgrade  1 Package

Total download size: 167 M
Downloading packages:
Delta RPMs disabled because /usr/bin/applydeltarpm not installed.
mssql-server-14.0.3022.28-2.x86_64.rpm                          | 167 MB   00:00:40
Running transaction check
Running transaction test
Transaction test succeeded
Running transaction
  Updating   : mssql-server-14.0.3022.28-2.x86_64 [#######################     ] 1/2
```

Figure 2-19. Updating SQL Server

When the update completes, you will be prompted to restart SQL Server using this command to complete the update:

```
sudo systemctl restart mssql-server
```

What if you would like to update SQL Server to a specific version? While Microsoft believes you should apply the latest updates, it is possible to update to a specific version if that version is later than the version you are currently running. This technique also is a method for you to update offline, as using the package manager update option will require an Internet connection.

So, if you were running the SQL Server 2017 GA version and wanted to update to SQL Server 2017 CU3 when CU4 is the latest update, you would follow this process:

- Download the SQL Server 2017 CU3 package (See this documentation page for a location of packages: `https://docs.microsoft.com/sql/linux/sql-server-linux-release-notes.`)

- Copy this package to your Linux server.

- Use the offline install method to install the SQL Server 2017 CU3 package.

What you cannot do is use this method to update SQL Server to a lower version than the version you are currently running. See the next section to learn how to update to a lower version of SQL Server.

Rolling Back to a Previous Update

While we believe you should not have issues using the latest updates for SQL Server, there may be a situation that comes up where you need to revert to a previous update of SQL Server. The process to roll back to a previous update is:

1. Find the package of the version you want to rollback in the SQL Server on Linux Release Notes at `https://docs.microsoft.com/sql/linux/sql-server-linux-release-notes`.

2. Copy the package to your Linux Server.

3. Use the following command to rollback:

   `sudo yum downgrade mssql-server-<version_number>.x86_64`

The problem with this process of using the downgrade command is that it requires an Internet connection as it downloads the package you specify.

So, if you need to do a rollback to a previous version offline, you would need to:

- Uninstall the current version using a command like sudo yum remove (Do not remove the /var/opt/mssql directory to retain all databases).

- Copy the package of the version you want to install.

- Perform an offline install of that new package.

Removing SQL Server

While we never want you to feel the need to uninstall SQL Server, you will likely find yourself removing SQL Server especially if you perform a lot of demonstrations, are performing special tests, or need to roll back to a previous version offline.

The basic syntax to remove SQL Server on RHEL is:

```
sudo yum remove -y mssql-server
```

Figure 2-20 shows the expected behavior when you uninstall SQL Server.

```
---> Package mssql-server.x86_64 0:14.0.3022.28-2 will be erased
--> Finished Dependency Resolution

Dependencies Resolved

================================================================================
 Package          Arch         Version          Repository                    Size
================================================================================
Removing:
 mssql-server     x86_64       14.0.3022.28-2   @packages-microsoft-com-mssql-server-2017   885 M

Transaction Summary
================================================================================
Remove  1 Package

Installed size: 885 M
Downloading packages:
Running transaction check
Running transaction test
Transaction test succeeded
Running transaction
  Erasing    : mssql-server-14.0.3022.28-2.x86_64                          1/1
  Verifying  : mssql-server-14.0.3022.28-2.x86_64                          1/1

Removed:
  mssql-server.x86_64 0:14.0.3022.28-2

Complete!
[thewandog@bwsql2017rhel ~]$ █
```

Figure 2-20. *Removing SQL Server*

At this point you have two choices:

1. You can completely remove SQL Server by removing the /var/opt/mssql directory, which will delete all system databases and any user databases stored in that directory. Run the following command to do this:

   ```
   sudo rm -rf /var/opt/mssql
   ```

2. Leave /var/opt/mssql intact. Any future installation would then just install the SQL Server binaries, not require mssql-conf, and leave all system databases intact.

The second option could be useful should you feel a need to cleanly install the SQL Server binaries because of some unexpected problem but keep all your data intact.

Summary

At this point, you should have SQL Server installed, understand where to find all the files that were installed, understand the methods and options to configure SQL Server, and know how to update SQL Server to the latest builds.

Let's go build a database and application that uses SQL Server on Linux!

CHAPTER 3

Building a Database and T-SQL Fundamentals

Now that you have installed SQL Server, the next step in your journey with SQL Server on Linux is to create a database. Then you will want to create tables, insert some data, and learn the fundamentals of the T-SQL language. Although this chapter covers basic T-SQL functionality, I've written the chapter from the perspective of a developer. For those of you who are experts with SQL Server and T-SQL, this chapter may seem like a review. But for those new to SQL Server, this chapter is essential, so you can build a foundation of knowledge about the T-SQL language and basic capabilities of SQL Server. To demonstrate SQL Server features in this chapter, I've chosen Visual Studio Code as the development tool to execute queries. Armed with this knowledge, you will be able to move to the next chapter to build an application, and learn more advanced T-SQL capabilities and new features of SQL Server 2017.

The T-SQL examples in this chapter can be found in the sample scripts provided with the book and are intended to be run in the sequence as you follow the chapter. I will use the sample scripts provided in this chapter in the next chapter to show you how to build an application and learn more advanced T-SQL language capabilities.

Setting Up Your Environment

In Chapter 2, I introduced you to the WideWorldImporters sample database created by Microsoft to help you explore the features of SQL Server. This sample database is provided in the form of a backup you can restore (which I showed you in Chapter 2 as a method to help verify your SQL Server installation). It is also available as a project, so you can execute all the commands to build the database from scratch. You can find the

© Bob Ward 2018
B. Ward, *Pro SQL Server on Linux*, https://doi.org/10.1007/978-1-4842-4128-8_3

documentation for this sample database at `https://docs.microsoft.com/sql/sample/world-wide-importers/wide-world-importers-documentation`. The source code for this sample database can be found on this GitHub repo: `https://github.com/Microsoft/sql-server-samples/tree/master/samples/databases/wide-world-importers`.

For the next two chapters, instead of restoring the backup, I will use a subset of the WideWorldImporters database and objects to create a database and tables from scratch. I have provided all the example scripts you need to use this subset of the WideWorldImporters database. Using this sample as a foundation allows me to show you the fundamentals of the T-SQL language, but also later in the book to expand your knowledge of other SQL Server features and the T-SQL language.

For all the examples in this chapter, I've chosen to use the Visual Studio Code development tool because it works on Windows, macOS, and Linux. Your first step in preparing for this chapter is to install Visual Studio Code from `https://code.visualstudio.com`. The examples in this chapter will use the Windows version of Visual Studio Code. However, all the examples will work on your preferred development platform, since Visual Studio code also runs no macOS and Linux.

After installing Visual Studio Code for Windows, I installed the **mssql** extension for Visual Studio Code. This extension provides rich features to assist when developing and executing T-SQL scripts in Visual Studio Code.

Tip   You might find it helpful after this chapter to go through the tutorial of using the mssql extension for Visual Studio code as documented at `https://docs.microsoft.com/sql/linux/sql-server-linux-develop-use-vscode`.

Figure 3-1 shows a search for the mssql extension to install it on Visual Studio Code. Notice the highlighted icon in the left-hand bar (the fifth icon down from the top), which is used to find and install extensions.

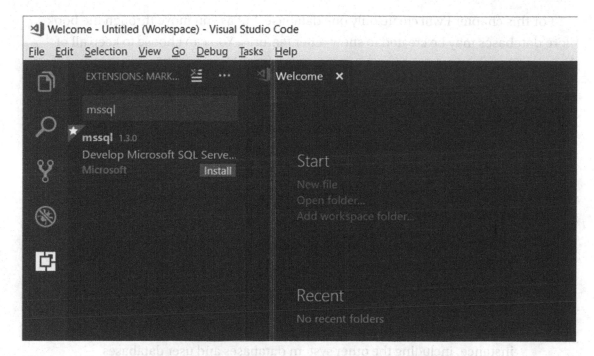

Figure 3-1. Installing the mssql extension in Visual Studio Code

When you first install Visual Studio Code, you have the choice of opening an existing folder for scripts you have created. So, create a new folder on you machine. On my Windows laptop I called this **c:\wwi**. Then copy all the example scripts for Chapter 3 into this folder. Now in Visual Studio Code, click on Open Folder. If you have been using Visual Studio Code, you already may have a workspace or other open folders. You can open this new local folder you created into your workspace, or just use the File Menu to open the folder directly to replace in the explorer area existing folders you may have opened. You should now be ready to create a database, create tables, and test out some fundamental T-SQL queries.

Creating a Database

SQL Server can host many databases for a single SQL Server installation (called an *instance*). SQL Server on Windows allows multiple instances per computer For SQL Server on Linux, there is only one instance allowed on a single Linux server (if you want to install more than one SQL Server instance on Linux, you need to use Docker containers. I will discuss in Chapter 11).

For this chapter I will create only one database, but as you move through the book more databases may be created to show other features. You can choose to keep all of these on the same SQL Server on Linux instance or put them on different ones.

System Databases

Before I show you how to create a database, I think it is important for you to know the details around what databases come with an SQL Server installation called *system databases*. The following list shows databases that come out of the box with a fresh install:

> **master**: By its name, this system database is the "root" of all databases and must exist for SQL Server to start. Master contains all types of SQL Server instance data that apply across all databases. One of the most important sets of data stored in master is information about all the other databases created for the instance, including the other system databases and user databases you create.

At any point in time, to see a list of all databases on an SQL Server instance, run this T-SQL query. You can find this query in the sample script **databases.sql**:

```
SELECT * FROM sys.databases
GO
```

Note   The keyword GO here is not a T-SQL statement. It is a special keyword recognized by tools to delimit a *batch*. A batch is a sequence of T-SQL statements that are sent to the server together from a client, but the server will execute each statement one at a time. Many users just execute one T-SQL statement in a batch.

You can run this statement from any database context because it uses the **sys** schema and a view called databases. I'll explain database context, schemas, and views as you move through the next two chapters. I'll talk more about system supplied views (also known as catalog views) and tables in Chapter 5.

model: The model system database is a *template*. When a user database is created, the contents of the model database are used to build the new user database. In many cases users leave this empty, as it was installed so your new user database would only contain system tables and objects. An example of this is a situation where you would like to create a standard set of user objects across any new user database that is created; you could place them into the model database.

tempdb: This system database is a *shared* database for all users of the SQL Server instance. It is shared because temporary objects that are created with a special syntax are stored here no matter what database context is used. In addition, other internal objects are placed in tempdb based on various conditions of query execution. In the next chapter, I'll talk about creating temporary objects (and mention what types of internal objects may appear in the tempdb database). In addition, the subject of the tempdb database will be discussed in later chapters, as it can be a significant factor in performance and managing the SQL Server instance. You can theoretically create user objects in this system database, but it is not recommended. That is because tempdb is recreated each time SQL Server starts (using the model database as a template).

msdb: This system database is used by SQL Server Agent for scheduling alerts and jobs and by other features such as SQL Server Management Studio, Service Broker, and Database Mail. Think of this as an application database used by SQL Server features. I do not recommend you put any user tables into this system database.

Resource: This is not the actual name of the database, but it is called the *Resource* database. This is a *hidden* system database that is read-only. SQL Server stores system objects (not data) in this database, such as system stored procedures, views, etc. When you query **sys.databases**, SQL Server understands how to get the databases view definition for the sys schema from the Resource database.

For a more detailed look at system databases, check out our documentation at: https://docs.microsoft.com/sql/relational-databases/databases/system-databases.

Creating a Login and User

The **sa** login is provided with SQL Server as the "root" account for complete control. Just like the root account in Linux, it is typically not a good practice to use the sa login for all your interaction with SQL Server.

So, I will create a new login called **sqllinux**, which I will use as the login to create the database and all objects for the rest of the chapter. But I first must connect to SQL Server as the sa login to create the sqllinux login. To do this with Visual Studio Code, I need to create a *connection profile* for the sa login.

If I hit the F1 key (or use the View/Command Palette from the menu in Visual Studio Code), I am presented with choices from the mssql extension for various tasks. If I choose the option called **MS SQL: Connect**, I'm presented with choices to Add a Connection Profile. In my scenario, I picked the name of my SQL Server on Linux (it could be an <IP address>,1433), used the system administrator login sa, put in the password for sa, but left the database name blank so when I connect I'll be put in the database context of master. I saved the name of the profile, so I can reuse it another time. If you go through these steps, Visual Studio code will also connect to the specified SQL Server. You can see the connection information in the bottom right-hand corner of the tool. Figure 3-2 shows the example on my SQL Server. The MSSQL means the editor is in MSSQL mode, which means the editor will assist me with various T-SQL commands and tasks.

Figure 3-2. *Visual Studio code editor in MSSQL mode and connected to SQL Server on Linux*

Use the sa login to create a login by using the following T-SQL statements as found in the example script **createlogin.sql**. I also add the sqllinux login to the dbcreator role so the sqllinux login has permissions to create databases. Feel free to change the password to one of your choice.

Tip   Unlike other SQL Server tools, Visual Studio Code requires you to create a file to run T-SQL statements.

```
USE master
GO
IF EXISTS (select * from sys.server_principals where name = 'sqllinux')
    DROP LOGIN [sqllinux]
GO
CREATE LOGIN [sqllinux] WITH PASSWORD=N'Sql2017isfast', DEFAULT_
DATABASE=[master]
GO
EXEC sys.sp_addsrvrolemember 'sqllinux', 'dbcreator'
GO
```

When I use the sqllinux login to create the database, it will automatically be mapped to a user in the database known as **dbo** (database owner).

To execute the remaining examples in this chapter, I need to create a new connection profile in Visual Studio code with the sqllinux login I just created. And now when I execute any example script, I use the connection profile for the sqllinux login.

Tip   I should stop at this point and give you a tip on connecting to your SQL Server on Linux. My SQL Server on Linux is running RHEL in a virtual machine on my laptop using Hyper-V for Windows 10. Using Hyper-V, I configured an Internal Network adapter, so I could bind a static IP address to that adapter in RHEL. Then on Windows 10, I edited the /windows/system32/drivers/etc/hosts file to put in the static IP address and the name bwsql2017rhel. Now from outside of the VM on my laptop, I can use bwsql2017rhel as a server name instead of having to put in an IP address and port 1433 to connect to my SQL Server on Linux. You may be using DNS or other methods to expose a logical name to your Linux Server. This technique allows me to connect to my Linux Server on my laptop regardless of the state of my wifi or ethernet adapter.

Creating a User Database

Creating your own database can be as easy as running the T-SQL statements as found in the sample script **ilovethedallascowboys.sql**:

```
USE master
GO
CREATE DATABASE ilovethedallascowboys
GO
```

(Yes, I'm a huge sports fan, and being from the Dallas/Ft. Worth area of Texas I'm a big Dallas Cowboys fan. Hopefully, other NFL fans will keep reading the rest of the book<g>).

The T-SQL syntax reference for **CREATE DATABASE** has so many options it will make your head spin. The most important choices when creating a database are file locations, number of files, and size.

As I stated in the previous section, the model database is a template, so when you run **CREATE DATABASE** without any options, SQL Server will use the definition and size of model to create the database. The only exceptions to this rule are the default locations of database and transaction log files, which I discussed in Chapter 2, can be set via the mssql-conf script. For SQL Server on Linux, the default location of these files will be stored in the /var/opt/mssql/data directory.

If you want to make a change to the definition of a database, SQL Server also provides an **ALTER DATABASE** T-SQL command (this is often used after creating a database to set various *database options*, which will be used in other parts of this book).

Let's look at how to use the mssql extension in Visual Studio Code to create the database for the WideWorldImporters sample. You may have restored the WideWorldImporters full backup in a previous chapter. If you have done this already, execute the **cleanup.sql** sample script using the sa login.

Note   Chapter 5 covers the tools for SQL Server, which include other options to create databases and manage SQL Server. I'm using Visual Studio Code in this chapter to show you as a developer how to use this tool to create databases, objects, and queries, and eventually an application in the next chapter.

I could just click on the highlighted icon to create a new file and call it createdb.sql. Figure 3-3 shows my editor for createdb.sql ready for me to now use the mssql extension to connect to SQL Server on Linux. (The samples don't include createdb.sql, since you will be typing in the statements).

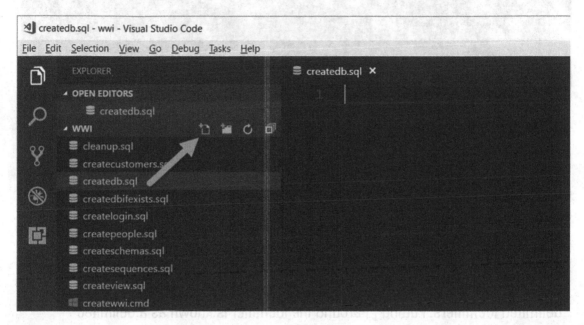

Figure 3-3. *Creating a new T-SQL script with the mssql extension in Visual Studio code*

I can now use the Visual Studio Code tool as a T-SQL editor to execute statements against SQL Server. In the next chapter, I'll switch the editor to a different language when I create the application.

Since I'm using the mssql extension in Visual Studio Code, I get a feature called Intellisense. The editor in Visual Studio Code will help guide me on the syntax of T-SQL statements and objects. Figure 3-4 shows an example of intellisense helping complete the syntax for **CREATE DATABASE:**

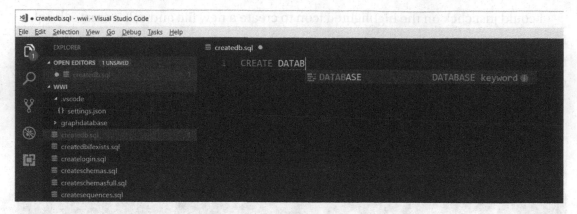

Figure 3-4. *Intellisense with the mssql extension*

Finish in the editor by typing in these T-SQL statements:

```
CREATE DATABASE [WideWorldImporters]
GO
```

Note   In this T-SQL statement, WideWorldImporters is known as an *identifier*. Identifiers are names that are not T-SQL statements. T-SQL allows regular and delimited identifiers. Putting [ ] around the identifier is known as a delimited identifier. You will find many different opinions about using regular vs. delimited identifiers in the SQL Server community. Many of the examples with the WideWorldImporters sample database use delimited identifiers, so I will use those in my sample scripts.

To execute this T-SQL batch, I can use the mssql extension by hitting F1 and selecting the **MS SQL: Execute Query** or use the shortcut keys <Ctrl>+<Shift>+<E>. Be sure to select the connection profile for sqllinux when executing the sample scripts in this chapter unless noted otherwise.

When I execute any query, Visual Studio Code will bring up another vertical pane in the editor to show the results. If any errors occur, they will also show in this pane. The message "Commands completed successfully" means the database was created. Figure 3-5 shows an example after creating the database.

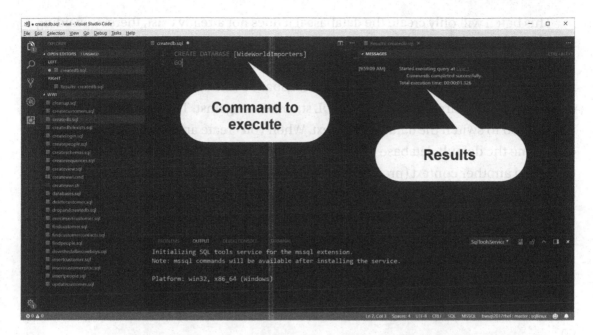

Figure 3-5. *Results of successful creation of a database using Visual Studio Code*

A better method to create this database is to use a set of T-SQL statements that looks like the following from the sample script **createdbifexists.sql**:

```
USE master
GO
IF NOT EXISTS (
    SELECT name
    FROM sys.databases
    WHERE name = N'WideWorldImporters'
)
CREATE DATABASE [WideWorldImporters]
GO
```

Tip   There is no requirement that T-SQL reserved words for the language be in upper case. However, it is a good practice to do this because it allows you and other readers of your scripts to quickly recognize what is T-SQL keyword and what is an identifier.

This batch will only create the database if it does not already exist, thereby avoiding an error if it does exist.

Notice also in the preceding code there is another batch with the statement **USE master**. I mentioned earlier the concept of database context, which means what database you are currently running T-SQL statements against. The **USE** T-SQL keyword is a method to switch the database context. When you create an SQL Server login, you can define the default database context for the login, and then use the USE keyword to change to another context (provided the login has permission in that database). In this example, changing to the master context is not actually required, but it is good practice to be in the context of master when you are creating or dropping databases.

Another option for creating a database if you plan to "get a clean slate" is to first drop the database and recreate it. Execute the following T-SQL statements as seen in the sample script **dropandcreatedb.sql**:

```
DROP DATABASE IF EXISTS [WideWorldImporters]
GO
CREATE DATABASE [WideWorldImporters]
GO
```

What do you get when you create a database in SQL Server on Linux? As I mentioned, SQL Server uses the model database as a template to create any new database. And since no options, file locations, or sizes were specified, the above command will create the WideWorldImporters database on SQL Server on Linux with two files in the /var/opt/mssql/data directory, each 8Mb in size:

> **WideWorldImporters.mdf**: This is the database file. A common convention, although not required, is to name the primary database file with a .mdf file extension. This file contains all the system tables used to store metadata about the database. The file is a collection of 8kb pages that will be used to store data about system tables, pages of data for user tables and indexes, and a series of pages for internal use by SQL Server to track file and allocation metadata. You will find out in later chapters in the book how to create multiple database files for a database.

WideWorldImporters_log.ldf: This is called the transaction log file (commonly used with a .ldf file extension). The transaction log is used to record changes to user and system data. In other database systems this is called a *journal*. Stored in a series of log blocks, the transaction log is used to ensure consistency and recovery of the database.

Tip   Linux is case sensitive for filenames. SQL Server will create file names, if you don't specify the file name, using the database name exactly specified by case. In Linux, navigating and finding these filenames is case sensitive.

Another thing you will love about SQL Server databases is that they are contained and portable. You will be able to back up a database and restore it to another SQL Server of the same major release or higher. And you can do this across Linux and Windows computers, since SQL Server is the same core database engine on both platforms. I'll cover more aspects to moving databases in Chapter 9.

If you want to first spend time understanding all the options when you create a database, visit the T-SQL reference documentation for the **CREATE DATABASE** command:

```
https://docs.microsoft.com/sql/t-sql/statements/create-database-sql-server-
transact-sql.
```

You can read more details about the **ALTER DATABASE** command and how to make changes to database options or metadata from this documentation page:

```
https://docs.microsoft.com/sql/t-sql/statements/alter-database-transact-sql.
```

Creating Tables

Creating a database provides the "shell" to contain your data. Within this shell are tables to store user data and indexes to help speed up access to the data or enforce integrity checks. Both tables and indexes require storage in the database in the form of pages, which are 8KB in size. These 8KB pages are comprised of rows and internal structures to physically describe the rows (and a page header on each page).

The logical format of rows in the pages for tables is defined by the definition of the table in terms of columns and types. This is also known as the *schema* of a table. That term can get somewhat confusing because there is also an object called a schema in SQL Server. A schema object is a namespace to uniquely define a collection of objects in a database, which can be tables and other objects such as indexes and stored procedures. Schemas provide a convenient method to decouple the ownership of objects by allowing permissions to be set on a schema that applies to all objects in the schema.

The options to create a table in SQL Server have grown over the years to include rich capabilities. I will start simple in this chapter. I will use two tables in the WideWorldImporters database sample in this chapter. I will show you how to create schemas, objects called sequences, and tables with objects called constraints. Later in the chapter, I'll show you to create other objects such as stored procedures and views. Then in the next chapter, I will take these sample definitions and show you how to use more advanced T-SQL capabilities.

Creating Schemas

In the WideWorldImporters database there are several schemas and several tables within each schema. Two tables that can be used to show fundamental capabilities of SQL Server are the [Application].[People] and the [Sales].[Customers] tables. The Application schema is used to store *reference* data. This is data that is typically infrequently modified but referenced by other tables that are more frequently modified. This is in line with normalized table designs. In this case, the People table is used to store information about a person, while other tables will reference these people in several ways. The Customers table contains information in columns that reference people who are customers for the WideWorldImporters company, and is part of the Sales schema.

In addition, in the next section I will show you how to build an object called a sequence, so I will create a schema for those objects as well.

The syntax to create schemas can be found in the sample script **createschemas.sql.** Execute this script or the following T-SQL statements to create all schemas:

```
USE [WideWorldImporters]
GO
IF EXISTS (select * from sys.schemas where name = 'Application')
    DROP SCHEMA [Application]
```

```
GO
CREATE SCHEMA [Application]
GO
IF EXISTS (select * from sys.schemas where name = 'Sales')
    DROP SCHEMA [Sales]
GO
CREATE SCHEMA [Sales]
GO
IF EXISTS (select * from sys.schemas where name = 'Sequences')
    DROP SCHEMA [Sequences]
GO
CREATE SCHEMA [Sequences]
GO
```

Creating Sequences

Sequence objects provide a capability to generate unique key values each time they are needed for data in a table. Another similar capability is called an identity column in SQL Server. Sequence objects are created independent of the table and have some desirable caching properties for performance. Sequence objects also are used in other database engines and make them a nice portable feature.

While Sequence objects can be shared across tables, I'll dedicate one sequence object for the two tables I'll be creating in this database (one for the People table and one for the Customers table). Execute the **createsequences.sql** sample script or the following T-SQL code to create the sequence objects:

```
USE [WideWorldImporters]
GO
DROP SEQUENCE IF EXISTS [Sequences].[PersonID]
GO
CREATE SEQUENCE [Sequences].[PersonID]
 AS [int]
 START WITH 1
 INCREMENT BY 1
 MINVALUE 0
 MAXVALUE 2147483647
```

```
 CACHE
GO
DROP SEQUENCE IF EXISTS [Sequences].[CustomerID]
GO
CREATE SEQUENCE [Sequences].[CustomerID]
 AS [int]
 START WITH 0
 INCREMENT BY 1
 MINVALUE 0
 MAXVALUE 2147483647
 CACHE
GO
```

The definition of the SEQUENCE object for [PersonID] says to start with a value of 1 and allow a maximum value to be the maximum number for an **int** datatype. The CACHE keyword helps improve performance of SEQUENCE values. You can read more about SEQUENCE objects in our documentation at `https://docs.microsoft.com/ sql/t-sql/statements/create-sequence-transact-sql`. Notice the min value is 0 but the sequence starts with 1. This allows me to use a value of 0 for the PersonID column without using the SEQUENCE object. The definition of the [CustomerID] starts with a value of 0.

I'll show you in the statements to create the tables how the sequence objects are used to supply unique key values anytime a row is inserted into either of the two tables.

Finally Creating the Tables

Now that I have created the schemas and sequences, I'm ready to create my two tables. Execute the following T-SQL statement or the sample script **createpeople.sql** to create the People table:

```
USE [WideWorldImporters]
GO
-- The table definition for the [Application].[People] table
--
DROP TABLE IF EXISTS [Application].[People]
GO
```

```sql
CREATE TABLE [Application].[People](
     [PersonID] [int] NOT NULL,
     [FullName] [nvarchar](50) NOT NULL,
     [PreferredName] [nvarchar](50) NOT NULL,
--   [SearchName]  AS (concat([PreferredName],N' ',[FullName])) PERSISTED
     NOT NULL,
     [IsPermittedToLogon] [bit] NOT NULL,
     [LogonName] [nvarchar](50) NULL,
     [IsExternalLogonProvider] [bit] NOT NULL,
     [HashedPassword] [varbinary](max) NULL,
     [IsSystemUser] [bit] NOT NULL,
     [IsEmployee] [bit] NOT NULL,
     [IsSalesperson] [bit] NOT NULL,
     [UserPreferences] [nvarchar](max) NULL,
     [PhoneNumber] [nvarchar](20) NULL,
     [FaxNumber] [nvarchar](20) NULL,
     [EmailAddress] [nvarchar](256) NULL,
     [Photo] [varbinary](max) NULL,
     [CustomFields] [nvarchar](max) NULL,
--   [OtherLanguages]  AS (json_query([CustomFields],N'$.OtherLanguages')),
     [LastEditedBy] [int] NOT NULL,
--   [ValidFrom] [datetime2](7) GENERATED ALWAYS AS ROW START NOT NULL,
--   [ValidTo] [datetime2](7) GENERATED ALWAYS AS ROW END NOT NULL
 CONSTRAINT [PK_Application_People] PRIMARY KEY CLUSTERED
(
     [PersonID] ASC
)
)
GO
-- Foreign key for a column within the People table referenced to the
   primary key
--
ALTER TABLE [Application].[People] WITH CHECK ADD CONSTRAINT
[FK_Application_People_Application_People] FOREIGN KEY([LastEditedBy])
REFERENCES [Application].[People] ([PersonID])
```

```
GO
-- The default value for PersonID is a SEQUENCE value
--
ALTER TABLE [Application].[People] ADD CONSTRAINT [DF_Application_People_
PersonID]  DEFAULT (NEXT VALUE FOR [Sequences].[PersonID]) FOR [PersonID]
GO
```

I realize this is a lot to consume, so let's unpack this. Look at the first column definition to understand how to read each column definition.

```
[PersonID] [int] NOT NULL
```

PersonID is the name of the column followed by the data type (integer) and then NULLability of the column (determines if the column can accept a NULL value or an explicit value required). The rest of the columns follow the same pattern with other data types and NULL designations.

For a complete (beware: there are so many options this is a long read) reference to the **CREATE TABLE** T-SQL command, see the documentation at `https://docs.microsoft.com/sql/t-sql/statements/create-table-transact-sql`. Some of these datatypes are interesting, including bit and the nvarchar and varbinary (max) column definitions. For a complete read on SQL Server data types, see our documentation at `https://docs.microsoft.com/sql/t-sql/data-types/data-types-transact-sql`.

There are four column definitions that do not appear very simple and are prefaced by the characters --. These characters are used for comments in any T-SQL code (You can also use /* <T-SQL code> */). I put comments here because in the next chapter I will uncomment these column definitions to show you other features and capabilities.

One of the great features of tools like the mssql extension in Visual Studio Code (or other tools to be discussed in Chapter 5) is to use color coding to distinguish keywords vs identifiers and comments. Figure 3-6 shows an example of the T-SQL command to create the People table in Visual Studio Code using the mssql extension.

```
≡ createpeople.sql ×
    1   USE [WideWorldImporters]
    2   GO
    3   -- The table definition for the [Application].[People] table
    4   --
    5   DROP TABLE IF EXISTS [Application].[People]
    6   GO
    7   CREATE TABLE [Application].[People](
    8       [PersonID] [int] NOT NULL,
    9       [FullName] [nvarchar](50) NOT NULL,
   10       [PreferredName] [nvarchar](50) NOT NULL,
   11   --  [SearchName]  AS (concat([PreferredName],N' ',[FullName]))
   12       [IsPermittedToLogon] [bit] NOT NULL,
   13       [LogonName] [nvarchar](50) NULL,
   14       [IsExternalLogonProvider] [bit] NOT NULL,
   15       [HashedPassword] [varbinary](max) NULL,
   16       [IsSystemUser] [bit] NOT NULL,
   17       [IsEmployee] [bit] NOT NULL,
   18       [IsSalesperson] [bit] NOT NULL,
   19       [UserPreferences] [nvarchar](max) NULL,
   20       [PhoneNumber] [nvarchar](20) NULL,
   21       [FaxNumber] [nvarchar](20) NULL,
   22       [EmailAddress] [nvarchar](256) NULL,
   23       [Photo] [varbinary](max) NULL,
   24       [CustomFields] [nvarchar](max) NULL
PROBLEMS    OUTPUT    DEBUG CONSOLE    TERMINAL
Initializing SQL tools service for the mssql extension.
Note: mssql commands will be available after installing the service.

Platform: win32, x86_64 (Windows)
```

Figure 3-6. *T-SQL syntax color coding with the mssql extension in Visual Studio Code*

Another aspect to this table definition is a concept called *constraints*. SQL Server provides the capability to declare various *integrity* checks when the table is defined (or altered) through a constraint.

For the People table, I can add a primary key to enforce unique values for each row for a specific column(s) through a constraint. A primary key constraint is implemented via an index, which by default is a **clustered index**. A clustered index is implemented by storing the pages for the data for the table at the base level of the index sorted by the columns in the clustered index. In this example, each row must contain a unique PersonID value. We will use the sequence object created earlier to ensure each PersonID value is unique.

In this example, the keyword ASC next to the [PersonID] column in the constraint definition indicates the clustered index will be sorted on the PersonID values in ascending key order.

There is another method to define a primary key in line with the table definition. For the above example, you could have declared the PersonID column as:

```
[PersonID] [int] NOT NULL PRIMARY KEY CLUSTERED
```

Another type of constraint is a *foreign key constraint* to ensure referential integrity for relationships between tables or between columns within the same table. In the preceding example, the LastEditedBy column is the PersonID value of another row in the table. To ensure that any data in the LastEditedBy column is a valid PersonID, you can declare a foreign key constraint by altering the table after it is created (you can also do this when the table is being created). Look at the following statement in the table definition set of statements. (Do not execute this. I'm showing you this, so you can see the details of the constraint.)

```
ALTER TABLE [Application].[People] WITH CHECK ADD CONSTRAINT [FK_
Application_People_Application_People] FOREIGN KEY([LastEditedBy])
REFERENCES [Application].[People] ([PersonID])
```

Unpacking this statement, the constraint ensures values in the LastEditedBy column always reference a row in the People table from the PersonID column. The WITH CHECK option at the beginning causes the statement to validate any existing data in the table for the constraint.

Another type of constraint can be a *default value* for a column if no value is specified when inserting a new row. A default value can be any value declared so that when you insert a row, if a value is not specified, the default one is used. Remember PersonID is a primary key column, which means every value must be unique. The intention of the PersonID is to be a key value that has no logical meaning but references each row for a person. The PersonID will be the way to physically identify each person in the People table without having to use a combination of columns (like FullName+....).

I can now use the sequence object I created in the previous section to create a constraint that will increment to the next SEQUENCE value for each row inserted into the People table for the PersonID column. Using the DEFAULT keyword allows me to insert rows into the People table, and each new PersonID will be populated by default from the SEQUENCE object. The ALTER TABLE statement in the preceding script to create the constraint for the default value looks like this:

```
ALTER TABLE [Application].[People] ADD CONSTRAINT [DF_Application_People_
PersonID]  DEFAULT (NEXT VALUE FOR [Sequences].[PersonID]) FOR [PersonID]
```

The NEXT VALUE FOR keyword is standard T-SQL syntax to indicate that the default value for any PersonID column for a new row will use the next value from the SEQUENCE object (e.g., 1,2,3...).

Here is the definition for the Customers table from the Sales schema. Execute this set of T-SQL statements or use the sample script **createcustomers.sql**:

```
USE [WideWorldImporters]
GO
-- The table definition for the [Sales].[Customer] table
--
DROP TABLE IF EXISTS [Sales].[Customers]
GO
CREATE TABLE [Sales].[Customers](
      [CustomerID] [int] NOT NULL,
      [CustomerName] [nvarchar](100) NOT NULL,
      [BillToCustomerID] [int] NOT NULL,
      [CustomerCategoryID] [int] NOT NULL,
      [BuyingGroupID] [int] NULL,
      [PrimaryContactPersonID] [int] NOT NULL,
      [AlternateContactPersonID] [int] NULL,
      [DeliveryMethodID] [int] NOT NULL,
      [DeliveryCityID] [int] NOT NULL,
      [PostalCityID] [int] NOT NULL,
      [CreditLimit] [decimal](18, 2) NULL,
      [AccountOpenedDate] [date] NOT NULL,
      [StandardDiscountPercentage] [decimal](18, 3) NOT NULL,
      [IsStatementSent] [bit] NOT NULL,
```

```
        [IsOnCreditHold] [bit] NOT NULL,
        [PaymentDays] [int] NOT NULL,
        [PhoneNumber] [nvarchar](20) NOT NULL,
        [FaxNumber] [nvarchar](20) NOT NULL,
        [DeliveryRun] [nvarchar](5) NULL,
        [RunPosition] [nvarchar](5) NULL,
        [WebsiteURL] [nvarchar](256) NOT NULL,
        [DeliveryAddressLine1] [nvarchar](60) NOT NULL,
        [DeliveryAddressLine2] [nvarchar](60) NULL,
        [DeliveryPostalCode] [nvarchar](10) NOT NULL,
        [DeliveryLocation] [geography] NULL,
        [PostalAddressLine1] [nvarchar](60) NOT NULL,
        [PostalAddressLine2] [nvarchar](60) NULL,
        [PostalPostalCode] [nvarchar](10) NOT NULL,
        [LastEditedBy] [int] NOT NULL,
--      [ValidFrom] [datetime2](7) GENERATED ALWAYS AS ROW START NOT NULL,
--      [ValidTo] [datetime2](7) GENERATED ALWAYS AS ROW END NOT NULL
 CONSTRAINT [PK_Sales_Customers] PRIMARY KEY CLUSTERED
(
        [CustomerID] ASC
),
 CONSTRAINT [UQ_Sales_Customers_CustomerName] UNIQUE NONCLUSTERED
(
        [CustomerName] ASC)
)
GO
-- Foreign Key Constraints
--
ALTER TABLE [Sales].[Customers]  WITH CHECK ADD  CONSTRAINT [FK_Sales_
Customers_AlternateContactPersonID_Application_People] FOREIGN KEY([Alterna
teContactPersonID])
REFERENCES [Application].[People] ([PersonID])
GO
ALTER TABLE [Sales].[Customers]  WITH CHECK ADD  CONSTRAINT [FK_Sales_
Customers_Application_People] FOREIGN KEY([LastEditedBy])
```

```
REFERENCES [Application].[People] ([PersonID])
GO
ALTER TABLE [Sales].[Customers]  WITH CHECK ADD  CONSTRAINT [FK_Sales_
Customers_BillToCustomerID_Sales_Customers] FOREIGN KEY([BillToCustomerID])
REFERENCES [Sales].[Customers] ([CustomerID])
GO
ALTER TABLE [Sales].[Customers]  WITH CHECK ADD  CONSTRAINT [FK_
Sales_Customers_PrimaryContactPersonID_Application_People] FOREIGN
KEY([PrimaryContactPersonID])
REFERENCES [Application].[People] ([PersonID])
GO
-- Default Value Constraint
--
ALTER TABLE [Sales].[Customers] ADD  CONSTRAINT [DF_Sales_Customers_
CustomerID]  DEFAULT (NEXT VALUE FOR [Sequences].[CustomerID]) FOR
[CustomerID]
GO
```

This is like the People table, with some comments for columns that I will
uncomment and showcase in the next chapter.

For the Customer table there are similar constraints to add, but with a few
differences:

- I added a UNIQUE constraint for the [CustomerName] column to
  ensure each customer name is unique. But I'll still use the CustomerID
  column, associated with a SEQUENCE, as the PRIMARY KEY.

Note   Indexes are created for the PRIMARY KEY and UNIQUE constraints.
Indexes help ensure the constraint definition is maintained but also can help with
performance to look up values depending on how much data is loaded into these
tables. I will cover more about using indexes for performance in Chapter 6.

- There are several FOREIGN KEY constraints that reference the
  [Application].[People].[PersonID] column.

Note   In the full WideWorldImporters sample, the Customers table has FOREIGN KEY references to other tables in the database, but I've left these out in this chapter to keep this example contained and simple.

Creating the Complete Database

Let's review the entire sequence of creating the schemas, sequence objects, tables, and constraints in this database.

When I usually build out a complete database definition with objects, I create a script to drive the entire execution of all T-SQL scripts. I've provided two example scripts you can use to create everything at once:

- **createwwi.sh** for macOS and Linux users

- **createwwi.cmd** for Windows users.

These scripts assume you have installed the sqlcmd utilities, sqlcmd is in your path, and require two command line parameters: server name and sa password. The sqllinux login is used and created in the createlogin.sql script. The password for that login is in that T-SQL script, so if you change it from what I have provided you will need to also change the shell or cmd script. If you are executing the createwwi.sh script on Linux, don't forget to execute chmod u+x createwwi.sh so you can execute the script.

Note   These scripts assume sqlcmd is in the path. For Windows, it should already be in the path after installation. For Linux, be sure to add this to your path using the following commands from the bash shell if you have not already:

```
echo 'export PATH="$PATH:/opt/mssql-tools/bin"' >>
~/.bash_profile

echo 'export PATH="$PATH:/opt/mssql-tools/bin"' >> ~/.bashrc

source ~/.bashrc
```

On Windows at a Powershell command prompt, the execution of createwwi.cmd looks like this in my environment.

```
.\createwwi bwsql2017rhel Sql2017isfast
```

From my Linux shell, here is an example execution of createwwi.sh run on my Linux server:

```
./createwwi.sh localhost Sql2017isfast
```

These shell and command scripts execute the following T-SQL scripts to create a login, database, and objects in the database:

1. **cleanup.sql**: I added this script, so you could run these scripts over and over. cleanup.sql is required to drop all databases from any previous executions. Even though the WideWorldImporters is dropped in step 3, if you have already created it in the context of the sqllinux login, you will not be allowed to drop and create the login again without dropping the database first.

2. **createlogin.sql**: Create the sqllinux login (while connected as the sa login).

3. **dropandcreatedb.sql**: Create the database. This will now make the sqllinux login the user dbo (database owner) in the WideWorldImporters databases when the context is changed to WideWorldImporters.

4. **createschemas.sql**: Create the schemas for all objects in the database.

5. **createsequences.sql**: Create the sequence objects to be used by the two tables.

6. **createpeople.sql**: Create the People table with constraints.

7. **createcustomers.sql**: Create the Customers table with constraints.

Now everything is ready for you to test out some T-SQL queries to insert data, query data, update and delete rows.

Building and Running Queries

I recommend creating and testing T-SQL queries you want to use for an application through a separate tool, so you can ensure there are no syntax errors and run as expected. It is far easier to debug your T-SQL commands outside of your application then weaved throughout the code. So, in this section of the chapter, I'll show you how to insert, update, delete, and view data using basic T-SQL statements. The example statements and scripts in this section assume you have run all the preceding scripts to create the database and objects. As with the scripts to create the database and objects in this chapter, I executed all the following T-SQL statements and scripts with the sqllinux login.

Inserting and Reading Data

For purposes of this chapter, I will talk about simple insert of data of single rows. You have several options to insert data in *bulk*, and I'll talk about those in other chapters of the book.

The basic T-SQL statement to insert data is **INSERT**. When you insert data into a table with foreign keys, you need to first insert rows into the base table. This means you should first insert any rows in the People table that are needed as foreign keys in the Customers table.

In the Customers table these columns are referenced back to the People table:

```
AlternateContactPersonID
LastEditedBy
PrimaryContactPersonID
```

When you insert a single row for a customer, you need to provide PersonID values for these columns. It could be all the same "person" but more likely it will be at least two or three different people. And if you remember in the People table, there is a LastEditedBy column that references another row in the People table. My strategy then is to create three rows in the People table, one is the "editor" of any rows in both tables, and then a primary and alternate contact ID for the customer.

Execute the following T-SQL statements or use the sample script **insertpeople.sql** to insert all three rows in the People table:

```
USE [WideWorldImporters]
GO
INSERT INTO [Application].[People]
([PersonID], [FullName], [PreferredName], [IsPermittedToLogon],
[LogonName], [IsExternalLogonProvider], [IsSystemUser],
[IsEmployee], [IsSalesPerson], [LastEditedBy])
VALUES (0, 'Robert Dorr', 'TheKraken', 1, 'rdorr', 0, 1, 1, 0, 0)
GO
INSERT INTO [Application].[People]
([FullName], [PreferredName], [IsPermittedToLogon],
[LogonName], [IsExternalLogonProvider], [IsSystemUser],
[IsEmployee], [IsSalesPerson], [LastEditedBy])
VALUES ('Slava Oks', 'thegodfather', 1, 'slavao', 0, 1, 1, 0, 0)
GO
INSERT INTO [Application].[People]
([FullName], [PreferredName], [IsPermittedToLogon],
[LogonName], [IsExternalLogonProvider], [IsSystemUser],
[IsEmployee], [IsSalesPerson], [LastEditedBy])
VALUES ('Tobias Ternstrom', 'theswede', 1, 'tobiast', 0, 1, 1, 0, 0)
GO
```

If you look at the syntax I used for the INSERT, I listed out specific columns and did not supply values for many of the columns defined to accept NULL values (i.e., optional columns).

To insert a single customer, I must know what the PersonID values are for my primary and alternate contacts for the customer. You can do this by reading rows from the People table using the T-SQL SELECT statement as seen in the script **findpeople.sql**:

```
USE [WideWorldImporters]
GO
SELECT [PersonID], [FullName] FROM [Application].[People]
GO
```

The result pane on the right side of Visual Studio will show the following result:

```
PersonID    FullName
--------    --------
0           Robert Dorr
1           Slava Oks
2           Tobias Ternstrom
```

Slava Oks will be the Primary Customer Contact, while Tobias Ternstrom is the Alternate Customer Contact, and Robert Dorr (aka "TheKraken") will continue to be my "editor."

Now I have the foundation to insert a new customer. Because the column [BillToCustomerID] references a valid [CustomerID], I use a feature called a *variable* to grab a SEQUENCE value, and then use it for both columns. Execute the following T-SQL statements or use the sample script **insertcustomer.sql**:

```
USE [WideWorldImporters]
GO
DECLARE @CustomerID INT
SET @CustomerID = NEXT VALUE for [Sequences].[CustomerID]
INSERT INTO [Sales].[Customers]
([CustomerID], [CustomerName], [BillToCustomerID], [CustomerCategoryID],
[PrimaryContactPersonID],
[AlternateContactPersonID], [DeliveryMethodID], [DeliveryCityID],
[PostalCityID],
[AccountOpenedDate], [StandardDiscountPercentage], [IsStatementSent],
[IsOnCreditHold],
[PaymentDays], [PhoneNumber], [FaxNumber], [WebsiteURL],
[DeliveryAddressLine1],
[DeliveryPostalCode], [PostalAddressLine1], [PostalPostalCode],
[LastEditedBy])
VALUES (@CustomerID, 'WeLoveSQLOnLinux', @CustomerID, 1, 1, 2, 1, 1, 1,
getdate(), 0.10, 0, 0, 30,
'817-111-1111', '817-222-2222', 'www.welovesqlonlinux.com', 'Texas',
'76182', 'Texas', '76182', 0)
GO
```

Notice for the [AccountOpenedDate]column I used **getdate()** to supply a value for datetime (getdate() provides the local datetime based on the computer where SQL Server is installed). This is an example of a built-in function that can be used with T-SQL queries. For more information about SQL Server functions, see our documentation at https://docs.microsoft.com/sql/t-sql/functions/functions.

Now I can read from the Customer table and join with the People table to get the name of a customer and their primary contact name from the T-SQL statements as seen in the sample script findcustomer.sql:

```
USE [WideWorldImporters]
GO
SELECT c.[CustomerName], c.[WebsiteURL], p.[FullName] AS PrimaryContact
FROM [Sales].[Customers] AS c
JOIN [Application].[People] AS p
ON p.[PersonID] = c.[PrimaryContactPersonID]
GO
```

The result of this query is as the following row:

```
CustomerName        WebsiteURL              PrimaryContact
------------        ----------              --------------
WeLoveSQLOnt...     www.welovesql...        Slava Oks
```

Updating and Deleting data

Now that you have learned examples of how to insert and retrieve rows from these tables, two other key operations of any application with SQL Server are the ability to update and delete rows. The syntax to perform this is amazingly simple.

Let's say you wanted to update the "WeLoveSQLOnLinux" company and change their website because they moved their site. Execute the following T-SQL statements or use the example script **updatecustomer.sql:**

```
USE [WideWorldImporters]
GO
UPDATE [Sales].[Customers]
SET WebsiteURL = 'www.sqlonlinux.com'
WHERE CustomerName = 'WeLoveSQLOnLinux'
GO
```

You may also want to delete a customer row with a T-SQL query like this from the sample script **deletecustomer.sql**:

```
USE [WideWorldImporters]
GO
BEGIN TRANSACTION
DELETE FROM [Sales].[Customers]
WHERE CustomerName = 'WeLoveSQLOnLinux'
ROLLBACK TRANSACTION
GO
```

I threw in another wrinkle for you. Notice the T-SQL commands **BEGIN TRANACTION** and **ROLLBACK TRANSACTION**. Effectively, all the T-SQL commands I have shown you have an implicit commit of a transaction. Using the BEGIN TRANSACTION syntax allows me to explicitly decide to commit or rollback (undo) my T-SQL command. In this case, the DELETE is executed, but the ROLLBACK TRANACTION undoes the change. For a thorough discussion of SQL Server transactions, see our documentation page at https://docs.microsoft.com/sql/t-sql/language-elements/transactions-transact-sql.

Building Views and Stored Procedures

SQL Server has built-in capabilities for other types of objects that help provide abstraction and containment of query logic. One of these objects is called a *view*, a common feature in many database systems. Views allow you to create an object based on a T-SQL SELECT statement from one or more tables.

For example, I could create a view based on the join I showed earlier between the Customer and People tables through the following T-SQL statements, as seen in the sample script **createview.sql**:

```
USE [WideWorldImporters]
GO
DROP VIEW IF EXISTS [Sales].[CustomerContacts]
GO
CREATE VIEW [Sales].[CustomerContacts]
AS
```

```
SELECT c.[CustomerName], c.[WebsiteURL], p.[FullName] AS PrimaryContact
FROM [Sales].[Customers] AS c
JOIN [Application].[People] AS p
ON p.[PersonID] = c.[PrimaryContactPersonID]
GO
```

Now I can execute a T-SQL statement for all columns in the view, as seen in the sample script **findcustomercontacts.sql**:

```
USE [WideWorldImporters]
GO
SELECT * FROM [Sales].[CustomerContacts]
GO
```

I get the same results as executing the join, but I've abstracted the logic to "find customer contacts" from users or applications. Views are very common when you want to shield some columns from a *base* table from users and allow them access to only certain columns.

Another type of object that is very common with SQL Server is a *stored procedure*. Using a stored procedure in SQL Server is often called *server-side programming*. Stored procedures can contain multiple T-SQL statements (and often can be lengthy and complex). This frees the application from having to include all the T-SQL statements in the code. Stored procedures also reduce network traffic from the client application and are efficiently cached in memory.

I can take the INSERT statement to insert a customer row and build a stored procedure like the following T-SQL statements, as seen in the sample script insertcustomerproc.sql:

```
USE [WideWorldImporters]
GO
DROP PROCEDURE IF EXISTS [Sales].[InsertCustomer]
GO
CREATE PROCEDURE [Sales].[InsertCustomer]
@PrimaryContactID INT, @AlternateContactID INT
AS
-- Find the normal editor with a known PersonID = 0
--
```

```
DECLARE @EditedBy INT
SELECT @EditedBy = PersonID FROM [Application].[People]
WHERE PersonID = 0

-- INSERT into Customers
-- Primary and Alternate Contacs are passed in as parameters
DECLARE @CustomerID INT
SET @CustomerID = NEXT VALUE for [Sequences].[CustomerID]
INSERT INTO [Sales].[Customers]
([CustomerID], [CustomerName], [BillToCustomerID], [CustomerCategoryID],
[PrimaryContactPersonID],
[AlternateContactPersonID], [DeliveryMethodID], [DeliveryCityID],
[PostalCityID],
[AccountOpenedDate], [StandardDiscountPercentage], [IsStatementSent],
[IsOnCreditHold],
[PaymentDays], [PhoneNumber], [FaxNumber], [WebsiteURL],
[DeliveryAddressLine1],
[DeliveryPostalCode], [PostalAddressLine1], [PostalPostalCode],
[LastEditedBy])
VALUES (@CustomerID, 'WeAllLoveSQLOnLinux', @CustomerID, 1, @PrimaryContactID,
@AlternateContactID, 1, 1, 1, getdate(), 0.10, 0, 0, 30,
'817-111-1111', '817-222-2222', 'www.welovesqlonlinux.com', 'Texas', '76182',
'Texas', '76182', @EditedBy)
GO
```

This procedure has built-in logic to find the LastEditedBy column and takes two parameters for the primary and alternate contacts.

To execute this procedure, you would run a T-SQL statement like the one found in the sample script execinsertcustomer.sql:

```
USE [WideWorldImporters]
GO
EXEC [Sales].[InsertCustomer] 1, 2
GO
```

To learn more about the power of stored procedures, see our documentation at https://docs.microsoft.com/sql/t-sql/statements/create-procedure-transact-sql.

Summary

In this chapter, I have shown the basics of creating a database and objects to go in the database. I've used the popular open-source, cross-platform tool Visual Studio Code for all the examples to show the fundamentals of T-SQL using the mssql extension. With this foundation of knowledge, I'll show you in the next chapter, using the same WideWorldImporters database example, how to build an application, learn more advanced T-SQL concepts, and explore new features that come with SQL Server 2017 on Linux.

CHAPTER 4

Building an Application and Advanced T-SQL

Now that you have learned how to create a database, tables, and execute basic T-SQL queries, it's time to write some code and build an application that connects to SQL Server on Linux. As in Chapter 3, I'll use Visual Studio Code as the development environment to build a node.js application.

The node.js application uses basic T-SQL queries based on the knowledge I showed you in Chapter 3. So, in the second part of this chapter, I'll show you more advanced T-SQL capabilities as well as new features that were shipped in SQL Server 2016 and 2017.

There are three resources I used as I wrote this chapter that I think you will also find useful:

- http://aka.ms/sqldev: Resources and tutorials on how to build applications for SQL Server in almost any language on multiple platforms

- https://code.visualstudio.com/docs/nodejs/nodejs-tutorial: Tutorials on how to build node.js applications using Visual Studio Code

- https://docs.microsoft.com/sql/linux/sql-server-linux-develop-use-vscode: A tutorial on how to use the mssql extension for Visual Studio Code

© Bob Ward 2018
B. Ward, *Pro SQL Server on Linux*, https://doi.org/10.1007/978-1-4842-4128-8_4

Setting Up Your Environment

In Chapter 3, I described how to setup an environment to run T-SQL queries using Visual Studio Code and the mssql extension. If you skipped Chapter 3 to come to this chapter, you will want to perform the following steps to install and configure what you need for this chapter's examples:

- Install the Visual Studio Code from `https://code.visualstudio.com/`.

- Install the mssql extension to Visual Studio Code by following the instructions found at `https://docs.microsoft.com/sql/linux/sql-server-linux-develop-use-vscode?view=sql-server-linux-2017#install-the-mssql-extension`.

- If you have not already installed the SQL command line utilities, including sqlcmd, download them for Windows from `www.microsoft.com/download/details.aspx?id=53591` or for Linux/macOS from `https://docs.microsoft.com/en-us/sql/linux/sql-server-linux-setup-tools`. Be sure that sqlcmd is in your path to run example scripts.

- Copy the sample scripts and code for Chapter 3 and Chapter 4 into a local directory you will open in Visual Studio Code. I called my local directory on Windows c:\wwi. If you have left your Chapter 3 environment available, then just copy all the Chapter 4 code and scripts into c:\wwi or whatever folder you created.

- Set up a connection profile for the sqllinux user. See the section titled "Creating a Login and User" in Chapter 3 for steps on how to do this.

- All the code and T-SQL scripts were intended to run in a sequence in this chapter as you follow along. To start clean, run the createwwi.sh (macOS or Linux) or createwwi.cmd (Windows) scripts that were provided in Chapter 3. These scripts use sqlcmd and have two arguments: server and sa password.

- Execute the T-SQL script **insertpeople.sql** and **insertcustomer. sql** from Chapter 3 to populate the People and Customers table. Also, execute the T-SQL script **insertcustomerproc.sql** to create a stored procedure that will be used in a node.js example later in the chapter.

The examples in this chapter will use the Windows version of Visual Studio Code both for SQL Server T-SQL commands as well as the Windows version of node.js. However, all the examples will work on your preferred development platform, since Visual Studio code and node.js exist on MacOS and Linux.

Because I'm building a node.js application, the other task I need to do is to install the necessary components to run node.js on my Windows laptop. I used the Windows installer package found at https://nodejs.org/en/download (I used all the defaults for the installation).

Building and Running a Data Application for SQL Server

There was a time years ago that the applications being built for SQL Server were written only in Visual Basic, C, or C++ using drivers that supported programming interfaces such as ODBC or OLE-DB. A few years ago, Microsoft made a conscious effort to expand programming interfaces to support a much wider variety of languages, interfaces, and platforms.

Today, it is possible to write a program to access SQL Server in almost every language you can think of. Whether you want to develop a program in Java, C#, PHP, or Python, SQL Server has the support you need. I don't try to remember all the programming language support anymore because of this nifty website called http:// aka.ms/sqldev.

Figure 4-1 shows the options as presented by the http://aka.ms/sqldev site.

Figure 4-1. *SQL Server programming language options*

As part of supporting these programming languages, SQL Server also supports several Object Relational Mapping (ORM) frameworks including Entity Framework, Hibernate ORM, Sequelize ORM, and Django. For a complete list of drivers and ORM framework support, see our documentation at `https://docs.microsoft.com/sql/connect/sql-connection-libraries`.

Using node.js with SQL Server

One of the more popular programming languages to build applications, especially on Linux, is node.js based on Javascript. Node.js supports connecting to any SQL Server through the Tabular Data Stream (TDS) protocol, the "data" language for SQL Server, from a component called **Tedious** (Microsoft is a major contributor to Tedious. You can find the open source at `https://github.com/tediousjs/tedious`), which is the node.js driver for SQL Server. The TDS protocol is supported by SQL Server and Azure SQL Server Database. The entire protocol is open and published at `https://msdn.microsoft.com/library/dd304523.aspx`.

Node.js supports programs to run on Windows, Linux, and MacOS. You can download the node.js platform of your choice at `https://nodejs.org`.

I will show you an example application using node.js (this is a simple example that displays output to the console. It doesn't display a web page) based on the samples provided by Microsoft at www.microsoft.com/sql-server/developer-get-started/node/windows.

Per the instructions in our documentation at www.microsoft.com/sql-server/developer-get-started/node/windows/step/2.html, I ran these programs to install the Tedious driver and prepare my environment to use node.js with SQL Server (you can execute these in the Integrated Terminal in Visual Studio Code) in the folder where I will save my program:

```
npm init -y
npm install tedious
npm install async
```

For a set of documentation references for using the Tedious driver to write programs for node.js with SQL Server, see the API documentation at http://tediousjs.github.io/tedious/index.html. Another source of examples can be found at https://github.com/tediousjs/tedious/tree/master/examples.

Connecting to SQL Server with node.js

Connecting to SQL Server with node.js relies on the **Connection** object from the Tedious driver. Get the full details of the object at http://tediousjs.github.io/tedious/api-connection.html. Following is the code I built to connect to SQL Server on Linux with the default database of WideWorldImporters, using the sqllinux login I created earlier in this chapter. Using the Visual Studio Code Editor, you can open the sample file **customerappconnect.js** to see this code. Using this file extension switches the editor to recognize JavaScript code:

```
var Connection = require('tedious').Connection;
var Request = require('tedious').Request;
var TYPES = require('tedious').TYPES;

// Create connection to database
var config = {
  userName: 'sqllinux',
  password: 'Sql2017isfast',
```

```
  server: 'bwsql2017rhel',
  options: {
      database: 'WideWorldImporters'
  }
}

console.log("Connecting to SQL Server");
var connection = new Connection(config);

// Attempt to connect to the SQL Server on Linux
connection.on('connect', function(err) {
  if (err) {
    console.log(err);
  } else {
    console.log('Connected to SQL Server successfully');
    connection.close();
  }
});
```

I can run this code in the Integrated Terminal (you can open the Integrated Terminal using the View Menu in Visual Studio Code) using the command:

```
node .\customerappconnect.js
```

Figure 4-2 shows the overall shape of things in Visual Studio.

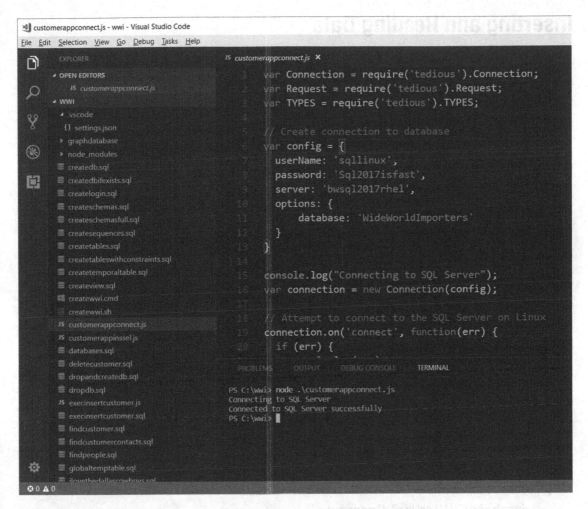

Figure 4-2. Connecting to SQL Server on Linux with a node.js program in Visual Studio Code

The results of running the code are shown in the bottom pane in Figure 4-2, and are as follows:

```
PS C:\wwi> node .\customerappconnect.js
Connecting to SQL Server
Connected to SQL Server successfully
```

In future examples, I'll often just show the results as text, without also showing the Visual Studio screenshot.

Inserting and Reading Data

Now that you have learned to connect to SQL Server using node.js, let's add in code to insert a row to the [Application].[People] table (a new row other than the ones used in the examples from Chapter 3) and another piece of code to get contacts from the Customer table.

Executing queries in node.js with Tedious requires the **Request** object. You can find the full details of the Request object at http://tediousjs.github.io/tedious/api-request.html.

This is a long piece of code to read, so I'll explain a few details at the end of the code fragment. This set of node.js code can be found in the sample file **customerappinssel.js**, and it appears as follows:

```
var Connection = require('tedious').Connection;
var Request = require('tedious').Request;
var TYPES = require('tedious').TYPES;
var async = require('async');

// Create connection to database
var config = {
  userName: 'sqllinux',
  password: 'Sql2017isfast',
  server: 'bwsql2017rhel',
  options: {
      database: 'WideWorldImporters'
  }
}

console.log("Connecting to SQL Server");
var connection = new Connection(config);

function Start(callback) {
  console.log('Starting...');
  callback(null, 'Travis Wright', 'radtravis', 'twright');
}
```

```
function Insert(FullName, PreferredName, Logon, callback) {
  console.log("Inserting '" + FullName + "' into Table...");

  request = new Request(
    'INSERT INTO [Application].[People] ([FullName], [PreferredName],
    [IsPermittedToLogon], [LogonName], [IsExternalLogonProvider],
    [IsSystemUser], [IsEmployee], [IsSalesPerson], [LastEditedBy]) VALUES
    (@FullName, @PreferredName, 1, @Logon, 0, 1, 1, 0, 0);',
      function(err, rowCount, rows) {
      if (err) {
          console.log(err);
          callback(err);
      } else {
          console.log(rowCount + ' row(s) inserted');
          callback(null);
      }
      });
  request.addParameter('FullName', TYPES.NVarChar, FullName);
  request.addParameter('PreferredName', TYPES.NVarChar, PreferredName);
  request.addParameter('Logon', TYPES.NVarChar, Logon);

  // Execute SQL statement
  connection.execSql(request);
}

function Read(callback) {
  console.log('Reading Customer Contacts...');

  // Read all rows from table
  request = new Request(
  'SELECT c.[CustomerName], c.[WebsiteURL], p.[FullName] AS PrimaryContact
  FROM [Sales].[Customers] AS c JOIN [Application].[People] AS p  ON
  p.[PersonID] = c.[PrimaryContactPersonID];',
  function(err, rowCount, rows) {
  if (err) {
      console.log(err);
      callback(err);
```

```
  } else {
      console.log(rowCount + ' row(s) returned');
      callback(null);
  }
});

// Print the rows read
var result = "";
request.on('row', function(columns) {
    columns.forEach(function(column) {
        if (column.value === null) {
            console.log('NULL');
        } else {
            result += column.value + " ";
        }
    });
    console.log(result);
    result = "";
});

// Execute SQL statement
connection.execSql(request);
}

function Complete(err, result) {
  if (err) {
      console.log(err);
  } else {
      console.log("Done!");
      connection.close();
  }
}

// Attempt to connect to the SQL Server on Linux
connection.on('connect', function(err) {
  if (err) {
    console.log(err);
    process.exit(1);
```

```
  } else {
    console.log('Connected to SQL Server successfully');

    // Execute all functions in the array serially
    async.waterfall([
      Start,
      Insert,
      Read
  ], Complete)
  }
});
```

If you are not familiar with node.js, the code flow can be hard to follow. The key piece of code that "fires off" the rest of the functions is found after the logic to connect with the **async** object:

```
async.waterfall([
      Start,
      Insert,
      Read
  ], Complete)
```

This code executes each function, starting with the Start function, serially allowing each function to pass on information to each other. The Complete function is the main function to run after the other functions have executed (or if an error occurs).

The syntax of the INSERT statement is also unique in that you can specify variables you bind from the program into the T-SQL statement:

```
'INSERT INTO [Application].[People] ([FullName], [PreferredName],
[IsPermittedToLogon], [LogonName], [IsExternalLogonProvider],
[IsSystemUser], [IsEmployee], [IsSalesPerson], [LastEditedBy]) VALUES
(@FullName, @PreferredName, 1, @Logon, 0, 1, 1, 0, 0);'
```

The parameters to the function Insert are used as the following bind variables to the INSERT statement @FullName, @PreferredName, and @Logon and defined using these statements:

```
request.addParameter('FullName', TYPES.NVarChar, FullName);
request.addParameter('PreferredName', TYPES.NVarChar, PreferredName);
request.addParameter('Logon', TYPES.NVarChar, Logon);
```

Here is the technique in the code to execute a T-SQL batch:

```
connection.execSql(request);
```

And the following code allows you to iterate through each column of each row of a result set from a T-SQL SELECT statement and bind to a variable, or in this case dump out the results to the console:

```
// Print the rows read
  var result = "";
  request.on('row', function(columns) {
      columns.forEach(function(column) {
          if (column.value === null) {
              console.log('NULL');
          } else {
              result += column.value + " ";
          }
      });
      console.log(result);
      result = "";
  });
```

You can also see in the Connection object, after a successful execution of these functions, the connection to SQL Server is closed:

```
function Complete(err, result) {
  if (err) {
      console.log(err);
  } else {
      console.log("Done!");
      connection.close();
  }
}
```

I executed this code from the command prompt like this:

```
node .\customerappinssel.js
```

The results are as follows:

```
PS C:\wwi> node .\customerappinssel.js
Connecting to SQL Server
Connected to SQL Server successfully
Starting...
Inserting 'Travis Wright' into Table...
1 row(s) inserted
Reading Customer Contacts...
WeLoveSQLOnLinux www.welovesqlonlinux.com Slava Oks
1 row(s) returned
Done!
```

Executing UPDATE and DELETE commands in node.js operates very similar
to executing an INSERT. You can see these examples in our documentation at www.
microsoft.com/sql-server/developer-get-started/node/windows/step/2.html.

Executing Stored Procedures

You can execute stored procedures using the same execSql() method by setting up a
request with the full T-SQL "EXEC <procedure name>" syntax. However, a more efficient
way to call stored procedures is via a remote procedure call (RPC) method as defined by
the TDS protocol. The Tedious driver supports this via a method called **callProcedure**().

Using the example T-SQL procedure **InsertCustomer** from the previous
chapter (remember at the beginning of this chapter I instructed you to execute the
insertcustomerproc.sql script), here is the node.js code to execute this procedure as an
RPC. You can find this code in the sample file **execinsertcustomer.js,** and it appears as
follows:

```
var Connection = require('tedious').Connection;
var Request = require('tedious').Request;
var TYPES = require('tedious').TYPES;

// Create connection to database
var config = {
  userName: 'sqllinux',
  password: 'Sql2017isfast',
```

```
    server: 'bwsql2017rhel',
    options: {
        database: 'WideWorldImporters'
    }
}

console.log("Connecting to SQL Server");
var connection = new Connection(config);

connection.on('connect', function(err) {
    // If no error, then good to proceed.
    console.log("Connected to SQL Server Successfully");
    InsertCustomer();
});

function InsertCustomer() {
    request = new Request("[Sales].[InsertCustomer]", function(err) {
    if (err) {
        console.log(err);}
    else
        console.log('Inserted new Customer');
    }
    );

    request.addParameter('PrimaryContactID', TYPES.Int, 1);
    request.addParameter('AlternateContactID', TYPES.Int, 1);
    request.on('requestCompleted', ()=>{connection.close();});
    connection.callProcedure(request);
}
```

To run this code, I ran this command:

```
node .\execinsertcustomer.js
```

The results should look like this from the Integrated Terminal in VS Code or your command shell:

```
PS C:\wwi> node .\execinsertcustomer.js
Connecting to SQL Server
Connected to SQL Server Successfully
Inserted new Customer
```

The method to close the connection uses the event programming model common to node.js applications. This line of code will close the connection when a request is completed (i.e., a query is completed).

```
request.on('requestCompleted', ()=>{connection.close();});
```

Enhancing Your Application

I covered just some of the fundamental methods to use node.js with Tedious to connect and run queries against SQL Server, including stored procedures. As you build up a production application, you will want to enhance it to take advantage of other methods with node.js.

Here are my recommendations to consider:

- A more efficient way to handle connections to open and close them frequently is a concept called *connection pooling*. Connection pooling is very common for SQL Server applications, and Tedious supports this through another object: `https://github.com/ tediousjs/tedious-connection-pool`.

- You may want the ability to control timeouts for logins and/or queries (the length of time to wait for a login or query). The Connection object provides options in the configuration to control these timeouts. The default is 15 seconds for both. You also may want the ability to cancel a query you have submitted to SQL Server manually, and the Connection object supports this through connection.cancel().

- There are a variety of other options you may want to use associated with the Connection object, such as encryption, IP addresses and port numbers, read intent for Availability Groups (which I will discuss later in Chapter 8), and more. They are all documented with the Connection object at `http://tediousjs.github.io/tedious/api- connection.html#function_newConnection`.

- Your application should be prepared to handle certain events based on execution of a query and/or stored procedure. See the documentation for handling doneProc and doneInProc events from the Request object at `http://tediousjs.github.io/tedious/api- request.html`.

- In addition, SQL Server may return both error and informational messages for any query execution. Be sure to handle these using the Connection object infoMessage and errorMessage events. See the Connection object details at `http://tediousjs.github.io/tedious/api-connection.html`.

- While you can use the T-SQL BEGIN TRANSACTION command as part of a batch within your application, the Tedious driver also provides interfaces for transactions. See the documentation for more details at `http://tediousjs.github.io/tedious/api-connection.html#function_beginTransaction`.

Go Big on T-SQL

In the previous chapter and with the node.js application, I showed you fundamental queries to create databases, tables, keys, constraints, and execute CRUD (create, read, update, and delete) operations against SQL Server on Linux.

Note   If you haven't heard this enough from me at this point, this entire set of T-SQL examples and scripts can run unchanged against SQL Server on Windows and Linux because the core SQL Server engine is the same on both platforms.

I decided when I outlined this book that it could not be a complete guide to SQL Server and T-SQL. That alone could take several books (and there are several out there on this topic). Rather, I wanted to include enough information for users new to SQL Server to get up and running on Linux, build up some capabilities, and understand what other options exist to go further.

In this section, I want to briefly talk about other features in the T-SQL language and the core database engine that can enhance your application and experience with SQL Server.

Creating and Using Temporary Objects

There could be situations where you want to create a temporary space for data that is unique per user without storing the data in your database and creating a design that must track data per user.

SQL Server provides this capability through a concept called a *temporary table* (also through *table variables*). All temporary objects are stored in a special system database called tempdb. The key word here is temporary. Tempdb is recreated each time SQL Server is started. So, even though you can store user tables in this database, I don't recommend this.

Temporary Tables and Table Variables

Temporary tables and table variables have the unique property of scope. When you create these objects, they are automatically destroyed when the stored procedure completes, or the user login session is disconnected.

Examples are the best way to show you how to do this. Let's use the InsertCustomers stored procedure created earlier in this chapter as an example to show you both temporary tables and table variables. Let's say you want to pull in sets of data to calculate the StandardDiscountPercentage or PaymentDays columns for a new customer. Depending on the data, there are several ways to do this. You could query data from the source table where these values exist and insert them into a temporary table. And then use the temporary table within the stored procedure to populate these values.

Here is a possible example. This assumes a source table called CustomerRates, which has columns called StandardDiscountPercentage, PaymentDays, and CustomerRegion. In addition, a region is passed into the procedure to look up the right data for the new customer. You can find example T-SQL statements in the sample script **insertcustomerproctemptable.sql**:

```
USE [WideWorldImporters]
GO
DROP TABLE IF EXISTS CustomerRates
GO
CREATE TABLE CustomerRates
(CustomerRegion NVARCHAR(30),
StandardDiscountPercentage [decimal](18,3),
PaymentDays INT
)
INSERT INTO CustomerRates VALUES ('Texas', 10.0, 30)
GO
DROP PROCEDURE IF EXISTS [Sales].[InsertCustomer]
```

```
GO
CREATE PROCEDURE [Sales].[InsertCustomer]
@PrimaryContactID INT, @AlternateContactID INT, @CustomerRegion
NVARCHAR(30)
AS
-- Declare local variables
--
DECLARE @StandardDiscountPercentage DECIMAL(18,3)
DECLARE @PaymentDays INT

-- Find the normal editor with a known PersonID = 0
--
DECLARE @EditedBy INT
SELECT @EditedBy = PersonID FROM [Application].[People]
WHERE PersonID = 0

-- Create a temporary table to store results for customer payment
information
--
CREATE TABLE #CustomerPayment
(StandardDiscountPercentage [DECIMAL](18, 3) NOT NULL,
PaymentDays INT NOT NULL
)
INSERT INTO #CustomerPayment SELECT StandardDiscountPercentage, PaymentDays
FROM CustomerRates
WHERE CustomerRegion = @CustomerRegion

SELECT @StandardDiscountPercentage = StandardDiscountPercentage,
@PaymentDays = PaymentDays FROM #CustomerPayment

-- INSERT into Customers
-- Primary and Alternate Contacs are passed in as parameters
DECLARE @CustomerID INT
SET @CustomerID = NEXT VALUE for [Sequences].[CustomerID]
INSERT INTO [Sales].[Customers]
([CustomerID], [CustomerName], [BillToCustomerID], [CustomerCategoryID],
[PrimaryContactPersonID],
```

```
[AlternateContactPersonID], [DeliveryMethodID], [DeliveryCityID],
[PostalCityID],
[AccountOpenedDate], [StandardDiscountPercentage], [IsStatementSent],
[IsOnCreditHold],
[PaymentDays], [PhoneNumber], [FaxNumber], [WebsiteURL],
[DeliveryAddressLine1],
[DeliveryPostalCode], [PostalAddressLine1], [PostalPostalCode],
[LastEditedBy])
VALUES (@CustomerID, 'WeLoveSQLOnLinuxToo', @CustomerID, 1,
@PrimaryContactID, @AlternateContactID, 1, 1, 1, getdate(),
@StandardDiscountPercentage, 0, 0, @PaymentDays,
'817-111-1111', '817-222-2222', 'www.welovesqlonlinux.com', 'Texas',
'76182', 'Texas', '76182', @EditedBy)
GO
```

I created this procedure to insert a new customer, so this example should work even with the execution of scripts from previous examples in this chapter.

I can now execute this procedure using the following T-SQL statements, which are also in the sample script **execinsertcustomertemp.sql**:

```
USE [WideWorldImporters]
GO
EXEC [Sales].InsertCustomer 1, 2, 'Texas'
GO
```

There could be more efficient methods to demonstrate the business logic for this example, but it is a convenient way to show you how to create and use a temporary table. In this example, when the procedure completes, the temporary table #CustomerPayment is destroyed.

Note   For performance optimization, SQL Server uses a technique called temporary table caching by default with some restrictions. See this excellent blog post on the topic: https://sqlperformance.com/2017/05/sql-performance/sql-server-temporary-object-caching.

Notice the use of the INSERT..SELECT syntax in the previous example to insert multiple rows in a single statement. Another method to populate the temporary table (which can also be used for user tables) is the SELECT..INTO syntax. In the example, you could have used the following syntax instead. SELECT..INTO will create the target table based on the definition of the columns from the source table, so there would be no need for CREATE TABLE.

```
SELECT StandardDiscountPercentage, PaymentDays INTO #CustomerRates
FROM CustomerRates
WHERE CustomerRegion = @CustomerRegion
```

For this same example, you could also use a table variable. The stored procedure fragment with a table variable looks like this:

```
DECLARE @CustomerRates table(
    StandardDiscountPercentage [DECIMAL] (18,3) NOT NULL,
    PaymentDays INT NOT NULL
);
INSERT INTO @CustomerRates SELECT StandardDiscountPercentage, PaymentDays
FROM CustomerRates
WHERE CustomerRegion = @CustomerRegion
```

Table variables and temporary tables both have their advantages and disadvantages. You must use table variables to enable a feature called *table valued parameters*. In general, table variables work fine with small sets of data, but you should use temporary tables when working with larger sets of data.

Remember that you may not even need temporary tables for the logic you are trying to build in a stored procedure or batch. There are performance considerations for many users concurrently using temporary objects, which I will discuss further in Chapter 6.

Other Temporary Objects

SQL Server provides capabilities to create *temporary stored procedures*, which have a scope and lifetime only for the duration of a SQL Server session. The syntax is the same for creating a stored procedure but with a twist of using the # symbol in front of

the procedure name, as in this T-SQL example, which I provided in the sample script
tempproc.sql:

```
CREATE PROCEDURE #tempproc
AS
SELECT @@VERSION
GO
```

Executing the procedure would be like any stored procedure using the #tempproc
name. Like temporary tables, a temporary stored procedure of the same name can be
created by multiple users concurrently, since each user would have a private version of
the procedure per their session. And like temporary tables, the definition of a temporary
stored procedure is kept in the tempdb database. There are a few reasons to use
temporary stored procedures, such as testing out a new procedure without storing it in a
user database or using it in a long T-SQL script to perform a task.

The other type of temporary object is a global temporary table or stored procedure.
Global temporary tables are defined by using the same syntax as temporary tables except
with an extra # character in front of the name, as in the following example:

```
CREATE TABLE ##globaltemp
(col1 INT, col2 INT)
GO
```

Because they are global, only one global temporary table of a given name can exist
at a time and their scope is across all active user sessions. A global temporary table is
stored in tempdb but is automatically destroyed when all users who have referenced the
global temporary table have disconnected.

It is also possible to create global temporary stored procedures. The have the same
characteristics in scope, visibility, and lifetime as global temporary tables.

Internal Usage of tempdb

When I've presented on the topic of tempdb, I've often called it the "garbage dump"
of SQL Server. I know the term has a negative meaning, but it is the reality for how
tempdb is used by SQL Server. What I've presented so far in this section are *user objects*
in tempdb. In other words, users decide now many objects and how much space they
consume.

SQL Server has other capabilities that require it to store pages of data in tempdb outside normal user tables. These include storage for versioning, spills for hash and sorts, and worktables. You normally don't worry about these because they are implemented within the SQL Server engine. The reality is that they can affect your application, especially when it comes to sizing tempdb correctly (or more importantly the performance of a query).

SQL Server provides mechanisms to examine the usage of tempdb between user and internal space at the file, session, and even task (query) level through Dynamic Management Views, which will be discussed in Chapter 5. If you are up for a detailed study on the topic of tempdb, you can listen into an in-depth talk I did at a major SQL Server user conference a few years back on YouTube at `https://youtu.be/SvseGMobe2w`.

Triggers

A trigger is a special kind of stored procedure that automatically executes when an event occurs in the database server. DML triggers execute when a user tries to modify data through a data manipulation language (DML) event such as INSERT, UPDATE, or DELETE statements.

Many years ago, before SQL Server supported declarative foreign key constraints, triggers were the recommended method to enforce referential integrity. Think of using a trigger in situations where you want some type of action to take place when data in a table is modified but you may not have complete control of what other queries could be modifying the table. You may build stored procedures to wrap all CRUD operations against your tables, but if you want to make sure some action takes place for other users not using your procedure, triggers could be a great solution.

There are other types of triggers as well. You can read more about them in our documentation at `https://docs.microsoft.com/sql/t-sql/statements/create-trigger-transact-sql`.

Analytic Queries

The examples I provided for SELECT statements were very simple, including joining tables and using a **WHERE** clause to filter results.

In many analytic type workloads, it is necessary to aggregate results or order them. Like other popular database engines, SQL Server provides T-SQL syntax to group rows with **GROUP BY** and ensure the results are specifically ordered with **ORDER BY**.

SQL Server also provides rich functions to perform on aggregations including aggregate functions (Ex. SUM) and analytic functions. You can read more about these at https://docs.microsoft.com/sql/t-sql/functions/aggregate-functions-transact-sql and https://docs.microsoft.com/sql/t-sql/functions/analytic-functions-transact-sql.

You can get more advanced and achieve great performance on complex aggregation queries by using a concept called w*indow functions*. Take a look at the documentation and examples at https://docs.microsoft.com/sql/t-sql/queries/select-over-clause-transact-sql.

I will show you some examples of analytic queries when I describe features like columnstore indexes in Chapter 6.

Complex Datatypes

In the example tables I've shown you in the previous chapter, I only used some of the most common datatypes including integers, characters, bit, and datetime values. Here is the People table definition for our reference as you read through this section and the rest of the chapter (this is meant as a reference and not to execute). If you have run the example scripts, the People table should exist in your database:

```
CREATE TABLE [Application].[People](
    [PersonID] [int] NOT NULL,
    [FullName] [nvarchar](50) NOT NULL,
    [PreferredName] [nvarchar](50) NOT NULL,
--    [SearchName] AS (concat([PreferredName],N' ',[FullName]))
    PERSISTED NOT NULL,
    [IsPermittedToLogon] [bit] NOT NULL,
    [LogonName] [nvarchar](50) NULL,
    [IsExternalLogonProvider] [bit] NOT NULL,
    [HashedPassword] [varbinary](max) NULL,
    [IsSystemUser] [bit] NOT NULL,
    [IsEmployee] [bit] NOT NULL,
    [IsSalesperson] [bit] NOT NULL,
    [UserPreferences] [nvarchar](max) NULL,
    [PhoneNumber] [nvarchar](20) NULL,
    [FaxNumber] [nvarchar](20) NULL,
```

```
      [EmailAddress] [nvarchar](256) NULL,
      [Photo] [varbinary](max) NULL,
      [CustomFields] [nvarchar](max) NULL,
--    [OtherLanguages]  AS (json_query([CustomFields],
      N'$.OtherLanguages')),
      [LastEditedBy] [int] NOT NULL,
--    [ValidFrom] [datetime2](7) GENERATED ALWAYS AS ROW START NOT NULL,
--    [ValidTo] [datetime2](7) GENERATED ALWAYS AS ROW END NOT NULL
 CONSTRAINT [PK_Application_People] PRIMARY KEY CLUSTERED
(
      [PersonID] ASC
)
)
```

SQL Server provides a rich set of datatypes beyond this including numeric, bigint, unicode, money, binary, special. variant, XML, and table (a special case that you can use with table-valued parameters. See https://docs.microsoft.com/sql/relational-databases/tables/use-table-valued-parameters-database-engine in our documentation for more information).

One special syntax on binary datatypes is in the table examples in this chapter:

```
[Photo] [varbinary](max) NULL,
```

Note the (max) syntax after the varbinary datatype where you would normally see a length. The normal maximum size of a row (or a column) in SQL Server is 8000 bytes, but a capability exists to store a value greater than this (the max is actually 2^31-1 bytes). This is called TEXT/IMAGE data and has a different storage mechanism than normal rows (a separate set of database pages than the pages where rows are stored). The legacy datatype names for these are text, image, and ntext. But you should use the modern syntax of the (max) specification with varchar, nvarchar, and varbinary.

In Chapter 3 in the section **Creating Tables**, I had comments on a few column definitions in the example tables, and one of them was this column:

```
[SearchName]  AS (concat([PreferredName],N' ',[FullName])) PERSISTED NOT
NULL,
```

This is an example of a *computed column*. A computed column has an expression based on other columns in the table and can be recognized by the **AS** syntax after the column name. Normally, computed columns are calculated any time you query the column with a SELECT statement. But if you use the **PERSISTED** keyword, SQL Server will store the computed expression as rows are inserted or updated from the referenced columns. Computed columns are in a way a form of *server-side programming* because you are creating data based on other data stored in the table. Computed columns make it easier to provide this type of programming in a declarative manner without writing separate procedures or trigger code.

String Functions

Application developers often need to perform operations against character data as strings. SQL Server provides a rich set of T-SQL functions to find and manipulate string data, which can be useful to enhance your stored procedure code. The **CONCAT** operation in the computed column example of the People table is an example of a T-SQL string function. Other functions exist to split (**STRING_SPLIT**), aggregate (**STRING_AGG**), find substring (**SUBSTRING**), format (**FORMAT**), and trim (**LTRIM** and **RTRIM**).

Other T-SQL Commands

The T-SQL language has become so powerful over the years, with rich capabilities beyond standard CRUD operations. While I will review some of the exciting recent new features in the next section, I encourage you to explore the entire T-SQL reference documentation. As a developer there may be other commands or features that will help your journey into building a rich data-driven application. For the complete reference, see our documentation at https://docs.microsoft.com/sql/t-sql/language-reference.

Exploring New SQL Server Capabilities

While SQL Server over the years has become a dominant relational database engine in the industry, today at Microsoft we think of SQL Server as a *modern data platform*. That is because we have extended the capabilities beyond the standard features of a typical relational database engine.

135

In this final section of the chapter, I will show you some of these new capabilities that have been introduced into the product in SQL Server 2016 and 2017.

JSON

In SQL Server 2008, we introduced a new XML datatype to store native XML data into a table column and provided operators to work against unstructured or semistructured data.

In SQL Server 2016, we recognized the popularity of JSON as a text format widely used in web applications and in NoSQL database systems.

Instead of creating a separate type like XML, SQL Server 2016 and 2017 provide T-SQL language commands to operate against JSON-formatted data stored in a character SQL Server column.

For an example, look at the People table and one of the columns I commented out:

```
[OtherLanguages]  AS (json_query([CustomFields],N'$.OtherLanguages'))
```

JSON_QUERY() is an example of a T-SQL function that allows you to extract an object or array from a JSON string. In this case, the object is OtherLanguages from the CustomFields column, which is defined as nvarchar(max) but the format of the data is JSON.

SQL Server support for JSON includes an **OPENJSON**() T-SQL function to convert JSON formatted data into rows and columns. Additionally, we have provided a new extension to the T-SQL SELECT statement called **FOR JSON**, which will take a standard column and row set of data and return the results as JSON-formatted data. The other JSON T-SQL functions are described in our documentation at https://docs.microsoft.com//sql/t-sql/functions/json-functions-transact-sql.

For a complete list of all SQL Server capabilities for working with JSON data, see our documentation at https://docs.microsoft.com/sql/relational-databases/json/json-data-sql-server.

Temporal Tables

A common scenario for some developers and data professionals is to store a history of changes or *versions* of rows in a table (which is another possible use for triggers).

Starting in SQL Server 2016, a new feature was introduced called *temporal tables* to solve the problem of storing a history of changes in the table but provide built-in, easy-to-use methods to retrieve a version of a row at point in time in the past.

A way to see this feature in action is through an example. Remember these two columns I commented out in the People and Customer tables.

```
[ValidFrom] [datetime2](7) GENERATED ALWAYS AS ROW START NOT NULL,
[ValidTo] [datetime2](7) GENERATED ALWAYS AS ROW END NOT NULL
```

When you combine these columns' definitions and add on other syntax to the table definition, you have defined a temporal table. I'm going to create a new People table definition to show the feature so as not to disrupt the existing table definitions from the examples in the previous and this chapter.

Here is the new People table definition with the full temporal syntax including the corresponding table, which is known as the *history* table. You can find these T-SQL commands in the sample script **createtemporaltable.sql**:

```
USE [WideWorldImporters]
GO
-- If you have already created the table we need to turn off system
versioning first
--
IF EXISTS (SELECT * FROM sys.objects where name = 'NewPeople')
    ALTER TABLE [Application].[NewPeople] SET (SYSTEM_VERSIONING = OFF)
GO
-- Drop the archive table if it exists
--
DROP TABLE IF EXISTS [Application].[NewPeople_Archive]
GO
DROP TABLE IF EXISTS [Application].[NewPeople]
GO
CREATE TABLE [Application].[NewPeople](
    [PersonID] [int] PRIMARY KEY NOT NULL,
    [FullName] [nvarchar](50) NOT NULL,
    [PreferredName] [nvarchar](50) NOT NULL,
    [SearchName]  AS (concat([PreferredName],N' ',[FullName]))
    PERSISTED NOT NULL,
    [IsPermittedToLogon] [bit] NOT NULL,
    [LogonName] [nvarchar](50) NULL,
    [IsExternalLogonProvider] [bit] NOT NULL,
```

```
    [HashedPassword] [varbinary](max) NULL,
    [IsSystemUser] [bit] NOT NULL,
    [IsEmployee] [bit] NOT NULL,
    [IsSalesperson] [bit] NOT NULL,
    [UserPreferences] [nvarchar](max) NULL,
    [PhoneNumber] [nvarchar](20) NULL,
    [FaxNumber] [nvarchar](20) NULL,
    [EmailAddress] [nvarchar](256) NULL,
    [Photo] [varbinary](max) NULL,
    [CustomFields] [nvarchar](max) NULL,
    [OtherLanguages]  AS (json_query([CustomFields],N'$.
    OtherLanguages')),
    [LastEditedBy] [int] NOT NULL,
    [ValidFrom] [datetime2](7) GENERATED ALWAYS AS ROW START NOT NULL,
    [ValidTo] [datetime2](7) GENERATED ALWAYS AS ROW END NOT NULL,
PERIOD FOR SYSTEM_TIME ([ValidFrom], [ValidTo])
)
WITH (SYSTEM_VERSIONING = ON ( HISTORY_TABLE = [Application].[NewPeople_
Archive]))
GO
```

With this defined, two tables exist in the database, the [Application].[NewPeople] table and the [Application].[NewPeople_Archive] table.

When a new row is inserted into the [Application].[NewPeople] table, the ValidFrom column will be assigned the current datetime for the transaction that inserted the row and the ValidTo column will be assigned the maximum value of a datetime2 type, which is 9999-12-31 (format of YYYY-MM-DD).

When this row is updated, the values of the row before the update are inserted into the [Application].[NewPeople_Archive] table but now with ValidTo set to the transaction time of the update. The updated row in [Application].[NewPeople] in the ValidFrom column will be assigned the transaction time of the update and ValidTo set to 9999-12-31. This now represents a history of the changes to this row based on the datetime2 columns.

The T-SQL SELECT statement has been extended to include a new **FOR SYSTEM_ TIME** clause to allow you to search for versions of the row based on a variety of options. SQL Server will automatically retrieve rows from the history table or current table based on the query. You don't have to know where your data exists. Just query the NewPeople table and use the FOR SYSTEM_TIME syntax to find a row for a given period. SQL Server will automatically retrieve the correct row from either the NewPeople or the NewPeople_ Archive table.

Any DELETE for a row in the table will cause the row to be inserted into the history table with the ValidTo set to the transaction time of the delete. The row in the current table will be deleted, but searches using the FOR SYSTEM_TIME will find historical rows.

A complete set of documentation on this feature can be found at `https:// docs.microsoft.com/sql/relational-databases/tables/temporal-tables#why- temporal`. There are also some very nice usage scenarios and examples at `https:// docs.microsoft.com/sql/relational-databases/tables/temporal-table-usage- scenarios`.

Graph Database

Some data models do not fit the traditional relationships, as seen by the example I've provided in this chapter. These scenarios include hierarchical data, complex many-to-many relationships, or complex interconnected data and relationships.

It is always possible to store and query data for these types of scenarios in SQL Server, but SQL Server 2017 introduces a new feature that makes it far easier to navigate these types of data relationships, called *graph database*.

Another example may help make it easier to understand this capability. Consider the diagram in Figure 4-3.

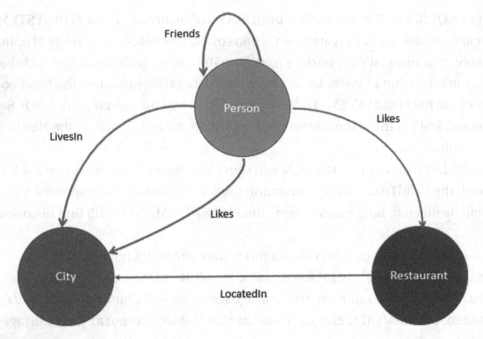

Figure 4-3. *A graph data model*

Designing out SQL Server tables to insert data and query on this model is possible but not natural for the T-SQL language.

SQL Server now provides extensions to the T-SQL language to make it possible to map models to tables and naturally find *matches* of information from the data.

Taking this model, I can build new tables that define *nodes* and *edges*. In the preceding diagram, the circles represent nodes and the relationships between them are edges.

Here is example T-SQL syntax to create these tables as seen in the sample script **graphtables.sql**:

```
-- Create a graph demo database
DROP DATABASE IF EXISTS graphdemo
GO
CREATE DATABASE graphdemo;
GO

USE   graphdemo;
GO
```

```
-- Create NODE tables
CREATE TABLE Person (
  ID INTEGER PRIMARY KEY,
  name VARCHAR(100)
) AS NODE;

CREATE TABLE Restaurant (
  ID INTEGER NOT NULL,
  name VARCHAR(100),
  city VARCHAR(100)
) AS NODE;

CREATE TABLE City (
  ID INTEGER PRIMARY KEY,
  name VARCHAR(100),
  stateName VARCHAR(100)
) AS NODE;

-- Create EDGE tables.
CREATE TABLE likes (rating INTEGER) AS EDGE;
CREATE TABLE friendOf AS EDGE;
CREATE TABLE livesIn AS EDGE;
CREATE TABLE locatedIn AS EDGE;
GO
```

Now I can insert some data using special T-SQL syntax to reference nodes when I insert data into the edge tables. See the sample script **graphinsert.sql** for an example to use this syntax:

```
USE graphdemo
GO
INSERT INTO Person VALUES (1,'John');
GO
INSERT INTO Restaurant VALUES (1, 'WeServeBigSteaks', 'Fort Worth')
GO
INSERT INTO likes VALUES ((SELECT $node_id FROM Person WHERE id = 1),
       (SELECT $node_id FROM Restaurant WHERE id = 1),9);
GO
```

Once I've inserted all the data, I can use a T-SQL query syntax like the following to find out what restaurants John likes or what his friends like. I've provided these statements in the sample script **graphquery.sql**:

```
USE graphdemo
GO
-- Find Restaurants that John likes
SELECT Restaurant.name
FROM Person, likes, Restaurant
WHERE MATCH (Person-(likes)->Restaurant)
AND Person.name = 'John';
GO
-- Find Restaurants that John's friends like
--
SELECT Restaurant.name
FROM Person person1, Person person2, likes, friendOf, Restaurant
WHERE MATCH(person1-(friendOf)->person2-(likes)->Restaurant)
AND person1.name='John';
GO
```

The second query will not find data until you go through the complete sample demo, which can be found at https://docs.microsoft.com/sql/relational-databases/graphs/sql-graph-sample.

Native Scoring

In SQL Server 2016, Microsoft did something unthinkable in the database community and industry. Instead of just creating a strategy to integrate data science and machine learning with SQL Server, we brought machine learning *to* SQL Server.

In SQL Server 2016, we built an architecture that allows for R scripts to be run co-located on the same SQL Server as the data, but the script was isolated from the SQL Server process. Furthermore, the R scripts were executed via a T-SQL stored procedure called **sp_execute_external_script.** No longer would data scientists have to pull huge amounts of data to a workstation that could be stale or unsecured. The data science model lives *inside SQL Server.* The performance ramifications in production were amazing. A great example of what is possible is the work Microsoft did to deliver 1 million predictions per second, https://blogs.technet.microsoft. com/dataplatforminsider/2016/10/11/1000000-predictions-per-second. In SQL Server 2017, we brought in the same type of support for machine learning with support for Python.

The problem is that SQL Server on Linux does not support this model in SQL Server 2017 (as of the CU4 release). Fortunately, another related feature was released in SQL Server 2017 that works on both Windows and Linux releases because it is built into the core database engine (and remember, the core database engine is the same on Windows and Linux). This feature is called *native scoring*. Native scoring is exposed through another T-SQL function called PREDICT.

Here is an example of the PREDICT syntax (This will not execute without going through the following sample tutorial):

```
DECLARE @model VARBINARY(MAX) = (SELECT TOP(1) native_model FROM dbo.
rental_models WHERE model_name = 'linear_model' AND lang = 'Python');
SELECT d.*, p.* FROM PREDICT(MODEL = @model, DATA = dbo.rental_data AS d)
WITH(RentalCount_Pred float) AS p;
GO
```

In order to completely understand this syntax, you will either need to go through the complete Python prediction model on SQL Server on Windows at https://microsoft. github.io/sql-ml-tutorials/python/rentalprediction or look at the sample in our documentation using a known set of data called **iris** at https://docs.microsoft.com/ sql/advanced-analytics/r/how-to-do-realtime-scoring.

The concept is that many data scientists perform a process called building a *trained model* on their workstations with test data. The T-SQL PREDICT function can take a trained model as input and execute machine learning code built inside the database engine to *run* the trained model. Native scoring has a huge performance boost advantage over running the models with R or Python with sp_execute_external_script.

Summary

You have learned in this chapter how to build a sample node.js application to access the database. In addition, you have learned other T-SQL capabilities to enhance your database or application. Finally, you have learned about new SQL Server capabilities introduced in SQL Server 2016 and 2017 to further enhance your database and application. In the next chapter, I'll show you a complete list of tools that will allow you to further explore the capabilities of SQL Server and manage your SQL Server database and installation. Having this knowledge of tools is important, as these tools will be used throughout the remaining chapters of the book.

CHAPTER 5

SQL Server Tools

SQL Server has a rich tradition of providing the tools any data professional needs. Tools give anyone the power to develop, interact, tune, manage, and troubleshoot applications and queries with SQL Server. Tools for SQL Server encompass far more than programs or utilities. SQL Server comes built-in with a rich set of capabilities that I will discuss in this chapter as part of the topic of tools.

All tools for SQL Server have a common bond. They use or provide interfaces through the T-SQL language. Tools that are separate programs all know how to connect and execute T-SQL queries through a driver or provider that uses the TDS protocol. In Chapters 2, 3, and 4, I introduced you to two tools to interact with SQL Server, sqlcmd and the mssql extension with Visual Studio Code.

In this chapter, I will show you graphical and command line tools to connect, run queries, and manage aspects of SQL Server. I'll also show you the built-in features of the SQL Server engine that provide insight into metadata, execution, performance, resources, and tracing. I'll show you other features that allow you to make configuration changes to SQL Server and databases and queries to affect behavior or provide more insight.

One crucial point as you explore this chapter is that existing tools that run on Windows computers work virtually unchanged to connect and interact with SQL Server on Linux. If you are a Windows user, you can continue to use tools like SQL Server Management Studio (SSMS). But if you are a macOS or Linux user, you will love our new strategy of providing cross-platform, open-source tools. I'll cover all of these in this chapter. I'll conclude the chapter by talking about tools to develop, build, and execute ETL packages with SSIS.

SQL Server provides other tools that are specific to features like security or high availability, and I'll discuss those in more detail in Chapters 7 and 8.

© Bob Ward 2018
B. Ward, *Pro SQL Server on Linux*, https://doi.org/10.1007/978-1-4842-4128-8_5

The intention of this chapter is to introduce you to the capabilities of these tools along with some examples. By showing you these tools now, you will be prepared to use them to explore other features and capabilities as you read the rest of the book. I will highlight in this chapter the names of sample script files I've provided that are companions to this book.

Command Line Tools

Tools that are run from the command line are simple but essential. I recommend you understand the command line tools that are available with SQL Server, because they provide the simplest, lightest method to interact with SQL Server.

Tip   Tools with graphical user interfaces such as SSMS provide powerful capabilities. But SSMS has more moving parts than a tool like sqlcmd. If someone said they were having problems connecting with SSMS on a Windows computer to SQL Server on Linux, I would ask whether they could connect with sqlcmd on the Linux server locally. This narrows down any problems with the graphical tool and networking issues.

The Microsoft strategy for command line tools is to ensure they are available on common client platforms including Windows, Linux, and macOS and in some cases make them an open-source project on GitHub.

In this section I'll talk about the following tools:

- sqlcmd (I showed you how to install and use some basics for this tool in Chapter 2.)

- bcp

- mssql-cli

- mssql-scripter

- sqlservr command line options

One tool not listed in this section is called DBFS, which will be covered in a later section on tools built inside the engine. A nice blog post written by SQL Server Linux expert Anthony Nocentino on DBFS can be found at `www.centinosystems.com/blog/sql/dbfs-command-line-access-to-sql-server-dmvs`. To keep track of all future advances in command line tools, refer to our documentation at `https://docs.microsoft.com/en-us/sql/tools/overview-sql-tools`.

sqlcmd

SQL Server has always provided a simple command line tool to submit T-SQL queries against the database engine. The evolution of these tools started with isql.exe and osql. exe for Windows, but in recent years we released a tool called sqlcmd.exe. This tool is compiled natively for Windows, Linux, and macOS and can be used as a client against any SQL Server for Windows or Linux (for example, you could connect with sqlcmd on a Linux client to a SQL Server on Windows). On all platforms, sqlcmd uses the Microsoft ODBC driver for SQL Server native to that operating system.

sqlcmd is installed by default when you install SQL Server on Windows. For SQL Server on Linux, you must install a separate package called **mssql-tools** (with a dependency on ODBC for Linux) as documented at `https://docs.microsoft.com/sql/linux/sql-server-linux-setup-tools`. For macOS, we use HomeBrew (`https://brew.sh`) to install the tools and ODBC drivers, as documented at `https://docs.microsoft.com/sql/linux/sql-server-linux-setup-tools#macos`.

sqlcmd offers two modes of execution: *interactive* or *script execution*. Either mode allows you to connect and run T-SQL query batches against any SQL Server, including SQL Server on Linux.

Like any good command line tool, there are many command line *switches* or options. If you execute T-SQL SELECT statements in sqlcmd, the results can be displayed in your console (stdout) or redirected to a file (using a command line option or *redirecting* the results of stdout).

Here is an example of a basic sqlcmd execution on the local Linux Server (hence I don't have to use the -S parameter for ServerName).

```
sqlcmd -Usqllinux
```

Figure 5-1 shows the results. Note the prompts that are provided within the sqlcmd tool. This is called the *sqlcmd editor*.

```
[thewandog@bwsql2017rhel ~]$ sqlcmd -Usqllinux
Password:
1> SELECT @@version
2> GO
```

```
--------------------------------------------------------------------------------------------
----------------------------------------------------------------------------
Microsoft SQL Server 2017 (RTM-CU4) (KB4056498) - 14.0.3022.28 (X64)
        Feb  9 2018 19:39:09
        Copyright (C) 2017 Microsoft Corporation
        Enterprise Edition: Core-based Licensing (64-bit) on Linux (Red Hat Enterprise Linux)

(1 rows affected)
1> █
```

Figure 5-1. Executing a query in sqlcmd on Linux using the sqlcmd editor

---

Note   I mentioned in Chapter 3 that the command GO is not a T-SQL command. Rather it is a special command recognized by a tool like sqlcmd to execute the batch of previously SQL command entered in the editor. The text GO is not sent to SQL Server.

At any sqlcmd line editor prompt, you can enter any valid T-SQL batch or a command (for example GO) recognized by the editor. A full list of sqlcmd editor commands is listed in our documentation at https://docs.microsoft.com/sql/tools/sqlcmd-utility#sqlcmd-commands or type in :HELP at the sqlcmd editor prompt.

For example, type in EXIT or QUIT to leave the editor. EXIT has a handy purpose where you can pass a query to EXIT(<query>) and the results of the query will be returned to the client, which is typically a script from the operating system shell.

The GO command has an optional parameter of GO (<n>), which indicates to run the T-SQL batch <n> times, one after the other.

In the last chapter, I created several scripts with a file extension of .sql (you are not required to use any file extension, but when you use .sql almost everyone understands what that means) and executed them within the Visual Studio Code Editor. I could have executed any of these with sqlcmd using the -i command line option. Any valid T-SQL or sqlcmd editor command can be put into the script.

I've provided the following T-SQL command in the sample script **getsqlversion.sql** with these statements:

```
SELECT @@version
GO
```

Tip @@version is a system-supplied variable that prints the version of SQL Server, edition, and operating system details. I consider this the most basic query to run against SQL Server, to ensure you can connect and run queries. You can see a complete list of system variables powered by the SQL Server Engine in our documentation at `https://docs.microsoft.com/en-us/sql/integration-services/system-variables`.

You can execute this script with sqlcmd from the bash shell with the following command:

```
sqlcmd -Usqllinux -igetsqlversion.sql
```

Figure 5-2 shows the result of executing this script with sqlcmd on Linux.

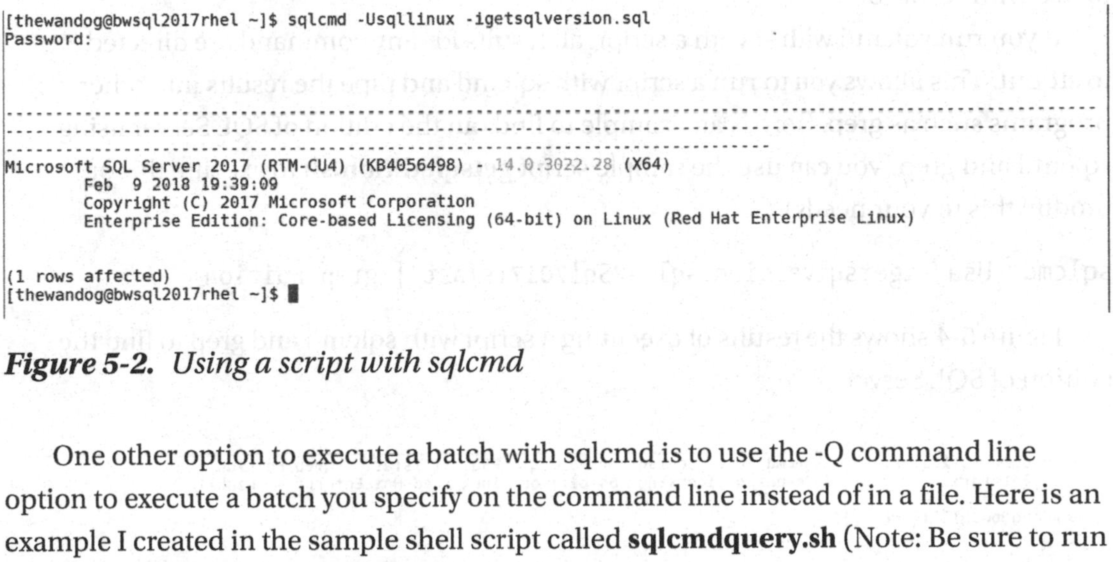

```
[thewandog@bwsql2017rhel ~]$ sqlcmd -Usqllinux -igetsqlversion.sql
Password:

--------------------------------------------------------------------------------
--------------------------------------------------------------------------------
--------------------------------------------------------------------
Microsoft SQL Server 2017 (RTM-CU4) (KB4056498) - 14.0.3022.28 (X64)
        Feb  9 2018 19:39:09
        Copyright (C) 2017 Microsoft Corporation
        Enterprise Edition: Core-based Licensing (64-bit) on Linux (Red Hat Enterprise Linux)

(1 rows affected)
[thewandog@bwsql2017rhel ~]$ 
```

Figure 5-2. *Using a script with sqlcmd*

One other option to execute a batch with sqlcmd is to use the -Q command line option to execute a batch you specify on the command line instead of in a file. Here is an example I created in the sample shell script called **sqlcmdquery.sh** (Note: Be sure to run `chmod u+x sqlcmdquery.sh` before executing this in a Linux shell):

```
sqlcmd -Usa -Q"SELECT @@version"
```

Note The -q option does the same thing as -Q but doesn't exit sqlcmd.

Figure 5-3 shows an example of using -Q with sqlcmd.

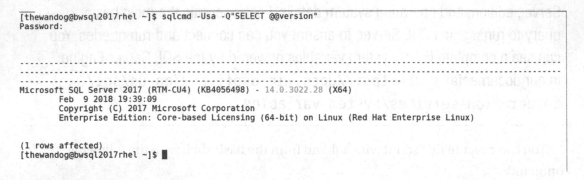

```
[thewandog@bwsql2017rhel ~]$ sqlcmd -Usa -Q"SELECT @@version"
Password:

--------------------------------------------------------------------------------------------------
--------------------------------------------------------------------------------------------------
---------------------------------------------------------------
Microsoft SQL Server 2017 (RTM-CU4) (KB4056498) - 14.0.3022.28 (X64)
        Feb  9 2018 19:39:09
        Copyright (C) 2017 Microsoft Corporation
        Enterprise Edition: Core-based Licensing (64-bit) on Linux (Red Hat Enterprise Linux)


(1 rows affected)
[thewandog@bwsql2017rhel ~]$ ▊
```

Figure 5-3. *Using the -Q option to execute a query with sqlcmd*

As with a script using -i, any valid T-SQL batch and sqlcmd editor command is valid to use with -Q or -q.

If you run sqlcmd with -i with a script, all results for any command are directed to stdout. This allows you to run a script with sqlcmd and pipe the results into other programs such as grep. Here is an example to find out the edition of SQL Server using sqlcmd and grep (you can use the sample script **getsqledition.sh** to execute this or modify this to your needs):

```
sqlcmd -Usa -igetsqlversion.sql -PSql2017isfast | grep Edition
```

Figure 5-4 shows the results of executing a script with sqlcmd and grep to find the edition of SQL Server.

```
[thewandog@bwsql2017rhel ~]$ sqlcmd -Usa -igetsqlversion.sql -PSql2017isfast | grep Edition
        Enterprise Edition: Core-based Licensing (64-bit) on Linux (Red Hat Enterprise Linux)

[thewandog@bwsql2017rhel ~]$ ▊
```

Figure 5-4. *Using sqlcmd with grep*

sqlcmd also provides a -o command line option to write all results and errors to a specific file.

Tip   One nice option (thank you Rathijit Sen for this tip) is the -p option, which prints out performance statistics from queries executed with sqlcmd. This includes the total time for SQL Server to execute queries and for the client to process them. Combined with SET STATISTICS TIME, which I will discuss later in this chapter, this can provide a nice option to determine how fast SQL Server can execute queries and how fast a client can process results over a network.

The full documentation for sqlcmd including all command line options can be found at `https://docs.microsoft.com/sql/tools/sqlcmd-utility`.

bcp

I demonstrated in Chapter 3 of this book how to insert data into SQL Server using the T-SQL INSERT statement. I showed you how to insert one row or use INSERT..SELECT or SELECT..INTO to insert multiple rows.

You might want to insert or *import* a very large number of rows based on data in a file stored outside of SQL Server. Or you may want to *export* data from SQL Server into a file. The bulk copy program (bcp) was designed for these types of tasks. Like sqlcmd, bcp has been built to run natively on Windows, Linux, and macOS and is installed when you install the tools that include sqlcmd using the **mssql-tools** package.

bcp relies on SQL Server ODBC driver extensions to bulk copy data in and out of SQL Server (see our documentation at `https://docs.microsoft.com/sql/relational-databases/native-client-odbc-extensions-bulk-copy-functions/sql-server-driver-extensions-bulk-copy-functions`). Therefore, you could also write an application that provides your own bulk copy functionality.

For import, the bcp tool will read a file you specify and transmit streams of data to SQL Server to be applied to a target table. For export, bcp will copy out streams of data from a table and write the data into a file.

The basic method to use bcp is to run this from a computer that can connect to SQL Server, either a remote computer or on the server itself. You specify command line options on how to connect to SQL Server, what database and tables you want to import into or export from, and an input or output file for the import or export. Input and output files can be all types of formats including the ability to be prescriptive on the datatypes within the file.

Let's use a simple example for a text formatted data in a file using the [Application].
[People] table example from Chapter 3. These examples assume you have created the
WideWorldImporters database and People table using scripts from Chapter 3 and
inserted data using commands from the **insertpeople.sql** script from Chapter 3. Since
you already have data in the People table, let's use bcp to export the data into a file using
a *native* format. (A native format will write out the data in binary form based on the
datatypes in the table. There are also command line options to write the data into a text
format). Here is the basic syntax to export a table as seen in the sample script **bcpout.sh**
(don't forget to run `chmod u+x bcpout.sh` to execute the script):

```
bcp [WideWorldImporters].[Application].[People] out people.dat -Usa -S
localhost -n
```

Figure 5-5 shows the results of running this bcp command on the Linux Server.

```
[thewandog@bwsql2017rhel ~]$ bcp [WideWorldImporters].[Application].[People] out people.dat -Usa -S localhost -n
Password:

Starting copy...

3 rows copied.
Network packet size (bytes): 4096
Clock Time (ms.) Total     : 1        Average : (3000.0 rows per sec.)
[thewandog@bwsql2017rhel ~]$
```

Figure 5-5. *Exporting data with bcp on a Linux Server*

You could delete the data from the People table and import the native formatted file
into SQL Server. But you first need to disable all the constraints on these tables before
executing the DELETE statement. Here is an example set of T-SQL commands I executed
from the sample script called **deletepeoplebeforeimport.sql**. This script will work
against the WideWorldImporters sample scripts from Chapter 3. You cannot use this
against the full WideWorldImporters sample backup.

Note   I disabled constraints including foreign key constraints from the Customers
table. If data existed in this table, disabling foreign key constraints is not
recommended, since you could violate logical referential integrity when inserting
new data. In addition, the bcp program itself will ignore constraints unless a
specific command line option is used. I disabled constraints in this example so I
could delete the existing rows.

```
USE [WideWorldImporters]
GO
ALTER TABLE [Sales].[Customers] NOCHECK CONSTRAINT ALL
GO
ALTER TABLE [Application].[People] NOCHECK CONSTRAINT ALL
GO
DELETE FROM [Application].[People]
GO
```

Now you can use bcp to import the data from the people.dat file created from the preceding export example (I've provided a sample bash shell script called **bcpin.sh**):

```
bcp [WideWorldImporters].[Application].[People] in people.dat -Usa -S
localhost -n
```

bcp has a rich set of command line options for both import and export scenarios. These include, but are not limited to, format files, import/export to text files, column and row delimiters, and performance options for hints and row batch sizes. For a complete list of command line options and examples, see the documentation at `https://docs.microsoft.com/sql/tools/bcp-utility`.

If you have the storage and are willing to copy your import files on the same computer as SQL Server (or an accessible file share for SQL Server on your network), you can use the T-SQL BULK INSERT to perform high speed imports. This command can significantly increase performance for an import, since the SQL Server engine will directly read the file and import the data into the target table. For more information about BULK INSERT, see the documentation at `https://docs.microsoft.com/sql/t-sql/statements/bulk-insert-transact-sql`. *Note*: at the time of the writing of this book, the BULK INSERT command on SQL Server on Linux requires sysadmin privileges.

mssql-cli

With the release of SQL Server on Linux, Microsoft launched a new strategy for tools used with SQL Server that is cross-platform (operating system) and produced through an open-source project. An example of one of these tools is **mssql-cli**. mssql-cli is a command line tool, like sqlcmd, to execute queries against SQL Server. mssql-cli is built using Python and is available on computers running Windows, Linux (including many distributions), and macOS operating systems.

To install mssql-cli, see the installation guide `https://github.com/dbcli/ mssql-cli/blob/master/README.rst#get-mssql-cli`. When we built mssql-cli, we created a GitHub project to allow open-source contributions (`https://github. com/dbcli/mssql-cli/`) and registered it as part of the dbcli initiative, which is a community of open-source projects towards better command line tools for databases.

While sqlcmd is a great simple command line tool for SQL Server, mssql-cli offers some advantages over sqlcmd, including:

- T-SQL intellisense

- Syntax highlighting

- Vertical format for query results

- Multi-line editor

- Configuration file to customize mssql-cli

- Environment variable support

One of the differences with mssql-cli from other SQL Server tools is that the GO keyword is not used to delimit a T-SQL batch. The mssql-cli editor allows you to execute one T-SQL command at a time by default. However, you use the multiline editor to create a multistatement T-SQL batch and then use the ";" character to end the batch.

You can launch mssql-cli with the following command:

```
mssql-cli -Usqllinux
```

Figure 5-6 shows an example of using mssql-cli on Linux to run a multi-statement T-SQL batch against the WideWorldImporters sample table I created in Chapter 3. (Note: results from this query assume you have populated data into these tables from previous chapters.)

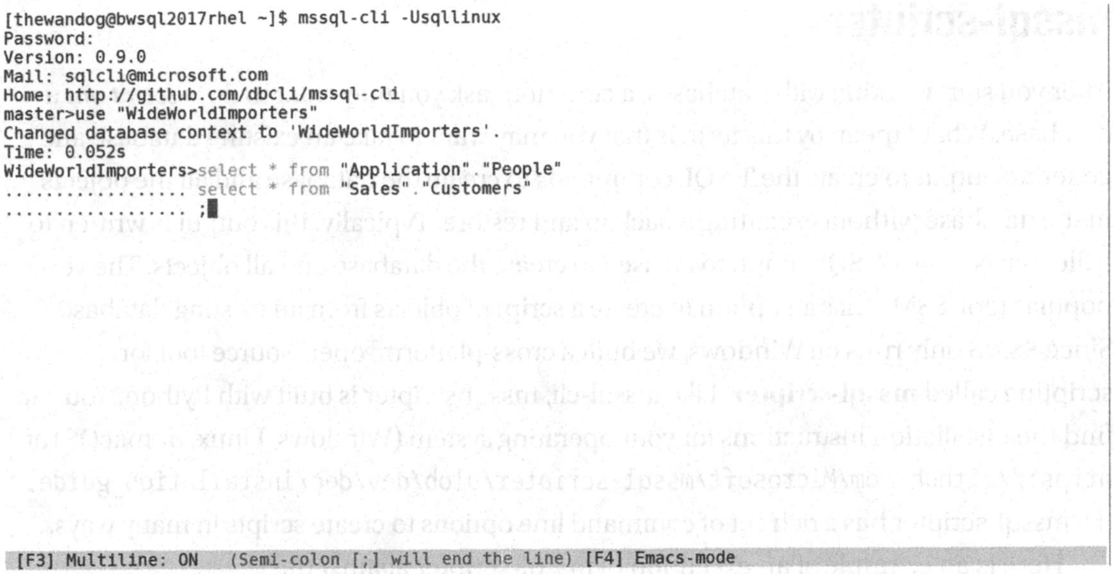

```
[thewandog@bwsql2017rhel ~]$ mssql-cli -Usqllinux
Password:
Version: 0.9.0
Mail: sqlcli@microsoft.com
Home: http://github.com/dbcli/mssql-cli
master>use "WideWorldImporters"
Changed database context to 'WideWorldImporters'.
Time: 0.052s
WideWorldImporters>select * from "Application"."People"
................. select * from "Sales"."Customers"
................. ;
```

```
[F3] Multiline: ON    (Semi-colon [;] will end the line) [F4] Emacs-mode
```

Figure 5-6. *Using mssql-cli on Linux*

While the options for the configuration file have not been completely documented at the time of the writing of this book, you can see the default configuration file (called **config**), which has comments inside it. The default configuration file is installed in the ~/**.config/mssqlcli** directory (~ means the home directory of the user logged in) on Linux and macOS and the **c:\users\<username>\AppData\Local\dbcli\mssqlcli** directory on Windows.

One of the strategies for new tools is to provide consistency in functionality and look and feel. Therefore, mssql-cli, the mssql Visual Studio Code extension, and SQL Operations Studio all use a common component called the SQL Tools Service for connection management, language support, query execution and result set processing. The SQL Tools Service is an open-source project. You can find out more information about the SQL Tools Service at `https://github.com/Microsoft/sqltoolsservice`.

mssql-cli was released in preview in December of 2017. There is some work to be done to fill in feature gaps compared with sqlcmd and other improvements. For example, there is no method today to pass in an input file or query for scripting or to pipe the results to stdout or a file. To view the roadmap for mssql-cli, see this documentation at `https://github.com/dbcli/mssql-cli/blob/master/doc/roadmap.md`.

mssql-scripter

After you start working with databases, a common task you may want to do is *script out* a database. What I mean by this term is that you may want to take an existing database and generate output to create the T-SQL commands to create the database and all the objects in the database without executing a backup and restore. Typically, this output is written to a file that is now a T-SQL script, to be used to create the database and all objects. The very popular tool, SSMS, has an option to create a script of objects from an existing database. Since SSMS only runs on Windows, we built a cross-platform, open-source tool for scripting called **mssql-scripter**. Like mssql-cli, mssql-scripter is built with Python. You can find the installation instructions for your operating system (Windows, Linux, or macOS) at https://github.com/Microsoft/mssql-scripter/blob/dev/doc/installation_guide. md. mssql-scripter has a rich set of command line options to create scripts in many ways.

Here is an example of an execution of mssql-scripter against the WideWorldImporters database from Chapter 3:

```
mssql-scripter -S localhost -d WideWorldImporters -U sqllinux -P
Sql2017isfast -f ./wwi.sql --logins --check-for-existence --display-progress
```

Figure 5-7 shows an example of the output from mssql-scripter to create a T-SQL script of the WideWorldImporters database and all its objects that I created in Chapter 3. Note some of the options I used to create logins, only create if the object does not exist, and to display progress during execution.

```
[thewandog@bwsql2017rhel ~]$ mssql-scripter -S localhost -d WideWorldImporters -U sqllinux -P Sql2017isfast
-f ./wwi.sql --logins --check-for-existence --display-progress
Scripting request: 7a9a22a6-829a-49b0-9906-fb4b653e611f plan: 9 database objects
Scripting progress: Status: Progress Progress: 0 out of 9 objects scripted
Scripting progress: Status: Progress Progress: 0 out of 9 objects scripted
Scripting progress: Status: Completed Progress: 1 out of 9 objects scripted
Scripting progress: Status: Completed Progress: 2 out of 9 objects scripted
Scripting progress: Status: Completed Progress: 3 out of 9 objects scripted
Scripting progress: Status: Completed Progress: 4 out of 9 objects scripted
Scripting progress: Status: Completed Progress: 5 out of 9 objects scripted
Scripting progress: Status: Completed Progress: 6 out of 9 objects scripted
Scripting progress: Status: Progress Progress: 6 out of 9 objects scripted
Scripting request submitted with request id: 7a9a22a6-829a-49b0-9906-fb4b653e611f
Scripting progress: Status: Progress Progress: 6 out of 9 objects scripted
Scripting progress: Status: Progress Progress: 6 out of 9 objects scripted
Scripting progress: Status: Progress Progress: 6 out of 9 objects scripted
Scripting progress: Status: Completed Progress: 7 out of 9 objects scripted
Scripting progress: Status: Progress Progress: 7 out of 9 objects scripted
Scripting progress: Status: Progress Progress: 7 out of 9 objects scripted
Scripting progress: Status: Progress Progress: 7 out of 9 objects scripted
Scripting progress: Status: Completed Progress: 8 out of 9 objects scripted
Scripting progress: Status: Completed Progress: 9 out of 9 objects scripted
Scripting request: 7a9a22a6-829a-49b0-9906-fb4b653e611f completed
[thewandog@bwsql2017rhel ~]$ ▎
```

Figure 5-7. *Using mssql-scripter to create a T-SQL script for all objects in the WideWorldImporters database*

Note   Using this method will not allow you to first create a login called sqllinux and then create the database and objects using the sqllinux login. You would need to create two different scripts: (1) One to create the sqllinux login that you would execute as sa and (2) one to create the database and objects that you would execute logged in as the sqllinux account.

You can now take the wwi.sql file and execute this as a script with a tool like sqlcmd using the -i option.

By default, mssql-scripter writes its output to stdout. Therefore, you can pipe the results of mssql-scripter to other tools. The **sed** program on Linux provides the ability to do "search and replace." Figure 5-8 shows an example of using mssql-scripter and sed to create a script of the WideWorldImporters database but change the database name to NewWideWorldImporters.

Execute this command to see the results:

```
mssql-scripter -S localhost -d WideWorldImporters -U sqllinux -P
Sql2017isfast --check-for-existence --display-progress | sed -e
"s/WideWorldImporters/NewWideWorldImporters/g" > new_wwi.sql
```

```
[thewandog@bwsql2017rhel ~]$ mssql-scripter -S localhost -d WideWorldImporters -U sqllinux -P Sql2017isfast
 --check-for-existence --display-progress | sed -e "s/WideWorldImporters/NewWideWorldImporters/g" > new_wwi.
sql
Scripting request: 5eee5728-f6cf-442a-8a05-e8f89be552c6 plan: 8 database objects
Scripting progress: Status: Progress Progress: 0 out of 8 objects scripted
Scripting progress: Status: Completed Progress: 1 out of 8 objects scripted
Scripting progress: Status: Completed Progress: 2 out of 8 objects scripted
Scripting progress: Status: Completed Progress: 3 out of 8 objects scripted
Scripting progress: Status: Completed Progress: 4 out of 8 objects scripted
Scripting progress: Status: Completed Progress: 5 out of 8 objects scripted
Scripting progress: Status: Progress Progress: 5 out of 8 objects scripted
Scripting request submitted with request id: 5eee5728-f6cf-442a-8a05-e8f89be552c6
Scripting progress: Status: Progress Progress: 5 out of 8 objects scripted
Scripting progress: Status: Progress Progress: 5 out of 8 objects scripted
Scripting progress: Status: Progress Progress: 5 out of 8 objects scripted
Scripting progress: Status: Completed Progress: 6 out of 8 objects scripted
Scripting progress: Status: Progress Progress: 6 out of 8 objects scripted
Scripting progress: Status: Progress Progress: 6 out of 8 objects scripted
Scripting progress: Status: Progress Progress: 6 out of 8 objects scripted
Scripting progress: Status: Completed Progress: 7 out of 8 objects scripted
Scripting progress: Status: Completed Progress: 8 out of 8 objects scripted
Scripting request: 5eee5728-f6cf-442a-8a05-e8f89be552c6 completed
[thewandog@bwsql2017rhel ~]$ ▌
```

Figure 5-8. *Using sed with mssql-scripter to create a script with a new database name*

For a complete list of mssql-scripter command line options, use the --help option or consult the documentation (which also includes some notable examples) at `https://github.com/Microsoft/mssql-scripter/tree/dev/doc`.

sqlservr Command Line Options

In Chapter 2 I showed you how to start and stop SQL Server using the systemctl program on Linux. It is also possible to start SQL Sever directly from the command line by executing the sqlservr program. Under normal circumstances you should not have to run sqlservr from the command line directly, but here are some possible reasons:

- SQL Server will not start with systemctl (Note: it is very likely that if SQL Server cannot be started with systemctl, starting it from the command line will not work either, but there could be some circumstances where this could help).

- You need to start SQL Server with a feature that is not available with configuration via the mssql-conf script. I will show you some of these options in Chapter 9.

To start SQL Server from the command line, you need to use the sudo command to run sqlservr in the context of the mssql Linux account (You must first stop SQL Server to run this):

```
sudo -u mssql /opt/mssql/bin/sqlservr
```

SQL Server will start and dump out the output of the ERRORLOG to stdout, which by default writes to the console. At this point, if you need to shut down SQL Server, you cannot use the systemctl program (systemctl stop mssql-server completes with no error). You will need to use one of two methods to shut down SQL Server:

1) Connect to SQL Server and execute the T-SQL **SHUTDOWN** command.

2) From the console when you execute **sqlservr**, type <ctrl>+<c>.

Figure 5-9 shows an example of the console after shutting down SQL Server with <ctrl>+<c>.

```
2018-04-07 09:33:00.13 spid25s     Parallel redo is started for database 'WideWorldImporters' with worker po
ol size [2].
2018-04-07 09:33:00.19 spid11s     Polybase feature disabled.
2018-04-07 09:33:00.19 spid11s     Clearing tempdb database.
2018-04-07 09:33:00.21 spid18s     A self-generated certificate was successfully loaded for encryption.
2018-04-07 09:33:00.22 spid18s     Server is listening on [ 'any' <ipv6> 1433].
2018-04-07 09:33:00.22 spid18s     Server is listening on [ 'any' <ipv4> 1433].
2018-04-07 09:33:00.22 Server      Server is listening on [ ::1 <ipv6> 1434].
2018-04-07 09:33:00.22 Server      Server is listening on [ 127.0.0.1 <ipv4> 1434].
2018-04-07 09:33:00.22 Server      Dedicated admin connection support was established for listening locally
on port 1434.
2018-04-07 09:33:00.24 spid18s     SQL Server is now ready for client connections. This is an informational
message; no user action is required.
2018-04-07 09:33:00.27 spid5s      Parallel redo is shutdown for database 'WideWorldImporters' with worker p
ool size [2].
2018-04-07 09:33:00.66 spid11s     Starting up database 'tempdb'.
2018-04-07 09:33:00.89 spid11s     The tempdb database has 1 data file(s).
2018-04-07 09:33:00.90 spid26s     The Service Broker endpoint is in disabled or stopped state.
2018-04-07 09:33:00.90 spid26s     The Database Mirroring endpoint is in disabled or stopped state.
2018-04-07 09:33:00.91 spid26s     Service Broker manager has started.
2018-04-07 09:33:00.93 spid5s      Recovery is complete. This is an informational message only. No user acti
on is required.
^C2018-04-07 09:33:05.38 spid5s      Always On: The availability replica manager is going offline because SQ
L Server is shutting down. This is an informational message only. No user action is required.
2018-04-07 09:33:05.38 spid5s      SQL Server shutdown due to Ctrl-C or Ctrl-Break signal. This is an inform
ational message only. No user action is required.
2018-04-07 09:33:05.38 spid5s      SQL Trace was stopped due to server shutdown. Trace ID = '1'. This is an
informational message only; no user action is required.
[thewandog@bwsql2017rhel bin]$ █
```

Figure 5-9. Shutting down sqlservr from the console

SQL Operations Studio

While SSMS is an extremely popular tool, it only works on Windows, so Linux and macOS users would have to install it with a virtualization program. As I mentioned earlier in this chapter when describing mssql-cli, when possible, we build new tools to run on multiple operating systems and be part of an open-source project.

For tools that require a graphical interface, the Visual Studio Code project provided a nice platform to build a cross-platform system. Coupled with the work we did for the SQL Tools Service, a new tool called SQL Operations Studio was born, forked from the Visual Studio Code open-source project.

Released as a preview tool in November 2017, SQL Operations Studio continues to receive monthly updates both from Microsoft and the community through a GitHub repo at https://github.com/Microsoft/sqlopsstudio. In true GitHub fashion, private builds are available on a more frequent basis, the entire source code is available for anyone to see or fork on their own, and all issues are filed through GitHub at https://github.com/Microsoft/sqlopsstudio/issues.

Installation

We have embraced the natural installation experience of each operating system. Windows comes with a .zip file or complete Windows installer experience. macOS users are provided a zip file, which works within the macOS Downloads experience, and Linux users can download a Debian or RPM package or a tar.gz file.

Figure 5-10 shows SQL Operations Studio after installing it on macOS.

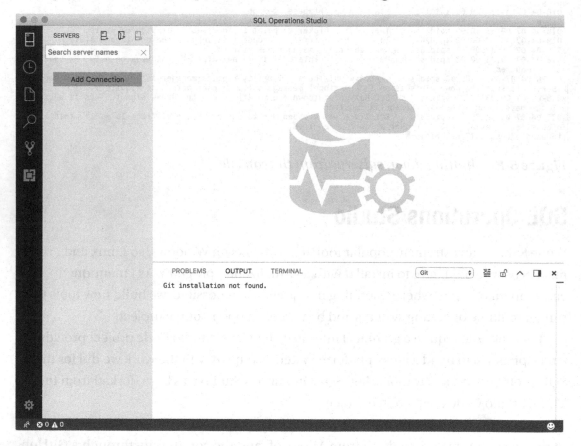

Figure 5-10. *SQL Operations Studio on macOS*

SQL Operations Studio provides these unique features:

- A T-SQL code editor built with Intellisense to execute queries
- Smart T-SQL code "snippets"
- Customizable dashboards through widgets
- Extensions to add on to the built-in base functionality
- Integrated Terminal (run shell commands without leaving the tool)

On my Windows laptop I've installed SQL Operations Studio. There are two things I want to do to get started with the tool: (1) Add a connection to SQL Server on Linux and (2) change settings for the background color and default font for the editor.

Figure 5-11 shows SQL Ops Studio on Windows before I add a connection to SQL Server.

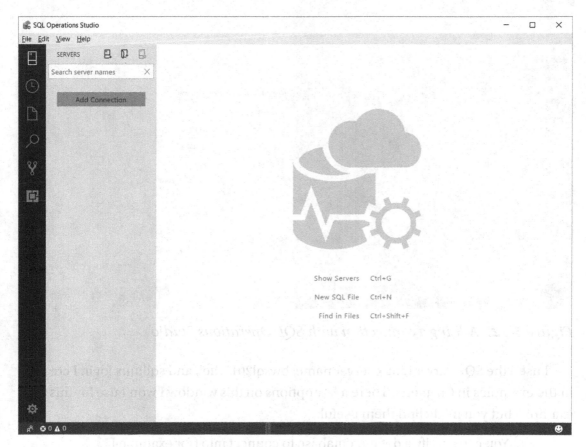

Figure 5-11. SQL Operations Studio on Windows

Now I'll select the blue button that says Add Connection. I get a new window to put in my server name, login, and password. Figure 5-12 shows the Connection profile window.

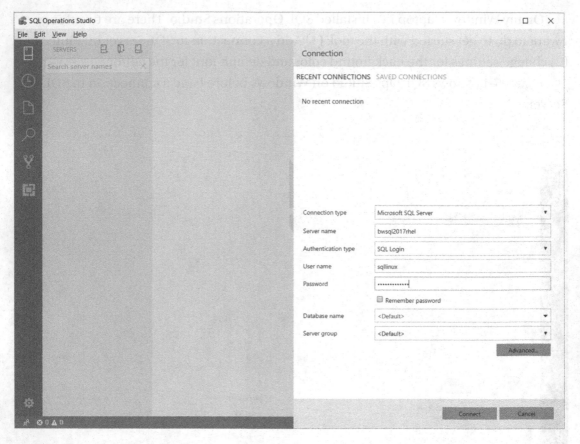

Figure 5-12. *Adding a connection with SQL Operations Studio*

I used the SQL Server Linux server name, bwsql2017rhel, and sqllinux login I created in the examples in Chapter 3. There a few options on this window I won't use for this example, but you might find them useful:

- You can specify a default database to connect into (for example I could have put in WideWorldImporters).

- You can create the concept of a Server Group, so you can manage and organize multiple SQL Servers into a unit.

- The Remember password option can be used so you do not have to specify the password each time you connect.

- The Advanced button provides additional options including login timeout (default is 15 seconds), Application Intent for read replicas in Availability Groups, and encryption settings.

After connecting to the SQL on Linux server, I'm presented with a pane on the left to explore and in the main window a Server dashboard with extensions. Figure 5-13 shows the default view after connecting to my SQL Server on Linux.

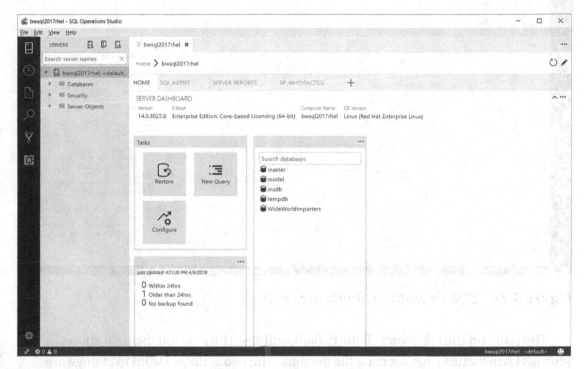

Figure 5-13. *The default view in SQL Operations Studio after connecting to SQL Server on Linux*

Configuration

The next thing I want to do is set some preferences to customize the tool. I do this by selecting the File/Preferences/Settings menu option. Preferences are customized by a file called **settings.json**. Figure 5-14 shows the interface in SQL Operations Studio to configure my preferences.

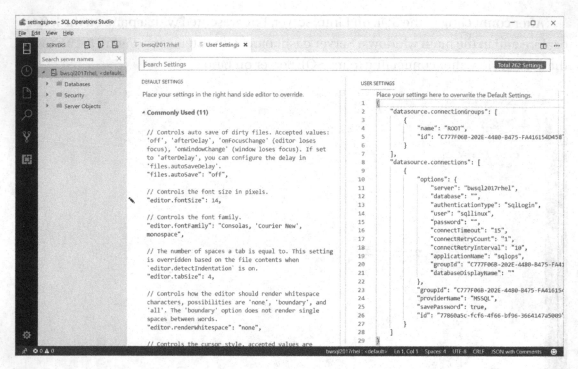

Figure 5-14. SQL Operations Studio user settings

The pane on the left shows all the default settings. The pane on the right shows settings I will include that override the defaults. The two settings I want to change are the default background color to black and the default font to display for the T-SQL code editor to a larger size. You can edit the user settings directly, but SQL Operations Studio includes a visual icon to help you copy the default settings into user settings and make changes. Figure 5-15 shows on the left pane how I clicked on the pencil icon and selected Edit to copy the settings for the editor fontsize, so I can make changes.

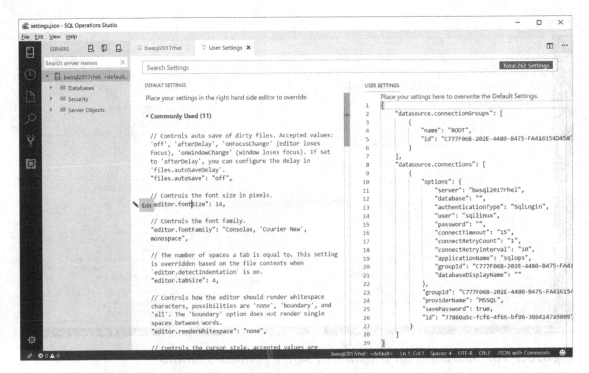

Figure 5-15. *Copying the default settings to make changes in SQL Operations Studio*

When I click Edit and Copy Settings, the setting will show up in the right pane and I can change the font size value. I then will save these settings by selecting Save from the File Menu. When I Save the font size, it automatically changes in the current window (because the font size applies to any editing in SQL Operations Studio).

The editor font size was easy to find on the default left pane, but what about the background color? At the top of the settings window is a Search edit box. I typed in the word Color in the Search edit box and it shows me the option to change the colorTheme of the Workbench. Figure 5-16 shows this example.

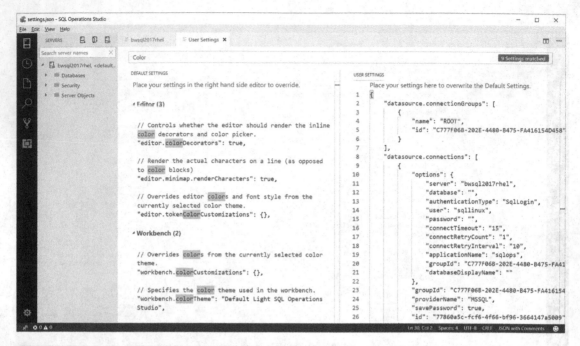

Figure 5-16. *Searching for a setting in SQL Operations Studio*

Now I can click the pencil icon near the workbench.colorTheme field and I'm presented with choices to change the theme. I selected Default Dark SQL Operations Studio. The color is instantly changed. Figure 5-17 shows the changes I made appear in the right pane for User Settings.

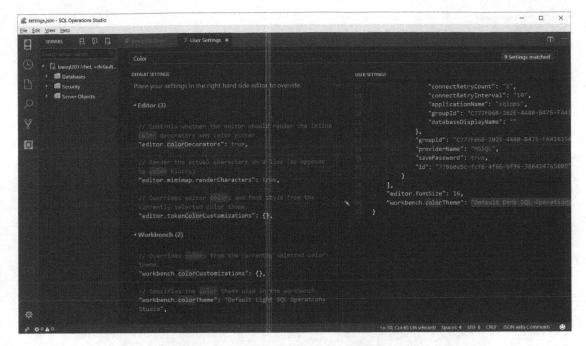

Figure 5-17. SQL Operations Studio with the new colorTheme

I saved my settings with the Save option from the File Menu and closed out the User Settings window.

Now that I have my settings saved to my preferences, let me show you a few basic features of SQL Operations Studio. For a complete walkthrough of the tool, I highly recommend this excellent community blog post: `https://www.mssqltips.com/sqlservertip/5339/new-sql-operations-studio-installation-and-overview`.

Object Explorer

Users of SSMS are familiar with a concept called **Object Explorer**. Object Explorer is a visual folder view of objects associated with SQL Server. You can traverse this view like typical folders by expanding or collapsing a tree view of objects including databases.

Figure 5-18 shows an example on my installation where I've expanded various objects from the Explorer tree.

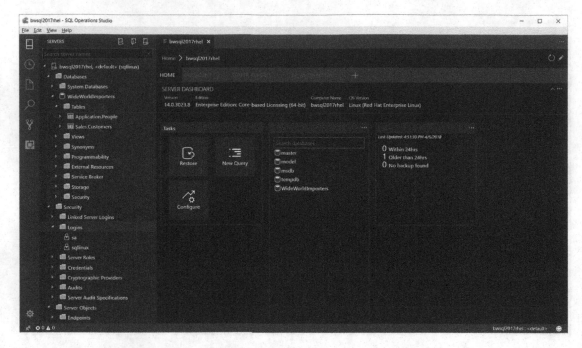

Figure 5-18. *Object Explorer in SQL Operations Studio*

SQL Operations Studio by default does not have the complete Object Explorer functionality as Windows users can see with SSMS, but I expect the functionality for this feature to grow over time.

Besides being able to navigate what objects are created with your SQL Server instance or database, you can right-click some objects for added functionality. For example, you can right-click a Server or a Database to edit a new T-SQL query or select Manage to see a dashboard. You can right-click a Table and view or edit data in a grid view. Figure 5-19 shows a grid where you can edit data directly for the [Application].[People] table created from the example in Chapter 3.

Figure 5-19. Editing table data in a grid view in SQL Operations Studio

Dashboards, Insights, and Extensions

By default, SQL Operations Studio has two dashboards: **Server** and **Database**. These dashboards are populated by objects called *widgets*. When you connect to SQL Server, by default, the Server dashboard is displayed with information about SQL Server, a widget for common tasks, a widget to find databases, and a widget on database backups. In Figure 5-20, you can see for my SQL Server I'm running Enterprise Edition (Core-based Licensing) for SQL Server on Red Hat Enterprise Linux. The widgets shown in Figure 5-20 are for tasks, a list of databases, and information about database backups.

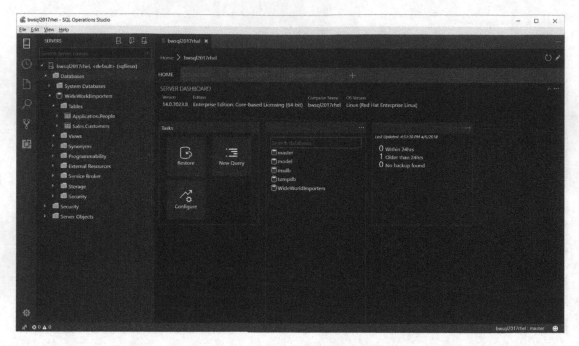

Figure 5-20. *The Server dashboard and widgets in SQL Operations Studio*

You can view the Server dashboard at any time by right-clicking the server name and selecting Manage.

You can view a similar dashboard about any database by right-clicking a database in the Object Explorer tree or on the list of databases on the Server dashboard and select Manage.

Figure 5-21 shows a dashboard for the example database WideWorldImporters I created in Chapter 3.

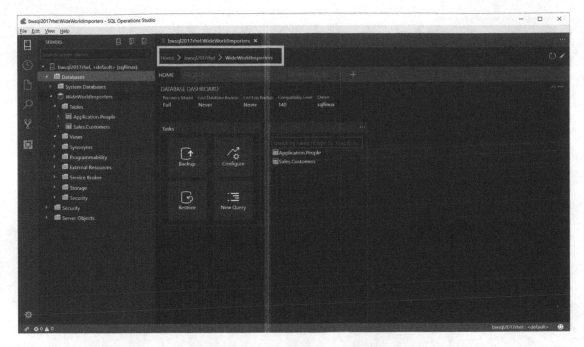

Figure 5-21. *The database dashboard for the WideWorldImporters sample database*

I've highlighted in red the context of the dashboards. When you select a database dashboard, it is stacked so that you can select the server name and go back to the Server dashboard. The database dashboard displays basic information about the database and displays a task and table list widget. I'll describe more about using SQL Operations Studio to back up and restore databases in a later chapter in this book.

One of the powerful aspects to SQL Operations Studio is the ability to customize its functionality. You can create other widgets to be displayed on a server or database dashboard. You can learn more about how to customize new widgets in our documentation at `https://docs.microsoft.com/sql/sql-operations-studio/tutorial-build-custom-insight-sql-server`. We have provided two built-in widgets you can add to a database dashboard for performance and table usage information. Figure 5-22 shows the database dashboard for the WideWorldImporters example database after enabling these widgets.

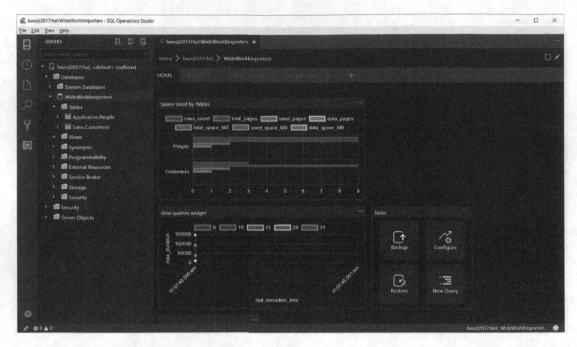

Figure 5-22. *Performance and table space usage widgets in a database dashboard in SQL Operations Studio*

You can learn how to enable these built-in widgets in our documentation at https://docs.microsoft.com/sql/sql-operations-studio/insight-widgets.

Another way to customize SQL Operations Studio is through the concept of *Extensions*. Think of extensions as methods to add your own dashboards outside of customizing the server and database dashboard. Extensions are add-ons like the concept of extensions in Visual Studio Code.

Extensions are built by the community or Microsoft and can be installed (or view what *is* installed) by selecting the Extensions icon in the far-left pane in SQL Operations Studio. Over time, I expect the list of extensions to become as robust as the marketplace found in Visual Studio Code.

Depending on what release of SQL Operations Studio, you may have some extensions already installed with the tool. For my installation, I have extensions for SQL Agent, Server Reports, and sp_whoisactive (an extremely popular T-SQL procedure used in the SQL Server Community). You can find these extensions next to the Home option, which is used to display the Server dashboard. You can find more information about extensions and how to create your own in our documentation at https://docs.microsoft.com/sql/sql-operations-studio/extensions.

T-SQL Query Editor

Perhaps the most common task you will use SQL Operations Studio for is to execute T-SQL queries. SQL Operations Studio provides a rich T-SQL query editor with similar functionality to the mssql extension for Visual Studio Code. And the quickest way to create and execute a query is to right-click the server or a database name and select the option for New Query.

Since SQL Operations Studio uses the SQL Tools Service, like the mssql extension for Visual Studio Code, it provides intellisense and features to aid in executing T-SQL queries. One feature I did not talk about in Chapter 3 with Visual Studio code is a concept called T-SQL snippets. T-SQL snippets provide templates for common tasks using T-SQL to aid in help completing T-SQL syntax.

To use T-SQL snippets, bring up the Query Editor using the New Query option or the keyboard shortcut <Ctrl>+<N>. Then type in the word **sql** and you will be presented a list of common T-SQL tasks such as creating a table. Figure 5-23 shows the T-SQL snippet to create a new table after picking **sqlCreateTable**.

Figure 5-23. *Using a T-SQL snippet in SQL Operations Studio*

Another excellent feature in the T-SQL editor is a concept called *Peek Definition*. Consider this scenario. You are using the T-SQL editor to execute an INSERT statement to insert a row into the [Application].[People] table from the WideWorldImporters database. The problem is you don't remember all the columns so are not sure of what columns names to list or how many values are required. Peek Definition allows you to see the table definition while completing the INSERT statement.

To use Peek Definition, highlight the table name in the T-SQL Query Editor and right-click to select Peek Definition. Figure 5-24 shows the interface of using Peek Definition to complete the INSERT statement.

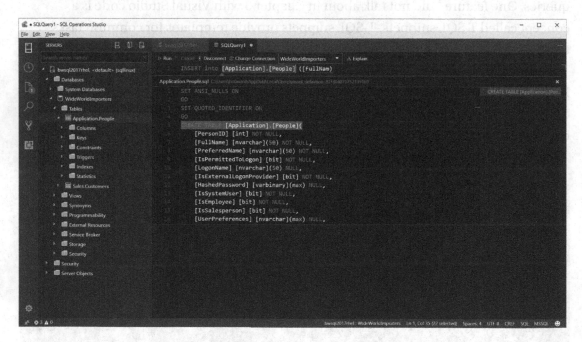

Figure 5-24. *Using Peek Definition with the T-SQL editor in SQL Operations Studio*

Other Features

SQL Operations Studio provides other functionality for data professionals. This includes an Integrated Terminal like Visual Studio Code, Source Code Control functionality, and a Task History for history of operations like Backup and Restore.

Like any useful tool, SQL Operations Studio has keyboard shortcuts for almost every interaction and allows you to customize the keyboard shortcuts. To learn more about keyboard shortcuts for SQL Operations Studio, see the documentation at `https://docs.microsoft.com/sql/sql-operations-studio/keyboard-shortcuts`.

At the time I wrote the chapter in this book, SQL Operations Studio was still in preview. Given the ability to extend this tool and the open-source capabilities for the community to contribute to the tool, I expect it will continue to grow in functionality and capability very rapidly as new major builds come out each month.

SQL Server Management Studio

Since 2005, the most popular tool in the world to interact with SQL Server is SQL Server Management Studio (SSMS). Prior to 2005, SQL Server provided a graphical interface tool called SQL Enterprise Manager. SSMS was an exciting new tool with rich capabilities based on a shell from Visual Studio. Since 2005, with each release of SQL Server, SSMS was enhanced to include a wide range of features and capabilities.

Historically, one of the issues with SSMS was that it was always bundled with the installation and release of a major version of SQL Server. This approach hampered our ability to make major enhancements to the tool on a frequent basis. Starting with SQL Server 2016, we made the decision to decouple SSMS from SQL Server. We also made a conscious effort to clean up a backlog of bugs, issues, and suggestions. We began this journey with a separate SSMS download in June of 2016, and now SSMS 17 is updated and enhanced monthly. You can always find the latest release of SSMS to download at `https://docs.microsoft.com/sql/ssms/download-sql-server-management-studio-ssms`. The biggest downside to SSMS as a tool for SQL Server on Linux users is that it can only be installed on computers with the Windows operating system. But for users of Windows, it is a powerful tool with rich capabilities. The great upside to SSMS is that connecting to SQL Server on Linux uses the same providers and libraries as is used for Windows, so connecting to SQL Server on Linux will feel the same as on Windows. It is a great compatibility story.

SSMS includes an Object Explorer, rich T-SQL editor, a T-SQL debugger, wizards to complete specific tasks, and reports for a range of SQL Server and database capabilities.

There has been a great deal of documentation, training, and information about SSMS that has been written over the years. A section in this chapter will never do it justice. I will cover some of the major features that you can use to interact with SQL Server on Linux with SSMS, and then provide other resources that cover the topic in more detail.

Figure 5-25 shows the default interface for SSMS with Object Explorer and a New Query editor window.

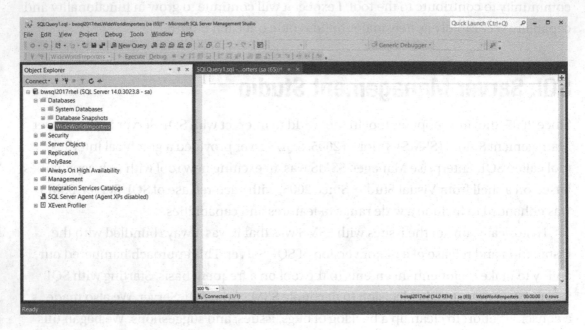

Figure 5-25. *The default SSMS interface*

Object Explorer

Like SQL Operations Studio, SSMS provides a visual interface to navigate objects for SQL Server. SSMS provides more options than SQL Operations Studio in Object Explorer, to include not just objects but features of SQL Server including Always On Availability Groups and Management Features. In addition, there are more options than in SQL Operations Studio when you right-click Object Explorer objects and features.

For example, Figure 5-26 shows options to create a T-SQL script to drop and create the WideWorldImporters example database.

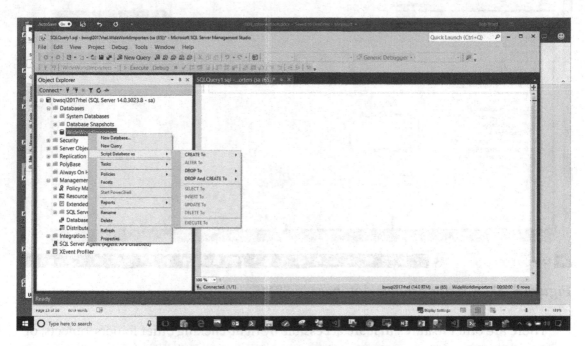

Figure 5-26. *Using SSMS to create a script to drop and create an existing database*

Another feature in SSMS through Object Explorer is the ability to create new objects like databases, tables, indexes, and other objects. If you right-click the Databases folder in Object Explorer, you have options to create or restore a new database. Figure 5-27 shows a new window that will appear when you right-click the Databases folder and select New Database.

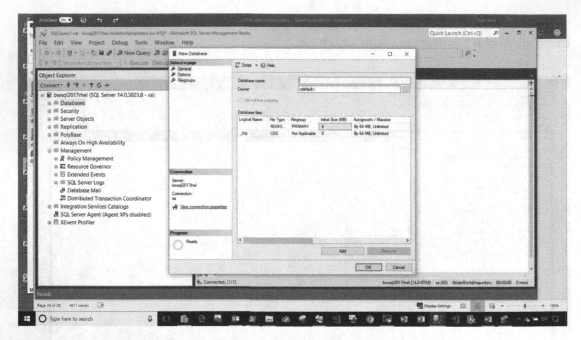

Figure 5-27. *Creating a new database in SSMS*

There are other features that are accessible by right-clicking other folders, objects, or features in SSMS.

One of the most powerful options when using right-click is Tasks for a database. Figure 5-28 shows all the types of tasks you can perform against a database with SSMS. Picking any of these options will present a new window or a *wizard* to lead you through performing one of these tasks. I'll describe some of these tasks as part of Chapter 9, either by using SSMS or the set of T-SQL commands to execute equivalent functionality.

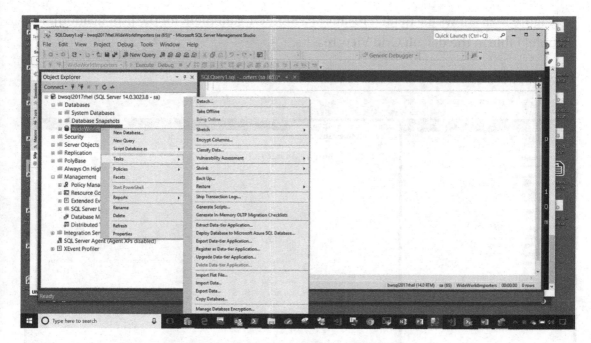

Figure 5-28. *Tasks available for databases in SSMS*

T-SQL Query Editor

Like SQL Operations Studio, SSMS provides a rich editor to create and design T-SQL queries. Features include color coding for identifiers, intellisense, and T-SQL snippets to aid in common T-SQL tasks. SSMS also allows you to open script files to execute T-SQL batches and save results to a grid view, text format, or a file. You also take results of a T-SQL SELECT statement and save them to a text file or a CSV (comma delimited) file.

Figure 5-29 shows the default results of a SELECT statement for the [Application]. [People] table in the default Grid View results.

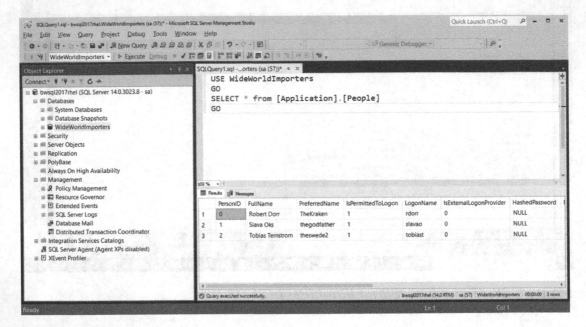

Figure 5-29. *Results of a query in the T-SQL editor in SSMS in grid view*

Notice the yellow status bar at the bottom of the SSMS screen shows context such as the server name, login of user connected, database context, total duration and total number of rows from the last executed query.

Reports

SSMS comes installed with a series of reports to view performance, disk usage, activity, and configuration of the SQL Server instance. Additionally, reports are available for databases to see space usage by object, indexes, and various statistics and performance specific to a database.

To execute a report, right-click the Server or a database, and select the Reports/ Standard Reports option.

Figure 5-30 shows the built-in report for Performance for all batches run on SQL Server on Linux instance since the server was started.

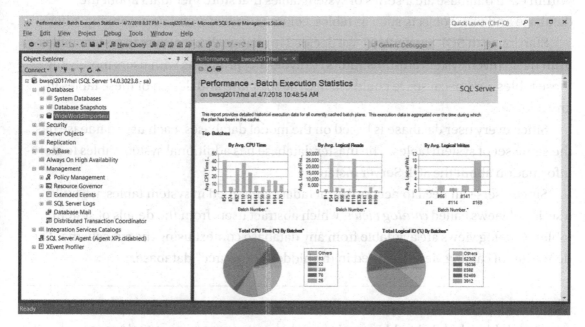

Figure 5-30. *The standard Performance Batch report in SSMS*

Reports can be an immensely powerful capability to gain insight into SQL Server and databases. While SSMS provides built-in reports, you can build our own custom report and integrate it into SSMS. You can read more about how to build custom reports in our documentation at `https://docs.microsoft.com/sql/ssms/object/custom-reports-in-management-studio`.

Tools Built into the Engine

One of the amazing stories of SQL Server is the number of *tools* that have been built into the core database engine. I call these "tools" because they are general-purpose features that are helpful for many various aspects to manage, monitor, and troubleshoot various scenarios for SQL Server. And since the core database engine is the same for SQL Server on Linux as Windows, most of these rich features work on Linux.

Keeping with the theme of consistency, most of the tools I will cover in this section are available through the T-SQL language. The open nature of T-SQL provides a natural method to expose rich tool functionality from the SQL Server engine.

System Tables and Catalog Views

Within each database are a series of system tables that store metadata about the database and other objects such as tables, columns, indexes, and users, among others.

Starting with SQL Server 2005, we decided to change direct access to system tables from users (even system administrators) to avoid any problems with users modifying these tables, and because we could change the structure and design of these tables in any release.

Since every user database is based on the model databases, each user database has the same set of system tables. The master database has additional system tables to store information about the SQL Server instance.

Since users still need to access the metadata contained in system tables, we built a series of views called *catalog views*, which abstract users from the details of system tables. Catalog views are available from any database context using the **sys** schema. The definition of catalog views is stored in the hidden "Resource" database.

Note   I'll provide some tips in Chapter 9 for some advanced techniques to access system tables, but it should never be needed under normal circumstances.

There are many features of SQL Server that require metadata to be stored in system tables. As of SQL Server 2017, there are approximately 300 catalog views spanning 30+ categories. You can see a complete list of catalog views by category in our documentation at `https://docs.microsoft.com/sql/relational-databases/system-catalog-views/catalog-views-transact-sql`. Our documentation also includes a very nice FAQ for common catalog view scenarios: `https://docs.microsoft.com/sql/relational-databases/system-catalog-views/querying-the-sql-server-system-catalog-faq`.

The most common categories I believe you will want to dive into are:

Object Catalog Views: Views about tables, columns, indexes, and other objects stored in the database

Databases and Files Catalog Views: Views about databases and files (I've used the sys.databases catalog view already in several examples.)

Security Catalog Views: Views about logins, roles, and users

There is even a catalog view to find a list of all catalog views! Execute the following T-SQL command from any database context from your favorite tool to get a list of all system objects:

```
SELECT name, type_desc FROM sys.system_objects
ORDER BY name
GO
```

Tip   Avoid building production applications or scripts that rely on SELECT * (all columns) from catalog views, because we may add columns to catalog view definitions in future releases of SQL Server.

Most of the results from this query that are type_desc = 'VIEW" are Catalog Views. I'll discuss shortly another type of special view called a *Dynamic Management View*.

Even though catalog views are stored in the hidden Resource database, you can see the T-SQL code for these views using the catalog view **sys.system_sql_modules**. The following T-SQL command can be used to find out the T-SQL view definition for the catalog view sys.databases:

```
SELECT * FROM sys.system_sql_modules
WHERE object_id = object_id('sys.databases')
GO
```

To comply with ISO standards, SQL Server also provides a series of catalog views known as System Information Schema Views. These views can easily be discovered because they belong to a special schema called INFORMATION_SCHEMA. You can get a complete list of these views in our documentation at https://docs.microsoft.com/sql/relational-databases/system-information-schema-views/system-information-schema-views-transact-sql.

Not all users can see everything in system catalog views. Policies for permissions for catalog views are a bit complex. You can read more about these permissions in our documentation at https://docs.microsoft.com/sql/relational-databases/security/metadata-visibility-configuration.

System Stored Procedures

SQL Server comes installed with a wide range of stored procedures called system stored procedures. Like catalog views, the definition and text of these procedures are stored in the hidden Resource database.

Many of the system stored procedures are used to manage and configure features and aspects of SQL Server. I introduced you to one of these system procedures in Chapter 2, called **sp_configure**, to configure SQL Server instance settings.

While most of the system stored procedures make changes, there is a series of general system stored procedures that provide information (in some cases using catalog views). These procedures have a known name format starting with the word **sp_help**. For example, this T-SQL command returns information like the catalog view sys.objects:

```
EXEC sp_help
GO
```

A full list of system stored procedures organized by category can be found in our documentation at https://docs.microsoft.com/sql/relational-databases/system-stored-procedures/system-stored-procedures-transact-sql.

Permissions or system stored procedures vary by the procedure. Consult the documentation of each procedure to see what permissions are required.

Dynamic Management Views

From the time I started working with SQL Server in 1993, there have been two *virtual tables* that provide information about the internal execution of SQL Server based on internal data structures in the engine: **sysprocesses** and **syslocks** (and stored procedures sp_who and sp_lock that reference them). These views take internal data structures for connections, queries, and locks and expose them in the form of rows and columns.

For many years these were the only views based on memory structures that could provide insight into the execution of the SQL Server engine. As I spent these years working in technical support, if I wanted insight into other memory structures within the engine, I would have to capture a user dump of the SQLSERVR.EXE process and use the Windows Debugger to manually inspect lists of structures. While it forced me to learn a great deal about the SQL Server engine, this was not an efficient way to troubleshoot SQL Server.

Then came along to the SQL Server team a guy named Slava Oks (can you see a trend here). Slava worked with a team of engineers to build the SQLOS platform, which is still part of the core engine architecture. Slava is an expert in debugging but had a goal to see how far he could solve problems with SQLOS without using a debugger. With the ideas from Slava, if you could connect to SQL Server, you could use T-SQL to "live debug" details of the SQL Server Engine.

The Views

Slava and team took the concept of virtual tables and expanded this into a series of views that exposed information from SQLOS structures such as tasks, threads, workers, and memory. This work led to other groups within the engine team exposing information about other structures.

In SQL Server 2005 we collected all these views into a new feature called Dynamic Management Views (DMV) and Dynamic Management Functions (DMF). You can query DMVs like any user or catalog view and you use DMFs as you would with any T-SQL function. (Note: DMFs, like functions, require parameters)

Tip   Intellisense is your friend when it comes to DMVs and DMFs. Typing in sys. dm_ will bring up a complete list of DMVs and DMFs supported in SQL Server.

These views from SQL Server 2005 still provide the core functionality of DMVs such as **sys.dm_exec_requests, sys.dm_os_tasks**, and **sys.dm_wait_stats**. In SQL Server 2017 on Linux and Windows, there are now approximately 240 DMVs and DMFs covering all aspects of the SQL Server engine.

DMVs and DMFs prove the open nature of T-SQL and the concept of exposing data as a table as a powerful tool to gain insight into any data, whether it be data from a user table, system table, or a list of structures that support the database engine.

A complete list of DMVs and DMFs can be found listed by category in our documentation at `https://docs.microsoft.com/sql/relational-databases/system-dynamic-management-views/system-dynamic-management-views`. DMVs and DMFs require the VIEW SERVER state permission, which can be assigned by sysadmin logins.

Many of these DMVs and DMFs are related and can be joined together. The SQL Server community over the years has published examples for different scenarios in various blogs and trainings. One of the most popular uses of DMVs comes from the community-developed stored procedure, sp_whoisactive, written by SQL Community Leader Adam Machanic (and is now extended into SQL Operations Studio). You can find details and downloads for sp_whoisactive from `http://whoisactive.com`.

Here is a list of my top ten DMVs and DMFs and example queries for each DMV/DMF:

> **dm_exec_requests**: A list of active queries and background requests. It is probably the most common DMV used today by SQL Server users.

The following query, found in the sample **dm_exec_requests.sql** file, shows a list of active user queries and details about the query including session_id (uniquely identifies a connection to SQL Server), status (is it running or waiting), command (what query is running), wait_type (if the query is waiting, what kind of resource), and wait_time (how long has it been waiting on a resource). You will also notice I join this DMV with sys.**dm_exec_sessions** so I only show the active "user" requests.

```
-- Get the session_id, status (RUNNING or SUSPENDED), command (what query),
wait_type (if waiting what resource?), and wait_time (how long waiting) for
active user requests
--
SELECT er.[session_id], er.[status], er.[command], er.[wait_type],
er.[wait_time]
FROM sys.dm_exec_requests er
INNER JOIN sys.dm_exec_sessions es
ON es.[session_id] = er.[session_id]
AND es.[is_user_process] = 1
GO
```

There are more columns in this DMV. Check out the complete options in our documentation at `https://docs.microsoft.com/sql/relational-databases/system-dynamic-management-views/sys-dm-exec-requests-transact-sql`. You can find a complete set of options for sys.dm_exec_sessions at `https://docs.microsoft.com/sql/relational-databases/system-dynamic-management-views/sys-dm-exec-sessions-transact-sql`. Wait types describe different scenarios where SQL Server requests can wait on a resource such as a lock, I/O, latch, and many others. The most comprehensive description of wait types and what they mean for your application can be found in this community blog run by my friend and SQL Server Community Leader Paul Randal `https://www.sqlskills.com/help/waits/`.

dm_exec_query_stats: A list of performance statistics based on queries currently cached. This is an extremely popular DMV for query performance. I like the example we have in our documentation, which I have provided in the sample script, **dm_exec_query_stats.sql**. This query is designed to show the Top <N> queries that account for the most CPU resource usage:

```
-- Get the top 5 queries by CPU usage. Show the query_hash, avg CPU time,
and T-SQL text
-- query_hash is a way to uniquely identify a query that could be executed
in more than one way but has as similar "pattern"
SELECT TOP 5 query_stats.query_hash AS "Query Hash",
    SUM(query_stats.total_worker_time) / SUM(query_stats.execution_count)
AS "Avg CPU Time",
    MIN(query_stats.statement_text) AS "Statement Text"
FROM
    (SELECT QS.*,
    SUBSTRING(ST.text, (QS.statement_start_offset/2) + 1,
    ((CASE statement_end_offset
        WHEN -1 THEN DATALENGTH(ST.text)
        ELSE QS.statement_end_offset END
            - QS.statement_start_offset)/2) + 1) AS statement_text
    FROM sys.dm_exec_query_stats AS QS
    CROSS APPLY sys.dm_exec_sql_text(QS.sql_handle) as ST) as query_stats
GROUP BY query_stats.query_hash
ORDER BY "Avg CPU Time" DESC
GO
```

This DMV stores query information in the form of hashes (uniquely identifies a query that is the same "pattern") and handles. Notice the use of the DMF **dm_exec_sql_text** to get the text of the SQL query.

You can find the complete documentation of dm_exec_query_stats at https://docs.microsoft.com/sql/relational-databases/system-dynamic-management-views/sys-dm-exec-query-stats-transact-sql. The documentation for dm_exec_sql_text can be found at https://docs.microsoft.com/sql/relational-databases/system-dynamic-management-views/sys-dm-exec-sql-text-transact-sql.

dm_os_waiting_tasks: A list of tasks (queries and background tasks) that are waiting on a resource. The DMV only shows requests that are waiting on a resource. Here is an example from the sample script **dm_os_waiting_tasks.sql** to show all user requests that are waiting on a resource (Note: If there are no user tasks waiting on a resource, this query will return 0 rows.):

```
-- Show all user requests that are waiting on a resource
--
SELECT wt.session_id, wt.wait_type, wt.wait_duration_ms
FROM sys.dm_os_waiting_tasks wt
INNER JOIN sys.dm_exec_sessions es
ON es.session_id = wt.session_id
AND es.is_user_process = 1
GO
```

You can find the documentation for this DMV at https://docs.microsoft.com/sql/relational-databases/system-dynamic-management-views/sys-dm-os-waiting-tasks-transact-sql.

dm_os_wait_stats: Another one of the most commonly used DMVs. This DMV records statistics about resource waits by type since SQL Server has started (or since the DMV stats have been cleared). Here is an example from the sample script **dm_os_wait_stats.sql** to show the average wait duration by wait_type for only wait types that have had any waits.

```
-- Show the number of waits by type and the avg wait time of that type
sorted by the highest avg wait types
-- Note that some waits are "normal" because they are part of background
tasks that naturally waits as part of its execution
SELECT wait_type, waiting_tasks_count, (wait_time_ms/waiting_tasks_count)
as avg_wait_time_ms
FROM sys.dm_os_wait_stats
WHERE waiting_tasks_count > 0
ORDER BY avg_wait_time_ms DESC
GO
```

You can find the documentation for sys.dm_os_wait_stats at `https://docs.`
`microsoft.com/sql/relational-databases/system-dynamic-management-views/sys-`
`dm-os-wait-stats-transact-sql`.

> **dm_io_virtual_file_stats**: This DMF is extremely helpful to gain
> insight into which database and files are seeing the most I/O and
> what type of average disk latency is occurring for a database and
> files associated with the database. Using a DMF in SQL Operations
> Studio shows the power of T-SQL Intellisense to help you provide
> the proper parameters for the function. Figure 5-31 shows an
> example of filling out the parameters for this DMF.

Figure 5-31. *T-SQL Intellisense in SQL Operations Studio to execute a DMF*

Here is an example query as found in the sample script **dm_io_virtual_file_stats.sql**
to see the database files by the highest average disk latency for reads:

```
-- Find the files and associated database that have the highest avg disk
latency for read operations
-- Use the DB_NAME() system function to find the database name from the id
in the DMF
-- Join with the sys.master_files catalog view to find the physical file
name from the file_id in the DMF
```

```
SELECT DB_NAME(ivfs.database_id), mf.physical_name, (ivfs.io_stall_read_ms/
ivfs.num_of_reads) as avg_io_read_latency_ms, ivfs.num_of_reads
FROM sys.dm_io_virtual_file_stats(null,null) ivfs
INNER JOIN sys.master_files mf
ON ivfs.database_id = mf.database_id
AND ivfs.file_id = mf.file_id
WHERE num_of_reads > 0
ORDER by avg_io_read_latency_ms DESC
GO
```

This DMF only provides the database_id and the file_id instead of names. I use the DB_NAME() system function to get the database name and the join with the catalog view sys.master_files to get the physical file name.

Figure 5-32 shows the results from the preceding query in SQL Operations Studio on my SQL Server on Linux server.

Figure 5-32. *Database files with highest average disk read latency on SQL Server on Linux*

You can find the documentation for this DMF at https://docs.microsoft.com/sql/relational-databases/system-dynamic-management-views/sys-dm-io-virtual-file-stats-transact-sql.

dm_os_memory_clerks: Memory is a valuable resource for SQL Server. SQL Server has a complex and powerful memory management system built into the engine. Various components within SQL Server consume memory and record memory usage through the concept of a *memory clerk*. This DMV will show memory usage by clerk across the SQL Server engine. The following example based on the sample script **dm_os_memory_clerks.sql** shows which memory clerks use the most memory at any point in time:

```
-- Find out which components in SQL Server are using the most memory
--
SELECT type, name, (pages_kb+virtual_memory_committed_kb+awe_allocated_kb)
total_memory_kb
FROM sys.dm_os_memory_clerks
ORDER BY total_memory_kb DESC
GO
```

Figure 5-33 shows the results of this query on my SQL Server on Linux immediately after startup.

Figure 5-33. *SQL Server memory clerks immediately after startup*

There is no detailed documentation on mapping different memory clerk types and what component of the SQL Server engine they belong to. Here are the most common ones I believe you will see consume the most memory on a typical SQL Server:

> MEMORYCLERK_SQLBUFFERPOOL: Buffer pool database pages. This is typically the largest consumer of memory.

> CACHESTORE_SQLCP: Plan cache for ad-hoc SQL Server queries

> CACHESTORE_OBJCP: Plan cache for SQL Server objects such as stored procedures

> CACHESTORE_COLUMNSTOREOBJECTPOOL: Memory consumed by columnstore indexes

> MEMORYCLERK_XTP: Memory for In-Memory OLTP memory optimized tables

You can find the complete documentation for this DMV at `https://docs.` `microsoft.com/sql/relational-databases/system-dynamic-management-views/` `sys-dm-os-memory-clerks-transact-sql`

> **dm_tran_locks**: A list of current locks held by active requests. This DMV could be helpful when you experience a blocking problem in SQL Server, to discover what locks are being held by a specific session, request, and query. Here is an example query as found in the sample script **dm_tran_locks.sql**:

```
-- Show locks are that requested or granted by active sessions and queries
--
SELECT resource_type, request_mode, request_request_id, resource_database_
id, resource_associated_entity_id, resource_type, resource_description
FROM sys.dm_tran_locks
GO
```

See the documentation for this DMV, including a good example about how to use this for a blocking scenario, at `https://docs.microsoft.com/sql/relational-` `databases/system-dynamic-management-views/sys-dm-tran-locks-transact-sql`.

dm_db_missing_index_details: I showed you in Chapter 3 how
to create constraints for building keys, which are implemented via
indexes. Indexes can also help boost query performance. As you
run SQL Server queries, the engine can recognize scenarios where
an index is not available and could help with performance. These
recommendations are available via this DMV. I will cover the
usage of this DMV and other performance tools in Chapter 6. Here
is an example query found in the sample script **dm_db_missing_
index_details.sql** to find all recommended missing indexes in
SQL Server.

```
-- Find the current recommended missing indexes for all databases and
objects
--
SELECT index_handle, database_id, object_id, equality_columns, statement
FROM sys.dm_db_missing_index_details
GO
```

This DMV is cleared after SQL Server is restarted. The complete documentation
for this DMV can be found at https://docs.microsoft.com/sql/relational-
databases/system-dynamic-management-views/sys-dm-db-missing-index-
details-transact-sql.

dm_os_sys_info: This DMV is a notable example of using T-SQL
interfaces to expose data in the format of a table from information
about the *system*, which is either the operating system, computer,
or SQL Server. This DMV will always return only one row.

There is so much cool information in this DMV. I've provided an example query to
list out a few columns, including a calculation to see how long SQL Server has been up
and running. You can find this example query in the sample script **dm_os_sys_info.sql**.

```
-- Retrieve information about the computer, the OS, and SQL Server
--
SELECT cpu_count, hyperthread_ratio, physical_memory_kb, committed_kb,
committed_target_kb, max_workers_count, datediff(hour, sqlserver_start_
time, getdate()) as sql_up_time_hours, affinity_type_desc, virtual_machine_
```

```
type_desc, softnuma_configuration_desc, socket_count, cores_per_socket,
numa_node_count, container_type_desc
FROM sys.dm_os_sys_info
GO
```

Some of the values from this DMV will be topics that will be discussed later in this book. For a complete description of the columns from this example query and all columns in the DMV, see our documentation at https://docs.microsoft.com/sql/relational-databases/system-dynamic-management-views/sys-dm-os-sys-info-transact-sql.

> **dm_os_ring_buffers**: There are a few DMVs that are not documented because they are not DMVs that are normally needed for typical management and monitoring of SQL Server. But one DMV that is not documented that I find to be helpful in some advanced scenarios is dm_os_ring_buffers. This DMV stores a memory bound set of *lists* ("ring" meaning when the list is full it wraps to the front) of detailed information for certain internal components of the SQL Server Engine. Each component (a ring buffer type) that builds a list exposed by this DMV has its own ring buffer.

This example query as found in the sample script **ring_buffer_types.sql** shows the possible ring buffer types (which could change with each release of SQL Server):

```
-- Find the distinct ring buffer types
--
SELECT DISTINCT(ring_buffer_type)
FROM sys.dm_os_ring_buffers
GO
```

One of the interesting ring buffer types is RING_BUFFER_EXCEPTION. Each ring buffer for a type is stored in a series of rows with a **record** field. Record fields are XML types. This example query found in the same script **dm_os_ring_buffers_exception. sql** is quite complex. Look at the comments in the T-SQL script to see how each field is either extracted from the XML record or found by joining with other data in the system:

```
-- Find all current error messages recorded by SQL Server in the ring
buffer
-- [record_timestamp] is calculated by taking the current timestamp in the
record (which is in clock ticks by milliseconds)
```

```
-- and subtracting this from ms_ticks in sys.dm_os_sys_info which is the
number of clock ticks in ms when SQL Server was started
-- and then adding this to the current datetime. This gives you the actual
datetime of the record
-- errorno, severity, and state are "shredded" from the XML record
-- errorno from the XML record is joined with sys.sysmessages to get the
error message string
-- Not all error messages are "errors". Anything less than severity 16 is
"informational"
DECLARE @current_ms_ticks INT
SELECT @current_ms_ticks=ms_ticks FROM sys.dm_os_sys_info
SELECT DATEADD(ms, (orb.timestamp-@current_ms_ticks), GETDATE()) as
[record_timestamp],
CAST(orb.record AS XML).value('(//Exception//Error)[1]', 'varchar(10)') as
[errorno],
CAST(orb.record AS XML).value('(//Exception/Severity)[1]', 'varchar(10)')
as [severity],
CAST(orb.record AS XML).value('(//Exception/State)[1]', 'varchar(10)') as
[state],
msg.description
FROM sys.dm_os_ring_buffers orb
INNER JOIN sys.sysmessages msg
ON msg.error = cast(record as xml).value('(//Exception//Error)[1]',
'varchar(255)')
AND msg.msglangid = 1033 -- This is for US English. Change this to your
language as needed
WHERE orb.ring_buffer_type = 'RING_BUFFER_EXCEPTION'
ORDER BY record_timestamp
GO
```

DBFS Tool

Many Linux users are more comfortable with the shell than a user interface and are also familiar with navigating the proc directory (virtual) filesystem (You can read more about procfs at https://en.wikipedia.org/wiki/Procfs). As part of Project Helsinki, we built an open-source tool that works like procfs for SQL Server catalog view and DMV data, called **dbfs**.

DBFS will query SQL Server on Linux for DMV data and produce the information into a directory structure with files. Each file will represent a snapshot of a specific catalog view or DMV. The tool will produce a text and JSON file for each catalog view and DMV. By default, dbfs runs in the background monitoring access to the files represented by catalog views and DMVs. When a user tries to access the content of the files, dbfs queries SQL Server to obtain the data to populate the file. This technique is like how procfs works for the Linux operating system.

To install dbfs, read the instructions on the GitHub project site at `https://github.com/Microsoft/dbfs`. I installed this on my RHEL VM and then followed the Quick Start instructions on the GitHub site to create a directory and configuration file.

The text files are formatted so Linux tools like awk, grep, and join can be used to query catalog view and DMV data very easily. Here is an example command using awk:

```
awk '{print $1, $2, $3, $4, $5}' dm_os_sys_info | column -t
```

Figure 5-34 shows an example of using awk to extract columns from the dm_os_sys_info dbfs file.

```
[thewandog@bwsql2017rhel server]$ awk '{print $1, $2, $3, $4, $5}' dm_os_sys_info | column -t
cpu_ticks          ms_ticks   cpu_count  hyperthread_ratio  physical_memory_kb
142918198191694    52698400   4          4                  6393856
[thewandog@bwsql2017rhel server]$ █
```

Figure 5-34. *Using awk with DBFS*

Extended Events

Prior to SQL Server 2008, the primary tool to trace events and the code execution of the SQL Server Engine was SQL Server Trace and the corresponding tool called SQL Profiler. While SQL Server Trace and SQL Server Profiler still exist today, this feature and tool are technically marked as deprecated (which means they may be removed at any point for a new release). It also means we are no longer making any enhancements to this feature and tool.

Note Deprecation of features is something we do across releases for features that we do not plan to enhance. In recent releases, even though we have marked features deprecated, we rarely remove them. Read more on this topic at `https://docs.microsoft.com/sql/database-engine/deprecated-database-engine-features-in-sql-server-2017`.

In SQL Server 2008, we embarked on a project called XEvent. Once again, I found myself after we shipped SQL Server 2005 in a conversation with Slava Oks about supportability and diagnostics. While SQL Server Trace and Profiler were popular, he knew the architecture of "server-side trace" had limitations, especially around scalability. Slava and the team that built SQLOS designed XEvent from the ground up and named the feature in SQL Server 2008, **Extended Events**. Extended Events is both a tracing library for developers of the SQL Server engine and a user feature for tracing. Developers of the SQL Server Engine can use the XEvent library to define instrumentation points, *events*, in their code. Users of SQL Server can then define ways to enable these events and consume information about them.

SQL Server 2008 was released with a base level of events, but not all the instrumentation points of SQL Server trace were available. In SQL Server 2012, we tried to ensure Extended Events included all the events from SQL Server trace and more. As of SQL Server 2017, there are 1,500+ events for users to consume to gain insight into the execution of queries, connections, various features, or internals of the SQL Server engine.

While DMVs provide insight into many aspects of the SQL Server engine, most of the DMVs provide a *snapshot* of data when you query them. Extended events allow you to trace details (including more than you can find in DMVs) and collect event data over time.

You can find all the documentation about Extended Events at `https://docs.microsoft.com/sql/relational-databases/extended-events/extended-events`.

Extended Event Objects

The fundamental objects for Extended Events are **events**, **targets**, and **actions**. Let me describe each of these in more detail:

> **Event**: Events are the instrumentation points in the SQL Server engine, as defined by developers of Microsoft. Think of events as important places in the code to trace execution. The documentation of events and their descriptions can be found by querying a DMV called **sys.dm_xe_objects** (object type = 'event'). Events have properties or columns. These are found by querying **sys.dm_xe_object_columns**. The following example query as found in the sample script **xe_events.sql** shows all the events and their columns sorted by event name:

```
-- List the XEvent events, description, and columns for each event and
description
--
SELECT xeo.name, xeo.description, xeoc.name, xeoc.description
FROM sys.dm_xe_objects xeo
INNER JOIN sys.dm_xe_object_columns xeoc
ON xeo.name = xeoc.object_name
WHERE xeo.object_type = 'event'
AND (xeo.capabilities IS NULL OR xeo.capabilities & 1 = 0) -- Filter out
private events
ORDER BY xeo.name, xeoc.name
GO
```

Notice in the preceding query I use a column from the DMV called capabilities. Some XEvent events, actions, and targets are considered *private*. Private XEvent objects cannot be used in user sessions because they support a feature of SQL Server, like SQL Server Auditing.

> **Target**: A target is a destination where events can be published and stored for consumption. Two fundamental target types are **event_file** (saving events to a file) and **ring_buffer** (saving events to a memory buffer that is not persisted after a server restart). There are other targets that have built-in "intelligence" such as a histogram target. A complete list of targets can be found in our documentation at https://docs.microsoft.com/ sql/relational-databases/extended-events/targets-for-extended-events-in-sql-server.

> **Action**: When an event is fired and published to a target, all the columns in the event are available (there are some columns that require a setting to have their data published because collecting the column could consume additional resources). Actions are data orthogonal to the columns for an event that can be captured as part of an event session. An example of an action is **sql_text**, which is the text of a T-SQL query. sql_text is not a column for every event, so this means in many cases you can capture the T-SQL query associated with an event, where without this action it would not be possible.

An excellent description of the sequence of how events, targets, and actions work together can be found in our documentation at https://docs.microsoft.com/sql/ relational-databases/extended-events/sql-server-extended-events-engine.

Usage and Scenarios

To use Extended Events, you must create a **session**. Sessions are persisted in system tables stored in the master database and exposed through catalog views. Once you create a session, you must start the session for the instrumentation points defined for the events to be *fired* and published to the defined target(s). At any point in time, you can stop the session and all events will no longer be fired, but the event definition is persisted in the master database. You can find all Extended Event definitions in the catalog view **sys.server_event_sessions**. You can find a list of all started Extended Event sessions from the **sys.dm_xe_sessions** DMV.

The following example query as found in the sample script **quicksessionstandard. sql** shows how to create an Extended Event session to collect basic information about SQL Server connections and queries (this event definition is based on the XEProfiler SQL Server Management Tool feature):

```
-- Create a XEvent session based on the XEProfiler feature in SSMS to
collect connections and queries
--
CREATE EVENT SESSION [QuickSessionStandardToFile] ON SERVER
ADD EVENT sqlserver.attention(
    ACTION(package0.event_sequence,sqlserver.client_app_name,sqlserver.
    client_pid,sqlserver.database_id,sqlserver.database_name,sqlserver.
    nt_username,sqlserver.query_hash,sqlserver.server_principal_
    name,sqlserver.session_id)
    WHERE ([package0].[equal_boolean]([sqlserver].[is_system],(0)))),
ADD EVENT sqlserver.existing_connection(SET collect_options_text=(1)
    ACTION(package0.event_sequence,sqlserver.client_app_name,sqlserver.
    client_hostname,sqlserver.client_pid,sqlserver.nt_username,sqlserver.
    server_principal_name,sqlserver.session_id)),
ADD EVENT sqlserver.login(SET collect_options_text=(1)
    ACTION(package0.event_sequence,sqlserver.client_app_name,sqlserver.
    client_hostname,sqlserver.client_pid,sqlserver.nt_username,sqlserver.
    server_principal_name,sqlserver.session_id)),
```

```
ADD EVENT sqlserver.logout(
    ACTION(package0.event_sequence,sqlserver.client_app_name,sqlserver.
    client_pid,sqlserver.nt_username,sqlserver.server_principal_
    name,sqlserver.session_id)),
ADD EVENT sqlserver.rpc_completed(
    ACTION(package0.event_sequence,sqlserver.client_app_name,sqlserver.
    client_pid,sqlserver.database_id,sqlserver.database_name,sqlserver.
    nt_username,sqlserver.query_hash,sqlserver.server_principal_
    name,sqlserver.session_id)
    WHERE ([package0].[equal_boolean]([sqlserver].[is_system],(0)))),
ADD EVENT sqlserver.sql_batch_completed(
    ACTION(package0.event_sequence,sqlserver.client_app_name,sqlserver.
    client_pid,sqlserver.database_id,sqlserver.database_name,sqlserver.
    nt_username,sqlserver.query_hash,sqlserver.server_principal_
    name,sqlserver.session_id)
    WHERE ([package0].[equal_boolean]([sqlserver].[is_system],(0)))),
ADD EVENT sqlserver.sql_batch_starting(
    ACTION(package0.event_sequence,sqlserver.client_app_name,sqlserver.
    client_pid,sqlserver.database_id,sqlserver.database_name,sqlserver.
    nt_username,sqlserver.query_hash,sqlserver.server_principal_
    name,sqlserver.session_id)
    WHERE ([package0].[equal_boolean]([sqlserver].[is_system],(0))))
ADD TARGET package0.event_file(SET filename=N'QuickSessionStandard.
xel',max_file_size=(5),max_rollover_files=(4))
WITH (MAX_MEMORY=8192 KB,EVENT_RETENTION_MODE=ALLOW_SINGLE_EVENT_LOSS,MAX_
DISPATCH_LATENCY=5 SECONDS,MAX_EVENT_SIZE=0 KB,MEMORY_PARTITION_MODE=PER_
CPU,TRACK_CAUSALITY=ON,STARTUP_STATE=OFF)
GO
```

This example query as found in the sample **start_xevent_session.sql** shows how to start the session created:

```
-- Start the XEvent session
--
ALTER EVENT SESSION [QuickSessionStandardToFile] ON SERVER STATE = start
GO
```

By default, a file target for an extended events session is stored in the /var/opt/ mssql/log directory.

There are several options when you create an Extended Event session, such as controlling memory and scalability. You can find the complete list of options in our documentation at `https://docs.microsoft.com/sql/t-sql/statements/create-event-session-transact-sql`. SQL Server also provides the capability of starting a session you create when SQL Server is first started, using the STARTUP_STATE option when you create the event definition (An example might be to trace database recovery at startup).

Once you create an Extended Event session, you can add events or alter the definition. You can find how to do this in our documentation at `https://docs.microsoft.com/sql/relational-databases/extended-events/alter-an-extended-events-session`.

One of the amazing built-in extended event sessions is the **system_health** session. I'll discuss how to use this session in Chapter 9.

Tools

Extended Events can be controlled and consumed using the T-SQL language. To view data from Extended Events targets that are memory-based, you can query the **dm_xe_session_targets** DMV. An example of how to view the XML data in a ring_buffer target can be found in our documentation at `https://docs.microsoft.com/sql/relational-databases/extended-events/targets-for-extended-events-in-sql-server#h2_target_ring_buffer`. File targets can be read with T-SQL, using the system function **sys.fn_xe_file_target_read_file,** which is documented at `https://docs.microsoft.com/sql/relational-databases/system-functions/sys-fn-xe-file-target-read-file-transact-sql`.

Application developers have the ability to read XEvent targets, including a "live" event stream target via the following object models: `https://msdn.microsoft.com/library/microsoft.sqlserver.management.xevent.aspx` and `https://msdn.microsoft.com/library/microsoft.sqlserver.xevent.linq.aspx`.

SSMS has user interface capability to create and managed Extended Events via Object Explorer. Figure 5-35 shows the Object Explorer tree for Extended Events in SSMS.

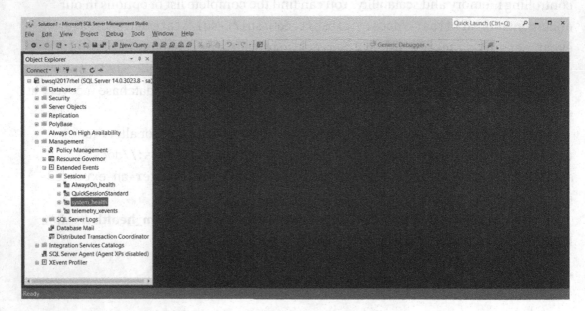

Figure 5-35. *The Extended Events Object Explorer tree view in SSMS*

SSMS allows you to create extended events, start event sessions, alter event sessions, and view extended event session target data via a grid view.

Recent builds of SSMS include the ability to view Extended Events data in a live stream like what you can do with SQL Server Profiler. This feature is called **XEProfiler**. To use XEProfiler, expand the icon from the Object Explorer tree in SSMS, right-click one of the two choices such as Standard, and select Launch Session. Figure 5-36 shows the result of using this feature to see connections and queries run against SQL Server on Linux.

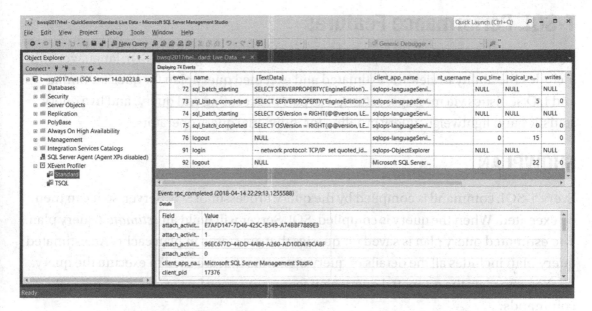

Figure 5-36. *Using XEProfiler with SSMS*

Whether you build your own T-SQL event or use XEProfiler, you will find *tracing* SQL Server queries extremely useful to debug how applications and tools work. For example, I used XEProfiler to debug how DBFS works to query SQL Server without having to look at the project source code.

There is an excellent demo and tutorial of how to use SSMS with Extended Events in our documentation at https://docs.microsoft.com/sql/relational-databases/ extended-events/quick-start-extended-events-in-sql-server.

There a several example scenarios in our documentation to use Extended Events, including:

> *Queries Holding Locks*: https://docs.microsoft.com/sql/ relational-databases/extended-events/determine-which- queries-are-holding-locks
>
> *Objects and Locks Held*: https://docs.microsoft.com/sql/ relational-databases/extended-events/find-the-objects- that-have-the-most-locks-taken-on-them
>
> *Monitor System Activity*: https://docs.microsoft.com/sql/ relational-databases/extended-events/monitor-system- activity-using-extended-events

T-SQL Performance Features

SQL Server comes with built-in performance statistics through the T-SQL language. This includes the ability to view the estimated and executed query plan for queries, timing and I/O statistics via messages returned as part of executing and query, and live query statistics and lightweight query profiling for individual query operators.

SHOWPLAN

Every T-SQL command is compiled by the query processor of SQL Server, so it can then be executed. When the query is compiled, SQL Server will build an *estimated* query plan. The estimated query plan is saved for queries that are stored in plan cache. An estimated query plan includes all the details of query operators that are used to execute the query.

You can view the estimated query plan for any query by first executing the T-SQL commands:

> **SET SHOWPLAN_ALL ON**: Return all the operators in the estimated query plan in the form of a table result set but do not execute the query.
>
> **SET SHOWPLAN_TEXT ON**: Return all the operators in the estimated query plan in the form of a text result but do not execute the query.
>
> **SET SHOWPLAN_XML ON**: Return all the operators in the estimated query plan in the form of an XML document. The format of the XML schema for SHOWPLAN is documented at http://schemas.microsoft.com/sqlserver/2004/07/ showplan/.

Note   T-SQL SET commands are used to turn ON and OFF a *setting*. If you use SET to turn ON a setting, that setting will be enabled for the lifetime of the session until you execute the same SET command to turn it OFF. Multiple settings can be enabled for a single SQL Server session. For a complete list of all T-SQL SET commands, see our documentation at https://docs.microsoft.com/sql/t-sql/statements/set-statements-transact-sql.

Figure 5-37 shows the example output when I use SET SHOWPLAN_XML ON with the query SELECT * FROM sys.databases:

```
SET SHOWPLAN_XML ON
GO
SELECT * FROM sys.databases
GO
```

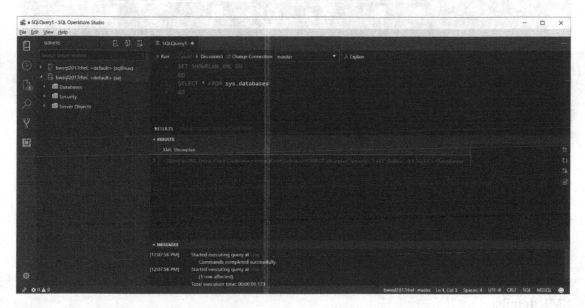

Figure 5-37.   *SET SHOWPLAN_XML in SQL Operations Studio*

If you click the XML results, SQL Operations Studio will open the XML document.

SQL Operations Studio automatically recognizes when you run SET SHOWPLAN_ XML and will generate a graphical version of the estimated plan in the QUERY PLAN tab next to RESULTS. Figure 5-38 shows the graphical query plan for SELECT * FROM sys. databases.

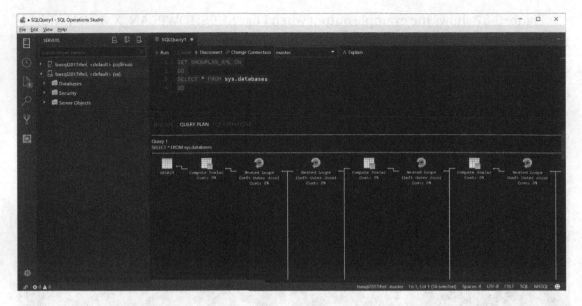

Figure 5-38. *Graphical Query Plan in SQL Operations Studio*

When you use a SET SHOWPLAN* command, it remains in effect for that session until you turn it off by using SET SHOWPLAN* OFF. SQL Operations Studio has another method to show the estimated query plan without using a SET command called *Explain*. If I execute SET SHOWPLAN_XML OFF and then type in SELECT * FROM sys.databases in the Query Editor, I can click Explain at the top of the Query Editor to get SHOWPLAN_XML details.

In addition, if I hover my cursor over any operator I can get further query operator details. Figure 5-39 shows the details of a query plan operator from the previous example.

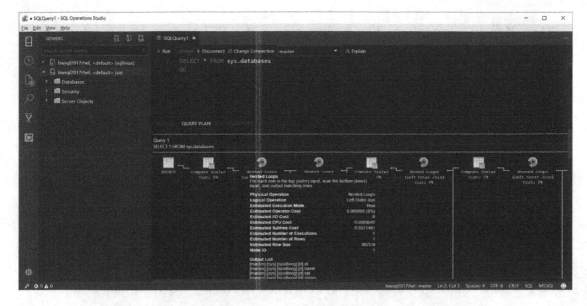

Figure 5-39. *Query Plan operator details in SQL Operations Studio*

Next to the QUERY PLAN tab in SQL Operations Studio is another option called TOP OPERATORS. TOP OPERATORS shows a table of query plan operators and statistics with each operator sorted by estimated cost of each operator.

While using the SET SHOWPLAN* T-SQL statements show the estimated query plan, you can use T-SQL to show the actual execution plan while executing the query. The actual execution plan is produced *after* the query is executed and includes important performance statistics about the execution of the query and each query plan operator.

You can see the *actual* execution plan for a query first executing the T-SQL command **SET STATISTICS XML** before the query. The schema for the resulting XML document is also available at http://schemas.microsoft.com/sqlserver/2004/07/showplan. Using this T-SQL command with SQL Operations Studio provides similar functionality as with the estimated plan, including a graphical view of the plan and top operator statistics. So, for example, while the estimated plan will show statistics like estimated rows for each query operator, the actual execution plan will show estimated and actual rows per query operator (estimates are produced when compiling the plan based on available statistics. Those statistics could be missing or out of date, which could result in scenarios where the actual values are different than estimates. This is a common performance problem when debugging query plans).

Tip   If query plan information is generated with a SET statement, it is returned to the application in the form of messages. Application developers who execute a SET statement to generate query plan details must be prepared to handle and process these messages.

SSMS provides similar functionality to SQL Operations Studio through *buttons* in the user interface called Display Estimated Execution Plan (estimated) and Include Actual Execution Plan (actual).

SET STATISTICS

You can also use T-SQL to gain insight into performance statistics including CPU, duration, and I/O performance for each statement in a batch. These T-SQL commands are:

> **SET STATISTICS TIME**: SQL Server will produce CPU and elapsed parse/compile and execution timings for each statement in batches after executing this command. Information is produced in the form of messages.

Figure 5-40 shows the message output in SQL Operations Studio from the following example query found in the sample **setstatstime.sql** (Note: Be sure to run SET SHOWPLAN_XML OFF before running the following command.):

```
SET STATISTICS TIME ON
GO
SELECT * FROM sys.databases
GO
```

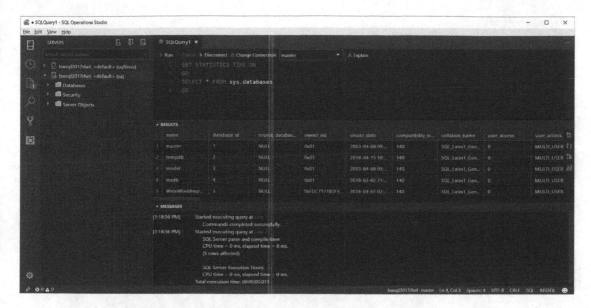

Figure 5-40. *SET STATISTICS TIME output in SQL Operations Studio*

SET STATISTICS IO: SQL Server will produce information about
logical (number of database pages read from cache) and physical
reads (number of database pages read from disk) for objects
referenced in each statement in batches after executing this
command. Information is produced in the form of messages.

Figure 5-41 shows the message output in SQL Operations Studio from the following
example query found in the sample **setstatsio.sql** (Note: For the following output, I had
first run SET STATISTICS TIME OFF to clear that setting.):

```
SET STATISTICS IO ON
GO
SELECT * FROM sys.databases
GO
```

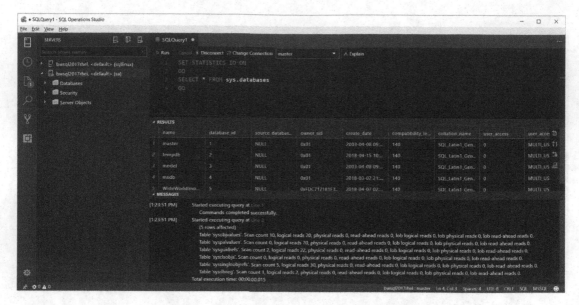

Figure 5-41. *SET STATISTIC IO output in SQL Operations Studio*

Note   read-ahead reads are also physical reads of database pages from disk.

Lightweight Query Profiling

It is possible to trace showplan information for each query by using Extend Events. The events **query_post_compilation_showplan** (estimated) and **query_post_execution_showplan** (actual) can be used to trace plans for queries in SQL Server. There are several columns available for these events as properties to the plan, including the XML document representation of the query plan.

While this information can be useful when investigating query performance problem, there can be substantial overhead to use these events on a production SQL Server.

Fortunately, we have a team at Microsoft called the Tiger Team (follow their work at https://twitter.com/mssqltiger). They built a new infrastructure and capability called *lightweight query profiling*, enabled with the global trace flag 7412 (remember with SQL Server on Linux, you can use the mssql-conf script to enable a trace flag).

An example of how to set this trace flag on Linux would be the following command:

```
sudo /opt/mssql/bin/mssql-conf traceflag 7412 on
```

See the documentation on how to set trace flags at `https://docs.microsoft.com/sql/linux/sql-server-linux-configure-mssql-conf#traceflags`.

After you enable this trace flag, you can now view actual execution plan information for any active query via the **sys.dm_exec_query_profiles** DMV (view operators and statistics in a table format) and the **sys.dm_exec_query_statistics_xml** DMF (view the plan as an XML document). We have done testing to show that lightweight query profiling has minimal impact on overall query performance, so it can be used in production environments. If you would like to trace query plan information using Extended Events with lightweight profiling, you can enable the **query_thread_profile** event, which also enables lightweight query profiling for all sessions. The query_thread_profile event includes columns about operators (nodes) but does not include the plan in the form of an XML document.

Lightweight profiling has another appealing feature in that the DMV and DMF can be used against queries currently in progress (live query profiling) so you don't have to wait for a query to complete.

> **Note**   dm_exec_query_profiles, dm_exec_query_statistics_xml, and query_thread_profile are also available for queries that have already completed when you enable the query_post_execution_showplan event. However, using query_post_execution_showplan overrides trace flag 7412 and will not use lightweight query profiling.

SSMS allows you to view the information from lightweight query profiling via a feature called Activity Monitor.

> **Note**   SSMS also includes a button to view query plan statistics for "live queries" called Include Live Statistics. This feature does not use lightweight query profiling.

Query Store

After we had shipped SQL Server 2008 (codename Katmai), I was approached by one of our chief architects for SQL Server, Conor Cunningham, about our techniques for performance troubleshooting in Technical Support and how we could improve them.

DMVs had become extremely popular by SQL Server 2008, and we continued to add more based on customer feedback and features we added to SQL Server. The biggest drawback to DMVs is that to capture a history of changes, you must *poll* DMV data by querying the DMV and save the results on a frequent basis (you also usually added a timestamp with each query against the DMV to note the history of rows over time). For example, to capture performance information about queries in cache, you could query sys. dm_exec_query_stats and save off the data every <n> seconds or minutes. This technique works but it is not elegant. We used this technique in technical support, along with tools like SQLTrace and Extended Events for performance troubleshooting with customers.

Conor came along with a new idea called *Query Disk Store*. His idea was to build into the SQL Server engine the ability to store performance information about queries, including changes over time directly into the database. This idea led to a new feature in SQL Server 2016 called **Query Store**.

Query Store is a database option that, when enabled, turns on code in the SQL Server engine to store information any time a new query is compiled, including the estimated query plan. In addition, when a query is executed, aggregate performance information is accumulated for the query. All this data is stored in a series of system tables in the database where Query Store is enabled. You can see query store data by querying a series of catalog views built on top of any data stored in memory or in the system tables.

Since the performance data is stored in the user database, this data is available after backing up and restoring the database.

Tip   Use the T-SQL command **DBCC CLONEDATABASE** to make a copy of the schema of a database without user data. This command captures all system table data, so it includes Query Store. This allows you to evaluate query store data offline without having to back up the entire user database. See more details about DBCC CLONEDATABASE at `https://support.microsoft.com/help/3177838/ how-to-use-dbcc-clonedatabase-to-generate-a-schema-and- statistics-only`.

Enabling query store for a database is as simple as running a T-SQL statement like the following:

```
ALTER DATABASE WideWorldImporters SET QUERY_STORE = ON
GO
```

Once you enable Query Store, the SQL Server engine will start collecting data in memory and system tables. By default, data is kept for 30 days and has a maximum size of 100MB. Both these, as well as other options, are configurable. You can find the available configuration options for Query Store in our documentation at `https://docs.microsoft.com/sql/relational-databases/performance/monitoring-performance-by-using-the-query-store#Options`.

You can find a list of query store catalog views in our documentation at `https://docs.microsoft.com/sql/relational-databases/system-catalog-views/query-store-catalog-views-transact-sql`. The views are very normalized, so I recommend you look at different Query Store key usage scenarios to see how to join these query store catalog views in our documentation at `https://docs.microsoft.com/sql/relational-databases/performance/monitoring-performance-by-using-the-query-store#Scenarios`.

You can enable a widget in SQL Operations Studio to view Query Store data, as found in our documentation at `https://docs.microsoft.com/sql/sql-operations-studio/tutorial-qds-sql-server?view=ssdt-18vs2017`.

SSMS comes built-in with Reports to view Query Store data. Figure 5-42 show the use of Query Store reports to find queries that consume the top resources.

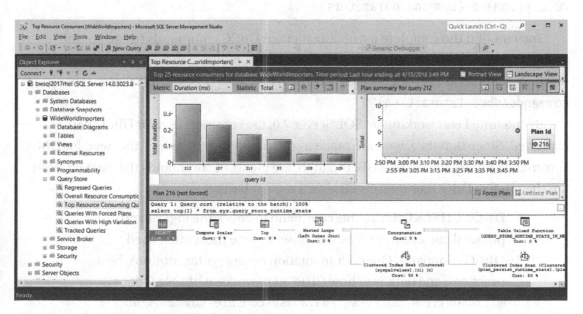

Figure 5-42. *Using Query Store Reports in SSMS*

Query store is a rich set of performance telemetry, and in many cases does not present a significant performance impact on a production server. Query store opens a range of possible performance tuning and investigation scenarios that were not previously possible without a large amount of extra work and code. Our documentation includes a discussion of Query Store usage scenarios such as performance regressions and A/B Testing at `https://docs.microsoft.com/sql/relational-databases/performance/query-store-usage-scenarios`.

I'll discuss another unique value to Query Store in Chapter 6 where we have added a feature to use the telemetry in Query Store to provide intelligent performance diagnostics and automation.

DBCC Commands

When I joined Microsoft in 1993, I already knew the SQL language well, based on the ANSI SQL Standard. I learned quickly that T-SQL was based on the ANSI standard but like other database engines had extended the command set for various purposes. One of the first unique T-SQL commands I learned was **DBCC** (Database Console Commands). The basic syntax of DBCC is:

```
DBCC <command>(command parameters)
```

You can find the complete list of documented DBCC commands (there are still many undocumented ones, but you should not rely on their behavior or existence) in our documentation at `https://docs.microsoft.com/sql/t-sql/database-console-commands/dbcc-transact-sql`.

By the time I was working on SQL Server 7.0, the command set for DBCC had exploded. Since that time, we have made a conscious effort to reduce the need for DBCC commands other than CHECKDB. But there are plenty of commands that remain. Here are the top five DBCC commands I use on a regular basis:

> **DBCC CHECKDB**: Use this command to check the logical and physical consistency of the database. It is the most often used DBCC command. Our documentation covers syntax, options, best practices, and details of how CHECKDB works at `https://docs.microsoft.com/sql/t-sql/database-console-commands/dbcc-checkdb-transact-sql`. You can also find a lot of information about CHECKDB and opinions about how often it needs to be run from the SQL Server community.

DBCC DROPCLEANBUFFERS: This command is extremely useful for testing disk I/O with SQL Server. This DBCC command will free up any database pages in memory so that any future SELECT statements must force pages to be read from disk. I use this command in demos and testing all the time to see how fast I can read database pages in from disk for a table or set of objects.

DBCC SHRINKDATABASE: Let's say you created a database of 100GB but you are only using 50GB of space within the files. Now you want to reduce the size of the database files on disk to 60GB without creating a new database and copying over data. DBCC SHRINKDATABASE can provide that functionality. You can find the syntax and options of this command in our documentation at `https://docs.microsoft.com/sql/t-sql/database-console-commands/dbcc-shrinkdatabase-transact-sql`.

DBCC TRACEON: The next section in this chapter is about trace flags, although I've mentioned trace flags a few times already in this book. I'll discuss the details of how to use this DBCC command to turn on and off trace flags in the next section. You can find the documentation of DBCC TRACEON at `https://docs.microsoft.com/sql/t-sql/database-console-commands/dbcc-traceon-transact-sql`.

DBCC HELP: While you can look up the syntax of DBCC commands in the documentation, SQL Server provides online help for DBCC with the DBCC HELP command. Run this command to see a list of all officially supported DBCC commands:

```
DBCC HELP('?')
GO
```

Run this command to see the syntax and options for DBCC CHECKDB:

```
DBCC HELP ('CHECKDB')
GO
```

> **Caution**   This is undocumented and could easily change in the future. If you enable trace flag 2588, it will enable DBCC HELP to show all DBCC commands in the code, even ones that are not supported. Again, you should use extreme caution with any undocumented DBCC command. They are not intended for production use and you could even cause problems for your SQL Server when using them unless you are guided by Microsoft.

Trace Flags

Trace flags can be used to enable a specific feature in SQL Server or gain insight into technical details that could be used for debugging or diagnostics.

Think of trace flags as *dynamic* decision points in the code of the SQL Server engine that can be used to turn on or off a capability or behavior.

Trace flags have a long history in SQL Server and were originally intended as debugging aids for the developers of the SQL Server engine. Developers wanted ways to turn certain behaviors on and off without rebuilding the code. Today, in the SQL Server source code there are hundreds of possible trace flags. However, the only official trace flags that are supported are either listed on this documentation page, `https://docs.microsoft.com/sql/t-sql/database-console-commands/dbcc-traceon-trace-flags-transact-sql` or in an official Microsoft Knowledge Base article.

Trace flags are enabled for a session or globally for all sessions. Some trace flags can only be enabled globally and must be turned on at the startup of SQL Server to be recognized by the code.

To enable a trace flag for a session, you use the T-SQL command **DBCC TRACEON**. To turn off a trace flag, you use the command **DBCC TRACEOFF**. If you use the special parameter -1 when turning on or off trace flags with DBCC TRACEON, the trace flags will be enabled globally for all sessions from that point forward. Trace flags can be turned on at SQL Server startup, to be enabled globally by using the mssql-conf script as documented at `https://docs.microsoft.com/sql/linux/sql-server-linux-configure-mssql-conf#traceflags`.

> **Note**   Like SQL Server for Windows, SQL Server for Linux supports startup trace flags with the sqlservr command line parameter -T. For SQL Server on Linux, I recommend you always use the mssql-conf script to set or unset startup trace flags.

You can view the status of all enabled trace flags by using the command **DBCC TRACESTATUS**.

Many documented trace flags end up in the product to enable a specific performance optimization or fix for a problem encountered by users. These changes often require trace flags to avoid causing problems for customers who do not need the behavior. In some cases, we have tried to use other methods to enable these types of enhancements such as ALTER DATABASE options or through commands like sp_configure.

Here are a few of common trace flags I often use that you can find in the documentation:

1222: Displays details of deadlock information in the SQL Server ERRORLOG in an XML format. You can find a discussion of locking and deadlocking topics, including details of the XML deadlock information from this traceflag, in our documentation at https://docs.microsoft.com/sql/relational-databases/ sql-server-transaction-locking-and-row-versioning- guide#Lock_Engine.

3226: By default, SQL Server writes out every successful backup operation to the ERRORLOG. For some customers, this is too much noise in the ERRORLOG. This trace flag will disable writing successful backup information to the ERRORLOG.

3608: This trace flag can only be used at startup. If trace flag is turned on, SQL Server will only recover the master database. It will not create tempdb unless you attempt to access a feature that requires tempdb (such as creating a temporary table). This command could be useful for advanced recovery scenarios and SQL Server startup troubleshooting.

4199: This trace flag is used to enable Query Optimizer fixes in cumulative updates. You can read more about how to use this trace flag in this Microsoft Knowledge Base article: `https://support.microsoft.com/help/974006/sql-server-query-optimizer-hotfix-trace-flag-4199-servicing-model`.

7752: Enables asynchronous loading of the Query Store. I recommend you turn this on when using Query Store in production to avoid any issues for users getting blocked when Query Store data is loaded into memory at the startup of a database.

3604: This one is not documented. It enables the output of some DBCC commands to be displayed as messages back to the client application. You should not need this for documented DBCC commands, but some that are undocumented require it to work (The prime example is DBCC PAGE).

Note   Another trace flag feature exists at the query level called QUERYTRACEON. This option only applies to a specific list of trace flags. You can read more about this trace flag option at `https://support.microsoft.com/help/2801413/enable-plan-affecting-sql-server-query-optimizer-behavior-that-can-be`.

SSIS for ETL

While bcp provides fundamental import/export capabilities, there are scenarios where you may need more complex functionality to extract, transform, and load (ETL) data. SQL Server comes with a feature to provide rich ETL capabilities in the form of SQL Server Integration Services (SSIS).

The first step to using SSIS is to install the SSIS package for Linux on either RHEL or Ubuntu (SQL Server 2017 does not provide an SSIS package for SUSE at the time of writing of this book). The installation process is like SQL Server and integrates with the package managers for RHEL (yum) and Ubuntu (apt-get). The SSIS installation process also requires a script called **ssis-conf** to complete the setup process.

You can follow the installation process and other aspects to deployment such as update and unattended install with our documentation at `https://docs.microsoft.com/sql/linux/sql-server-linux-setup-ssis`.

When you install SSIS on Linux, we do not create a systemd service. Rather, a Linux program called **dtexec** is installed in the **/opt/ssis** directory. dtexec is the program used to execute SSIS packages on a Linux server. Like SQL Server, dtexec uses the SQLPAL architecture to allow the same code that runs SSIS on Windows to run on Linux.

Creating a Package

SSIS on Linux requires a package to execute an ETL scenario. Packages are created and saved into a file format that is based on XML, called the Data Transformation Services Package (DTSX) file format. The complete format is documented at `https://msdn.microsoft.com/library/gg587140.aspx`.

Creating a package by editing a DTSX formatted file directly is complex. Therefore, there are methods to create SSIS packages with a tool using SQL Server Data Tools (SSDT) on Windows or developing a program using the .Net package Microsoft.SqlServer.Dts.Runtime. For more information about building programs to create and run packages, see our documentation at `https://docs.microsoft.com/sql/integration-services/integration-services-programming-overview`.

SQL Server Data Tools

SSDT works within the Visual Studio IDE development experience. SSDT installs within an existing Visual Studio installation. If you don't have Visual Studio, when you install SSDT a minimal version of the Visual Studio environment is installed. Therefore, SSDT is completely free to use to create SSIS packages on a Windows computer. You can find the complete instructions to download and install SSDT in our documentation at `https://docs.microsoft.com/sql/ssdt/download-sql-server-data-tools-ssdt`.

Building the Package

SSDT comes with a project type called an Integration Services project. When you create a new Integration Services project, you are presented with a visual designer to build a package. Figure 5-43 shows an example of the Package Designer in a new Integration Services Project.

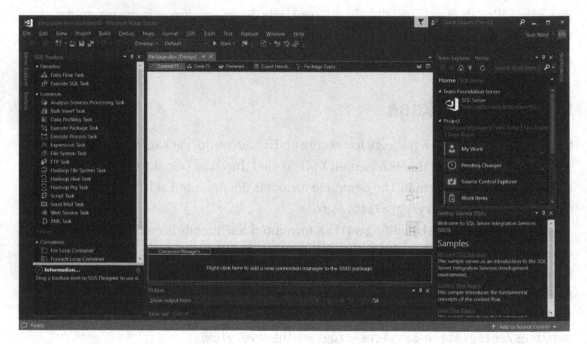

Figure 5-43. *The Package Designer with an Integrated Services project in SSDT*

SSIS Packages have many options and features to connect to data sources to extract and load data. In addition, packages can contain a wide variety of data flow tasks that allow for rich transformations.

I'll create a simple example to show how to build a package and execute it on the Linux Server using dtexec. In this example, I'm going to build a package that will extract all data from the People table from the WideWorldImporters example I showed you in Chapter 3 and write out the data to a text file on the Linux Server.

Using SSDT, I created a new Project called an Integration Services project (I selected Project from the New Menu of the tool and found this project type under Installed/ Business Intelligence). Figure 5-44 shows the interface to start a new Integration Services project.

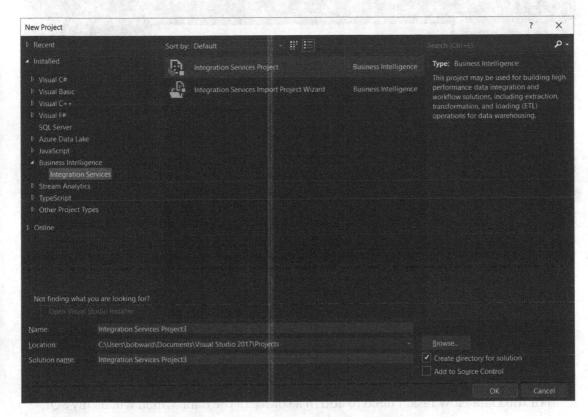

Figure 5-44. A new Integration Services project in SSDT

After selecting this project type, I'm presented with the Package Designer screen as shown in Figure 5-43. To perform the simple example of extracting data and writing this data to a file, the first step on the main Package Designer screen is to create a new Data Flow task. I can do this by selecting the Data Flow Task in the SSIS toolbar on the left-hand side of the Designer and dragging and dropping the icon into the main designer window, which by default is called the Control Flow designer.

Figure 5-45 shows my screen after adding a Data Flow Task to my Control Flow for this package.

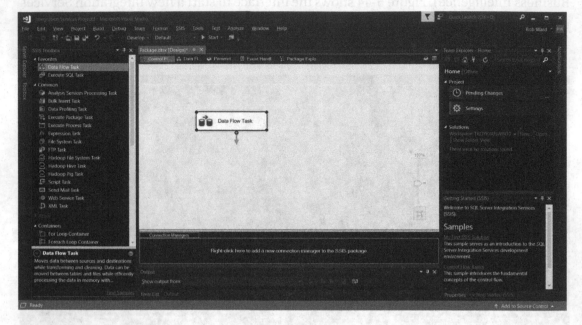

Figure 5-45. *A Data Flow Task added to the Control Flow of the SSIS Package*

In the tab next to the Control Flow Designer is the Data Flow Designer. I can see the design for this Data Flow Task by double-clicking the rectangle shape called Data Flow Task.

For the Data Flow Task, I need to add in a source of the data, which will be my SQL Server on Linux, and a destination, which will be a flat file. For the source of the data, I will need an ODBC source, since I'm going to run the package on the Linux Server. First, I found the **ODBC Source** from the Other Sources category in the SSIS Toolbar and drag/dropped this into my designer window. Figure 5-46 shows my screen after adding an ODBC Source to the Data Flow Task.

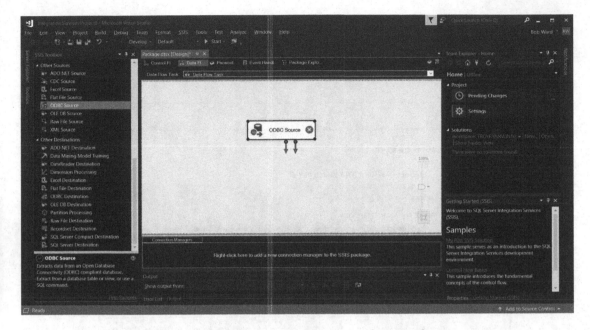

Figure 5-46. *Adding an ODBC Source to the Data Flow Task*

Now I need to configure the ODBC source to point to my SQL Server on Linux server and my example WideWorldImporters database. I'll do this by right-clicking the ODBC Source and selecting Edit. I selected New on the next window for the ODBC Connection Manager. This brings up another window, where I will pick the New button again to build a new connection.

On this screen, I will use an ODBC *connection string*. Connection strings are a method to provide all the necessary information to connect to SQL Server on Linux (or any other ODBC based data source). For this example, my connection string looks like this:

```
Driver={ODBC Driver 17 for SQL Server};server=bwsql2017rhel;database=WideWo
rldImporters;uid=sa
```

Connection strings are common ways for programmers to supply connection information for SQL Server. You can learn more about all the connection strings options for ODBC in our documentation at https://docs.microsoft.com/sql/connect/odbc/dsn-connection-string-attribute.

On this screen I'll also supply the login of sa and the sa password. Figure 5-47 shows my screen before I hit OK to create this new connection.

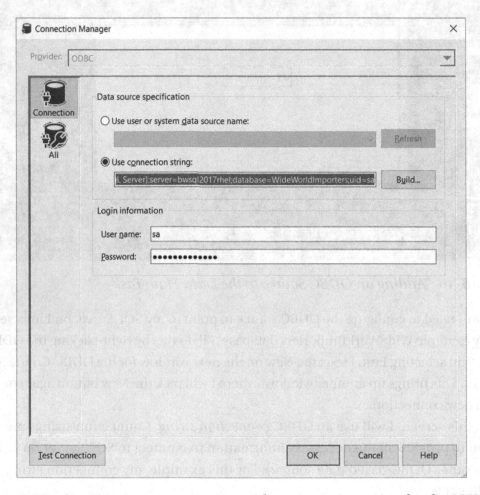

Figure 5-47. *Creating a new connection with a connection string for the SSIS package*

Note   To use this connection string on your windows computer within your package, you must install the ODBC Driver 17 for SQL Server on your Windows computer. You can download this package from `https://docs.microsoft.com/sql/connect/odbc/download-odbc-driver-for-sql-server`

Once you hit OK, you can select the Table Name in the Name of the table of the view field on the ODBC Source screen. I selected the "Application"."People" table for this example. To simply this example, I need to exclude columns from this table that are varbinary(max) or varchar(max), which are the HashedPassword, UserPreferences, Photo, and CustomFields columns. There are methods to include these columns for extraction to a file using Data Conversion tasks. To exclude these columns, I need to pick the Columns option on the left-hand side of the ODBC Source Window and uncheck these column names, then hit the OK button.

Now I'm ready to set up the Flat File Destination. From the SSIS Toolbar, drag the Flat File Destination icon on the canvas where the ODBC Source exists.

You can now take the blue arrow from the ODBC Source shape and connect it to the Flat File Destination. Right-click and select Edit to provide the File information. Select the New button, keep the default of Delimited for format, and hit OK. You will be presented with a window to put in a File Name (this will be the name of the new file created on the Linux Server, which by default will be the directory where you execute dtexec).

I put in a File Name of people.txt and selected the Unicode checkbox.

Now select the Mappings option on the Flat File Destination Editor page. The Editor will automatically map column names to field names for the file. Hit OK on this screen. When you have completed this, the screen looks like Figure 5-48.

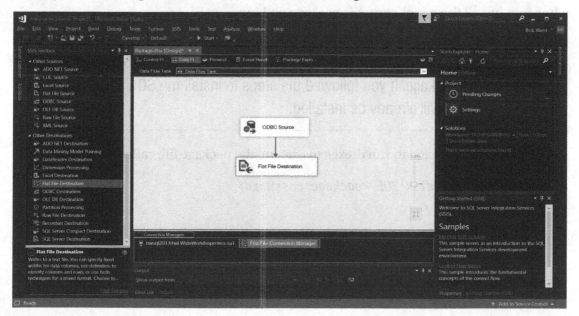

Figure 5-48. *A Data Flow Task with source and destination*

I have one last step before I copy the package to my Linux server. By default, the package is encrypted for sensitive information in the package like passwords and usernames. For purposes of this example, I'm going to change the properties of the Package to protect it via a password.

When you click in the canvas of the designer, there should be a pane at the lower right-hand corner of the tool for Properties. It may be currently on a Data Flow Task. If so, I clicked on the down arrow button next to that task and selected Package. I scrolled down the list of properties and changed the ProtectionLevel to EncryptSensitiveWithPassword, and supplied a password in the PackagePassword field. I will need this password any time I want to open the package or execute it, including when I execute it on Linux.

Executing a Package

To execute this package, I need to copy it from my Windows computer to the Linux Server. I can conveniently use MobaXterm to do this or a program like scp or winscp. Package files from SSDT are stored by default in the <user>\Projects directory, so I used the tool to save the package (.dtsx file) to a location like c:\temp on my computer.

I then copied the file (Package.dtsx) to my home directory on my Linux Server.

Now I'm ready to execute the package using the dtexec program that is installed when you install the mssql-server-is package on Linux.

Note   You must first install the Microsoft ODBC Driver 17 for SQL Server on Linux to execute this package. If you followed the steps to install the SQL Server tools (sqlcmd, …), this will already be installed.

Here is the command to run dtexec to execute the package file called Package.dtsx:

```
dtexec /F Package.dtsx /DE <package password>
```

Figure 5-49 shows the results of executing dtexec on Linux.

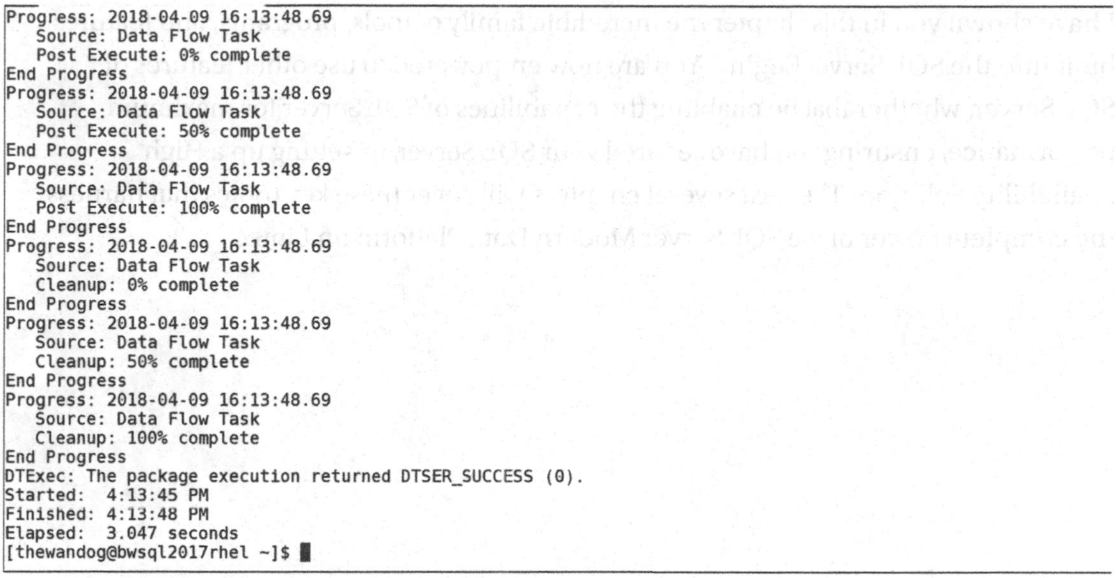

```
Progress: 2018-04-09 16:13:48.69
    Source: Data Flow Task
    Post Execute: 0% complete
End Progress
Progress: 2018-04-09 16:13:48.69
    Source: Data Flow Task
    Post Execute: 50% complete
End Progress
Progress: 2018-04-09 16:13:48.69
    Source: Data Flow Task
    Post Execute: 100% complete
End Progress
Progress: 2018-04-09 16:13:48.69
    Source: Data Flow Task
    Cleanup: 0% complete
End Progress
Progress: 2018-04-09 16:13:48.69
    Source: Data Flow Task
    Cleanup: 50% complete
End Progress
Progress: 2018-04-09 16:13:48.69
    Source: Data Flow Task
    Cleanup: 100% complete
End Progress
DTExec: The package execution returned DTSER_SUCCESS (0).
Started:  4:13:45 PM
Finished: 4:13:48 PM
Elapsed:  3.047 seconds
[thewandog@bwsql2017rhel ~]$ █
```

Figure 5-49. *Executing dtexec on Linux*

The file people.txt was created in my home directory. You can also examine the XML details of the Package.dtsx file created for this package.

Go Further with SSIS

To learn more about SSIS on Linux, including capabilities and limitations, see our documentation at https://docs.microsoft.com/sql/linux/sql-server-linux-migrate-ssis.

To learn more about SSIS overall, see our main documentation page at https://docs.microsoft.com/sql/integration-services/sql-server-integration-services.

To learn about typical usage scenarios for SSIS, see our documentation page at https://msdn.microsoft.com/en-us/library/ms137795(v=sql.105).aspx.

Summary

I have shown you in this chapter the incredible family of tools, programs, and features built into the SQL Server Engine. You are now empowered to use other features of SQL Server, whether that be enabling the capabilities of SQL Server for maximum performance, ensuring you have secured your SQL Server, or setting up a High Availability Solution. The next several chapters will cover these key topics that harness the complete power of the SQL Server Modern Data Platform on Linux.

CHAPTER 6

Performance Capabilities

If you are going to provide a data platform that is competitive in the industry and can handle the largest enterprise workloads on the planet, the database engine must be fast. The engine must be fast, built-in. It must provide capabilities for configuration, and tuning for users and developers to use computing resources to their maximum. It must provide features that allow users to accelerate performance beyond expectation with little or no application changes. And finally, a world-class data platform should come with built-in capabilities to adapt and autotune common query performance problems.

SQL Server on Linux has all of this and more. If you have read all the chapters of the book to this point, I've shown the basics of deployment and how to create a database and application. I've also shown the vast set of tools and features for maximizing the investment of SQL Server. In this chapter, I want to describe the major performance capabilities of the SQL Server data platform. My goal for this chapter is that anyone reading this will understand how to achieve the best performance possible for a database application using SQL Server on Linux.

I'll first describe the built-in capabilities of the SQL Server database engine that are the foundation required to achieve maximum performance. Then I'll discuss the various configuration choices to achieve the best performance possible including configuration of the SQL Server instance, database, and Linux Operating System. I'll provide a section in this chapter on performance tuning, so you can ensure you are using resources for SQL Server most efficiently and at maximum capacity. I'll then discuss features in SQL Server that allow an application to accelerate performance beyond traditional database application functionality. And finally, I'll conclude the chapter by discussing new features in SQL Server that provide automation to adapt and autotune query performance.

In 2017 at the Microsoft Ignite Conference, I gave a presentation on SQL Server Performance capabilities called **Experience Microsoft SQL Server 2017: The fast and the furious**. I encourage you to watch this presentation as a supplement to this chapter. You can find this video at `https://channel9.msdn.com/Events/Ignite/Microsoft-Ignite-Orlando-2017/BRK3109`.

229

© Bob Ward 2018
B. Ward, *Pro SQL Server on Linux*, https://doi.org/10.1007/978-1-4842-4128-8_6

For examples in this chapter, we will use the full WideWorldImporters database. So, before you proceed, you need to copy the WideWorldImporters backup to your Linux Server. You will restore it in the chapter and then use it for various examples. To copy in this example, use the following command on your Linux Server if it is connected to the Internet:

```
wget https://github.com/Microsoft/sql-server-samples/releases/download/
wide-world-importers-v1.0/WideWorldImporters-Full.bak
```

I have provided the following scripts to help you restore this sample on your Linux server:

> **cpwwi.sh**: Copies the WideWorldImporters-Full.bak file into /var/opt/mssql
>
> **restorewwi_linux.sql**: Restores the WideWorldImporters database
>
> **restorewwi.sh**: Executes the restorewwi_linux.sql script with sqlcmd

Remember that the scripts are available by clicking the Download source code button on the Apress.com catalog page for this book. The URL for that page is www.apress.com/us/book/9781484241271.

Note   I often refer in this chapter to some of the objects in this database, so it is helpful to see the complete set of T-SQL scripts that make up the database. I have provided a script called **wwi.sql** in the examples that provides the database definition and all objects.

Performance Built In

We built the SQL Server database engine to be fast and scale to the needs of the largest database workloads on the planet. I wrote this section of the chapter, not to require any action, but to give the reader the understanding of what is *possible* with SQL Server. The SQL Server on Linux database engine is built to understand how to dynamically scale and maximize CPU, I/O, and memory resources of a computer, virtual machine, or container. Users may be reading this book to learn about SQL Server and decide whether it's a data platform they can rely on to run their business or be the data source for a new application. This section is intended to help provide the information necessary to answer those questions.

You don't have to go any further to understand what is possible with SQL Server then to just look at our TPC benchmark performance. SQL Server on Linux currently has the two best performance results for a 1TB TPC-H benchmark, which measures analytic query performance. (You can read more about TPC benchmarks at http://www.tpc.org and you can see the specific benchmarks results I mention for TPC-H at http://www.tpc.org/3331 and http://www.tpc.org/3327.)

SQL Server 2017 on Linux is based on some amazing work our engineering team did in SQL Server 2016. As a supplement to this section of the chapter, I encourage you to read the blog series called SQL Server 2016 It Just Runs Faster at https://blogs.msdn.microsoft.com/bobsql/tag/it-just-runs-faster and the 2016 Microsoft Ignite presentation I gave on the same subject at https://channel9.msdn.com/Events/Ignite/2016/BRK3043-TS.

SQL Server Built-in Scalability

I described in Chapter 1 as part of the architecture of SQL Server the SQLOS component. SQLOS is built to provide scheduling and memory services to the SQL Server engine. All SQL Server engine components use SQLOS to create and execute tasks executed by a pool for worker threads. SQL Server engine components are required to use SQLOS services for scheduling using a non-preemptive system. Using this type of scheduling system allows SQLOS to minimize kernel context switches and maximize CPU resource usage and efficiency.

To provide these services, SQLOS creates a list of *schedulers* based on the number of detected logical CPUs and assigns a group of worker threads from an overall pool to each scheduler. As new tasks are created to execute a unit of work (for example, a login or a query), they are assigned to run on a worker thread on a specific scheduler. Furthermore, the scheduling system is designed to detect and take advantage of NUMA computer architectures through *nodes*. Nodes and CPUs provide a natural scaling unit for SQLOS and SQL Server. SQLOS can allow worker threads to run on any CPU within a NUMA node but avoid cross-node boundaries to reduce foreign memory access. Recognition of NUMA nodes and CPUs allows SQL Server to spread worker threads across CPUs to provide maximum scalability. Furthermore, SQL Server can partition internal data structures and lists by node and/or CPU to ensure the code does not encounter bottlenecks for high, concurrent user workloads.

SQLOS exposes scheduler, node, and CPU information through these DMVs:

> **dm_os_schedulers**: This DMV lists out the schedulers used by SQL Server for worker thread scheduling, including statistics of how many workers are running or how many tasks are waiting for a worker thread from the pool. Figure 6-1 shows example output from this DMV on my SQL Server on Linux on a virtual machine with four logical CPUs: (Note: you can use the example script **dm_os_schedulers.sql** to see this output for your SQL Server).

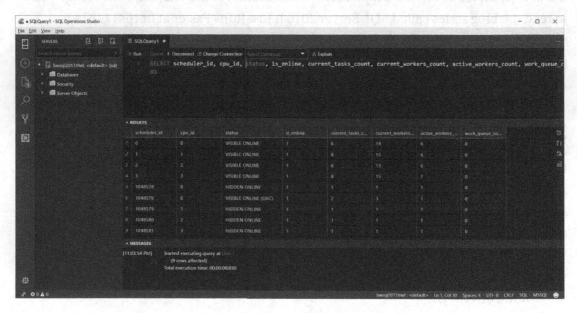

Figure 6-1. *dm_os_schedulers on a four CPU virtual machine running SQL Server on Linux*

The four schedulers with a status of VISIBLE ONLINE are *normal* schedulers used to run SQL Server tasks and workers. HIDDEN schedulers are used to schedule work for some background and other tasks such as backups. You can find the complete documentation of this DMV at https://docs.microsoft.com/sql/relational-databases/system-dynamic-management-views/sys-dm-os-schedulers-transact-sql.

dm_os_nodes: This DMV lists out all detected NUMA nodes on the server running SQL Server. Even servers that don't have NUMA nodes will have a node_id=0. Node_id=64 is for a special node reserved for the Dedicated Administrator Connection (DAC). I'll talk more about DAC in a later chapter in this book.

SQLOS exposes tasks, workers, and threads through these DMVs:

dm_os_workers: This DMV lists out all worker threads that are either executing or can execute a task for SQL Server. Worker threads for SQL Server are created in a pool grouped by scheduler. SQL Server will assign worker threads from the pool to execute an incoming task (instead of dedicating a thread for every request). By default, the configuration of **max worker threads** = 0 (which means *dynamic*). The value of 0 means SQL Server creates a maximum pool of worker threads based on formulas as documented at https://docs.microsoft.com/sql/database-engine/configure-windows/configure-the-max-worker-threads-server-configuration-option. The sys.dm_os_sys_info DMV lists the current max worker threads calculated value. For most scenarios, you should be able to leave the max worker threads configuration value to 0 and let SQL Server calculate the value. However, in some cases, you may want to override the default by using the system procedure sp_configure to change max worker threads to a fixed value. I'll discuss this choice later in the chapter.

dm_os_tasks: Any *unit of work* in SQL Server is a task. Any login, query, or background task is a task. Think of a task as a function in the SQL Server to execute code in the SQL Server engine. Tasks are run by worker threads. It is possible in some situations that a task will need to wait for a worker thread. In these situations, the task will be listed in this DMV and the wait_type for the task in dm_os_waiting_tasks will be THREADPOOL. A larger list of tasks waiting on THREADPOOL could present a problem in SQL Server. I documented some information on THREADPOOL waits many years ago in this blog post: https://blogs.msdn.microsoft.com/

psssql/2009/11/24/doctor-this-sql-server-appears-to-
be-sick/. My friend Paul Randal has another great description
of how to address THREADPOOL waits in his blog post https://
www.sqlskills.com/help/waits/threadpool/. When a task is
bound to a worker thread, it becomes a *request* and will appear in
sys.dm_exec_requests.

Because modern NUMA and CPU architectures can support more than eight
physical cores per CPU, we introduced a feature called **Auto Soft NUMA** in SQL Server
2016, so SQL Server can logically partition nodes and CPUs within its code to provide
better scalability.

To understand how SQL Server detects CPU and NUMA nodes (and uses Auto Soft
NUMA), let's look at an example. I have a machine in the labs of Microsoft with four
NUMA nodes, one CPU socket per node, and 24 cores per socket (hyperthreading is not
enabled, so a total of 96 CPUs).

When I install SQL Server on this computer, the ERRORLOG file detects the CPU and
cores with the following entries, as shown in Figure 6-2.

```
2018-04-22 10:51:58.04 Server      Microsoft SQL Server 2017 (RTM-CU6) (KB4101464) - 14.0.3025.34 (X64)
        Apr  9 2018 18:00:41
        Copyright (C) 2017 Microsoft Corporation
        Enterprise Edition: Core-based Licensing (64-bit) on Linux (Red Hat Enterprise Linux)
2018-04-22 10:51:58.04 Server      UTC adjustment: -7:00
2018-04-22 10:51:58.04 Server      (c) Microsoft Corporation.
2018-04-22 10:51:58.04 Server      All rights reserved.
2018-04-22 10:51:58.04 Server      Server process ID is 4124.
2018-04-22 10:51:58.04 Server      Logging SQL Server messages in file '/var/opt/mssql/log/errorlog'.
2018-04-22 10:51:58.04 Server      Registry startup parameters:
        -d /var/opt/mssql/data/master.mdf
        -l /var/opt/mssql/data/mastlog.ldf
        -e /var/opt/mssql/log/errorlog
2018-04-22 10:51:58.05 Server      SQL Server detected 4 sockets with 24 cores per socket and 24 logical processors per socket, 96 total logical proce
ssors; using 96 logical processors based on SQL Server licensing. This is an informational message; no user action is required.
2018-04-22 10:51:58.05 Server      SQL Server is starting at normal priority base (=7). This is an informational message only. No user action is requi
red.
2018-04-22 10:51:58.05 Server      Detected 1238240 MB of RAM. This is an informational message; no user action is required.
```

Figure 6-2. *The SQL Server ERRORLOG entries detecting available CPUs*

Auto Soft NUMA will be enabled if SQL Server detects more than eight physical cores
per CPU. SQL Server will then attempt to partition NUMA nodes (logical within SQL
Server) to get as close as possible to eight CPUs per node. Figure 6-3 shows how Auto
Soft NUMA has partitioned the 96 CPUs across four NUMA nodes on this computer
logically within SQL Server.

```
2018-04-22 10:51:59.11 Server        Automatic soft-NUMA was enabled because SQL Server has detected hardware NUMA nodes with greater than 8 physical co
res.
2018-04-22 10:51:59.20 Server        Buffer pool extension is already disabled. No action is necessary.
2018-04-22 10:51:59.34 Server        InitializeExternalUserGroupSid failed. Implied authentication will be disabled.
2018-04-22 10:51:59.35 Server        Implied authentication manager initialization failed. Implied authentication will be disabled.
2018-04-22 10:51:59.35 Server        Successfully initialized the TLS configuration. Allowed TLS protocol versions are ['1.0 1.1 1.2']. Allowed TLS ciph
ers are ['ECDHE-ECDSA-AES128-GCM-SHA256:ECDHE-ECDSA-AES256-GCM-SHA384:ECDHE-RSA-AES128-GCM-SHA256:ECDHE-RSA-AES256-GCM-SHA384:ECDHE-ECDSA-AES128-SHA25
6:ECDHE-ECDSA-AES256-SHA384:ECDHE-ECDSA-AES256-SHA:ECDHE-ECDSA-AES128-SHA:AES256-GCM-SHA384:AES128-GCM-SHA256:AES256-SHA256:AES128-SHA256:AES256-SHA:A
ES128-SHA:!DHE-RSA-AES256-GCM-SHA384:!DHE-RSA-AES256-GCM-SHA256:!DHE-RSA-AES256-SHA:!DHE-RSA-AES128-SHA'].
2018-04-22 10:51:59.40 Server        The maximum number of dedicated administrator connections for this instance is '1'
2018-04-22 10:51:59.40 Server        Node configuration: node 0: CPU mask: 0x0000000000000ff:0 Active CPU mask: 0x00000000000000ff:0. This message prov
ides a description of the NUMA configuration for this computer. This is an informational message only. No user action is required.
2018-04-22 10:51:59.40 Server        Node configuration: node 1: CPU mask: 0x000000000000ff00:0 Active CPU mask: 0x000000000000ff00:0. This message prov
ides a description of the NUMA configuration for this computer. This is an informational message only. No user action is required.
2018-04-22 10:51:59.41 Server        Node configuration: node 2: CPU mask: 0x0000000000ff0000:0 Active CPU mask: 0x0000000000ff0000:0. This message prov
ides a description of the NUMA configuration for this computer. This is an informational message only. No user action is required.
2018-04-22 10:51:59.41 Server        Node configuration: node 3: CPU mask: 0x00000000ff000000:0 Active CPU mask: 0x00000000ff000000:0. This message prov
ides a description of the NUMA configuration for this computer. This is an informational message only. No user action is required.
2018-04-22 10:51:59.41 Server        Node configuration: node 4: CPU mask: 0x000000ff00000000:0 Active CPU mask: 0x000000ff00000000:0. This message prov
ides a description of the NUMA configuration for this computer. This is an informational message only. No user action is required.
2018-04-22 10:51:59.41 Server        Node configuration: node 5: CPU mask: 0x0000ff0000000000:0 Active CPU mask: 0x0000ff0000000000:0. This message prov
ides a description of the NUMA configuration for this computer. This is an informational message only. No user action is required.
2018-04-22 10:51:59.41 Server        Node configuration: node 6: CPU mask: 0x00000000000000ff:1 Active CPU mask: 0x00000000000000ff:1. This message prov
ides a description of the NUMA configuration for this computer. This is an informational message only. No user action is required.
2018-04-22 10:51:59.41 Server        Node configuration: node 7: CPU mask: 0x000000000000ff00:1 Active CPU mask: 0x000000000000ff00:1. This message prov
ides a description of the NUMA configuration for this computer. This is an informational message only. No user action is required.
2018-04-22 10:51:59.42 Server        Node configuration: node 8: CPU mask: 0x0000000000ff0000:1 Active CPU mask: 0x0000000000ff0000:1. This message prov
ides a description of the NUMA configuration for this computer. This is an informational message only. No user action is required.
2018-04-22 10:51:59.42 Server        Node configuration: node 9: CPU mask: 0x00000000ff000000:1 Active CPU mask: 0x00000000ff000000:1. This message prov
ides a description of the NUMA configuration for this computer. This is an informational message only. No user action is required.
2018-04-22 10:51:59.42 Server        Node configuration: node 10: CPU mask: 0x000000ff00000000:1 Active CPU mask: 0x000000ff00000000:1. This message pro
vides a description of the NUMA configuration for this computer. This is an informational message only. No user action is required.
2018-04-22 10:51:59.42 Server        Node configuration: node 11: CPU mask: 0x0000ff0000000000:1 Active CPU mask: 0x0000ff0000000000:1. This message pro
vides a description of the NUMA configuration for this computer. This is an informational message only. No user action is required.
```

Figure 6-3. ERRORLOG entries for NUMA and CPU mapping

Auto Soft NUMA is enabled by default, but you can disable this for any reason (perhaps you suspect it is causing a performance problem) through ALTER SERVER CONFIGURATION. You can read more about Auto Soft NUMA in our documentation at `https://docs.microsoft.com/sql/t-sql/statements/alter-server-configuration-transact-sql`. To understand how to read the mappings in the ERRORLOG for the "CPU Mask" to see which CPUs are mapped to specific NUMA nodes, see this blog post where I talk more about Auto Soft NUMA and how to interpret CPU mappings: `https://blogs.msdn.microsoft.com/bobsql/2016/11/29/how-it-works-it-just-runs-faster-auto-soft-numa`.

Since SQLOS controls scheduler and thread execution, it is possible to assign SQL Server worker threads to specific NUMA nodes and/or CPUs. This process is called *affinity*. I'll discuss more about affinity in later sections of this book.

Dynamic Memory and Cache Management

SQL Server is built to adapt but also maximize computing resources. Memory can be one of the most important resources for database performance. SQL Server provides a robust memory management system for important resources such as database pages (buffers) and cached T-SQL queries and plans. SQL Server also manages memory for other internal needs and is tracked through a system of memory clerks. (One of the Dynamic Management Views I called out in Chapter 5 was dm_os_memory_clerks.)

Another amazing aspect of SQL Server's memory management is *dynamic memory*. SQL Server has built-in capabilities to grow and shrink its memory footprint based on demand for memory. You will find that after installing SQL Server without creating any new database, the engine will consume approximately 600MB of memory on Linux. Then as you create databases, load data, and execute queries, SQL Server will grow its memory consumption until it reaches designed limits. For many years when I was in technical support for SQL Server on Windows, I would often hear complaints from my Windows colleagues that SQL Server is "leaking" memory. What they were observing was the natural dynamic growth of SQL Server's memory consumption. SQL Server will not grow its memory consumption forever, causing possible memory problems on Linux. SQL Server is gated by two memory limits that are configurable. I'll discuss these settings in a later section in this chapter.

One of the methods in which SQL Server can shrink its memory footprint is that the largest memory consumers within the SQL Server engine are *caches*. These cache consumers are the **Buffer Pool** and **Plan Cache**.

The Buffer Pool is a cache of database pages including data, index, and system pages. Since all database pages are backed by database files, it is possible at any point in time to either free up a database page that is *clean* (not modified) or write a *dirty* database page to disk to free it up for another page.

The Plan Cache is a separate set of memory cache for queries including their query plans. SQL Server will cache query plans for ad hoc queries and objects like stored procedures so that they will not have to be compiled for each execution. Not all query execution plans are cached. For more details on this topic, read our documentation at https://docs.microsoft.com/sql/relational-databases/query-processing-architecture-guide#execution-plan-caching-and-reuse.

Here is an easy test to see how SQL Server will grow its memory usage dynamically through the buffer pool. Note: If you have already restored the WideWorldImporters backup or created it from previous chapters, the following steps will drop the database and restore the full sample backup.

1. If you have not done so already, drop the WideWorldImporters sample with these T-SQL commands from any SQL tool:

    ```
    USE [master]
    GO
    DROP DATABASE IF EXISTS [WideWorldImporters]
    GO
    ```

2. Restart SQL Server on Linux with this command from the Linux shell:

```
sudo systemctl restart mssql-server
```

3. Let's observe the amount of memory consumed by the sqlservr process and the memory used within the SQL Server Engine.

Run the top command from the Linux shell.

```
top
```

Look for memory consumed by the sqlservr process under the RES column. Figure 6-4 shows that on my Linux VM the sqlservr process consumes approximately 570MB.

```
top - 21:15:32 up 20:35,  1 user,  load average: 0.02, 0.02, 0.05
Tasks: 127 total,   2 running, 125 sleeping,   0 stopped,   0 zombie
%Cpu(s):  0.2 us,  0.2 sy,  0.0 ni, 99.6 id,  0.1 wa,  0.0 hi,  0.0 si,  0.0 st
KiB Mem :  7992468 total,  5462736 free,   814988 used,  1714744 buff/cache
KiB Swap:  5242876 total,  5242876 free,        0 used.  6873004 avail Mem

  PID USER      PR  NI    VIRT    RES    SHR S  %CPU %MEM     TIME+ COMMAND
13214 mssql     20   0 3034388 573420   5272 S   1.0  7.2   0:07.10 sqlservr
  677 root      20   0   21524   1200    972 S   0.3  0.0   0:04.46 irqbalance
13314 thewand+  20   0  161972   2256   1580 R   0.3  0.0   0:00.07 top
    1 root      20   0  193572   6684   4168 S   0.0  0.1   0:03.96 systemd
    2 root      20   0       0      0      0 S   0.0  0.0   0:00.02 kthreadd
    3 root      20   0       0      0      0 S   0.0  0.0   0:00.21 ksoftirqd/0
    5 root       0 -20       0      0      0 S   0.0  0.0   0:00.00 kworker/0:0H
    7 root      rt   0       0      0      0 S   0.0  0.0   0:00.02 migration/0
    8 root      20   0       0      0      0 S   0.0  0.0   0:00.00 rcu_bh
    9 root      20   0       0      0      0 S   0.0  0.0   0:03.11 rcu_sched
   10 root       0 -20       0      0      0 S   0.0  0.0   0:00.00 lru-add-drain
   11 root      rt   0       0      0      0 S   0.0  0.0   0:00.34 watchdog/0
   12 root      rt   0       0      0      0 S   0.0  0.0   0:00.27 watchdog/1
   13 root      rt   0       0      0      0 S   0.0  0.0   0:00.03 migration/1
   14 root      20   0       0      0      0 S   0.0  0.0   0:00.04 ksoftirqd/1
   16 root       0 -20       0      0      0 S   0.0  0.0   0:00.00 kworker/1:0H
   17 root      rt   0       0      0      0 S   0.0  0.0   0:00.26 watchdog/2
   18 root      rt   0       0      0      0 S   0.0  0.0   0:00.34 migration/2
   19 root      20   0       0      0      0 S   0.0  0.0   0:00.11 ksoftirqd/2
   20 root      20   0       0      0      0 R   0.0  0.0   1:19.88 kworker/2:0
   21 root       0 -20       0      0      0 S   0.0  0.0   0:00.00 kworker/2:0H
   22 root      rt   0       0      0      0 S   0.0  0.0   0:00.25 watchdog/3
   23 root      rt   0       0      0      0 S   0.0  0.0   0:00.01 migration/3
   24 root      20   0       0      0      0 S   0.0  0.0   0:00.03 ksoftirqd/3
```

Figure 6-4. *Memory consumed by sqlservr after initial startup*

Now run the following T-SQL command to see how much total memory the SQL Server engine consumes within its own memory management. This T-SQL batch is provided in the example script **sqlmem.sql:**

```
-- Find the total memory used within the SQL Server Engine, the total
amount of buffer pool usage,
-- and the target that SQL Server believes it can grow to
--
```

```
SELECT counter_name, cntr_value FROM sys.dm_os_performance_counters
WHERE object_name = 'SQLServer:Memory Manager'
AND counter_name IN ('Database Cache Memory (KB)', 'Total Server Memory
(KB)', 'Target Server Memory (KB)')
GO
```

sys.dm_os_performance_counters is a Dynamic Management View (DMV) used to query certain performance statistics across the SQL Server Engine. On Windows, these values are also exposed by a tool called Performance Monitor. For Linux, I can just query the data directly with T-SQL.

Tip   To find out the complete list of SQL Server performance counter objects and their descriptions, you can use this reference in our documentation: `https://docs.microsoft.com/sql/relational-databases/performance-monitor/use-sql-server-objects`.

Let me show the results on my Linux Server so you can observe this on your own system. Figure 6-5 shows the results of running this T-SQL batch.

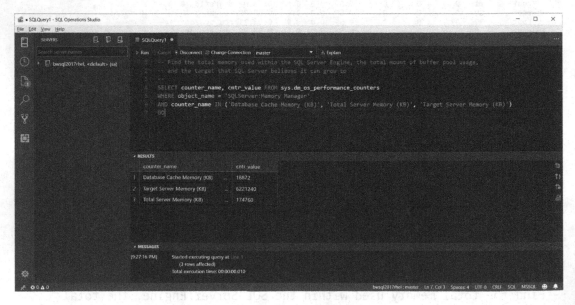

Figure 6-5.   *Examining SQL Server memory statistics*

Database Cache Memory (KB) is the amount of memory used by the buffer pool. At startup on this server, it is only approximately 18MB.

Target Server Memory (KB) is the potential amount of memory SQL Server can grow to. Think of this as the ceiling of memory used within the SQL Server engine. In this example, it is approximately 6.2GB.

Total Server Memory (KB) is the amount of memory used within the SQL Server engine, which is approximately 174MB.

Why then did top show the sqlservr process consuming 500+MB? This is because the difference between Total Server Memory (KB) and what top is showing is a fairly fixed amount of memory allocated by the sqlservr process on Linux, not related to SQL Server's engine memory consumers like the buffer pool (including SQLPAL). As the amount of memory SQL Server allocates grows, this difference should remain fairly constant.

Now let's continue by showing a quick example of how SQL Server can dynamically grow its memory usage through the buffer pool:

- Restore the full WideWorldImporters sample database using the sample script **restorewwi.sh**.

- Run the following T-SQL command, which will force SQL Server to read in all database pages from the WideWorldImporters database into the buffer pool:

```
USE master
GO
DBCC CHECKDB(WideWorldImporters) WITH TABLOCK
GO
```

- Run the same **top** command you did previously and the preceding T-SQL query to look at dm_os_performance_counters.

On my Linux server, the top command shows SQL Server's memory increased to approximately 1.3GB (looking at the RES column). The Database Cache Memory (KB) increased to approximately 430MB, The Total Server Memory (KB) increased to approximately 720MB, and the Target Server Memory (KB) increased slightly. These increases line up with the fact that the WideWorldImporters database has about approximately 400MB of database pages.

Efficient I/O Processing

SQL Server uses efficient methods to read and write database pages and transaction log records to maximize performance and ensure durability and consistency. This includes read-ahead reading, write-ahead logging, checkpoint processing, and data compression.

In addition, since SQL Server has its own caching mechanisms, the engine uses Direct I/O by enabling the O_DIRECT flag when opening database and transaction log files on Linux to bypass file system caches. You can read more about O_DIRECT at `http://man7.org/linux/man-pages/man2/open.2.html`.

Read-Ahead

Each database page is 8KB in size. It would be inefficient if SQL Server tried to only read a single database page from a database file each time it needed to read data from disk. Instead, SQL Server uses a mechanism called read-ahead to pull in database pages to the buffer pool. The thinking is that these pages will likely be needed by the query currently executing, so it would be more efficient to pull them into cache because a larger read size is more efficient than a larger number of smaller reads. Scenarios where read-ahead is used in SQL Server are situations where several rows spanning multiple pages are scanned from a table or index. How can you tell if SQL Server is using read-ahead to read database pages? There are several methods:

- Use the SET STATISTICS IO T-SQL statement in the session where the query reading pages is executed.

- Use Extended Events to track the event **file_read_completed**.

You can also see the overall use of read-ahead in SQL Server using the DMV **dm_os_performance_counters**, using the object_name = 'SQLServer:Buffer Manager' and counter_name = 'Readahead pages/sec'.

SQL Server can only read multiple pages from a database file that are contiguous, so the size of a read-ahead may vary depending on how pages are organized in a table or index. Therefore, if a table or clustered index is fragmented where many of the pages containing the data are not contiguous in the database file, read-ahead reads are not as effective. I'll discuss index fragmentation and how to manage it in Chapter 9. There are some limits to read-ahead reads. The maximum size of a read-ahead in SQL Server 2017 Enterprise edition is 1MB. This number will be lower in other editions of SQL Server.

There is also a limit to how many pages SQL Server will attempt to read asynchronously as it performs read-ahead for pages that have been ready yet in buffer pool. This maximum is larger in the Enterprise edition (5,000) than other editions (128).

Here is an example to see how SQL Server will use read-ahead for a typical scan of table data. This assumes you restored the full WideWorldImporters database:

1. Create and start an extended event session using the following T-SQL set of statements. These statements can be found in the sample script **tracesqlreads.sql:**

```
CREATE EVENT SESSION [tracesqlreads] ON SERVER
ADD EVENT sqlserver.file_read_completed(SET collect_path=(1)
    ACTION(sqlserver.database_name,sqlserver.sql_text)
    WHERE ([sqlserver].[database_name]=N'WideWorldImporters'))
ADD TARGET package0.event_file(SET filename=N'tracesqlreads')
WITH (MAX_MEMORY=4096 KB,EVENT_RETENTION_MODE=ALLOW_SINGLE_EVENT_
LOSS,MAX_DISPATCH_LATENCY=30 SECONDS,MAX_EVENT_SIZE=0 KB,MEMORY_
PARTITION_MODE=NONE,TRACK_CAUSALITY=OFF,STARTUP_STATE=OFF)
GO
ALTER EVENT SESSION [tracesqlreads] ON SERVER STATE=START
GO
```

For this extended event session, I use a file target to write out the extended events data.

2. Execute the following T-SQL batches from your favorite SQL Server tool. I'll use SQL Operations Studio. These statements can be found in the sample script **sqlreadahead.sql:**

```
USE [WideWorldImporters]
GO
DBCC DROPCLEANBUFFERS
GO
SET STATISTICS IO ON
GO
SELECT COUNT(*) FROM Sales.Invoices WITH (INDEX=1)
GO
```

In this example, I use the DBCC DROPCLEANBUFFERS statement to force SQL Server to read all pages needed for the query from disk. I then use SET STATISTICS IO so that SQL Server will return messages with I/O statistics for the SELECT statement. For the T-SQL SELECT statement to read data, I use a *query hint* for force SQL Server to scan all pages from the clustered index of the Sales.Invoices table. You can read more about query hints in our documentation at `https://docs.microsoft.com/sql/t-sql/queries/hints-transact-sql-query`. Figure 6-6 shows the I/O statistics from the SELECT statement on my Linux server.

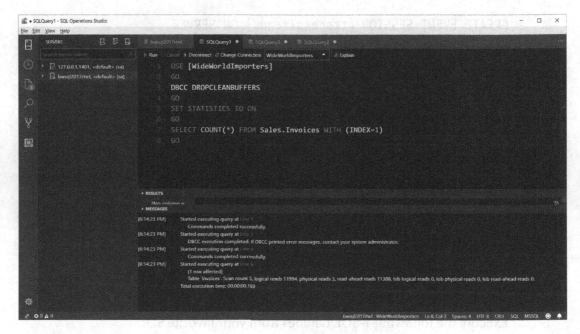

Figure 6-6. *I/O statistics for SQL Server read-ahead reads*

Physical reads are single-page reads. Read-ahead reads are the number of times SQL Server attempted to read more than one page when reading from the database file.

3. Now I can use the results of the extended events session to see what sizes were used for read-ahead reads. First, I need to stop the extended events session with the following T-SQL statement:

```
ALTER EVENT SESSION [tracesqlreads] ON SERVER STATE=STOP
GO
```

4. Now I use the following T-SQL statement to read the results from the extended events session using the **fn_xe_file_target_read_file** system stored procedure. You can find this T-SQL batch in the sample script **readxefile.sql**:

```
SELECT [database_name] = xe_file.xml_data.value('(/event/action[@
name="database_name"]/value)[1]','[nvarchar](128)'),
[read_size] = CAST(xe_file.xml_data.value('(/event/data[@
name="size"]/value)[1]', '[nvarchar](128)') AS INT),
[file_path] = xe_file.xml_data.value('(/event/data[@name="path"]/
value)[1]', '[nvarchar](128)')
--xe_file.xml_data
FROM
(
SELECT [xml_data] = CAST(event_data AS XML)
FROM sys.fn_xe_file_target_read_file('/var/opt/mssql/log/
tracesqlreads*.xel', null, null, null)
) AS xe_file
GO
```

This system procedure returns the extended events data in the form of XML. The preceding query shows an example of how to *shred* XML data into columns and rows. Some of the results of this session on my Linux Server can be seen in Figure 6-7.

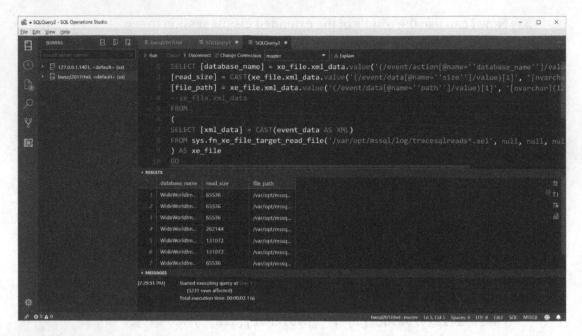

Figure 6-7. *Extended events for read sizes from SQL Server read-ahead reads*

The read_size column is measured in bytes. You can see that several reads are 64KB, while some are larger including 246KB and 128KB.

Write-Ahead Logging

When SQL Server needs to modify data on pages in the buffer pool, performance would not be optimal if SQL Server had to wait for all changes for each database page to be written to disk for the T-SQL statement that required the change (such as an INSERT statement). Since each database includes a transaction log, if SQL Server ensures all changes are written to the transaction log file, it does not have to write database pages immediately.

This concept is called write-ahead logging (this concept is also known as the WAL protocol). Provided SQL Server ensures all modifications for a committed transaction are written to the transaction log on disk, all transactions will be *consistent* even if the changes to the database page are not written to disk should SQL Server or the Linux server terminate unexpectedly.

This architecture allows for T-SQL statements that modify data to operate as fast as changes can be *hardened* to the transaction log. This means for applications that rely on performance of database modifications (such as OLTP heavy applications), placing the transaction log file on an extremely fast storage system is important.

SQL Server does offer a feature called **delayed durability**, which allows transactions to complete without waiting for the transaction log changes to be written to disk. However, the tradeoff for performance is possible data loss. You can read more about SQL Server transaction durability options in our documentation at `https://docs.microsoft.com/sql/relational-databases/logs/control-transaction-durability`.

Transaction log writes are performed by a background task called LOG WRITER (you can see this background task looking for the row in dm_exec_requests where command = LOG WRITER). For scalability purposes, we enhanced SQL Server 2016 to use multiple LOG WRITER tasks per NUMA node. You can read more about this concept in this blog post: `https://blogs.msdn.microsoft.com/bobsql/2016/06/03/sql-2016-it-just-runs-faster-multiple-log-writer-workers/`.

Checkpoint, LazyWrites, and Eager Writes

If SQL Server never wrote modified database pages (also called *dirty pages*) to the database data file on disk, the transaction log would grow endlessly and require a large amount of disk space. Furthermore, recovering an SQL Server database if it were restarted could take an exceptionally long time because all changes must be replayed from the transaction log.

SQL Server uses several techniques to write database pages to disk. All these techniques are based on a similar principal to read-ahead so that databases pages that are contiguous are written together, resulting in efficient, larger writes.

By default, SQL Server 2017 uses a method of writing database pages called **indirect checkpoint.** Indirect checkpoint uses a *target recovery time* to make decisions on when to collect dirty database pages and write them to the corresponding database data file. This concept is to reliably ensure that if the database must be restarted, the database can be recovered (transactions rolled forward and rolled back) in a known interval of time. The target recovery time is configured using the ALTER DATABASE T-SQL statement using the TARGET_RECOVERY_TIME option. The default is one minute. SQL Server also offers an option for **automatic checkpoints**, which was the default behavior prior to SQL Server 2016. Automatic checkpoints use the sp_configure option **recovery interval** and can result in I/O write behaviors that are not smooth but can have spikes. Indirect checkpoints are designed to result in a smoother I/O pattern for writes but could have an impact on heavy OLTP type applications. Indirect checkpoints are performed by a background task called RECOVERY WRITER (you can see this background task by looking for the row in dm_exec_requests where command = RECOVERY WRITER).

Automatic checkpoints are performed by a background task called CHECKPOINT (you can see this background task by looking for the row in dm_exec_requests where command = CHECKPOINT).

SQL Server can also generate checkpoints for other types of internal operations and events. For a complete read on the topic of database checkpoints, see our documentation at `https://docs.microsoft.com/sql/relational-databases/logs/database-checkpoints-sql-server`. You can track indirect checkpoints by looking for the value in dm_os_performance_counters where object_name = SQLServer:Buffer Manager and counter_name = Background writer pages/sec. You can track automatic checkpoints by looking for the value in dm_os_performance_counters where object_name = SQLServer:Buffer Manager and counter_name = Checkpoint pages/sec.

When SQL Server needs to free up memory for new database pages to be read into the buffer pool because all existing memory is being used, some database pages that need to be freed could be dirty. All dirty pages that need to be freed must be written to disk. SQL Server uses the WAL protocol for these writes to ensure database consistency. It is possible some of these dirty pages are part of uncommitted transactions, so transaction log records must be first written so these uncommitted transactions can be properly rolled back if necessary during recovery. Any activity to write out dirty pages during buffer pool management operation is called a **lazywrite**. Lazywrites will be performed by either a background task called LAZY WRITER (you can see this background task by looking for the row in dm_exec_requests where command = LAZY WRITER) or *in line* with SQL Server worker threads that are attempting to allocate memory. You can track lazywrite activity by looking for the value in dm_os_performance_counters where object_name = SQLServer:Buffer Manager and counter_name = Lazy writes/sec.

Some scenarios with SQL Server involve a larger number of database page modifications such as bulk insert, SELECT..INTO, or INSERT..SELECT. Rather than flooding checkpoint processes, SQL Server will use a technique called *Eager Write*s to trigger writes for dirty pages vs. waiting for a checkpoint. There is no special background process for eager writes because they occur as a part of the bulk operation.

Data Compression

To support maximizing your memory footprint, SQL Server supports data compression for database pages and rows. Compression by its nature allows you to fit more data from database pages into the buffer pool cache, offset with the cost of uncompressing data when you need to read data. Another more interesting form of compression is used when you create columnstore indexes, which I will discuss later in this chapter. For more information about data and row compression, see our documentation at `https://docs.microsoft.com/sql/relational-databases/data-compression/data-compression`.

Parallel Processing

Why use one thread when two can do it faster? That is the philosophy of parallel processing in SQL Server. SQL Server has parallel processing capabilities across the engine and for many different purposes and scenarios.

The most common scenario is *parallel query processing*. When compiling a query to build a query plan, SQL Server can decide that a specific type of operation (e.g., Index Scan) could be run faster if run by multiple tasks (worker threads). Parallel query processing traditionally gets a "bum rap" by many in the SQL Server community because queries that use parallel processing can consume more CPU resources. While it is true that any time SQL Server chooses to use operators for parallel query processing, there is likely a tuning opportunity, there are several scenarios where using parallel queries is a preferable option. Most of these scenarios are related to data warehouse applications.

I will discuss configuration options for controlling the number of tasks involved in parallel query processing and other parallel operations later in this chapter.

Let's look at an example of how to observe parallel query processing using a T-SQL SELECT statement that has to scan a clustered index to retrieve a larger number of rows. This example assumes you have already restored the full WideWorldImporters sample as mentioned at the start of this chapter.

Use SQL Operations Studio with the following T-SQL batch, which can be found in the sample script **sqlqpparallel.sql**:

```
USE [WideWorldImporters]
GO
SET STATISTICS XML ON
GO
SELECT COUNT(*) FROM Sales.Invoices WITH (INDEX=1)
GO
```

Figure 6-8 shows the results, including a visual representation of the query plan.

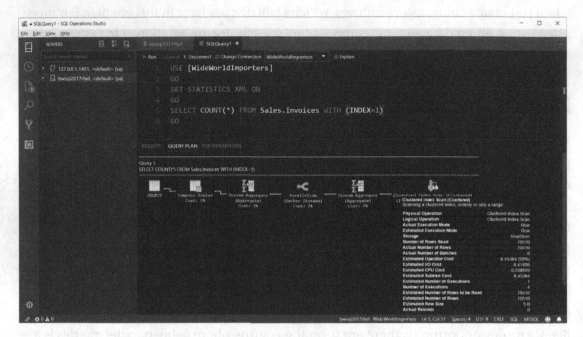

Figure 6-8. *A parallel query plan on SQL Server on Linux*

In this figure, notice two indicators of a parallel query plan:

- The Parallelism operator

- The Number of Executions for the Clustered Index Scan is 4. Since the Clustered Index Scan is the first execution in the query, a Number of Executions = 4 indicates 4 worker threads are used to scan the clustered index.

Parallel execution is used in other areas of SQL Server, including but not limited to:

- **Creating Databases**: SQL Server will create one worker thread for each unique disk volume for creating database and transaction log files.

- **Backup/Restore**: SQL Server will create multiple worker threads to read or write to database files, and multiple worker threads to read or write to the database backup.

- **DBCC CHECKDB**: By default, DBCC CHECKDB will use multiple worker threads to check the consistency of the database. Trace flag 2528 can be used to disable the use of parallel worker threads to execute CHECKDB.

- **Building Indexes**: Creating or rebuilding indexes uses multiple worker threads.

- **SELECT..INTO/INSERT..SELECT**: These "bulk" T-SQL statements can use multiple worker threads to read source tables and populate target tables.

- **Recovery**: SQL Server can use multiple worker threads to roll forward transactions as part of database recovery.

- **Statistics**: Statistics can now be updated in parallel. See the following blog post for more details: `https://blogs.msdn.microsoft.com/sql_server_team/boosting-update-statistics-performance-with-sql-2014-sp1cu6/`.

Configuration for Maximum Performance

While SQL Server "out of the box" can meet the performance needs of many applications, configuration options exist for the SQL Server instance, a database, and the Linux kernel that can help you maximize performance.

These include options to configure the SQL Server instance through mssql-conf, the T-SQL system procedure sp_configure, and the T-SQL ALTER SERVER CONFIGURATION T-SQL statement.

Note   As with any change in configuration, I highly recommend you test your application and workload before making any changes to the configuration options I talk about in this section.

SQL Server Instance Configuration

Some configuration settings for SQL Server can impact maximum performance of your application. These include settings for memory, parallel execution, processor affinity, tracing, threads, plan cache, and tempdb files.

Note   Configuration setting changes with sp_configure and ALTER SERVER CONFIGURATION may require a restart of SQL Server to take effect. Check the SQL Server documentation on sp_configure at `https://docs.microsoft.com/sql/database-engine/configure-windows/server-configuration-options-sql-server` or ALTER SERVER CONFIGURATION at `https://docs.microsoft.com/sql/t-sql/statements/alter-server-configuration-transact-sql` for more details.

- **Memory**: SQL Server on Linux by default will only allocate 80% of the physical memory on the Linux Server it is installed on, to help avoid swapping of the sqlservr process. On systems with larger amounts of RAM, leaving 20% of memory could be considered a waste. Therefore, the mssql-conf script can be used to change this setting with the **memorylimitmb** option. You should be careful setting this value too high, or you may encounter problems on Linux with the **oom killer**. You can read more about how the oom killer works on Linux at `https://unix.stackexchange.com/questions/153585/how-does-the-oom-killer-decide-which-process-to-kill-first`.

The SQL Server engine also has its own memory limit configuration settings by using the **sp_configure** system stored procedure. The *ceiling* for the SQL Server Engine is set by the **max server memory**. By default the value is 0, which is equivalent to the 80% memorylimitmb number. SQL Server will grow its memory usage to this ceiling, as discussed previous in this chapter. While it is common on SQL Server on Windows to set the **max server memory** setting to a number other than 0, since the memorylimitmb configuration exists on Linux, it is very possible to leave max server memory to 0. SQL Server also has a floor, under which SQL Server will not shrink its memory footprint. You can configure this setting with the **min server memory** setting with sp_configure. I typically only use the min server memory setting on servers where I have other programs running so I can "lock in" SQL Server from shrinking its memory too low.

Note   The memorylimitmb value does not account for memory needed by components outside the SQL Server engine, such SQL Server Agent, the SQLPAL, and Host Extension. SQL PAL and Host Extension should not require that much memory outside the SQL Server engine. For SQL Server Agent, you should perform testing to see how much memory agent jobs require.

For complete details on these server memory configuration options, see our documentation at `https://docs.microsoft.com/sql/database-engine/configure-windows/server-memory-server-configuration-options`.

- **Parallel Execution**

I discussed in the previous section of this chapter the various scenarios where SQL Server will execute tasks in parallel. Two instance configuration settings that are available through the sp_configure system procedure are: **max degree of parallelism** and **cost threshold for parallelism**.

max degree of parallelism is used to control the maximum number of parallel tasks that will be used for operators in a query plan, index build operations, DBCC CHECKDB, parallel inserts, online column modifications, and statistics updates. The default value is 0, which means SQL Server determines the best number of concurrent parallel tasks to use for a specific operation based on available CPUs to SQL Server. The ideal setting for this configuration value has been a long debate in the SQL Server community. One of the problems with finding an ideal value is that different workloads may work better with higher values of max degree of parallelism. For example, data warehouse workloads using columnstore indexes may achieve maximum performance with a higher number of parallel tasks. For SQL Server applications with a high number of concurrent users, especially ones that include OLTP workloads, it may be necessary to change the default of max degree of parallelism. My experience and testing shows this is only necessary when SQL Server is configured to run on servers with greater than eight CPUs. When I was in technical support at Microsoft, we created the following Knowledge Base Article to give more guidance on setting max degree of parallelism: `https://support.microsoft.com/help/2806535/recommendations-and-guidelines-for-the-max-degree-of-parallelism-confi`. If you struggle with setting this value, take heart that there are database options and query level hints available to override this SQL Server instance setting. For more details on the max

degree of parallelism option, see our documentation at `https://docs.microsoft.`
`com/sql/database-engine/configure-windows/configure-the-max-degree-of-`
`parallelism-server-configuration-option`.

The "cost threshold for parallelism" setting is used to control when the SQL Server
optimizer chooses whether to use parallel tasks in a query plan based on cost. The
default value of 5 can work for many workloads. However, this default was established
based on testing by the SQL Server engineering team back in the days of SQL Server 7.0.
Therefore, almost all SQL Server experts agree this default value should be much higher.
In fact, the SQL Server documentation at `https://docs.microsoft.com/sql/database-`
`engine/configure-windows/configure-the-cost-threshold-for-parallelism-`
`server-configuration-option` states: "While the default value of 5 is retained for
backwards compatibility, it is likely that a higher value is appropriate for current
systems. Many SQL Server professionals suggest a value of 25 or 30 as a starting point,
and to perform application testing with higher and lower values to optimize application
performance."

- **Process Affinity**

As described earlier in this chapter, SQL Server automatically takes advantage
of multicore and NUMA architectures. There could be some scenarios where you
want to only allow the SQL Server core engine and its worker threads to run on
specific NUMA nodes and/or CPUs. You can achieve this by using the ALTER SERVER
CONFIGURATION T-SQL command. One scenario could be that other processes are
running on the Linux Server that you want to ensure get enough CPU resources, so you
will restrict SQL Server to only certain NUMA nodes and/or CPUs.

For example, assume you had Linux Server with eight CPUs. The following T-SQL
command will only allow SQL Server to scheduler worker threads on CPUs 4-7 (CPUs
start with 0):

```
ALTER SERVER CONFIGURATION SET PROCESS AFFINITY CPU = 4 TO 7
GO
```

The effect of this command is dynamic and immediate, and does not require a restart
of SQL Server. At this point, to switch back to allow SQL Server to run on all available
CPUs, execute the following T-SQL statement:

```
ALTER SERVER CONFIGURATION SET PROCESS AFFINITY CPU = AUTO
GO
```

For maximum performance, we have found during testing that *if you plan to allow SQL Server to run on all available CPUs*, you should set the affinity to all nodes or CPUs on your system. For example, if you had a 4 NUMA node system, then you would set affinity to all nodes like the following T-SQL statement:

```
ALTER SERVER CONFIGURATION SET PROCESS AFFINITY NUMANODE = 0 TO 3
GO
```

Note   Some threads execute in the context of the SQLPAL or the Host Extension that are not scheduled worker threads. They will not adhere to using ALTER SERVER CONFIGURATION, but their execution should not consume as much CPU as SQL Server worker threads.

For more examples of setting process affinity, see our documentation at `https://docs.microsoft.com/sql/t-sql/statements/alter-server-configuration-transact-sql`.

- **Tracing**

I mentioned earlier in the book the legacy tracing feature SQL Server Trace. Several releases ago we put in a *default trace* that captures some basic information when configuration options are changed in SQL Server and tracing of object modifications. While some of this information may be useful to you, I recommend you turn off this configuration option, called **default trace enabled**, through sp_configure. Every small amount of performance can help, and this functionality is deprecated, so could be removed in a future release. See our documentation on how to do this at `https://docs.microsoft.com/sql/database-engine/configure-windows/default-trace-enabled-server-configuration-option`.

- **Threads**

I have touched on the concept of worker threads and the fact that SQL Server has a pool of these threads to service the needs of tasks such as logins and queries. SQL Server primes this pool at startup and grows and shrinks the number of threads as needed. In order to avoid consuming too many resources, SQL Server has a maximum on the number of threads in the pool. By default, SQL Server calculates this maximum based on the number of detected CPUs on the Linux Server. You can see this calculated value in the sys.dm_os_sys_info.max_workers_count column. The formula for this value can be found in our documentation at `https://docs.microsoft.com/sql/database-engine/configure-windows/configure-the-max-worker-threads-server-configuration-option`.

In most circumstances where this worker pool calculation is not enough to service the workload of the application, the problem is a concurrency issue such as many threads blocking on a resource. However, there are some situations where increasing the default value could boost a high-volume, multiuser workload. Use the **sp_configure** system procedure to change the **max worker threads** configuration value for these situations. You will need to restart SQL Server for this to take effect. Use the documentation resource in this section for the complete syntax.

- **Plan Cache**

The plan cache can be a precious resource to ensure a maximum number of queries and objects are cached to avoid frequent query compilations. Some application workloads unavoidably use many *single-user ad hoc queries*. These are T-SQL statements that are not in the form of procedure objects, are not *parameterized*, and typically are only executed one time. In order to minimize the amount of memory for these type of queries, you can enable the **optimize for ad hoc workloads** configuration option with sp_configure. This will minimize the memory impact of these types of ad hoc queries. You can determine whether your application workload matches the need for this option and how to configure it in our documentation at `https://docs.microsoft.com/sql/database-engine/configure-windows/optimize-for-ad-hoc-workloads-server-configuration-option`.

- **Tempdb Files**

I discussed the use of tempdb in Chapter 4 as part of a discussion on the use of temporary tables. Because the unique usage of tempdb involves a frequent allocation and deallocation of database pages, using a single tempdb database file can cause concurrency issues with system database pages used to track allocation information with any reasonable multiuser workload.

In order to make these concurrency scenarios more scalable, you can improve access to these system database pages by creating multiple database files for the tempdb database. SQL Server on Linux only provides a single tempdb database file by default when you install SQL Server. Therefore, on any Linux Server with greater than one CPU, you should plan to create additional tempdb database files.

My friend Denzil Ribero from the SQL Server Customer Advisor Team created a nice T-SQL script you can use to add multiple tempdb files for our Linux Server installation. This script can be found at `https://github.com/denzilribeiro/sqlunattended/blob/master/AddTempdb.sql`. You can read more about how to decide the size and number of tempdb files in our documentation at `https://docs.microsoft.com/sql/relational-databases/databases/tempdb-database` and this Knowledge Base article at `https://support.microsoft.com/help/2154845/recommendations-to-reduce-allocation-contention-in-sql-server-tempdb-d`.

Database Options

While the previous section covered some of the more interesting performance configuration choices that affect the SQL Server instance, you can also make changes at the database level to help the performance of your application. All of these options are configured using the T-SQL ALTER DATABASE statement.

- **PARAMETERIZATION**: I discussed in the previous section how to minimize the plan cache footprint for ad hoc queries. One reason why ad hoc queries can bloat the plan cache is that they are not parameterized. Parameterization involves caching a single query plan for queries that are almost exactly the same except for parameters in the WHERE clause of a T-SQL statement.

  SQL Server by default contains logic to perform *simple* parameterization on ad hoc queries. Simple parameterization does not cover a wide range of queries. Therefore, it is possible to use the ALTER DATABASE option SET PARAMETERIZATION FORCED. Using this database option will cause SQL Server to cast a wider net on possible queries to parameterize. So, how would you know whether this database option is one to consider? Consider these important points:

  - Applications that submit queries that are not parameterized are characterized typically by a high query compile rate. You can examine the dm_os_performance_counters DMV where object_name = SQLServer:SQL Statistics and counter_name = SQL Compilations/sec.

- What is "high"? Well, the second symptom of a possible lack of query parameterization is a high CPU utilization for SQL Server. This is because a high compilation rate for queries results in a higher rate of SQL CPU utilization.

- You can use the DMV dm_exec_query_stats to find which queries are in plan cache that are the same except for literal values using a concept called query hash. You can run a query like the following (which can be found in the example script **queryhash.sql**) T-SQL batch:

```
-- Find out what queries hash to the same value but are
different in cache
--
SELECT dest.text, deqs.query_hash, count (*) query_count
FROM sys.dm_exec_query_stats deqs
CROSS APPLY sys.dm_exec_sql_text(deqs.sql_handle) AS dest
GROUP BY (query_hash), dest.text
ORDER BY query_count DESC
GO
```

If you run this query and only find the highest counts to be 2 or 3, then you probably don't have any issues. But if the counters for these queries are much higher, then you could boost your performance by investigating parameterization of queries.

- The preceding query is very quick to use but only finds queries whose plans are in cache. What if, due to memory pressure, there are plans that could be candidates for parameterization but are not in cache. This is where Query Store can be valuable. Check out this example in our documentation on how to use Query Store to identify ad hoc workloads: https://docs.microsoft.com/sql/relational-databases/performance/query-store-usage-scenarios.

One comment about this database option: even if you find the need for query parameterization, the best method to resolve the problem is to fix the application. However, if you cannot change the application, using this option could prove beneficial. As with any option that is not the default, be careful arbitrarily changing this. While using this option can reduce query compilations, using this option will force many queries to now have the same compiled plan. That may not be the best option for some applications.

- **READ_COMMITTED_SNAPSHOT**

A common performance problem for SQL Server application is *blocking*. While I always recommend anyone encountering a blocking problem attempt to investigate the cause and resolve the issue, there is a database option that can provide relief and possibly even be a solution. First, I recommend you read this section in our documentation to understand the fundamentals of locking and *row versioning*, `https://docs.microsoft.com/sql/relational-databases/sql-server-transaction-locking-and-row-versioning-guide`.

One of the common blocking scenarios involves readers and writers blocking each other for common data, especially when these readers and writers are involved in long running transactions. One option to avoid these scenarios is to use ALTER DATABASE and SET READ_COMMITTED_SNAPSHOT ON. When you use this database option, readers in the context of this database will see a snapshot or version of the data as of the start of the T-SQL SELECT statement, as opposed to using locks. There is some overhead required to use this database option within the database page and in tempdb. This specific documentation link discusses more the requirements to use row versioning: `https://docs.microsoft.com/sql/relational-databases/sql-server-transaction-locking-and-row-versioning-guide#Row_versioning`.

Applications can also use snapshots, and you can read more on snapshots and row versions in our documentation at `https://docs.microsoft.com/dotnet/framework/data/adonet/sql/snapshot-isolation-in-sql-server#understanding-snapshot-isolation-and-row-versioning`.

- **SCOPED CONFIGURATION**

One of the nice feature additions starting in SQL Server 2016 is to set configuration options at the database level, which previous were only available at the instance level or through a trace flag.

For example, the server configuration option max degree of parallelism can be overridden at the database level using ALTER DATABASE SCOPED CONFIGURATION SET MAXDOP = <value>. (Note: max degree of parallelism is also an option that can be configured at the query level through query hints.)

Another option to consider using is QUERY_OPTIMIZER_HOTFIXES. This is equivalent to using trace flag 4199 to enable query optimizer hotfixes, which I discussed in Chapter 5 in the section "Trace Flags." The different here is that you can enable optimizer hotfixes for only queries that run in the database where you set this option ON.

The full set of options that can be set with ALTER DATABASE SCOPED CONFIGURATION can be found in our documentation at `https://docs.microsoft.com/sql/t-sql/statements/alter-database-scoped-configuration-transact-sql`.

Linux Kernel Configuration

I have shown you SQL Server instance and database configuration options. These options apply to SQL Server on Windows and Linux. Is there any special tuning for the Linux kernel that I would recommend you use for SQL Server? The answer is yes, but it is not as complicated as you might think.

SQL Server is an application that will maximize CPU, memory, and I/O resources. Therefore there are several Linux kernel options we found to be helpful as we built SQL Server and worked with customers during Community Technology Preview (CTP) builds.

The full list of these options is included in this section of our documentation, Performance best practices and configuration guidelines for SQL Server 2017 on Linux, `https://docs.microsoft.com/sql/linux/sql-server-linux-performance-best-practices`.

You may look at these configuration options and decide to change them based on your workload. We found these options to help SQL Server maximize performance on Linux across most application workloads.

As you look through these options, consult the documentation for your Linux distribution and the proper method to make changes. It is possible on some Linux distributions that these options are already set to recommended settings. For example, I've found that on Red Hat Enterprise Linux, the **throughput-performance** profile via the **tuned-adm** feature is the default, which contains many of our recommended settings (Note: run `man tuned-adm` on your RHEL system to learn more about RHEL profiles).

A few other important points about Linux and machine configuration:

- Pay close attention to BIOS settings related to energy and power consumption. For maximum performance, be sure your BIOS settings use the maximum power possible.

- For SQL Server on Linux running in a virtual machine, consult your virtual machine provider on the proper settings for virtual CPUs, NUMA, and other machine related settings. The only setting you cannot use with SQL Server on Linux is any configuration for a virtual machine that supports *dynamic memory*.

One last comment about OS configuration: on Windows, there are two configuration settings that affect SQL Server performance: **locked pages in memory** (you can read more at `https://docs.microsoft.com/sql/database-engine/configure-windows/enable-the-lock-pages-in-memory-option-windows`) and **instant file initialization** (you can read more at `https://docs.microsoft.com/sql/relational-databases/databases/database-instant-file-initialization`). For SQL Server on Linux, neither of these options is required. There is no concept of **locked pages in memory** as it exists on Windows for Linux (i.e., there is no AWE API equivalent in Linux). Using the memorylimitmb option can avoid memory issues and paging of the sqlservr process. In addition, SQL Server uses Linux API calls when creating files where the behavior of instant file initialization is the default behavior. Note: SQL Server still is required to zero the transaction log file as it does on Windows, to properly recognize the end of the transaction log during recovery. For more information, see Anthony Nocentino's blog post `http://www.centinosystems.com/blog/sql/instant-file-initialization-in-sql-server-on-linux`.

Tuning for Success

You have seen the built-in performance capabilities of SQL Server. I've shown you some of the important SQL Server, database, and Linux configuration options. Armed with this knowledge, there are a few other important topics to tune your SQL Server database, objects, and applications I believe everyone using SQL Server should know. This includes physical placement of database and transaction log files, creating the right indexes, keeping statistics accurate and up to date, and techniques for developers to ensure their application is using SQL Server to its best potential.

Files and File Groups

I showed you in Chapter 3 how to create a database and gave a brief description of the default files that come with a database, a database file (usually ending with a file extension of .mdf), and a transaction log file (usually ending with a file extension of .ldf).

In many situations, using a single database file and a single transaction log file adequately serves the needs of an SQL Server database. However, this chapter is about tuning, so I've provided in this section guidance on how to maximize I/O performance using file placement, filegroups, and planning for file growth.

I should also comment that if you decide to host multiple databases on an SQL Server instance, you should consider spreading out the files from each database across multiple disks or using a hosted disk storage system that is configured to strip I/O across a series of drives. I typically place system databases on the default database file location and am not as concerned about disk performance except for the tempdb database. It is common practice to place tempdb database files on a separate disk from other system databases. Our documentation has a good example of how to move tempdb files to a different path at `https://docs.microsoft.com/sql/relational-databases/ databases/move-system-databases#Examples`.

Separate Data and Transaction Log Files

I almost always recommend a single transaction log file. There is no performance benefit in having more than one transaction log file. If you decide to stay with just one database file, I do recommend you place the database file and transaction log file on different disks. That has been a traditional recommendation for SQL Server databases for many years. One of the primary reasons for this recommendation is the nature of I/O usage patterns between the database file and transaction log file. Writes to the database file are characterized as *random* I/O. While SQL Server writes in contiguous pages to the database file, it could write to pages anywhere in the file. Writes to the transaction log are always sequential. SQL Server always appends log blocks when writing to the transaction log file. Furthermore, it is very possible for SQL Server to concurrently write to database files through checkpoint tasks (such as RECOVERY WRITER) and the transaction log through the LOG WRITER task. Therefore, you will almost always achieve better I/O performance by separating database file writes from transaction log writes on different disks.

Another important benefit in separating database and transaction log files is recoverability. It is possible to perform advanced recovery if the database file is lost but the current transaction log is available (assuming you are using a full recovery model; find more about the full recovery model at https://docs.microsoft.com/sql/relational-databases/backup-restore/recovery-models-sql-server#RMov) and vice versa.

The syntax I used in earlier chapters to create the database did not specify file names or file paths. If you generate the script for the full WideWorldImporters sample database, you will see this syntax:

```
CREATE DATABASE [WideWorldImporters]
 CONTAINMENT = NONE
 ON  PRIMARY
( NAME = N'WWI_Primary', FILENAME = N'/var/opt/mssql/data/
WideWorldImporters.mdf' , SIZE = 1048576KB , MAXSIZE = UNLIMITED,
FILEGROWTH = 65536KB ),
 FILEGROUP [USERDATA] DEFAULT
( NAME = N'WWI_UserData', FILENAME = N'/var/opt/mssql/data/
WideWorldImporters_UserData.ndf' , SIZE = 2097152KB , MAXSIZE = UNLIMITED,
FILEGROWTH = 65536KB ),
 FILEGROUP [WWI_InMemory_Data] CONTAINS MEMORY_OPTIMIZED_DATA  DEFAULT
( NAME = N'WWI_InMemory_Data_1', FILENAME = N'/var/opt/mssql/data/
WideWorldImporters_InMemory_Data_1' , MAXSIZE = UNLIMITED)
 LOG ON
( NAME = N'WWI_Log', FILENAME = N'/var/opt/mssql/data/WideWorldImporters.
ldf' , SIZE = 102400KB , MAXSIZE = 2048GB , FILEGROWTH = 65536KB )
GO
```

Note the FILENAME parameter is used to specific the path and physical name of the file. To separate the transaction log, you would mount a directory from a separate disk and specify a path to the transaction log on that disk. I'll show you an example of how to do this using filegroups in the next section.

Using Multiple Database Files and Filegroups

For a single database, I have described several processes and scenarios where concurrent tasks write to the database such as checkpoints, lazy writes, and eager writes. However, it is more common to see multiple concurrent readers for database pages. These read scenarios could be multiple users executing queries that require database pages to be read from disk or a single query executed with parallel operators.

If you store database files on a storage system that is striped and optimized for concurrent I/O, you may just be able to use one database file. However, many production databases for SQL Server use multiple database files and a concept called **filegroups**.

A filegroup is a logical grouping of database files. After you create a database with a filegroup with multiple database files, SQL Server will allocate pages in these files using a *round-robin, proportional fill* algorithm. Round-robin means SQL Server will allocate groups of pages from a database file and then to other files in the filegroup. Proportional fill means SQL Server attempts to perform these allocations so that the spaces used across the database files are fairly evenly spread.

Once you create a filegroup, you can then designate one or more tables or indexes to the named filegroup. By default, each database has a built-in filegroup called PRIMARY. All system tables are stored in the files associated with the PRIMARY filegroup.

The most common configuration for production databases is to create one database file of smaller size for the PRIMARY filegroup and one or more named filegroups for a collection of tables and/or indexes. Filegroups provide other advantages from a management point of view. You can backup, restore, run consistency checks, and manage the filegroup as a unit.

Let's look at an example of how to create a database with a separate filegroup for data across multiple files on multiple disks, along with a transaction log on a separate disk.

First, I need to add disks to my Linux Server. I've mentioned before that I'm using a Linux Virtual Machine with Hyper-V for Windows. For Hyper-V on Windows, you can follow the instructions on how to add hardware such as controllers and disks to our virtual machine in our documentation at `https://docs.microsoft.com/azure/virtual-machines/linux/attach-disk-portal`.

Once I've added my hardware, I need to configure my new disks in the Linux Operating System and mount directories on these disks. My virtual machine already had two disks: one for the standard files for Linux and one specifically mounted for the /var/opt directory where the standard SQL Server database files exist. For this example

I've added four new disks: one to hold three new database files, which will be in their own filegroup, and one for the transaction log. If you have not configured disks within Linux before, I found this documentation on how to do this in an Azure Virtual Machine invaluable: https://docs.microsoft.com/azure/virtual-machines/linux/add-disk.

For my virtual machine, when I was finished configuring disks and mounting the directories to them, the final configuration looked like Figure 6-9.

```
[thewandog@bwsql2017rhel data1]$ df -H
Filesystem              Size  Used Avail Use% Mounted on
/dev/mapper/rhel-root    48G   27G   21G  57% /
devtmpfs                4.1G     0  4.1G   0% /dev
tmpfs                   4.1G     0  4.1G   0% /dev/shm
tmpfs                   4.1G  9.5M  4.1G   1% /run
tmpfs                   4.1G     0  4.1G   0% /sys/fs/cgroup
/dev/sde1                33G   34M   33G   1% /data3
/dev/sda1               1.1G  233M  831M  22% /boot
/dev/sdd1                33G   34M   33G   1% /data2
/dev/sdc1                33G   34M   33G   1% /data1
/dev/sdf1                33G   34M   33G   1% /log
/dev/sdb                135G  3.8G  124G   3% /var/opt
tmpfs                   819M     0  819M   0% /run/user/1000
[thewandog@bwsql2017rhel data1]$ 
```

Figure 6-9. Using multiple disks in Linux for SQL Server

In my example, the /dev/sdb disk is the second disk I created for my virtual machine where I mounted the /var/opt directory. When I installed SQL Server, the system databases were copied to /var/opt/mssql/data. This is also where I'll put my PRIMARY filegroup database file.

Table 6-1 provides a list of the other disks and their mounted directories. I created each of these virtual disks to be 30GB in size for purposes of this example.

Table 6-1. Disks and Their Mounted Directories

Disk	Mounted Directory	Purpose
/dev/sdc1	/data1	Database File
/dev/sdd1	/data2	Database File
/dev/sde1	/data3	Database File
/dev/sdf1	/log	Transaction Log

Tip   As described in the preceding documentation on adding disks to Linux, it is important to update the /etc/fstab file with these disks, so they are mounted after any reboot. In addition, be sure to change the permissions for these directories to the mssql group and user by executing `sudo chown mssql:mssql <directory>`.

With these disks created and directories mounted, I can now create my database like the following T-SQL statement found in the example **bigdb.sql**:

```sql
USE [master]
GO
CREATE DATABASE [big dB]
 ON  PRIMARY
( NAME = N'bigdb_Primary', FILENAME = N'/var/opt/mssql/data/bigdb.mdf' ,
SIZE = 5GB , MAXSIZE = 100GB, FILEGROWTH = 65536KB ),
 FILEGROUP [USERDATA]  DEFAULT
( NAME = N'bigdb_UserData_1', FILENAME = N'/data1/bigdb_UserData_1.ndf' ,
SIZE = 10GB , MAXSIZE = 30GB, FILEGROWTH = 65536KB ),
( NAME = N'bigdb_UserData_2', FILENAME = N'/data2/bigdb_UserData_2.ndf' ,
SIZE = 10GB , MAXSIZE = 30GB, FILEGROWTH = 65536KB ),
( NAME = N'bigdb_UserData_3', FILENAME = N'/data3/bigdb_UserData_3.ndf' ,
SIZE = 10GB , MAXSIZE = 30GB, FILEGROWTH = 65536KB )
 LOG ON
( NAME = N'big_Log', FILENAME = N'/log/bigdb_log.ldf' , SIZE = 10GB ,
MAXSIZE = 30GB , FILEGROWTH = 65536KB )
GO
```

Looking at this CREATE DATABASE statement, you can see I have placed the PRIMARY filegroup on the default location /var/opt/mssql/data; three database files in the USERDATA filegroup on the /data1, /data2, and /data3 directories; and the transaction log file on the /log directory. I've chosen arbitrary sizes for these files, but when you create a database for production you will want to spend time carefully determining the initial best size for these files. I will discuss the MAXSIZE and FILEGROWTH parameters in the next section, but planning for the initial sizes of your files is important to overall performance. See the guide at `https://docs.microsoft.`

com/sql/relational-databases/databases/estimate-the-size-of-a-database
in our documentation for best practices on estimating size of data and database and
transaction log file size.

Also note the syntax for the USERDATA filegroup

```
FILEGROUP [USERDATA] DEFAULT
```

The keyword DEFAULT means that this filegroup is the default location for all user
objects created in the database (system objects must go in the PRIMARY filegroup).

Note   If you don't specify a user FILEGROUP as DEFAULT, all tables and indexes
by default will be placed in the PRIMARY FILEGROUP. However, T-SQL provides
syntax to explicitly place tables and indexes on a specific user FILEGROUP using
the ON keyword. See this section of our documentation for examples and more
information on filegroups: `https://docs.microsoft.com/sql/relational-`
`databases/databases/database-files-and-filegroups#filegroups`.

Let's add in a table and populate data to see how SQL Server will spread the database
pages across the files in the USERDATA filegroup. Execute the following T-SQL batches
from the example **bigtab.sql:**

```
USE [bigdb]
GO
DROP TABLE IF EXISTS [bigtab]
GO
CREATE TABLE [bigtab] (col1 INT, col2 CHAR (7000) NOT NULL)
GO
SET NOCOUNT ON
GO
DECLARE @x INT
SET @x = 0
WHILE (@x < 100000)
BEGIN
    INSERT INTO [bigtab] VALUES (@x , 'x')
    SET @x = @x + 1
END
```

```
GO
SET NOCOUNT OFF
GO
```

This script creates a table that holds one row per page. The col2 column is padded to 7,000 characters no matter what value is inserted into the column. The script performs a loop inserting 100,000 rows (which should also be 100,000 pages) into the table.

I can now use the following script from the DMV **dm_db_file_space_usage** (use the example script **dm_db_file_space_usage.sql**) to see how SQL Server spreads the allocation of pages across the three files in the USERDATA filegroup:

```
USE [bigdb]
GO
SELECT file_id, FILEGROUP_NAME(filegroup_id) filegroup, total_page_count,
allocated_extent_page_count
FROM sys.dm_db_file_space_usage
GO
```

Figure 6-10 shows the spread of pages across the files for the database when I executed this script with SQL Operations Studio.

Figure 6-10. *Using dm_db_file_space_usage to see allocation of pages across files in a filegroup*

The total_page_count is the total possible pages in each file. If you multiply these numbers by 8192 (the size of a database page) you will see file_id = 1 is 5GB, while the other files are 10GB. The allocated_extent_page_count is the number of pages allocated in each file. The 368 pages for the PRIMARY file group are pages for allocation structures and system table pages. The approximately 33,000 pages in each file of the USERDATA filegroup are for the 100,000 pages allocated for the bigtab table plus allocation pages and pages for the clustered index b-tree that are not data.

Tip   Use the icons to the right in the Results pane of SQL Operations Studio to turn this result into a chart. Click the 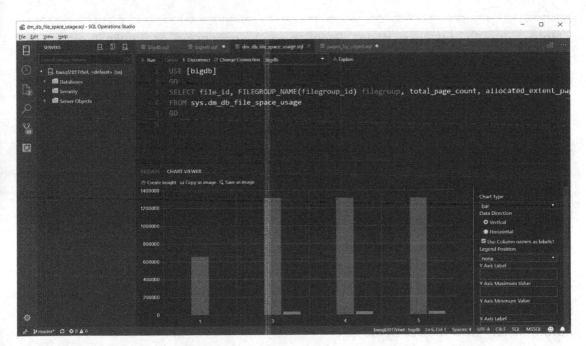 icon and pick the chart type of bar. Figure 6-11 shows the bar chart of the preceding results.

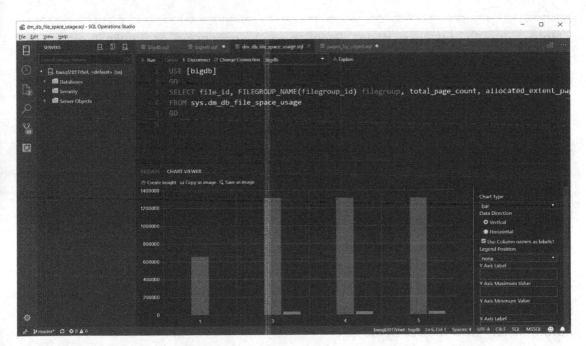

Figure 6-11. *Using SQL Operations Studio to show a bar chart of page allocations across files in the database*

Another way to view page allocations across files by objects is with the undocumented DMF **dm_db_database_page_allocations.** Use the following T-SQL batch found in the example script **pages_by_object.sql** to see the allocation of pages across files in the database, organized by object:

```
USE [master]
GO
SELECT OBJECT_NAME(object_id), count(*) total_pages_allocated
FROM sys.dm_db_database_page_allocations(DB_ID('bigdb'), NULL, NULL, NULL,
'DETAILED')
GROUP BY object_id
ORDER BY total_pages_allocated DESC
GO
```

Note   dm_db_database_page_allocation can be expensive, as it pulls in many pages into the buffer pool and can take a long time to execute.

If you want to learn more about the architecture of pages and extents for SQL Server, check out our documentation at https://docs.microsoft.com/sql/relational-databases/pages-and-extents-architecture-guide.

Planning for File Growth

When I worked in Technical Support in a galaxy far, far away, one of the most common emergency calls I received from customers was running out of space in the database. Thankfully, the SQL Server Engineering team introduced the concept of *autogrow* for SQL Server database and transaction log files. By default, when you create a database, if SQL Server runs out of space in either the database or transaction log file, it will automatically grow the size of the file.

While this can avoid emergency out of space problems (it doesn't of course avoid out of disk space problems) within the database and transaction log files, there can be a performance penalty. This is because any "autogrow" typically occurs within the context of a user transaction executing a query that requires page allocations (and a file growth is required to create more space for a new page).

As I've mentioned previously in this chapter, SQL Server on Linux can allocate file space very quickly for database files so an autogrow for a database file can be fast. However, even a fast autogrow can add seconds or longer to a user transaction, and that user transaction could be holding on to resources that can lead to a blocking problem. Furthermore, the transaction log must be written with a stamp of data so SQL Server can understand the "tail of the log," so growing the transaction log file may take some time. Again, growing the transaction log may need to take place in the context of a user transaction, which may be holding resources that can lead to a blocking problem. One other factor of frequent growth of the transaction log is that it can lead to an issue with virtual log file (VLF) fragmentation, which you can read more about at `https://docs.microsoft.com/sql/relational-databases/sql-server-transaction-log-architecture-and-management-guide#physical_arch`.

My recommendation is that you absolutely configure your database and transaction log files to allow an autogrow value. The last thing you want is for the database to run out of space because of an unexpected event and cause a production outage when plenty of disk space exists. However, you should do careful planning first to choose a size of database and transaction log files to account for possible usage and required growth of the database. The FILEGROWTH parameter when specifying a file path and size is used to determine how autogrow will work for a database or transaction log. You must choose a value that balances the need for a fairly fast autogrow operation but avoids a large number of autogrow operations. The default FILEGROWTH sizes are 64MB for database and transaction log files, and that value could be a particularly good one for many databases. I have found through my experience that managing the size of growth for the transaction log is usually most important. See this documentation page for more detailed guidance on the topic: `https://docs.microsoft.com/sql/relational-databases/logs/manage-the-size-of-the-transaction-log-file`.

I also recommend you monitor when an autogrow occurs on your system, to decide if you need to resize the actual database or transaction log size. I'll address how to monitor the size of the transaction log as part of your backup strategy in Chapter 9.

Indexes

I showed you in Chapter 3 how to create indexes to enforce uniqueness for primary keys and other columns (e.g., a UNIQUE constraint) in a table design. Indexes serve another important purpose in SQL Server: query performance. Using indexes to speed up query performance is a common technique with any database platform. Having said that, the simplest way to build indexes when first creating your database is to create indexes to:

- Enforce primary key constraints

- Enforce other unique constraints (you can read more about unique constraints at `https://docs.microsoft.com/sql/relational-databases/tables/create-unique-constraints`).

- Ensure proper performance for any foreign key constraint lookups. These will almost always be nonclustered indexes, so I'll discuss them later in the section.

So, the base set of indexes you will build is all based on your key design. After that, the process is about deciding what other indexes might help boost query performance, balanced with the cost to maintain them.

I could spend an entire chapter on index selection and recommendations, but I'm also a believer in making these decisions simple. We do have a fairly thorough guide in our documentation on index design, which you can use as a reference at `https://docs.microsoft.com/sql/relational-databases/sql-server-index-design-guide`.

In this section of the chapter, I will provide practical guidance to creating indexes, both clustered and nonclustered. I'll also show you examples, tools to help in selection, and discuss a few other index types that are interesting to use. I'll discuss one special type of index called a columnstore index later in this chapter. I also discuss managing indexes to keep them healthy and performing well over time (in Chapter 9).

In this chapter, as I talk about indexes it is difficult not to discuss some concepts about query processing and query plan operators. Here are some excellent resources to guide you to understand more about these concepts:

- The Query Processing Architecture Guide at `https://docs.microsoft.com/sql/relational-databases/query-processing-architecture-guide`.

- Showplan Operators Reference at `https://docs.microsoft.com/sql/relational-databases/showplan-logical-and-physical-operators-reference`.

Clustered Indexes

When you create tables, you typically are going to have a primary key on every table. Therefore, the only decision to make about how to implement the primary key with an index is whether it should be **clustered** or **nonclustered**. Both index types are organized using a b-tree of pages. The primary difference is that a clustered index has the actual data pages as its leaf-level of the b-tree, while the leaf level of a nonclustered index *points* to the data pages. A table can only have one clustered index and the data is sorted on the columns of the clustered index.

I personally recommend you create a clustered index for each table. But your primary key does not have to be implemented with a clustered index. The vast majority of primary keys are enforced with clustered indexes, but I'll list a few reasons why you may not want to do that.

Kimberly Tripp is one of the most popular MVPs in the SQL Server community and specializes in query performance and index design. I've heard here say many times before that choosing the right clustered index is the most important step in index design.

I also believe though in making this decision simple. Here is my practical advice on clustered index choices.

- Create a clustered index for every table in your database. The two exceptions to this rule are tables with a small number of rows (it could be faster to scan a heap than traverse a clustered index) and memory optimized tables (memory optimized tables do not support a clustered index).

Tip   There are some scenarios for bulk import where you may want to ensure the table is empty with a clustered index to boost performance. Read our documentation guidance on the topic when performing large bulk inserts into tables: `https://docs.microsoft.com/sql/relational-databases/import-export/prerequisites-for-minimal-logging-in-bulk-import`.

- If you use a generated column for a primary key (such as a SEQUENCE object or identity property), build a clustered index on that column unless you have a heavy concurrent OLTP application. In this scenario you might encounter a problem called PAGELATCH waits because all users will be trying to insert rows at the "end of the table," since the clustered index is sorted on a key value that increases with each insert. Find a column or set of columns to build the clustered index that logically represents the primary key that allows inserts and updates to be more spread out across the index.

- Build a clustered index on the primary key for a set of columns that is *narrow*. Narrow means to avoid building clustered indexes on columns that are hundreds of bytes. A name column that is 200 bytes is not a good choice for a clustered index. One major reason for this is that any nonclustered index has to carry around the keys of the clustered index in its b-tree.

- Use a clustered index on columns you often will join with other tables. This is why a clustered index on the primary key is a good choice especially with tables that have foreign key that reference back to your primary key. In these normalized table designs, it is common to join primary and foreign key columns for production queries.

- While it is possible to create a nonunique clustered index, I believe these situations are fairly rare. Which is also way I don't recommend creating clustered indexes on columns that can accept NULL values.

- If you choose multiple columns to support a clustered index, add them in order based on their distinct values and how queries typically query them. As an example, a clustered index for a last and first name should be created with last name followed by first name, since last name is often more selective than first name.

- You can specify a sorting (ASC, which is default, or DESC) with each column in the clustered index. I would choose DESC if you think it will help to avoid PAGELATCH contention and also is a natural order for sorting data with ORDER BY clauses in SELECT statements.

Nonclustered Indexes

So, let's say you have created a clustered index for almost all tables to support a primary key. In the exceptions where you might create hotspots for a clustered index key, you have used a nonclustered index to support some primary keys. In these cases, unless the table is small, I recommend you find another column or combination of columns to create a clustered index.

As I mentioned in the previous section, any foreign key is a natural choice for a nonclustered index. This is because it is common for applications to query data between two tables with a primary and foreign key using a JOIN on the foreign key column.

Now that you have built all of our indexes based on key design, you have choices to build nonclustered indexes for other columns for your tables. See the next section for tools to help guide you in these decisions.

The following are considerations for you as you tune and make decisions on other nonclustered indexes:

- Indexes can require updates as you modify data. If you have a clustered index, any modifications to the clustered key columns require updates to all nonclustered indexes (since the leaf level of the nonclustered index uses clustered index key values to "point" to the data). In addition, any modification to a column that is part of a nonclustered index would require updates to pages in the nonclustered index. The same concept applies for any deletes of rows of data in the base table as this represents a modification to columns that could affect nonclustered indexes. The net result is a balancing act of creating nonclustered indexes to improve performance when searching for data vs. the need to maintain nonclustered index with modifications.

- Examine your most commonly executed queries that have the most impact on application performance and tune for these. Consider these query patterns that are candidates to use nonclustered indexes:

  - Look for columns in WHERE clauses, especially ones where you are looking for a specific unique value with =

  - Look for columns in ORDER BY clauses. If SQL Server can't use an index to find data that is sorted, it will have to use a SORT operator. Sorts aren't necessarily a bad thing but can be expensive if there is a great deal of data to sort.

273

- Look for opportunities for *covering indexes*. A covering index includes all the columns in the index that make up a SELECT statement. If you have a particularly important query that only requires columns a, b, and c and you build an index on these three columns, there is no need to query data pages to retrieve these column values. One technique to create a covered index is to create an index with included columns, which you can read more about at https://docs.microsoft.com/sql/relational-databases/indexes/create-indexes-with-included-columns.

- Nonclustered indexes that are not used for a primary key or unique constraint are often not defined as unique. For example, columns used in a foreign key by their nature are not unique for each row in a table, so therefore will not be unique.

Looking at WideWorldImporters

Let's look at how Microsoft built the WideWorldImporters database to see an example of index design. Use the following T-SQL script to see what indexes are included in the WideWorldImporters design for the Orders table (this script is found in the example **wwi_indexes.sql**):

```
USE [WideWorldImporters]
GO
SELECT o.name as table_name, i.name as index_name, i.type_desc, i.is_
primary_key, i.is_unique, c.name as column_name
FROM sys.objects o
INNER JOIN sys.indexes i
ON o.object_id = i.object_id
AND o.type = 'U'
AND o.name = 'Orders'
INNER JOIN sys.index_columns ic
ON ic.index_id = i.index_id
AND ic.object_id = i.object_id
```

```
INNER JOIN sys.columns c
ON ic.column_id = c.column_id
AND c.object_id = i.object_id
ORDER BY table_name, index_name
GO
```

This script uses SQL Server catalog views to determine what indexes, the type, and columns in the index for the Orders table. Figure 6-12 shows the results of this query.

Figure 6-12. Finding indexes for a table in SQL Server

In this output, you can see that the clustered index is the primary key on OrderID, which is a column generated by a SEQUENCE. You can see from the index name that the other nonclustered indexes are on columns that are foreign keys to other tables.

I'll show you in the next section how to use tools to determine if another nonclustered index would help query performance based on a specific SQL Server T-SQL statement.

Use the Tools

SQL Server provides several tools to assist in determining whether an index will be helpful to boost query performance:

- *Missing index* DMVs such as dm_db_missing_index_details (which you can read more about at https://docs.microsoft.com/sql/relational-databases/system-dynamic-management-views/sys-dm-db-missing-index-details-transact-sql): I mentioned this DMV in an earlier chapter. While I don't recommend blindly implementing all suggestions found in this DMV, it is absolutely worth looking into any results found to see if these indexes could help performance.

- Missing index information located in the XML SHOWPLAN (the XML schema can be found at http://schemas.microsoft.com/sqlserver/2004/07/showplan): I'll show you an example below of how to use this information on a query by query basis.

- The Database Tuning Advisor tool: This tool seems forgotten in the SQL Server world but has the capability of recommending indexes based on an individual query or a *workload* based on a trace of SQL Server queries, data from the Query Store, or queries currently found in plan cache. The only downside of this tool for Linux users is that the tool is only available today to run on a computer running Windows. You can read more about the Database Tuning Advisor tool at https://docs.microsoft.com/sql/relational-databases/performance/start-and-use-the-database-engine-tuning-advisor.

Let me show you an example of how to spot a missing index in a XML SHOWPLAN after executing a query using the [Sales].[Orders] table from the full WideWorldImporters sample. Execute the following T-SQL statement in SQL Operations Studio (this query can be found in the example script **orders_missing_index.sql**):

```
USE [WideWorldImporters]
GO
SELECT CustomerID, COUNT(*)
FROM [Sales].[Orders]
```

```
WHERE [OrderDate] = '2013-01-01'
GROUP BY CustomerID
GO
```

My goal for this query was to get a count of customer orders by customer on a given order date. The problem is there is no index on OrderDate to find a specific set of orders for a given date value. Therefore, SQL Server must scan the entire clustered index to filter out the rows for a specific date. Furthermore, SQL Server has to perform a sort to satisfy the aggregation for a GROUP BY.

Figure 6-13 shows the results of SET STATISTICS IO, because SQL Server must scan the entire clustered index.

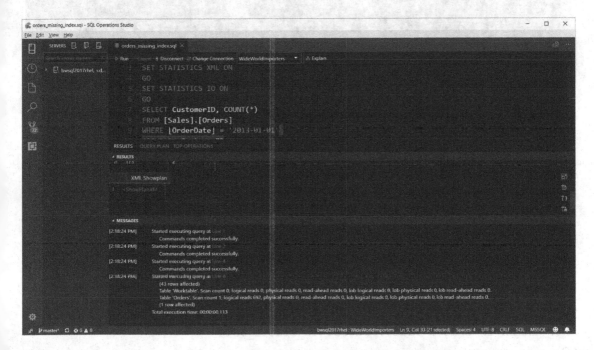

Figure 6-13. *IO statistics to scan the clustered index of the Orders table*

If you click the results of the XML Showplan, you will see a section on Missing Indexes. Figure 6-14 shows the Missing Indexes section of this plan.

Figure 6-14. *The Missing Indexes section of an SQL Server XML SHOWPLAN*

The query optimizer in SQL Server when compiling the plan can detect a possible index that would help query performance (the query optimizer also is responsible for adding rows to the missing index DMVs). In this case, the recommendation is to create an index on the OrderDate columns but also including the Customer ID column.

Therefore, you can now execute this T-SQL statement to create the nonclustered index (also found in the example **ncl_orders_date.sql**):

```
USE [WideWorldImporters]
GO
DROP INDEX IF EXISTS Sales.Orders.NCL_Orders_Date
GO
CREATE NONCLUSTERED INDEX NCL_Orders_Date ON Sales.Orders (OrderDate)
INCLUDE (CustomerID)
GO
```

If I now run the query from orders_missing_index.sql again, Figure 6-15 shows the improvement in IO statistics with fewer physical reads.

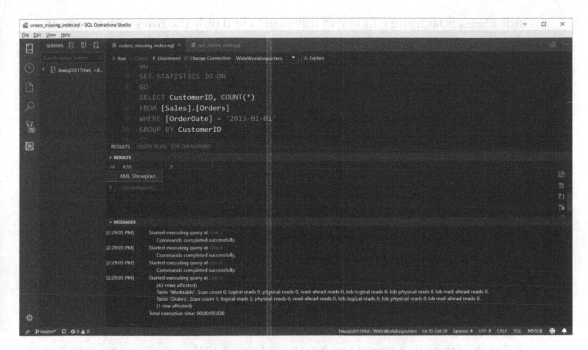

Figure 6-15. *Improved IO statistics after adding an index*

Figure 6-16 shows the new query plan if you select the QUERY PLAN option next to RESULTS.

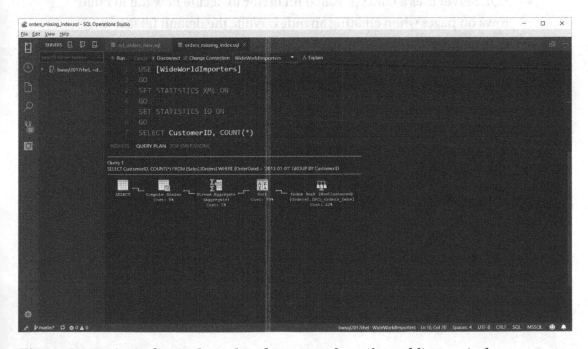

Figure 6-16. *An Index Seek used in the query plan after adding an index*

An Index Seek is far more efficient in this case to find only the rows with the exact OrderDate requested vs. scanning the entire clustered index.

Index Types and Other Considerations

There are a few other index types that can be helpful for performance and consideration about parameters when creating indexes:

- **Filtered indexes** allow you to create a nonclustered index using a WHERE clause to build the index with only a specific set of data. This can be extremely helpful to reduce the size of an index and fits well for sets of queries with specific criteria that don't change. You can read more about this feature at `https://docs.microsoft.com/sql/relational-databases/indexes/create-filtered-indexes`.

- **Indexed Views** are indexes on an SQL Server view but are unique because a clustered index on a view will be stored just like a table. Think of this like a *stored result set* based on a T-SQL view. You can read more about indexed views at `https://docs.microsoft.com/sql/relational-databases/views/create-indexed-views`.

- SQL Server uses a concept called **fill factor** to decide how full to build rows on pages when creating an index. While the default fill factor may be fine for many workloads, it is possible that you may want to adjust the default or change the fill factor for a specific index to avoid a lot of *page splits*. You can read more about choosing a fill factor for an index for SQL Server and why page splits may cause performance problems at `https://docs.microsoft.com/sql/relational-databases/indexes/specify-fill-factor-for-an-index`.

Statistics

The query processor in SQL Server is *all about statistics*. What I mean by that is the query processor often makes decisions on compiling a query plan based on available statistics about values of rows (uniqueness of rows) in a table, column(s), and indexes.

Statistics on Indexes and Columns

Any time an index is created or rebuilt, SQL Server builds a set of statistics on the key columns of the index. A *histogram* is built on the leading column of an index. There are other statistics called *density* that are calculated based on the combination of all columns in the index. The decisions of the query processor to build an optimal query plan are only as good as available statistics.

By default, statistics are calculated through *sampling*, which means SQL Server will not examine every row in an index to build statistics but rather build statistics based on sampling of data. And for most workloads, this default sample algorithm works fine. But there are situation where I've seen better query plans built when using an option called FULLSCAN (which means to completely scan all rows in the index or table when building statistics).

It is also possible to create statistics on one or more columns without an index. In fact, SQL Server will automatically create statistics on single columns for certain types of queries (assuming a database option is enabled which I'll discuss later in this section of the chapter). There are some interesting scenarios where manually creating statistics can benefit query plan selection without incurring the overhead of an index. The complete guide to statistics including details of what a histogram looks like can be found in our documentation at `https://docs.microsoft.com/sql/relational-databases/statistics/statistics`.

I've not found anyone who is an SQL Server expert debate that you don't need statistics, ones that come from an index, automatically created by SQL Server, or scenarios where you would create your own manually. The largest debate is: (1) Is sampling good enough? (2) When and how should I update them?

For the first question, SQL Server automatically decides what the right sample rate is, depending on how many rows are in the table or index. You can change the sampling rate or specify FULLSCAN after statistics are created by using the UPDATE STATISTICS T-SQL statement. How would you know whether you need to change the sampling rate or even use FULLSCAN? One scenario where the default sampling of statistics by SQL Server may not give you the best performance is documented by our CSS team at Microsoft at `https://blogs.msdn.microsoft.com/psssql/2010/07/09/sampling-can-produce-less-accurate-statistics-if-the-data-is-not-evenly-distributed`. In this scenario, the histogram that is mentioned was produced using the DBCC SHOW_STATISTICS (see `https://docs.microsoft.com/sql/t-sql/database-console-commands/dbcc-show-statistics-transact-sql` for more information) T-SQL statement (there is a new DMV called **dm_db_stats_histogram** you can also use for this purpose). If digging into histograms is not your thing, then the time to consider making this change is when you believe a query could be performed better and you encounter a cardinality estimation problem. I'll discuss cardinality estimation in one of the next sections of this chapter. In my experience, the default sampling by the query optimizer works for many workloads.

I'll discuss strategies for updating of statistics in the next section of this chapter and in Chapter 9.

Automation and Statistics

As you modify data in your tables, statistics may not accurately reflect your changes. There is a nice solution for you though. By default, every database created in SQL Server has a database option called AUTO_UPDATE_STATISTICS. When this database option is enabled (which is the default), SQL Server will maintain statistics (using the default sampling algorithm) automatically. The automation is based on a formula that has evolved over the years but is fundamentally based on the amount of changes made to a table and/or index.

The threshold for kicking in the automation to update statistics was updated in recent releases of SQL Server to more accurately reflect large table sizes. You can read more about this threshold in this Knowledge Base Article: `https://support.microsoft.com/help/2754171/controlling-autostat-auto-update-statistics-behavior-in-sql-server`. In addition, a new DMV called **dm_db_stats_properties** can be used to track when and how statistics are updated (automatically or manually) for a specific statistic. Even when this database option is set, you can disable automatic updating of a specific statistic using the system procedure **sp_autostats**. Automatic statistics are typically done *inline*, which means statistics are updated as part of a T-SQL statement "behind the scenes" in the engine (like a SELECT). You also have the option to have statistics updated asynchronously by setting the AUTO_UPDATE_STATISTICS_ASYNC database option. The default for this option is OFF. I recommend you leave this off unless you specifically have situations where synchronous update statistics are causing performance problems for a given set of queries. In my experience it is better to pay the penalty of a specific query having to wait while stats are updated (because that query will benefit) than having statistics updated asynchronously.

Some customers have found that even with this database option set to automatically update statistics, it is not frequent enough for their workload (and you cannot change the frequency threshold). Therefore, you always have the option to use the T-SQL statement **UPDATE STATISTICS**, or the system procedure **sp_updatestats**. I've seen some customers schedule jobs to run these commands on a frequent basis to ensure statistics are frequently up to date. Here is the tradeoff. If statistics are modified, SQL Server may choose to recompile a query plan the next time a query is executed after the statistics are updated. Therefore, frequent updates to statistics could cause a large number of query recompilations, which overall may be a performance problem for your application.

Tip   If you have a maintenance window (say weekly) where you can afford to update statistics WITH FULLSCAN on all statistics, then go for it! You will get some recompiles afterward but probably will have the best possible query plans produced. Most customers can't afford to do this, so there is a balance between where you let SQL Server update statistics using automation and picking some statistics critical to your application to update manually.

You can read more about updating statistics manually in our documentation at `https://docs.microsoft.com/sql/t-sql/statements/update-statistics-transact-sql`.

As I've mentioned already, it is possible to create statistics outside of indexes. And fortunately, SQL Server has a database option, called AUTO_CREATE_STATISTICS, which is on by default for all databases you create. With this option enabled, the query optimizer in SQL Server will create statistics on columns that are not already part of a statistic in an index or another statistic. I highly recommend you leave this option enabled. You can tell which statistics were automatically created by SQL Server using a query against system catalog views, as described in our documentation at `https://docs.microsoft.com/sql/relational-databases/statistics/statistics` (we name these statistics with a _WA prefix).

Tip   When running benchmark tests, use the **sp_createstats** stored procedure to create statistics on columns not already in a statistic vs. waiting for the optimizer to automatically create statistics.

Cardinality Estimation

One of the key reasons for keeping statistics up to date and accurate is the concept of *cardinality estimation*. Cardinality in terms of SQL Server query processing is the unique number of values for a given set of rows. SQL Server estimates the cardinality when compiling a query plan to make decisions on how to build the plan. This could be a decision to use an index or not, join order, and other decisions.

The most visible view of cardinality estimation comes from looking at the XML SHOWPLAN for a query and looking at **EstimateRows** in the XML plan. In some cases, SQL Server may compile a query plan that is not optimal if the EstimateRows are different than the **ActualRows**. Although inaccurate statistics can be a cause for these numbers to be off, there are some query patterns where SQL Server may need to make a *guess* on cardinality estimation (guess means use a fixed number from the code). These include missing statistics, use of table variables, local variables, and other query predicates.

For a complete read on the importance of cardinality estimation, see our documentation at `https://docs.microsoft.com/sql/relational-databases/performance/cardinality-estimation-sql-server`.

In addition, SQL Server Management Studio has some very cool tools to analyze cardinality estimation problems. See this blog post by the very capable Pedro Lopes from the SQL Server Tiger Team at `https://blogs.msdn.microsoft.com/sql_server_team/new-in-ssms-query-performance-troubleshooting-made-easier`.

Tips for Developers

I couldn't leave the topic of Tuning for Success without providing some advice to developers based on my experience over the years on important tips on using SQL Server for maximum performance.

Use the Power of T-SQL

Based on my experience both in technical support and the SQL Server Engineering team, I've seen many developers not maximize the power of the T-SQL language.

Some examples include:

- Executing multiple SELECT statements to retrieve multiple rows when executing a single SELECT statement to retrieve all the rows in one statement. But be careful on the flip side of this problem. In almost every case, your T-SQL SELECT statements should have a WHERE clause defining criteria for a subset of rows you need from a table. There are definitely exceptions when the table is exceedingly small, but in almost every case your application wants to avoid the dreaded SELECT * FROM <table> without a WHERE clause because it will retrieve more data than intended.

- The same concept applies for UPDATE or DELETE statements. If you need to update 100 rows, you don't want to execute 100 UPDATE statements for each row but rather execute one UPDATE statement with the right WHERE clause to cover the 100 rows.

- If you need to aggregate or sort results in your application, don't pull all the rows into your client application and then aggregate or sort. Use the T-SQL GROUP BY or ORDER BY clauses for SELECT statements to let SQL Server do the aggregation or sort (and remember indexes can be important to ensure these operations are executed at optimal performance).

- If your application needs to execute a series of T-SQL statements as part of a logical function, transaction, or business operation, consider creating a stored procedure. Executing many T-SQL statements against an SQL Server vs. executing a single stored procedure is an example of what I call a *chatty* application. Using a stored procedure is also called *server-side programming* in SQL Server. Server-side programming reduces network traffic and allows SQL Server to more effectively compile plans for the stored procedure.

Connections, Transactions, and Deadlocks

- I mentioned in Chapter 3 when discussing a node.js application that you should consider using connection pooling for your application. You can read more about connection pooling in our documentation at `https://docs.microsoft.com/dotnet/framework/data/adonet/sql-server-connection-pooling`. While connection pooling can enhance the performance of your application, you should still consider whether you need to open and close connections in the application often. I've seen developers use the pattern of open/<execute query>/close often in applications. Connection pooling greatly reduces the overhead of such patterns, but there is some logic in SQL Server to "reset" a connection. This doesn't mean you have to keep a connection open for the lifetime of your application, but it also means that frequently opening and closing connections is not a best practice.

- Transactions are common to ensure a logical group of T-SQL statements are committed together. However, one of the most common mistakes I've seen by developers is to begin a transaction and then execute code where a delay in committing the transactions is out of the control of the developer. For example, you may begin a transaction, start executing T-SQL statements, but then provide a graphical user interface input to the user while the transaction is active. The life of the transaction is now in the hands of the user, which could be the length of a coffee break! The result is most likely a major performance problem in the form of a blocking problem. There is an older article we built in Technical Support that can still be a good resource to identify the cause of blocking problems at `https://support.microsoft.com/help/224453/inf-understanding-and-resolving-sql-server-blocking-problems`.

Tip   I've also seen the opposite problems with transactions, where applications never group statements in a transaction but execute each statement as a transaction. Grouping modifications in a transaction can improve performance because each commit of a transaction requires a flush to the transaction log.

- Deadlocks are problems that are almost always caused by the application. I say this from pure experience. And the most common deadlock cause is acquiring locks in an inconsistent manner based on the order of how you query and modify data in concurrent connections. Read our documentation on locking to gain more insight on the cause of deadlocks and how to diagnose them at `https://docs.microsoft.com/sql/relational-databases/sql-server-transaction-locking-and-row-versioning-guide#Lock_Engine`.

Process Your Results!

Another application pattern I've seen from experience that can cause performance problem is result set processing. When you execute a T-SQL SELECT statement to extract rows from SQL Server, your application should be *processing* the rows immediately. Processing means executing the necessary steps in your code to iterate through the rows returned from SQL Server. There should not be any delay in between processing rows. Why? Because SQL Server can potentially hold resources (locks) while it is waiting for the client application to process the entire result set, which can lead to unexpected blocking problems. One of the key indicators in SQL Server of this behavior is a wait type called ASYNC_NETWORK_IO. See a great description of this problem from Paul Randal on this blog post: `https://www.sqlskills.com/help/waits/async_network_io/`.

Set Your Application Name

The DMV **dm_exec_sessions** has a column called program_name. The value of this column for user connections is filled in based on the Application Name specified by the application connecting to SQL Server. Since dm_exec_session is easily joined with dm_exec_requests, and dm_exec_requests is often a central DMV to analyze performance problems, having the program_name unique identify your application can help pinpoint issues specific to your application vs. other connections with SQL Server such as tools. To learn more about how to set the Application Name, see the example in our documentation `https://docs.microsoft.com/dotnet/api/system.data.sqlclient.sqlconnectionstringbuilder.applicationname`.

Accelerating Performance

SQL Server has features that require some configuration or T-SQL statements to adopt but have some incredible possible returns on investment to accelerate performance of your queries and application. These include Partition Tables and Indexes, Columnstore Indexes, and In-Memory OLTP. Each of these can be used for various scenarios but they all have one thing in common: boosting performance for mission critical applications.

Partitioned Tables and Indexes

Some data naturally can be *sliced* via a set of criteria for a column. In other words, it is possible to naturally partition a table horizontally to a set of rows. Having this capability can provide some very compelling performance and management capabilities.

SQL Server allows you to specifically create partitions on tables and indexes using the following concepts:

- **Partition function**: An object you create that allows you to specify a range of values that define the number of partitions and their range (boundaries)

- **Partition scheme**: A T-SQL statement to define what FILEGROUPs are defined to be used by the partition function. It is common to map partitions to one or more user FILEGROUPs. Since you can backup and manage FILEGROUPs individually, mapping a partition to multiple FILEGROUPs allows you to manage partitions individually.

- **Partition column**: The column in the table used to define values for the partition and used by the partition function. A common type of column used in partitions is a datetime, because many customers use partitions to divide up a table based on a set of rows over a period of time.

So, why use partitions? Do they really provide any performance benefit? The number one factor to use partitions for performance reasons is a concept called *partition elimination*. The best way to see this is to use look at an example.

The WideWorldImporters sample database contains two tables that are partitioned. How do I know? Run the following T-SQL statement found in the example script **partitioned_tables.sql**:

```
USE [WideWorldImporters]
GO
SELECT *
FROM sys.tables AS t
JOIN sys.indexes AS i
    ON t.[object_id] = i.[object_id]
    AND i.[type] IN (0,1)
JOIN sys.partition_schemes ps
    ON i.data_space_id = ps.data_space_id
GO
```

This query will return results for two tables: CustomerTransactions and SupplierTransactions. If you generate the script for all objects in the WideWorldImporters database as I've described in the book, you won't see the details of partition functions and schemes by default. For SQL Server Management Studio, you need to enable an option first under the Tools/Options menu to have script generation pick up partition details (as of the time of this writing, mssql-scripter does not support partition details but there is a GitHub issue filed to include this).

Note   The **wwi.sql** sample I've provided includes all the objects including partition details.

Using this method, you will see the details of partitions for the [Sales]. [CustomerTransactions] table first through this partition function and scheme:

```
CREATE PARTITION FUNCTION [PF_TransactionDate](date) AS RANGE RIGHT FOR
VALUES (N'2014-01-01T00:00:00.000', N'2015-01-01T00:00:00.000', N'2016-01-
01T00:00:00.000', N'2017-01-01T00:00:00.000')
GO

CREATE PARTITION SCHEME [PS_TransactionDate] AS PARTITION [PF_
TransactionDate] TO ([USERDATA], [USERDATA], [USERDATA], [USERDATA],
[USERDATA], [USERDATA])
GO
```

The partition function defines a partition based on a date type column with five partitions, each one a calendar year in size. The RANGE RIGHT syntax means the fifth partition is any value >= 2017-01-01. The partition scheme in this case maps all partitions based on the partition function to the USERGROUP filegroup. It is very possible to create multiple filegroups and map the partition across them. That could be a valuable technique to span partitions across multiple disks or to allow for management possibilities such as "backup a partition" because it is possible to back up a filegroup separately.

So, the partition function defines how to partition the data values. The partition scheme defines how to take those values and place them in specific filegorups.

Now let's look at the definition of the [Sales].[CustomerTransactions] table to see how the partition is used and how indexes and the table are placed on the partition scheme:

```
CREATE TABLE [Sales].[CustomerTransactions](
      [CustomerTransactionID] [int] NOT NULL,
      [CustomerID] [int] NOT NULL,
      [TransactionTypeID] [int] NOT NULL,
      [InvoiceID] [int] NULL,
      [PaymentMethodID] [int] NULL,
      [TransactionDate] [date] NOT NULL,
      [AmountExcludingTax] [decimal](18, 2) NOT NULL,
      [TaxAmount] [decimal](18, 2) NOT NULL,
      [TransactionAmount] [decimal](18, 2) NOT NULL,
      [OutstandingBalance] [decimal](18, 2) NOT NULL,
      [FinalizationDate] [date] NULL,
      [IsFinalized]  AS (case when [FinalizationDate] IS NULL then
      CONVERT([bit],(0)) else CONVERT([bit],(1)) end) PERSISTED,
      [LastEditedBy] [int] NOT NULL,
      [LastEditedWhen] [datetime2](7) NOT NULL,
 CONSTRAINT [PK_Sales_CustomerTransactions] PRIMARY KEY NONCLUSTERED
(
      [CustomerTransactionID] ASC
)WITH (PAD_INDEX = OFF, STATISTICS_NORECOMPUTE = OFF, IGNORE_DUP_KEY = OFF,
ALLOW_ROW_LOCKS = ON, ALLOW_PAGE_LOCKS = ON) ON [USERDATA]
) ON [PS_TransactionDate]([TransactionDate])
```

```
GO
CREATE CLUSTERED INDEX [CX_Sales_CustomerTransactions] ON [Sales].
[CustomerTransactions]
(
        [TransactionDate] ASC
)WITH (PAD_INDEX = OFF, STATISTICS_NORECOMPUTE = OFF, SORT_IN_TEMPDB = OFF,
DROP_EXISTING = OFF, ONLINE = OFF, ALLOW_ROW_LOCKS = ON, ALLOW_PAGE_LOCKS =
ON) ON [PS_TransactionDate]([TransactionDate])
GO
```

The nonclustered index for this table is based on the CustomerTransactionID
but is aligned on the partition that is based on the TransactionDate column. The
clustered index is also aligned on the TransactionDate column. This means the data
in the CustomerTransactions table is partitioned by SQL Server in its metadata, based
on the date ranges defined in the partition function. Partition schemes and functions
are independent objects and can be reused. In fact, if you look at the [Purchasing].
[SupplierTransactions] table, it uses the same partition functions and schemes.

Now let's see a query example where partitions help with performance. SQL Server
has the ability to recognize the column involved in a query is part of a partition function
and can therefore target specific partitions and eliminate others. This allows SQL Server
to reduce the number of pages required to satisfy a query.

Execute the following T-SQL statement found in the example query
customertransactions_partition.sql:

```
USE [WideWorldImporters]
GO
SET STATISTICS IO ON
GO
SET STATISTICS XML ON
GO
SELECT COUNT(*) FROM Sales.CustomerTransactions
WHERE TransactionDate between '2013-01-01' and '2014-01-01'
GO
```

The results for SET STATISTICS IO ON should look like the following:

Table 'CustomerTransactions'. Scancount 2, logical reads 123, physical reads 0, read-ahead reads 0, lob logical reads 0, lob physical reads 0, lob read-ahead reads 0.

If you were to scan the entire table, you would see the number of logical reads required is twice the amount required here. Yet when you look at the execution plan, you can see from Figure 6-17 that an Index Scan is required.

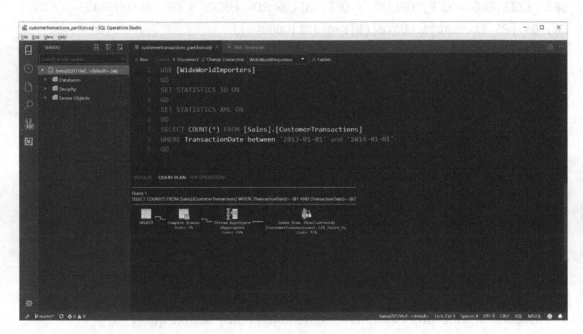

Figure 6-17. *The Query Plan used for a query with partitions*

If you drill into the details of the XML SHOWPLAN from these results, you will find this unique section called RunTimePartitionSummary, as seen in Figure 6-18.

Figure 6-18. *Partition statistics in an XML SHOWPLAN*

The RunTimePartitionSummary XML node shows that two partitions out of the five possible were accessed to satisfy this query, including partitions 1 and 2. This explains why even though the query plan showed an Index Scan, the entire index was not needed to satisfy the requirements of the query. That is an example of partition elimination and explains one of the performance benefits of using partitions.

I made partitions sound simple, and they can be. However, they may be more complex to use to fit the needs of your application. Use the following resources to learn more about partitions:

- Our documentation on partitions at https://docs.microsoft.com/sql/relational-databases/partitions/partitioned-tables-and-indexes.

- A very nice blog post on partition elimination by MVP Kendra Little: https://littlekendra.com/2015/11/17/did-my-query-eliminate-table-partitions-sql-server.

- An excellent blog post by a close friend and top MVP who is both knowledgeable and passionate about partitions, Kimberly Tripp: `https://www.sqlskills.com/blogs/kimberly/sqlskills-sql101-partitioning/` (Note: Kim says outright that partitions are not about performance but more about manageability. I think her point, if you read this closely, is that partitions are not the answer to all performance problems, but they can provide performance benefits. She also mentions the concept of partitioned views, which I didn't cover in this section of the book.)

Columnstore Indexes

Perhaps one of the coolest, but also practical, features to be introduced into SQL Server to accelerate performance is columnstore indexes. A **Columnstore** is data that is logically organized as a table with rows and columns, and physically stored in a *column-wise* data format. A **Rowstore** is both logically and physical organized and stored in a *row-wise* format. Row-wise is the standard format for SQL Server tables and indexes. Columnstore indexes help accelerate performance through column-wise structure, efficient compression, data elimination, and batch mode execution.

The concept of columnstore has been around a bit, but it did not make its way into SQL Server until SQL Server 2012 (the compression algorithms are common to the Vertipaq engine used for products like PowerPivot and SQL Server Analysis Services). One common misnomer I've heard about columnstore indexes is that it is an "in-memory technology." A columnstore index is stored on disk and is compressed in-memory and on disk. If the columnstore index can all fit in memory, then of course performance will be optimal, but it is not required that the entire columnstore index fit on disk. It is the compression of columnstore indexes that allows more of the data to fit into memory that makes it an efficient feature of SQL Server.

How it Works

To better understand how columnstore works, let me introduce you to a few additional terms:

rowgroup: A group of rows that are compressed together into a columnstore format at the same time

segment: A slice of a column of data within the rowgroup

Each rowgroup contains one segment for each column that makes up the columnstore index. SQL Server first slices the data into rowgroups, and then compresses each segment within that group.

clustered columnstore index: The entire table is stored as a columnstore index. In this scenario, you cannot create a normal clustered index, but you can create normal nonclustered indexes to support UNIQUE constraints.

nonclustered columnstore index: A set of columns that make up the index is stored as a columnstore index over the base table (which could have a normal clustered index).

delta rowgroup: A clustered index internally used to store data for a columnstore index until enough data is populated in the index to allow it to be compressed. Turns out that magic number is 102,400 rows. You don't create a delta rowgroup; SQL Server does this automatically. Therefore, it is not going to make much sense to use columnstore indexes on tables that have less than 102,400 rows. Once a delta rowgroup reaches this magic size, it is compressed into a columnstore rowgroup.

My colleague at Microsoft, Sunil Agarwal, is the "godfather" of columnstore indexes ever since it first appeared in SQL Server 2012. We chatted about the fundamentals of columnstore indexes and he showed me this basic visualization of how columnstore is structured, as seen in Figure 6-19.

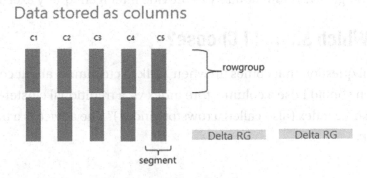

Figure 6-19.   *The basic structure of columnstore indexes*

In this diagram, if you build a clustered columnstore index on a table with columns C1...C5, this would be the structure of the clustered columnstore index.

Even though a columnstore index requires a copy of the data for columns it contains, SQL Server uses efficient compression techniques, so the overhead is less than you might expect. The performance benefits can be enormous. Sunil summarized for me three fundamental benefits of columnstore:

- **Compression**: Clustered columnstore indexes are the primary storage for the table. We have seen some customers achieve up to 10× compression ratios on their base table data. These compression ratios help you fit more of your data in physical memory. And SQL Server will only uncompress the data you need when you need it. Furthermore, compression algorithms can be more efficient when compressing data in a column-wise fashion.

- **Data elimination**: Since data is stored in a column-wise format, SQL Server can skip columns you are not accessing through your query. Furthermore, SQL Server has the ability to understand which rowgroups of columns segments are required for your query and only access the required rowgroups. This is a concept called *rowgroup elimination*.

- **Batch Mode execution**: Batch mode execution is a technique used by the query processor to process rows together with query processor operators vs. one row at a time. This style of execution can provide a boost to query performance. In addition, you will see a new feature in SQL Server 2017 called adaptive query processing that can take advantage of this functionality to provide intelligent query execution.

When and Which Should I Choose?

The first natural question that comes up when I talk to customers about columnstore indexes is: when should I use a columnstore index vs. a traditional clustered or nonclustered b-tree index (also called a rowstore index)? The advice is a bit simpler than you might think.

First, you need to consider whether a clustered columnstore index is right for your workload. Clustered columnstore indexes are best used for data warehouse scenarios where the workload is mostly read based. Most data warehouses have a large number of rows (> 100,000 rows) so clustered columnstore indexes fit very well for *fact* tables and *dimension* tables with a minimum of 102,400 rows (there is a good description of fact and dimension tables at this resource `https://en.wikipedia.org/wiki/Data_warehouse`).

Want some proof of clustered columnstore index performance? All the TPC-H benchmarks produced by Microsoft use them. You can also see this demo, where I show you the performance differences of using clustered columnstore indexes using the popular tool PowerBi on YouTube: `https://youtu.be/Y27OnS42yL8?list=PL-_k_UrAvrYvJh21uc8xebV18YW8sfpHE`. You can try this demo yourself by using my scripts from GitHub at `https://github.com/Microsoft/bobsql/tree/master/demos/rhelsummit2018/columnstore`.

Let's say you don't have a data warehouse so you will not use a clustered columnstore index. What about a nonclustered columnstore index? A nonclustered columnstore index fits nicely into scenarios that involve operational or OLTP workloads but some columns may be involved in queries that are *range queries*. A range query is one that typically you know will involve finding a fairly large number of rows (typically 100 or more) vs. a *seek query*, which is typically targeting one or a few rows. If you know you have queries on operational workloads that will require requesting a large number of rows for specific columns, consider creating nonclustered columnstore indexes. Using nonclustered columnstore indexes in this scenario is often called *Hybrid Transactional Analytical Processing* (HTAP). I've also seen it called real-time operational analytics.

There is an excellent table in the documentation that summarizes your choice on whether a columnstore index may be right for your workload, and which type of index may be best for your workload, at `https://docs.microsoft.com/sql/relational-databases/indexes/columnstore-indexes-design-guidance#choose-the-best-columnstore-index-for-your-needs`. Nothing beats experimentation and testing, and I always recommend you do this with columnstore indexes.

Columnstore in Action

To see a clustered columnstore index in action, let's look at the WideWorldImportersDW example database.

Note   This demo requires the WideWorldImportersDW sample database as found at `https://github.com/Microsoft/sql-server-samples/releases/download/wide-world-importers-v1.0/WideWorldImportersDW-Full.bak`. So you can copy the backup from another machine or run the following command to download the backup directly in your Linux server: `wget https://github.com/Microsoft/sql-server-samples/releases/download/wide-world-importers-v1.0/WideWorldImportersDW-Full.bak`. I've also provided the cpwwidw.sh, restore_wwidw_linux.sql, and restorewwidw.sh scripts to help you copy and restore this example.

Use the following T-SQL statement as found in the example script **wwidw_cci.sql** to find out which tables have clustered columnstore indexes in the WideWorldImportersDW database:

```
USE [wideworldimportersdw]
GO
SELECT OBJECT_NAME(object_id) as table_name, name, type_desc
FROM sys.indexes
-- type = 5 means clustered columnstore index
WHERE type = 5
GO
```

Figure 6-20 shows the results using SQL Operations Studio.

Figure 6-20. *Clustered columnstore indexes in the WideWorldImportersDW database*

Now let's run some queries against the Sales table (which is the Fact schema) to see how column and rowgroup elimination works. First, let's find out how many rows exist in the entire Fact.Sales table using the following T-SQL statement (found in the example script **fact_sales_count.sql**):

```
USE [wideworldimportersdw]
GO
SELECT COUNT(*) FROM Fact.Sale
GO
```

You should get a result of 228,265 rows. Many tables in data warehouse databases that are fact tables use datetime columns because it is common to store warehouse data over time. For the Fact.Sales table, there are two datetime columns, but the data is sorted by the column, [Delivery Date Key]. Here lies the magic of rowgroup elimination for clustered columnstore indexes. SQL Server has metadata for the range of values for each segment in the rowgroup. If the data is sorted on a specific column, SQL Server can then skip certain rowgroups based on the criteria of the query. Try running the following T-SQL statement as found in the example script **fact_sales_all.sql:**

```
USE [wideworldimportersdw]
GO
SET STATISTICS IO ON
GO
SET STATISTICS XML ON
GO
SELECT * FROM Fact.Sale
WHERE [Delivery Date Key] >= '2016-01-01'
GO
```

If you look at the results of SET STATISTICS IO, you should see something like this:

```
Table 'Sale'. Scan count 1, logical reads 0, physical reads 0, read-ahead
reads 0, lob logical reads 240, lob physical reads 0, lob read-ahead reads 0.
Table 'Sale'. Segment reads 2, segment skipped 5.
```

The value of **lob logical reads** is the amount of data in cache SQL Server needs to read from the clustered columnstore index to satisfy this query (Note: if you didn't specify a WHERE clause, the lob logical reads in this case would be approximately 805). SQL Server stores columnstore indexes as LOB data, which is why this counter is used to measure reads. The second set of output that shows segment reads and segments skipped is misleading. This should really read "rowgroups read" and "rowgroups skipped." This means there are seven total rowgroups for this clustered columnstore index, but because of rowgroup elimination SQL Server was able to skip five of them.

Now execute this T-SQL statement as found in the example script **fact_sales_query.sql:**

```
USE [wideworldimportersdw]
GO
SET STATISTICS IO ON
GO
SET STATISTICS XML ON
GO
```

```
SELECT [Customer Key], Quantity
FROM Fact.Sale
WHERE [Delivery Date Key] >= '2016-01-01'
GO
```

In this example, I only request two columns (or segments) and use the same WHERE clause. The SET STIATISTICS IO results now look like the following:

```
Table 'Sale'. Scan count 1, logical reads 0, physical reads 0, read-ahead
reads 0, lob logical reads 36, lob physical reads 0, lob read-ahead reads 0.
Table 'Sale'. Segment reads 2, segment skipped 5.
```

The same number of rowgroups is skipped but because I only used two columns, I need fewer segments, hence the significant lower number of reads required. This is the power of columnstore. SQL Server can greatly speed up queries for large scans of data in a data warehouse scenario because of both column and rowgroup elimination.

Sunil has an excellent blog post describing rowgroup elimination and how to interpret the SET STATISTICS IO output at https://blogs.msdn.microsoft.com/sql_server_team/columnstore-index-performance-rowgroup-elimination.

Tips

To effectively use columnstore indexes, there a few topics you need to review, understand, and implement.

- **Data loading**: Review and plan for data loading properly by reading this section of our documentation: https://docs.microsoft.com/sql/relational-databases/indexes/columnstore-indexes-data-loading-guidance.

- **Fragmentation**: Follow this guidance in our documentation for defragmentation: https://docs.microsoft.com/sql/relational-databases/indexes/columnstore-indexes-defragmentation.

- **Partitions**: You can combine partitions with columnstore indexes specially to help with manageability. See our documentation guidance at https://docs.microsoft.com/sql/relational-databases/indexes/columnstore-indexes-design-guidance#use-table-partitions-for-data-management-and-query-performance.

- **Improving performance**: To ensure maximum performance, read
  through these recommendations in our documentation: https://
  docs.microsoft.com/en-us/sql/relational-databases/
  indexes/columnstore-indexes-design-guidance#use-table-
  partitions-for-data-management-and-query-performance and
  https://docs.microsoft.com/en-us/sql/relational-databases/
  indexes/columnstore-indexes-query-performance#columnstore-
  performance-explained.

Customer Stories and Resources

Columnstore really makes a difference. Check out these customer case studies and other
resources:

- Sunil Agarwal Presentation on Customer Stories: https://channel9.
  msdn.com/Events/Ignite/2016/BRK2083, https://channel9.msdn.com/
  Events/Ignite/Australia-2017/DA343, and https://groupby.org/
  conference-session-abstracts/successful-production-
  deployments-with-columnstore-index-in-sql-server-2016/

- One of the most comprehensive studies of columnstore by Niko
  Neugebauer on this blog through various posts at http://www.
  nikoport.com/columnstore/

- Blog posts (mostly by Sunil) on columnstore on the SQL
  Server Engine blog at https://blogs.msdn.microsoft.com/
  sqlserverstorageengine/tag/columnstore-index

Columnstore indexes are such a powerful feature to accelerate performance in SQL
Server. And the amazing story is that it **does not require any application changes**.
Columnstore is not for every workload, but it may be right for you. I always recommend
that customers investigate to see how columnstore indexes can help boost SQL Server
query performance.

In-Memory OLTP

As far back as 2007, the SQL Server engineering team embarked on a journey to build
high-speed, low-latency, Online Transaction Processing (OLTP) into SQL Server. Things
kicked into full gear around 2010 with a project called **Hekaton**. Hekaton in Greek

means 100, and the goal from the onset was to achieve a 100× performance boost in OLTP transactions vs. traditional SQL Server techniques. As of SQL Server 2017, the reality is that we have seen amazing performance with this feature but to a maximum of about 30× performance from a traditional OLTP application. But we have seen some great stories including one customer who was able to achieve 1.2 million batch requests/second for a highly scalable OLTP application. You can see their story and what is possible at `https://blogs.msdn.microsoft.com/sqlcat/2016/10/26/how-bwin-is-using-sql-server-2016-in-memory-oltp-to-achieve-unprecedented-performance-and-scale/`.

Fundamentals

First and foremost, read this page in the documentation for the basic requirements to use the In-Memory OLTP feature: `https://docs.microsoft.com/sql/relational-databases/in-memory-oltp/requirements-for-using-memory-optimized-tables`.

In-Memory OLTP is a feature of SQL Server and is available in both Standard and Enterprise editions (Standard edition does have some limitations). In-Memory OLTP has seen major advances in functionality and fewer restrictions since it first was introduced as a feature in SQL Server 2014. This feature is made up of these components:

- The Hekaton engine
- A Memory Optimized FILEGROUP
- Memory Optimized Tables
- Indexes for Memory Optimized Tables—Hash or Nonclustered
- Natively Compiled Stored Procedures

The Hekaton Engine

Built inside of the SQL Server database engine is "an engine with an engine" for In-Memory OLTP. It is comprised of a series of Dynamic Linked Libraries that implement the logic for In-Memory OLTP transactions. There is a component for compilation, runtime, and an engine. These components interoperate with the rest of the SQL Server engine such as query processing and transaction logging. However, there are other components that are independent of the SQL Server engine for things like checkpoint and garbage collection. All of the Hekaton components still rely on the SQLOS subsystem and on Linux into the Host Extension for any native Linux kernel services (e.g., I/O).

You normally don't see any of these components of the Hekaton engine because the concept is that it is all built-in. However, when you start examining some of the details of DMVs like dm_exec_requests, you will start to see new tasks when you use T-SQL to create a memory optimized FILEGROUP and memory optimized tables.

For example, the WideWorldImporters database has a memory optimized FILEGROUP and memory optimized tables. So when you restore that example database, you will see tasks in sys.dm_exec_requests where the command column = XTP_CKPT_ AGENT' or 'XTP_THREAD_POOL' and others.

Note   XTP stands for eXtreme Transaction Processing and is another internal name for In-Memory OLTP. You may see several diagnostic objects and messages that start with HK (Hekaton) or XTP. These are all related to the In-Memory OLTP components.

Two of the key design principles of In-Memory OLTP are:

- All data is stored in memory (but has a durable option through the transaction log and checkpoint files) and **has to fit into memory**.

- Access to data is optimized using a "lock and latch free" set of algorithms and row versioning. In-Memory OLTP uses an optimistic concurrency methodology to prevent locking problems and internally uses techniques to avoid internal thread concurrency issues. Modifications to memory optimized tables use a row versioning scheme to avoid additional transaction conflicts (this row versioning scheme is the not the same as SQL Server snapshot isolation and does not use tempdb).

I've briefly mentioned locks in previous sections of this chapter as this is the primary mechanism to ensure transaction consistency for SQL Server applications. I've not mentioned the concept of *latches*, which is an internal mechanism of SQL Server to protect the physical integrity of database pages between multiple threads and is also used for other thread concurrency protection schemes in the engine. One of the key design principles for In-Memory OLTP to achieve low latency and high speed is to avoid the use of any locks or latches in the "Hekaton Engine". (Hekaton also avoids the use of *spinlocks* in its code, which is another internal thread concurrency mechanism).

In-Memory OLTP is not a feature you enable with a specific option. You use this feature by:

1. Creating a Memory Optimized FILEGROUP

2. Creating and using one or more memory optimized tables in your database (including the choice of indexes)

3. Optionally creating one or more natively compiled stored procedures

Let's take a look at each of these in more detail.

Memory Optimized FILEGROUP

The first step to use In-Memory OLTP in a database is to create a special FILEGROUP for memory optimized tables. Let's look at an example of this using the WideWorldImporters example. If you generate the script to create the database based on the backup/restore (see the following documentation on how to do this: `https://docs.` `microsoft.com/sql/ssms/tutorials/scripting-ssms#script-databases`) you will see this T-SQL statement:

Note   If you don't have SQL Server Management Studio, remember the **mssql-scripter** tool (you can get this tool at `https://github.com/Microsoft/` `mssql-scripter`) on Linux can be used to generate scripts for SQL Server. I've also provided the complete script for the WideWorldImporters database in the example script **wwi.sql**.

```
CREATE DATABASE [WideWorldImporters]
CONTAINMENT = NONE
ON  PRIMARY
( NAME = N'WWI_Primary', FILENAME = N'/var/opt/mssql/data/
WideWorldImporters.mdf' , SIZE = 1048576KB , MAXSIZE = UNLIMITED,
FILEGROWTH = 65536KB ),
 FILEGROUP [USERDATA]  DEFAULT
```

```
( NAME = N'WWI_UserData', FILENAME = N'/var/opt/mssql/data/
WideWorldImporters_UserData.ndf' , SIZE = 2097152KB , MAXSIZE = UNLIMITED,
FILEGROWTH = 65536KB ),
 FILEGROUP [WWI_InMemory_Data] CONTAINS MEMORY_OPTIMIZED_DATA  DEFAULT
( NAME = N'WWI_InMemory_Data_1', FILENAME = N'/var/opt/mssql/data/
WideWorldImporters_InMemory_Data_1' , MAXSIZE = UNLIMITED)
 LOG ON
( NAME = N'WWI_Log', FILENAME = N'/var/opt/mssql/data/WideWorldImporters.
ldf' , SIZE = 102400KB , MAXSIZE = 2048GB , FILEGROWTH = 65536KB )
GO
```

Notice this part of the CREATE DATABASE statement:

```
FILEGROUP [WWI_InMemory_Data] CONTAINS MEMORY_OPTIMIZED_DATA  DEFAULT
( NAME = N'WWI_InMemory_Data_1', FILENAME = N'/var/opt/mssql/data/
WideWorldImporters_InMemory_Data_1' , MAXSIZE = UNLIMITED)
```

The special syntax here is CONTAINS MEMORY_OPTIMIZED DATA. Notice the FILENAME is not the name of a file but rather the path to a directory. This syntax tells SQL Server that this database will be enabled to store memory optimized tables. SQL Server uses the path for this special FILEGROUP to create directories to store checkpoint files. Checkpoint files are files that store durable memory optimized table data that is not active in the transactions log. In fact, the durability of memory optimized tables is the combination of what is stored in checkpoint files and the part of the transaction log since the last database checkpoint.

You can read more about the memory optimized FILEGROUP in our documentation at https://docs.microsoft.com/sql/relational-databases/in-memory-oltp/ the-memory-optimized-filegroup and checkpoint files for memory optimized tables at https://docs.microsoft.com/sql/relational-databases/in-memory-oltp/ durability-for-memory-optimized-tables.

Memory Optimized Tables

Once you have created a memory optimized FILEGROUP for a database, you can create memory optimized tables in the database. Memory optimized tables look and feel like *normal* (often called disk based) in a database except you use an extension to the T-SQL syntax with the CREATE TABLE statement.

Let's use the WideWorldImporters sample database again to see an example. Using the feature in SQL Server Management Studio to script a table (see the documentation at https://docs.microsoft.com/sql/ssms/tutorials/scripting-ssms#script-tables), generate the script for the [Warehouse].[VehicleTemperatures] table:

```
CREATE TABLE [Warehouse].[VehicleTemperatures]
(
        [VehicleTemperatureID] [bigint] IDENTITY(1,1) NOT NULL,
        [VehicleRegistration] [nvarchar](20) COLLATE Latin1_General_CI_AS
        NOT NULL,
        [ChillerSensorNumber] [int] NOT NULL,
        [RecordedWhen] [datetime2](7) NOT NULL,
        [Temperature] [decimal](10, 2) NOT NULL,
        [FullSensorData] [nvarchar](1000) COLLATE Latin1_General_CI_AS NULL,
        [IsCompressed] [bit] NOT NULL,
        [CompressedSensorData] [varbinary](max) NULL,
 CONSTRAINT [PK_Warehouse_VehicleTemperatures]  PRIMARY KEY NONCLUSTERED
(
        [VehicleTemperatureID] ASC
)
)WITH ( MEMORY_OPTIMIZED = ON , DURABILITY = SCHEMA_AND_DATA )
GO
```

Notice the extended syntax for the WITH option. MEMORY_OPTIMIZED = ON tells SQL Server this will be a memory optimized table.

Memory optimized tables have two types, and you use the DURABILITY option to specify which type:

> SCHEMA_AND_DATA: This option ensures the durability of both the schema (table definition) and the data through checkpoint files and the transaction log.

> SCHEMA_ONLY: This option ensures the durability of only the schema not user data. This means that if SQL Server is shut down for any reasons after inserting data, all data will be lost. This may sound like an awfully bad thing, but there could be scenarios where you need to *cache* data and don't care if the data

is persisted. This type of memory optimized table offers the fastest possible performance, since changes are not recorded in the transaction log.

Memory optimized tables have one particularly important characteristic. All of the data in these types of tables must fit into memory. SQL Server will use memory resources outside the normal buffer pool for memory optimized data. This means that if you use memory optimized tables in SQL Server, there will be competing resources for memory between disk-based tables using the buffer pool and memory optimized tables. There are limits to how much memory SQL Server will allow for memory optimized tables but there are also ways to restrict memory usage through resource governor. See our documentation for more details at `https://docs.microsoft.com/sql/relational-databases/in-memory-oltp/bind-a-database-with-memory-optimized-tables-to-a-resource-pool`.

It is important to know that memory optimized tables can co-exist with disk-based tables in a database. Disk-based tables will be stored with the standard SQL Server buffer pool and database files. Memory optimized tables are stored in memory in a separate memory area managed by SQL Server and durable through checkpoint files and the transaction log (Note: all transactions in a database for disk-based and memory optimized tables are stored in the same transaction log).

The fact that memory optimized tables must fit memory is not really the performance benefit. Even disk-based tables are pulled into the buffer pool from disk. The key performance benefit is *optimized* access to data in memory, hence the name. And the optimization benefit is truly seen with concurrent access to memory optimized tables. I don't recommend you measure the true benefit of memory optimized tables with a single user example. It's all about concurrent, optimized access to data.

Indexes

Memory optimized tables are internally structured differently than disk-based tables. They do not use the same 8KB database page and row structure concept. Those internals are not meant to be something you should concern yourself with as you use this feature, but it is useful to know especially when it comes to understanding indexes.

Memory optimized tables do not have a clustered index. Instead, indexes are used only for access to data. Two types of indexes are available for memory optimized tables:

> **Hash**: A index of hashed values on the key columns. This can be very efficient when you are almost always executing queries for single row lookups. Hash indexes can be efficient but also can be difficult to decide how to configure and maintain.

> **Nonclustered**: A b-tree structure like disk-based table nonclustered indexes. I recommend you use a nonclustered index as the default index type and then do tuning to see if a hash index is better for your workload.

You can use many indexes across columns of a memory optimized table, but you must always have one index (hash or nonclustered) that is defined as the primary key.

As you explore how memory optimized tables work, I think these two resources can be valuable:

- A white paper on Internals of In-Memory OLTP written by Kalen Delaney at `https://docs.microsoft.com/sql/relational-databases/in-memory-oltp/sql-server-in-memory-oltp-internals-for-sql-server-2016`

- An Inside In-Memory OLTP presentation I did that can be found on YouTube at `https://www.youtube.com/watch?v=P9DnjQqEOGc`

Natively Compiled Stored Procedures

Standard T-SQL statements are allowed with memory optimized tables with some restrictions (See this documentation for restrictions: `https://docs.microsoft.com/sql/relational-databases/in-memory-oltp/transact-sql-constructs-not-supported-by-in-memory-oltp`). This concept is called *interpreted* T-SQL.

To accelerate performance even further, we created a concept called a *natively compiled* stored procedure. The concept is that you can create a stored procedure using a special T-SQL syntax so that SQL Server will compile and build a Dynamic Link Library (DLL) to represent all the T-SQL queries in the stored procedure.

All the code to execute the query normally compiled into query plans is baked into the DLL. This allows for incredibly fast speed when executing a natively compiled stored procedure.

If you use the techniques I've described previously in this chapter to generate the script of an object, you can see from this fragment of the stored procedure [Website].[RecordColdRoomTemperatures] the syntax of a natively compiled stored procedure:

```
CREATE PROCEDURE [Website].[RecordColdRoomTemperatures]
@SensorReadings Website.SensorDataList READONLY
WITH NATIVE_COMPILATION, SCHEMABINDING, EXECUTE AS OWNER
AS
BEGIN ATOMIC WITH
(
      TRANSACTION ISOLATION LEVEL = SNAPSHOT,
      LANGUAGE = N'English'
)
    BEGIN TRY
.
.
.
```

The WITH NATIVE_COMPILATION extension is the key to creating a natively compiled stored procedure.

The combination of a memory optimized table with natively compiled stored procedures provides the maximum possible performance capabilities of In-Memory OLTP. Natively compiled procedures are not for every scenario and have some limits on T-SQL statements. See this documentation for any limits to using certain aspects of T-SQL with natively compiled procedures: https://docs.microsoft.com/sql/relational-databases/in-memory-oltp/transact-sql-constructs-not-supported-by-in-memory-oltp.

Usage Scenarios

If you have enough memory to fit the data and need a high-speed, scalable, OLTP solution, memory optimized tables may be a good fit for you. Use this place in our documentation to estimate the memory needs of your memory optimized tables: https://docs.microsoft.com/sql/relational-databases/in-memory-oltp/estimate-memory-requirements-for-memory-optimized-tables.

In-Memory OLTP has more uses than your traditional INSERT, UPDATE, DELETE type of SQL application. Consider these other examples:

- Data ingestion applications, especially internet of things (IoT) scenarios

- Caching and session state data

- Replacing tempdb usage

- Extract Transform Load (ETL) scenarios

Check out our documentation for more guidance on these scenarios and some customer case study examples: `https://docs.microsoft.com/sql/relational-databases/in-memory-oltp/overview-and-usage-scenarios`.

The Intelligent SQL Server Engine

I've presented in this chapter all the amazing performance capabilities either built into the SQL Server Engine or available through configuration settings or additional features like Columnstore indexes. In SQL Server 2017, we made decisions to start investing in features that provide more *intelligence* into the SQL Server engine, to help boost performance for applications and reduce the time to resolve performance problems. One of these features is built into the Query Processing Engine and another is built into the engine when the Query Store feature is enabled.

Adaptive Query Processing

While the query processor in SQL Server is an amazing component of the engine and is designed to build the best possible query plans balanced with keeping compile times quick, patterns exist where the query processor is limited in decisions it can make. And many of these scenarios involve limitations based on cardinality estimation.

So, in SQL Server 2017, instead of always "chasing our tails" and trying to fix these cardinality issues, we built functionality to have the query processor *adapt* to query execution issues and correct them "on the fly."

This family of features is called **adaptive query processing** (which is actually part of a wider set of functionalities planned for SQL Server called *intelligent query processing*).

In SQL Server 2017, we have enabled three different scenarios for adaptive query processing:

- Batch mode memory grant feedback
- Batch mode adaptive join
- Interleaved execution

If you remember in the earlier section on columnstore indexes, I touched on the topic of *batch mode* processing. This means that for the first two scenarios, adaptive query processing will only work when the query processor uses batch mode. In SQL Server 2017, this means only for scenarios for columnstore indexes.

The concept for the first scenario, batch mode memory grant feedback, is that SQL Server will adapt its memory allocation for memory grants if it detects a query has executed and used an incorrect memory grant. Subsequent executions of the query will adapt to a new grant, thereby avoiding a performance problem. This detection is built into the query processor and does not require a recompilation of the query.

The second scenario is an example of SQL Server adapting by creating a new query plan operator that is *intelligent* to adapt. The new operator is called an *Adaptive Join* operator. The concept is that SQL Server can defer deciding a particular type of join method to use when joining tables until after it has read data to decide which join method is best.

The third scenario involves the SQL Server query optimizer adapting itself during the compilation of a query plan for a multistatement table valued function, which has challenges for cardinality estimation. The optimizer will pause optimization, gather more accurate cardinality information, and resume optimization to adapt to a better query plan.

To see adaptive query processing in action, download the examples files for this chapter from the **aqp** directory and follow the instructions in the readme.md file.

Note   This demo requires the WideWorldImportersDW sample database as found at `https://github.com/Microsoft/sql-server-samples/releases/download/wide-world-importers-v1.0/WideWorldImportersDW-Full.bak`. So you can copy the backup from another machine or run the following command to download the backup directly in your Linux server: `wget https://github.com/Microsoft/sql-server-samples/releases/download/wide-world-importers-v1.0/WideWorldImportersDW-Full.bak`. I've also provided the cpwwidw.sh, restore_wwidw_linux.sql, and restorewwidw.sh scripts to help you copy and restore this example.

When you go through the demo for adaptive joins, as found in the **aqp_adaptivejoin. sql** example script, display the actual execution plan for the final query of the demo. Your query plan should look something similar to Figure 6-21.

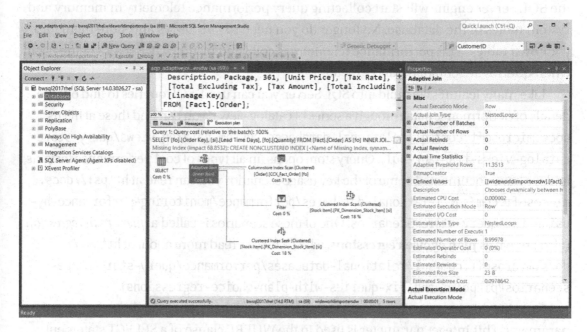

Figure 6-21. *An adaptive join as part of adaptive query processing*

Note the Adaptive Join operator has an Actual Join Type, which in this case is Nested Loops based on the values of data at the time of the query execution. In the demo script, the previous query had a join type of Hash Join.

Adaptive query processing is enabled in the SQL Server query processor if you are using database compatibility 140. This is the default compatibility level if you create a new database with SQL Server 2017. I'll talk about database compatibility for upgrade and migration scenarios in a later chapter in the book on migration.

The lead Program Manager for this area of the product, Joe Sack, has a really nice video on YouTube you can watch to see the complete demo and hear from him on the aspects of this feature: https://www.youtube.com/watch?v=szTmo6rTUjM.

Automatic Tuning

When I first saw early builds of SQL Server 2017, one of the features that caught my eye immediately was **Automatic Tuning** with an option called Automatic Plan Correction.

SQL Server 2017 was released in October of 2017 right on the heels of one of my favorite releases, SQL Server 2016. In SQL Server 2016, we brought to the product a new feature called **Query Store**. When Query Store is enabled for a database via ALTER DATABASE, the SQL Server engine will start collecting query performance telemetry in memory and system tables in the database. No longer do you need to *poll* DMVs and store them into your own tables. This performance telemetry is collected by the SQL Server engine itself when queries are compiled and executed.

Like many features we build into SQL Server, you can use T-SQL queries to find out the details of performance data through a series of catalog views (you can find these at `https://docs.microsoft.com/sql/relational-databases/system-catalog-views/query-store-catalog-views-transact-sql`). Query store opens up all types of cool performance insights, and we have documented some of the key usage scenarios you can read at `https://docs.microsoft.com/sql/relational-databases/performance/monitoring-performance-by-using-the-query-store#Scenarios`. One of these scenarios is called a *query plan regression* (also known as **plan choice regressions**, which you can read more about at `https://docs.microsoft.com/sql/relational-databases/performance/query-store-usage-scenarios#pinpoint-and-fix-queries-with-plan-choice-regressions`).

Imagine this scenario. You have a stored procedure that takes a single integer parameter. This integer parameter is used in the WHERE clause of a SELECT statement in the stored procedure. The first time the stored procedure is compiled, the plan for this procedure is inserted into cache based on the value of the parameter from the first execution of the procedure. And this plan may be a good plan for most users. Now for unexpected reasons, perhaps memory pressure, the plan is evicted from cache. Let's say a user then executes the procedure through an application but this time with a different integer parameter value. This could result in a different query plan that leads to poor performance (for example, the new plan could involve an index scan that is not optimal for all executions). Compiling a plan for a stored procedure based on the parameter value is called *parameter sniffing*. This concept is discussed in our **Query Processing Architecture Guide** in the documentation (which in itself is a cool read at `https://docs.microsoft.com/sql/relational-databases/query-processing-architecture-guide`). Parameter sniffing is designed to be a good thing, but in some situations where the data in the table associated with the parameter is skewed, a performance problem could occur.

So, in SQL Server 2016, you can use our reports in SQL Server Management Studio or run queries against Query Store catalog views to see whether a query plan regression has caused a performance problem. Now SQL Server 2017 comes along with some automation. Why not bake into the engine some automation behind the rich telemetry of Query Store? Turns out the folks in our engineering team that own the Query Store feature were already working on these kinds of features in the cloud for Azure SQL Database. Using our cloud-first approach for engineering, we started working on these features in Azure, tested and verified their functionality, and then brought them to SQL Server 2017.

I have a demo you can try yourself (surprise! It uses the WideWorldImporters database) for SQL Server on Linux using SQL Operations Studio. I encourage you to go through the entire example, which can be found in the **autotune** directory for the examples for this chapter or on my GitHub site at `https://github.com/Microsoft/bobsql/tree/master/demos/sqlserver/sqllinux/autotune`. Just follow the instructions in the readme.md file. When you run this demo you will notice I used the charting feature for SQL Operations Studio I showed you earlier in this chapter in a new way. Figure 6-22 shows an example of the chart from SQL Operations Studio after Automatic Tuning corrected a query plan regression problem from the demo.

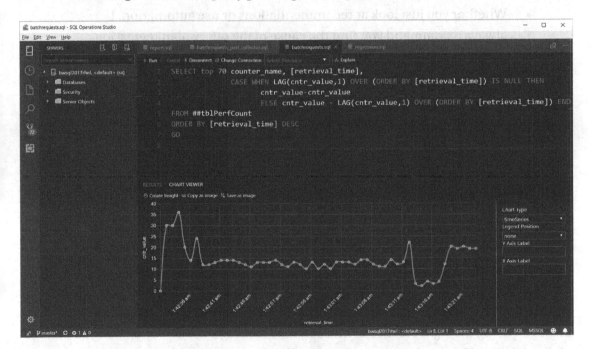

Figure 6-22. Automatic Tuning demonstrated with SQL Operations Studio

The chart shown in Figure 6-22 measures batch requests/sec, which is a standard method to measure SQL Server query throughput. Note how performance goes down on the right-hand side of the chart but automatically picks back up to expected levels quickly.

Almost everyone I've shown this demo to has been amazed. My recommendation to use this feature is the following:

- Enable Query Store and configure it to your needs. See our documentation on best practices at `https://docs.microsoft.com/sql/relational-databases/performance/best-practice-with-the-query-store`.

- Monitor any recommendations we have for you by examining the DMV, **dm_db_tuning_recommendations**.

- If you are comfortable with our recommendations, experiment with turning on Automatic Plan Correction using this T-SQL syntax:

```
ALTER DATABASE current
SET AUTOMATIC_TUNING ( FORCE_LAST_GOOD_PLAN = ON );
```

- Whether you just look at recommendations or use automation, I always recommend you find the cause of the query plan regression problem and take a more long-term corrective action.

If you want to follow along and watch me demonstrate Automatic Tuning with SQL Server on Linux, catch this demo video I posted on the SQL Server YouTube Channel, `https://youtu.be/Sh8W7IFX390`.

Summary

My intent in this chapter was to make sure you understand what is possible for performance for SQL Server on Linux. I've covered the built-in capabilities of performance that you can trust from SQL Server, from scalability on your laptop to the largest enterprise servers in the industry. I've shown you important configuration choices both for SQL Server and Linux. And I've talked about how tuning can be achieved using the right balance of indexes, maintaining statistics, and taking advantage of the right T-SQL usage in your application. You have also seen how to take advantage of new technology to accelerate performance from columnstore indexes to intelligent performance capabilities such as Automatic Tuning. Armed with this knowledge, it's time to ensure you understand how to secure your SQL Server and learn important security features and options when running on Linux.

CHAPTER 7

Security in SQL Server

The second major pillar of the SQL Server data platform and engine is security. SQL Server 2017 not only comes with a rich set of features to meet your security needs but has been recognized for being the least vulnerable database platform over almost the last decade. Figure 7-1 is the one of the standard visuals I use to show an overview of the SQL Security feature suite (many in the industry call this *defense in depth*) and a chart showing the rating of SQL Server vs. the competition on vulnerabilities.

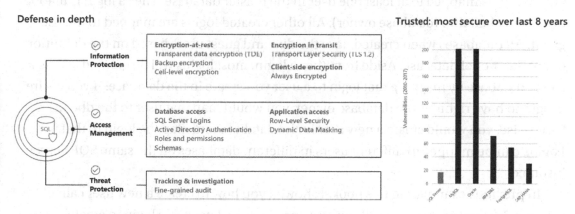

Figure 7-1. SQL Server Defense in depth

The bar chart on the right isn't something Microsoft made up. It comes from the National Institute of Standards and Technology Comprehensive Vulnerability Database (https://www.nist.gov/programs-projects/national-vulnerability-database-nvd) and it explains how seriously we take security.

In this chapter I will show you the various security features that make up the defense in depth story. Security can be more than just a software feature, so I recommend you also read this section in our documentation about how to secure your SQL Server including physical security: https://docs.microsoft.com/sql/relational-databases/security/securing-sql-server.

© Bob Ward 2018
B. Ward, *Pro SQL Server on Linux*, https://doi.org/10.1007/978-1-4842-4128-8_7

Logins and Users

So far in this book I've shown you two examples of SQL Server logins (sa and a login called sqllinux I created), which are identifications used to connect to SQL Server and execute queries. Both of these logins are examples of connecting to SQL Server using *SQL Server Authentication*. SQL Server authentication requires a name and a password. Applications use the name and password to connect to SQL Server. It is the simplest and most compatible method to connect to an SQL Server, whether it be on Windows, Linux, or even Azure. The biggest downside is that you must maintain a separate authentication set of objects from ones you might be using for other authentication purposes (such as Active Directory). I'll show you in the next section of this chapter how to set up and use Active Directory Authentication on Linux.

While *logins* are objects at the SQL Server instance level, databases also have *users*. There is a connection between a login and users in a database. Every login created with SQL Server is mapped to at least one user in the master database. The sa login is mapped to a user called **dbo** (database owner). All other created logins are mapped to the user **guest**. All databases when created have the dbo and guest users based on the definition out of the model database. Aside from the sa login, most logins will be granted access to a user database by mapping that login to a user you create in the database. If you desire a login to have rights as the database owner, you would map that user to the dbo user. Otherwise, you would create a new user in the database and map the login to that user. Logins can be mapped to different users in different databases on the same SQL Server instance.

In previous examples in this book, I showed you how to create a new user called sqllinux. Instead of mapping sqllinux to a specific user, I used this login to create a database called WideWorldImporters. Using a login (if you place the login in the dbcreator role) to create a database automatically maps that login to the dbo user of the database that was created. By default, as a security best practice, the guest user is revoked access to connect for a user database (it must be enabled for the system database msdb). What this means is that if you create a new login and try to access a database where your login has not been mapped to a user, then your access will fail with an error like the following:

> *Msg 916, Level 14, State 1, Line 1*
>
> *The server principal "sqllinux" is not able to access the database "WideWorldImporters" under the current security context.*

So let's follow the steps you would use to create logins and users for any database you create:

- First, I highly recommend you not use the sa login to create new databases for production. If you are just developing or experimenting with SQL Server, then using sa is fine.

- So, to create your first database, create a new login using the T-SQL CREATE LOGIN statement. I showed you an example of how to do this and give proper permissions to this login to create a database in Chapter 3 of the book like this (this script is found in the examples with Chapter 3 called **createlogin.sql**). Execute this script connected as the sa login.

Tip   For any production system you should consider password expiration and complexity. Read our documentation for guidance on these topics at `https://docs.microsoft.com/sql/relational-databases/security/password-policy`.

```
USE master
GO
IF EXISTS (select * from sys.server_principals where name = 'sqllinux')
    DROP LOGIN [sqllinux]
GO
CREATE LOGIN [sqllinux] WITH PASSWORD=N'Sql2017isfast', DEFAULT_
DATABASE=[master]
GO
ALTER SERVER ROLE dbcreator ADD MEMBER sqllinux
GO
```

In this example, I added this login to a server role to allow it to create databases. I'll discuss more details about roles later in this chapter. This login will now be mapped to the user dbo and will have all the privileges given to the dbo user in that database.

> **Note**   In Chapter 3 I used the legacy system procedure sp_addsrvrolemember.
> This is perfectly fine to use but technically it is deprecated. Here I use the new
> ALTER SERVER ROLE syntax.

- Create a new database connected as the sqllinux login using the
  following T-SQL statement as found in the example **createdb.sql**:

```
USE [master]
GO
DROP DATABASE IF EXISTS [SecureMyDatabase]
GO
CREATE DATABASE [SecureMyDatabase]
GO
```

- Run this T-SQL statement as found in the example **whichuserami.sql**
  to find out what database user the sqllinux login is mapped to:

```
USE [SecureMyDatabase]
GO
SELECT SUSER_NAME() as current_login, USER_NAME() as
current_database_user
GO
```

Figure 7-2 shows the results with SQL Operations Studio.

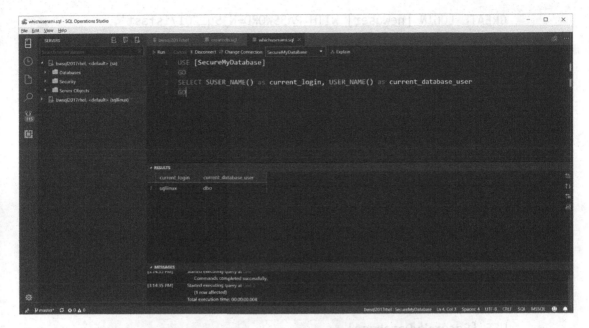

Figure 7-2. *Login and user for sqllinux after creating the database*

For this example I used two built-in SQL Server functions to find out the current connected login and database user. Since the sqllinux login created the database, it is automatically mapped to the dbo user.

- Now let's create a user in the database that will not be the database owner. The first step is to create a new login that will have a default database of [SecureMyDatabase]. Use the following T-SQL batch as found in the example script **createnewuserlogin.sql** connected as the **sa** login (Note: it is possible to grant permissions to the sqllinux login to create new logins):

```
USE [MASTER]
GO
USE master
GO
IF EXISTS (select * from sys.server_principals where
name = 'newuser')
    DROP LOGIN [newuser]
GO
```

```
CREATE LOGIN [newuser] WITH PASSWORD=N'Sql2017isfast',
DEFAULT_DATABASE=[SecureMyDatabase]
GO
```

At this point if you tried to log in as the newuser login, you would get an error like this:

```
Cannot open user default database. Login failed. Login failed for user
'newuser'.
```

This is because the newuser login is not mapped to any user in the [SecureMyDatabase] database.

- So, the next step is to create a user in the database connected as the dbo user, which is the sqllinux login. Connected as sqllinux executes the following T-SQL batch, which can be found in the example script **createuser.sql:**

```
USE [SecureMyDatabase]
GO
CREATE USER newuser FOR LOGIN newuser
GO
```

Note   You don't have to map users to the same name as a login, but it does make it easier to manage and understand.

- Now let's **connect as the newuser login** and run the **whichuserami.sql** script again using SQL Operations Studio. Figure 7-3 shows what the results should look like.

Figure 7-3. *The newuser login and user*

If the user called newuser is not a database owner, what can this user do? What permission and access do this login and user have now? I'll cover that in a later section. First, I want to show you a different method for login authentication called Active Directory Authentication.

Active Directory Authentication

SQL Server authentication is simple and easy to use. However, most users in an organization of any size have login accounts that are part of a company infrastructure such as an Active Directory domain. Using a *single sign-on* is not only efficient but more secure, as you don't have to manage different accounts to use corporate resources and SQL Server. SQL Server on Windows has provided this method for many years called Windows Authentication.

Active Directory is an extremely popular identity-based management system even for organizations that use Linux Servers. Linux provides the necessary packages and software to join an Active Directory domain. SQL Server can take advantage of this functionality using Kerberos to authenticate an Active Directory user, much like Windows Authentication. Users can now login to the Linux Server or any computer that can join the domain and log in to SQL Server without using a separate SQL login.

How it Works

Active Directory Authentication involves the following commands and objects:

realm: A command on Linux that allows you to join a Linux server to an Active Directory domain. realm requires you to install the realmd package. The term *realm* comes from the Kerberos concept, Kerberos realm.

Ticket Granting Ticket (TGT): an encrypted file that is a *ticket* sent to a Ticket Granting Server (TGS) to request access to services in the domain (such as SQL Server). The TGS functionality is implemented by a Windows Domain Controller.

kinit: a Linux command used to obtain and cache a TGT for a domain user

Service Principal Name (SPN): a unique identifier for a service (such as SQL Server) in the Active Directory

keytab: A file on Linux used to store encrypted keys used to validate incoming Kerberos authentication requests

Domain Controller: A Windows Server that provides Active Directory Domain Services for an Active Directory Domain

My colleague Vin Yu, one of the key program managers for SQL Server on Linux and containers, has an excellent diagram, as seen in Figure 7-4, which shows the flow how Kerberos works to support Active Directory Authentication with SQL Server.

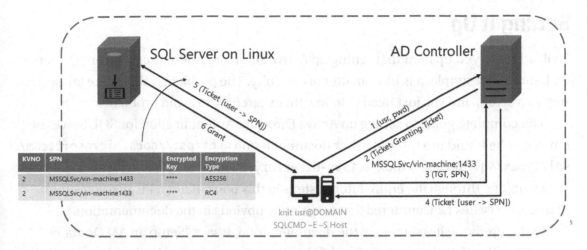

Figure 7-4. *SQL Server Active Directory Authentication flow on Linux*

Let me explain this flow to understand how Kerberos authentication works with SQL Server on Linux:

1. The user logs into the domain on a Linux client executing kinit with the domain user account and password. kinit will send the user and password to the Domain Controller (DC).

2. The DC will issue a TGT after it verifies this is a valid domain user with correct password. This same process would happen if you logged into your Windows computer with your domain account.

3. Now you need to connect to SQL Server with a tool like sqlcmd. exe. The -E parameter says to use Windows authentication. The client will use the TGT along with the SPN for the SQL Server service to send to the DC when trying to connect to a SQL Server on Linux using AD authentication with a tool like sqlcmd.exe.

4. The DC then sends back a ticket which the client can now use for authentication to SQL Server.

5. The sqlcmd program can now use the ticket provided by the DC to attempt to authenticate a connection to SQL Server. SQL Server will use the keys (listed in the table) to verify the ticket is valid to connect to SQL Server, along with ensuring the domain account has a created login in SQL Server.

6. SQL Server will grant the request to connect to SQL Server.

Setting it Up

I will admit to you up front that setting up Active Directory Authentication for SQL Server on Linux is not simple. It is not a matter of difficulty. The problem is that there are several steps involved, and you just need to follow them carefully to avoid problems.

The complete guide to setting up Active Directory Authentication for SQL Server on Linux can be found in a tutorial in our documentation at `https://docs.microsoft.com/sql/linux/sql-server-linux-active-directory-authentication`.

I won't go through the entire tutorial steps in this book. Rather, I'll give you some pointers on issues I encountered that may not be obvious in the documentation.

In the Prerequisites section of the documentation, it says "Setup an AD Domain Controller (Windows) on your network." You might be in an organization that already had an Active Directory system. If so, you will need to show this section of the documentation to your network administrators to have the Active Directory configured for SQL Server Active Directory Authentication: `https://docs.microsoft.com/sql/linux/sql-server-linux-active-directory-authentication?#createuser`.

You may be like me, where you want to demonstrate this capability; I set up my own Windows Server in a Virtual Machine as a domain controller with my own Active Directory. Setting my own AD and Domain Controller was simpler than I thought but I had help. This blog post is excellent to show you how: `https://blogs.technet.microsoft.com/canitpro/2017/02/22/step-by-step-setting-up-active-directory-in-windows-server-2016/`.

Here are some other issues I ran into that may help you as you set up AD Authentication for SQL Server on Linux.

When I tried to join the SQL Server to the domain like this command in the documentation

```
sudo realm join contoso.com -U 'user@CONTOSO.COM' -v
```

I ran into three issues:

1. I had to change the hostname of my Linux Server from its default using a command like this:

    ```
    hostnamectl -set-hostname bobsqllinux
    ```

I should have done this already when I installed RHEL on my VM (and in fact Azure does this automatically). It turns out that when I install RHEL, putting in a hostname other than the default is optional.

2. I had to install missing packages (the documentation says you might have to do this) like this:

```
sudo yum -y install oddjob oddjob-mkhomedir sssd samba-common-
tools
```

3. When the command to join the domain worked, I received some error messages that I found out can be ignored. A successful join of the domain looked like Figure 7-5.

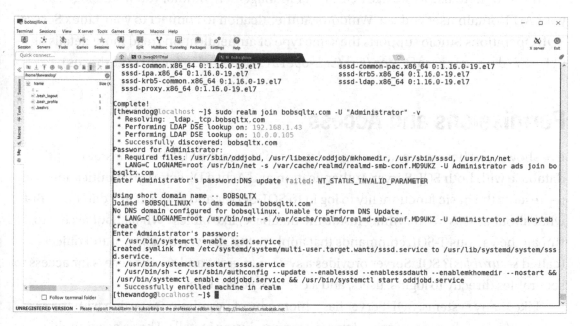

Figure 7-5. *A successful join to the domain of Linux Server*

In addition, while I can use kinit on the Linux server to "login to the domain" as described in the documentation, I wanted to login through ssh to my Linux Server using my AD domain account. I encountered an Access Denied error until I ran this command:

```
realm permit -all
```

Note   You can use realm permit to only allow logins to specific AD users instead of all users.

Using AD Authentication

Once I went through the steps in the documentation and maneuvered around the preceding issues, I was able to successfully use a command like this:

```
sqlcmd -E
```

and was able to successfully start executing queries logged in as an AD user to SQL Server.

If you want to use a tool like SQL Server Management Studio, you would log in as your AD Domain user and use Windows Authentication to connect to your Linux Server. SQL Operations Studio supports the same type of authentication (read more details at https://docs.microsoft.com/sql/sql-operations-studio/enable-kerberos).

Permissions and Access

I've shown you how to create logins and users to access the SQL Server instance and database with both SQL Server Authentication and Active Directory Authentication. This represents the basic functionality to log in to SQL Server and connect to a database. But what about access to everything inside the database, like tables? What about access to run all the various T-SQL commands that apply to SQL Server, databases, and objects (called *securables*)? SQL Server provides a system to grant and revoke access for access to securables directly to logins, users, and a concept called roles.

Like many systems, SQL Server has a hierarchy of permissions starting with the sa account (remember you specified the sa account during install). The sa account (like root in Linux) is *supreme* when it comes to permissions. I'll discuss a technique where you can disable the sa account to make your SQL Server more secure once you have installed SQL Server (see the section on Roles and Permissions).

If you want a deep dive into all the securable options for SQL Server, take a look at this pdf *poster* at https://aka.ms/sql-permissions-poster.

Grant and Revoking Access

T-SQL provides two statements to grant and revoke access to securables: respectively, GRANT and REVOKE. A complete list of possible securables can be found in the documentation of the T-SQL GRANT statement at https://docs.microsoft.com/sql/t-sql/statements/grant-transact-sql.

By default, logins and users will have some form of basic access to a certain set of securables. The process of securing SQL Server and all of your securables will be:

- Decide what securables and access a specific login and/or user needs and use the GRANT command to grant these logins and users access.

- Decide if you want to revoke access to some securables for some logins and/or users.

While you can use the GRANT command to grant access to securables to specific logins and/or users, it may be more effective to grant access to a concept called *roles* and then revoke access to specific logins and/or users based on your security needs.

In addition, instead of granting access to roles to specific objects, it can be more efficient to group objects into schemas and grant access to the schema. I've discussed the concept of schemas in previous chapters of the book while describing the fundamentals of creating objects like tables and views.

Roles and Permissions

Roles provide a convenient method to grant (or revoke) access to a group of logins or users. SQL Server comes with a series of built-in roles that have already been granted certain permissions.

Permissions define what operations are allowed for a given login, user, or role at the SQL Server instance level or database level. A complete list of possible permissions can be found in our documentation at `https://docs.microsoft.com/en-us/sql/relational-databases/security/permissions-database-engine`. I'll show you examples of permissions that are defined by default for built-in roles and then talk about how you can make changes for permission per your security needs. Permissions also are organized into a hierarchy. Our documentation has a very good visual diagram to view this at `https://docs.microsoft.com/sql/relational-databases/security/permissions-hierarchy-database-engine`.

Server Roles

SQL Server provides a set of roles that have permission for operations that apply across the SQL Server instance for logins. You can see a list of these roles in our documentation at `https://docs.microsoft.com/sql/relational-databases/security/authentication-access/server-level-roles`.

Let me call out a few of these server roles worth noting:

sysadmin: Logins that are members of this role can perform any operation for SQL Server. Therefore, it is critical to minimize which logins are members of this role. By default, the sa login is a member of this role. However, as the sa login, you can create a new login, add it to the sysadmin role, and then disable the sa login. This could provide an extra layer of security to avoid unwanted users from trying to guess the sa password. You can use the ALTER SERVER ROLE T-SQL command as documented at `https://docs.microsoft.com/sql/t-sql/statements/alter-server-role-transact-sql` to add logins to server roles.

dbcreator: Members of this role have permissions to create, alter, and drop databases. While it is possible to assign login rights to create their own database (and they would now automatically become the database owner), the problem with this role is that members have permissions to alter or drop *any database*, not just ones they own. Another technique to allow a login to own their own database is to create the database as a member of the sysadmin role, and then assign a new login the rights as database owner. I'll show you how to do this in the next section, "Database Roles."

Sysadmin and dbcreator are examples of *fixed* server roles. This means the permissions for these roles cannot be changed. The documentation at `https://docs.microsoft.com/sql/relational-databases/security/authentication-access/server-level-roles#permissions-of-fixed-server-roles` has a diagram that shows the permissions for fixed server roles.

public: This is the default role for any new login created for SQL Server. The public server role is not fixed, so the permissions for the role can be changed. By default, the public role has permissions for CONNECT, which means any login has the right to connect to SQL Server and VIEW ANY DATABASE, which means any login has the right to see what databases exist on the SQL Server instance. You would use the T-SQL command GRANT to add new permissions for the public server role or REVOKE to take any default permissions away.

Your strategy can vary, but effectively the process from a server perspective to create logins and users can look like the following:

1. Create the necessary logins for your SQL Server with CREATE LOGIN.

2. Assign specific logins to server roles based on your decision on what type of server access and operations they should be able to perform. I recommend that one of these logins become added to the sysadmin role, so you do not rely on the sa login to perform all sysadmin options.

3. Leave all other users with the default permission for the public server role.

4. Create your database from the sysadmin role member.

Note   My examples show using the sqllinux login as part of the dbcreator role, because the login that creates the database becomes the database owner by default. However, as I've indicated, anyone with the dbcreator role has authority to affect other databases. If you want one login to create and own all databases, then using this technique is fine. If you have separate database owners, you will not want to use this technique.

---

5. Use the ALTER AUTHORIZATION T-SQL command to make your designated login become the database owner. I'll talk more about this in the next section, "Database Roles."

ALTER AUTHORIZATION is a method to change the ownership of a securable in SQL Server. You can read more about how to use this statement at https://docs.microsoft.com/sql/t-sql/statements/alter-authorization-transact-sql.

6. The database owner now has permissions to add other logins to the database, assign them to specific roles, and give them specific permissions based on their needs.

It is also possible to create your own server roles and assign members and permissions to them. You can use the T-SQL CREATE SERVER ROLE command to create your own server roles.

Database Roles

Just like server roles, each database has built-in roles that define certain permissions to perform necessary operations in a database.

As I mentioned in the previous section, one of the most important roles in each database is called **db_owner**, and the user dbo is assigned membership to that role. A list of fixed database roles and their permissions are listed in our documentation at `https://docs.microsoft.com/sql/relational-databases/ security/authentication-access/database-level-roles`. These roles exist for your convenience, to manage a database. For example, the database role **db_datareader** gives any member the permission to read data from all user tables in the database. Many customers will choose to assign specific permissions to schemas to specific users.

Or another method is to create your own database role for a specific set of security needs, assign users to that new database role, and then assign specific permissions to certain schemas to that database role. You will see in the next section that another advantage of creating your own database roles is to apply them to row level security and dynamic data masks.

Like the server role, public, each database has a public role. Every user created in the database is automatically a member of the public database role. And by default, permissions for default users are to view most system catalog views in the database but that is just about it.

Let's go through an example using the WideWorldImporters database (I recommend you restore the WideWorldImporters full database "from scratch" per instructions I've provided in previous chapters first).

1. Let's add the login sqllinux, and this time make it the owner of the database using the ALTER AUTHORIZATION T-SQL command. Use the example script **createdbownerlogin.sql** connected as sa, like the following T-SQL statements:

```
USE master
GO
IF EXISTS (select * from sys.server_principals where name =
'sqllinux')
    DROP LOGIN [sqllinux]
GO
```

```
CREATE LOGIN [sqllinux] WITH PASSWORD=N'Sql2017isfast',
DEFAULT_DATABASE=[master]
GO
ALTER AUTHORIZATION ON DATABASE::WideWorldImporters to sqllinux
GO
```

2. Create the other server login for the **appuser** login using
   createappuserlogin.sql connected as sa, like the following T-SQL
   statements:

```
USE [MASTER]
GO
USE master
GO
IF EXISTS (select * from sys.server_principals where name =
'appuser')
    DROP LOGIN [appuser]
GO
CREATE LOGIN [appuser] WITH PASSWORD=N'Sql2017isfast',
DEFAULT_DATABASE=[WideWorldImporters]
GO
```

3. Create the appuser user, which will be bound to the appuser
   server login, using **createappuser.sql** connected as the **sqllinux**
   login, like the following T-SQL statements:

```
USE [WideWorldImporters]
GO
DROP USER IF EXISTS appuser
GO
CREATE USER appuser FOR LOGIN appuser
GO
```

4. Create the db role, add the appuser database user to it, and
   assign it CONTROL privileges to the Application Schema using
   createdbrole.sql connected as the **sqllinux** login, like the
   following T-SQL statements:

```
USE [WideWorldImporters]
GO
IF (SELECT IS_ROLEMEMBER('Application_Users', 'appuser')) IS NOT
NULL
    ALTER ROLE Application_Users DROP MEMBER appuser
GO
DROP ROLE IF EXISTS Application_Users
GO
CREATE ROLE Application_Users
GO
ALTER ROLE Application_Users ADD MEMBER appuser
GO
GRANT CONTROL ON SCHEMA::Application TO Application_Users
GO
```

Notice how I used the GRANT T-SQL statement here with the option
CONTROL. GRANT allows you to grant permissions to objects including schemas.
In this case, GRANT CONTROL gives ownership of the Application schema in the
WideWorldImporters database to any member of the Application_Users role. You can
read more about GRANT CONTROL in the documentation at https://docs.microsoft.
com/sql/t-sql/statements/grant-database-principal-permissions-transact-sql.

5. To see how these permissions work, execute the queries in
   appuserquery.sql connected as the **appuser** login, like the
   following T-SQL statements:

```
use [WideWorldImporters]
go
SELECT * from [Application].People
GO
SELECT * from [Sales].[Customers]
GO
```

Figure 7-6 shows the results using SQL Operations Studio.

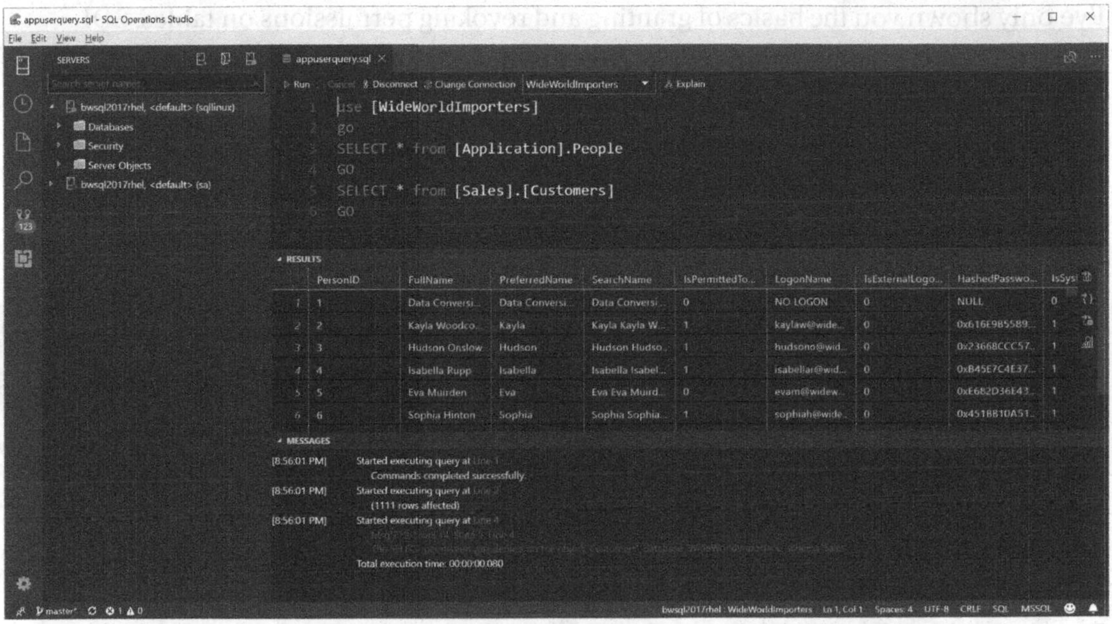

Figure 7-6. *Schemas and objects the appuser login has access to*

You can see that the appuser has access to a table in the Application Schema but gets an error when trying to access a table in a schema it is not granted to.

Besides the basic permissions for a schema and/or user to an object like a table, you can also assign permissions to a specific set of columns in a table and/or view. See the syntax for the GRANT T-SQL statement in the documentation for more information: https://docs.microsoft.com/sql/t-sql/statements/grant-transact-sql.

Application Roles

One interesting security feature that may appeal to developers is application roles. Application roles allow applications to use a password only known to the application and set permissions specific to the application independent of the login used to connect from the application.

You can read more about application roles at https://docs.microsoft.com/sql/relational-databases/security/authentication-access/application-roles.

Other Permissions

I've only shown you the basics of granting and revoking permissions on tables. SQL Server allows you to assign permissions on a wide range of objects and specific T-SQL statements. In some cases, these permissions only apply if you are using a specific feature of SQL Server. For example, you can assign permissions for aspects of Availability Groups only if you have enabled that feature. For a complete list of possible permission examples, see our documentation at `https://docs.microsoft.com/sql/t-sql/statements/grant-transact-sql#examples`.

Tip   Want to test out permissions for a user you have created without actually logging in as the user? Check out the EXECUTE AS T-SQL statement in our documentation at `https://docs.microsoft.com/sql/t-sql/statements/execute-as-clause-transact-sql`.

Row Level Security

One highly requested feature landed in SQL Server 2016, Row Level Security (RLS). Instead of just being able to assign permissions on objects or statements that apply across all rows of a table, you can now assign permissions for certain rows of data. You actually had a way to achieve this before using a view, but now you can assign permissions to a set of rows directly to tables. Furthermore, RLS provides additional functionality to block operations before or after they execute.

The best way to understand RLS is to see it in action. I found a great example on GitHub from our team on RLS, using the WideWorldImporters database at `https://github.com/Microsoft/sql-server-samples/tree/master/samples/databases/wide-world-importers/sample-scripts/row-level-security`. I made a few modifications, which you can find in **rls.sql**. This example will set up row level security for users based on sales territory data for customers. The concept is that only application users who are part of a given sales territory should be able to see sales for their territory and not sales data for other territories. The database owner should see all data.

Let me walk through the T-SQL statements in this script and explain how it works (Connect as sa when running this script to make it simple):

1. Create the login for this RLS example:

```
USE master
GO

IF NOT EXISTS (SELECT 1 FROM sys.server_principals WHERE
name = N'GreatLakesUser')
BEGIN
    CREATE LOGIN GreatLakesUser
    WITH PASSWORD = N'SQLRocks!00',
        CHECK_POLICY = OFF,
        CHECK_EXPIRATION = OFF,
        DEFAULT_DATABASE = WideWorldImporters;
END
GO
```

2. Create the user to map to the login you just created and add this user to a role already defined in WideWorldImporters:

```
USE WideWorldImporters;
GO
DROP USER IF EXISTS GreatLakesUser
GO
CREATE USER GreatLakesUser FOR LOGIN GreatLakesUser
GO
ALTER ROLE [Great Lakes Sales] ADD MEMBER GreatLakesUser
GO
```

WideWorldImporters comes built-in with database roles that will map to *sales territories,* as found in the Customer sales data found in the [Sales].[Customers] table based on cities for customer sales.

3. In order to apply RLS, you need to create an SQL Server *function*, which will be used to apply to any query to determine what rows the user can access. Then you have to create a security policy that maps to the function you have created.

```
-- Drop the security policy and function if they exist
--
DROP SECURITY POLICY IF EXISTS [Application].
FilterCustomersBySalesTerritoryRole
GO
DROP FUNCTION IF EXISTS [Application].DetermineCustomerAccess
GO

-- Create the function to apply for RLS
--
CREATE FUNCTION [Application].DetermineCustomerAccess(@CityID int)
RETURNS TABLE
WITH SCHEMABINDING
AS
RETURN (SELECT 1 AS AccessResult
          WHERE IS_ROLEMEMBER(N'db_owner') <> 0
           OR IS_ROLEMEMBER((SELECT sp.SalesTerritory
                            FROM [Application].Cities AS c
                            INNER JOIN [Application].
                            StateProvinces AS sp
                            ON c.StateProvinceID =
                            sp.StateProvinceID
                            WHERE c.CityID = @CityID) + N' Sales')
                            <> 0
        )
GO

-- The security policy that has been applied is as follows:
--
CREATE SECURITY POLICY [Application].
FilterCustomersBySalesTerritoryRole
```

```
ADD FILTER PREDICATE [Application].DetermineCustomerAccess
(DeliveryCityID)
ON Sales.Customers
GO
```

Let me explain how the function works. The function takes in a CityID value and finds the SalesTerritory name of the city from the Cities and StateProvinces table. The function concatenates the word 'Sales' to the end of the name. So any CityID that falls in the GreatLakes territory would return GreatLakesSales. The security policy takes the DeliveryCityID values from the [Sales].[Customers] when a user tries to query the [Sales]. [Customers] table. This means if I'm logged in as the GreatLakesUser, which is a member of the GreatLakesSales role, only rows with the DeliveryCityID from the Customers table that map to the GreatLakes region will be returned to the user.

4. Connected still as sa (which is a database owner), find out how many rows are in the [Sales].[Customers] table and note the count:

```
SELECT COUNT(*) FROM Sales.Customers; -- and note count
GO
```

When I run this, I get 663 rows.

5. Now grant permissions to the GreatLakesSales role to query the [Sales].[Customers] table, *impersonate* the GreatLakesUser, and see how many rows are in the table:

```
GRANT SELECT, UPDATE ON Sales.Customers TO [Great Lakes Sales];
GO
-- impersonate the user GreatLakesUser
EXECUTE AS USER = 'GreatLakesUser'
GO

-- Now note the count and which rows are returned
-- even though we have not changed the command

SELECT COUNT(*) FROM Sales.Customers;
GO
```

When I run the query this time, I **only see 77 rows**. The other rows are part of other sales territories, which is why the GreatLakesSales role member cannot even see they exist.

6. To revert the impersonation, use the following T-SQL statement in
    the **rls.sql** script:

```
-- Revert back to logged in user
--
REVERT
GO
```

Row Level Security is a great feature in the suite of security capabilities for SQL
Server and is fully managed by T-SQL statements independent of the application. Find
out more of the details of RLS and how it works in our documentation at https://docs.
microsoft.com/sql/relational-databases/security/row-level-security.

Dynamic Data Masking

Dynamic data masking is another great security feature that landed starting in SQL
Server 2016 and works the same for SQL Server on both Windows and Linux. It is
another great security feature that doesn't require any application changes or logic.

The concept behind dynamic data masking is to provide T-SQL commands that allow
you to supply masking rules to sensitive data and control the ability to see sensitive data
unmasked to specific users. The feature is *dynamic* because you can make changes via
T-SQL, and application queries will see different results with no changes required.

Another example is a great way to see how this works. And again, there is an example
I can borrow and modify from the Microsoft WideWorldImporters sample scripts
as found at https://github.com/Microsoft/sql-server-samples/tree/master/
samples/databases/wide-world-importers/sample-scripts/dynamic-data-masking.

Note   This example works fine if you have run the preceding example for
row-level security or if you have not done those examples. It does assume you
have restored the WideWorldImporters full sample database, as I've shown you in
other examples in this book.

I've taken the above GitHub example, modified this, and pulled this into the example
script **ddm.sql**. The concept is that *privileged* users (like dbo) can see sensitive data
in the [Purchasing].[Suppliers] such as bank account information but a nonprivileged

user will not be able to see that sensitive data. A privileged user is one who usually has permissions to access almost anything in the database (or server) vs. a nonprivileged user who usually has only specific permissions needed for their job or tasks.

Using the generated **wwi.sql** script I've provided in samples, you can see the definition of the [Purchasing].[Suppliers] and how masking is defined:

```
CREATE TABLE [Purchasing].[Suppliers](
    [SupplierID] [int] NOT NULL,
    [SupplierName] [nvarchar](100) NOT NULL,
    [SupplierCategoryID] [int] NOT NULL,
    [PrimaryContactPersonID] [int] NOT NULL,
    [AlternateContactPersonID] [int] NOT NULL,
    [DeliveryMethodID] [int] NULL,
    [DeliveryCityID] [int] NOT NULL,
    [PostalCityID] [int] NOT NULL,
    [SupplierReference] [nvarchar](20) NULL,
    [BankAccountName] [nvarchar](50) MASKED WITH (FUNCTION = 'default()')
    NULL,
    [BankAccountBranch] [nvarchar](50) MASKED WITH (FUNCTION =
    'default()') NULL,
    [BankAccountCode] [nvarchar](20) MASKED WITH (FUNCTION = 'default()')
    NULL,
    [BankAccountNumber] [nvarchar](20) MASKED WITH (FUNCTION =
    'default()') NULL,
    [BankInternationalCode] [nvarchar](20) MASKED WITH (FUNCTION =
    'default()') NULL,
    [PaymentDays] [int] NOT NULL,
    [InternalComments] [nvarchar](max) NULL,
    [PhoneNumber] [nvarchar](20) NOT NULL,
    [FaxNumber] [nvarchar](20) NOT NULL,
    [WebsiteURL] [nvarchar](256) NOT NULL,
    [DeliveryAddressLine1] [nvarchar](60) NOT NULL,
    [DeliveryAddressLine2] [nvarchar](60) NULL,
    [DeliveryPostalCode] [nvarchar](10) NOT NULL,
    [DeliveryLocation] [geography] NULL,
    [PostalAddressLine1] [nvarchar](60) NOT NULL,
```

```
    [PostalAddressLine2] [nvarchar](60) NULL,
    [PostalPostalCode] [nvarchar](10) NOT NULL,
    [LastEditedBy] [int] NOT NULL,
    [ValidFrom] [datetime2](7) GENERATED ALWAYS AS ROW START NOT NULL,
    [ValidTo] [datetime2](7) GENERATED ALWAYS AS ROW END NOT NULL,
 CONSTRAINT [PK_Purchasing_Suppliers] PRIMARY KEY CLUSTERED
(
    [SupplierID] ASC
)WITH (PAD_INDEX = OFF, STATISTICS_NORECOMPUTE = OFF, IGNORE_DUP_KEY = OFF,
ALLOW_ROW_LOCKS = ON, ALLOW_PAGE_LOCKS = ON) ON [USERDATA],
 CONSTRAINT [UQ_Purchasing_Suppliers_SupplierName] UNIQUE NONCLUSTERED
(
    [SupplierName] ASC
)WITH (PAD_INDEX = OFF, STATISTICS_NORECOMPUTE = OFF, IGNORE_DUP_KEY = OFF,
ALLOW_ROW_LOCKS = ON, ALLOW_PAGE_LOCKS = ON) ON [USERDATA],
    PERIOD FOR SYSTEM_TIME ([ValidFrom], [ValidTo])
) ON [USERDATA] TEXTIMAGE_ON [USERDATA]
WITH
(
SYSTEM_VERSIONING = ON ( HISTORY_TABLE = [Purchasing].[Suppliers_Archive] )
)
GO
```

Note the use of this syntax on some of the columns involved with banking data:

```
[BankAccountName] [nvarchar](50) MASKED WITH (FUNCTION = 'default()') NULL,
```

The MASKED WITH syntax is the T-SQL extension to define data masks. What can be defined in the (FUNCTION =) after the WITH clause defines the mask including the type of mask. The syntax after FUNCTION defines the type of mask. The default mask has rules of how to mask certain characters depending on the column type. For example, character column gets masked with the character 'X' and integers get masked with a 0. You can see the list of mask types in our documentation at https://docs.microsoft.com/sql/relational-databases/security/dynamic-data-masking#defining-a-dynamic-data-mask (which includes the ability to define your own custom mask).

Let's go through an example to see this in action using some of the statements in the **ddm.sql** script (connect as sa for all of these steps):

1. Connect as sa and create a new login.

```
-- Demonstrate Dynamic Data Masking
--
-- Make sure to connect using a privileged user such as the
   database owner or sysadmin
IF NOT EXISTS (SELECT 1 FROM sys.server_principals WHERE name
= N'GreatLakesUser')
BEGIN
    CREATE LOGIN GreatLakesUser
    WITH PASSWORD = N'SQLRocks!00',
        CHECK_POLICY = OFF,
        CHECK_EXPIRATION = OFF,
        DEFAULT_DATABASE = WideWorldImporters;
END
GO
```

2. Create a user to map to the login, add them to one of the defined roles in the database, and grant read permissions to the role.

```
USE WideWorldImporters
GO
DROP USER IF EXISTS GreatLakesUser
GO
CREATE USER GreatLakesUser FOR LOGIN GreatLakesUser
GO
ALTER ROLE [Great Lakes Sales] ADD MEMBER GreatLakesUser
GO

-- grant SELECT rights to role
GRANT SELECT ON Purchasing.Suppliers TO [Great Lakes Sales];
GO
```

3. Try to read data from the [Purchasing].[Suppliers] table.

```
-- select with current UNMASK rights (NOTE row count and data
values), assuming you are connected using a privileged user
SELECT SupplierID, SupplierName, BankAccountName,
BankAccountBranch, BankAccountCode, BankAccountNumber FROM
Purchasing.Suppliers
```

You will see all the data for all the columns.

4. Impersonate the GreakLakesUser user and run the query again.

```
-- impersonate the user GreatLakesUser
EXECUTE AS USER = 'GreatLakesUser'
GO
```

```
-- select with impersonated MASKED rights (NOTE row count and
data values)
SELECT SupplierID, SupplierName, BankAccountName,
BankAccountBranch, BankAccountCode, BankAccountNumber FROM
Purchasing.Suppliers
GO
```

The results now are masked for certain columns even though you can see all rows.
Figure 7-7 shows the results from SQL Operations Studio.

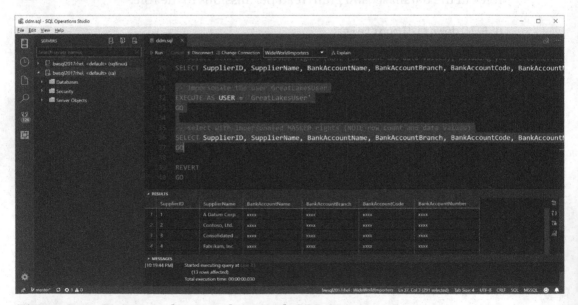

Figure 7-7. *Dynamic data masking with SQL Server on Linux*

Learn more about dynamic data masking in our documentation at `https://docs.`
`microsoft.com/sql/relational-databases/security/dynamic-data-masking`.

SQL Server and Encryption

Encryption of data can be important to any security scheme. However, not all
applications using SQL Server need to use encryption. Using any of the features for
encryption with SQL Server will require some overhead (such as additional CPU usage),
so that has to be considered in your overall security plan.

SQL Server supports several features that enable customers to secure *data at
rest*, *data in transit*, and *connections*. Data at rest is SQL Server data stored in files
and backups. You want to ensure data is encrypted so that attackers cannot read data
outside of the SQL Server process (for example, if someone stole the hard drive with
SQL Server database files on it). In addition, some applications would like the ability to
ensure all data, end-to-end, is encrypted from an SQL Server client application to SQL
Server and back.

SQL Server on Windows relies on Crypto API to encrypt and decrypt data with
routines like BCryptEncrypt (see `https://docs.microsoft.com/windows/desktop/`
`api/bcrypt/nf-bcrypt-bcryptencrypt` for more info). If you remember in the details
of the SQLPAL architecture in Chapter 1, API calls that need Linux Kernel support will
go through the Host Extension. I spoke with Mitchell Sternke, our engineering lead on
security for SQL Server on Linux, to understand how we are able to support encryption
on Linux. In order to support cryptography APIs, we use the OpenSSL set of libraries
on Linux (see `https://www.openssl.org` for more information). One slight twist to the
architecture, as described by Mitchell, is that we deploy a special DLL in SQL Server 2017
for SQL Server on Windows (called secforwarder.dll), which when running on Windows
simply calls the Windows Crypto API support. But with SQLPAL on Linux, Crypto API
calls are forwarded to the Host Extension to call any necessary OpenSSL routines. We
use OpenSSL for all types of security needs, including support for TLS (and even for
Kerberos support).

SQL Server Keys and Certificates

When using techniques with SQL Server to encrypt data on SQL Server, you need to become familiar with the following objects, which are all created using T-SQL:

> **Service master key:** SQL encryption has a hierarchy, and it all starts with the service master key. The service master key is automatically generated by SQL Server at installation. All other keys and encryption of data will rely on the existence of this key. Therefore, if you are going to use SQL Server encryption, one of the very first things you absolutely need to do is back up this key to a secured location. Why? Because this is the top of the hierarchy of encryption; if this key were lost (e.g., the hard drive was damaged where SQL Server is installed), you would not be able to decrypt any data you encrypted. Ouch! Furthermore, when you back this up you use a password. You need to secure that password because you will need it to restore a backup of the key. You can read more about how to do this and the service master key at `https://docs.microsoft.com/sql/relational-databases/security/encryption/service-master-key`. The service master key will be used to encrypt other keys such as the database master keys and linked server passwords.

Note   Encrypted connections and a feature called Always Encrypted do not rely on this hierarchy.

> **Database master key:** This is a key protected by the service master key that is used to protect certificates and other objects in a database. To use functionality like Transparent Data Encryption (TDE) and encrypted backups, you will create a database master key in the master database. To encrypt column data (not Always Encrypted columns), you will create a database master key in a user database. You can read more about database master keys at `https://docs.microsoft.com/sql/t-sql/statements/create-master-key-transact-sql`. Just like the server master

key, once you create a database master key you should back it
up immediately. See our documentation on how to do this at
https://docs.microsoft.com/sql/relational-databases/
security/encryption/back-up-a-database-master-key.

SQL Server certificate: The third layer in the encryption hierarchy
is a certificate. A certificate will be protected by the database
master key and is used to encrypt other objects such as database
encryption keys (used for TDE), backups, and other keys used to
encrypt columns. You can use SQL Server to create a self-signed
certificate or load a certificate from a trusted authority. And like
the other objects I've discussed, you should back up any created
certificates because you will need to perform operations like
restoring an encrypted backup. You can read more about SQL
Server certificates at https://docs.microsoft.com/sql/t-sql/
statements/create-certificate-transact-sql.

Note   Extensible Key Management (EKM) is not currently supported on SQL
Server on Linux. Be sure to stay up to date with the release notes for any updates
to unsupported features at https://docs.microsoft.com/sql/linux/sql-
server-linux-release-notes#Unsupported.

Armed with this fundamental knowledge, let's look at some of the encryption
features available for SQL Server on Linux.

Transparent Data Encryption

TDE is a feature for SQL Server where data and transaction log files are encrypted as
they are written to disk. The encryption key (a database encryption key) to encrypt and
decrypt these files is maintained with the master database. This allows the database
engine to completely access the encrypted data on disk, but any program or user outside
the engine would not be able to get access to unencrypted data.

What is really nice about this feature is all the functionality for certificates and encryption is built into SQL Server. Here are the basic steps for using TDE:

1. Create a database master key in the master database using T-SQL.

2. Create a certificate protected by the database master key using T-SQL.

3. Create a database encryption key for the database you are using TDE for, protected by the certificate using T-SQL. A database encryption key is a special key used only for TDE. You can read more about the use of database encryption keys at `https://docs.microsoft.com/sql/t-sql/statements/create-database-encryption-key-transact-sql`.

4. Use ALTER DATABASE to enable TDE for the database.

SQL Server will then start encrypting data in the background to disk. Subsequent new writes to disk are encrypted as they are written. One key aspect to using this feature is that you should back up the certificate and keys. You will need these if you need to attach this database on another server or restore a backup. Any backup of the database is also encrypted for a database that has TDE enabled.

You can read more about setting up TDE on SQL Server on Linux at `https://docs.microsoft.com/sql/linux/sql-server-linux-security-get-started#enable-transparent-data-encryption`. You can also read more about TDE in general at `https://docs.microsoft.com/sql/relational-databases/security/encryption/transparent-data-encryption`.

Encrypting Database Backups

If you don't use TDE for a database, you also have the ability to encrypt your database backups. The process to do this is pretty much the same as TDE. You create a database master key (or use one you have already created), create a certificate, and then use the T-SQL BACKUP command specifying the certificate you created. Like TDE, we recommend you backup the database master key and certificate, as you will need them to restore the backup.

The example and steps to encrypt a database backup for SQL Server on Linux can be found at `https://docs.microsoft.com/sql/linux/sql-server-linux-security-get-started#configure-backup-encryption`. And you can find the complete documentation about backup encryption at `https://docs.microsoft.com/sql/relational-databases/backup-restore/backup-encryption`.

Encrypting Connections

SQL Server also supports encrypting data transferred between clients and the SQL Server engine across a network connection. SQL Server on Linux uses Transport Layer Security (TLS) to encrypt any data transmitted from a SQL Server client application or from the server. SQL Server on Linux currently supports TLS 1.2. You have options to force all connections to be encrypted by SQL Server (*server initiated*) or specific clients to request encryption from their application (*client initiated*).

The certificates and objects for encrypting connections are independent of the keys and certificates used inside SQL Server to encrypt data (i.e., the service master key, ...). As with other encryption and certificate functionality I've described to this point, encryption and certificate services used by SQL Server are provided by the Linux Operating System.

In order to configure SQL Server for encrypted connections, you will use a combination of the **openssl** program (which should be installed on your Linux server) and the **mssql-conf** configuration script that comes when you install SQL Server.

If you choose a client-initiated encrypted connection, each of the tools provided by Microsoft has an option to choose an encrypted connection. In addition, applications can add "**Encrypt=True**" to their connection string.

Sometimes the option to choose an encrypted connection with our tools is a bit hidden. Figure 7-8 shows the connection options for SQL Operations Studio.

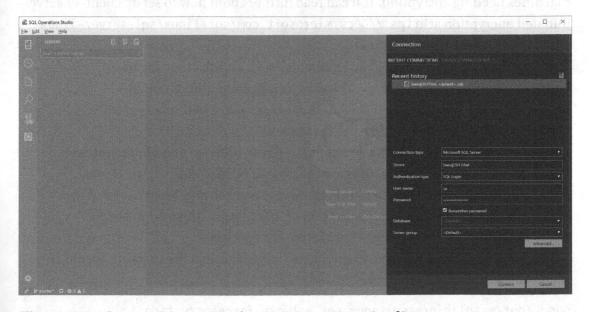

Figure 7-8. *Connection options for SQL Operations Studio*

If you click the Advanced button, you are presented with a new screen where you can pick the option to Encrypt the connection, as seen in Figure 7-9.

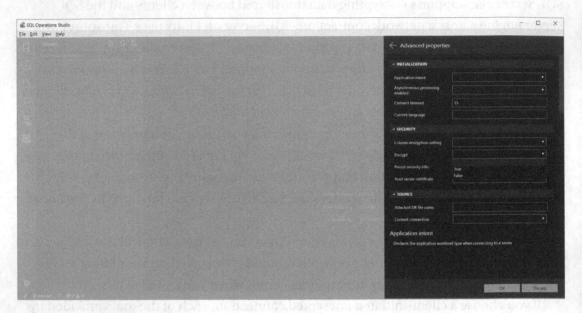

Figure 7-9. *Selecting option to encrypt a SQL Server connection*

SQL Server provides steps in the documentation on how to configure SQL Server with **openssl** and **mssql-conf** as well as instructions on how to configure client machines needing encryption. You can read further about how to set up client- or server-initiated encryption at `https://docs.microsoft.com/sql/linux/sql-server-linux-encrypted-connections`.

Furthermore, there are specific requirements for certificates to be used with this feature. See our documentation for certificate requirements at `https://docs.microsoft.com/sql/linux/sql-server-linux-encrypted-connections#requirements-for-certificates`.

Read through the instruction carefully for server-initiated encryption (force all connections) at `https://docs.microsoft.com/sql/linux/sql-server-linux-encrypted-connections#server-initiated-encryption` and client-initiated encryption at `https://docs.microsoft.com/sql/linux/sql-server-linux-encrypted-connections#client-initiated-encryption`.

If you read through these instructions you will notice that the steps are absolutely identical except for this one step:

```
sudo /opt/mssql/bin/mssql-conf set network.forceencryption 1
```

350

A value of 1 is used to force all connections to be encrypted, while a value of 0 is for client-initiated encryption scenarios.

Our documentation includes a few errors you might encounter using encrypted connections at `https://docs.microsoft.com/sql/linux/sql-server-linux-encrypted-connections#common-connection-errors`. Figure 7-10 shows an example of the error you will get when you try to use an encrypted connection but you have not set up encryption on SQL Server.

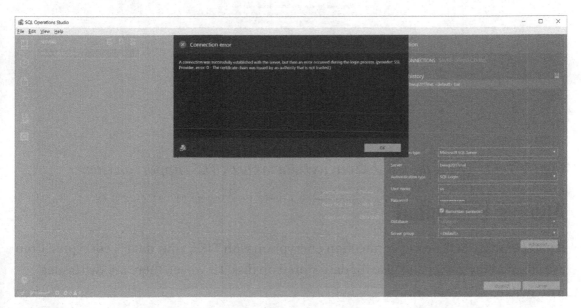

Figure 7-10. *An error connecting to SQL Server when encryption is not configured*

One note of guidance in our documentation is that your client machine has to support TLS 1.2. I honestly have never even concerned myself with whether my client computers support TLS 1.2, so I did a bit of research and found this very handy website to test my version of TLS, `https://www.ssllabs.com/ssltest/viewMyClient.html`. Figure 7-11 shows the results on my Windows laptop.

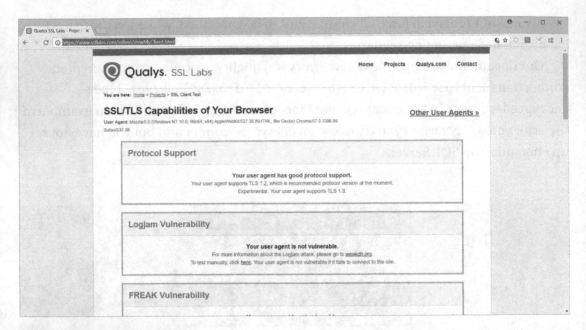

Figure 7-11. Using the ssllabs.com website to check TLS support on client

Always Encrypted

If you combine SQL Server connection encryption with TDE, your data is encrypted from the client to the server and also for data stored on disk. However, there are two issues with just these solutions:

- Data is not encrypted in memory in database pages.

- There is no separation of control over the keys for encryption, since the SQL Server Administrators control the encryption keys and certificates.

SQL Server has a feature to fill some of these gaps and provide an end-to-end encryption solution called **Always Encrypted**. The best way to describe Always Encrypted is with a diagram. Figure 7-12 shows the overall architecture of Always Encrypted.

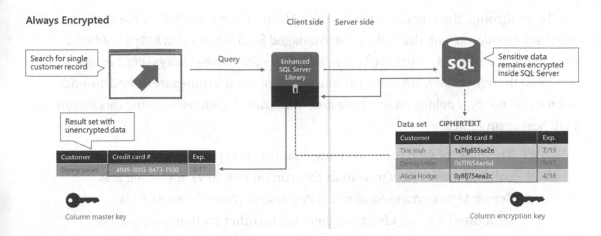

Figure 7-12. Always encrypted in SQL Server on Linux

On the Server side of this diagram is your database, with columns in tables you deem necessary to encrypt.

The process to set up Always Encrypted is to create a *column master key* where you supply the location of the key from a key store provider (hence separate of key administration). Then you create a *column encryption key* for column(s) you want to encrypt, specifying the column master key. While SQL Server administrators will create the column encryption key, the column master key is provided by someone else who manages a *key store* separate from SQL Server. So the only way to read encrypted data with this method is to use an application that has an SQL Server library that supports Always Encrypted and the location of the column master key. This means that even SQL Server administrators would not be able to decrypt the columns you choose. SQL Server administrators are needed to set up the database to encrypt certain columns, but they don't have full control to decrypt the data.

The application and the owners of the column master key have complete control over decryption. Furthermore, the data in the columns that are encrypted are encrypted in the application, across the connection to SQL Server, and in the data columns, whether they are in memory or written to disk. SQL Server will store metadata such as the encrypted column encrypted keys and only the location of the key store for the column master key.

Examples of SQL Server libraries that support Always Encrypted are https://docs. microsoft.com/sql/connect/odbc/using-always-encrypted-with-the-odbc-driver and https://docs.microsoft.com/sql/connect/php/using-always-encrypted-php-drivers.

To go through the process of configuring Always Encrypted, follow the steps in the documentation with the SQL Server Managed Studio Wizard at `https://docs.microsoft.com/en-us/azure/sql-database/sql-database-always-encrypted`.

Even though this is a very elegant solution to provide a transparent, end-to-end solution to encrypt column data, there are some considerations for using this feature for SQL Server on Linux:

- The only method today to create column encryption keys and specify column master keys uses tools that run on Windows, including SQL Server Management Studio and Powershell (Note: Powershell is supported now on Linux but there are no other methods supported currently native to Linux). SSMS comes with a cool wizard to walk you through the process at `https://docs.microsoft.com//sql/relational-databases/security/encryption/configure-always-encrypted-using-sql-server-management-studio`.

- Depending on how you configure Always Encrypted, there could be some limitations on how you are able to execute queries on columns that are encrypted (especially when you are searching for a value or range of values). See these types of restrictions in our documentation at `https://docs.microsoft.com/sql/relational-databases/security/encryption/always-encrypted-database-engine#feature-details`.

- There are some features that do not work with Always Encrypted, such as temporal tables and In-Memory OLTP.

- There could be some penalty in performance and extra storage required for columns that are encrypted.

Even with these limitations and potential performance penalty, you could have some data in your database (social security numbers, credit card data, ..) that is too sensitive to risk a breach or even risk users with SQL Server administrator access having access to this data. In these situations, Always Encrypted provides a complete end-to-end solution along with a clear separation of roles on encrypting and decrypting the data.

Encryption Summary

Figuring out how to use encryption with SQL Server can be a bit overwhelming. Let me summarize my recommendations on how to traverse our encryption features:

- No matter what type of encryption feature you decide to choose, always back up the service master key and all of your keys associated with encryption.

- You have to decide whether you actually really need encryption for your application. Many customers I've talked with decide not to use encrypted connections or Always Encrypted but almost always encrypt their backups.

- If you use SQL Server to create any keys or certificates, back them all up and store them in a separate location from your data backups. Consider any key or certificate as valuable as your data.

- TDE has some overhead on performance for I/O operations. However, if you have any concerns about anyone being able to access your data files outside of SQL Server, you should strongly consider using it. SQL Server databases on a laptop could be a good example (could be a second line of defense from Windows BitLocker).

- Always Encrypted is a great feature but it is not for all applications and databases. If you need a complete end-to-end encryption scheme and want to separate management of keys from the database, then Always Encrypted could be the right fit for you. Take advantage of the cloud by using Azure Key Vault as your key store provider. Check out how to do this at `https://docs.microsoft.com/azure/sql-database/sql-database-always-encrypted-azure-key-vault`.

Data Classification and Auditing

The introduction in May of 2018 of new rules for General Data Protection and Regulation (GDPR) in the European Union (see the official website at `https://ec.europa.eu/commission/priorities/justice-and-fundamental-rights/data-protection/2018-reform-eu-data-protection-rules_en`) has brought new attention to the topics of data classification, vulnerability, and data auditing.

The Microsoft SQL Server Engineering team recognizes these needs and has provided general guidance for organizations to prepare and handle GDPR regulations through the following document: http://aka.ms/gdprsqlwhitepaper.

In addition to guidance, SQL Server provides tools and features to assist in these areas, including SQL Server Management Studio and T-SQL commands to help with tagging and auditing.

Data Classification

An important aspect to understanding what data is stored in SQL Server is to be able to classify data according to an *information type* and *sensitivity level*. Examples of information types include Banking, Credentials, Health, and SSN. Examples of sensitivity levels are Public, Confidential, and Confidential GDPR. These types and sensitivity levels are fixed within the SQL Server Management Studio tool using the **Classify Data** functionality. This is also known as the **SQL Data Discovery and Classification** feature, as documented at https://docs.microsoft.com/sql/relational-databases/security/sql-data-discovery-and-classification.

You can access this feature in SSMS through the Tasks option when you right-click a database in Object Explorer in SSMS. Here is an example of this, as seen in Figure 7-13.

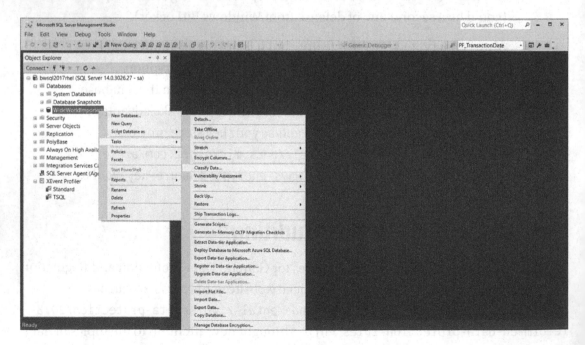

Figure 7-13. *SQL data dictionary and classification for SQL Server on Linux*

This feature has a fixed set of T-SQL statements that implement a dictionary of column names that might match information types and sensitivity levels. This dictionary is then matched against the current database. Figure 7-14 shows the results on SSMS for the WideWorldImporters Sample database.

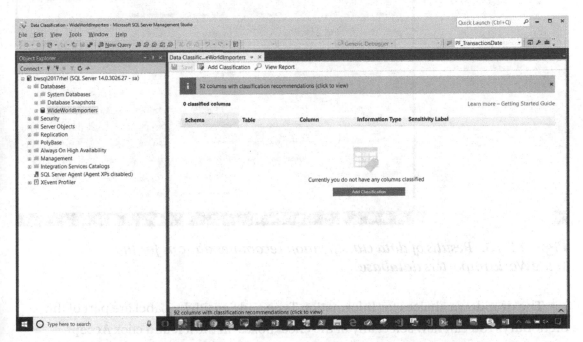

Figure 7-14. *Classification results for the WideWorldImporters database*

At the top of the report on the right-hand side, it shows 92 columns were found that match the dictionary for possible classification. Let's drill into the results and see why. If you click that gray bar at the top to see recommendations, your results should look like Figure 7-15.

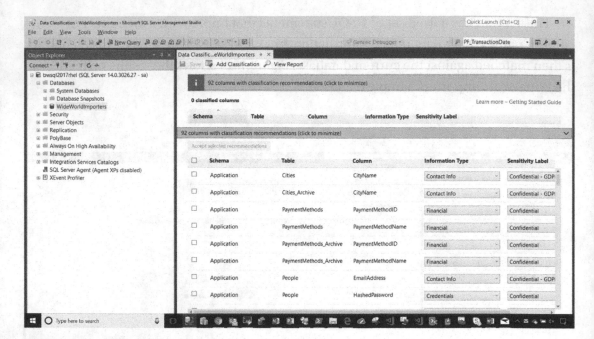

Figure 7-15. *Results of data classification recommendations for the WideWorldImporters database*

The dropdown choices for Information Type and Sensitivity Label are part of the dictionary. You can now select any of the checkboxes on the left and click **Accept selected recommendations**. The tool will save your changes once you click the Save icon. Now you can select the View Report option at the top of this screen to view a report of your classification choices and Sensitivity Labels.

Figure 7-16 shows a report from my WideWorldImporters database when I checked all columns and accepted the default recommendations.

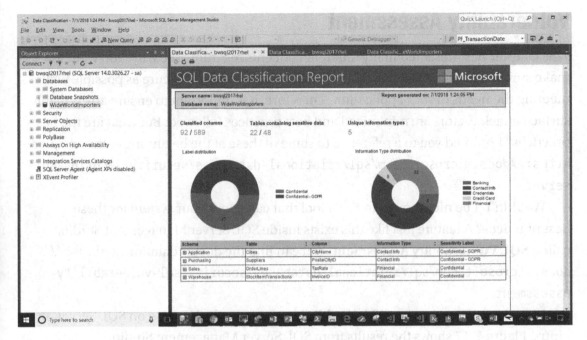

Figure 7-16. *Default classification report for WideWorldImporters*

Currently, this tool only works in SQL Server Management Studio. And the types, labels, and rules are fixed. However, all the logic behind this tool uses features of SQL Server as described in the documentation at `https://docs.microsoft.com/sql/relational-databases/security/sql-data-discovery-and-classification`.

The dictionary rules are a series of T-SQL statements you can capture using XEProfiler (as I described in Chapter 5). The classification types and labels are saved using a system stored procedure called **sp_addextendedproperty** (read more at `https://docs.microsoft.com/sql/relational-databases/system-stored-procedures/sp-addextendedproperty-transact-sql`). Using this procedure will save the data in system tables so you can retrieve them later. The point is, you can create our own classification scheme using this system stored procedure and the Extended Properties feature of SQL Server.

Vulnerability Assessment

This chapter has presented many different concepts regarding security. You want to make sure to configure SQL Server and your database to be as secure as possible while meeting the needs of your application. Therefore, it is important to ensure any possible surface attack vectors are minimized and best practices followed. But what are the best practices? I pointed you to a reference to some of these at the beginning of this chapter at `https://docs.microsoft.com/sql/relational-databases/security/securing-sql-server`.

Wouldn't it be nice though to run a tool that can check your system for these best practices? A feature just like this exists inside SQL Server Management Studio, called **SQL Vulnerability Assessment**. You can find the documentation at `https://docs.microsoft.com/sql/relational-databases/security/sql-vulnerability-assessment`.

I ran this tool against the WideWorldImporters sample database on SQL Server on Linux. Figure 7-17 shows the results from SQL Server Management Studio.

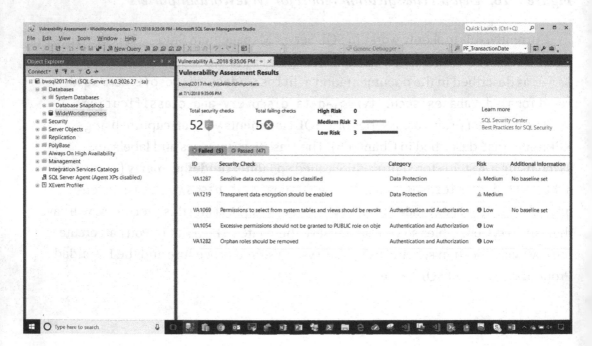

Figure 7-17. *SQL Server vulnerability assessment on the WideWorldImporters database*

As you can see from the rules that Failed, built into the Assessment tool, reviews metadata in the database involving areas such as classifying columns, enabling TDE, and ensuring authorization to objects and using roles follow best practices.

Even though this tool exists today only in SQL Server Management Studio, the tool displays for each rule the T-SQL statement used to check the security practice both for rules that pass and ones that fail.

Figure 7-18 shows an example of how to see the T-SQL query behind one of the rules that is flagged as a Low Risk for the WideWorldImporters database.

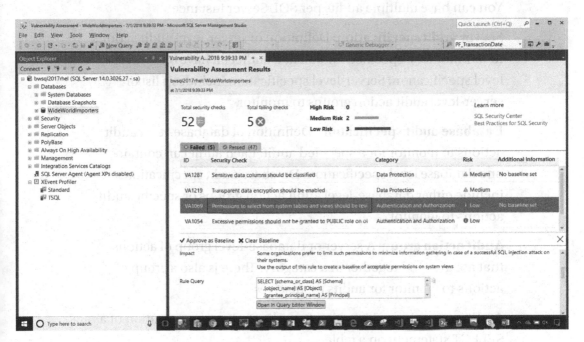

Figure 7-18. *Vulnerability assessment T-SQL query details*

Since the Vulnerability Assessment tool uses a series of T-SQL queries, I used the XEProfiler in SQL Server Management Studio and saved all queries in the **vulnassess.csv** example file for you to review and use in your own system.

In order to see assessments that apply to the SQL Server instance, use the tool against a system database like master.

SQL Server Audit

The final piece in the puzzle to secure your SQL Server is the ability to audit access to SQL Server and your data. SQL Server provides built-in capabilities to audit all aspects of access to the server instance and your database. The SQL Server Audit feature is implemented using **Extended Events**, which was described in Chapter 5. SQL Server Audit is made up of the following components:

> **Audit**: A monitored result of server or database level audit actions. You can have multiple audits per SQL Server instance.

> **Server audit specification**: Definition of server-level audit actions to monitor for a specified audit. Each audit can have one server level specification. Server-level specification includes a list of server-level audit action groups to monitor.

> **Database audit specification**: Definition of database-level audit actions to monitor for a specified audit. Each audit can contain one database level specification. Database audit specifications include either database-level audit action groups or specific audit actions to monitor.

> **Audit action group**: A server or database-level group of actions that are grouped together in a category. There is also a group of actions to monitor for audits themselves.

> **Audit action**: A specific action to audit, such as the execution of a SELECT statement on a table

> **Target**: The location where results of the audit are saved. For SQL Server on Linux, the only supported target is a file.

The process to use SQL Server Audit is the following:

1. Create the audit and define the target like the following T-SQL statement, as found in the example script **createsqlaudit.sql** connected as sa:

```
USE MASTER
GO
IF EXISTS (SELECT * FROM sys.server_audits WHERE name =
'AuditSQLServer')
```

```
BEGIN
    ALTER SERVER AUDIT AuditSQLServer WITH (STATE = OFF)
    DROP SERVER AUDIT AuditSQLServer
END
GO
CREATE SERVER AUDIT AuditSQLServer
    TO FILE (FILEPATH ='/var/opt/mssql')
GO
```

Tip   When you drop an audit, the previous target files are not automatically deleted. If you plan to run these demos more than once, you should delete the previous audit files in the target path.

---

2. Add in a server audit specification for successful logins with the following T-SQL statement, as found in the example script **addserveraudit.sql** (connect as sa when running this):

```
USE MASTER
GO
IF EXISTS (SELECT * FROM sys.server_audit_specifications WHERE
name = 'AuditSQLServerSpec')
BEGIN
    ALTER SERVER AUDIT SPECIFICATION AuditSQLServerSpec WITH
    (STATE = OFF)
    DROP SERVER AUDIT SPECIFICATION AuditSQLServerSpec
END
GO
CREATE SERVER AUDIT SPECIFICATION AuditSQLServerSpec
FOR SERVER AUDIT AuditSQLServer
    ADD (SUCCESSFUL_LOGIN_GROUP)
WITH (STATE = ON)
GO
```

The SUCCESSFUL_LOGIN_GROUP is an example of a server-level audit action group. You can find more examples in our documentation at https://docs.microsoft.com/sql/relational-databases/security/auditing/sql-server-audit-action-groups-and-actions.

3. Let's now add in a database audit specification to track who is trying to read from any table in the Sales schema in the WideWorldImporters database, using the following T-SQL statement as found in the example script **adddbaudit.sql** (connect as sa when running this):

```
USE [WideWorldImporters]
GO
IF EXISTS (SELECT * FROM sys.database_audit_specifications
WHERE name = 'AuditWWISpec')
BEGIN
    ALTER DATABASE AUDIT SPECIFICATION AuditWWISpec WITH
    (STATE = OFF)
    DROP DATABASE AUDIT SPECIFICATION AuditWWISpec
END
GO
CREATE DATABASE AUDIT SPECIFICATION AuditWWISpec
FOR SERVER AUDIT AuditSQLServer
ADD (SELECT ON SCHEMA::[Sales] BY public)
WITH (STATE = ON)
GO
```

You can read about other database audit actions in our documentation at https://docs.microsoft.com/en-us/sql/relational-databases/security/auditing/sql-server-audit-action-groups-and-actions#database-level-audit-actions.

4. Now turn on the audit using the following T-SQL statement, as found in the example script **startsqlaudit.sql** (connected as sa):

```
USE MASTER
GO
ALTER SERVER AUDIT AuditSQLServer WITH (STATE = ON)
GO
```

5. Let's test the audit. Connect to your Linux server as sa and run the following T-SQL statement, as found in the example script **readsalescustomers.sql**:

```
USE [WideWorldImporters]
GO
SELECT * FROM [Sales].[Customers]
GO
```

6. Now we can use the system procedure **sys.fn_get_audit_file** to read the audit trace by executing the following T-SQL statement, as found in the script **readauditlogs.sql** (connected as sa):

```
USE [WideWorldImporters]
GO
SELECT event_time, action_id, session_id, object_name, server_
principal_name, database_principal_name, statement, client_ip,
application_name
FROM sys.fn_get_audit_file ('/var/opt/mssql/auditsqlserver*.*',
default,default)
GO
```

The results should look similar to Figure 7-19.

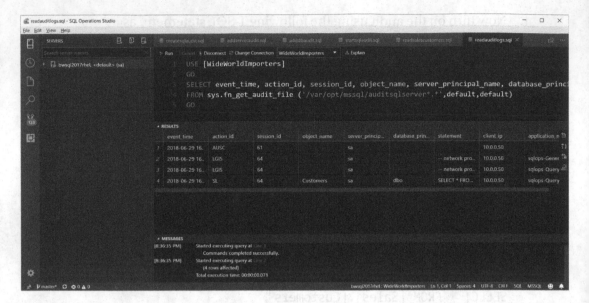

Figure 7-19. *SQL Server Audit example*

The action_id column comes from values as found in the DMV **sys.dm_audit_actions**. In this case, AUSC = AUDIT SESSION CHANGED, which is the audit to start the audit trace. LGIS = LOGIN SUCCEEDED, which is for the new connection by sa to run the query against WideWorldImporters (there is another login because of the nature of how SQL Operation Studio connects. You can see that from the application_name. It's another great reason to Application Name your application!). The action_id SL = SELECT, which shows the trace of dbo running a SELECT statement to access the Customers table. Notice the audit also includes data like the IP address of the client. The complete set of columns for sys.fn_get_audit_file is documented at https://docs.microsoft.com/sql/relational-databases/system-functions/sys-fn-get-audit-file-transact-sql.

Note   SQL Server Management Studio provides user interface options to create and manage audits and view audit logs. Read more at the following resources:

https://docs.microsoft.com/sql/relational-databases/security/auditing/create-a-server-audit-and-server-audit-specification #SSMSProcedure

https://docs.microsoft.com/sql/relational-databases/security/auditing/view-a-sql-server-audit-log#SSMSProcedure.

The complete list of T-SQL statements, DMVs, and catalog views related to audit can be found in our documentation at `https://docs.microsoft.com/sql/relational-databases/security/auditing/sql-server-audit-database-engine#creating-and-managing-audits-with-transact-sql`.

Given how important auditing can be, there are options with SQL Server Audit to ensure SQL Server will shut down or not start if auditing fails for any reasons. Read more about this and other considerations for SQL Server Audit at `https://docs.microsoft.com/sql/relational-databases/security/auditing/sql-server-audit-database-engine#creating-and-managing-audits-with-transact-sql`.

Summary

You have now been through an extensive study of performance and security for SQL Server on Linux. In this chapter I covered the fundamentals of logins and users, discussed using Active Directory Authentication, showed you how to set up Permissions and Access, described the different options for encryptions of data and network connections, and concluded the chapter by showing you features for data classification and auditing. The next important topic to build out a production SQL Server story is high availability and disaster recovery (HADR).

CHAPTER 8

High Availability and Disaster Recovery for SQL Server

While performance and security are critical features that any world-class database engine and platform must provide, production workloads and databases need high availability and features that support a robust disaster recovery plan. SQL Server is a database platform that includes rich features and options for both high availability and disaster recovery needs.

In this chapter, I will cover the three most important functional areas for both high availability and disaster recovery included with SQL Server on Linux:

- Backup and Restore
- Always On Failover Cluster Instance
- Always On Availability Groups

One other solution I will not cover in this book is called *Log Shipping*, which you can read more about at https://docs.microsoft.com/sql/linux/sql-server-linux-use-log-shipping. Another great resource related to this topic is called *Business Continuity*, which you can read at https://docs.microsoft.com/sql/linux/sql-server-linux-business-continuity-dr.

Backup and Restore

I love this quote from our documentation: "The SQL Server availability features do not replace the requirement to have a robust, well tested backup and restore strategy, the most fundamental building block of any availability solution" (you can read this at https://docs.microsoft.com/sql/linux/sql-server-linux-business-continuity-dr#sql-server-2017-scenarios-using-the-availability-features).

That pretty much sums up the importance of backups. Here is a quote I've always used: "Your data is only as good as your backups." In 25 years of experience working with SQL Server, I've never seen anything else taken more for granted then having a solid backup strategy. I've worked with customers who have run their entire production business with SQL Server for *months* without a good backup. And of course, it just takes the first time you have a failure where you need a backup to realize how important it truly is.

Let's explore then the fundamentals and details of backing up and restoring databases in SQL Server on Linux, including an important related topic, database recovery.

Database Backup

I've not shown you an example of a backup yet, but we have used the T-SQL RESTORE statement to restore the WideWorldImporters database backup (you may be tired of doing that at this point in the book). Furthermore, I did talk about encrypting backups in Chapter 7. The fundamentals of backing up your database are quite simple. It is the mechanics of developing a good backup strategy to meet the needs of our application and business that is more complex.

Full Database Backup

Let's start the discussion of backups with an easy example using the WideWorldImporters database. Let's say you just want to take a backup of the current state of the database. You could do that with this T-SQL statement connected as sa (or a database owner or a member of the db_backupoperator role) with your favorite SQL Server tool (or whatever database owner you may be using from examples in the book). This statement is found in the example **backupwwi.sql:**

```
BACKUP DATABASE WideWorldImporters
TO DISK = '/var/opt/mssql/data/wwi.bak'
WITH INIT, STATS=5, CHECKSUM
GO
```

The results of running this in SQL Operations Studio look like Figure 8-1.

Figure 8-1. *A full database backup of the WideWorldImporters database*

The result of this statement is a *full database backup* of the WideWorldImporters database written to a file called /var/opt/mssql/data/wwi.bak (there is no requirement on the file extension. I use .bak as a method to help me know the type of file). By default, SQL Server will write backup files to the /var/opt/mssql/data directory, but you can change this with mssql-conf (see our documentation at `https://docs.microsoft.com/sql/linux/sql-server-linux-configure-mssql-conf#backupdir`). A full database backup contains all the allocated pages from database files, the active transaction log, and metadata about the backup. The internal format of an SQL Server backup is defined by the Microsoft Tape Format (MTF) protocol. This is not an open source protocol, and you really don't need to know the internals of what is in the backup format (but if you are really, really interested, this website has the original protocol documented at `http://laytongraphics.com/mtf/MTF_100a.PDF`).

> **Tip**   Want to see some of the details of MTF? Enable trace flags 3216 and 3605 and you can see these details in the ERRORLOG file. Trace flag 3216 is not documented or supported, so I do not recommend using this in production. Remember mssql-conf can be used to set trace flags, as discussed in our documentation at `https://docs.microsoft.com/sql/linux/sql-server-linux-configure-mssql-conf#traceflags`.

I used a few options with this BACKUP DATABASE command that are fairly common:

> **TO DISK**: DISK is a type of backup device and is the most common one used. We technically support TAPE (unfortunately, I spent a great deal of my career dealing with SQL Server tape backup problems for customers. I know, showing my age) and a type called **URL**. URL is a nice feature that allows you to back up a database directly to Azure Blob Storage. See `https://docs.microsoft.com/sql/relational-databases/tutorial-sql-server-backup-and-restore-to-azure-blob-storage-service` in our documentation for more information. The path for a disk backup can be any valid Linux path, including mounted drives from networks or local disks. The only requirement is that the mssql user must have permissions to write to the target directory.

> **WITH INIT**: SQL Server by default allows you to save multiple backups into a single file. Using INIT basically overwrites anything in the current file if it already exists. If you didn't specify INIT, the default would be to append the current backup to the end of the file.

> **Tip**   You may also want to consider using FORMAT as well with INIT to completely start a new formatted backup file. I've seen situations where I wanted to back up over an existing file on disk, but the backup file was damaged. I needed to use FORMAT and INIT to completely start a new file (or remove the existing file on disk first).

STATS=5: STATS is a "progress indicator" option by percent compete. I included this to demonstrate backups are executed by parallel workers. I'll discuss what I mean by this when talking more about the results just following this. STATS can also be handy if you have an exceptionally long backup to run on-demand to see its progress.

CHECKSUM: By default, SQL Server uses a checksum algorithm to ensure database pages are physically consistent after being written to disk. I'll talk more about this later in the book. Based on this same concept, backup files can also have a checksum.

Using this option does two things:

1. If the database is enabled for a checksum with the PAGE_VERIFY option, the backup operation will verify database page checksums as it reads each page. If the checksum fails, the backup will fail (unless the CONTINUE_AFTER_ERROR option is used).

2. A checksum is computed for the entire backup file and stored with the backup MTF formatted file. I'll talk about how this can be effectively used to verify backup files using RESTORE later in the chapter.

You can enable checksum for all backups by default by using the **backup checksum default** server configuration option, as documented at https://docs.microsoft.com/sql/database-engine/configure-windows/backup-checksum-default.

Besides the "stats" messages in the result of the BACKUP command, the other messages indicate how many database pages were backed up for each filegroup and transaction log of the database. This can give you a feel for the size of the backup. Remember only allocated pages are backed up, so backups are generally not as large as the database files themselves. In addition, the last message indicates how many total pages were backed up in the database, the total duration for the backup to execute, and a rate of backup speed.

Other metadata and information about the backup are recorded in the ERRORLOG with a message like this:

```
Database backed up. Database: WideWorldImporters, creation date(time):
2018/06/29(01:36:22), pages dumped: 60981, first LSN: 626:25064:2, last
LSN: 627:18664:1, number of dump devices: 1, device information: (FILE=1,
TYPE=DISK: {'/var/opt/mssql/data/wwi.bak'}). This is an informational
message only. No user action is required.
```

Tip   Some users find having these messages with every backup command makes for a noisy ERRORLOG. Therefore, you can use trace flag 3226 to suppress backup (and restore) messages in the ERRORLOG.

In addition to the ERRORLOG, backup information is also recorded in the **msdb** database in tables like **backupfile**, **backupfilegroup**, and **backupmediaset**, among others.

I said that backups are done with parallel worker threads and the results from Figure 8-1 prove it. I say this because the main backup worker thread is the one displaying the stats information, while other workers read from database files and write to the target device. The interleaved results demonstrate this behavior. Typically, SQL Server will create one worker thread for reading for each unique disk across all files for the database and one worker thread for writing for each unique disk for target database backup files (you can partition out the backup by specifying multiple files even across multiple disks).

There are several options for the BACKUP DATABASE command. You can see all of them in our documentation at https://docs.microsoft.com/sql/t-sql/statements/backup-transact-sql. One option that may be interesting to use is COMPRESSION. SQL Server will compress the backup file to help reduce space requirements. There are some considerations when using COMPRESSION with TDE, and the preceding documentation reference contains the details.

Database backups are completely online, which means that you can actively use the database during a backup.

Note Technically there are some operations that can block a backup and vice versa. These include ALTER DATABASE and other operations that need an exclusive database lock.

The BACKUP DATABASE T-SQL statement also allows you to only back up specific files or filegroups. There could be scenarios for large databases where creating a full database backup takes too long for your business needs. Therefore, if you have multiple files or use secondary filegroups, you can create your backups in stages. The preceding documentation reference for the BACKUP DATABASE command describes how to back up files or filegroups. Carefully read through the process for backing up specific files or filegroups before using this as a backup strategy.

Recovery Models

I've described in the book that the transaction log is a record of changes to the database (much like a journal). Before I describe the concept of backing up the transaction log, I should first describe a concept called a *recovery model*. A recovery model dictates how transaction log space is managed and what kind of *media recovery* is possible. Media recovery determines what options exist to recover a database from backup media should the database and/or transaction log files become damaged or unusable. This translates into what kind of exposure you are willing to accept for data loss. SQL Server supports the following recovery models:

> **Simple:** Space in the transaction log is reclaimed automatically after a period of time based on transactions that are complete (also called *log truncation*). You cannot back up the transaction log with this model. Your data loss exposure is that you might lose changes since your last database backup because not all transactions in the transaction log are saved. This would of course only occur if the database and transaction log files became damaged or unusable (for example, the disk holding these files becomes damaged). Use this recovery model for scenarios where you only plan to back up the full database, typically for smaller databases where data loss for changes in between backups are acceptable.

Full: This is the default recovery model. With this model, all media recovery options are possible because the transaction log is never automatically reclaimed. All transactions are saved in the transaction log until a transaction log backup is taken. In fact, one of the most common issues I've seen with customers who say their transaction log file keeps growing unexpectedly is that they are using full recovery but have never backed up the transaction log. With full recovery, you can recover to any point in time based on your sequence of database and transaction log backups. Full recovery also allows you to use features such as Always On Availability Groups, which are not allowed for databases using the simple recovery model. Use this model for production databases where you want to minimize data loss exposure.

Bulk logged: This recovery model is a good fit for databases where you often bulk insert. This model works just like a Full recovery model except it allows bulk copy operations to be minimally logged reducing the amount of space in the transaction log. Minimally logged operations allow for fast and efficient bulk operations. You can read more about minimally logged operations at https://docs.microsoft.com/sql/relational-databases/ import-export/prerequisites-for-minimal-logging-in- bulk-import. This recovery model though does have a data loss exposure for bulk operations, since the most recent transaction log backup. This model also does not allow options like point-in-time restore, nor can it be used with Always On Availability Groups.

For a complete read on SQL Server recovery models, see our documentation at https://docs.microsoft.com/sql/relational-databases/backup-restore/ recovery-models-sql-server.

Transaction Log Backup

If you plan to use the Full recovery model, then you don't want to always have to back up the full database as the only way to recover from situations like disk failures. Furthermore, as I described, you don't want the transaction log file to keep growing until you run out of disk space. Therefore, SQL Server provides an option with the BACKUP LOG T-SQL statement to back up the transaction log. In order to back up the transaction log, you first must have executed one BACKUP DATABASE statement.

Most of the options exist for BACKUP LOG just like BACKUP DATABASE. You have the option to not use the WITH INIT option here to keep all of your log backups in a single file, or use WITH INIT to keep them in separate files.

While a full database backup contains all the current allocated pages and the current active transaction log, a transaction log backup contains all the changes in the transaction log since the *last transaction log backup* (or the last database backup if it is the first log backup). Therefore, transaction log backups are typically collected in a *log chain*. Consider the example in Figure 8-2 for a log chain.

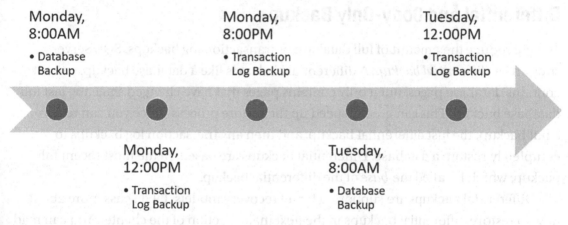

Figure 8-2. *A log chain example*

The transaction log backup on Monday at 12:00PM contains all changes in the transaction log since the Database Backup at 8:00AM. The Monday 8:00PM transaction log backup contains all changes in the log backup at 12:00PM. The Tuesday 12:00PM transaction log backup contains all the changes since the Monday 8:00PM transaction log backup.

I'll talk more about understanding how to apply the sequence of a log chain of backups in the next section on Restore. Your data loss exposure when using transaction log backups are any changes made in between log backups. Therefore, you must make a business decision on how often to back up the transaction log based on your data loss exposure requirements (Note: Later in this chapter we will talk about using other technologies like Always On Availability Groups to minimize this exposure even further).

The common terms in the industry related to these decisions are called *Recovery Time Objective* (RTO) and *Recovery Point Objective* (RPO). RTO is a targeted duration of time to restore an application after a disruptive event. RPO is the maximum amount of changes lost for a time interval the application can accept after a disruptive event. So, for example if your RTO is four hours and RPO is 15 minutes, you will need to ensure you create log backups every 15 minutes and devise a scheme where you can restore a database backup and a series of log backups in 4 hours.

One interesting scenario I'll discuss during the next section on restore is a Tail-Log Backup. You can read more information about Transaction Log Backups in our documentation at `https://docs.microsoft.com/sql/relational-databases/backup-restore/transaction-log-backups-sql-server`.

Differential and Copy-Only Backup

To help reduce the amount of full database or transaction log backups, SQL Server supports a *differential backup*. A differential backup is like a database backup, since it contains database pages, but it only contains pages that have changed since the last full database backup. This can greatly speed up the restore process, since you can restore a full backup, the last differential backup, and then any transaction log backups to completely restore a database. Differential backups are based on the most recent full backup, which is called the *base* of the differential backup.

Differential backups are supported for all recovery models. I'll discuss more about how to restore differential backups in the next major section of the chapter. You can read more about differential backups in our documentation at `https://docs.microsoft.com/sql/relational-databases/backup-restore/transaction-log-backups-sql-server`.

A *copy-only backup* is a database or log backup that does not affect the sequence of backups, the log chain, or differential base. There could be situations where you want to create a database or log backup independent of a backup strategy already in place. Use the WITH COPY_ONLY option of the T-SQL BACKUP statement to create a copy-only backup. Read more about copy-only backups in our documentation at `https://docs.microsoft.com/sql/relational-databases/backup-restore/copy-only-backups-sql-server`.

Database Snapshots

I had no great place in this book to add in the concept of a database snapshot, but adding it here with backups seems logical because it can be part of a high-availability solution. Database snapshots also can be used during RESTORE, so I'll introduce the topic first here.

Database Snapshots are a read-only, static view of a database at a point in time. They provide a great method to have a view of your data or revert from a mistake based on a specific point in time, rather than having to restore a sequence of backups using point-in-time restore.

Database snapshots are stored as a file on disk using a concept called *sparse files*. This means that when you first create a snapshot, it is small in size. As you make changes to the database, the original version of database pages is copied to the snapshot. This means the more changes that occur over time, the larger the snapshot. You use database snapshots just like databases. SQL Server will attempt to obtain database pages from the snapshot first. If they don't exist in the snapshot, it means the pages were not changed from the original database and the page is retrieved from the database itself. Snapshots are not a substitute for your backup strategy but are very convenient for interesting situations. For example, if you are going to make major changes to a database for a project, create a database snapshot. If you make a major mistake, you can quickly revert the database with the snapshot. If you don't need it, you can easily just drop the snapshot.

Pages written to the snapshot file can add an I/O performance cost to SQL Server database operations, so I recommend you keep snapshot files on separate disks from SQL Server database and transaction log files.

You can read more about creating snapshots, further benefits, and limitations of snapshots in our documentation at https://docs.microsoft.com/sql/relational-databases/databases/database-snapshots-sql-server.

VDI and Snapshot Backup

SQL Server supports a special device not listed in the standard documentation, called a *virtual device*. The Virtual Device Interface (VDI) is a specification for developers to build applications that can accept a backup as a stream of data from SQL Server to a program. The program can then process the stream of data in any number of ways. You can find an example of how to build a VDI application at https://github.com/Microsoft/sql-server-samples/tree/master/samples/features/sqlvdi-linux.

The BACKUP T-SQL statement supports VDI backups using a TO VIRTUAL_DEVICE option. In addition, VDI backups support a concept called *snapshot backups.* Snapshot backups allow a VDI program to copy the SQL Server database and log files directly to another storage device instead of relying on a stream of data from the backup from SQL Server. SQL Server recognizes the WITH SNAPSHOT option for BACKUP and will freeze I/O on all files until the VDI application acknowledges the snapshot (like a file copy) is complete.

An older blog post but a good one explaining how VDI works can be found at `https://blogs.msdn.microsoft.com/sqlserverfaq/2009/04/28/informational-shedding-light-on-vss-vdi-backups-in-sql-server/`.

There are a few specifics to using VDI backups on SQL Server on Linux. Read about these details in our documentation at `https://docs.microsoft.com/sql/linux/sql-server-linux-backup-vdi-specification`.

The complete VDI specification for developers can be found at `https://www.microsoft.com/download/details.aspx?id=17282`. (Don't be shocked when you open this file after unzipping it. It is called vbackup.chm, which is an old Microsoft Help format, and the file says SQL Server 2005 specification. It is still valid for SQL Server 2017!)

System Database Backup

System databases, except for tempdb, can be backed up like any other user database. The question is should you backup system databases? The answer is yes, but I recommend you really only need a full database backup of system databases and you may not need to do them often. For example, unless you change the model database, just back it up after installation and you may never need to back it up again.

I will discuss in the next section a method to rebuild system databases as they were after installation, but it is far simpler to restore a system database backup, and it provides a method to restore any changes made within them. You can read more about backup and restore of system databases in our documentation at `https://docs.microsoft.com/sql/relational-databases/backup-restore/back-up-and-restore-of-system-databases-sql-server`.

Database Restore and Recovery

SQL Server provides several options to restore database backups, sequence of database differential, and log backups, and other methods to restore portions of a database such as piecemeal and page restore. In this section, I'll review all of these options plus information about restoring and recover of system databases. Part of restore is running recovery of the database, and since I've not addressed that topic in the book, this is a good time to review how database recovery works and how it affects both restore and database startup. As a reference point, a great overview of all the restore options is in our documentation at https://docs.microsoft.com/sql/relational-databases/backup-restore/restore-and-recovery-overview-sql-server.

Database Recovery

In order to ensure transactions are consistent between what is recorded in the transaction log and database pages on disk, SQL Server will run recovery against a database in certain situations. I discussed before in the book the concept of Write Ahead Logging (WAL). Because of this method of durability, at any point in time there could be transactions that are in the transaction log that are not reflected on database pages on disk. Furthermore, there could be transactions in the transaction log that are not committed but are reflected on database pages on disk (because of, e.g., a Lazy Write).

When SQL Server has to restore a backup or bring a database online, it will examine the transaction log to see whether it should reconcile these possible inconsistencies between the log and database pages. The transaction log is the *source of truth* in this process. This process of recovery is done in the following phases, as described in Figure 8-3.

Figure 8-3. *Phases of database recovery*

Analysis: SQL Server will find which pages may have been dirty since the last checkpoint and the state of uncommitted transactions. SQL Server uses this analysis to properly execute the other phases of recovery, redo and undo.

Redo: Start at the oldest active transaction and redo any committed transactions in the transaction log that are not reflected on databases pages listed in the transactions (this is also called rolling forward transactions). SQL Server can perform this operation in parallel with multiple worker threads, which is an optimization we made in SQL Server 2016 to accelerate recovery performance.

Undo: Start with the oldest active transactions in the log and make sure that any transactions that are not committed are **not** reflected in database pages listed in the transactions (this is also called rolling back).

SQL Server understands how to compare a transaction in the transaction log and whether it is reflected on a database page by looking at something called a *log sequence number* (LSN). Each transaction is stamped with an LSN, and any database page that is modified has the LSN of the transaction that modified it. LSN values are incremented sequentially. Therefore, it is easy to compare an LSN in the log and a database page and know whether that change was applied or not.

In some situations for Enterprise Edition, SQL Server can use *fast recovery*, where it can allow the database to become online after the redo phase as locks are obtained for undo operations. That situation does not apply to restore but for situations where the database is brought online, like crash recovery of SQL Server (after an unexpected shutdown).

Understanding the concept of recovery is important for restore sequences to know when recovery is applied to transactions that are contained in database or log backups.

Restoring a Database

Let's start looking at restore with some basics of restoring a full database backup. Using the backup you created earlier in the chapter (wwi.bak), execute the following T-SQL statement as found in the example script **restorewwiheaderonly.sql**:

```
RESTORE HEADERONLY FROM DISK = '/var/opt/mssql/data/wwi.bak'
GO
```

This option for restore will examine the backup file (the MTF format) and return information that is contained in the metadata header of the backup file. This is helpful to find out information about what is contained in a backup (especially if you are not sure what is in the backup).

Figure 8-4 shows the results of this command.

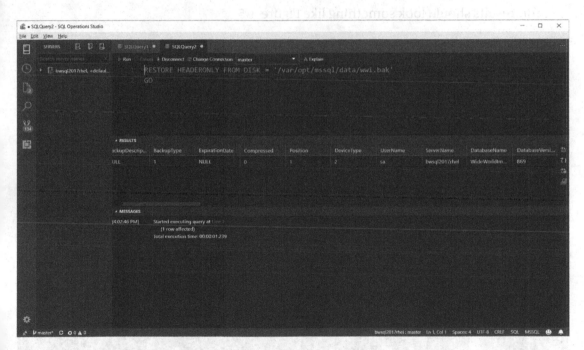

Figure 8-4. *RESTORE HEADERONLY in SQL Server*

In these results, BackupType = 1 is a full database backup. There are many other fields in this result set that describe the backup, including when the backup was taken and what options where used (like WITH CHECKSUM).

One of the pieces of metadata in a database backup is the original file path of all the database and log files. When you restore a backup, SQL Server will attempt to create these files to build the database in the exact file path location when the database was backed up. This might create a problem for you if you are attempting to restore a backup where the original file paths don't exist (and you cannot create them). Therefore, you will have to use syntax supported by the RESTORE T-SQL statement to move the database and/or log files. But how do you know what the files and original paths are to move? This is where the following very handy option for RESTORE exists, called FILELISTONLY. Execute the following T-SQL statement as found in the example **restorewwifilelistonly.sql**:

```
RESTORE FILELISTONLY FROM DISK = '/var/opt/mssql/data/wwi.bak'
GO
```

You results should look something like Figure 8-5.

Figure 8-5. *RESTORE FILELISTONLY in SQL Server*

You can see from the results the logical names of the files and the physical file paths. So, let's say you wanted to restore this backup, but instead of putting the database in their original file paths you needed them to be created in a different directory.

Here is an example of how to do this with the following T-SQL statement, found in the example **restorewwimove.sql**:

```
RESTORE DATABASE WideWorldImporters
FROM DISK = '/var/opt/mssql/data/wwi.bak'
WITH MOVE 'WWI_Primary' to '/var/opt/mssql/WideWorldImporters.mdf',
MOVE 'WWI_UserData' to '/var/opt/mssql/WideWorldImporters_UserData.ndf',
MOVE 'WWI_Log' to '/var/opt/mssql/WideWordImporters.ldf',
MOVE 'WWI_InMemory_Data_1' to '/var/opt/mssql/WideWordImporters_InMemory_
Data_1',
REPLACE
GO
```

The results of this T-SQL statement should look like Figure 8-6.

Figure 8-6. *Moving files while restoring a database*

In this example I've restored the database, so the files are created in the /var/opt/ mssql directory instead of /var/opt/mssql/data. Also note the use of the REPLACE keyword since the database already exists. Using this keyword will cause SQL Server to delete the existing database and files and restore the new one.

Tip If you are restoring a database for disaster recovery purposes, I do not recommend using REPLACE. Instead, restore the database backup to a new name, keeping the original database. This is my own personal recommendation, because I've seen customer situations where the original database had some damage but the backup was invalid. Using REPLACE causes SQL Server to delete the original database before it restores the backup. If the backup fails, now you have no way to try to recover what was in the original database.

Earlier in this chapter I mentioned the use of the CHECKSUM option for backups. One nice advantage of using this feature is that you can verify the checksum of the backup media without restoring the entire database using the RESTORE VERIFYONLY option. If RESTORE VERIFYONLY comes back without an error, it is not a guarantee the restore will be work successfully including recovery (the only way to know for sure a backup will restore is to restore it, even on another server), but it does guarantee the backup media was not damaged after the backup was created.

Complete Database Restore

Let's use an example to look at a possible complete restore sequence based on backup options we have discussed in this chapter. Consider the following sequence of events in Figure 8-7.

Figure 8-7. *Database backup sequence before a crash*

At Tuesday at 1:00PM an event occurs where the database files are damaged, but in this example the current transaction log file is intact. How can you recover from this event and will you lose data? Provided the transaction log is really valid, you could end up with no data loss. Here is how and why.

Because we have a database backup and a series of log backups, we can do the following:

1. Back up the current "tail of the log." You can do this with the BACKUP T-SQL statement using the NO_RECOVERY option.

2. Restore the full database backup from the backup file wwi.bak. The difference here from the RESTORE examples I've shown you is that you will use the WITH NO_RECOVERY. SQL Server will actually apply redo logic after restoring the backup but not undo. When the restore is finished, the database is not available yet to use.

3. Restore the differential backup from the backup file wwi_diff1.bak. As with step #2, you will need the WITH NO_RECOVERY option. The database is still not available yet for use.

4. Restore the transaction log backup from the backup file wwi_log3.bak. This time use the RESTORE LOG statement, using WITH NO_RECOVERY. The database is still not available yet for use.

5. Restore the tail of the log backup you created in Step #1. Again, use RESTORE LOG WITH NO_RECOVERY. The database is still not available for use.

6. Execute the RESTORE DATABASE command but only with the WITH RECOVERY option to fully recover the database and bring it to a consistent state. The database should now be available with no data loss.

And because I created transaction log backups, even if the differential backup were not valid, I could restore all the log backups in sequence.

Let's see this in action by simulating a series of changes in the WideWorldImporters database with log and differential backups. For these examples, connect as sa or another sysadmin login you have created. To ensure these commands run correctly, run all of them from a tool like sqlcmd one at a time or use the same connection in a tool like SQL Operation Studio.

1. First, restore the WideWorldImporters full sample, as I've described in previous chapters, to its original state. I've included the **restorewwi.sh** and **restorewwi_linux.sql** scripts used in previous chapters.

2. It turns out the WideWorldImporters database is set for the SIMPLE recovery model, but we want to use the FULL recovery model for our examples. Execute the following T-SQL statement to change the recovery model to FULL for WideWorldImporters, as found in the example script **wwisetfull.sql**:

```
USE master
GO
ALTER DATABASE WideWorldImporters SET RECOVERY FULL
GO
```

Note   Databases using the simple recovery model have all types of recovery options except using transaction log backups, since you cannot create a transaction log backup using the simple recovery model. See our documentation for more information about complete database restores for a simple recovery model database at `https://docs.microsoft.com/sql/relational-databases/backup-restore/complete-database-restores-simple-recovery-model`.

---

3. Create a full database backup for the WideWorldImporters by executing the **backupwwi.sql** script as found earlier in this chapter:

```
USE master
GO
BACKUP DATABASE WideWorldImporters
```

```
TO DISK = '/var/opt/mssql/data/wwi.bak'
WITH INIT, STATS=5, CHECKSUM
GO
```

4. Execute the following T-SQL statements to create a new table in the WideWorldImporters database as found in the example script **letsgomavs.sql**:

```
USE WideWorldImporters
GO
DROP TABLE IF EXISTS letsgomavs
GO
CREATE TABLE letsgomavs (player char(50), number int)
GO
```

5. Now back up the transaction log to simulate the backup for Monday at 12:00PM by executing the following T-SQL statement found in the example script **backupwwilog1.sql**:

```
USE master
GO
BACKUP LOG WideWorldImporters TO DISK = '/var/opt/mssql/data/wwi_
log1.bak'
WITH INIT, CHECKSUM
GO
```

6. Now insert a row into the table I created using the following T-SQL statements found in the example script **insertdirk.sql**:

```
USE WideWorldImporters
GO
INSERT INTO letsgomavs VALUES ('Dirk Nowitski', 41)
GO
```

7. Now let's do another backup simulating the log backup for Monday at 8:00PM by executing the following T-SQL statement found in the example script **backupwwilog2.sql**:

```
USE master
GO
BACKUP LOG WideWorldImporters TO DISK = '/var/opt/mssql/data/wwi_
log2.bak'
WITH INIT, CHECKSUM
GO
```

8. Another insert into the table using the following T-SQL statements found in the example script **insertdennis.sql**

```
USE WideWorldImporters
GO
INSERT INTO letsgomavs VALUES ('Dennis Smith Jr.', 1)
GO
```

9. Now create a differential database backup using the following T-SQL statement found in the example script **backupwwidiff.sql**:

```
USE master
GO
BACKUP DATABASE WideWorldImporters
TO DISK = '/var/opt/mssql/data/wwi_diff1.bak'
WITH INIT, DIFFERENTIAL, CHECKSUM
GO
```

10. One more insert into the letsgomavs table (I'm building up my roster!) using the following T-SQL statement found in the example script **insertdeandre.sql**:

```
USE WideWorldImporters
GO
INSERT INTO letsgomavs VALUES ('DeAndre Jordan', 6)
GO
```

11. One last log backup simulating the backup on Tuesday at 12:00PM
     using the following T-SQL statement found in the example script
     backupwwilog3.sql

```
USE master
GO
BACKUP LOG WideWorldImporters TO DISK = '/var/opt/mssql/data/wwi_
log3.bak'
WITH INIT, CHECKSUM
GO
```

12. Now let's do one last insert, which according to our timeline is
     before Tuesday at 1:00PM, using the following T-SQL statement
     found in the example script **insertluka.sql**:

```
USE WideWorldImporters
GO
INSERT INTO letsgomavs VALUES ('Luka Doncic', 77)
GO
```

13. Now let's say at the simulated Tuesday 1:00PM time the database
     becomes unavailable, but you believe the disk holding the
     transaction log is intact. We definitely need these transactions to
     ensure the Dallas Mavericks NBA roster looks good (especially
     Luka, our #1 pick). The first step is to back up the current tail of the
     log using the following T-SQL statement, as found in the example
     script **backupwwitailoflog.sql**:

```
USE master
GO
BACKUP LOG WideWorldImporters TO DISK = '/var/opt/mssql/data/wwi_
tailoflog.bak'
WITH INIT, NO_TRUNCATE, CHECKSUM
GO
```

14. You have several recovery paths at this point. We could recover our data from the initial backup to any point in time in the sequence of backups and transactions. I don't want any data loss and I want to be up and running as fast as possible. Execute the following T-SQL statements as found in the example script **restorewwiall.sql:**

```
USE master
GO
RESTORE DATABASE WideWorldImporters FROM DISK = '/var/opt/mssql/
data/wwi.bak'
WITH REPLACE, NORECOVERY
GO
RESTORE DATABASE WideWorldImporters FROM DISK = '/var/opt/mssql/
data/wwi_diff1.bak'
WITH NORECOVERY
GO
RESTORE LOG WideWorldImporters FROM DISK = '/var/opt/mssql/data/
wwi_log3.bak'
WITH NORECOVERY
GO
RESTORE LOG WideWorldImporters FROM DISK = '/var/opt/mssql/data/
wwi_tailoflog.bak'
WITH NORECOVERY
GO
RESTORE DATABASE WideWorldImporters WITH RECOVERY
GO
```

15. If all is successful, I expect my four players still to be in my database. Verify this by executing the following T-SQL statement **mavstothenbafinals.sql:**

```
USE WideWorldImporters
GO
SELECT * FROM letsgomavs
GO
```

The results should look like Figure 8-8.

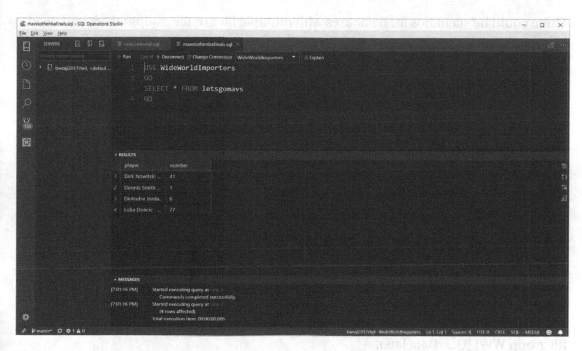

Figure 8-8.   *Recovering data using a series of backups in SQL Server*

That was a long sequence to go through, but it demonstrates how to use a series of backups to meet your RTO and RPO requirements. The one issue with the scheme I showed you is that the database is offline during the entire RESTORE sequence until the very last step (fast recovery doesn't work with restore). There are other methods for you to restore in a more online fashion, as described in the next section.

Another option for a restore sequence is a *point-in-time* restore. Point-in-time restores are available when using the RESTORE LOG T-SQL syntax. When you use a point-in-time restore, you specify with options WITH STOPAT=<time>, RECOVERY (since you will be recovering the database with this statement). You can restore an entire database and log backup sequence and then use a point-in-time restore as the final RESTORE LOG statement. Check out our documentation and examples for point-in-time restores at `https://docs.microsoft.com/sql/relational-databases/backup-restore/restore-a-sql-server-database-to-a-point-in-time-full-recovery-model`.

File, Piecemeal, and Page Restore

There could be scenarios for databases with multiple files or filegroups where you need to only restore a specific file or filegroup without having to restore the entire database, provided you have a file or filegroup backup you have created. You can restore files or filegroups offline or online (online is available for Enterprise Edition only). To see examples and scenarios to restore files or filegroups see the documentation at `https://docs.microsoft.com/sql/relational-databases/backup-restore/file-restores-full-recovery-model`.

If you have full database backups like the sequence I showed you in the previous section, it is possible to restore a database in phases called a *piecemeal restore*. A piecemeal restore allows you to bring filegroups online in phases vs. the entire database. This could be an interesting part of your RTO strategy because it is possible you can define RTO now at the filegroup level.

For example, for the sequence in the previous section for restoring the WideWorldImporters database, we could have changed up the restore sequence to something different. We could restore the primary filegroup first and then the secondary filegroup WWI_UserData later.

Note   A memory optimized data filegroup must be backed up and restored with the primary filegroup. Therefore, you need to create a database backup including the primary and memory optimized data filegroup and another backup including your secondary filegroups.

Using this technique allows users to access the data that's stored in primary filegroup faster, while the WWI_UserData filegroup can come online at a later time. Online piecemeal restores are only supported on the Enterprise edition. You can read more about piecemeal restores for a full recovery model database in our documentation at `https://docs.microsoft.com/sql/relational-databases/backup-restore/example-piecemeal-restore-of-database-full-recovery-model`.

The final example of a more granular restore option is a *page level restore*. This option allows you to restore specific pages in the database, should they become damaged. And the great part of this feature is that it can be done online (Enterprise edition only). Consider a scenario where a specific page or set of pages is reported to be damaged (either through an Msg 824 error, which I'll explain more in Chapter 9, or from DBCC CHECKDB).

You could use the methods I've described so far in this chapter to restore from a database, differential, file, filegroup, and/or log backups. Or you could use these backups to restore only the pages you need from them. You still need a valid log backup sequence to apply any changes to the pages after they are restored from a database backup. This is an extremely attractive feature to speed up your RTO if you can identify the problem to only a set of database pages.

It turns out SQL Server has some tools to help guide you. First, in the msdb database a table exists called **suspect_pages** that contains only pages that were found by SQL Server to be damaged. Second, SQL Server Management Studio has a tool called the Database Recovery Advisor, which provides recommendations based on the backup history found in msdb to guide you through point-in-time restores and database page restores. You can read more about this tool in our documentation at `https://docs.microsoft.com/sql/relational-databases/backup-restore/restore-and-recovery-overview-sql-server#DRA`.

You can read the complete guide to restoring pages in our documentation at `https://docs.microsoft.com/sql/relational-databases/backup-restore/restore-pages-sql-server`.

System Database Restore

I mentioned in the section on Backups in this chapter that you can backup master, model, and msdb like user databases. Let's take each system database and talk about the process to restore them from backups.

> **msdb**: This is the easiest of the three to restore, since SQL Server can start up even if this database is not accessible or is damaged. So, the process to restore msdb is just like any user database while SQL Server is running.

Tip   How do I know this? It is easy to test. First, shut down SQL Server. Then simply rename the msdbdata.mdf file and restart SQL Server. You can use this method to test out how SQL Server behaves if any system database is not available.

---

model: If a problem exists with the model database where it is still accessible, then you should be able to restore the database while SQL Server is online. However, if the model database cannot be started, SQL Server will attempt to start but immediately shutdown. Fortunately, there is a nice trick here to restore msdb in this situation. Enable trace flag 3608 (which says don't open any databases except for master) with mssql-conf and then start SQL Server. You should be able to go in and restore an msdb backup. After you do this, shut down SQL Server, disable the trace flag, and restart the service.

master: Like model, if the master database is available, you can restore a backup of master but only after starting SQL Server in "single user mode" (our documentation tells you how to do this at `https://docs.microsoft.com/sql/linux/sql-server-linux-troubleshooting-guide#start-sql-server-in-minimal-configuration-or-in-single-user-mode`). SQL Server will shut down by default after a restore of master. If the master database is not available, SQL Server fails to start immediately. In some cases, you can still restore a backup of master if you start SQL Server in "single user mode" and enable trace flag 3607 (this trace flag tells SQL Server to not recover master).

What if a backup is not available for any of these databases and you need them to function properly? There is an option to rebuild system databases from their original state at installation. The system databases are stored in one of the .sfp files I mentioned in Chapter 2. The method to rebuild these is documented at `https://docs.microsoft.com/sql/linux/sql-server-linux-troubleshooting-guide#rebuild-system-databases`. The process effectively uses a command line option for sqlservr called **-- force setup**. The problem with rebuilding system databases is that all of them are rebuilt together. If you have backups of some system databases, you could always rebuild a system database and then restore the backups you have. It is easy to forget that system databases like msdb do hold important information such as backup history and SQL Server agent job definitions.

Model is typically not a problem unless you have made changes to it (which is a good reminder to back up any T-SQL scripts you have used to modify model), but master is an issue. Losing the master database means you have lost logins, linked servers, and information about databases. But again, any object like a login you have created should be saved in a T-SQL script and backed up separately. And all user databases can be recognizable again by attaching them. You can read about how to attach a database in our documentation at `https://docs.microsoft.com/sql/relational-databases/databases/attach-a-database`.

Always On Failover Cluster Instance

Having backups to restore is essential for any high availability and disaster recovery strategy, there are other options that compliment backups but also provide better high availability. SQL Server provides features in a suite called *Always On* (I'm going to try and use the right terms for this chapter. Allan Hirt, a prominent MVP and HADR expert, always keeps me honest on these terms). One solution provides high availability for SQL Server instance failures across a cluster using a shared storage for data. Protection of the data must be done through a non-Microsoft hardware solution for the shared storage and SQL Server backups. High availability using this solution is called *Always On Failover Cluster Instance.* Always On Failover Cluster Instance and Always On Availability Groups (described in the next section) have one theme in common. The functionality of these features on Linux is pretty much the same as SQL Server on Windows, but the *configuration is different.* This is due to the differences in software components required to make these technologies work in Linux vs. Windows. Having said this, the way Always on Failover Clustering and Always On Availability Groups work under the covers with Linux is perhaps one of the areas that is more different than I've encountered in my journey with SQL Server on Linux. SQL Server engine functionality is exactly the same, but the manner in which Linux handles concepts like failover is in some cases quite different than Windows.

Many thanks for this and the next section of the chapter from my colleagues at Microsoft who specialize in HADR, including Sourabh Agarwal, Mihaela Blendea, Pradeep M, Brooks Remy, and Arnav Singh. Without them, I could not have navigated the complexity and functionality of Always On for SQL Server on Linux.

How It Works

For many years SQL Server has provided a failover cluster solution in conjunction with Windows Server Failover Clustering (WSFC). Always On Failover Cluster Instance (I'm going to call this FCI or SQL FCI for the rest of this chapter) for SQL Server on Linux relies on a similar solution that is open source, called *Pacemaker* (you can read more about the origins and details of Pacemaker at `http://clusterlabs.org/pacemaker/doc`). Pacemaker and its components such as *Corosync* are implemented by the various Linux distributions in various add-ons. For example, RHEL supports a component called *HA Add-On* (the details of the HA Add-On can be found at `https://access.redhat.com/documentation/en-us/red_hat_enterprise_linux/7/pdf/high_availability_add-on_overview/Red_Hat_Enterprise_Linux-7-High_Availability_Add-On_Overview-en-US.pdf`).

Note One learning for me as part of working with customers is that the RHEL HA Add-On can require a separate purchase from the standard RHEL license. SLES has the same concept for their HA extension. You can read more about SLES at `https://www.suse.com/products/highavailability`.

An SQL FCI is a set of SQL Server instances across a number of computers (nodes) that can participate in a failover high-availability solution called a cluster. However, with FCI, only one SQL Server instance is actively using the databases on shared storage among the nodes.

This diagram from the documentation at `https://docs.microsoft.com/sql/linux/sql-server-linux-shared-disk-cluster-concepts#the-clustering-layer`, as seen in Figure 8-9, describes the layers of software interacting with hardware to support an FCI for SQL Server on Linux.

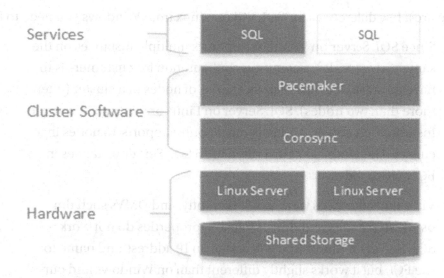

Figure 8-9. *FCI software and hardware components for SQL Server on Linux*

Looking more at Figure 8-9, Corosync is a framework for communications between Linux Servers or *nodes* that Pacemaker uses. In order for Pacemaker components to make decisions to failover resources across nodes based on a failover condition, a *resource agent* is required. A resource agent is similar to a resource DLL used in WSFC, which is used for health checks for failover, to handle the coordination of SQL Server FCI on Windows. The SQL Server resource agent for Linux is installed with the *mssql-server-ha* package.

Note   The SQL Server resource agent is now available on GitHub as an open-source project at `https://github.com/Microsoft/mssql-server-ha`. Since our resource agent is open-source, other vendors can build HADR solutions that work with SQL Server on Linux to provide high-availability functionality as an alternative to Pacemaker. One such example is HPE Serviceguard. You can read more about HPE Serviceguard at `https://www.hpe.com/us/en/product-catalog/detail/pip.hpe-serviceguard-for-linux.376220.html#`.

A great documentation reference for Always On FCI can be found at `https://docs.microsoft.com/sql/linux/sql-server-linux-ha-basics#pacemaker-for-always-on-availability-groups-and-failover-cluster-instances-on-linux`.

There are a few differences for SQL FCI on Linux from Windows you need to know:

- Since SQL Server on Windows supports multiple instances on the same server (node), a common configuration for customers is to have multiple SQL FCIs across a series of nodes in a cluster (often more than two nodes). SQL Server on Linux only supports a single instance on a server. And Pacemaker only supports 16 nodes in a cluster. Therefore, you are limited to 16 SQL Server instances in an FCI across nodes.

- Virtual IP addresses work a bit differently, and DMVs such dm_ os_cluster_nodes and dm_os_cluster_properties do not work on SQL Server on Linux. You will assign an IP address and name to the FCI, but it works slightly different than on Windows and our documentation as I referenced earlier describes how to set this up.

- You need to copy the service master encryption key manually from the primary node to all nodes, as SQL Server runs on each node as a local user called mssql.

- SQL Server FCI on Windows supports the tempdb database on a local disk (such as a fast SSD disk). This is not supported on SQL Server on Linux. All system databases must be in the /var/opt/mssql/data directory, which will be on the shared storage for the FCI.

- Pacemaker clusters have a concept called *fencing* or STONITH (Shoot the Other Node in the Head). You have to love Linux! This concept is required for Pacemaker clusters in production and is how the cluster manages poorly behaved nodes to not affect the entire cluster (hence the term fencing to fence off a node). Window Failover Clusters do not have this concept. I'll mention STONITH again in the section on Always On Availability Groups.

Note   At the time of writing of this book, STONITH is not supported with Hyper-V or Azure Virtual Machine. You can disable this, but Pacemaker is not officially supported without it. Microsoft expects to resolve this issue in the future so stay tuned to the documentation for updates.

Setup and Configuration

While the setup of SQL Server on Linux simply just beats the experience on Windows, setting up an FCI with SQL Server on Linux is quite frankly challenging. Windows Clustering provides graphical wizards and validation tools and processes. The experience on Linux is all command line driven, involves several different steps, and can be error prone.

The overall outline of the setup process for SQL Server FCI on Linux is as follows:

- Set up and configure your Linux server on at least two servers (nodes). Designate which ones will be *primary* and *secondaries*.

- Install SQL Server on Linux on each node and specific "add-ons" for HA depending on the Linux distribution.

- Create your user database(s) on the primary node.

- Prepare SQL Server on each node:

  - Stop and disable SQL Server on secondary nodes (systemctl has a disable option).

  - Create a new SQL Server login on the primary node and grant permissions to execute the system procedure sp_server_diagnostics by placing this login in the sysadmin role.

  - Stop and disable SQL Server on the primary node.

- Make sure each node has a unique computer name and add all nodes with IP addresses and names to the /etc/hosts file on all nodes.

- Configure shared storage to be used across all nodes and then move the databases from the primary node, including system databases, to shared storage. Shared storage for production scenarios is typically on a separate Linux server or external storage device. SQL Server supports the following shared storage protocols:

  - iSCSI: `https://docs.microsoft.com/sql/linux/sql-server-linux-shared-disk-cluster-configure-iscsi`.

  - NFS: `https://docs.microsoft.com/sql/linux/sql-server-linux-shared-disk-cluster-configure-nfs`.

  - SMB: `https://docs.microsoft.com/sql/linux/sql-server-linux-shared-disk-cluster-configure-smb`.

- Install and configure Pacemaker on all nodes. This will include providing Pacemaker with information about the SQL Server login you created earlier.

- Install the SQL Server resource agent on all nodes. The SQL Server resource agent utilizes the system procedure sp_server_diagnostics for failover decisions. I'll discus sp_server_diagnostics in the next section.

- Create FCI resources in a resource group for storage (your shared storage) and networking. As part of this, you will be creating an FCI IP address that can be used to connect to SQL Server as part of the FCI instead of the node IP address.

- Create the FCI resource using the resource group.

- Bring the FCI online.

- You should now be able to connect to the FCI IP address for SQL Server. You can manually failover SQL Server to ensure connectivity works. Pacemaker provides the functionality to manually failover, as seen in our documentation at `https://docs.microsoft.com/sql/ linux/sql-server-linux-shared-disk-cluster-operate`.

Not much of an outline; more like a book, right? Each step is carefully documented at `https://docs.microsoft.com/sql/linux/sql-server-linux-shared-disk-cluster-configure`. SQL Server on Windows Failover Clustering has almost as many steps, but there are tools to make this faster and help validate the details.

The bottom line is back to the theme I mentioned at the top of this section. SQL Server FCI on Linux is robust and provides a great instance high-availability solution on Linux just as it does on Windows. It just takes a bit more careful preparation and time to set up and configure.

Note   It is possible to add or remove a node from the SQL Server FCI after you have installed and configured. See our documentation on the steps for RHEL at `https://docs.microsoft.com/sql/linux/sql-server-linux-shared-disk-cluster-red-hat-7-operate#add-a-node-to-a-cluster`.

---

sp_server_diagnostics and failover

One of the main purposes for an SQL FCI is to keep the SQL Server instance as highly available as possible should a problem occur with the SQL Server instance or node hosting the instance. So how does Pacemaker (or WSFC for that matter) understand when a failover should occur, specific to SQL Server? The concept of a resource agent as I described earlier in this chapter defines that protocol.

And the SQL Server resource agent (much like the resource DLL in Windows) uses the system stored procedure **sp_server_diagnostics** to make this happen. This system procedure is another example of a *special* system stored procedure, because the source code for this stored procedure is not T-SQL but C++ code baked into the engine. The beauty of using this system stored procedure is that the SQL Server engine can include health checks about the engine itself (not just whether the instance is running) to help make decisions for a failover. sp_server_diagnostics is one of the coolest features we have produced for the engine. For example, sp_server_diagnostics produces health state information that is available to users even if Always On technologies are not used. I'll discuss how in Chapter 9.

The architecture for how sp_server_diagnostics works in conjunction with a failover is called the *flexible failover policy*. The concept is that there are levels of failover decision from the highest (Level 1 = SQL Server is "down") to the lowest (Level 5 = "query processing" is not healthy but SQL may be running). A complete list of the failover policies and how to configure them can be found at `https://docs.microsoft.com/sql/sql-server/failover-clusters/windows/failover-policy-for-failover-cluster-instances`. sp_server_diagnostics produces information about the health of SQL Server that line up with these policies. The details of health information provided by sp_server_diagnostics are documented at `https://docs.microsoft.com/sql/relational-databases/system-stored-procedures/sp-server-diagnostics-transact-sql`.

Since SQL Server on Linux is not as tightly coupled with Pacemaker as it is on Windows with WSFC; not all policies apply and the method in which you configure them is different.

Let me explain each of these policies (these policies will also apply to Always On Availability Groups). The lower the policy *number*, the less granular the check is to decide to failover the cluster. Each policy as you go to higher numbers is inclusive of all the policies before it.

1 – SERVER_UNRESPONSIVE_OR_DOWN: Fail if the SQL Server instance is unresponsive (unable to establish a connection) or down (the process is not running)

3 - Policy 1 + SERVER_CRITICAL_ERROR: Fail if sp_server_diagnostics detects a *critical system* error. **This is the default policy.** A critical system error includes conditions like long-running spinlock contention problems and non-yielding scheduler issues.

4 – Policy 1, 3, + SERVER_MODERATE_ERROR: Fail if sp_server_diagnostics detects a *resource* error. Resource errors are conditions like extremely low available SQL Server memory (memory managed by the engine).

5 – Policy 1,3,4 + SERVER_ANY_QUALIFIED_ERROR: Fail if sp_server_diagnostics detects a *query_processing* error. A query_processing error is a condition that prevents basic query processing like an exhaustion of worker threads.

Again each policy builds on the other, so policy 5 includes all the sp_server_ diagnostics errors. Notice, there is no policy 2 listed. Policy 2 only exists in the Windows architecture as it relates to how a resource DLL works. For many users, the default policy=3 is fine. I don't see many reasons to use policy 1 unless for some scenario where policy 3 is causing an undesirable failover occurrence. Using policy 4 or 5 is worth investigating because there are situations where SQL Server is running and will not failover with the default policy but there is a pretty serious problem with running the application (such as worker thread exhaustion), so the appearance that SQL Server is "down" occurs. In these situations, a failover might free up the problem and make SQL Server more highly available.

Tip   sp_server_diagnostics maintains a log (an Extended Events file) of health information that can be useful to investigate the cause of a failover (or lack of a failover). This file is kept in the "log" directory with the ERRORLOG files (default is / var/opt/mssql/log).

The flexible failover policies with Pacemaker are called *monitoring policies* and are configured with a program called **pcs** (pcs is used in the steps I outlined to set up and configure an SQL FCI). As I stated, the default policy is 3. Here is an example command to configure the policy to 1:

```
pcs resource update <fci_resource_name> meta monitor_policy=1
```

When a decision to failover is decided by Pacemaker, it uses a concept called *quorum* to decide if the cluster is healthy and which node to failover to (unless you manually fail it over to a specific node). The idea is that more than half of the nodes must be healthy to keep the cluster alive (although there is a way to keep a cluster alive with only two nodes). You can read more about Pacemaker and quorum at https://access.redhat.com/documentation/en-us/red_hat_enterprise_linux/7/html/high_availability_add-on_overview/ch-operation-haao. (You may need a Red Hat subscription to read this documentation).

As part of the concept of quorum, Pacemaker (using Corosync) has a method to ensure that nodes don't access the same shared resource, to avoid data corruption (although this would never be a problem with SQL Server database and log files, since SQL Server uses advisory locking in the Host Extension so two SQL Server processes cannot open the same database and/or log files at the same time. You can read more about advisory locking at https://www.quora.com/Linux-What-is-the-difference-between-advisory-lock-and-mandatory-lock). As I mentioned earlier in this chapter, the method to keep the cluster healthy is called fencing. And the component to implement fencing is called STONITH. STONITH can remove a node from the cluster to ensure two nodes don't access the same shared resource, or stop the entire cluster if that cannot be guaranteed. It is possible to configure STONITH with power supplies to literally shut down a computer. If you are used to WSFC, you should read up on how quorum and fencing work with Pacemaker on Linux.

The following are other good resources I found to understand Pacemaker and Corosync further:

- http://www.juliosblog.com/pacemaker-101-2/

- https://access.redhat.com/documentation/en-us/red_hat_enterprise_linux/7/html/high_availability_add-on_overview/s1-pacemakeroverview-haao

Always On Availability Groups

While Always On FCI is a great technology to protect the high availability of the SQL Server instance, there are two shortcomings to this approach:

- Storage becomes a central point of failover, so you need to have another solution (perhaps hardware) to protect from data storage outages.

- Other SQL Server instances in the cluster cannot actively be used, since only one SQL Server can access databases on the shared storage at one time.

SQL Server offers another feature as an alternative called *Always On Availability Groups*. I'll often use the term *AG(s)* for Always On Availability Groups for the rest of the chapter. An AG provides fault tolerance and high availability at the database level and provides for greater access to data. In this section of the chapter, I'll discuss how the technology works and provide you a detailed walkthrough on how to setup, configure, and test an AG.

I'll also discuss other aspects to AGs, which include database health detection, performance considerations, how data can be read on other nodes, automatic repair capabilities, and new functionality that does not require cluster software. For those of you who have used SQL Server AGs on Windows, the core functionality is the same, but the configuration and setup and a few behavior differences exist on Linux. I'll do my best to distinguish those during the rest of the chapter.

How it Works

The journey for AGs started back in SQL Server 2005 with a feature called Database Mirroring. In SQL Server 2012 we made some fairly major revisions to that original architecture and launched the Always On family, including FCI and Availability Groups (we had FCI before but did not call it Always On).

Like Database Mirroring, an AG does not require a shared storage architecture and instead tracks changes in the transaction log and transmit these changes to other SQL Server instances.

An AG consists of one or more databases that are replicated to one more of SQL Servers and is a unit of failover. The original SQL Server where transactions begin is called a *primary replica*. A SQL Server receiving changes is called a *secondary replica*. You will see that for SQL Server on Linux, a third type of replica is required when clustering is introduced with the AG, called a *configuration replica*.

As it turns out all the software components to support an AG are in SQL Server itself. In order to support the concept of an automatic failover with an AG, clustering software comes into play. For Windows, that software is WSFC. For SQL Server on Linux, similar to an FCI as described in the previous section, the Pacemaker software stack is used.

Our documentation has a very good visualization to show you how the various pieces of SQL Server support the fundamentals of replicas in an AG. Consider the diagram in Figure 8-10.

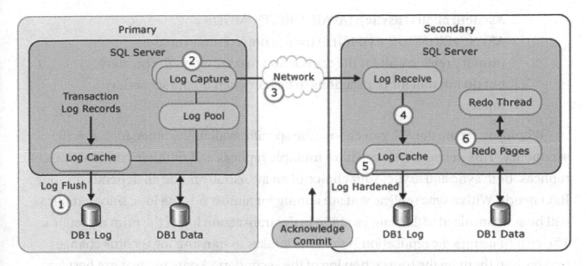

Figure 8-10. *The architecture and data synchronization flow of an Always On Availability Group*

As you can see in this diagram, SQL Server will capture transaction log changes on a Primary and transmit them over a separate communication channel (called a database mirroring endpoint) to the Secondary replica. On the Secondary replica, the changes are first hardened to the local transaction log and then separately any necessary redo recovery operations are applied. And one of the great advantages of an AG because this is not a shared storage solution, is that connections can be made to the secondary replica and data can be read after redo recovery is applied to the changes. You can read more about this architecture and detailed data flow in our documentation at https://docs.microsoft.com/sql/database-engine/availability-groups/windows/monitor-performance-for-always-on-availability-groups#BKMK_DATA_SYNC_PROCESS.

Synchronization Options

AGs offer two synchronization options, also called *availability modes*, for secondary replicas:

> **Synchronous (sync):** (AVAILABILITY_MODE = SYNCHRONOUS_COMMIT) a transaction on the primary replica wait for the transaction to commit on the primary and for log records associated with the transaction to be hardened on the secondary replica

Asynchronous (async): (AVAILABILITY_MODE = ASYNCHRONOUS_COMMIT) transaction commits on the primary replica wait for the transaction to commit on the primary but do not wait for transactions to be hardened on the secondary replica

When you create the AG, you choose the specific availability mode for a specific secondary. This means an AG can have multiple replicas and multiple combinations of replicas, both sync and async. Your choice of an availability mode all depends on your RPO needs. With a sync replica, you are aiming for almost no data loss, since a replica will be synchronized with changes made in the transaction log of the primary replica. The cost of using sync replication is the time it takes to transmit log records changes and harden them on the transaction log of the secondary. Async replicas are best for applications that don't require the most up to the minute changes but still want to read data on a secondary replica that is close to the primary. Another use for async replicas is for disaster recovery scenarios where the replica is on a network with latencies that won't make it a candidate for a sync replica.

Closely associated with the availability mode of an AG is the *failover mode*. I'll discuss this in the next section of the chapter.

Clustering and Availability Groups

AGs by themselves provide the mechanism to keep replicas up to date with changes from the primary. However, to make the AG *highly available*, intelligence is needed to decide if the primary is not available to switch to a secondary replica. This intelligence is provided by clustering software much like with an FCI. And like a FCI, for SQL Server on Linux, the Pacemaker software stack is used to provide clustering failover capabilities. When you create an AG and specify a sync replica, you can also choose the option FAILOVER_MODE=AUTOMATIC. When you choose this option, SQL Server together with Pacemaker can decide to failover to a secondary replica, provided that replica *is completely synchronized* with all changes currently made on the primary replica transaction log. In this case, synchronized means that all committed transactions on the primary are hardened on the transaction log of the secondary. Then, if a failover needs to occur, recovery is run on the secondary to allow all transactions to be consistent, so the secondary can now server as a primary. When clustering software combined with the SQL Server Resource Agent decides to failover to the secondary replica, this replica becomes the new primary.

Prior to SQL Server 2017, if a secondary sync replica went offline or it was not synchronized with the primary, SQL Server would allow transactions to continue on the primary, but SQL Server would not allow an automatic failover to occur because the secondary replica may not be in sync. The DMV **sys.dm_hadr_database_replica_states** can be used to determine the current synchronization status of the AG, as documented at https://docs.microsoft.com/sql/relational-databases/system-dynamic-management-views/sys-dm-hadr-database-replica-states-transact-sql.

SQL Server on Linux does not possess the same integration as it does with Windows Failover Clustering, so the policies and logic to ensure automatic failover can be a bit different. Starting with SQL Server 2017 CU1, SQL Server introduces a new replica type called a *configuration replica*, which is used to help make decisions to provide high availability and data protection when only a primary and only one secondary sync replica are configured. It is important to know that the configuration replica can be an SQL Server Express edition, which is a free license of SQL Server. In addition, SQL Server 2017 introduced a new AG option called REQUIRED_SYNCHRONIZED_SECONDARIES_TO_COMMIT. For SQL Server on Linux, this option is established when you configure the Pacemaker cluster for the AG. It determines how many replicas are required to ensure for proper data protection and high availability. For SQL Server on Linux, this setting is automatically configured when the cluster is set up for the AG but can be overridden using Pacemaker commands.

Note   This same option exists for SQL Server 2017 on Windows for AGs, but the default is 0, which is the behavior prior to SQL Server 2017 as I described earlier. This behavior means that transactions on the primary replica will continue even if configured secondary replicas are not available, but automatic failover is not allowed. You can set this to a value > 0 to force transactions on the primary to wait until one or more secondary replicas are available and synchronized.

You can read more about how to configure this option or the various configuration combinations required for high availability and data protection at https://docs.microsoft.com/sql/linux/sql-server-linux-availability-group-ha. A very common setup for many users will be a primary replica, a single sync replica, and a configuration replica (and possibly several async replicas that do not factor into the equation for requirements for high availability and data protection). This can provide a good cost-effective option for high availability and data protection. However, the behavior by default is much like prior to SQL Server 2017 if the secondary goes offline: the primary continues but automatic failover is not possible. If you change the REQUIRED_SYNCHRONIZED_SECONDARIES_TO_COMMIT to 1 in this configuration, it provides the best data protection option but not maximum high availability. In this scenario, transactions on the primary will wait until the secondary is synchronized. Furthermore, in a case where an automatic failover occurs to the secondary, the new primary must wait until the new secondary is online and synchronized. A more highly available data protection scheme would be a single primary replica and two sync secondary replicas.

Cluster decisions are done similar to FCI using sp_server_diagnostics and the flexible failover policies I described in an earlier section of the chapter. I'll discuss one additional failover logic option called database health detection later in this chapter.

My colleague in the engineering team, Sourabh Agarwal, gave me a few other tips on AGs for SQL Server on Linux that are different than SQL Server on Windows:

- You cannot set up an AG on a SQL Server instance with FCI installed as you can on Windows. This is an option we may look to support in the future, but it is not supported for SQL Server 2017.

- Due to the method in which STONITH and fencing work, you should not include an async replica in the Pacemaker cluster. I will show you later in this chapter how to add your AG replicas into the cluster. Do not add an async replica into the cluster, as the cluster will face issues when STONITH is enabled. This will not affect cluster operations, since you cannot automatically failover to an async replica.

- Most operations for the cluster cannot be done via T-SQL, such as a manual failover operation. You must use Pacemaker commands, and I will show you how later in this chapter. The one exception to this statement is a *forced failover*. You will use T-SQL for this situation, which is described in our documentation at `https://docs.microsoft.com/sql/linux/sql-server-linux-availability-group-failover-ha`.

Distributed Availability Groups

A unique concept provided by SQL Server AGs is a *distributed availability group*. A distributed availability group is a special type of availability group that spans two availability groups. Consider the diagram in Figure 8-11, which can be found in the Microsoft documentation at `https://docs.microsoft.com/sql/database-engine/availability-groups/windows/distributed-availability-groups#understand-distributed-availability-groups`.

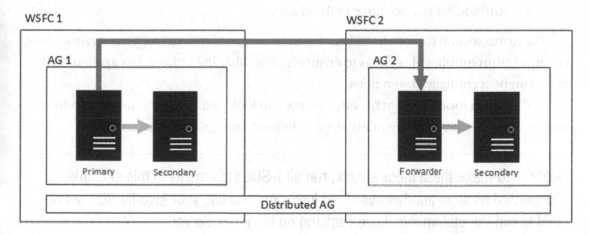

Figure 8-11. *A distributed availability group for SQL Server on Linux*

The concept is that both the secondary replica for availability group AG1 and the primary replica for availability group AG2 receive updates from the AG1 primary replica. Distributed availability groups provide AG functionality for multisite remote configurations such as organizations with data centers in remote locations. Check out various scenarios to use distributed availability groups in our documentation at `https://docs.microsoft.com/sql/database-engine/availability-groups/windows/distributed-availability-groups#distributed-availability-group-usage-scenarios`.

Setup and Configuration

The steps to set up an availability group for high availability and data protection are at a high level the following (follow along in the documentation at `https://docs.microsoft.com/sql/linux/sql-server-linux-availability-group-configure-ha`).

1. Install Linux and SQL Server on Linux on each *node* that
    participates in the AG set of *replicas* (a node that participates
    in the AG). The minimum number on Linux replicas to ensure
    data protection and high availability is three: a primary replica, a
    secondary replica, and a configuration replica.

2. Create and Configure the AG across these SQL Servers replicas.

3. Create the cluster using Pacemaker.

4. Add the AG as a resource to the cluster.

There are several choices based on the architecture of replicas for your environment.
The minimum number of replicas to ensure high availability is three, but again one of
these can be a configuration replica.

Let's look in more detail at how this works and looks using an example. I should be
honest up front that there are many steps to follow to complete this example.

Note   To make these steps simple, run all T-SQL statements in this example
connected as sa or another sysadmin login. You can use your favorite SQL Server
tool to run the statements. I used sqlcmd on the Linux Server.

Install Linux and SQL Server

1. I installed three VMs on Azure with RHEL 7.5: bwsqllinuxag1,
    bwsqllinuxag2, and sqllinuxcfgag (I made this VM only a two
    CPU to save costs). I put all of these VMs in the Azure Resource
    Group bwsqllinuxags, so they are automatically part of the same
    virtual network (vnet). I'll call each of these servers *nodes* and
    replicas. bwsqllinuxag1 is the primary replica, bwsqllinuxag2 is the
    secondary replica, and sqllinuxcfgag is the configuration replica.

    •   I opened up port 22 on all of these so I could use ssh clients from
        my laptop.

    •   Run sudo yum -y update to get all packages up to date.

- Configure the hosts file on each server (Note: be sure the Linux Server has a valid hostname in /etc/hostname other than localhost) to contain all the IP addresses and hostnames of each server. For my Azure Virtual Machines, this is the Private IP of each VM, since they are all on the same virtual network in Azure. My /etc/hosts file looks like this on each server, as in Figure 8-12.

```
[thewandog@bwsqllinuxag2 ~]$ sudo cat /etc/hosts
127.0.0.1   localhost localhost.localdomain localhost4 localhost4.localdomain4
::1         localhost localhost.localdomain localhost6 localhost6.localdomain6
172.17.0.6 bwsqllinuxag1
172.17.0.5 bwsqllinuxag2
172.17.0.7 sqllinuxcfgag
```

***Figure 8-12.** Example /etc/hosts file*

2. Install SQL Server. Since I've used RHEL for my servers, I've followed the instructions as I documented in Chapter 2. You can also find these in the documentation at https://docs. microsoft.com/sql/linux/quickstart-install-connect-red-hat. Be sure to install SQL Server, open up firewall ports, and install the command line tools for Linux. Both bwsqllinuxag1 and bwsqllinuxag2 are running the Enterprise edition, while sqllinuxcfgag is using SQL Express Edition.

Create and Configure the AG across these SQL Servers Replicas

Note   It is possible to perform some of steps in this section using SQL Server Management Studio (SSMS). Learn more at https://docs.microsoft.com/ sql/linux/sql-server-linux-create-availability-group#create-the-availability-group. I'm going to show you the complete set of steps using all bash shell scripts and T-SQL

1. Enable the AG for SQL Server on Linux on each node with the following command run from the bash shell, as found in the example script **enableag.sh** (remember, you must execute chmod u+x to execute an .sh script):

```
sudo /opt/mssql/bin/mssql-conf set hadr.hadrenabled 1
sudo systemctl restart mssql-server
```

2. An extended events session exists to track AG states. Start this session on each node using the following T-SQL statement, as found in the example script **enableagxe.sql**:

```
ALTER EVENT SESSION  AlwaysOn_health ON SERVER WITH (STARTUP_
STATE=ON);
GO
```

3. Create login and users for the database mirroring endpoint **on each replica** using the following T-SQL statements as found in **dbmloginuser.sql**:

```
CREATE LOGIN dbm_login WITH PASSWORD = 'Sql2017isfast'
GO
CREATE USER dbm_user FOR LOGIN dbm_login
GO
```

4. In Chapter 7 you learned about master keys and certificates in SQL Server and that knowledge is about to pay off. As I said at the top of this section, AGs communicate over *database mirroring endpoints.* Authentication over these endpoints is achieved using certificates in SQL Server. So the first step is to create a certificate on the **primary replica** (in my scenario that is **sqllinuxag1**) using the following T-SQL statement, as found in the example script **primaryagcert.sql** (substitute in your own password):

```
CREATE MASTER KEY ENCRYPTION BY PASSWORD = 'Sql2017isfast'
GO
CREATE CERTIFICATE dbm_certificate WITH SUBJECT = 'dbm'
GO
BACKUP CERTIFICATE dbm_certificate
    TO FILE = '/var/opt/mssql/data/dbm_certificate.cer'
    WITH PRIVATE KEY (
            FILE = '/var/opt/mssql/data/dbm_certificate.pvk',
            ENCRYPTION BY PASSWORD = 'Sql2017isfast'
)
GO
```

5. When this is successful, it will not return any results. Now you
    have a certificate (dbm_certificate.cer) file and a private key
    (dbm_certificate.pvk) file created on the primary node replica.
    You will need to copy these files into the same locations (/var/
    opt/mssql/data) on all nodes. Using the same certificate protected
    by the same key allows all nodes to authenticate with each other
    over the communication endpoint. First, you will copy the files
    into the home directory of the Linux user created for the Azure
    VM like the following commands, as found in the example script
    copycertkeys.sh:

    ```
    sudo scp /var/opt/mssql/data/dbm_certificate.cer thewandog@
    bwsqllinuxag2:
    sudo scp /var/opt/mssql/data/dbm_certificate.pvk thewandog@
    bwsqllinuxag2:
    ```

You will be prompted for passwords to copy these files. This example copies the files
from the primary replica to the secondary replica. **Do the same thing but replace the
target server with the name of the host for the configuration replica**. Now these files
should exist on the other replica nodes in the home directory.

6. These files need to now be moved to the /var/opt/mssql/data
    directory on each replica node and have permissions changed
    to mssql:mssql like the following shell script, as found in the
    example **movecertkeys.sh. This script should be run from the
    bash shell on the secondary and configuration replica nodes**.

    ```
    sudo mv dbm_certificate.cer /var/opt/mssql/data
    sudo chown mssql:mssql /var/opt/mssql/data/dbm_certificate.cer
    sudo mv dbm_certificate.pvk /var/opt/mssql/data
    sudo chown mssql:mssql /var/opt/mssql/data/dbm_certificate.pvk
    ```

7. Now you will use the following T-SQL statements as found in
secondaryagcert.sql to create the keys and certificates on the
secondary and **configuration** nodes referencing these files
copied to each node. Notice, for these statements I create the
certificate from the files copied from the primary replica but use
the DECRYPTION keyword to decrypt the certificate to be used by
SQL Server.

```
CREATE MASTER KEY ENCRYPTION BY PASSWORD = 'Sql2017isfast'
GO
CREATE CERTIFICATE dbm_certificate
    AUTHORIZATION dbm_user
    FROM FILE = '/var/opt/mssql/data/dbm_certificate.cer'
    WITH PRIVATE KEY (
    FILE = '/var/opt/mssql/data/dbm_certificate.pvk',
    DECRYPTION BY PASSWORD = 'Sql2017isfast'
)
GO
```

8. Now you need to create an endpoint for communication. AGs
communicate on a different port than the standard SQL Server
port for logins and T-SQL queries. As I said in an earlier step,
this endpoint is called a *database mirroring endpoint*. Use the
following T-SQL statements as found in **endpoint.sql** on the
primary and secondary replicas. Because we are using SQL Server
Express for the configuration replica, we will need a slightly
different version, which I'll show you in the next step. You don't
have to use port 5022, but it is a common port to use for database
mirroring endpoints.

```
CREATE ENDPOINT [Hadr_endpoint]
    AS TCP (LISTENER_IP = (0.0.0.0), LISTENER_PORT = 5022)
    FOR DATA_MIRRORING (
        ROLE = ALL,
        AUTHENTICATION = CERTIFICATE dbm_certificate,
        ENCRYPTION = REQUIRED ALGORITHM AES
        )
```

```
GO
ALTER ENDPOINT [Hadr_endpoint] STATE = STARTED
GO
GRANT CONNECT ON ENDPOINT::[Hadr_endpoint] TO [dbm_login]
GO
```

9. If the configuration replica is using the SQL Server Express
    edition, then the ROLE value can only be a WITNESS. Use
    the following T-SQL statement as found in the example script
    cfgendpoint.sql:

```
CREATE ENDPOINT [Hadr_endpoint]
    AS TCP (LISTENER_IP = (0.0.0.0), LISTENER_PORT = 5022)
    FOR DATA_MIRRORING (
        ROLE = WITNESS,
        AUTHENTICATION = CERTIFICATE dbm_certificate,
        ENCRYPTION = REQUIRED ALGORITHM AES
        )
GO
ALTER ENDPOINT [Hadr_endpoint] STATE = STARTED
GO
GRANT CONNECT ON ENDPOINT::[Hadr_endpoint] TO [dbm_login]
GO
```

10. A subtle comment in our documentation states the port specified
    for the database mirroring connection needs to be open in the
    firewall on Linux. I ran the following command to see what ports
    were open with the firewall on each of my nodes:

```
sudo firewall-cmd --list-ports
```

The only port listed was 1433, which is the main port for SQL Server connections and
queries. So I ran the following commands from the bash shell as found in the example
script **dbmirrorfirewall.sh** (make sure the shell script is marked for execute with chmod
u+x dbmirrorfirewall.sh):

```
sudo firewall-cmd --zone=public --add-port=5022/tcp --permanent
sudo firewall-cmd --reload
```

417

11. Now it's time to create the availability group using the following
T-SQL statements found in the example script **createag.sql**. This
T-SQL script should be run on the **primary replica** (which in my
example is bwsqllinuxag1):

```
CREATE AVAILABILITY GROUP [footballag]
   WITH (CLUSTER_TYPE = EXTERNAL)
   FOR REPLICA ON
    N'bwsqllinuxag1' WITH (
       ENDPOINT_URL = N'tcp://bwsqllinuxag1:5022',
       AVAILABILITY_MODE = SYNCHRONOUS_COMMIT,
       FAILOVER_MODE = EXTERNAL,
       SEEDING_MODE = AUTOMATIC,
       SECONDARY_ROLE (ALLOW_CONNECTIONS = ALL)
       ),
    N'bwsqllinuxag2' WITH (
       ENDPOINT_URL = N'tcp://bwsqllinuxag2:5022',
       AVAILABILITY_MODE = SYNCHRONOUS_COMMIT,
       FAILOVER_MODE = EXTERNAL,
       SEEDING_MODE = AUTOMATIC,
       SECONDARY_ROLE (ALLOW_CONNECTIONS = ALL)
       ),
    N'sqllinuxcfgag' WITH (
       ENDPOINT_URL = N'tcp://sqllinuxcfgag:5022',
       AVAILABILITY_MODE = CONFIGURATION_ONLY
       )
GO
ALTER AVAILABILITY GROUP [footballag] GRANT CREATE ANY DATABASE
GO
```

Once you run this command, the availability group should appear in the **sys.
availability_groups** and **sys.availability_replicas** catalog views on the primary replica.
One problem you may notice is that the primary replica immediately starts connecting
to the secondary replicas even when they are not ready to accept these connections.
Therefore, you might see messages like the following in the ERRORLOG on the primary
replica:

A connection timeout has occurred while attempting to establish a
connection to availability replica 'bwsqllinuxag2' with id [D36B7503-2EFB-
467C-AD8A-4CE2B9E63958]. Either a networking or firewall issue exists, or
the endpoint address provided for the replica is not the database mirroring
endpoint of the host server instance.
A connection timeout has occurred while attempting to establish a
connection to availability replica 'sqllinuxcfgag' with id [AC5F02C0-A481-
4760-BA44-BF7E9FF83F9D]. Either a networking or firewall issue exists, or
the endpoint address provided for the replica is not the database mirroring
endpoint of the host server instance.

This does not mean the CREATE AVAILABILITY GROUP failed. It just means the
secondaries are not set up yet. Follow the next step and you will see how.

12. Setup the availability groups on the secondary and configuration
    replica by running the following T-SQL statements, as found in
    joinag.sql on both the secondary and configuration replicas:

Note   The GRANT statement is not allowed on the configuration replica, so only
run the ALTER AVAILABILITY GROUP statement on a configuration replica.

```
ALTER AVAILABILITY GROUP [footballag] JOIN WITH (CLUSTER_TYPE = EXTERNAL)
GO
-- Do not run this statement on the configuration replica
ALTER AVAILABILITY GROUP [footballag] GRANT CREATE ANY DATABASE
GO
```

When these statements are executed, the primary, secondary, and configuration
replica are "connected." You will see these statements in the ERRORLOG on the primary
replica:

A connection for availability group 'footballag' from availability replica
'bwsqllinuxag1' with id [B8438077-BA82-4AD1-A5B6-6601ECA82C9E] to
'bwsqllinuxag2' with id [D36B7503-2EFB-467C-AD8A-4CE2B9E63958] has been
successfully established. This is an informational message only. No user
action is required.

A connection for availability group 'footballag' from availability
replica 'bwsqllinuxag1' with id [B8438077-BA82-4AD1-A5B6-6601ECA82C9E]
to 'sqllinuxcfgag' with id [AC5F02C0-A481-4760-BA44-BF7E9FF83F9D] has been
successfully established. This is an informational message only. No user
action is required.

13. You are almost there! Remember the definition of an availability
group is one or more databases that are replicated to another
node and a unit of failover. So far, all that has been created is three
SQL Server instances that know how to communicate with each
other. So the first step is to choose a database(s) for the AG and
create a full database backup. Run the following T-SQL statements
connected to the primary replica, as found in the example **dbag.sql**:

```
CREATE DATABASE [cowboysrule]
GO
ALTER DATABASE [cowboysrule] SET RECOVERY FULL
GO
BACKUP DATABASE [cowboysrule] TO DISK = N'/var/opt/mssql/data/
cowboysrule.bak'
GO
```

14. Now add the database to the availability group by running the
following T-SQL statement on the **primary replica**, as found in
the example script **dbjoinag.sql**:

```
ALTER AVAILABILITY GROUP [footballag] ADD DATABASE [cowboysrule]
GO
```

15. Because we created the availability group with an option called
SEEDING_MODE = AUTOMATIC, SQL Server will automatically
create the new database and copy over any data to secondary
replicas. You can see this by running the following T-SQL
statement on the secondary replica, as found in the example script
listdbs.sql:

```
SELECT name FROM sys.databases
GO
```

If all works well, **cowboysrule** will show up in this list. And because we used the option SECONDARY_ROLE previously when creating the availability group, we can even read from the cowboysrule database on the secondary replica.

Congratulations! You have just created and set up an Always On Availability Group for SQL Server on Linux. There is only one thing left to show you. How does a failover work in this situation? If you dare, go to the next sections to set up a Pacemaker cluster and add the AG to the cluster.

Create the Cluster Using Pacemaker

Note   To go further with this example you must have a subscription with Red Hat, because the High Availability Add-On is required to allow Pacemaker to work in production.

Follow along with the steps I'll show to create a Pacemaker cluster for RHEL in our documentation at `https://docs.microsoft.com/sql/linux/sql-server-linux-availability-group-cluster-rhel`.

Note   As stated in our documentation, production Pacemaker clusters requires STONITH, but in these examples I will disable STONITH. That is because it is not currently supported in Azure Virtual Machine (but the work to make this supported is happening as I write this chapter!)

1. **On each node**, run the following command from the bash shell and put in your subscription user name and password (it is possible that for your own Linux Server you have already done this):

   ```
   sudo subscription-manager register
   ```

2. Your subscription that includes the High Availability Add-On has a poolid associated with it. You can use the following command from the bash shell to find that poolid. The name of the feature is "Red Hat Enterprise Linux High Availability (for RHEL Server)":

   ```
   sudo subscription-manager list --available
   ```

3. Using the poolid, run the following command from the bash shell **on each node** to attach the right subscription. For privacy reasons, I have not listed my poolid, but the command looks like

```
sudo subscription-manager attach --pool=<pool id>
```

4. Now enable the repository so you can install Pacemaker by running the following command from the bash shell on all nodes:

```
sudo subscription-manager repos --enable=rhel-ha-for-rhel-7-
server-rpms
```

5. Pacemaker requires communication between nodes, so open up firewall ports with the following command from the bash shell on all nodes:

```
sudo firewall-cmd --permanent --add-service=high-availability
sudo firewall-cmd --reload
```

6. Now it's time to install Pacemaker on all nodes using the following from the bash shell:

```
sudo yum install pacemaker pcs fence-agents-all resource-agents
```

7. Pacemaker installs a user on Linux that requires a password. Run this command from the bash shell on all nodes to create the password. Be sure to provide the same password on all nodes:

```
sudo passwd hacluster
```

8. Run the following commands from the bash shell on all nodes to enable and start Pacemaker services:

```
sudo systemctl enable pcsd
sudo systemctl start pcsd
sudo systemctl enable pacemaker
```

9. Now it's time to create the cluster. Run commands from the bash shell like the following but put in your nodes you set up earlier in the example and the password you established for Pacemaker in Step 7 (your password goes after the -p parameter in the script). I've provided an example script called **createcluster.sh** you can use as a template. In this example, footballcluster is the name of the cluster but you can put in your own name. You only need to run this on the **primary node**:

```
sudo pcs cluster auth bwsqllinuxag1 bwsqllinuxag2 sqllinuxcfgag
-u hacluster -p Sql2017isfast
sudo pcs cluster setup --name footballcluster bwsqllinuxag1
bwsqllinuxag2 sqllinuxcfgag
sudo pcs cluster start -all
```

The output of running this command should look similar to Figure 8-13.

```
bwsqllinuxag2: Authorized
Destroying cluster on nodes: bwsqllinuxag1, bwsqllinuxag2, sqllinuxcfgag...
sqllinuxcfgag: Stopping Cluster (pacemaker)...
bwsqllinuxag1: Stopping Cluster (pacemaker)...
bwsqllinuxag2: Stopping Cluster (pacemaker)...
bwsqllinuxag2: Successfully destroyed cluster
bwsqllinuxag1: Successfully destroyed cluster
sqllinuxcfgag: Successfully destroyed cluster

Sending 'pacemaker_remote authkey' to 'bwsqllinuxag1', 'bwsqllinuxag2', 'sqllinuxcfgag'
bwsqllinuxag1: successful distribution of the file 'pacemaker_remote authkey'
bwsqllinuxag2: successful distribution of the file 'pacemaker_remote authkey'
sqllinuxcfgag: successful distribution of the file 'pacemaker_remote authkey'
Sending cluster config files to the nodes...
bwsqllinuxag1: Succeeded
bwsqllinuxag2: Succeeded
sqllinuxcfgag: Succeeded

Synchronizing pcsd certificates on nodes bwsqllinuxag1, bwsqllinuxag2, sqllinuxcfgag...
sqllinuxcfgag: Success
bwsqllinuxag1: Success
bwsqllinuxag2: Success
Restarting pcsd on the nodes in order to reload the certificates...
sqllinuxcfgag: Success
bwsqllinuxag1: Success
bwsqllinuxag2: Success
sqllinuxcfgag: Starting Cluster...
bwsqllinuxag2: Starting Cluster...
bwsqllinuxag1: Starting Cluster...
[thewandog@bwsqllinuxag1 ~]$ ▋
```

Figure 8-13. *Creating a Pacemaker cluster on Linux*

> **Note**   pcs (pacemaker configuration system) is a command line interface to interact with the Pacemaker cluster. Get used to using it, as it will be helpful in many scenarios and is used in some cases where T-SQL would be used with AGs on SQL Server on Windows.

10.   You might remember I told you in earlier chapters that we have separated the installation process for SQL Server into packages. Well now it's time to install another one. This package is the SQL Server HA Resource Agent, which has been developed to interact with Pacemaker and something I mentioned earlier in this chapter. Install this agent on all nodes using the following command from the bash shell:

```
sudo yum install mssql-server-ha
```

11.   As I mentioned earlier, STONITH is not supported today on Azure Virtual Machine so I'm going to disable this using the following command from the bash shell on the primary node:

> **Note**   The pcs program exists on all clusters, but command execution can be done on any cluster in the node because pcs commands apply to the entire cluster.

```
sudo pcs property set stonith-enabled=false
```

12.   The documentation recommends setting a few pacemaker properties-related failover timeouts and refresh check intervals. I recommend you adhere to these recommendations, running the following commands from the bash shell as found in the example script **clusterproperties.sh** on the primary node. These recommendations and details behind them can be found at https://docs.microsoft.com/sql/linux/sql-server-linux-availability-group-cluster-rhel.

```
sudo pcs property set cluster-recheck-interval=2min
sudo pcs property set start-failure-is-fatal=true
```

Add the AG as a Resource in the Cluster

We have the AG created in SQL Server and the Pacemaker cluster created on all nodes. To tie the systems together, we need to create a resource in the cluster associated with the AG.

1. We need an SQL Server login for the SQL Server resource agent. Execute the following T-SQL statements **on all nodes**, found in the example script **pacemakerlogin.sql**. This script also grants the minimum permissions for the agent to execute and access proper SQL Server resources:

```
USE [master]
GO
CREATE LOGIN [pacemakerLogin] with PASSWORD= N'Sql2017isfast'
GO
GRANT ALTER, CONTROL, VIEW DEFINITION ON AVAILABILITY
GROUP::footballag TO pacemakerLogin
GO
GRANT VIEW SERVER STATE TO pacemakerLogin
GO
```

2. The resource agent needs to know what login and password to use. Therefore, you need to execute the following commands from the bash shell **on all nodes**, as found in the example **sqlrgagentlogin.sh**:

```
echo 'pacemakerLogin' >> ~/pacemaker-passwd
echo 'Sql2017isfast' >> ~/pacemaker-passwd
sudo mv ~/pacemaker-passwd /var/opt/mssql/secrets/passwd
sudo chown root:root /var/opt/mssql/secrets/passwd
sudo chmod 400 /var/opt/mssql/secrets/passwd # Only readable
by root
```

3. Create the AG resource with the cluster using the same name as
    the AG in SQL Server by executing the following commands from
    the bash shell on any node:

```
sudo pcs resource create ag_cluster ocf:mssql:ag ag_
name=footballag meta failure-timeout=60s master notify=true
```

Note   The version of the documentation at the time of the writing of this book
uses a failure-timeout of 30s but then earlier in the documentation it says to use
60s, so I made the change here when creating the resource.

4. SQL Server Availability Groups on Linux have a concept called
    a listener, so you can connect to a virtual IP address vs. the IP
    address of each node. This concept is integrated with SQL Server
    and Windows Server Failover Cluster. We will use a similar
    concept on Linux, but the virtual IP is part of the Pacemaker
    design. Therefore, choose an IP address similar to your Azure VMs
    but not a physical IP address. Then execute a command from the
    bash shell like the following:

```
sudo pcs resource create virtualip ocf:heartbeat:IPaddr2
ip=172.17.0.100
```

Note   SQL Server AGs support the concept of a listener. A listener abstracts a
client application from knowing the physical name or IP address of the primary
replica. This is very powerful, especially in a failover scenario when a secondary
replica becomes the new primary. You can read more about AG listeners at
https://docs.microsoft.com/sql/database-engine/availability-
groups/windows/listeners-client-connectivity-application-
failover#AGlisteners. Furthermore, you can read more about AG listeners
on SQL Server on Linux at https://docs.microsoft.com/sql/linux/sql-
server-linux-availability-group-overview#the-listener-under-
linux.

5. Now add a colocation constraint and ordering constraint to ensure the primary replica and virtual ip run on the same node by running the following commands from the bash shell on any node:

```
sudo pcs constraint colocation add virtualip ag_cluster-master
INFINITY with-rsc-role=Master
sudo pcs constraint order promote ag_cluster-master then start
virtualip
```

You have now completed the exercise to create a highly available Always On Availability Group on SQL Server on Linux. No sweat, right? Is there a better way to do this? The answer is yes. It is called an Ansible Playbook. It reminds me of my senior year in college when we worked all semester in a course to build a Fortran program for a statistical simulation model. After we turned in all of our assignments, the very last week of the semester the professor showed us how to build the same program in one day using a language called GPSS. We of course all asked him why? The answer was simple. He wanted us to understand the internals of creating statistic simulation models but also to understand to look for efficient methods to do the same task. Hard lesson. Ansible is all about that. We have produced an open source Ansible Playbook to install SQL Server, a Pacemaker cluster, and an AG at `https://github.com/Microsoft/sql-server-samples/tree/master/samples/features/high%20availability/Linux/Ansible%20Playbook`.

Let's Test it

In this section, let's connect to SQL Server and test our new setup we just completed for an AG with a cluster. There are two tests I would like to run on this new setup: (1) Add some data to the primary replica database and see it show up on the secondary replica and (2) test how failover works to the secondary and back to the primary.

Testing Data Replication

1. Run the following T-SQL statements as found in the example
    createandinsert.sql connected to the <virtual IP address>,1433 to
    create a table on the primary replica and insert data:

```
USE [cowboysrule]
GO
DROP TABLE IF EXISTS wewillwintheeast
GO
CREATE TABLE wewillwintheeast (col1 int)
GO
INSERT INTO wewillwintheeast VALUES (1)
GO
```

Note   Just like the other nodes, you can add an entry into /etc/hosts with a string name associated with the virtual IP address and use that to connect without having to specify the port number.

---

2. Connect directly to the secondary replica and run the
    following T-SQL statements as found in the example script
    querysecondary.sql, to prove you are connected to the secondary
    server and the preceding changes were replicated from the
    primary:

```
SELECT @@SERVERNAME
GO
USE [cowboysrule]
GO
SELECT * FROM wewillwintheeast
GO
```

The results should be you secondary replica (mine is bwsqllinuxag2) and a result of one row.

Testing Failover

The simplest method to ensure that failover will work between the primary and secondary replica is to execute a *manual failover*.

In SQL Server on Windows, you can use T-SQL commands to manually failover a replica with AGs. However, for Linux, you must use the pcs program with Pacemaker. You can read all about operating the cluster on Linux in our documentation at https://docs.microsoft.com/sql/linux/sql-server-linux-availability-group-failover-ha. Let's give it a try.

1. First, we need a way to see the current state of replicas from a failover perspective. Execute the following T-SQL statement, as found in the example script **checkreplicas.sql**:

```
SELECT ar.replica_server_name, hars.role_desc,
hars.operational_state_desc
FROM sys.dm_hadr_availability_replica_states hars
JOIN sys.availability_replicas ar
ON hars.replica_id = ar.replica_id
GO
```

In my environment, the results look like Figure 8-14.

```
[thewandog@bwsqllinuxag1 ~]$ sqlcmd -Usa -icheckreplicas.sql
Password:
replica_server_name
                                                        role_desc
        operational_state_desc
------------------------------------------------------------------------------------
------------------------------------------------------------------------------------
------------------------------------------------- -----------------------------------
----- ---------------------------------------------------
bwsqllinuxag1
                                                        PRIMARY
        ONLINE
bwsqllinuxag2
                                                        SECONDARY
    NULL
sqllinuxcfgag
                                                        SECONDARY
    NULL
(3 rows affected)
```

Figure 8-14. Replica states for AGs on SQL Server on Linux

2. Now it's time to try a failover using the pcs program. Run the following command from the bash shell on any node, putting in the name of your secondary node (mine is bwsqllinuxag2):

```
sudo pcs resource move ag_cluster-master bwsqllinuxag2 --master
```

3. The documentation calls out that the nature of Pacemaker is to add a colocation constraint after performing a manual failover that can cause issues, so execute the following command from the bash shell on any node:

```
sudo pcs constraint remove cli-prefer-ag_cluster-master
```

4. To make sure the failover worked properly, execute the same **checkreplicas.sql** script but this time on the secondary node. The results in my environment look like Figure 8-15.

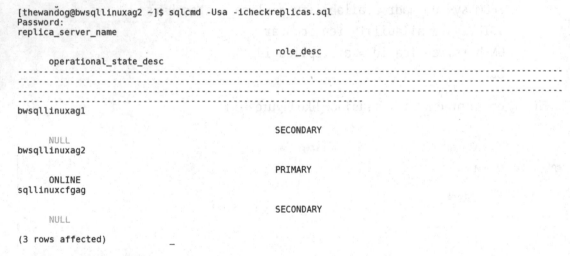

Figure 8-15. *Replica states after a failover*

You can see now the secondary has become the primary and the primary the secondary. You can repeat the steps 2 and 3 above now to fail back to the primary replica. Use the same pcs command as above in step 2 to move the resource but this time put in the name of the primary like the following code example (be sure to also run the same command to remove the colocation constraint):

```
sudo pcs resource move ag_cluster-master bwsqllinuxag1 --master
```

Note   I've noticed on my setup it seems to take a bit longer to fail back to the primary then failing over the secondary, so when you fail back give it a longer time to check on states.

Congratulations! If you have made it this far you successfully have set up a Highly Available Always On Availability Group for SQL Server on Linux and tested its functionality. Why do I call it Highly Available? You will find out in a section towards the end of this chapter. Let's look at other aspects of AGs to conclude this chapter.

Database Health Detection

I mentioned in the section on FCI as well as an earlier section on AGs the concept of how failover is detected using sp_server_diagnostics and flexible failover policies. You may have noticed that those policies are at an SQL Server *instance* level. The problem with using instance level logic for AGs is that AGs are a database level of failover.

Therefore, SQL Server has a concept called *Database Health Detection*. By using an option for CREATE AVAILABILITY GROUP (or ALTER) called DB_FAILOVER, SQL Server will monitor if a database goes offline and start a failover. The default is OFF, but I recommend using this option to ensure a failover occurs if the database is not accessible. All databases in the AG are monitored as part of this feature.

There are a few nuances and limits to the feature, which you can read about at `https://docs.microsoft.com/sql/database-engine/availability-groups/windows/sql-server-always-on-database-health-detection-failover-option`.

Performance Considerations

One common question I hear from customers about the use of a synchronous replica with AGs is whether performance of the application running transactions against the primary will be affected. And the answer is yes. The more important question is whether the performance impact can be negligible and still achieve the benefit of high availability. That answer is definitely yes.

The three biggest factors in performance for AGs are:

- The rate of transactions run against the primary replica

- The speed in which transactions can be hardened on the primary and secondary replica transaction log files (disk I/O is usually the biggest factor)

- The speed of connectivity between the primary and secondary replicas

You have complete control over using the fastest hardware for disks on both the primary and secondary for transaction log and the speed of network devices between replicas.

Therefore, the biggest concern may be transaction rates to the primary. The two scenarios where I've seen some bottleneck issues are:

- A high rate of exceedingly small single statement transactions by a large number of concurrent users

- Large index builds and rebuilds

The first issue can be mitigated by grouping statements together into logical transactions (this is a good practice for transaction performance independent of AGs). The second issue is trickier and may require you to carefully schedule index builds and rebuilds, use partitioning to build indexes in smaller chunks, and also evaluate whether you need to build or rebuild an index.

Take a look through this part of our documentation to see common methods to monitor the performance of availability groups to look for possible bottlenecks in the synchronization process: `https://docs.microsoft.com/sql/database-engine/availability-groups/windows/monitor-performance-for-always-on-availability-groups#BKMK_SCENARIOS`.

One thing you can count on is that Microsoft has worked to streamline the code that handles AGs. You can read more about the performance optimization work we did starting in SQL Server 2016 at `https://blogs.msdn.microsoft.com/sqlserverstorageengine/2016/09/26/sql-server-2016-it-just-runs-faster-always-on-availability-groups-turbocharged/`.

Readable Secondaries

One of the biggest advantages of Always On Availability Groups over an FCI, besides the fact that you don't need shared storage, is that the secondary replicas for the AG can be *actively used*. You can read from secondary replica data, run backups on the databases on a secondary replica, and even perform integrity checks like DBCC CHECKDB. Furthermore, you can configure client applications to be routed automatically to a readable secondary replica, thereby offloading workloads from the primary.

Note   Readable secondaries are only available with SQL Server Enterprise edition. The Standard edition provides for basic availability groups but does not allow you to read from the secondary replica. You can read more about basic availability groups at `https://docs.microsoft.com/sql/database-engine/availability-groups/windows/basic-availability-groups-always-on-availability-groups`.

The data available to read on the secondary replica is only based on committed transactions that have been hardened and redone in the secondary transaction log. Any data based on active transactions is not available. Furthermore, if there is latency in moving transactions to a secondary (which you may see more with asynchronous replicas), there could be a difference in data you are trying to read from the secondary replica.

There are other considerations when using readable secondary replicas, including how statistics are handled, possible blocking situations, and overall consuming of resources on the SQL Server, which can affect secondary replication redo performance. I encourage you to read through these details at `https://docs.microsoft.com/sql/database-engine/availability-groups/windows/active-secondaries-readable-secondary-replicas-always-on-availability-groups#bkmk_Performance`.

Last, since we have shipped SQL Server 2017 we have been able to pinpoint a few performance optimizations that can help with conflicts between parallel redo worker threads and readable secondary queries. Read more about this at `https://blogs.msdn.microsoft.com/sql_server_team/sql-server-20162017-availability-group-secondary-replica-redo-model-and-performance/` and be sure to keep up to date on the latest cumulative updates for further enhancements.

Automatic Page Repair

Another slick feature and great advantage with AGs is the fact that the secondary replica can hold valid database pages even when a page becomes damaged on the primary. Given this fact, if a database page becomes damaged on the primary, why not take advantage of the good page on the secondary? That is exactly what SQL Server provides with a feature called *Automatic Page Repair*.

Here is how it works. If the primary replica detects that a database page from a database in the AG is damaged (for example a checksum error on a page), it will request to all secondaries for a valid copy of the page. When the transaction log records associated with the page are redone on the secondary, the secondary will send the valid page back to the primary, which will restore it online. Furthermore, there is no need to enable the feature. It works by default with AGs. OK, you have to admit that is incredibly cool!

Furthermore, if a secondary replica encounters a damaged page during redo, it can request a valid copy of the page from the primary. This is another great feature to help with your RTO and RPO needs of SQL Server and it is all built into the SQL Server engine (however, this feature is only available with SQL Server Enterprise edition).

Read more about Automatic Page Repair at `https://docs.microsoft.com/sql/sql-server/failover-clusters/automatic-page-repair-availability-groups-database-mirroring`.

Clusterless Availability Groups

As we built SQL Server 2017 and enabled AG capabilities for SQL Server on Linux (with the new CLUSTER_TYPE=EXTERNAL), we realized we could introduce the capabilities of using AGs without a cluster component, either with WSFC or Pacemaker.

We call this new concept a *Clusterless Availability Group*. Consider the architecture diagram I introduced earlier in this chapter. All the software components exist to ship log changes to replicas without any clustering software required. The difference is that without clustering software, the AG is not highly available, because there is no automatic failover capability.

However, you may have a scenario where you would like to set up an AG because you want to allow workloads for readers (say reporting users) to access a series of secondary replicas but you don't need the AG to be highly available. We call this concept in SQL Server 2017 *read-scale routing*.

Furthermore, because the core database engine is the same code on Windows and Linux, and the core software components for AGs are in the engine, you can set up a primary and set of replicas *across Windows and Linux,* hence a cross-platform AG.

Think of it this way. When you went through the example in the previous section to set up an AG, once you created the AG and joined the secondaries, SQL Server was ready to ship log blocks to replicas. If you changed the CREATE AVAILABILITY GROUP statement to use CLUSTER_TYPE = NONE like this

```
CREATE AVAILABILITY GROUP [footballag]
   WITH (CLUSTER_TYPE = NONE)
   FOR REPLICA ON
    N'bwsqllinuxag1' WITH (
       ENDPOINT_URL = N'tcp://bwsqllinuxag1:5022',
       AVAILABILITY_MODE = SYNCHRONOUS_COMMIT,
       FAILOVER_MODE = EXTERNAL,
       SEEDING_MODE = AUTOMATIC,
       SECONDARY_ROLE (ALLOW_CONNECTIONS = ALL)
       ),
    N'bwsqllinuxag2' WITH (
       ENDPOINT_URL = N'tcp://bwsqllinuxag2:5022',
       AVAILABILITY_MODE = SYNCHRONOUS_COMMIT,
       FAILOVER_MODE = EXTERNAL,
       SEEDING_MODE = AUTOMATIC,
       SECONDARY_ROLE (ALLOW_CONNECTIONS = ALL)
       ),
    N'sqllinuxcfgag' WITH (
       ENDPOINT_URL = N'tcp://sqllinuxcfgag:5022',
       AVAILABILITY_MODE = CONFIGURATION_ONLY
       )
GO
ALTER AVAILABILITY GROUP [footballag] GRANT CREATE ANY DATABASE
GO
```

you would be creating a clusterless availability group. It is that simple.

Summary

In this chapter, I have talked about the fundamentals of high availability and recovery through backup and restore, but also discussed the more advanced yet powerful features to meet the needs of your RTO and RPO requirements through Always On Failover Cluster Instance and Always On Availability Groups. One interesting angle for high availability is using Docker containers with Kubernetes. I discuss this new capability in the last chapter of the book.

Move on to the next chapter to talk about the important concepts of Monitoring and Managing your SQL Server on Linux.

CHAPTER 9

Managing and Monitoring SQL Server

After reading through the first eight chapters of this book you have learned the necessary fundamentals to install SQL Server on Linux, deploy a database and application, and set yourself up for success by understanding the fundamentals of our tools, performance, security, and high availability.

It is one thing to get an application deployed that uses SQL Server, but what are the key aspects to managing, maintaining, and monitoring SQL Server? That is what this chapter is about.

In fairness, I've covered some of the aspects of managing and monitoring throughout the book, including chapters on tools, performance, and high availability (certainly learning how to back up and restore a database is a key aspect to managing SQL Server).

This chapter extends that knowledge by covering topics that I have not discussed before on how to manage the SQL Server instance, your database, and objects within the database.

In the second part of the chapter, I'll talk about monitoring SQL Server including these topics:

- Monitoring SQL performance

- Using an amazing but little known feature called the System Health Session to monitor SQL Server health

- Learning a new and creative way to monitor transaction log backups

- A review of Linux tools I like to use to monitor performance

- Unique aspects to troubleshooting SQL Server problems

© Bob Ward 2018

B. Ward, *Pro SQL Server on Linux*, https://doi.org/10.1007/978-1-4842-4128-8_9

As you start reading through the sections on Management of the SQL Server instance, database, and objects, be sure to keep in mind an important lesson I've learned from my experience with SQL Server: *test your management strategy*. Most developers will focus on testing the application, which is vital to a successful deployment, but typically I see management tasks, like rebuilding an index, never get tested. How long will an index rebuild take on your largest table? You won't know unless you test it. In addition to testing, be sure to have a well-defined *change control and auditing process* for any changes made to the SQL Server instance configuration, database, objects, or the Linux operating system. Understanding what and who makes changes to a production SQL Server environment is important in my experience, especially when it comes to troubleshooting a problem and trying to answer the inevitable question "What changed?"

I have to admit I had fun writing this chapter because it contains some interesting history of my journey at Microsoft with SQL Server and my interactions with some of the smartest people I've ever known to build rich features for managing and monitoring SQL Server.

Managing the SQL Server Instance

SQL Server provides rich capabilities to manage the SQL Server instance after deployment, using tools like mssql-conf, the T-SQL statement ALTER SERVER CONFIGURATION, and the system stored procedure sp_configure. We honestly built SQL Server so that you should not have to spend a great deal of time configuring the instance after installation, but most production environments have some configuration changes that makes sense for their application. I've discussed these capabilities and options in previous chapters of the book. I've briefly listed these capabilities again in this section of the chapter for completeness.

In addition, in this section I'll spend time talking about SQL Server instance configuration options I have not mentioned at this point in the book, including:

- Creating SQL Server Agent jobs

- Using Resource Governor to control resource usage for users

- Using the Dedicated Admin Connection for emergency situations

- Using the sqlservr command line for special scenarios

Changing Server Configuration Options

I've discussed in previous chapters three methods to change the default configuration of the SQL Server instance. I've included this list purely as a review to ensure you know what options exist for SQL Server instance configuration:

> **mssql-conf:** A bash shell script used for configuration options that cannot be done through a T-SQL connection. I've shown you several examples in the book, but the full list of options can be found at https://docs.microsoft.com/sql/linux/sql-server-linux-configure-mssql-conf. I recommend anytime you use this feature, you create a script and track all executions for change control.

> **ALTER SERVER CONFIGURATION:** This is a T-SQL statement used to make instance level configuration changes. I've shown you in past chapters two examples for this statement: PROCESS AFFINITY and SOFTNUMA. A complete list of options for this statement can be found at https://docs.microsoft.com/sql/t-sql/statements/alter-server-configuration-transact-sql.

> **sp_configure:** This is a system stored procedure used to modify various types of instance level configuration options. I showed you in previous chapters some of the more important options related to performance, security, and high availability. There are other options, but the ones I've covered so far in the book I consider the most important. The complete list of options for sp_configure can be found at https://docs.microsoft.com/sql/database-engine/configure-windows/server-configuration-options-sql-server. The documentation talks about how some configuration options require a restart of SQL Server. All options require the T-SQL statement RECONFIGURE to take effect.

Note   I also covered in previous chapters the ALTER DATABASE SCOPED CONFIGURATION T-SQL statement that allows you to configure options at the database level that are normally reserved for an instance level modification.

Creating an SQL Server Agent Job

SQL Server Agent is a scheduling service that is installed when you deploy SQL Server on Linux. SQL Server Agent provides the capabilities to create *jobs* and then schedule the execution of jobs with various frequency options. Jobs execute via a series of *job steps*. A job step defines a specific set of T-SQL statements to execute in the job.

Note   SQL Server Agent before SQL Server 2017 CU4 required a separate package. Starting with 2017 CU4, SQL Server Agent is bundled with the mssql-server package. In addition, SQL Server on Linux only offers a job step that includes a set of T-SQL statements. SQL Server on Windows includes several *subsystems* that support other types of job steps.

The first step to be able to use SQL Server Agent is to enable this as a feature, using mssql-conf by running the following commands from the bash shell:

```
sudo /opt/mssql/bin/mssql-conf set sqlagent.enabled true
sudo systemctl restart mssql-server
```

At this point, you can now create SQL Server Agent jobs via T-SQL system stored procedures (e.g., **sp_add_job**), with an extension to SQL Operations Studio, or with SQL Server Management Studio (SSMS).

Our documentation has a very nice example of creating a job via the T-SQL system stored procedures to back up a database on a daily basis, at https://docs.microsoft. com/sql/linux/sql-server-linux-run-sql-server-agent-job#create-a-job-with-transact-sql.

An example of using SSMS to create a job can be seen at https://docs.microsoft. com/sql/linux/sql-server-linux-run-sql-server-agent-job#create-a-job-with-ssms.

Figure 9-1 shows an example of using the SQL Agent extension in SQL Operations Studio to create a new job.

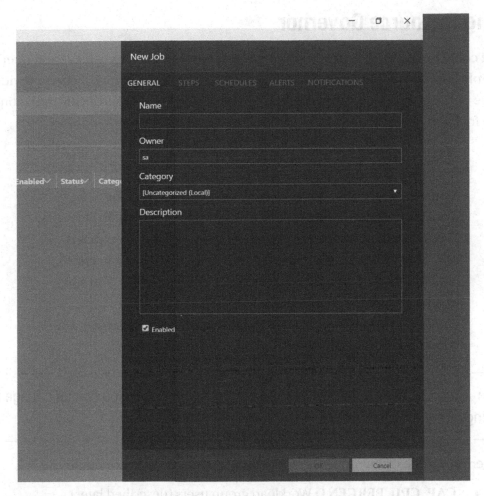

Figure 9-1. *Using SQL Operations Studio to create an SQL Agent job*

Since SQL Server Agent supports jobs that can execute any T-SQL statement or set of statements in a series of steps, you can use SQL Server Agent to perform any task you want to run on a schedule or ad hoc basis.

Linux users may just prefer to use the **cron** system (https://en.wikipedia.org/wiki/Cron) to schedule commands that can execute T-SQL commands using a program like sqlcmd to execute T-SQL scripts. My recommendation is that if you just need to run T-SQL statements for any application need or task, use SQL Server Agent. If you need to run other Linux commands or shell scripts with T-SQL scripts together as a unit, I would use cron.

441

Using Resource Governor

There could be scenarios where you want to control the resources of users and queries for applications for SQL Server related to CPU, memory, and I/O. SQL Server provides a feature to control these resources called *Resource Governor*. Resource Governor consists of the following objects:

> **Resource Pool:** A resource pool defines the constraint specified on physical resources such as CPU, memory, and I/O. Two pools come with SQL Server installed: (1) **internal**, which is used for background and system tasks and worker threads for SQL Server; and (2) **default**, which is a predefined pool for user tasks that is the "default" if no user-defined pools are created. You can create your own user-defined resources pools through T-SQL. You can read more about resource pools at `https://docs.microsoft.com/sql/relational-databases/resource-governor/resource-governor-resource-pool`.

Note   You can change the settings for the default pool, but you cannot change the settings for the internal pool.

Here are some of the properties for a resource pool you can configure:

- **CAP_CPU_PERCENT:** Workload group users (described later) associated with this pool will be capped for CPU utilization for any SQL Server worker thread usage.

- **MAX_MEMORY_PERCENT:** Workload group users associated with this pool will be capped on memory grants (hashes, sorts, ...) related to query execution. This setting does not affect memory allocated for buffer pool or any other cache.

- **AFFINITY:** This is an interesting setting. Using this setting for NUMA node(s) and CPU(s) will direct any workload group user associated with this pool to only run on the designed node(s) or CPU(s). This is an excellent technique to direct specific applications to only run on specific NUMA node(s) or CPU(s). This is also a more granular method to "affinitize" SQL Server than server configuration options (resource group affinity runs within the constraints of the affinity of the SQL Server instance).

- **MAX_IOPS_PER_VOLUME:** This setting controls the maximum physical IO operations per second (IOPS) for workload group users associated with this pool per unique disk volume. Unique disk volume means unique physical disk based on files for the database. The big "gotcha" for this setting is that it only applies to any I/O operation executed under the context of a *user task*. That means any I/O under the context of a background task (Log Writer, Recovery Writer, Checkpoint, ...) will not honor this setting (and you cannot change the internal pool setting to which they belong).

Pools also support "min" settings for CPU, memory, and I/O. Things can get a bit interesting if you start to play with minimum and maximum settings. Our documentation has a nice table that describes the effective settings, should you decide to do this. Read more at `https://docs.microsoft.com/sql/relational-databases/ resource-governor/resource-governor-resource-pool`.

> **Workload groups:** A workload group is a container of user tasks that are assigned to a resource pool. A workload group is the method to group a set of users together to restrict resource usage. Two workload groups are installed by default, internal and default, which are mapped to the corresponding resource pools by the same name. You can create your own workload group through T-SQL. If you don't create a user-defined workload group, all logins will be mapped to the default workload group (which is mapped to the default resource pool). You can read more about workload groups at `https://docs.microsoft.com/ sql/relational-databases/resource-governor/resource- governor-workload-group`.

Workload groups allow you to specify settings at a more granular level than the pool they are associated with. For example, you can configure REQUEST_MAX_MEMORY_ GRANT_PERCENT to specify the maximum memory grant for workload group users. This is applied within the maximum already established for the pool.

Note   There is a good description of memory grants by one of our top developers, Jay Choe, at `https://blogs.msdn.microsoft.com/sqlqueryprocessing/2010/02/16/understanding-sql-server-memory-grant`.

One unique setting for a workload group is MAXDOP. I've discussed parallel query execution in a previous chapter and how you can configure the maximum workers applied to a query plan operator through sp_configure, ALTER DATABASE, and even a query hint. Workload groups allow you to specify a MAXDOP setting for all users in the group. Using a combination of these MAXDOP settings can perhaps get confusing. Here is guidance on how the order of precedence is applied for MAXDOP:

- MAX_DOP as a query hint is honored as long as it does not exceed workload group MAX_DOP.

- MAX_DOP as a query hint always overrides sp_configure 'max degree of parallelism'.

- The MAXDOP at the database scope overrides (unless it is set to 0) the max degree of parallelism set at the server level by sp_configure. Query hints can still override the database scoped MAXDOP in order to tune specific queries that need different setting. All these settings are limited by the MAXDOP set for the Workload Group.

- Workload group MAX_DOP overrides sp_configure 'max degree of parallelism'.

- If the query is marked as serial (MAX_DOP = 1) at compile time, it cannot be changed back to parallel at run time regardless of the workload group or sp_configure setting.

The documentation has a complete list of workload group settings at `https://docs.microsoft.com/sql/t-sql/statements/alter-workload-group-transact-sql#arguments`.

> **Classification functions:** A classifier function is a T-SQL function that binds a login to a user-defined workload group. You build a T-SQL function (with a known template) and assign a specific login (or group of logins) to a workload group. This allows SQL

Server to know how to map resource restrictions to a login for a specific workload group and resource pool. You can read more about classifier functions at https://docs.microsoft.com/sql/relational-databases/resource-governor/resource-governor-classifier-function.

I found this simple but easy to use demo built by my colleague Travis Wright on GitHub at https://github.com/twright-msft/mssql-test-scripts/blob/master/Administration/resource-governor.sql to show the basics of how to use Resource Governor for I/O.

Note   Linux has an operating system concept similar to Resource Governor for control of resources for processes called Linux control groups (*cgroups*). cgroups are independent of SQL Server but since SQL Server is a Linux process, SQL Server should be able to run when cgroups are being used to control SQL Server resources such as CPU or I/O. You can read more about cgroups at http://man7.org/linux/man-pages/man7/cgroups.7.html.

Resource Governor is technically enabled for default and internal pools without any user intervention. However, if you want to have modifications to the default pool take effect or create your own pool and workload groups, you must enable Resource Governor for these new configurations using the following T-SQL statement:

```
ALTER RESOURCE GOVERNOR RECONFIGURE;
GO
```

Using the Dedicated Admin Connection

When I worked for Microsoft technical support years ago before SQL Server 2005, I would occasionally have to help a customer on a critical problem where SQL Server appeared to be *hung* (no connection or query is allowed to SQL Server). It was around this timeframe that often my colleagues in support, Robert Dorr and Keith Elmore, would produce some amazing innovative ideas on how to troubleshoot complex problems. In fact, some of the best ideas we produced were done when the three of us would take a walk after lunch around the Microsoft Texas Campus in Irving, Texas.

(Note: We carried on this tradition for many years dating from the mid-1990s all the way to the present day. As the three of us are on different teams, this now happens far less often.)

One of those days, Robert Dorr was talking to us about another customer incident where SQL Server appeared to be hung. He said, "there has to be a better way to figure these out." And indeed this discussion led to supportability improvements for errors in the ERRORLOG when these conditions can occur (see this older blog post by Robert at https://blogs.msdn.microsoft.com/psssql/2008/03/28/how-it-works-non-yielding-resource-monitor/).

As part of this conversation, we all three agreed that if the SQL Server engine cannot accept new logins or queries, why can't we have a special *dedicated* connection to SQL Server that has limited capabilities but can be used to connect to SQL Server to investigate and possibly even fix a SQL Server hang. Thus was born a feature in SQL Server 2005 called Dedicated Admin Connection (DAC).

DAC is supported by a separate TCP port (1434) for SQL Server and operates on a different SQLOS scheduler. Therefore, if SQL Server cannot respond to new requests due to a scheduler or standard port issue, it may be possible to connect with DAC, and at minimum run queries against DMVs to find out a possible cause of the problem before you need to restart SQL Server. In addition, it may even be possible to find the cause and free up the problem without having to restart. I'll talk about an example shortly.

First, let's see how to connect with DAC. Run the following command with sqlcmd from the bash shell on the Linux Server:

```
sqlcmd -Usa -Sadmin:localhost
```

Notice the syntax for the Servername uses the prefix **admin**.

Note   sqlcmd on Windows supports the -A option, which forces the use of DAC but that is not supported on Linux. However, you can use the admin: prefix on any SQL Server tool, including sqlcmd, SQL Operations Studio, and SSMS.

You are now presented with the sqlcmd editor, but how do you know if this worked and you connected with DAC?

Run the following T-SQL statements as found in the example script **amidac.sql**:

```
-- What is my session id?
SELECT @@spid
go
-- List out the current connections, their endpoint, and port
SELECT dec.session_id, e.name, dec.local_tcp_port
FROM sys.dm_exec_connections dec
JOIN sys.endpoints e
ON e.endpoint_id = dec.endpoint_id
GO
```

I ran this script with the following command from the bash shell:

```
sqlcmd -Usa -Sadmin:localhost -iamidac.sql
```

The results should look similar to the following:

```
------
   51

(1 rows affected)
session_id  name                          local_tcp_port
----------- ----------------------------- --------------
        51 Dedicated Admin Connection    1434

(1 rows affected)
```

Notice the nifty server variable @@SPID to find out your current session id. Then you can find your session in the list of connections (in this example it is the only connection). I introduced you to the concept of an endpoint with Always On Availability Groups. DAC has its own endpoint automatically created, typically hosted off port 1434. You can see this session is using that port.

There is only one active DAC connection allowed at a time (hence the term Dedicated). And you can connect with DAC remotely. I personally believe if you feel the need to use DAC you should use it locally with an ssh session. I say this because if there are remote connectivity issues to your Linux Server, you won't know if the SQL Server connectivity problem is a result of a connectivity issue over the network or with the server itself (and if you can't get an ssh session, there is likely a larger problem than SQL Server).

Here is another rarely known secret about DAC. I mentioned in a previous chapter that while you can see a list of system tables as a user, you cannot by default read directly from these tables. You should be using system catalog views.

Try the following T-SQL statements using DAC and with a connection without DAC:

```
USE master
GO
SELECT * FROM sys.sysschobjs
GO
```

sys.sysschobjs is one of the system tables that powers catalog views like sys.objects. When you run this query when not using DAC, you get this error

```
Msg 208, Level 16, State 1, Server bwsql2017rhel, Line 1
Invalid object name 'sys.sysschobjs'.
```

However, if you use DAC, you will be able to read any system table directly. It is a neat trick, but to be honest I don't see much of a need for you to do this in production. It can be interesting to use to learn more about SQL Server internals, but we don't publish the schema definition for system tables.

Tip   You can examine the text of system catalog views through **sys.system_sql_ modules** to figure out how system tables work.

You can't run anything you want over DAC. We built DAC to only have a certain set of resources that should reliably allow you to connect to SQL Server in emergency situations and perform critical, but minimal operations. When should you use DAC? I recommend only using DAC when you cannot connect to SQL Server even with a local sqlcmd connection on the Linux Server. Once you connect, query DMVs like dm_exec_ requests to get a basic sense of the connections and queries are running.

One scenario where you may be able to resolve a problem with DAC is the following:

1.   The maximum number of worker threads is being used.

2.   All worker threads are blocked on a lead blocker.

3. The lead blocker is not giving up its resources. For example, you could have a session that starts a transaction, runs queries that obtain locks, but never commits. All workers may be blocked waiting for this transaction and session to complete.

4. Since all worker threads are busy, SQL Server cannot service any new connections or queries because there are no worker threads available.

5. However, you could connect with DAC and terminate the leader blocker using the T-SQL KILL statement, thus freeing up all the blocked workers. The T-SQL KILL statement requires higher than usual privileges, and rightly so. You can read more about the T-SQL KILL statement and scenarios it may make sense to use for your server at `https://docs.microsoft.com/sql/t-sql/ language-elements/kill-transact-sql`.

You can read about more about DAC, including limits and how to connect remotely, at `https://docs.microsoft.com/sql/database-engine/configure-windows/ diagnostic-connection-for-database-administrators`.

sqlservr Command Line Options

In Chapter 8 I briefly talked about a technique to rebuild system databases that use a command line option for the sqlservr program. You typically start SQL Server with systemctl, but sqlservr is a program that can be launched from the shell directly. And there are a range of command line options, mostly undocumented, that can be used with sqlservr. You can see the list by running this command from the bash shell (be sure to stop SQL Server first if it is already running):

```
sudo -u mssql /opt/mssql/bin/sqlservr --help
```

Your results should look like the following:

```
usage: sqlservr [OPTIONS...]

Configuration options:
  -T<#>                Enable a traceflag
  -y<#>                Enable dump when server encounters specified error
  -k<#>                Checkpoint speed (in MB/sec)
```

```
Administrative options:
  --accept-eula              Accept the SQL Server EULA
  --pid <pid>                Set server product key
  --reset-sa-password        Reset system administrator password. Password
                             should
                             be specified in the SQLSERVR_SA_PASSWORD
                             environment variable.
  -f                         Minimal configuration mode
  -m                         Single user administration mode
  -K                         Force regeneration of Service Master Key
  --setup                    Set basic configuration settings and then
                             shutdown.
  --force-setup              Same as --setup, but also reinitialize master and
                             model databases.

General options:
  -v                         Show program version
  --help                     Display this help information
```

The functionality for many of these options can be done with another documented method. For example, -T for setting a trace flag can be achieved using mssql-conf.

There are two options worth calling out that can be useful for troubleshooting and emergency situations:

> **-m:** Start SQL Server in *single user mode*. When you start SQL
> Server with this option, only one user can connect to SQL Server.
> One common use for -m is a scenario where you need to restore
> the master database. You must first start SQL Server with -m in
> order to restore master. A more interesting, advanced, and quite
> frankly dangerous scenario is to modify system tables or access
> the mssqlsystemresource database. If you start SQL Server with
> -m and use DAC to connect to SQL Server, you will be given
> access to directly modify a system table. Before we shipped SQL
> Server 2005, the plan was to completely lock down any access to
> system tables. Working in technical support, I just knew some

scenario would come up where we would need this capability.
The compromise was to provide read access to system tables using
DAC and modify access with -m and DAC. And sure enough,
there have been a few times over the years where in an emergency
situation I needed this capability.

But beware! Once you modify a system table, SQL Server marks a bit in the database
structure so that any time you open the database, a warning is put in the ERRORLOG
stating database system tables have been directly modified. You are completely in
an unsupported state at that point. However, Microsoft may have you do this to work
around some critical problem and they can help you get back into a supported state.

An example of starting SQL Server in single user mode is the following command
from the bash shell:

```
sudo -u mssql /opt/mssql/bin/sqlservr -m
```

One issue with single user mode is what I call a *race to connect*. When you start SQL
Server in single user mode, the first sysadmin to connect *wins*. Therefore you can restrict
who can connect by application name using an option after the -m parameter. Here is an
example to restrict only sysadmin users using the program sqlcmd can connect:

```
sudo -u mssql /opt/mssql/bin/sqlservr -m"SQLCMD"
```

See our documentation for more information on starting SQL Server in single user
mode at https://docs.microsoft.com/sql/database-engine/configure-windows/
start-sql-server-in-single-user-mode.

> **-f:** This option indicates to start SQL Server in *minimal
> configuration mode*. Minimal configuration mode includes single
> user mode plus it restricts other SQL Server functionality or
> configures SQL Server in a *minimal method*. For example, SQL
> Server will use default server configuration information to start
> the server in case you have made a server configuration change
> that prevents SQL Server from running or starting. The best
> example I can think of for this option is the server configuration
> option 'max server memory'. If you set this value too low, in some
> cases, SQL Server does not have enough memory to allow a

connection or startup properly. Starting SQL Server in minimal
configuration mode will set 'max server memory' to its default,
allowing you to connect and change it to a correct value. You can
read more about starting SQL Server in minimal configuration
mode at `https://docs.microsoft.com/sql/database-engine/`
`configure-windows/start-sql-server-with-minimal-`
`configuration`.

Note   SQL Server containers run SQL Server by using the sqlservr program
directly.

Managing Databases

After deploying your database you will at some point have to perform some management
of the database, whether it is making changes at the database level or file level. In this
section, I'll review those key topics including Moving Databases, Managing Files, Detach
and Attaching Databases, important ALTER DATBASE scenarios, and a very interesting
discussion on repairing databases (I think you will like this section with some internals
on database states and checksum).

Moving Databases

One common operation you may need to perform after you create a database and have
it running in production is to move the database and transaction log files to a new
directory or new disks. There may be several reasons you need to move the files, such as
disk maintenance or disk upgrade scenarios. One common method to move one or more
files is the following:

1. Change the database to an offline state by executing the following
    T-SQL statement

    ```
    ALTER DATABASE <dbname> SET OFFLINE
    ```

This shows the ability to control database state without shutting down SQL Server.

2. Move the intended files on the Linux Server to your intended
    target directory or disk.

3. Indicate to SQL Server the new location of the file. For each file
    you move, run the following T-SQL statement:

```
ALTER DATABASE <dbname> MODIFY FILE ( NAME = logical_name,
FILENAME = 'new_path\os_file_name' )
```

4. Change the database state back to ONLINE using the following
    T-SQL statement:

```
ALTER DATABASE <dbname> SET ONLINE
```

SQL Server will bring the database online and run recovery (as it always does when a database is brought online).

You also may have a need to move the system databases. You can read more about the procedure to do this in our documentation at `https://docs.microsoft.com/sql/relational-databases/databases/move-system-databases`. The only exception to this documentation for SQL Server on Linux is to move the master database. In order to move the master database on SQL Server on Linux, you need to use the mssql-conf script as documented at `https://docs.microsoft.com/sql/linux/sql-server-linux-configure-mssql-conf#masterdatabasedir`.

Managing Files

There could be other scenarios to manage database and/or transaction log files, including adding new files, removing existing files, or adding more space to existing files.

Before I review the process for these operations, one of the most fundamental tasks you may need regarding files is to understand the space used by files. To see space usage for the database, use the system procedure **sp_spaceused**. To view the size of the transaction log and space used within the transaction log, you can use the legacy method with the T-SQL statement **DBCC SQLPERF(LOGSPACE)** or query the new DMV for SQL Server 2017 **sys.dm_db_log_stats.**

Another alternative is to use the new SERVER REPORTS extension in SQL Operations Studio to view space usage across databases split by data and transaction log usage. Figure 9-2 shows an example.

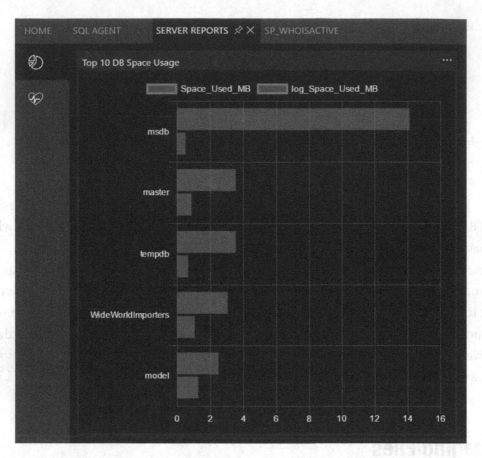

Figure 9-2. *Database space usage in SQL Operations Studio*

Adding a database file to a database is pretty simple via the T-SQL **ALTER DATABASE** statement using the **ADD FILE** option. You can read more about this at https://docs.microsoft.com/sql/relational-databases/databases/add-data-or-log-files-to-a-database. Even though adding transaction log files is possible for a database, there is almost no benefit to adding a second transaction log file, so I don't recommend it.

Note   You shouldn't have much of a need to add a database file to a system database, except for tempdb. When you need to add a file for tempdb, you should ensure you (1) add the file with exact same size and autogrow options as all other files and (2) enable the AUTOGROW_ALL_FILES for tempdb using ALTER DATABASE if is not enabled already.

There could be situations where you need to remove a file from a database, but that file must be empty before it can be removed via **ALTER DATABASE** using the **REMOVE FILE** option. You can learn more about removing files at https://docs.microsoft.com/sql/relational-databases/databases/delete-data-or-log-files-from-a-database and how to empty a file at https://docs.microsoft.com/sql/relational-databases/databases/shrink-a-file.

You can also use ALTER DATABASE with the MODIFY FILE option to increase the size of a file for a database. Learn more in our documentation at https://docs.microsoft.com/sql/relational-databases/databases/increase-the-size-of-a-database.

Note   One common issue you may encounter with any execution of ALTER DATABASE that affects files is that it will block BACKUP statements or be blocked by any active BACKUP.

Detaching and Attaching Databases

I've talked about how to move a database by moving the database and transaction log files. I've also talked about how to recover a database using backup and restore in earlier chapters. However, backup and restore can also be used to *transport* a database to another server and is the preferred method to do that.

SQL Server also offers an alternative to transport a database by detaching and attaching the database. Detaching a database will shut down the database and remove the metadata about the database in the master system database but does NOT remove the files (which a DROP DATABASE would do).

Note   For security purposes, never attach a database you do not trust or know the source.

You can detach a database using the following T-SQL statement:

> **Note**   The following examples assume you have restored the full
> WideWorldImporters database, as I've described in previous chapters using `wget`
> `https://github.com/Microsoft/sql-server-samples/releases/`
> `download/wide-world-importers-v1.0/WideWorldImporters-Full.bak`.

```
EXEC sp_detach_db 'WideWorldImporters', 'true'
GO
```

At this point the database and log files for the WideWorldImporters database remain in their current location on disk. You could then copy these files to another Linux Server running SQL Server and attach them. Run the following T-SQL statement, which is found in the example script **attachwwi.sql**:

```
CREATE DATABASE WideWorldImporters
    ON (FILENAME = '/var/opt/mssql/data/WideWorldImporters.mdf'),
    (FILENAME = '/var/opt/mssql/data/WideWorldImporters_UserData.ndf'),
    (FILENAME = '/var/opt/mssql/data/WideWorldImporters.ldf'),
    (FILENAME = '/var/opt/mssql/data/WideWorldImporters_InMemory_Data_1')
    FOR ATTACH
GO
```

Note in this example I provided all the files for the WideWorldImporters database and the folder for the Memory Optimized checkpoint files. In this example, you could have changed the name of the database when you attach. You could have also placed the files in different paths and attach from the new paths.

> **Note**   SQL Server has a legacy system procedure called sp_attach_db but it is
> marked deprecated, so use the CREATE DATABASE using the FOR ATTACH option.

While you normally need all of the original files to attach the database, there a few hidden tricks

1. If the database was cleanly shut down by doing a detach when no active transactions exist and there is only one transaction log file, it is possible to leave out the transaction log file when you attach the database and SQL Server will build a new one automatically.

2. If the database was cleanly shut down by doing a detach when no active transactions exist and there are multiple transaction log files, SQL Server offers the CREATE DATABASE option FOR ATTACH_REBUILD_LOG.

You should only detach a database that is ONLINE and healthy. A database that is in a state called SUSPECT (because recovery failed for someone reason) cannot be detached. However, if you take a database offline that is SUSPECT and then drop this database, the files remain. Then if you try to attach this database, it will fail. If you ever find yourself in this situation, you can use what I call the *Paul Randal attach method*, named after my good friend Paul Randal, who is one of the top experts when it comes to tips and tricks for salvaging and repairing databases. You can read Paul's technique for this situation at https://www.sqlskills.com/blogs/paul/creating-detaching-re-attaching-and-fixing-a-suspect-database.

Note   I'll add in the hidden secret of the attach option ATTACH_FORCE_REBUILD_LOG. It is undocumented and completely unsupported but still works. It could also be used in a desperate situation to attach a database when the transaction log files are missing or damaged.

ALTER DATABASE Usage Scenarios

To this point I've described in this book many different purposes and scenarios to use ALTER DATABASE. The following are a few more SET options you might find useful:

- **EMERGENCY:** I'll discuss this option in the next section on Repairing Databases. This comes in handy if the database cannot come online.

- **[READ_ONLY | READ_WRITE]:** If you would like to prevent any changes to a database, you can set it to READ_ONLY. This might come in handy if you want to provide a copy of a database to another user or developer so can they read the data, but you want to make sure they don't make any changes to ensure a consistent copy of the data. Using READ_WRITE marks the database available for changes.

- **PAGE_VERIFY:** In Chapter 8, I discussed the concept of a database checksum. I'll talk more about it in the next section on Repairing Databases. This is the option to change the default, which is CHECKSUM (which I recommend you use). The other options are TORN_PAGE_DETECTION (a form of page verification that is not as robust as CHECKSUM) and NONE (turn off all page verification).

- **WITH [ROLLBACK AFTER | ROLLBACK IMMEDIATE | NO_WAIT]:** Some ALTER DATABASE scenarios require an exclusive lock on the database. This option is called a *termination clause*. If that exclusive lock is blocked by other users, this SET option gives you choices on what behavior should occur for those active users. ROLLBACK_ AFTER <time> will terminate and rollback any active transactions after a period of time. ROLLBACK IMMEDIATE takes this action immediately. NO_WAIT means that the ALTER DATABASE will fail if it must wait on active users. For a list of what options can use this clause see our documentation at `https://docs.microsoft.com/ sql/t-sql/statements/alter-database-transact-sql-set- options?view=sql-server-2017&tabs=sqlserver#SettingOptions.`

- **[SINGLE_USER | RESTRICTED_USER |MULTI_USER]:** By default, SQL Server allows multiple users to interact with a database. However, you can restrict access to only a single user or restricted users. It is common to use the termination clause when using SINGLE_USER or RESTRICTED_USER. RESTRICTED_USER only allows future access to the database to members of the db_owner or sysadmin roles.

All ALTER DATABASE SET options can be found in our documentation at `https:// docs.microsoft.com/sql/t-sql/statements/alter-database-transact-sql-set- options?view=sql-server-2017&tabs=sqlserver#arguments.`

Repairing Databases

Over my career at Microsoft I've seen scenarios where a database or pages in a database become damaged or unavailable to access. I call the technique to get the database or portions of it back online and available *repairing* a database. As I mentioned earlier in the documentation on attaching, there is probably no one outside of Microsoft (and perhaps inside) that knows the "ins and outs" of repairing databases like Paul Randal. There is a reason behind this.

Around the timeframe of the development of SQL Server 2000, I was visiting the Microsoft campus and the SQL Server Engineering team. I had gained a reputation with the engineering team for expertise and skills on DBCC CHECKDB, database corruption, and repairing databases. On this visit I was introduced to a new developer named Paul Randal. This would not only begin a journey for Paul and me to work together on various features of the SQL Server product (many of these which landed in SQL Server 2005) but also a great friendship. Paul became a major champion for ensuring SQL Server had the supportability features needed by Microsoft Support and our customers. Paul and I have remained great friends along with his wife Kimberly Tripp (and with many of the folks that work for their company SQLskills). If fact, one of my favorite events at which to speak about SQL Server is called SQLIntersection, which occurs twice a year run by Paul and Kim.

The following section has Paul's imprint all over it from his work in the SQL Engineering team. Furthermore, he has an incredible series of blog posts on the topics of repairing databases and recovering databases (among the other topics on just about everything about the SQL Server Engine). One of the things that make Paul's blog so unique is that he shows examples for you to try yourself. His blog can be found at `https://www.sqlskills.com/blogs/paul`. With the encouragement of others like Paul, I started to blog myself (along with Robert Dorr) when I worked in technical support. And many of the older blog posts Robert and I both wrote about recovery and repair still exist today at `https://blogs.msdn.microsoft.com/psssql`. I don't blog as much on these topics as I did before, but Robert and I maintain our own blog now at `http://aka.ms/bobsql`.

Enough with the walk down memory lane and shameless advertising of blogs. In this section, I'll talk about how to repair and recover databases in situations where a restore of a backup is not possible.

Database States

I've referenced a few times in the book the fact that a database can be OFFLINE or ONLINE and even a state called SUSPECT.

The difference between the state of SUSPECT and one called RECOVERY_PENDING is important when evaluating why a database cannot be accessed. The state of a database can be found at any time by querying the **sys.databases.state_desc** column in the master database. A list of all possible states can be found in our documentation at `https://docs.microsoft.com/sql/relational-databases/system-catalog-views/ sys-databases-transact-sql`.

When a database is first *started*, either through SQL Server startup, a RESTORE, attach, or bringing it online via ALTER DATABASE, the state of the database is set to ONLINE if no issues occur. However, there can be some intermediate states to get ONLINE. Furthermore, some issues can cause the state of the database to go a different direction, not go ONLINE, and cause it to become inaccessible.

Figure 9-3 shows a state diagram of these various states and actions that can cause a state to occur.

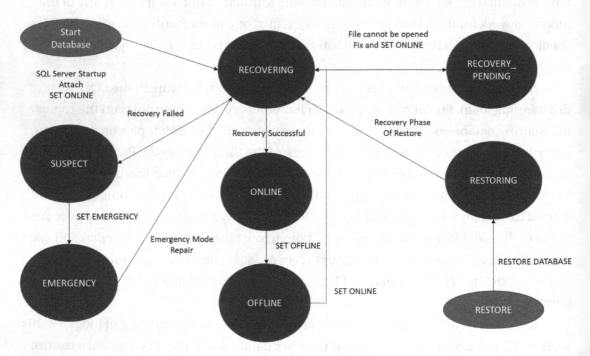

Figure 9-3. *States of a database in SQL Server*

Let me explain some of the states and flow to gain a better understanding of how you can act in scenarios where the state of the database does not go to ONLINE.

- Anytime the database is started, it always starts at the RECOVERING phase.

- If the files for the database cannot be opened (e.g., a permission problem or a file is missing), the state goes to RECOVERY_PENDING. You may be able to easily fix the problem by finding the right file or setting the correct permission. Using ALTER DATABASE to set the state to ONLINE will cause it to go back to RECOVERING. If recovery is successful, the state will go to ONLINE. Check the ERRORLOG for error messages that pinpoint the cause of the RECOVERY_PENDING state (which file and what operating system error).

- If recovery is not successful (for several different reasons), the state of the database will be set to SUSPECT. You can use a technique called *emergency mode repair* to potentially repair the database. I'll describe that technique later in this section.

Note   SQL Server has a really cool technique that can avoid a SUSPECT state should it find it encounter an error on a page during recovery (like a checksum failure, which I'll describe more next). This is called *deferred transactions*, which you can read more about at `https://docs.microsoft.com/sql/relational-databases/backup-restore/deferred-transactions-sql-server`.

- Note that during a RESTORE DATABASE, the state of the database is RESTORING and then the state moves to RECOVERING during the recovery phase of the database restore.

More About Checksum

I've mentioned the concept of a database checksum several times in the book. Checksum is an important concept added in SQL Server 2005 to indicate a database page has been altered after it has been written to disk. If SQL Server finds a database page has been altered and fails a checksum, the following error will be written to the ERRORLOG:

```
Msg 824, SQL Server detected a logical consistency-based I/O error:
incorrect checksum (expected: 0xdec71ff7; actual: 0xb0499fcf). It occurred
during a read of page (<pageid>)...
```

In addition, an entry is written into the **suspect_pages** found in the msdb database. Remember, this is a condition that can trigger an automatic page repair for Always On Availability Groups. Over the years, I've had questions about how a checksum really works, so I'll describe it here. Figure 9-4 shows a diagram I've created to give a sense for the basics of a checksum.

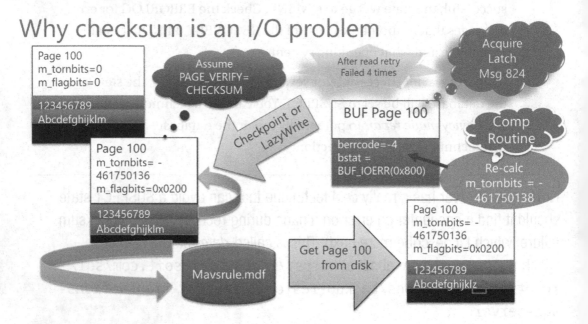

Figure 9-4. *How a checksum works in SQL Server*

Let me explain the flow. If the PAGE_VERIFY=CHECKSUM is set for a database (the default for SQL Server), when a page is written to disk, SQL Server will compute a checksum value (based on a mathematical calculation of the bits on the page) and store this in the header of the page. When SQL Server reads the page from disk, it recalculates the checksum. If the calculated checksum does not match what is in the page header, a checksum failure has been encountered.

Notice though in the diagram that it says, "After read retry failed 4 times." This is because if a checksum failure is encountered, SQL Server will attempt to retry the read up to four times before it signals a true checksum failure. Our SQL Engineering team found that in some cases transient hardware issues can arise where a retry of the read would work (but 4 was typically the threshold where it would always fail). If a retry of the read is successful, the query that was trying to read the page succeeds, but you will see Msg 825 in the ERRORLOG.

Note   An Msg 824 is a *logical* failure when reading or writing a database page. There are a few other logical checks besides a checksum calculation. For example, SQL Server always compares the pageid value in the page header to the actual page SQL Server believes it is reading. Msg 823 is raised should SQL Server encounter a physical error when reading or writing a page. For example, if an operating system error occurred when reading a page, Msg 823 would occur and not Msg 824.

There is one flaw with the checksum algorithm worth noting. The checksum is calculated based on what is stored in the database page *at the time it is written*. If the database page was damaged in memory, the checksum will be based on the already damaged page and will never raise an error. SQL Server does have an algorithm to occasionally verify a checksum even when it is memory by background processes. When this process detects a checksum failure on a page in memory, it will raise Msg 832 to the ERRORLOG. You can read more about this verification on how to resolve it from this Microsoft Knowledge Base article https://support.microsoft.com/help/2015759/how-to-troubleshoot-msg-832-constant-page-has-changed-in-sql-server.

Fixing a page that fails with a checksum error can be done by restoring a backup, restoring the page from a backup, or repairing it with DBCC CHECKDB (which will result in losing the data on the page).

DBCC CHECKDB Repair

I've discussed in Chapter 8 the DBCC CHECKDB command to check the consistency of a database. CHECKDB does include reading pages from disk, so checksum verification on every page is part of that execution.

If DBCC CHECKDB encounters any failure when checking the consistency of the database, it is possible to repair the database using this T-SQL statement. There are two options for repairing a database with CHECKDB:

> **REPAIR_REBUILD:** If it's possible to repair the database by only rebuilding or repairing an index, REPAIR_REBUILD can correct errors found when executing CHECKDB.
>
> **REPAIR_ALLOW_DATA_LOSS:** If SQL Server detects errors in CHECKB that can only be repaired by deallocating a page(s),

which could result in data loss, this option can be used. By its name, when you use this option you are doing so with the knowledge that you may lose data. CHECKDB is very good about reporting out details on which pages are being deallocated and how many. Restoring from a good backup is always the best mode of recovery (or failing over to a valid secondary replica), but in some cases repairing a database with CHECKDB is your only choice, even though you may encounter some data loss.

The documentation is fairly good about going through some of these scenarios, which you can read at `https://docs.microsoft.com/sql/t-sql/database-console-commands/dbcc-checkdb-transact-sql`. In addition, the output of running CHECKDB indicates which repair option is the minimal required to resolve all errors found at the completion of CHECKDB. I can tell you from years of experience a few observations about using repair for CHECKDB:

- There are some errors that cannot be repaired.

- I rarely run into customer situations where REPAIR_REBUILD was a valid solution. If you have database damage (commonly known as *corruption*. An example of corruption is a checksum failure I have described earlier in this chapter), it is typically going to result in some data loss. Not always, but typically.

- I've seen some cases where I had to run several iterations of CHECKDB with repair options to resolve all errors.

- CHECKDB can be run in a transaction with repair options so you can run repair and then rollback if necessary.

- If you are deciding whether you should restore a backup or run repair, consider what is *known* vs. *unknown*. If you have a valid backup to restore but you lose a day of work, that may be far better and a faster method to resolve the situation because it is known. Trying to repair a damaged database and trying to figure out what pages you lost related to known business value and data can take a very long time. I've been in situations where I've given guidance to a customer to do both. Restore the backup to a different database while trying repair options.

Consider reviewing Paul Randal's blog post tag he calls "CHECKDB from every angle" at `https://www.sqlskills.com/blogs/paul/category/checkdb-from-every-angle` for some really great information about DBCC CHECKDB.

Note   I still get a question from customers and users of SQL Server whether Microsoft has some magical set of tools no one knows about that allows us to *patch* databases. The transparent truth is we used to. In a galaxy, far, far away, I used to use some programs that allowed me to "fix bits" on database pages. It was still very time consuming and costly, and I rarely used it. The tool doesn't exist anymore and there is no benefit in recreating it. You can read Paul's blog posts about an undocumented DBCC command that allows for "bit fixing." However, don't rely on this. We don't really test this (it could crash the server or cause irreparable damage), it requires tons of time to use, requires an extensive knowledge of the internal page structures of SQL Server (which we don't document and have changed over time and will continue to change), and we may remove it at any time.

Emergency Mode Repair

Consider the database state in the preceding diagram (Figure 9-3) called SUSPECT. SQL Server has attempted to run recovery, but a failure has occurred that is not recoverable (e.g., the transaction log file is damaged). Prior to Paul coming to Microsoft, this was one of the uglier scenarios for me to help customers with. Paul invented in SQL Server 2005 a concept called *emergency mode repair*. The concept is to change the database state to EMEGENCY using ALTER DATABASE <dbname> SET EMERGENCY.

This will give you access to the database to then run DBCC CHECKDB using the REPAIR_ALLOW_DATA_LOSS option. SQL Server will recognize the transaction log is not accessible and will *rebuild the transaction log* and run recovery. Paul describes the process in this blog post at `https://www.sqlskills.com/blogs/paul/checkdb-from-every-angle-emergency-mode-repair-the-very-very-last-resort`.

It sounds pretty easy and simple, which it is. Here is the problem. Since the transaction log must be rebuilt, you have no idea what transactions were in the log that needed to be rolled forward or undone. So even though DBCC CHECKDB is *clean*, you could easily have logical inconsistency in your database (e.g., imagine the accidental credit of 1 million dollars into a bank account, which may be there but you don't know it!).

This is why it is a last resort and definitely not a replacement for a restore of a good backup. Despite these warnings, I would find myself in Microsoft support using this technique frequently because these customers did not have a valid backup to restore.

I have one other comment about the use of the EMERGENCY state of a database. While you can use the emergency mode repair option, I've seen other situations where setting the state of a database to EMERGENCY allowed me to access the database and copy out (for example with bcp) critical tables to a business. Keep this in mind as part of your toolkit for database salvage operations.

RESTORE with CONTINUE_AFTER_ERROR

I mentioned Chapter 8 that a backup would fail to restore if it was created using the WITH CHECKSUM option and a checksum failure occurred on the backup media itself.

In that magical supportability release of SQL Server 2005, we added an option to RESTORE called CONTINUE_AFTER_ERROR. In most cases, this option will allow the RESTORE to complete even if an error (like a checksum) occurs. At this point, it is completely a "toss of the coin" whether the database can be used or salvaged. However, it is possible only a small portion of the backup (even a single bit) media has a problem, so this option could help you recover much of your database.

Finding the Cause of Corruption

Through the years as I worked on customer cases in Microsoft support involving database corruption, I would always (and rightly so) be asked "What caused this?" I can tell you from 25 years of experience that the number one cause of database corruption is a system problem, most of the time from the I/O system.

Here is an interesting technique you can use to help prove it. If you run DBCC CHECKDB or encounter a checksum failure and have a sequence of database and transaction log backups that span the timeframe of the problem, restore them on a separate server. If the database and transaction log backups are valid, and you restore them in a sequence that spans the error but the restore sequence does not show the error, then the problem must be on the original database in the form of a damaged page, either in memory or on disk.

I actually did have a customer follow this sequence many years back on a case, and a restore sequence showed the same error. This turned out to be a bug in SQL Server, which we found and fixed immediately.

What was more common is that the restore sequence did not show the problem. And after a period of time, the customer would tell us an update to the drivers and firmware of the hardware made the problem go away (or a replacement of hardware components).

Managing Objects

Like databases, once you create tables, indexes, and server-side code like stored procedures, you will inevitably have to manage these objects. This section covers some examples of management tasks you may have to perform, such as altering tables, truncating tables, dealing with index fragmentation, and altering server-side code.

Managing Tables

In this section I'll discuss two aspects of managing tables: altering tables by altering columns and properties; and truncating tables, which can be a very efficient method to *clear* a table.

Altering Tables

After you create tables for your database, there could be scenarios where you want to modify the definition or properties of a table. You always have the option to copy out the data of a table, drop the current table, create a new table definition, and import back in your data.

However, SQL Server provides an ALTER TABLE statement to modify the definition or properties about the table. One of the most common usages to alter a table is to make changes to columns. With ALTER TABLE you can add, drop, or change the definition of columns within some limits. Making modifications to columns though has some implications. The following are options to use with ALTER TABLE to make changes to column definitions and those implications:

> **ADD <column>:** You can add column(s) to a table that will be defined in order at the end of the table. Any column you add must either allow NULL values or you must specify a DEFAULT

467

CONSTRAINT as part of adding the column, to provide default values for each row for the new column. Adding a column with a default value on a table with a large number of rows can take some time to complete (because it is like executing an INSERT on each row) and generate a large number of log records.

ALTER COLUMN <column>: You can change the type of a column and it size. Changing the type must follow the rules of possible data type conversion for SQL Server, which can be found at `https://docs.microsoft.com//sql/t-sql/data-types/data-type-conversion-database-engine`. Changing the size of a column is possible provided the new size is larger than the current size definition (e.g., you can change a varchar(100) to varchar(200) but not to varchar(10)).

DROP COLUMN <column>: You are allowed to drop a column in the table except for columns that are part of constraints such as primary keys. You must drop these constraints first, which is also possible with ALTER TABLE. Note that dropping a column is fully logged (like a DELETE), so this operation on a table with large number of rows may take some time and generate a large number of log records.

There is a range of other properties for the table you can adjust with ALTER TABLE, such as partitioning, constraints, lock escalation, and triggers. You can see the complete list of options to use with ALTER TABLE at `https://docs.microsoft.com/sql/t-sql/statements/alter-table-transact-sql#arguments`.

By default, an ALTER TABLE execution blocks just about every other query (or is blocked by other queries). This is because an ALTER TABLE by default obtains a Schema Modification lock (Sch-M). The problem is that even the simplest SELECT statement requires a Schema Stability Lock (Sch-S), which is not compatible with a Sch-M lock. Fortunately, SQL Server allows some scenarios with ALTER TABLE to avoid a Sch-M lock and allow operations to execute *online* with an option called WITH (ONLINE=ON) as part of the ALTER TABLE syntax. You can read more about which operations are allowed to run online with ALTER TABLE as part of the documentation of the WITH (ONLINE=ON) option at `https://docs.microsoft.com/sql/t-sql/statements/alter-table-transact-sql#arguments`.

You can read all the details of the ALTER TABLE statement in our documentation at `https://docs.microsoft.com/sql/t-sql/statements/alter-table-transact-sql`.

Truncating Tables

Consider a situation where you need to delete all the rows in an existing table. Perhaps you are using a table as part of an Extract, Transform, and Load (ETL) process. Part of this process requires you to *clear* the table in SQL Server and refresh it with new data. You could use the T-SQL DELETE statement, but this can be expensive because SQL Server has to log the change of the delete of every row. SQL Server does use a process called *ghosted records* to speed up deletes, but using a DELETE to remove 1 million rows from a table when that is all the rows in the table is not efficient.

Therefore, SQL Server provides the **TRUNCATE TABLE** statement to remove all the rows in a table in a much more efficient manner. When you execute a TRUNCATE TABLE statement, SQL Server will deallocate extents (a collection of eight consecutive pages) and only log these deallocations. Therefore a TRUNCATE TABLE statement is very fast and uses a minimal amount of log space (but can still be run in the context of a transaction and therefore be rolled back). In addition, deallocation of pages for operations like TRUNCATE TABLE are faster because SQL Server uses a concept called *deferred drop*. You can read more about deferred drop and logging of TRUNCATE TABLE from a blog post by Paul Randal at `https://www.sqlskills.com/blogs/paul/a-sql-server-dba-myth-a-day-1930-truncate-table-is-non-logged`.

You can read more details about how TRUNCATE TABLE works, including limits and restrictions, in our documentation at `https://docs.microsoft.com/sql/t-sql/statements/truncate-table-transact-sql`.

Managing Indexes

Once you have created indexes for your tables, you may decide to create other indexes, as I discussed in Chapter 6. In some situations, you may decide a specific index choice you originally made doesn't make sense anymore. In these cases, you can use the **DROP INDEX** statement to drop a specific index. Just keep in mind that I did recommend in Chapter 6 that in most cases you want a clustered index for a table, so if you decide to drop a clustered index you will want to replace it with a new clustered index with a different set of columns. This blog post is an older but still very appropriate one by Kimberly Tripp on looking at usages of indexes and whether it makes sense to keep ones you have already created, at `https://www.sqlskills.com/blogs/kimberly/spring-cleaning-your-indexes-part-i`.

It would be incredible if you simply built the indexes you needed for a table and never had to worry about them again for the life of your database and application. And for a database that is mostly read-only, that could be partially true. However, almost every application modifies data and indexes must be updated and changed along with the data in most cases. SQL Server handles that type of modification for indexes automatically. However, because of some data changes over time, you may need to *maintain* your indexes either by rebuilding or reorganizing them. In this section, I'll talk about the process to rebuild and reorganize an index, along with a small section about the ability to modify some properties of an index. In any of these situations, SQL Server provides the **ALTER INDEX** T-SQL statement to maintain existing indexes. However, first I need to discuss in more details the concept of index fragmentation.

Note   One really cool solution from one of the best experts in the SQL Server community, Ola Hallengren, includes scripts to help automate index maintenance at `https://ola.hallengren.com/sql-server-index-and-statistics-maintenance.html`.

Index Fragmentation

As you modify data, especially inserting and delete new rows, the indexes you have created may become fragmented. I briefly mentioned the concept of *fragmentation* in a previous chapter on performance capabilities on indexes. There are two types of fragmentation:

> **Logical or Extent Fragmentation:** Logical fragmentation is the percentage of pages that are logically linked together but out of physical order. For example, a clustered index has at the *leaf level* a linked list of database pages representing the data. Ideally, all these pages would be ordered in the list by pageid so that they are physically in order and contiguous in the database file. If you remember from Chapter 6, I talked about how SQL Server can only read multiple pages at one time if they are physically contiguous in the file. If you run an SQL Server query that needs

to scan several pages in the clustered index, SQL Server is limited on its ability to efficiently read multiple pages unless they are in physical order. Extent fragmentation is the same concept except it applies to tables without clustered indexes (heaps) and how pages are ordered within IAM pages.

Page Compactness: Page compactness is a term I created for the book, and you may not see this term be represented as part of the concept of fragmentation. I call this part of fragmentation because the more pages of an index (or data for a clustered index) are sparsely filled with rows, or less compact, the more pages it can take to service the need of a query. This can lead to higher than desired level of pages required across all queries taking up space in the buffer pool and requiring more I/O. However, there is a balance here. If pages were 100% full (compacted), inserting new rows could require *page splits*, which could lead to more logical fragmentation. Therefore, ideally, leaving some space available on pages is desirable but not to the level where most pages are empty. When you create, rebuild, or reorganize an index, you can make smart choices about how to leave space in index pages with an option called *fillfactor*. I like this blog post by Kimberly Tripp to learn more about fillfactor, at `https://www.sqlskills.com/blogs/kimberly/database-maintenance-best-practices-part-ii-setting-fillfactor`.

Note   Fragmentation in an index may not affect application performance, especially Logical Fragmentation. Logical fragmentation mostly affects T-SQL queries involving scans of pages vs. a seek to a specific page. Therefore, just because you detect fragmentation in an index does not mean you have to always rebuild or reorganize the index. Having said that, in my experience almost every production SQL Server environment deploys a plan to keep indexes from staying fragmented, to ensure the maximum possible performance of all types of T-SQL queries.

SQL Server provides a method to look at both aspects of fragmentation through a DMV called **sys.dm_db_index_physical_stats**. The column **avg_fragmentation_in_ percent** tracks Logical or Extent fragmentation and **avg_page_space_used_in_percent** tracks how full pages are across the index.

So the question comes up, how to resolve issues related to fragmentation? I recommend you look at two options provided by SQL Server to maintain an existing index: *Rebuild an index* or *Reorganize an index*.

Rebuilding an Index

Rebuilding an index through ALTER INDEX using the **REBUILD** option involves dropping the existing index and creating a new index based on the existing index definition, so it will require extra space in the database to rebuild the index (Note: ALTER INDEX and CREATE INDEX have an option called **SORT_IN_TEMPDB** to store sort results as part of the index rebuild in tempdb vs. the user database). Rebuilding the index will reorder pages in physical order to remove fragmentation and compact pages based on the specified fillfactor. In addition, rebuilding the index will create a new set of fresh statistics for the index.

By default, an index rebuild is an *offline* operation that will block existing queries. However, like ALTER TABLE, ALTER INDEX using REBUILD provides an option to rebuild an index *online* using the WITH ONLINE=ON option. This allows queries to execute at the same time the index is being rebuilt. In addition, SQL Server provides an option called a *resumable* online index rebuild option with the **RESUMABLE=ON** option. Using this option allows you to pause an index rebuild and resume it where it left off. Some possible scenarios this can helpful to you are:

- Pause an index rebuild that is consuming many resources for SQL Server affecting overall performance. This allows you to resume the index rebuild at a later point in time as opposed to having to cancel the index rebuild and run the entire process.

- Execute the index rebuild in chunks. For example, you could rebuild the index in 25% increments over time. The catalog view **index_resumable_operations** can be used to track the progress of resumable online index rebuilds. You can read more about this catalog view at https://docs.microsoft.com/sql/relational-databases/system-catalog-views/sys-index-resumable-operations.

Here is a simple example of a resumable online index rebuild using the full WideWorldImporters sample database. Execute the following T-SQL statement as found in the example **resumablerebuild.sql** to see an example of rebuilding an index online with the resumable option:

```
USE WideWorldImporters
GO
ALTER INDEX PK_Purchasing_PurchaseOrders
ON [Purchasing].[PurchaseOrders]
REBUILD
WITH (ONLINE = ON, RESUMABLE = ON);
GO
```

ALTER INDEX using REBUILD can take advantage of parallelism, and follows the rules as with queries to decide MAXDOP. The ALTER INDEX statement offers a MAXDOP hint. In addition, ALTER INDEX offers an option called **ALL** to rebuild all indexes for the specified table in a single transaction.

Reorganizing an Index

An alternative to rebuilding the index is reorganizing the index. An index reorganization is an online operation and uses existing index pages to compact pages and shuffle pages to move them into physical order. You use the ALTER INDEX with the REORGANIZE option to reorganize an index.

Reorganizing an index provides a great option to help with index fragmentation but does not update statistics for the index. In addition, ALTER INDEX with REORGANIZE has options to use ALL to reorganize all indexes for the table and also allows you to specify a fillfactor. Paul Randal has a great blog post to describe the difference between rebuilding and reorganizing an index at `https://www.sqlskills.com/blogs/paul/sqlskills-sql101-rebuild-vs-reorganize`.

Adaptive Index Defragmentation

You can use the guidance from the documentation to decide to rebuild or reorganize an index, as described at `https://docs.microsoft.com/sql/relational-databases/indexes/reorganize-and-rebuild-indexes`. However, thanks to the smart folks in SQL Engineering known as the Tiger Team, you can use a script to create a stored procedure that is *intelligent* to decide whether to rebuild or reorganize your indexes. This script and its concept are called Adaptive Index Defragmentation. You can read more about this script, its features, and download it at `https://github.com/Microsoft/tigertoolbox/tree/master/AdaptiveIndexDefrag`.

Modifying an Index

It is possible to change some of the properties of an index without requiring the index to be rebuilt. This includes options like locking behavior (e.g., ALLOW_PAGE_LOCKS) and statistics options (e.g., STATISTICS_NORECOMPUTE). Most options for ALTER INDEX do require changes to the index structure as seen previously in the examples for rebuilding and reorganizing an index. For a full list of options for ALTER INDEX, see our documentation at `https://docs.microsoft.com/sql/t-sql/statements/alter-index-transact-sql#arguments`.

Maintaining Columnstore Indexes

I discussed the amazing performance feature called Columnstore indexes in Chapter 6. Even though Columnstore indexes are organized differently than rowstore indexes, they still can require maintenance. Here are some resources to use when deciding how to maintain Columnstore indexes:

- Check out the documentation on defragmentation of Columnstore indexes at `https://docs.microsoft.com/sql/relational-databases/indexes/columnstore-indexes-defragmentation`.

- Here is a discussion on how to defragment a Columnstore index using ALTER INDEX REORGNIZE at `https://docs.microsoft.com/sql/relational-databases/indexes/columnstore-indexes-defragmentation#use-alter-index-reorganize-to-defragment-a-columnstore-index-online`.

- Here are more details on how to rebuild a Columnstore index at `https://docs.microsoft.com//sql/relational-databases/indexes/columnstore-indexes-defragmentation#rebuild`.

- Look at the T-SQL examples on rebuilding and reorganizing Columnstore indexes at `https://docs.microsoft.com/sql/t-sql/statements/alter-index-transact-sql#examples-columnstore-indexes`.

Managing Server-Side Code

I've shown examples in this book so far to create T-SQL *server-side code* including procedures, views, functions, and triggers. Once you have created these objects you may need to modify or even drop them. Each type of object supports a corresponding ALTER and DROP T-SQL version of the CREATE syntax.

Anytime you ALTER a server-side programming object such as a stored procedure, that object will be recompiled the next time it is executed and stored in cache.

New to SQL Server 2016 SP1 and SQL Server 2017 is a new syntax you should consider using for your scripts to create these types of objects. It is called CREATE or ALTER. With this new syntax, you can create a single script to create or modify your object instead of having one script to create and another to modify, or having to drop and create each time you want to make a change.

For example, the following T-SQL statement creates a stored procedure called **howboutthemcowboys** if it does not exist, or modifies it if already exists. No need to use a DROP statement. You can find this statement in the example script **howboutthemcowboys.sql**:

```
USE WideWorldImporters
GO
CREATE or ALTER PROCEDURE howboutthemcowboys
AS
BEGIN
SELECT 'Back to the Super Bowl in 2019'
END
GO
```

You can read more about how to use CREATE or ALTER object in our documentation at https://docs.microsoft.com/sql/t-sql/statements/create-procedure-transact-sql.

Monitoring SQL Server

Managing the SQL Server instance, database, and objects is important to keep your SQL Server healthy and running at peak performance. But how do you know in some situations whether some management decisions are needed? You need to be able to monitor key performance information and aspects of SQL Server to be proactive and make smart management decisions.

In this section of the chapter, I'll talk about various methods to monitor SQL Server performance using SQL Server features, how to use an incredibly cool feature called the System Health session, how to monitor Transaction Log Backups, and my take on Linux tools to monitor the health of the operating system and server.

I'll pause here to make an important statement that may seem obvious to you but is quite frankly neglected by many. **It is critical to establish a performance baseline for your SQL Server**. You can monitor SQL Server daily, but you won't know if you are seeing a possible problem, especially with performance, unless you establish and save baselines for your workload, so you can compare. How do you know you are having a performance problem if you don't know what good performance looks like?

Monitoring SQL Server Performance

While the SQL Server database platform comes built-in with many great features that empower performance monitoring, there is no better substitute for an overall monitoring solution than from our partners who specialize in monitoring. You can find a complete list of these partners at `https://docs.microsoft.com/sql/sql-server/ partner-monitor-sql-server`.

Many of the features and capabilities used by these partners are built on a vast array of tools I covered in Chapter 5 including features built in the database engine. In this section, I will review some of these tools and features and the fundamental methods to use them to monitor the performance of SQL Server.

Running or Waiting

I mentioned earlier in this chapter one of my longtime colleagues and friend, Keith Elmore. Like Robert Dorr, I worked side by side with Keith at Microsoft technical support for many years and Keith remains a great friend today. I always looked to Keith when it came to understanding how to tackle performance problems with SQL Server (and I still do today).

Keith built some training for technical support several years ago and the philosophy he used for this training was simple but brilliant. Keith coined the term that SQL Server performance problems can be categorized as *Running* or *Waiting*.

Running equates to CPU utilization. Monitoring the CPU utilization of all processes on the server was important, to know whether any performance problems are related to the SQL Server process or some other process. If the CPU utilization for SQL Server appears to be high such that it might affect performance, then you need to drill into what T-SQL queries are executing that are consuming the most CPU. If no queries are consuming the most CPU, then a problem could exist with a background process or with a spinlock contention problem (I briefly mentioned spinlocks when I discussed In-Memory OLTP in Chapter 6). Tracing the queries that might account for a high CPU scenario could be done with DMVs such as dm_exec_query_stats or Query Store.

Waiting as it relates to SQL Server is a scenario where a SQL Server user task may be waiting on a specific *wait type*, which equates to waiting for a specific resource. Since multiple users could all be competing for similar resources, a waiting scenario could involve multiple users waiting on another user who is waiting on a resource (in terms of a wait type known as a lock, this is often called a *blocking chain*). I mentioned the concept of a wait type in Chapter 5 when I discussed the DMVs dm_exec_requests, dm_os_waiting_tasks, and dm_os_wait_stats.

Armed with this knowledge you could not only tackle almost any SQL Server performance problem but would know how to proactively monitor SQL Server performance by monitoring CPU utilization and wait types across users and for the SQL Server instance.

Using DMVs to Monitor Performance

Following Keith's lead on looking at CPU utilization or waiting scenarios, you first need to be able to monitor CPU utilization of all processes on the Linux Server including sqlservr. Look in a section later in this chapter for tools and package for Linux to monitor CPU of all processes.

Assuming you are focusing on the CPU utilization of SQL Server, you can use the DMV **dm_exec_query_stats** to find out which queries based on cached plans have used the highest CPU utilization. In addition, you can use the DMVs **dm_exec_requests** and **dm_os_waiting_tasks** to find out which tasks are waiting on other tasks or specific resources. The DMV **dm_os_wait_stats** gives a picture of what are the highest wait resources across the SQL Server instance. I provided examples on how to use each of these DMVs in Chapter 5. In addition, don't forget about monitoring queries live using Lightweight Query Profiling including the DMV **dm_exec_query_profiles**. I mentioned this feature in Chapter 5, but here is a link as a reminder for you to read more about monitoring queries live, at `https://docs.microsoft.com/sql/relational-databases/` `system-dynamic-management-views/sys-dm-exec-query-profiles-transact-sql`. I look towards a future where we can just turn this on by default, so you can always see live query information all the time!

You also will want to monitor the overall performance of SQL Server from a workload and throughput perspective. I've mentioned in previous chapters the DMV **dm_os_ performance_counters** that can be used for this purpose. This DMV is initialized at SQL Server startup and then kept up to date by the SQL Server engine as it is running. Remember this DMV has a very normalized structure where the row values describe the specific counters to measure instead of column names.

The following T-SQL statement, as found in the example **dm_os_performance_ counters.sql**, returns all counters for the object called **SQLServer:SQL Statistics** at any point in time for the SQL Server instance:

```
SELECT * FROM sys.dm_os_performance_counters
WHERE object_name = 'SQLServer:SQL Statistics'
ORDER BY counter_name
GO
```

We built performance counters for SQL Server to integrate with the Windows Performance Counters System (see more information at `https://docs.microsoft.com/` `windows/desktop/perfctrs/performance-counters-reference`). A common method to view these counters is with the Windows Performance Monitor Tool (commonly known as *perfmon*). Since the Windows Performance Counter system does not work on Linux Operating Systems, you can query the SQL Server performance counters through the **dm_os_performance_counters** DMV. A description of all the possible SQL Server performance counters is described in our documentation at `https://docs.microsoft.` `com/sql/relational-databases/performance-monitor/use-sql-server-objects`.

When you view SQL Server performance counters with the perfmon tool on Windows, the rates of counter values are automatically displayed. For example, the counter_name **Batch Requests/sec** is a rate of workload throughput for SQL Server. But the rate is presented as a cumulative value. In order to find out the true rate, you must perform a calculation using T-SQL. Look at the following excellent blog post to see how to use information in the DMV to understand how to perform the correct calculations: `https://blogs.msdn.microsoft.com/psssql/2013/09/23/interpreting-the-` `counter-values-from-sys-dm_os_performance_counters`. In addition, you can look at the example scripts from the Automatic Tuning example from Chapter 6 (found in the auto_tune directory) on how to generate a correct rate for Batch Requests/sec.

There are 1600+ SQL Server performance counters to choose from. The following in Table 9-1 are the top five counter areas I recommend you always monitor (and then add from there other ones that suit your needs).

Table 9-1. *My top 5 SQL Server Performance Counters to Monitor*

object_name	counter_name	description
SQLServer:SQL Statistics	Batch Requests/Sec	Rate of T-SQL batches executed on SQL Server
SQLServer:Memory Manager	Total Server Memory (KB)	The total amount of memory allocated by the SQL Server engine
SQLServer:Wait Statistics	All counters	This allows you to track the major categories from dm_os_wait_stats
SQLServer:General Statistics	User Connections	The current number of active users connected to SQL Server
SQLServer:SQL Errors	All counters	I had to choose only 5, so why not monitor the total number of errors. A huge spike may indicate a severe SQL Server or application problem.

So how will you know what you are monitoring is good or bad? There could be some obvious signs. For example, if SQL Server is consuming 100% CPU constantly, that is usually not a good sign but maximizing your CPU resource is a goal. The only way to know for sure is to set a baseline based on DMV information by saving the DMV collection (even during testing) and then monitoring any major changes over time. Don't forget to keep multiple baselines as you make changes to your database, application, or even updates to SQL Server.

Using the Query Store to Monitor Performance

As I mentioned in Chapter 5, if you enable Query Store you now have historical performance information for queries compiled and executed stored in your database. This will include information about total execution time, CPU time, and information about wait statistics.

The largest benefit to Query Store is that you don't have to *poll* DMVs and save their output, as Query Store information is persisted to your database (in fact the default is to keep 30 days of performance information). The drawback to Query Store is that the information is stored per database. If you have multiple databases on your SQL Server instance, you would have to consolidate this information to get an instance-wide view of performance of SQL Server.

As I mentioned in Chapter 5, our documentation has some excellent examples of how to execute queries against the Query Store. You can find these at `https://docs. microsoft.com/sql/relational-databases/performance/monitoring-performance- by-using-the-query-store#Scenarios`. Included here are queries you can edit to your needs that run against the Query Store to look at a baseline and monitor for changes. But remember the advantage of Query Store: your history is built-in! Let's say you started your production workload on Monday, August 1, 2018 and enabled Query Store. By default, you now get 30 days of historical information (you can configure the history timeline). At any point in time, you can run queries against the Query Store and compare them to historical dates including your baseline date. This is because everything has a timestamp in the Query Store (remember it is UTC datetime).

Using Extended Events for Performance

Having the Query Store for automatic history of performance is a great asset to your monitoring toolkit. Once you start monitoring with DMVs or the Query Store, it could be possible that you need to track the exact execution of specific queries and other information like the execution plan of the query. Remember, the DMVs and the Query Store will not track the actual execution plan of a query. And Query Store aggregates execution information about queries and plans rather than tracking each execution.

Lightweight Query Profiling could really be a benefit for these situations to get the actual execution plan of specific running queries. However, there may be situations where you need to *trace* query execution and possibly other key events related to performance as you monitor SQL Server. There is where Extended Events comes into play as a great technology for detailed tracing. I discussed many aspects of Extended Events in Chapter 5, including examples of how to find all the possible events to trace.

Want a way to get started quickly with Extended Events? Use the XEProfiler that comes built into SSMS. You can read more about using XEProfiler at `https://docs. microsoft.com/sql/relational-databases/extended-events/use-the-ssms-xe- profiler`.

XE Profiler creates Extended Event sessions called QuickSessionStandard and QuickSessionTSQL. Use these as a base to create your own sessions that have other events you want to trace. You can use SSMS to right-click one of these sessions and script out the definition of it to create your own. Figure 9-5 shows an example of how to do this.

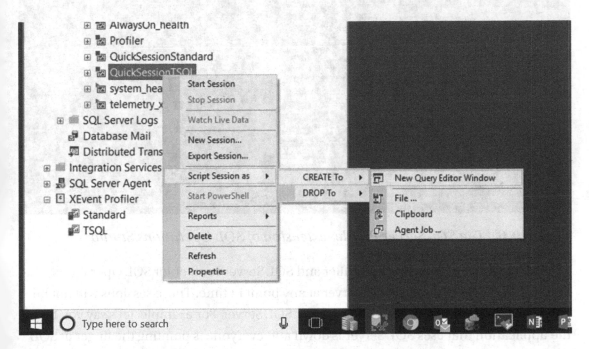

Figure 9-5. Scripting the QuickSessionTSQL Extended Events session

Notice in this figure a session called Profiler. That session is similar to the functionality of XEProfiler and comes from a new extension to SQL Operations Studio called SQL Server Profiler (not to be confused with the actual tool called SQL Server Profiler). You can read more about this extension at https://docs.microsoft.com/ sql/sql-operations-studio/sql-server-profiler-extension. Figure 9-6 shows an example of this extension in action against an SQL Server instance on Linux.

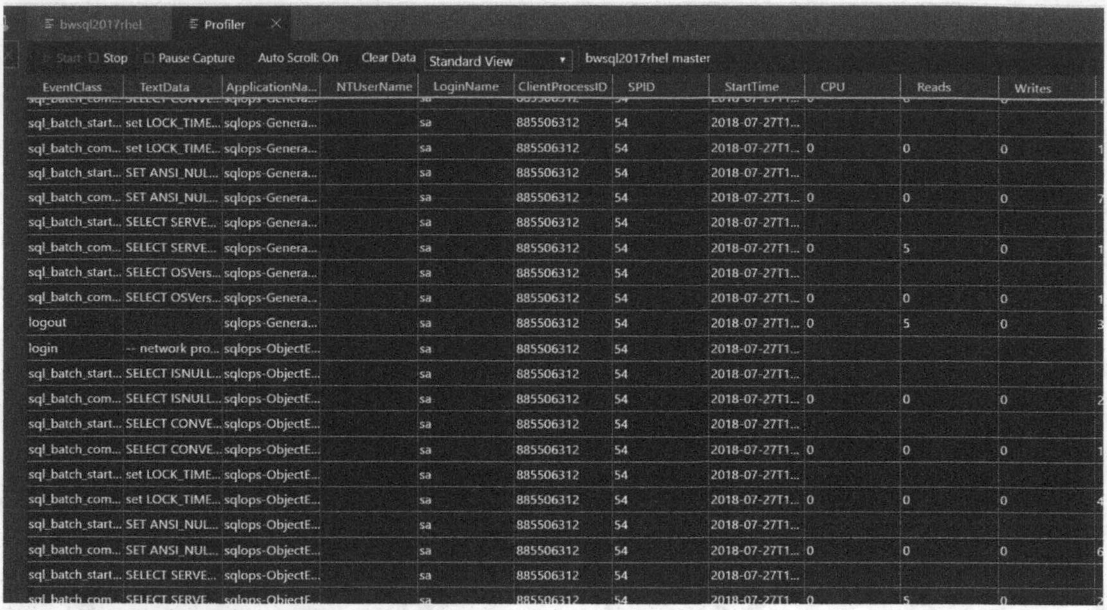

Figure 9-6. *The SQL Server Profiler extension of SQL Operations Studio*

I like to think of tools like XEProfiler and SQL Server Profiler for SQL Operations Studio as a quick live look at SQL Server at any point in time. These sessions will not be expensive and could give you a quick look at SQL Server. For example, let's say you hear the application that uses SQL Server is down and everyone is pointing the finger at SQL Server. These tools could quickly tell you whether the application is sending queries to SQL Server and are they executing within a reasonable timeframe. If no queries are coming to SQL Server, then the problem could be networking or an application issue.

But Extended Events can also be used as a detailed tracing mechanism to supplement your monitoring needs, especially if you detect a possible problem. Let me give you a quick example. Let's say you suspect fragmentation is occurring due to a large number of page splits. So you monitor the DMV **dm_os_performance_counters** for the counter called Page Splits/sec and confirm your suspicion. Wouldn't it be nice to track what queries are executing when a page split occurs?

The following T-SQL statement will create an Extended Events session to do just that (this session definition can be found in the example script **tracepagesplits.sql**).

```
CREATE EVENT SESSION [tracespagesplits] ON SERVER
ADD EVENT sqlserver.page_split(
ACTION (sqlserver.session_id, sqlserver.sql_text, sqlserver.client_app_name,
sqlserver.database_id))
```

```
ADD TARGET package0.event_file(SET filename=N'pagesplits.xel')
WITH (MAX_DISPATCH_LATENCY=5 SECONDS,STARTUP_STATE=OFF)
GO
```

You can now see what sessions, queries, application name, and databases are involved in the page split. The page_split events include the pageid that was split.

Using the System Health Session

Extended Events was launched as part of the SQL Server 2008 release. At that time, I worked in Microsoft technical support and thought we could leverage Extended Events by creating a default session that would capture important *health* information about SQL Server. Thus was born the system_health Extended Events session. You can read about the original version of this in this blog post: `https://blogs.msdn.microsoft.com/psssql/2008/07/15/supporting-sql-server-2008-the-system_health-session`. One of the limitations with this early version is that the session wrote data to a ring_buffer target so when SQL Server was restarted, the information collected was lost.

With the launch of SQL Server 2012, we revised the method in which failure detection worked with clustering via the sp_server_diagnostics system procedure, which I described in Chapter 8. My colleague in support, Robert Dorr, was a huge part of defining how sp_server_diagnostics worked. In addition, Bob took the time to revamp the system_health session to include sp_server_diagnostics information and to have a file target added to the session.

This is really a major advancement, as now by default any SQL Server has a set of Extended Event files that includes health information about SQL Server, including but not limited to:

- sp_server_diagnostics output

- Memory diagnostics

- Deadlocks

- Non-yielding problems

- Latch waits over 15 seconds

- Certain preemptive waits over five seconds

- Critical errors

Robert Dorr has a good blog post discussing this new system_health session at `https://blogs.msdn.microsoft.com/psssql/2012/03/08/sql-server-2012-true-black-box-recorder`.

These files are by default stored in the /var/opt/mssql/log directory. Look for the set of files that match the pattern system_health*.xel. Use the following T-SQL statement as found in the example **readsystemhealth.sql** to read all the events in the current system health session. I included a conversion to your local time but also left in the original UTC time in the query.

```
SELECT DATEADD(minute, DATEDIFF(minute,getutcdate(),getdate()), timestamp_utc)
as local_datetime, *
FROM sys.fn_xe_file_target_read_file('/var/opt/mssql/log/system_health*.xel',
NULL, NULL, NULL)
ORDER BY local_datetime DESC
GO
```

On my Linux Server, the results looked like Figure 9-7 from SQL Operations Studio.

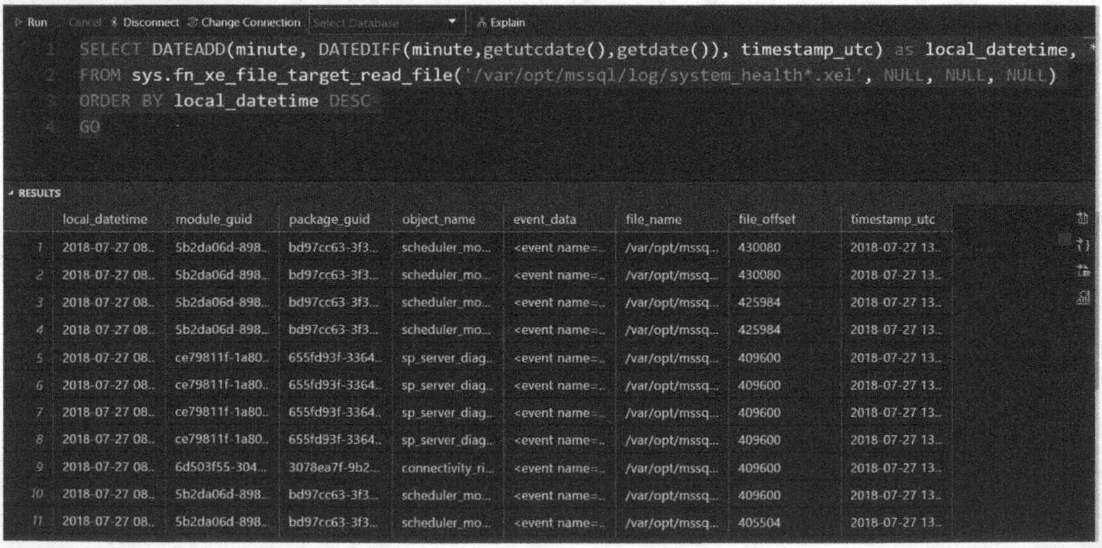

Figure 9-7. *Results from reading the system_health Extended Events session*

Smart Log Backups

In some cases, monitoring activities like backups can be linked to performance. In Chapter 8 I talked about how to back up the transaction log. The examples I talked about in this chapter showed a schedule of log backups based on a time frequency. This technique has been used for many years and works for many production workloads. One problem with this technique is that applications can generate unexpected spikes of transaction log activity resulting in possible autogrowth of the transaction log. I've described earlier in the book how autogrowth of the transaction log can possibly lead to blocking and performance problems.

Fortunately, SQL Server has a technique to perform a *smarter log backup*, One of my colleagues in SQL Server Engineering (who still works for Microsoft but with a bit broader scope now), Parikshit Savjani, wrote an excellent blog post on how to perform a smart log backup based on the DMF **dm_db_log_stats**. You can read the details at https://blogs.msdn.microsoft.com/sql_server_team/smart-transaction-log-backup-monitoring-and-diagnostics-with-sql-server-2017.

Linux Tools for Monitoring

While SQL Server provides a rich set of tools for monitoring, it is important to also monitor the operating system hosting SQL Server. If you have experience using Linux, you probably have a set of tools and programs you use all the time to monitor Linux.

Below is a list of tools and commands I've discovered to be useful from both my experience using Linux and from others in the SQL Server Engineering team.

> **top:** top is a core Linux program to display a real-time view of processes and overall CPU and memory of the Linux Server, and I've used it in previous chapters. top should be installed by default on almost all Linux distributions. top is interactive in the sense that it refreshes constantly. You have to type 'q' to exit the program. Here is a glimpse of part of the output of top on my Linux RHEL Server as seen in Figure 9-8.

```
top - 10:03:20 up 2 days,  2:14,  2 users,  load average: 0.00, 0.01, 0.05
Tasks: 177 total,   2 running, 175 sleeping,   0 stopped,   0 zombie
%Cpu(s):  0.2 us,   0.2 sy,  0.0 ni, 99.5 id,  0.1 wa,  0.0 hi,  0.0 si,  0.0 st
KiB Mem : 7992460 total,  4562388 free,  1816200 used,  1613872 buff/cache
KiB Swap: 5242876 total,  5242876 free,        0 used.  5884668 avail Mem

  PID USER      PR  NI    VIRT    RES    SHR S  %CPU %MEM     TIME+ COMMAND
17260 mssql     20   0 9929076   1.5g   6896 S   1.3 19.4  54:14.25 sqlservr
    1 root      20   0  193608   6752   4156 S   0.0  0.1   0:14.54 systemd
    2 root      20   0       0      0      0 S   0.0  0.0   0:00.07 kthreadd
```

Figure 9-8. *The output of the top program on Linux*

> **iotop:** iotop is a program similar to top but focused only on I/O. iotop may not be installed by default, so first execute this command from the bash shell:
>
> ```
> sudo yum install -y iotop
> ```
>
> Running iotop requires sudo, and I recommend using the -o parameter, which shows only the active I/O from the system. Run the following command from the bash shell:
>
> ```
> sudo iotop -o
> ```
>
> Figure 9-9 shows the output of iotop on my Linux Server.

```
Total DISK READ :     0.00 B/s | Total DISK WRITE :     3.89 K/s
Actual DISK READ:     0.00 B/s | Actual DISK WRITE:     0.00 B/s
  TID  PRIO  USER     DISK READ  DISK WRITE  SWAPIN     IO>    COMMAND
83617 be/4 root        0.00 B/s    0.00 B/s  0.00 %  0.08 % [kworker/1:1]
17537 be/4 mssql       0.00 B/s    3.89 K/s  0.00 %  0.00 % sqlservr
```

Figure 9-9. *The output of the iotop program on Linux*

> **htop:** htop is a program similar to top with a bit more *flair*. One of the programs I use on Windows Server is Task Manager. I can get quick visual view of CPU utilization by processor. htop provides that type of look and feel plus details of process resource usage. I've found that htop is not likely installed on most Linux systems by default. Therefore, to install this on RHEL, run these commands from the bash shellL
>
> ```
> sudo wget dl.fedoraproject.org/pub/epel/7/x86_64/Packages/e/epel-
> release-7-11.noarch.rpm
> sudo rpm -ihv epel-release-7-11.noarch.rpm
> sudo yum install -y htop
> ```

To execute htop, just run the following command:

```
htop
```

Figure 9-10 shows a part of the htop output on my Linux Server, which has four CPUs.

```
  1 [                                          0.0%]   Tasks: 34, 211 thr; 1 running
  2 [||                                        1.3%]   Load average: 0.00 0.01 0.05
  3 [|                                         0.7%]   Uptime: 04:37:31
  4 [|                                         0.7%]
Mem[|||||||||||||||                      1.29G/7.62G]
Swp[                                       0K/5.00G]

  PID USER       PRI  NI  VIRT   RES    SHR S CPU% MEM%   TIME+   Command
 1892 mssql       20   0 3331M 1018M  6668 S  0.7 13.0  3:02.99 /opt/mssql/bin/sqlservr
14211 thewandog   20   0  119M  2284  1504 R  0.7  0.0  0:00.23 htop
 1958 mssql       20   0 3331M 1018M  6668 S  0.7 13.0  1:24.87 /opt/mssql/bin/sqlservr
10891 mssql       20   0 3331M 1018M  6668 S  0.7 13.0  0:00.32 /opt/mssql/bin/sqlservr
 3876 mssql       20   0 3331M 1018M  6668 S  0.0 13.0  0:15.27 /opt/mssql/bin/sqlservr
 4415 mssql       20   0 3331M 1018M  6668 S  0.0 13.0  0:01.25 /opt/mssql/bin/sqlservr
 3881 mssql       20   0 3331M 1018M  6668 S  0.0 13.0  0:02.61 /opt/mssql/bin/sqlservr
```

Figure 9-10. *htop on Linux*

sar: sar (System Activity Report) has been around for a long time on UNIX and Linux systems. It uses the /proc filesystem to gather information into a report. Therefore, sar is a good program to see operating system resources such as CPU, memory, and I/O over time even across server restarts. There are many options with sar and you can see all of them by executing the following command:

```
man sar
```

Figure 9-11 shows a part of the default sar output on my Linux server.

```
[thewandog@bwsql2017rhel ~]$ sar
Linux 3.10.0-862.9.1.el7.x86_64 (bwsql2017rhel)        07/30/2018       _x86_64_       (4 CPU)

02:03:13 PM       LINUX RESTART

02:10:01 PM       CPU    %user    %nice   %system   %iowait   %steal    %idle
02:20:01 PM       all     0.13     0.00      0.08      0.06     0.00    99.73
02:30:01 PM       all     0.12     0.00      0.07      0.05     0.00    99.76
02:40:01 PM       all     0.14     0.00      0.08      0.06     0.00    99.72
02:50:01 PM       all     0.13     0.00      0.09      0.06     0.00    99.73
03:00:01 PM       all     0.13     0.00      0.09      0.07     0.00    99.72
03:10:01 PM       all     0.13     0.02      0.13      0.08     0.00    99.63
03:20:01 PM       all     0.14     0.00      0.09      0.07     0.00    99.70
03:30:01 PM       all     0.12     0.00      0.09      0.07     0.00    99.72
03:40:01 PM       all     0.13     0.00      0.08      0.05     0.00    99.73
```

Figure 9-11. *default sar output on Linux*

dstat: dstat is a program that combines the functionality of several programs such as vmstat, iostat, and ifstat. dstat may not be installed on your Linux Server, so you can install it by running this command:

```
sudo yum install -y dstat
```

When you execute dstat it immediately starts producing output scrolling across the screen from your ssh session. Figure 9-12 shows part of the output from dstat on my Linux server.

```
[thewandog@bwsqlrhel ~]$ dstat
You did not select any stats, using -cdngy by default.
----total-cpu-usage---- -dsk/total- -net/total- ---paging-- ---system--
usr sys idl wai hiq siq| read  writ| recv  send|   in   out | int   csw
  1   0  99   0   0   0|1115B   16k|   0     0 |   0     0 | 109   767
  0   0  99   0   0   0|   0     0 |3135B 7972B|   0     0 |  82   752
  0   0 100   0   0   0|   0     0 | 106B  228B|   0     0 |  41   715
  0   0 100   0   0   0|   0     0 | 106B  212B|   0     0 |  55   743
  0   0 100   0   0   0|   0     0 | 106B  196B|   0     0 |  64   728
  0   0 100   0   0   0|   0    48k|3029B 7972B|   0     0 | 101   800
  0   0 100   0   0   0|   0     0 | 106B  244B|   0     0 |  43   707
  0   0 100   0   0   0|   0     0 | 106B  212B|   0     0 |  48   701 ▌
```

Figure 9-12. dstat output on Linux

LinuxKI: Patrick Kilfoyle joined our SQL Engineering team during Project Helsinki and brought to us a wealth of experience on Linux. One of Patrick's skills is Linux kernel performance tuning. I asked him what interesting "low-level" tools he used for performance tuning. He quickly pointed me to LinuxKI. According to the GitHub project site, LinuxKI is "an opensourced advanced mission critical performance troubleshooting tool for Linux." I consider it "low-level" because it uses Linux kernel trace data to help drill into complex performance workload situations. Patrick uses it at Microsoft to dig into complex SQL Server performance tuning problems at the Linux kernel level. You can download and learn more about LinuxKI on the GitHub project site at `https://github.com/HewlettPackard/LinuxKI`.

SQL Server Troubleshooting

Throughout the book so far, I have introduced you to tools, techniques, and features that could be used for the purposes of troubleshooting problems with SQL Server on Linux.

Having said that, there are a few troubleshooting topics worth covering in this chapter that I have not discussed at this point in the book. This includes dump files, core dump files, and PSSDiag. I want to personally thank two of the top experts currently in Microsoft support on SQL Server on Linux, Pradeep M and Suresh Kandoth, for the content in this section.

Dump Files

When some error conditions occur with SQL Server such as an Access Violation, the database engine will produce a dump file and entry in the ERRORLOG. The dump file is useful for Microsoft technical support to investigate the cause of the problem. In most cases, when a dump file is generated, SQL Server has *handled* the error or exception, produced the dump file, and properly terminated the worker thread (which is like a severe error causing possibly a connection to be terminated and transactions rolled back).

The dump files are saved in the same directory where the ERRORLOG files reside, which is by default /var/opt/mssql/log. You will recognize dump files (often called minidump files) by the file pattern SQLDump<n>.mdmp. These files are formatted to be read by the Windows Debugger, as any dump file generated by SQL Server uses the minidump format for Windows.

There is also a technique sometimes used by Microsoft support to manually generate a dump file to gain more insight into the SQL Server process. You can do this yourself by executing the following T-SQL statement:

Note   Do not run this on a production server unless instructed by Microsoft. This command is not officially supported and is only to be run for advanced diagnostic purposes.

```
DBCC STACKDUMP
GO
```

When you run this command, the ERRORLOG file will have a "stack dump header" that looks similar to the following text

```
spid51      **Dump thread - spid = 0, EC = 0x000000067EDA1290
spid51      *
spid51      * User initiated stack dump.  This is not a server exception dump.
spid51      *
spid51      ***Stack Dump being sent to /var/opt/mssql/log/SQLDump0001.txt
spid51      * *********************************************************************
            ************
spid51      *
spid51      * BEGIN STACK DUMP:
spid51      *   07/30/18 22:05:25 spid 1
spid51      *
spid51      * StackDump (all)
```

In the /var/opt/mssql/log directory will be three files:

> **SQLDump0001.txt:** Text file with information about the reason for the dump and important data structures

> **SQLDump0001.log:** A portion of the ERRORLOG near when the dump was created

> **SQLDump0001.mdmp:** The minidump file of the SQL Server process. Remember, this file is generated by SQL Server running within the SQLPAL architecture, so it's a representation of a minidump for SQLSERVR.EXE Windows process.

At this point, you can load the SQLDump0001.dmp file with the Windows Debugger (windbg). You can learn more about the Windows Debugger at https://docs.microsoft.com/windows-hardware/drivers/debugger/getting-started-with-windows-debugging. Reading dump files with the Windows Debugger definitely requires advanced skills. Again, these files are generated for diagnostics purposes to be used by Microsoft technical support and SQL Server Engineering. However, it is possible to use the Windows Debugger along with the Microsoft public symbol server to look at call stacks associated with the reason for the dump (e.g., Access Violation) and possibly determine if the problem may be fixed already by Microsoft or a general idea of where in the code the problem is occurring and avoid it.

Core Dump Files

In some rare situations, SQL Server cannot handle an exception or critical error. On Linux, when a process crashes and cannot handle the exception, a *core dump* is typically generated. A core dump represents a dump of the entire process memory of a Linux process. (I always wanted to know why it is called core dump and found out that the term comes from older UNIX systems that used magnetic core memory.)

For SQL Server, we wanted to provide rich diagnostics and control how a core dump is generated, should the sqlservr Linux process encounter what normally would result in a Linux core dump.

If you remember, in Chapter 1 I talked about how SQL Server on Linux has two processes. One of the processes is the *watchdog* process that forks the child process, the actual SQL Server database platform. In addition, I talked about some of the files installed with SQL Server in the /opt/mssql/bin directory. This directory contains the sqlservr binary but also some other files including a shell script called **handle-crash.sh** and a program called **paldumper**.

The flow of a core dump for SQL Server then looks like the following:

- The *watchdog* sqlservr process listens on a signal if the child process crashes.

- When signaled, the watchdog process will invoke the handle-crash.sh script.

- handle-crash.sh invokes the paldumper program to generate the core dump.

Other information is collected in addition to the core dump and compressed into a .tbz2 file.

Let's see this in action using the following example:

Note   Do not try this in production, as it will terminate the sqlservr process unexpectedly.

---

1. Make sure SQL Server is running.

2. Find the process ID of the child process. Use the following command from the bash shell:

   ```
   ps -auxf | grep sqlservr
   ```

3. The second process listed for sqlservr is the actual sqlservr engine or child process.

4. Run the following command to kill the process:

```
sudo kill -s SIGSEGV <pid>
```

This command sends a signal to the sqlservr process that it is not prepared to handle and therefore it will terminate unexpectedly. The watchdog process is signaled and the aforementioned process kicks in. You can observe the core dump being generated if you run the following command within a few seconds of executing the kill command:

```
sudo systemctl status mssql-server
```

Figure 9-13 shows an example on my Linux Server.

```
 mssql-server.service - Microsoft SQL Server Database Engine
   Loaded: loaded (/usr/lib/systemd/system/mssql-server.service; enabled; vendor preset: disabled)
   Active: active (running) since Mon 2018-07-30 22:59:03 CDT; 6s ago
     Docs: https://docs.microsoft.com/en-us/sql/linux
 Main PID: 8218 (sqlservr)
   CGroup: /system.slice/mssql-server.service
           ├─8215 sh /opt/mssql/bin/compress-dump.sh /var/opt/mssql/log/core.sqlservr.6563.temp /var...
           ├─8216 tar cjf /var/opt/mssql/log/core.sqlservr.07_30_2018_22_58_57.6563.work -C /var/opt...
           ├─8217 bzip2
           ├─8218 /opt/mssql/bin/sqlservr
           └─8220 /opt/mssql/bin/sqlservr
```

Figure 9-13. *A core dump being generated for SQL Server on Linux*

Three files are created in the /var/opt/mssql/log directory:

> core.sqlservr.<datetime>.<pid>.txt – Contains information about the reason for the creash

> core.sqlservr.<datetime>.<pid>.json – JSON version of the .txt file

> core.sqlservr.<datetime>.<pid>.tbz2 – Compressed file containing the core dump and other diagnostic data for Microsoft Technical Support and SQL Engineering.

PSSDiag

Soon after SQL 2000 released, one of the pillars of the SQL Server community, Ken Henderson, joined the Technical Support team at Microsoft. Ken loved innovation and along with another super smart colleague of mine in support, Bart Duncan, they built a tool called PSSDiag to automate the collection of diagnostic information for SQL Server support cases. This includes performance monitor data, log files, SQL Server DMV data, and other files commonly needed for customer support cases.

Note   Ken passed away several years ago, but his influence is felt today. It is ironic that I'm mentioning him in this book. I actually had the privilege of co-authoring a book with him called *SQL Server 2005 Practical Troubleshooting*. I thought of my experience working with Ken, who authored many books, when I thought about authoring this book. Ken also was a huge influence on me getting started to speak at customer events such as the PASS Summit. And of course, we were also friends because he was a huge Dallas Cowboys fan! Bart still works for Microsoft in Engineering and I see him from time to time when both of us happen to be visiting Redmond.

PSSDiag has become one of the most widely used tools by Microsoft Technical Support for SQL Server in history. Therefore, as the support team was preparing for the release of SQL Server on Linux, they built a version of PSSDiag that could work on Linux. Working in conjunction with the SQL Customer Advisory Team (CAT), PSSDiag was built to collect information about the Linux operating system along with SQL Server diagnostic data. You can read more about how to download this tool yourself to see how it works and the details the tool collects, at this blog post: `https://blogs.msdn.microsoft.com/sqlcat/2017/08/11/collecting-performance-data-with-pssdiag-for-sql-server-on-linux`.

Summary

This chapter concludes the main *heart* of the book, as it provides to you important information to prepare yourself to manage and monitor an SQL Server once you have built your database and deployed your application. For those of you looking to migrate an older version of SQL Server or another database product such as ORACLE or PostgreSQL, you will want to read Chapter 10 to gain insight and guidance for migration. Or you could move ahead to the final chapter of the book where I'll describe and discuss how SQL Server works with Docker Containers.

Migrating to SQL Server on Linux

Some of you reading this book are building a new database and will use the previous chapters in this book to create a new database(s) and application. However, some of you have existing databases either on SQL Server or other database products and are looking to migrate to SQL Server on Linux. This chapter is intended for you. However, even if you are not performing a migration, I think you'll be interested in looking over this chapter, which is broken down into these sections:

- *Migrating from SQL Server*: In this section I'll talk about tools and considerations for migrating from a previous version of SQL Server to SQL Server on Linux.

- *Migrating from Oracle*: In this section, I'll discuss the mechanics of migrating from Oracle on Linux to SQL Server on Linux.

- *Migrating from PostgreSQL*: In this section, I'll give you my opinions on a comparison of features between SQL Server and PostgreSQL. I'll also give some tips and resources on how to migrate your database from PostgreSQL to SQL Server on Linux.

- *Post Migration Considerations*: Once you have migrated from SQL Server or another database product, you should take into consideration several post migration steps and actions to ensure a great experience with SQL Server on Linux.

Tip Keep up to date with the team that owns the migration strategy for SQL Server and Azure Data Services on their blog at `https://blogs.msdn.microsoft.com/datamigration`.

© Bob Ward 2018
B. Ward, *Pro SQL Server on Linux*, https://doi.org/10.1007/978-1-4842-4128-8_10

Migrating from SQL Server

Since we have launched SQL Server on Linux, I've encountered some customers who are currently using a previous version of SQL Server on Windows but are now considering a move to SQL Server on Linux. This chapter is for you. I'll discuss the overall process for migration, tools to use to prepare the migration, and tools and techniques to execute the migration.

Figure 10-1 represents a picture of the overall migration process from a previous release of SQL server to SQL Server on Linux.

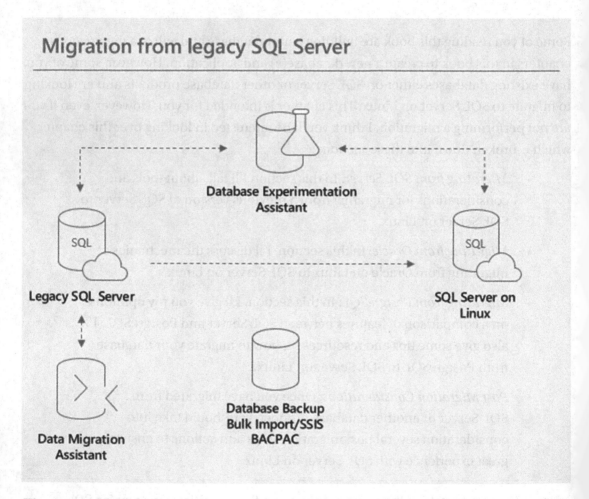

Figure 10-1. *The migration process from a previous release of SQL Server to SQL Server on Linux*

In this section, I will talk about the components that can assist you to migrate from older releases of SQL Server to SQL Server on Linux. Microsoft provides tools to prepare you to migrate to SQL Server on Linux, called **Data Migration Assistant** and **Database Experimentation Assistant**. I'll also discuss how to execute a migration of your database(s) using a database backup, export and import data with bulk import or SSIS packages, or a Data-Tier application file (called a BACPAC file).

When you have completed reading these sections for preparation and execution of your migration, be sure to not miss the section of this chapter on Post Migration Considerations to learn about next steps once the migration is completed.

Preparing for the Migration

Based on Figure 10-1, preparation to migrate one or more databases to SQL Server on Linux centers on the use of two tools:

> **Data Migration Assistant**: The Data Migration Assistant (DMA) tool is free to download and can be used to assess the configuration of the SQL Server instance and your databases, to point out potential problems that could occur after the migration and also point out new features that might help you when you start using SQL Server on Linux. In addition, this tool will look to see possible features being used on SQL Server on Windows that are not supported on SQL Server on Linux.

Note   The DMA can be used to migrate your data and also has capabilities to migrate to Azure SQL Database and SQL Server in Azure Virtual Machine. You can read the full list of DMA functionality and features, including links to download the tool, at `https://docs.microsoft.com/sql/dma/dma-overview`.

> **Database Experimentation Assistant**: Assessing static
> configuration details of your instance or databases is very helpful
> to make your migration smoother. However, most users are also
> concerned about performance of queries when migrating to a
> new version of SQL Server, such as SQL Server 2017 on Linux.
> The Database Experimentation Assistant (DEA) tool can help
> you trace, execute, and compare query workloads between two
> versions of SQL Server.

Let's take a look at the capabilities of each of these tools to prepare you for migrating your databases to SQL Server on Linux.

Data Migration Assistant

The DMA tool includes capabilities to check for the compatibility of your configuration of SQL Server, your database, and T-SQL objects such as stored procedures in your database matched to the target version of SQL Server for your migration.

Note   For checks on the use of incompatible T-SQL, DMA can only check objects in your database like stored procedures. It does not check T-SQL compatibility of the code in your application.

In addition, DMA can look for possible new features in your target SQL Server version that you could improve your use of SQL Server such as columnstore indexes. Finally, if the target version of SQL Server is Linux, DMA can check to see if you are using a feature that is not supported for SQL Server on Linux, like SQL Server Replication.

Currently, the rules that support compatibility, new features, and feature parity are not publicly documented. However, I talked to Venkata Raj Pochiraju and Sreraman Narasimhan from the team that built DMA and they gave me insight into the type of coverage that is supported by DMA.

Tip   You can gain some insight into how DMA checks for compatibility, new features, and feature parity by using a tool like XEProfiler to trace the queries used by DMA. I often use XEProfiler and Extended Events to "debug" what tools do.

Compatibility Issues include rules like:

- Using legacy T-SQL statements like COMPUTE instead of replacement functionality like T-SQL ROLLUP

- The use of older DBCC commands like DBCC DBREINDEX instead of ALTER INDEX.

- Warnings for the use of older data types like TEXT or IMAGE instead of using the new varchar(max) or varbinary(max) types.

New Features recommendations include suggestions for use of features like:

- Using columnstore indexes to accelerate analytic performance

- Using security features like Always Encrypted, TDE, and dynamic data masking

Feature parity rules include a check for any use of the following features, which as of the writing of this book are not supported for SQL Server on Linux (see `https://docs.microsoft.com/sql/linux/sql-server-linux-release-notes#Unsupported`).

Showing you an example for this tool is more difficult, since I would need to show you how to build an SQL Server instance on Windows and database that causes several of these rules to fire. It turns out the WideWorldImporters database, which was built for SQL Server 2016, doesn't really hit any problems worth calling out. I even went back to use the older example database we published for SQL Server 2008, AdventureWorks, and it didn't really uncover any issues either.

However, I've talked to customers who have found the tool very helpful to assess a legacy SQL Server and point out possible issues to migrate to SQL Server on both Windows and Linux.

Figure 10-2 shows an example screen you are presented when you build a new Database Migration Assistant project and choose SQL Server 2017 on Linux as your target.

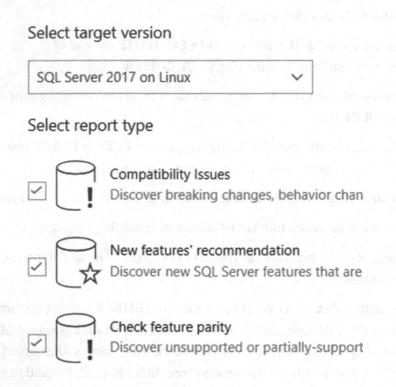

Select target version

SQL Server 2017 on Linux   ⌄

Select report type

Compatibility Issues
Discover breaking changes, behavior chan

New features' recommendation
Discover new SQL Server features that are

Check feature parity
Discover unsupported or partially-support

Figure 10-2. *Assessment choices for migration to SQL Server on Linux*

I highly encourage anyone migrating from older versions of SQL Server to SQL Server on Linux to use DMA and study the results carefully before executing the migration. Be sure to read through these resources related to DMA:

- Best Practices for running Data Migration Assistant, at `https://docs.microsoft.com/sql/dma/dma-bestpractices`

- Read more about analyzing DMA results using PowerShell at `https://docs.microsoft.com/sql/dma/dma-consolidatereports#import-assessment-results-into-a-sql-server-database`.

- Use the PowerBI sample reports at `https://docs.microsoft.com/sql/dma/dma-powerbiassesreport` to gain analysis for assessments of a large number of databases.

Tip   Assess databases at scale in an unattended mode using the dmacmd.
exe utility. For details on how to use dmacmd.exe, look at `https://blogs.`
`msdn.microsoft.com/datamigration/2016/11/08/data-migration-`
`assistant-how-to-run-from-command-line/`.

Database Experimentation Assistant

Doing as much testing as possible for performance of your SQL Server application is one of
the most critical aspects to a successful migration. DEA can be a very powerful tool to help
you achieve that goal. The goal is to use DEA to tell you what queries from your application
will run better, worse, or the same on the target new version of SQL Server. In addition,
DEA can tell you if any queries might fail, for example due to a compatibility issue.

All of the DEA documentation is currently on the Data Migration blog in these posts:
`https://blogs.msdn.microsoft.com/datamigration/tag/dea/`.

To use DEA correctly, it is possible you will need up to four SQL Server instances:

- The *source* SQL Server to capture your workload

- Two *target* SQL Servers to replay the captured workload traces

- One SQL Server to store *analysis* and run reports (you need a
  database to store the results, so it could actually exist on one of the
  target SQL Server instances)

The basic flow to use DEA is as follows:

1. Back up the database on the source SQL Server.

2. **Capture** a trace of your workload using the DEA tool, which can use
   SQL Server Trace or Extended Events. SQL Server Trace is required
   if you are capturing a workload on a SQL Server version earlier
   than SQL Server 2012, because Extended Events does not have the
   required events in SQL Server 2008. DEA does support SQL Server
   2005 as a source SQL Server version, and Extended Events did not
   exist in that release, so you must use SQL Server Trace.

   In order to make the best use of the DEA tool, you need to capture a
   trace of your workload that is representative of the application. The
   DEA tool allows for captures of five minutes to up to three hours.
   You may have a test server where you can capture a trace for your
   application or you may need to do it on the production SQL Server.

3. Prepare replying traces by restoring the backup in step #1 to two
    target SQL Server instances:

    Target Server #1 is a version of SQL Server that is the same as the source
    from the captured trace in Step #2. You generally do not want to use your
    production SQL Server.
    Target Server #2 is the new version of SQL Server you are migrating towards,
    which can be SQL Server on Linux.
    You should set up these SQL Server instances with very identical environments
    in terms of CPU, memory, disk speeds, and SQL Server configurations.

4. Use the DEA tool to **replay** the captured trace from Step #2 on
    both target SQL Servers. The DEA tool will ask for a location to
    save a trace of the replay.

5. Use the DEA tool to **analyze** the two captured replay traces so you can
    compare performance or possible errors from queries in the trace.
    The DEA tool will prompt you for an SQL Server database to store the
    analysis results and the location of the replayed traces from Step #4.

Figure 10-3 shows the DEA tool initial screen to perform all of these steps.

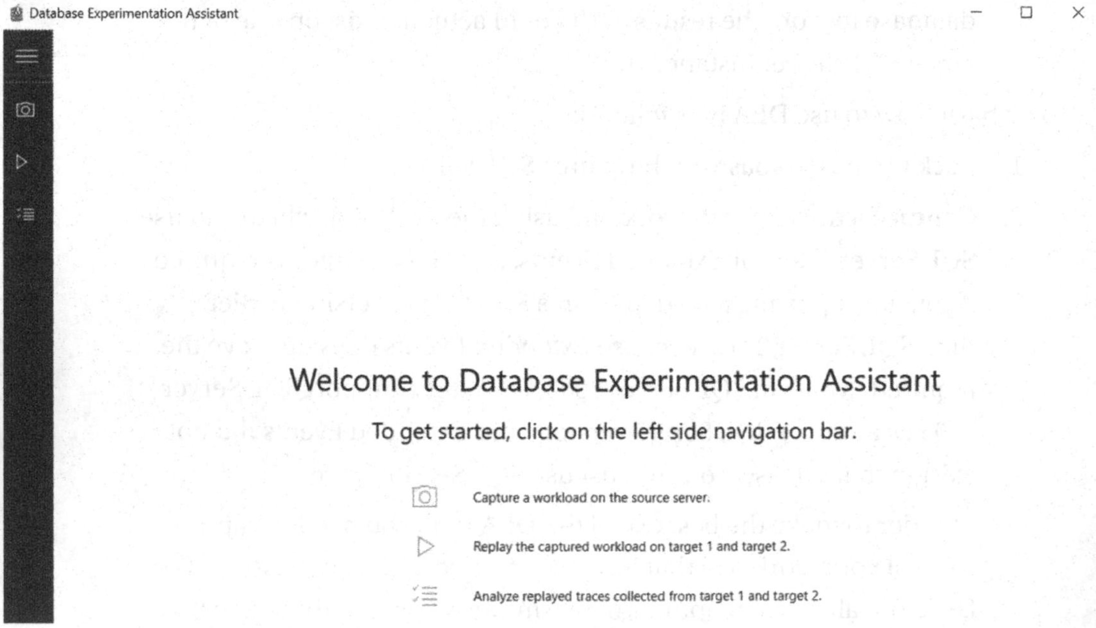

Figure 10-3. The Database Experimentation Assistant tool

Earlier versions of DEA required you to use a feature in SQL Server called Distributed Replay. You can still use that method but as of DEA version 2.6, you can use the *InBuilt* replay method. The InBuilt replay method internally uses a tool called **ostress.exe**. Perhaps you remember in the last chapter I mentioned a colleague of mine at Microsoft named Keith Elmore? Many years ago, when Keith first joined Microsoft in Technical Support, he quickly saw the need to stress SQL Server with multiple concurrent threads executing queries or a T-SQL script. Keith has always been a brilliant programmer, so he built a tool called ostress.exe, which uses ODBC. Keith and Robert Dorr collaborated further to expand ostress.exe to be able to replay captured traces of SQL Server workloads. Keith and Robert bundled these tools together into a toolkit called RML Utilities. RML Utilities is free to download at `https://www.microsoft.com/download/details.aspx?id=4511`. Unfortunately, ostress.exe and RML Utilities do not run natively on Linux (we have an internal version of ostress.exe running using SQLPAL but it is not something ready to release at this time) but if you still have Windows clients that can connect to SQL Server on Linux, you may find the use of ostress.exe and RML Utilities to be a very nice set of tools.

Using DEA with SQL Server on Linux requires some special configuration. Mollee Jain, a developer for the DEA tool, gave me these instructions that are required to make DEA work for Linux (Mollee's intention is to get this into the Data Migration blog).

You have to set up folder permissions to allow for replay to create files on the Linux Server. The user can set this up in many different ways, but mounting a shared folder may be the easiest way to progress because it doesn't require firewall reconfiguration.

- To mount a shared folder in the Linux system with uid + gid specified, you can use a command like the following using CIFS:

```
sudo mount.cifs //DEA/LinuxShare /var/opt/mssql/
LinuxShare -o user=sqladmin,vers=2.0,dir_mode=0777,
file_mode=0777,uid=996,gid=994
```

Note   there are several methods to set up your Linux Server to write files to your Windows Server. One method is to use Samba, which you can learn more about at `https://app.pluralsight.com/library/courses/advanced-network-system-administration-lfce/table-of-contents`.

- Within the DEA replay step, they will need to provide the Linux path if they are replaying to Linux (i.e., /var/opt/mssql/LinuxShare).

There are several aspects of DEA to consider when capturing and replaying traces and using reports for assessments. The DEA set of blogs have good examples and tips as you go through the exercise of using this tool to assess the performance and execution of your workload and application with SQL Server on Linux. I would recommend these specific blog posts:

- *Overview of using DEA*: https://blogs.msdn.microsoft.com/ datamigration/2017/03/24/dea-2-0-how-to-use-database- experimentation-assistant/

- *The latest features of DEA 2.6*: https://blogs.msdn.microsoft.com/ datamigration/2018/08/06/release-database-experimentation- assistant-dea-v2-6/

- *FAQ for Capture*: https://blogs.msdn.microsoft.com/ datamigration/2017/03/24/dea-2-0-capture-trace-faq/

- *FAQ for Replay*: https://blogs.msdn.microsoft.com/ datamigration/2017/03/24/dea-2-0-replay-faq/

- *FAQ for Analysis*: https://blogs.msdn.microsoft.com/ datamigration/2017/03/24/dea-2-0-analysis-faq

Executing the Migration

Now that you have done preparation work for the migration, it is time to migrate your database(s) to SQL Server on Linux. You have the following options to perform a migration:

- Restore a database backup.

- Copy data with bulk copy or SSIS package.

- Export and Import with BACPAC.

Note   SQL Server Management Studio comes with a feature called Copy Database, which is not supported to copy from SQL Server on Windows to SQL Server on Linux.

Let's look at each option in more detail with examples.

Restore a Database Backup

Restoring a backup from SQL Server on Windows is one of the beautiful stories of compatibility on SQL Server on Linux. You are allowed to restore a backup of SQL Server, all the way back to SQL Server 2005, to SQL Server 2017 on Linux. You can actually attach a database as well, following the process for attaching database as far back as SQL Server 2005.

Note   The "pain-free" upgrade path to restore a backup or attach a database can go as far back as SQL Server 2008. However, technically you can restore or attach an SQL Server 2005 backup or database file but there are some limitations and possible issues you should consider. You can read more about this at `https://docs.microsoft.com/sql/database-engine/install-windows/supported-version-and-edition-upgrades-2017#SupportFor2005`.

I've shown you examples of how to restore a backup throughout the book, and you have seen the process is very simple.

1. Copy the backup file to the SQL Server on Linux sever or place on a mounted directory that can be accessed by the Linux Server.

2. Ensure the ownership of the file has the mssql group and mssql owner permissions.

3. Use the T-SQL RESTORE command from any valid tool that can connect to SQL Server on Linux.

Note   The database backup has the paths of the files stored in the metadata of the backup. Therefore, you must always use the WITH MOVE options of the T-SQL RESTORE statement to move the database and transaction log files into their new location. And the new location must be set up to be accessed by the mssql user account on Linux.

Even though I've shown you this example in previous chapters, let's review one more time the process to restore the WideWorldImporters sample database to SQL Server on Linux.

1. Copy the WideWorldImporters sample database on the Linux
   server with the following command from the bash shell:

   ```
   wget https://github.com/Microsoft/sql-server-samples/releases/
   download/wide-world-importers-v1.0/WideWorldImporters-Full.bak
   ```

2. Run the following commands from the bash shell as found in the
   example script **cpwwi.sh** to copy the backup into the /var/opt/
   mssql directory:

   ```
   sudo cp WideWorldImporters-Full.bak /var/opt/mssql
   sudo chown mssql:mssql /var/opt/mssql/WideWorldImporters-Full.bak
   ```

3. Run the following command to restore the database from any
   valid SQL Server tool as found in **restorewwi_linux.sql** (Note: I've
   provided a bash shell script **restorewwi.sh** to run this SQL script
   using sqlcmd on the Linux server):

   ```
   restore database WideWorldImporters from disk = '/var/opt/mssql/
   WideWorldImporters-Full.bak' with
   move 'WWI_Primary' to '/var/opt/mssql/data/WideWorldImporters.
   mdf',
   move 'WWI_UserData' to '/var/opt/mssql/data/WideWorldImporters_
   UserData.ndf',
   move 'WWI_Log' to '/var/opt/mssql/data/WideWorldImporters.ldf',
   move 'WWI_InMemory_Data_1' to '/var/opt/mssql/data/
   WideWorldImporters_InMemory_Data_1'
   go
   ```

The restore will execute and run a series of *upgrade steps*, typically changes to system
tables required for the new version of SQL Server, to finish the restore the database since
the WideWorldImporters example was backed up with SQL Server 2016 on Windows.
The output of the RESTORE execution should look like the following:

```
Processed 1464 pages for database 'WideWorldImporters', file 'WWI_Primary'
on file 1.
Processed 53096 pages for database 'WideWorldImporters', file 'WWI_
UserData' on file 1.
```

Processed 33 pages for database 'WideWorldImporters', file 'WWI_Log' on file 1.

Processed 3862 pages for database 'WideWorldImporters', file 'WWI_InMemory_Data_1' on file 1.

Converting database 'WideWorldImporters' from version 852 to the current version 869.

Database 'WideWorldImporters' running the upgrade step from version 852 to version 853.

Database 'WideWorldImporters' running the upgrade step from version 853 to version 854.

Database 'WideWorldImporters' running the upgrade step from version 854 to version 855.

Database 'WideWorldImporters' running the upgrade step from version 855 to version 856.

Database 'WideWorldImporters' running the upgrade step from version 856 to version 857.

Database 'WideWorldImporters' running the upgrade step from version 857 to version 858.

Database 'WideWorldImporters' running the upgrade step from version 858 to version 859.

Database 'WideWorldImporters' running the upgrade step from version 859 to version 860.

Database 'WideWorldImporters' running the upgrade step from version 860 to version 861.

Database 'WideWorldImporters' running the upgrade step from version 861 to version 862.

Database 'WideWorldImporters' running the upgrade step from version 862 to version 863.

Database 'WideWorldImporters' running the upgrade step from version 863 to version 864.

Database 'WideWorldImporters' running the upgrade step from version 864 to version 865.

Database 'WideWorldImporters' running the upgrade step from version 865 to version 866.

```
Database 'WideWorldImporters' running the upgrade step from version 866 to
version 867.
Database 'WideWorldImporters' running the upgrade step from version 867 to
version 868.
Database 'WideWorldImporters' running the upgrade step from version 868 to
version 869.
RESTORE DATABASE successfully processed 58455 pages in 1.351 seconds
(338.027 MB/sec).
```

Any backup from a previous version of SQL Server restored to a newer version
will retain the *database compatibility* of the previous version. See the section on Post
Migration Considerations for a discussion on database compatibility.

For very large databases (100GB or more, which is my definition of very large for the
purposes of migration), restoring a backup is the fastest method to migrate to SQL Server
on Linux.

Copy Data with Bulk Copy or SSIS Package

There could be some reasons why you do not want to restore the database backup to
migrate to SQL Server on Linux. Perhaps for the migration process you want to make
changes to existing object definitions in the database. You could do this after you restore
a backup. Or you could create a new database perhaps with new file definitions, create
new objects, and then use SQL Server tools to export data out of the existing SQL Server
database and import the data into the new database structures.

For SQL Server on Windows, you can use the bcp program to export the data, copy
the files to the Linux Server, and use bcp on Linux to import the data into your new
databases. I introduced the bcp program in a previous chapter on tools, but you can also
read more about bcp at `https://docs.microsoft.com/sql/linux/sql-server-linux-migrate-bcp`.

You might have a more complex Extract, Transform, and Load (ETL) process to
migrate to a new SQL Server database on Linux. In this case, consider creating an SQL
Server Integration Services (SSIS) package. While you must use tools on a Windows
client to create an SSIS package, SQL Server on Linux supports executing SSIS packages
on the Linux server. You can read more about SSIS on Linux at `https://docs.microsoft.com/sql/linux/sql-server-linux-migrate-ssis`.

Export and Import with BACPAC

A third option to migrate an existing SQL Server database to SQL Server on Linux is a Data-Tier package file called an *BACPAC* file. BACPAC files are very portable and can be used to migrate to other platforms such as Azure. A BACPAC file is a package and contains the definition or schema of the database, files, and the objects (such as tables and indexes). In addition, the package contains exported versions of the data contains in user tables.

BACPAC files are created using either SQL Server Management Studio via a visual interface wizard or the program **sqlpackage**. You can now use sqlpackage on Windows, macOS, or Linux from https://docs.microsoft.com/sql/tools/sqlpackage. BACPAC files are created by using options via these tools to *export* the package. You can read more about exporting a BACPAC file at https://docs.microsoft.com/sql/relational-databases/data-tier-applications/export-a-data-tier-application. The same set of tools can be used to *import* the package. Importing the package will execute the package, which includes creating the database, creating files, all objects, and importing all data. You can read more about the import process at https://docs.microsoft.com/sql/relational-databases/data-tier-applications/import-a-bacpac-file-to-create-a-new-user-database.

The following is an example command to run sqlpackage on SQL Server on Windows from Powershell to export a BACPAC file for a database:

```
.\sqlpackage /A:Export /ssn:<sql server> /sdn:<database> /tf:c:\temp\wwi.bacpac
```

Here is an example of executing sqlpackage on the same Windows client to import the package into the SQL Server on Linux target:

```
.\sqlpackage /A:Import /tsn:<Linux SQL instance> /tdn:<target db name>
/sf:c:\temp\wwi.bacpac /tu:sa /tp:<sa password>
```

You don't need to create the database on the SQL Server on Linux instance. sqlpackage will do that when executing everything in the bacpac file.

Migrating from Oracle

You may be reading this book looking to migrate from another database platform, like Oracle, to SQL Server on Linux. In this section of the book, I will not cover a comparison of features between Oracle and SQL Server. I've done my best up until this point in the book to describe all the features and functionality of SQL Server on Linux to educate you and prepare you for its capabilities, should you be looking to migrate from Oracle.

In this section, I'm going to assume you have made this decision to migrate or are looking to test a migration, so you can evaluate how your application will behave and perform with SQL Server on Linux. While there could be several methods to export data from Oracle allowing you to create your own database on SQL Server on Linux and import your data, SQL Server provides a free tool to assist in migrating from Oracle. This tool is called the **SQL Server Migration Assistant** (SSMA).

SSMA supports many different data platform sources, including Oracle, DB2, MySQL, and SAP ASE, to migrate to several different target Microsoft database platforms including SQL Server on Linux. To get a complete list of sources and targets for SSMS, see our documentation at `https://docs.microsoft.com/sql/ssma/sql-server-migration-assistant#supported-sources-and-target-versions` and `https://docs.microsoft.com/sql/linux/sql-server-linux-migrate-ssma`. I will use SSMA for the rest of this chapter describing the preparation and execution of migration from Oracle.

For a complete reference on SSMA, see our documentation at `https://docs.microsoft.com/sql/ssma/sql-server-migration-assistant`. When you have completed reading these sections for preparation and execution of your migration from Oracle, be sure to see the section of this chapter on Post Migration Considerations.

Preparing for the Migration

Because the SSMA tool only runs on Windows, you will need three computing environments capable of being connected together to migrate from Oracle to SQL Server on Linux:

- Your Linux server running Oracle

- A new Linux server running SQL Server on Linux

- A Windows client to run the SSMA tool

The Windows client running SSMA must be capable of connecting to each server over TCP/IP, so you need to be sure to open up any firewall ports to allow remote connectivity. To use SSMA, the Oracle server and the SQL Server do not have to be able to connect to each other.

To prepare for the migration using SSMA, you will need to install the SSMA tool on your preferred Windows client. Follow the instructions carefully in our documentation, as there are dependencies from other components (such as Oracle client software) to allow SSMA to work. You can read these details in our documentation at `https://docs.microsoft.com/sql/ssma/oracle/installing-ssma-for-oracle-client-oracletosql`.

In addition, since you are migrating to SQL Server, you will want to create the database and files ahead of time following the best practices and performance recommendations I've outlined in the book.

One last important comment: you need to measure the performance of your Oracle workload carefully with existing tools used with Oracle and document these. You will want to compare this baseline to your application with SQL Server after doing the migration.

Executing the Migration

The SSMA tool works on a concept called a project. The migration process using a project looks like the following:

1. Create a SSMA project and configure settings.

2. Connect to an Oracle server.

3. Connect to SQL Server on Linux.

4. Map schemas between Oracle and SQL Server (or use the default.)

5. Convert the Oracle schemas, including your ability to choose which objects. This documentation has an excellent description of what can and cannot be converted from Oracle: `https://docs.microsoft.com/sql/ssma/oracle/converting-oracle-schemas-oracletosql`. At this point, SSMA saves the project information in the form that can be converted into T-SQL statements to SQL Server to migrate the select Oracle schema and objects.

6. Load the converted objects into SQL Server. You can let SSMA do this or save the information to a T-SQL script and then run the script (including modifying it to your needs) against SQL Server with any valid SQL Server tool.

7. Migrate the data, using SSMA to SQL Server on Linux.

This complete process is documented at `https://docs.microsoft.com/sql/ssma/oracle/migrating-oracle-databases-to-sql-server-oracletosql`.

You will love the fact that our engineering team who owns SSMA has built a step by step tutorial on how to use SSMA to migrate from Oracle to SQL Server on Linux. Therefore, you can set up your own environment and follow each step in our documentation at `https://docs.microsoft.com/sql/ssma/oracle/sql-server-linux-convert-from-oracle`. This tutorial uses objects from the HR example schema, which comes with every Oracle installation.

I went through the tutorial myself using three virtual machines in Azure (one for Oracle, one for SQL Server on Linux, and one for the Windows machine running SSMA). It worked as advertised, with a few important points to note:

- The tutorial does not make it clear in the prerequisites that you need a third computing environment running Windows for SSMA if your Oracle server to migrate is running Linux.

- If SQL Server Agent is not running on SQL Server on Linux, you will get a warning that server-side migration is not possible. Server-side migrations are not supported on SQL Server on Linux, so this can be ignored.

- The tutorial uses Oracle 12c, but I've done this with Oracle 11 XE (free version) as well. When I connect to the Oracle instance with SSMA, since I was using the XE edition, the name of the Oracle instance is XE and the login is SYSTEM.

- The tutorial says to pick a target of SQL Server 2017 (Linux) – Preview, but the latest version of SSMA just has SQL Server 2017 as a choice (it is no longer in Preview for Linux).

- Since SSMA using SQL Server on Linux as a target does not support server-side migration, the Oracle server and the SQL Server on Linux don't have to be able to communicate with each other. The SSMA Windows client connects with each server to transmit data.

Figure 10-4 shows the final result of my migration of the HR schema from Oracle 11 XE to SQL Server on Linux using SSMA.

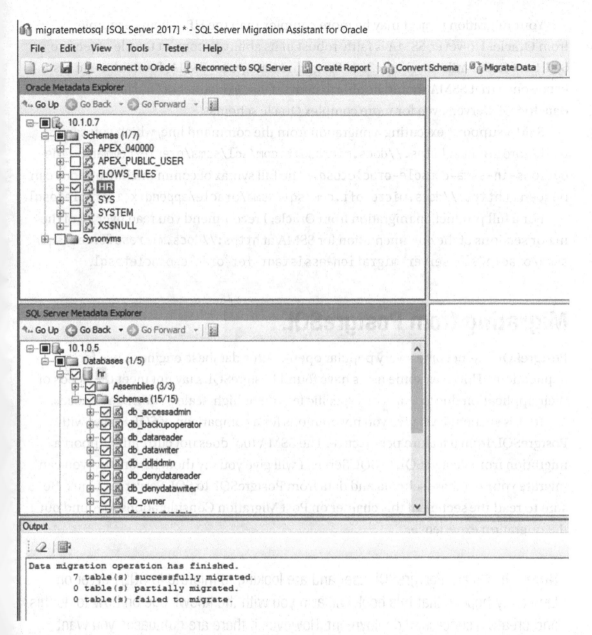

Figure 10-4. *A successful migration from Oracle to SQL Server on Linux using SSMA*

Your migration project may be more complex than the HR schema example from Oracle. However, SSMA is fairly robust in its ability to convert Oracle objects to SQL Server. Shamik Ghosh, the lead Program Manager for SSMA, has told me in his experience that SSMA should be able to convert 90+% or better of Oracle objects and data to SQL Server, even for more complex Oracle schemas.

SSMA supports executing a migration from the command line, which you can read more about at `https://docs.microsoft.com/sql/ssma/oracle/command-line-options-in-ssma-console-oracletosql`. The full syntax of command line options can be seen at `https://docs.microsoft.com/sql/ssma/oracle/appendix-1-oracletosql`.

For a full production migration from Oracle, I recommend you read over all of the major sections of the documentation for SSMA at `https://docs.microsoft.com/sql/ssma/oracle/sql-server-migration-assistant-for-oracle-oracletosql`.

Migrating from PostgreSQL

PostgreSQL has become a very popular open-source database engine to use for applications. However, some users have found PostgreSQL may not meet the needs of their application due to a lack of a specific feature or high-scale performance needs.

In this section, I will give you my opinions for a comparison of SQL Server with PostgreSQL from a feature perspective. The SSMA tool does not currently support a migration from PostgreSQL to SQL Server. I will give you my thoughts on how you can migrate your database schema and data from PostgreSQL to SQL Server on Linux. Be sure to read the section of this chapter on Post Migration Considerations to round out the migration experience.

Note   If you are PostgreSQL user and are looking to migrate to SQL Server on Linux, my hope is that this book will arm you with the knowledge on how to do this and create a successful deployment. However, if there are databases you want to keep with PostgreSQL, I highly encourage you to look at the managed service for PostgreSQL in Azure at `https://docs.microsoft.com/en-us/azure/postgresql/`.

How Does PostgreSQL Compare with SQL Server?

I call this section "the case for SQL Server." I've not used PostgreSQL in the past, so I will not claim to be an expert on using it. To write this chapter, I installed PostgreSQL on RHEL and performed some basic testing of its functionality. In addition, I did some research on features and functionality of SQL Server I've talked about in this book and looked to see if the same capabilities exist with PostgreSQL. To be transparent, I used the following resources for this research:

- The main PostgreSQL site that includes an overview at `https://www.postgresql.org/about/`

- The PostgreSQL version 10 documentation at `https://www.postgresql.org/files/documentation/pdf/10/postgresql-10-A4.pdf` (Note: I did not choose to use version 11, which is currently in beta.)

- The following PostgreSQL tutorials: `http://www.postgresqltutorial.com/` and `http://www.tutorialspoint.com/postgresql`

- A beginner primer to PostgreSQL at `https://zaiste.net/postgresql_primer_for_busy_people/`

- The Wikipedia site for PostgreSQL at `https://en.wikipedia.org/wiki/PostgreSQL`

- An excellent slide deck talking about the PostgreSQL architecture at `http://people.inf.elte.hu/kiss/14kor/korszcru-ea-01-postgre.pdf`

Note   My evaluation of PostgreSQL is based on the core open-source version that is documented in the aforementioned resources. Since PostgreSQL is open source, there are distributions of PostgreSQL modified by other organizations such as EnterpriseDB (`https://www.enterprisedb.com/`) and Crunchy Data (`https://www.crunchydata.com/`). There is even a huge list of PostgreSQL derived distributions and forks at `https://wiki.postgresql.org/wiki/PostgreSQL_derived_databases`. I have not used these resources to compare SQL Server on Linux.

In addition to this research, I reviewed my comparison with two engineers at Microsoft, Michal Primke and Harini Gupta, who work on our Azure for PostgreSQL service, and they agreed with all the points in the following comparison.

Rather than try to do an exhaustive comparison, I researched what features and functionality SQL Server has that is not in PostgreSQL or is better than PostgreSQL in my opinion. In this section I'll list this comparison by the following areas: Core Database Engine, The SQL Language, Tools, Performance, Security, HADR, and Management and Monitoring. If you don't see an SQL Server feature I've discussed in this book listed in this section, it is because pgsql has equivalent functionality or I could not find enough of a difference between the two systems to highlight it. I've provided this to give you my perspective on the unique value SQL Server on Linux can bring to your application vs. using PostgreSQL.

Note   From this point forward in the chapter, I'll refer to PostgreSQL as **pgsql** (you would too if you had to type in PostgreSQL each time).

Core Database Engine

There are several aspects built into the core database engine that are different than pgsql, distinguishable enough to call them out:

- **Threads vs. processes**

The pgsql documentation states the architecture for the server is based on a set of processes and not threads. All pgsql work is done via separate processes. All the background tasks (such as the checkpointer process) are processes. Each connection to pgsql results in the fork of a new process. In my testing on RHEL, each forked process to support a new connection requires around 5MB (this could mean that even 300 concurrent idle connections would require ~1.5GB of memory). I've read that the overhead to fork a new process is not heavy and requiring 5MB per connection in a process is not expensive. SQL Server is one single Linux process called sqlservr and uses threads to support all background tasks and a worker pool of threads to support connections and queries.

I was surprised to see the forked process architecture but then I remembered my early career out of college using Ingres, which had this same design. Pgsql was derived from the original Ingres database engine. So which architecture is better? On Windows, using threads is a proven better method than using multiple processes. I personally feel our TPC benchmark performance speaks for itself on the performance and scalability of SQL Server on Linux vs. pgsql. You can see the latest TPC-H #1 benchmark result for SQL Server on Linux at `http://www.tpc.org/3331`.

- **CPU and NUMA assignment**

SQL Server provides built-in functionality to control what CPUs and/or NUMA nodes SQL Server threads will use for execution. In addition, SQL Server uses a capability called Auto Soft NUMA to promote scalability on dense core socket systems. Pgsql does not offer any of these capabilities in the database engine.

- **Multiple files and write ahead logging file placement**

Pgsql has a concept called a *tablespace*. This is similar to the SQL Server filegroup object, as it allows you to place objects in a different location on disk than the default database directory. However, you cannot specify multiple files to spread out the I/O load for a tablespace as you can with SQL Server. Pgsql has its own method of creating files that support the database, which you do not have control over. There is only one directory for a specific tablespace and therefore objects related to a tablespace are limited to a single directory on disk.

Furthermore, there is no method to separate the location for transaction log (called write ahead logging or wal) data *per database* in pgsql. SQL Server allows you to specify the exact location for the transaction log for each database. Pgsql states in their best practices documentation to move the location of the wal directory by moving the directory pg_wal. However, all wal data for all databases goes to this directory.

- **Database size control**

Databases created with pgsql are not created with a fixed size and can grow until you run out of disk space or hit a limit based on any Linux space restrictions. As you have seen from reading this book, SQL Server allows you granular control over the size of files for the database and transaction log including initial size, maximum size, and autogrow parameters.

- **Checksum**

Pgsql does support the concept of checksum for database pages. However, you must specify whether you want this option when you first initialize pgsql with initdb. Furthermore, the documentation at `https://www.postgresql.org/docs/current/static/app-initdb.html` states "...Enabling checksums may incur a noticeable performance penalty." Checksum in pgsql cannot be controlled per database. SQL Server enables checksum on a database by default, and we do this because it will not incur a significant performance penalty. Furthermore, we allow you to turn this on or off at any time at a database scope.

- **Buffer Pool cache**

Both SQL Server and pgsql have a buffer pool cache concept. However, pgsql also does not open database files using the O_DIRECT option (i.e., direct I/O). Therefore, the Linux kernel buffers all file I/O in file system cache for pgsql, thereby almost doubling the amount of memory needed for database pages (Note: this does depend on how you configure pgsql for shared buffer cache using the shared_buffers setting).

- **Plan cache**

SQL Server can cache ad hoc T-SQL statements and even auto-parameterize them. Pgsql only caches prepared statements and PL/pgSQL code.

- **Temporal tables**

Temporal tables are a built-in feature of SQL Server. The base pgsql distribution does not support this. After doing some research, I found that pgsql can support temporal tables with a *custom extension*, which is found at `https://pgxn.org/dist/temporal_tables/`. The problem is that this extension is not one of the standard extensions documented with the core pgsql documentation at `https://www.postgresql.org/docs/current/static/contrib.html`. Therefore, I'm not sure about the reliability or the support of this extension. You can read more about temporal tables for SQL Server at `https://docs.microsoft.com/sql/relational-databases/tables/temporal-tables`.

- **Graph database**

There is no equivalent in pgsql to the SQL Server graph database functionality with T-SQL support for node and edge table types and the new MATCH syntax. Most examples I've seen with pgsql talk about using recursive common table expression (CTE) queries to achieve this functionality. However, that is the actual reason we built the new graph database feature: to make it simpler to design natural graph data models using tables vs. writing complex queries. You can read more about graph database with SQL Server at `https://docs.microsoft.com/sql/relational-databases/graphs/sql-graph-overview`.

- **Native scoring**

pgsql supports the ability to write server-side code using Python as language (using CREATE FUNCTION). As I've mentioned in the book, SQL Server 2017 on Windows supports built-in R and Python code with SQL Server, but it's not supported by SQL Server on Linux today (believe me, it's coming!). One nice feature built into the SQL Server engine I have mentioned in a previous chapter is called *native scoring*. Native scoring allows you to take as input a persisted machine learning model and use the new T-SQL PREDICT statement to execute high-speed scalable predictions applications. pgsql does not offer a native scoring capability. You can read more about native scoring with SQL Server at https://docs.microsoft.com/sql/advanced-analytics/sql-native-scoring.

The SQL Language

After studying the pgsql SQL language there are many similarities to T-SQL (which could make the migration process to SQL Server easier than I first thought), but a few differences stood out to me worth calling out:

- **T-SQL batches**

One method to avoid a *chatty* application is to use T-SQL batches. T-SQL batches allow you to send multiple T-SQL statements in one trip to SQL Server, and the database engine processes each T-SQL statement. pgsql does not offer this concept. Each SQL statement is sent separately even if an application attempts to execute multiple statements. In the psql tool, each SQL statement must be separated by a semicolon.

- **Stored procedures**

Server-side programming in pgsql is done using a language called PL/pgSQL, which uses SQL statements (Note: in SQL Server, all statements are called T-SQL whether they are part of ANSI SQL or statements specific to SQL Server). In version 10 of pgsql, the only PL/pgSQL to write a server-side program is a *function* using CREATE FUNCTION (which doesn't allow for transactions). In transparency, I've read that version 11 of pgsql, now in beta, plans to support CREATE PROCEDURE PL/pgSQL statement. In version 10, I've seen several examples of functions in pgsql return a VOID type to simulate a procedure.

- **IDENTITY column property**

Pgsql supports a SEQUENCE object, just like I've shown you in the book using T-SQL Sequences are a SQL standard (so this will make a SEQUENCE object very portable to migrate to SQL Server). However, SEQUENCE objects are created separately from columns and then bound to one or more columns. SQL Server offers a simpler approach to the same concept using the identity property for a specific column.

Tools

I think you now remember the very long chapter on tools (Chapter 5). That chapter was long for a reason. I believe SQL Server has an amazing tools story: both features built into the engine and programs outside the engine. Here are a few specific areas for tools where I think SQL Server on Linux shines compared with pgsql:

- **Dynamic Management Views (DMVs)**

DMVs are one of the most powerful features of SQL Server to gain live, dynamic insight into the execution of the SQL Server database engine. pgsql has similar capabilities, but I've observed through my research several significant differences in favor of DMVs.

- Our DMVs have memory information in detail. Pgsql only supports looking at buffer cache information from a pg_buffercache view.

- pg_stat_statements, which is an equivalent feature to the DMV dm_exec_requests, is not on by default. The docs for pgsql say that enabling this feature can cause performance overhead, can be saved across restarts, but doesn't contain execution plan information where dm_exec_query_stats provides the estimated query plan (as does Query Store).

- pg_stat_activity is equivalent to the DMV dm_exec_requests except that it is not "live" because it is refreshed based on information from each process (default refresh rate is 500ms but that can be configured). SQL Server DMVs are "on-demand." You can query the state of the system anytime and you get the real-time view of the system at that time.

- Pgsql provides blocking information about processes and locks in the view pg_locks. The pid of the process waiting on a lock can be seen in this view. However, this information is not found in pg_stat_activity. The SQL Server DMV dm_exec_requests provides blocking information (including the blocking task) and you can also see all detailed locks in the DMV dm_tran_locks.

- SQL Server provides DMVs for all core engine functionality and for just about every feature included in SQL Server (in fact, SQL Server includes ~243 DVMs in SQL Server on Linux). Pgsql provides mostly dynamic system activity through the statistics collector and covers only the core database engine.

- SQL Server provides a DMV to recommend missing indexes with dm_db_missing_index_details. Pgsql does not offer an index recommendation feature built into the database engine.

You can read more about DMVs for SQL Server at https://docs.microsoft.com/sql/relational-databases/system-dynamic-management-views/system-dynamic-management-views.

- **ERRORLOG**

pgsql does have a logging facility to a file and is very configurable. However, by default the SQL Server ERRORLOG contains a rich set of information (especially at startup) about the configuration of SQL Server, the OS, and databases. When I was in technical support, I could tell a customer a lot about their system just by reading ERRORLOG files. The default pgsql log contains only errors.

- **Query Store**

I simply love the power of the Query Store, one of my favorite features launched with SQL Server 2016. While pgsql has a similar feature to view query performance information via a view called pg_stat_statements, I believe Query Store is superior for several reasons.

- The Query Store is saved with a backup of the database, since the Query Store is tied to a database. Pgsql statistics are server wide and can be persisted, but I found no way to export or back them up for separate analysis.

- pg_stat_statements contains query execution statistics and is available via a supported extension but requires a server restart to enable. Query Store can be enabled online for your needs at any time via ALTER DATABASE. Query Store also supports richer configuration parameters to control the collection of queries, including CAPTURE_MODE=AUTO (only store the queries that matter) and history (number of days to keep data).

- Query Store includes wait statistics per query but pgsql statistics for waits are tied to the overall process in pg_stat_activity.

- Pg_stat_statements can be saved across server restarts but there is no date/time stamp for queries. So you cannot run a historical analysis of queries over time to find out the differences and perform analysis like query plan regressions. Furthermore, the estimated plan is saved with Query Store for each plan for a specific query over time. Pg_stat_statements does not contain any query plan information.

- Query Store captures query information even when a query fails. There is no mention in pgsql documentation whether pg_stat_statements save query information if a query fails.

- Query Store captures information about compilation and execution time. Pg_stat_statements does not breakdown information on compilation vs. execution.

You can read all the details about Query Store in SQL Server at `https://docs.microsoft.com/sql/relational-databases/performance/monitoring-performance-by-using-the-query-store`.

- **Live query statistics**

There is no method to see the current query level information about a query while it is in progress in pgsql through pg_stat_statements. SQL Server provides the ability to see per query plan operator execution statistics as a query is executing in progress. You can read more about live query statistics for SQL Server at `https://docs.microsoft.com/sql/relational-databases/performance/live-query-statistics`.

- **DBCC commands**

The most unique DBCC command that does not have an equivalent feature in pgsql is CHECKDB. I've read discussions in my research that pgsql doesn't need a consistency checker, since page checksum is now supported (as of pgsql 9.3). However, as I've said in this book, if pages become damaged in memory, a page checksum will not detect it (although SQL Server even has some minimal detection for this scenario). Remember DBCC CHECKDB is online because SQL Server supports the concept of database snapshots. You can read more about DBCC CHECKDB for SQL Server at `https://docs.microsoft.com/sql/t-sql/database-console-commands/dbcc-checkdb-transact-sql`.

- **SSIS**

SQL Server offers as part of the license for SQL Server an ETL system called SQL Server Integration Services (SSIS), which I've outlined in the book. pgsql does not come with any rich, built-in ETL system like SSIS. You can read more about SSIS on Linux at `https://docs.microsoft.com/sql/linux/sql-server-linux-migrate-ssis`.

- **DBCC CLONEDATABASE**

While pgsql offers methods to create a new database based on a source database (i.e., clone), there is no method to create a new database based on a source database *and include statistics and performance information.* SQL Server offers this capability with DBCC CLONEDATABASE. You can read more about DBCC CLONEDATABASE at `https://docs.microsoft.com/sql/t-sql/database-console-commands/dbcc-clonedatabase-transact-sql`.

- **Intellisense and mssql extension for query editing**

Pgsql has a free GUI tool to perform administration tasks and execute SQL queries called pgAdmin. There are several differences between SSMS and SQL Operations Studio and pgAdmin, but pgAdmin is a reasonably good tool. One difference that stood out to me was SSMS and SQL Operations Studio support for intellisense for T-SQL query design vs. the autocomplete feature for pgAdmin. I believe the Microsoft Intellisense feature is far richer to aid with the syntax and object selection for T-SQL vs. autocomplete for pgAdmin. SQL Operations Studio and mssql-cli both support intellisense functionality via the mssql extension that also is provided with the Visual Studio Code editor.

You can read more about intellisense in SSMS at `https://docs.microsoft.com/sql/relational-databases/scripting/intellisense-sql-server-management-studio` and the mssql extension at `https://docs.microsoft.com/sql/linux/sql-server-linux-develop-use-vscode#install-the-mssql-extension`.

Performance

Chapter 6 of this book discusses in detail the performance capabilities of SQL Server. I believe SQL Server has a long, proven track record of performance both with customer testimonials and TPC benchmarks. In fact, one of our first SQL Server on Linux production customers has a testimonial that performance of SQL Server compared with pgsql is what convinced them to migrate. You can read their story at `https://customers.microsoft.com/doclink/dv01`. I've listed out in this section my perspective on the unique capabilities of SQL Server for performance as compared with pgsql.

- **Scalability and TPC benchmarks**

I've demonstrated and talked extensively about scalability for performance for SQL Server. Performance for SQL Server and scalability are best demonstrated with TPC benchmarks. SQL Server dominates TPC benchmarks. In fact, SQL Server on Linux has the top 1TB (`http://www.tpc.org/3331`) TPC-H benchmark official results. As I've discussed in the book these benchmarks matter for two reasons:

1. The benchmarks measure the potential capability of a database to process an application workload.

2. Microsoft is not allowed to post their own benchmarks, based on the rules of the TPC council. Our partners such as HPE and Lenovo are the ones posting the benchmarks to show the performance capabilities of our database platform combined with their hardware. To this date, no hardware vendor has chosen to post a TPC benchmark for pgsql.

- **Read-ahead**

SQL Server has many built-in capabilities in the engine to boost query performance. I've described how read ahead accelerates query scan performance. Pgsql does not support read ahead capabilities. There is an older blog written on SQL Server read ahead (some details may be a bit out of date but it paints the picture) at `https://blogs.msdn.microsoft.com/craigfr/2008/09/23/sequential-read-ahead/`.

- **Parallel queries**

The pgsql documentation makes this statement: "Many queries cannot benefit from parallel query, either due to limitations of the current implementation or because there is no imaginable query plan which is any faster than the serial query plan" (`https://www.postgresql.org/docs/10/static/parallel-query.html`). Remember, these are run by processes so inter process communication is required vs. SQL Server, which shares information in a process across threads.

SQL Server supports parallel queries and many queries can benefit from this capability (especially analytic queries using technologies like clustered columnstore indexes). Furthermore, SQL Server supports parallel queries for operations like SELECT INTO and INSERT SELECT.

- **Query hints and options**

pgsql does not support query level hints and options but SQL Server has this capability. You can read more about query hints for SQL Server at `https://docs.microsoft.com/sql/t-sql/queries/hints-transact-sql-query`.

- **Columnstore indexes**

I've described the amazing performance power of columnstore indexes in this book for analytic workloads. Pgsql does not have columnstore index capabilities. I did find this custom extension for pgsql at `https://pgxn.org/dist/cstore_fdw/` but I cannot tell if it is widely used or supported.

- **In-Memory OLTP**

I've also described the performance capabilities of memory optimized tables for OLTP workloads with SQL Server. pgsql does not contain In-Memory OLTP capabilities. You can read more about In-Memory OLTP for SQL Server at `https://docs.microsoft.com/sql/relational-databases/in-memory-oltp/in-memory-oltp-in-memory-optimization`.

- **Adaptive Query Processing and Automatic Tuning**

I described the new performance capabilities of SQL Server called Adaptive Query Processing (AQP) and Automatic Tuning. Pgsql does not have these capabilities, as far as I have seen from my research. You can read more about AQP at `https://docs.microsoft.com/sql/relational-databases/performance/adaptive-query-processing`. You can read more about Automatic Ytuning in a blog post I wrote at `https://cloudblogs.microsoft.com/sqlserver/2018/06/11/sql-server-automatic-tuning-around-the-world/`.

Security

Security is so important for a data platform product, and I made a case for you in this book about how SQL Server has all the capabilities you need to secure your data. In this section, I'll point out the unique aspects that make SQL Server a superior database product in my opinion in the area of security vs pgsql.

- **Least vulnerable database product**

According to the National Institute of Standard and Technology (NIST), SQL Server has the least number of security vulnerabilities in the industry. The chart as seen in Figure 10-5 shows the trends over the last eight years.

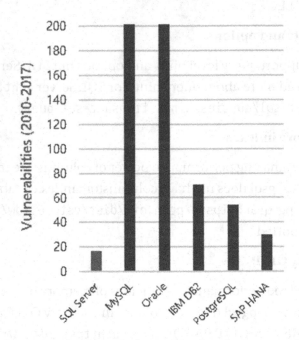

Figure 10-5. *SQL Server is the least vulnerable database over the last eight years.*

We didn't make up these statistics. You can read more about this data at `https://nvd.nist.gov/`.

- **Active Directory authentication**

While pgsql does support GSSAPI-based authentication, there is no specific mention in the pgsql documentation that it supports GSSAPI authentication for an Active Directory system. Active Directory is one of the most popular identity systems in the industry and SQL Server on Linux supports. You can read more about Active Directory authentication for SQL Server on Linux at `https://docs.microsoft.com/sql/linux/sql-server-linux-active-directory-authentication`.

- **Transparent Data Encryption (TDE)**

SQL Server provides encryption of data at rest using TDE. Pgsql does not provide any built-in encryption for database and wal log files at rest. You can read more about TDE for SQL Server at `https://docs.microsoft.com/sql/relational-databases/security/encryption/transparent-data-encryption`.

- **Always Encrypted**

I described in Chapter 7 the new end-to-end security feature called Always Encrypted, which integrates SQL Server providers with the database engine to encrypt data end-to-end but place the control of keys in the hands of application developers and users. pgsql does not have a built-in end-to-end encryption feature like Always Encrypted.

- **Dynamic data masking (DDM)**

DDM for SQL Server allows a SQL Server administrator to define masking rules using T-SQL vs. encoding the rules in an application. The feature is called dynamic because applications can pick up new masks on data after the T-SQL statements are applied to SQL Server. pgsql does not currently support a dynamic data masking feature.

- **Auditing**

SQL Server provides built-in security auditing uses the foundation of extended events. pgsql does not provide any built-in security audit capabilities. In my research, I did find this custom extension for auditing for pgsql on GitHub at `https://github.com/pgaudit/pgaudit` but I cannot tell how widely this is used or supported.

- **Data classification and vulnerability assessment**

The recent GDPR regulations have many users looking closer at both data classification and possible vulnerabilities in their data platform. SQL Server provides built in capabilities and tools for both data classification (read more at `https://docs.microsoft.com/sql/relational-databases/security/sql-data-discovery-and-classification`) and vulnerability assessments (read more at `https://docs.microsoft.com/sql/relational-databases/security/sql-vulnerability-assessment`). Pgsql does not provide any built-in capabilities for either data classification or vulnerability assessments.

HADR

I described in this book how important high availability and disaster recovery features and processes are for a production database platform. In this section, I'll highlight some of the unique differences between SQL Server and pgsql regarding HADR.

- **Backup and Restore**

  - SQL Server backups support checksums but that is not supported with pgsql. SQL BACKUP WITH CHECKSUM verifies the checksum during the backup. SQL Server has RESTORE VERIFYONLY to verify the checksums.

  - There is no encryption option for backups for pgsql where SQL Server supports encrypted backups.

  - SQL Server supports the Virtual Device Interface (VDI) for backup streaming to external programs, including the support for snapshot backups. The pg_dump program for pgsql does support streaming the output using a "pipe" with Linux to another program, but VDI is a complete protocol interface allowing for rich third-party backup solutions.

  - SQL Server supports differential backups but pgsql does not have this concept. You can read more about differential backups in SQL Server at `https://docs.microsoft.com/sql/relational-databases/backup-restore/differential-backups-sql-server`.

  - SQL Server supports restores of filegroups, partial restores, and page restores online, which are not supported in pgsql.

- **Startup and parallel recovery**

  - I've described in the book the process for SQL Server recovery of a database at startup including the analysis, redo, and undo phases. SQL Server supports the concept of fast recovery to allow database users to access the database after the redo phase while maintain locks on the necessary resources as undo executes. Pgsql does not offer this functionality.

- SQL Server also uses parallel works for the redo phase of recovery, thereby speeding up the overall recovery process. Pgsql does not offer parallel redo recovery of databases.

- **Disaster recovery**

If you lose a database tablespace in pgsql (for example you put it on a separate disk that fails) the entire pgsql cluster may not start. This is according to the pgsql documentation at `https://www.postgresql.org/docs/10/static/manage-ag-tablespaces.html`. Any SQL Server user database failure to start for any reason will not result in an instance startup failure.

- **Database snapshots**

pgsql does not offer any functionality like the SQL Server database snapshot, which is a sparse version of the original database and only grows as changes are made to the original database. You can read more about SQL Server database snapshots at `https://docs.microsoft.com/sql/relational-databases/databases/database-snapshots-sql-server`.

- **Failover clustering and Availability Groups**

Pgsql offers both shared disk and transaction log based HADR solutions and integrates with clustering system software such as Pacemaker. The resource agent to use with Pacemaker must be installed from a different location at `https://github.com/ClusterLabs/resource-agents/blob/master/heartbeat/pgsql`. All resources on how to install the resource agent and integrate with Pacemaker can be found at `https://wiki.postgresql.org/wiki/Ecosystem:Pacemaker`. After looking through this functionality of pgsql, two differences stood out for me

1. The granularity of failover detection for SQL Server uses flexible failover policies and the sp_server_diagnostics system procedure. In addition, SQL Server supports database health as a component to detect the need for a failover. I did not see pgsql offer this level of failure detection to trigger a failover built inside the database engine. You can read more about flexible failover for SQL Server at `https://docs.microsoft.com/sql/database-engine/availability-groups/windows/flexible-automatic-failover-policy-availability-group`.

529

2. SQL Server provides a capability for automatic page repair with Availability Groups, where pgsql does not offer this feature with their streaming replication technology.

Management and Monitoring

The final area where I've compared SQL Server with pgsql is various management and monitoring features. The following are areas I feel SQL Server shines and provides more robust functionality than pgsql.

- **SQL Server Agent**

SQL Server provides a built-in job scheduling engine, which can be especially handy to schedule database maintenance tasks. pgsql does not offer a built-in job scheduler system. You can read more about how to use SQL Server Agent on Linux at `https://docs.microsoft.com/sql/linux/sql-server-linux-run-sql-server-agent-job`.

- **Resource Governor**

SQL Server provides a built-in feature to control resources for users and applications including CPU, I/O, and memory. In addition, Resource Governor allows you to control the max degree of parallelism at an application level and affinitize applications to CPUs or NUMA nodes. Pgsql does not have built-in features that compare with Resource Governor. Most uses of pgsql use Linux cgroups to control the pgsql cluster resources but you cannot tie this assignment to applications. You can read more about SQL Server Resource Governor at `https://docs.microsoft.com/sql/relational-databases/resource-governor/resource-governor`.

- **Dedicated Admin Connection (DAC)**

As I've described in the book, should SQL Server become inaccessible for any reason, but the SQL Server instance is still running, you may be able to connect with DAC, collect diagnostics, and in some cases resolve the problem. Should pgsql become hung for any reason, there is no method to access the engine without stopping and restarting pgsql. You can read more about DAC for SQL Server at `https://docs.microsoft.com/sql/database-engine/configure-windows/diagnostic-connection-for-database-administrators`.

- **Attaching and detaching a database**

Since SQL Server allows you to control and establish specific files for your database and transaction log, you have the capability to detach a database, copy or move your files to another SQL Server, and attach these files for a new database. Pgsql does not offer any capabilities like detach and attach for SQL Server.

- **Recovery and repair**

For page checksum failures, pgsql does offer the ability to clean up damaged pages by initializing them from a query or the background vacuum process. SQL Server offers richer repair capabilities such as DBCC CHECKDB REPAIR and emergency mode repair to rebuild the transaction log. In addition, if SQL Server recovery encounters a checksum error, recovery will continue, skipping the damaged page using deferred transactions.

- **Online maintenance**

SQL Server supports the concept of an online index build so that users are not blocked while the index is being built (or rebuilt). pgsql does not offer this functionality. In addition, SQL Server supports the concept of a resumable index rebuild, so you can pause and continue a large index rebuild task. You can read more about online index operations for SQL Server at https://docs.microsoft.com/sql/relational-databases/indexes/perform-index-operations-online.

- **Index reorganization**

Indexes in SQL Server and pgsql can become fragmented. Both SQL Server and pgsql offer a method to defragment an index by rebuilding the index (only SQL Server can do this online). However, only SQL Server offers a different, less intrusive method to defragment an index by reorganizing the index. You can read more about index reorganization with SQL Server at https://docs.microsoft.com/sql/relational-databases/indexes/reorganize-and-rebuild-indexes.

- **System health session**

While SQL Server (Extended Events) and pgsql (dtrace) offer rich tracing capabilities, only SQL Server automatically uses tracing to save information about key events regarding the health of SQL Server, called the system health session. Included in the system health session is output of the sp_server_diagnostics stored procedure, which is used to make health decisions for failover. You can read more about the system health session in SQL Server at https://docs.microsoft.com/sql/relational-databases/extended-events/use-the-system-health-session.

Executing the Migration

Just like a migration from Oracle, to migrate from PostgreSQL I recommend you first perform the following steps:

1. Assess and capture a baseline of performance for your current application using PostgreSQL.

2. Decide if you want to make any changes to the definition of tables, indexes, or server-side code as part of your migration.

3. Install SQL Server on Linux.

4. Create a new database with the appropriate sizes of the database and transaction log to accommodate the current size of the PostgreSQL database and to account for transactions to insert data into tables.

A migration from PostgreSQL will typically involve three areas:

- Migrating the schema or definition of all objects such as table, indexes, views, and server-side code

- Migrating data

- Migrating any maintenance scripts or jobs

Through my research I found a few tools written by software vendors you can purchase to help you with migrating the schema and object definitions, but nothing I could find is free to download.

So instead, I found these two resources that talk about migrating from SQL Server to pgsql. By studying these examples, you should be able identify possible issues you will encounter when migrating from pgsql to SQL Server:

1. This blog post at https://www.devbridge.com/articles/ migrating-from-mssql-to-postgresql/ talks about a user experience migrating from SQL Server to pgsql.

This is very useful to read because it shows many of the SQL language differences between the two systems. You can use this knowledge as you migrate to SQL Server.

2. The GitHub project `https://github.com/lorint/AdventureWorks-for-Postgres` for AdventureWorks is an excellent resource.

The user took the SQL Server sample database AdventureWorks from SQL Server 2014 as found at `https://github.com/Microsoft/sql-server-samples/releases/tag/adventureworks` to migrate it to pgsql. I have a few remarks after looking through this project.

- The project uses the following zip file, `https://github.com/Microsoft/sql-server-samples/releases/download/adventureworks/AdventureWorks-oltp-install-script.zip`, which has the T-SQL script to create the AdventureWorks database and a series of .csv files to load the data for SQL Server.

- Compare the T-SQL script with the install.sql found in the pgsql GitHub project so you see fundamental differences on how to create tables, indexes, schemas, and datatypes.

- The user was forced to create functions returning VOID for T-SQL stored procedures, since pgsql does not have a stored procedure concept. You should be able to take functions from pgsql that return void and change them to SQL Server stored procedures.

- The project has a program written in Ruby to convert the CSV files to be able to load the data in pgsql. While you could look at this code to do the reverse with CSV files generated from a program like pgdump, consider that SSIS supports a pgsql ODBC driver. Therefore, you would build an SSIS package to export data from pgsql into your SQL Server on Linux. Pgsql supports ODBC drivers (see `https://www.postgresql.org/ftp/odbc/versions/msi/` for downloads). Then see this documentation for how to use SSIS with ODBC data sources: `https://docs.microsoft.com/sql/integration-services/data-flow/extract-data-by-using-the-odbc-source`.

Post Migration Considerations

Once you have migrated to SQL Server, you will want to consider several changes for the SQL Server instance and databases you have migrated. There could be many tasks you need to work on post migration, but in this section I've narrowed it to ones I feel most important that can affect the success of your experience on SQL Server on Linux. In this section, I'll discuss performance, HADR, database compatibility, and application compatibility. Database compatibility only applies if you have migrated from an earlier version of SQL Server. All other topics are very applicable to your migration from any database platform to SQL Server on Linux.

Optimizing Performance Post Migration

This book contains a very lengthy chapter on performance (Chapter 6) for a good reason. Performance is one of the most critical aspects to a successful application using a data platform like SQL Server. Therefore, after you have migrated to SQL Server on Linux, you want to be sure to optimize performance. Everything I discussed in Chapter 6 applies to your use of SQL Server on Linux. In this section, I'll call out some specific areas you want to look at after you have migrated.

First, our documentation contains an excellent set of performance-related post migration topics at `https://docs.microsoft.com/sql/relational-databases/ post-migration-validation-and-optimization-guide`. Let me start by making some comments on these recommendations:

- **Change in CE version**: CE stands for cardinality estimation, and I mentioned this topic in Chapter 6 on performance. I'll defer commenting on this topic until the section later in this chapter on database compatibility.

- **Change in cardinality estimation**: You'll want to address changes in cardinality estimation. See "Using Database Compatibility" later in this chapter for specific advice.

- **Parameter sniffing**: This is another topic I talked about in Chapter 6 on performance. This guidance is more for awareness and how to deal with situations for *parameter sensitive plans*. If you remember, in

Chapter 6 I talked about the new feature called Automatic Tuning to detect and even fix query plan regression problems that can occur in some situations because of parameter sniffing.

- **Missing indexes**: I discussed this topic in Chapter 6 on performance. Always take a look at recommended missing indexes but always investigate each recommendation to make sure it makes sense for your database.

- **Predicates and filter of data**: This section talks about various *query patterns* that would prevent SQL Server from generating an optimal query plan to search based on *filters*. A filter is just another word for using a WHERE clause in a T-SQL statement. An example of a filter that could prevent the ability of SQL Server to seek for rows using an index (vs. scanning the entire index or table) is a WHERE clause comparing a column with a variable or value that is not the same data type and requires an implicit data conversion.

- **Table valued functions**: This is a topic I did not cover in the book to this point. Table valued functions (TVFs) give you the ability to create a T-SQL function that returns a table type. The documentation discusses how this concept could be an alternative to a view, since a TVF can have multiple statements but a view only allows one T-SQL statement. Be careful using a Multi-Statement TVF (MSTVF), since statistics used for query plan choices use a fixed value. Having said this, the new AQP feature I discussed in Chapter 6 can help with estimating the correct statistics for a MSTVF.

There are other considerations for performance I think you should keep in mind after a migration to SQL Server on Linux, including indexes, baselines and monitoring, and using new features.

Rebuild Existing Indexes and Build New Indexes

I don't necessarily have the evidence to back up this statement, but I'll say it anyway. Any time you upgrade or migrate to a newer version of SQL Server, always rebuild all of your indexes. It just gives you a *clean slate* on index organization and statistics.

After you migrate, it is also a good opportunity to investigate whether you should consider changing your current indexes, removing unneeded indexes, or adding new indexes. Use the guidance from Chapter 6 on possible missing indexes. If you are migrating from another database platform, you definitely want to take a look at the right index strategy for your new tables. While tools like SSMA can convert indexes from a platform like Oracle to SQL Server, you should ensure these indexes are still the right ones for your workload, including clustered indexes and nonclustered indexes.

Establish New Baselines and Performance Monitoring Strategy

In Chapter 6, I talked about the important of performance baselines and monitoring. I also discussed in that chapter the importance of capturing performance baseline data on your previous system before the migration. A tool like DEA allows you to do this for SQL Server and compare future performance before the migration.

After the migration is a good time to check on the performance of your application compared with previous baselines, whether it is SQL Server or another database platform. In addition, as I mentioned at the top of the chapter, compare your overall system utilization on SQL Server on Linux with your previous system. It is very possible the overall system utilization may be different on SQL Server on Linux, but you should be on the lookout for radically different observations. If you migrate to SQL Server on Linux and your application results in a 100% CPU utilization of the Linux server (and sqlservr consumes all of this), you need to carefully study whether you have enough CPUs for your workload or whether T-SQL queries may not be optimally tuned.

Once you are satisfied with the new performance of SQL Server after the migration, it is a great time to establish new baselines. This is where a feature like Query Store can become extremely useful, since it automatically captures historical information about query performance.

You also need to ensure you have the right monitoring strategy in place for performance. If you are migrating from SQL Server on Windows, many of the great SQL Server features exist to monitor query performance, but you will need to establish new methods to observe performance of the Linux operating system compared with Windows.

If you are coming from a different database platform, you will need to set up your system for using built-in SQL Server features to monitor query performance such as DMVs, Extended Events, and Query Store.

Enable New Features for Performance

Once you have migrated to SQL Server on Linux, are comfortable with performance, and have new baselines established, before you "turn on" production you may consider also looking at using new features for performance, including but not limited to:

- Columnstore indexes

- In-Memory OLTP

- Partitions (this is not necessarily a new feature if you are migrating from SQL Server, but you may not have been using this. Users from other data platforms will definitely want to consider partitions).

- Automatic Tuning

Review back to Chapter 6 for more details on these features and how and when to best use them.

Design Your Security and HADR Strategy

Ensuring performance meets your needs after the migration is critical to success. But as I've described in other chapters in the book, security and HADR can be just as important. Review these chapters to see what security features you should use and how you should set up logins and users. Perhaps you can take this opportunity to use Active Directory authentication.

For HADR, having a backup strategy is fundamentally required. But you also may use the migration as an opportunity to set up Always On Availability Groups as a new HADR strategy.

Using Database Compatibility

Each SQL Server database can operate at a *database compatibility* level on each version of SQL Server. When a database is created on a specific version of SQL Server, that database takes on the default database compatibility level for that SQL Server version. I have to admit, it can get a bit confusing on the numbering system for database compatibility levels compared with the name of the SQL Server version. For example, the default database compatibility level for SQL Server 2017 is 140. The reason for 140 is to match the version number of SQL Server. For example, the version number of SQL Server 2017 starts with 14, so the compatibility levels match the engine version *major number*.

> **Note**   You can find the full engine version using the T-SQL statement SELECT @@VERSION or using one of the options for the T-SQL @@SERVERPROPERTY system function like ProductVersion. The full product version is made up of a major. minor.build.revision number. In most cases, we do not use the minor number (exception SQL Server 2008R2). The build equates to a major build release of SQL Server like RTM, Cumulative Update, or GDR. The revision is an internal mechanism to update builds once we are close to releasing a build as part of a RTM, Cumulative Update, or GDR release.

The full table of the default database compatibility level that matches the SQL Server release and version are documented at https://docs.microsoft.com/sql/t-sql/statements/alter-database-transact-sql-compatibility-level#arguments. As each new major release of SQL Server comes to market, a new default database compatibility is established. Any database restored from a previous release will retain the default database compatibility level of that previous release. You didn't realize it, but every time you restored the WideWorldImporters sample in previous chapters of this book, this database retained the database compatibility level of 130. You can see this by running the following T-SQL statement after restoring WideWorldImporters:

```
SELECT name, compatibility_level FROM sys.databases WHERE name =
'WideWorldImporters'
GO
```

The results should look like

```
Name                             compatibility_level

-----------------------------    -------------------

WideWorldImporters               130
```

You can use the ALTER DATABASE T-SQL statement to change the compatibility level of any database, as documented at https://docs.microsoft.com/sql/t-sql/statements/alter-database-transact-sql-compatibility-level.

I've given you the mechanics of a database compatibility level, but I haven't explained its purpose. Database compatibility level is used for two reasons:

1. Enable new functionality
2. Backward compatibility

Enabling New Functionality with Database Compatibility

Some enhancements, typically around query processing, are introduced when using a database compatibility level. For example, starting with database compatibility level 140, new functionality for query processing is enabled when a database is set to this compatibility level. I described this new functionality, called Adaptive Query Processing, in Chapter 6. You can expect Microsoft in the future to enable new query processing functionality using database compatibility.

Here are other examples of query processing enhancements introduced with database compatibility:

Cardinality estimation: A new cardinality estimation (CE) model is enabled when the database is using compatibility level 120 or later (introduced in SQL Server 2014). I discussed the impact of the new CE model in Chapter 6. I've also mentioned previously in this book that you can revert to the older CE model with a database compatibility level of 120 or later if you use the ALTER DATABASE option called LEGACY_CARDINALITY_ESTIMATION.

Query processing fixes: Database compatibility level 130 includes query processing hotfixes that were previously only enabled with trace flag 4199. Database compatibility 140 level includes query processing hotfixes introduced in the timeframe between SQL Server 2016 (compatibility level 130) and SQL Server 2017 (compatibility level 140). I discussed this concept previously in the book, but for review you can read more about enabling these fixes at https://docs.microsoft.com/sql/t-sql/database-console-commands/dbcc-traceon-trace-flags-transact-sql#4199.

Parallel bulk operations: SELECT INTO queries for databases under compatibility level 120 or higher can run in parallel. INSERT SELECT queries for databases under compatibility level 130 or higher can run in parallel.

There are other examples, and you can read through them starting at this place in the documentation: `https://docs.microsoft.com/sql/t-sql/statements/ alter-database-transact-sql-compatibility-level#differences-between- compatibility-level-130-and-level-140`. This starts a series of tables that describes the differences in behavior between compatibility levels.

Using Database Compatibility for Backward Compatibility

Database compatibility can be used to perform *some* level of protection of backward compatibility for queries and functionality of your application. All of the backward compatibility differences are listed in the documentation for each compatibility level (see the last documentation link I provided previously). Let me give you can example.

If you are using database compatibility level 110 or lower, a T-SQL query using a concept called common table expression (CTE) allows duplicate column names. However, starting with database compatibility level 120, duplicate column names would result in an error and the query would fail.

There are two areas where database compatibility has no effect on possible breaking changes:

- Discounted features or functionality
- Changes outside the scope of a database at the SQL Server instance level

One of the areas that database compatibility can be of great help is performance. Starting with database compatibility level 130, any changes or features that could result in a change to a query plan should only happen with the new compatibility level. This provides a safer approach for applications that upgrade to a newer release of SQL Server but retain the previous database compatibility level.

I recommend you read through all of our documentation on using compatibility level for backward compatibly at `https://docs.microsoft.com/sql/t-sql/statements/ alter-database-transact-sql-compatibility-level#using-compatibility-level- for-backward-compatibility`.

Migrate SQL Server Instance Objects

If you are migrating a database from a previous version of SQL Server to SQL Server on Linux, you may have to migrate *objects* outside the scope of the database, including:

> **Logins**: Remember, only SQL Standard security and Active Directory authentication is supported. If you have Windows domain logins, you will need to configure Active Directory authentication to allow them access to SQL Server on Linux.

> **SQL Server Agent jobs**: Remember, the only type of jobs that work with SQL Server on Linux are general jobs that have T-SQL job steps. You will have to find alternate solutions for other jobs with job steps that are outside the scope of T-SQL.

> **Linked servers**: Only SQL Server to SQL Server linked servers are supported, but you can define those using T-SQL system procedures to add linked servers. You can read more about this in the documentation at `https://docs.microsoft.com/sql/relational-databases/linked-servers/linked-servers-database-engine`. Unfortunately, with SQL Server 2017 on Linux, you cannot use distributed transactions over linked servers and only SQL Standard security is supported.

Using New Features

I've worked with customers who have migrated from one version of SQL Server to the next who are doing this just to keep up to date with the latest SQL Server version or because the version they are currently using is out of support. In these situations, what can get lost after the migration is to take advantage of new features. SQL Server 2016 and 2017 come with new features you might easily miss, including:

- Columnstore indexes (introduced in SQL Server 2012 but in SQL 2017 I consider this feature at its peak)
- In-Memory OLTP (introduced in SQL Server 2014 but many restrictions are removed by SQL Server 2017)

- Graph database
- JSON support
- Temporal tables
- Native scoring

I've covered these in previous chapters of the book, so I encourage you to go back and review these to see if they make sense for your application needs after the migration (or you may choose to use some of these as part of the migration).

Using an Existing Application Against SQL Server on Linux

It is one thing to migrate your objects and data, but what about your application developed to use SQL Server. The good news is that whether you are migrating from SQL Server or another database platform, our server-side programs such as stored procedures are typically part of the migration process I've described in this chapter.

However, if you have queries embedded in your application, such as ad hoc queries, or use a programming interface such as Object Relational Mapping (ORM), which typically generates queries, migration of the application may be more difficult.

The great news is that SQL Server supports just about every popular programming language interface on the market today, including C#, Java, Node.js, PHP, Python, Ruby, and C++. You can see a complete list of programming interfaces supported for SQL Server on Windows, macOS, and Linux at `https://docs.microsoft.com/sql/linux/sql-server-linux-develop-connectivity-libraries`. And if you are using an application against a previous version of SQL Server, there is a high chance your application will work with SQL Server on Linux with very few changes.

Note   The type of breaking changes that may affect your SQL Server application will be more related to database compatibility and any differences in features not supported by SQL Server on Linux. Keep up to date with feature differences for SQL Server on Linux in our release notes at `https://docs.microsoft.com/sql/linux/sql-server-linux-release-notes`.

The challenge if you are migrating an application that connected to a database platform other than SQL Server is to make the necessary changes to use the programming interface native to that platform. For example, in Chapter 4 I showed you how to use node.js and the tedious driver to connect to SQL Server. The tedious driver does not work with Oracle. So you may have a program written in node.js that uses something like the node-oracleb driver (see more about this driver at `https://github.com/oracle/node-oracledb`). The classes and methods may be similar between tedious and node-oracleb, but likely there are enough differences that this will require code changes, testing, and design. Don't forget to check out differences in how the drivers work even in the same programming language for concepts like connection pooling, results processing, concepts like cursors, and error conditions (e.g., deadlocks may be handled differently across database platforms).

Summary

I hope this chapter gave you the right information to make the necessary decisions to migrate to SQL Server on Linux. It is only appropriate to complete this book by talking about a technology that is currently gaining steam as a popular environment to deploy applications and databases, called containers.

CHAPTER 11

SQL Server and Containers

The concept of virtual machines has been around for some time, but at Microsoft I really didn't see customers start to use SQL Server as a database platform on virtual machines until around the 2006 to 2007 timeframe. Even when virtual machine environments such as Hyper-V and VMWare started to become popular, I was skeptical SQL Server would run well in a guest virtual machine. Today, SQL Server is probably deployed in virtual machines far greater than on a bare metal computer.

I see containers as the new virtual machine. But the excitement and adoption of containers with application and database platforms like SQL Server are growing faster than I ever saw with virtual machines.

In this chapter, I'm going to provide you with an introduction to containers, and then a fairly deep discussion and set of examples of how to use containers with SQL Server. Then I'll conclude the chapter with a fun example of using SQL Server on macOS (Mac users probably thought I had ignored them in this book) and a discussion of how to use SQL Server in the container platform called Kubernetes. I think you will enjoy this chapter. It was one of my favorite chapters to write in the book.

Introduction to Containers

While virtual machines are best defined as *hardware virtualization*, containers (or containerization) are defined as *operating system virtualization*. A virtual machine consists of a complete operating system (guest) running on a host machine (bare metal hardware). Therefore, it is common for a host machine to host several virtual machines. Each virtual machine could be running a different guest operating system.

545

© Bob Ward 2018
B. Ward, *Pro SQL Server on Linux*, https://doi.org/10.1007/978-1-4842-4128-8_11

Containers rely on a single host operating system (which could be a virtual machine) sharing kernel resources. This makes containers more lightweight than virtual machines. Even though containers share a single operating system kernel, containers are isolated from each other. I love the following visual diagram as seen in Figure 11-1, which I found at `https://i.stack.imgur.com/exIhw.png` to show the difference between containers and virtual machines.

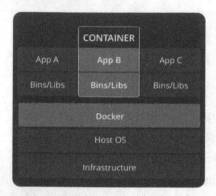

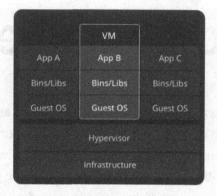

CONTAINERS

Containers are an abstraction at the app layer that packages code and dependencies together. Multiple containers can run on the same machine and share the OS kernel with other containers, each running as isolated processes in user space. Containers take up less space than VMs (container images are typically tens of MBs in size), and start almost instantly.

VIRTUAL MACHINES

Virtual machines (VMs) are an abstraction of physical hardware turning one server into many servers. The hypervisor allows multiple VMs to run on a single machine. Each VM includes a full copy of an operating system, one or more apps, necessary binaries and libraries - taking up tens of GBs. VMs can also be slow to boot.

Figure 11-1.   Containers vs. virtual machines

In addition, this stackoverflow.com post is a great description of the differences between virtual machines and containers: `https://stackoverflow.com/questions/16047306/how-is-docker-different-from-a-virtual-machine`. One comment about this posting: the posting describes the use of a Union File System (UnionFS) called AuFS. UnionFS is an important concept for Docker containers because it supports a layered file system. Current releases of Docker still use a UnionFS, but now use a system called OverlayFS. You can read more about OverlayFS at `https://docs.docker.com/storage/storagedriver/overlayfs-driver`.

Docker containers are created using *images*, which specify the contents of the filesystem and what runs in the container. A container then is an instance of an image. You can run multiple containers based on the same image. A *Dockerfile* specifies the contents of the Docker image. Docker provides functionality to *build* a Docker image from a Dockerfile specification. In addition, Docker supports functionality to build multicontainer applications using a tool called *compose*. I'll show you more about Docker images, files, and compose in the next section, using SQL Server as an example.

Docker containers have the following characteristics:

- **Portable:** Any Docker image you build can be run anywhere Docker containers are supported, including multiple operating systems and public and private clouds. I've run Docker containers on Windows, Linux, macOS, and Azure.

- **Lightweight:** As I've stated, Docker containers don't include an entire operating system like a virtual machine. Docker containers share kernel resources and therefore are more lightweight than virtual machines.

- **Consistent:** Container images allow you to deploy a consistent version of your application or database system like SQL Server. I'll talk more about how this benefits SQL Server later in the chapter.

- **Efficient:** Docker containers provide a mechanism for faster deployment, less downtime, and easier updates. I'll explain how this benefits SQL Server in the next section.

Docker uses two main components to help you manage Docker containers:

- **Docker client:** This is a program called **docker**, which you will use with several options to build images and pull, run, start, stop, and manage containers. You will learn more about these Docker concepts through the examples in the chapter.

- **Docker daemon:** The Docker client communicates with the daemon program, which does all the work as instructed by the client to build images and manage and run containers.

Docker containers use a concept called *namespaces* to isolate one container from each other (you can read more about the use of namespaces at https://docs.docker.com/engine/docker-overview/#the-underlying-technology). Even though containers are isolated, they can still communicate with each other (over TCP/IP example). Use the Docker documentation as your complete reference for containers at https://docs.docker.com. For your reference, please consider reading these other excellent resources I found on containers: http://theearlybirdtechnology.com/2017/08/12/docker-cheatsheet/ and https://www.quora.com/What-exactly-is-a-base-image-in-Docker.

Let's dive right in to explain how you can use containers with SQL Server and database applications.

How to use SQL Server with Containers

In this section of the book, I'm going to show you practical examples of the fundamental concepts of containers I've introduced you to in the opening section. I will show you how to deploy a simple container with SQL Server, use containers to show how to minimize downtime for updates, build and deploy an image using a Dockerfile, and finally implement a multicontainer deployment with SQL Server and an application.

One thing to remember as you read this section: SQL Server on Linux does not support multiple instances (this is called named instances on Windows) on the same server, so containers is the method to use should you want to run multiple SQL Server instances on the same Linux server.

During the time I was writing this book, my colleague Vin Yu and I built a series of free, self-paced labs for SQL Server on Linux and Docker containers at `https://github.com/Microsoft/sqllinuxlabs`. Vin built the labs to explorer Docker containers (found at `https://github.com/Microsoft/sqllinuxlabs/tree/master/containers`). I will use pieces of this lab in this section to show you how to use SQL Server with containers. (I've added a few scripts as examples with the book that you can use with these labs.) I may not go in the exact order of Vin's labs every time, and I'll explain a few more details behind the commands you will run to see SQL Server containers in action.

To show you these examples, I created a new Azure Virtual Machine running RHEL 7.5. (My VM size is a Standard D16s v3 [16 vcpus, 64 GB memory] but you can do this with a smaller sized VM. Just make sure to have at least 4 vpus and 16GB RAM). I then ran the following commands from the bash shell to update the VM, install the git package, and then *clone* the Github repo to get scripts and instructions:

```
sudo yum -y update
sudo yum install git
git clone https://github.com/Microsoft/sqllinuxlabs.git
```

Now let's install the Docker engine so we can go through other examples in the rest of the chapter by running the following commands from the bash shell:

```
sudo yum install -y yum-utils device-mapper-persistent-data lvm2
sudo yum-config-manager --add-repo https://download.docker.com/linux/
centos/docker-ce.repo
sudo yum install http://mirror.centos.org/centos/7/extras/x86_64/Packages/
pigz-2.3.3-1.el7.centos.x86_64.rpm
sudo yum install docker-ce
```

> **Note**   The standard Docker package for RHEL is a paid version called Docker
> Enterprise Edition (you can read more at `https://docs.docker.com/`
> `install/linux/docker-ee/rhel`). For the purposes of this lab and the
> examples in the book, I am going use the free Docker Community Edition, which is
> built for CentOS but is compatible to work on RHEL. You can read more about the
> Docker Community Edition at `https://docs.docker.com/install/`.

Now start the Docker engine with the following command from the bash shell:

```
sudo systemctl start docker
```

You can use the following command as well to have Docker start on a reboot:

```
sudo systemctl enable docker
```

Now I am ready to show you how to deploy SQL Server with a container.

Deploy and Run the SQL Server Image

In this section, I'll show you the basics of deploying containers with SQL Server and how
to update SQL Server using containers.

Docker Container SQL Server Basics

Let's learn first the basics of deploying a container with SQL Server and interacting with
it. Containers are instances of an *image*. Microsoft has published a series of images on
the Docker Hub at `https://hub.docker.com/r/microsoft/mssql-server-linux/`.
Docker images can be stored in a private *registry* or in a public domain like Docker Hub.
You can even use the cloud for a private container registry such as the Azure Container
Registry, which you can read more about at `https://azure.microsoft.com/services/`
`container-registry`.

The Microsoft-published images for SQL Server on Docker Hub include images for
SQL Server 2017 from RTM all the way to the latest CU and GDR updates. These images
are based on a *base image* of Linux Ubuntu 16.04 with SQL Server Developer edition.
This does not mean you have to deploy these images only on an Ubuntu Linux server.
The Docker image we have built using Ubuntu can run on any platform Docker supports,
because the base Linux kernel is the same across Linux distributions. In fairness, if you

need to rely on a Linux-specific distribution functionality, our image based on Ubuntu may not work for you. In this case, you may need to build an image with a Dockerfile. Furthermore, if you want to use a Docker image with another edition of SQL Server, look through our documentation at `https://docs.microsoft.com/sql/linux/sql-server-linux-configure-docker#production`.

Note   You can build your own Docker container image for SQL Server with RHEL as the base image, using a Dockerfile. See our example at `https://github.com/Microsoft/mssql-docker/blob/master/linux/preview/RHEL/Dockerfile`. Microsoft is working on publishing Docker images that include Linux distributions like RHEL in the future.

In this chapter, I run all Docker commands as root using sudo. You may configure Docker so that you can use Docker commands as a non-root user. See this documentation (`https://docs.docker.com/install/linux/linux-postinstall/#manage-docker-as-a-non-root-user`) for more information.

The method to deploy the SQL Server Docker Hub container image is with one of two methods:

- Use the Docker client program with the *pull* option like the following command from the bash shell:

  ```
  sudo docker pull microsoft/mssql-server-linux:2017-latest
  ```

- *Run* a Docker container specifying one of the SQL Server images, which if it does not already exist will first pull the image and then run the container.

  ```
  sudo docker run -e 'ACCEPT_EULA=Y' -e \ 'SA_
  PASSWORD=YourStrong!Password' \
  -p 1500:1433 --name sql1 \
  -d microsoft/mssql-server-linux:2017-latest
  ```

If you first pull the image, the second option to run the container will run the container image you have pulled down. Both of these methods require an Internet connection from your Linux server.

Tip   The following stackexchange.com post at `https://serverfault.com/`
`questions/701248/downloading-docker-image-for-transfer-to-`
`non-internet-connected-machine` has a great description on the *offline*
experience for deploying containers. Docker provides the ability to pull an image
to an Internet-connected machine, save the image to a tar file, copy the tar file to
your Linux server, and then use docker load to import the tar file into an image you
can use to run a container.

Let's use the second method to run the container, which will automatically pull
the Docker image for SQL Server with the latest CU update. I wanted to put in my sa
password, so I took the preceding command in the nano editor, changed the string
for my sa password, and then pasted the result into the bash shell like the following
command:

```
sudo docker run -e 'ACCEPT_EULA=Y' -e 'SA_PASSWORD=Sql2017isfast' \
    -p 1500:1433 --name sql1 \
    -d microsoft/mssql-server-linux:2017-latest
```

If the command is successful, you will see results like the following (if this is the first
time you have attempted to run an SQL Server container image). You can see that the
Docker image cannot be found locally, so it will be pulled first from the Docker Hub so a
docker pull is run implicitly.

```
Unable to find image 'microsoft/mssql-server-linux:2017-latest' locally
2017-latest: Pulling from microsoft/mssql-server-linux
f6fa9a861b90: Pull complete
da7318603015: Pull complete
6a8bd10c9278: Pull complete
d5a40291440f: Pull complete
bbdd8a83c0f1: Pull complete
3a52205d40a6: Pull complete
6192691706e8: Pull complete
1a658a9035fb: Pull complete
344203922c4b: Pull complete
5975df51ff07: Pull complete
```

```
Digest: sha256:97d2a9cd87ecfab641f24be254e03a45b8d551355e21516c0460da7daf8b
526e
Status: Downloaded newer image for microsoft/mssql-server-linux:2017-latest
66e7e043e41683af4e1f419df41417e7fb3c19f8013b2d9d3e5c69a5d03ec3f8
```

The best way to know if your container is running successfully is to run the following command from the bash shell:

```
sudo docker ps
```

On my Linux server, the results look like the following:

```
CONTAINER ID              IMAGE                                      COMMAND
CREATED                   STATUS          PORTS                      NAMES
a01c1c991cec              microsoft/mssql-server-linux:2017-latest
"/opt/mssql/bin/sqls..."   About a minute ago   Up About a minute
 0.0.0.0:1500->1433/tcp   sql1
```

Let's break down the docker run command parameters I just used.

The parameters for -e are used for environment variables that are required to run SQL Server (similar to what you specify when you run the mssql-conf script as part of deploying SQL Server on Linux), including accepting the EULA and specifying a sa password. (Note: These variables are passed to the sqlservr program.)

The -p parameter is used for *port mapping*. SQL Server listens on port 1433, but using that port for the container could conflict with port 1433 on the host Linux server or other Docker containers for SQL Server So, this parameter maps port 1500 to port 1433 in the container. I'll show you how to use the mapped port when connecting to SQL Server in the container.

The –name parameter allows you to specify a user-friendly name to interact with the container with other Docker commands.

The -d parameter says to run the container in the background (i.e., detached) so the docker run command will come back to the bash shell prompt but start the container in the background.

The final parameter is the name of the Docker image, which in this case is **microsoft/mssql-server-linux:2017-latest.** Docker will try to find this image locally on the Linux server. If it does not exist, it will attempt to first pull that image from the Docker Hub as you saw in the results of the docker run command previously.

You can run the following command from the bash shell to see the Docker image for SQL Server is now stored locally:

```
sudo docker images
```

The results on my Linux server look like the following:

```
REPOSITORY                        TAG                      IMAGE ID
CREATED               SIZE
microsoft/mssql-server-linux      2017-latest              c90c3ab55158
13 days ago           1.44GB
```

Now that the Docker container is running, you will want to connect to SQL Server. Let's use the following two methods:

1. Interact with the container using a Docker command to run a bash shell with the following command:

    ```
    sudo docker exec -it sql1 bash
    ```

You should now have a shell prompt that looks something like this:

```
root@66e7e043e416:/#
```

In this example, 66e7e043e416 is the container ID and becomes the server name as found in the T-SQL statement @@SERVERNAME.

This is a bash shell that allows you to run commands within the container (pretty cool, right?). Run the following command to use sqlcmd (The SQL Server images include the sqlcmd tool) within the container to connect to SQL Server (put in your sa password):

```
/opt/mssql-tools/bin/sqlcmd -U SA -P 'Sql2017isfast'
```

> **Note**   While it is interesting to interact directly with the container using the bash shell, most of the interactions you will have with a container will be using programs *outside* the container. Be careful making any changes inside the container itself unless you are making changes to data or files on a persisted volume (which I will describe later in this chapter). Any changes to the container not on persisted storage will be lost should you remove the container. You will see in the following examples I show you how to run sqlcmd both inside the container and outside the container. But in these examples I'm making changes to an SQL Server database that is on a persisted storage volume.

Type **exit** in sqlcmd and type in **exit** to leave this shell.

2. The second method is to use an SQL Server tool outside the container to connect with the SQL Server in the container. On this Azure VM, I installed the SQL Server tools per the following documentation (`https://docs.microsoft.com/sql/linux/ quickstart-install-connect-red-hat#tools`) so I can use sqlcmd to connect to SQL Server in the container. Since the container is mapped to port 1500 and I'm connecting on the local Linux server, I can run a command from the bash shell like the following:

```
sqlcmd -S localhost,1500 -Usa -PSql2017isfast
```

> **Note**   You can connect to SQL Server in the container on another computer that can access the Linux host server by using the IP address of the Linux host server with port 1500 for the -S parameter. This port must be open from the firewall.

Now from the sqlcmd prompt, run the following T-SQL statement:

```
SELECT @@version
GO
```

Your results should look like the following, which shows SQL Server *thinks* it is running on Ubuntu but the host is really RHEL:

```
----------------------------------------------------------------------
----------------------------------------------------------------------
----------------------------------------------------------------------
----------------------------------------------------------------------
Microsoft SQL Server 2017 (RTM-CU9-GDR) (KB4293805) - 14.0.3035.2 (X64)
        Jul  6 2018 18:24:36
        Copyright (C) 2017 Microsoft Corporation
        Developer Edition (64-bit) on Linux (Ubuntu 16.04.5 LTS)
```

Type **exit** to leave sqlcmd.

You can stop the container with the following command from the bash shell:

```
sudo docker stop sql1
```

To see all containers, even ones that are not running, you can use the following command from the bash shell:

```
sudo docker ps -a
```

You results should look something like the following:

```
CONTAINER ID        IMAGE                                          COMMAND
CREATED             STATUS                            PORTS        NAMES
66e7e043e416        microsoft/mssql-server-linux:2017-latest
"/opt/mssql/bin/sqls..."  About an hour ago   Exited (0) 2 minutes ago
sql1
```

Docker containers include any files or data you have created or modified while running the container. You can start and stop the container and the data you have created will be persisted for the lifetime of the container. However, if you remove the container, all data in the container will be lost. But there is a method to persist any data in the container in a way, so the data is saved even if the container is removed. Let's look at an example that could prove useful to update SQL Server to minimize downtime. Before you proceed, remove the previous container and image using the following commands from the bash shell:

```
sudo docker rm sql1
sudo docker rmi microsoft/mssql-server-linux:2017-latest
```

Updating SQL Server Using Containers

To update SQL Server on Linux to a new cumulative update on RHEL, you would normally run a command like `sudo yum update mssql-server`. This command will pull down the latest cumulative update, shut down SQL Server, apply the new binaries, and then start SQL Server. If the update runs smoothly, it should not take a considerable amount of time, but containers offer a different method. Let me show you how with an example. For this section, I'll be using the WideWorldImporters sample database, so with my new Azure VM, I first ran this command from the bash shell to pull down this sample backup:

```
wget https://github.com/Microsoft/sql-server-samples/releases/download/
wide-world-importers-v1.0/WideWorldImporters-Full.bak
```

The first step is to run a container (which will pull down the image) based on SQL Server 2017 for Linux CU8 with the following command from the bash shell (as found in the example script **dockerruncu8.sh**), with a slight twist from the previous section:

```
sudo docker run -e 'ACCEPT_EULA=Y' -e 'MSSQL_SA_PASSWORD=Sql2017isfast'
-p 1401:1433 -v sqlvolume:/var/opt/mssql --name sql1 -d microsoft/mssql-
server-linux:2017-CU8
```

There are three differences in how I ran this Docker container from the previous section:

1. I used the -v parameter to map a volume on the Linux host to the /var/opt/mssql directory inside the container. This means that any data stored in /var/opt/mssql in the container will be persisted on the Linux Server.

Tip   Run the following command to find out the actual directory on the Linux host server where this data is stored:

```
sudo docker inspect volume sqlvolume
```

---

2. I used a different image for SQL Server: in this case, SQL Server 2017 CU8 (which at the time I wrote this chapter is *not* the latest update of SQL Server).

3. I used port 1401 instead of 1500 to connect to this SQL Server.

Now let's restore the WideWorldImporters backup in the new container. The first step is to copy the backup from my home directory on the Linux server host *into the container*. I will do this by running the following command from the bash shell (which is also found in the example script **dockercopy.sh**):

```
sudo docker cp WideWorldImporters-Full.bak sql1:/var/opt/mssql
```

To restore the database, I will use the docker exec command to run sqlcmd inside the container with a T-SQL statement. Run the following command from the bash shell, as found in the example script **docker_restorewwi.sh**:

```
sudo docker exec -it sql1 /opt/mssql-tools/bin/sqlcmd  -S localhost -U SA
-P 'Sql2017isfast' -Q 'RESTORE DATABASE WideWorldImporters FROM DISK = "/
var/opt/mssql/WideWorldImporters-Full.bak" WITH MOVE "WWI_Primary" TO "/
var/opt/mssql/data/WideWorldImporters.mdf", MOVE "WWI_UserData" TO "/var/
opt/mssql/data/WideWorldImporters_userdata.ndf", MOVE "WWI_Log" TO "/var/
opt/mssql/data/WideWorldImporters.ldf", MOVE "WWI_InMemory_Data_1" TO "/
var/opt/mssql/data/WideWorldImporters_InMemory_Data_1"'
```

Now let's run a query to make sure we can access data in this database. This time I'll use sqlcmd from the Linux host (I'm showing you both ways of accessing SQL Server in the container). Use the following command from the bash shell as found in the example script **dockerquery.sh**:

```
sqlcmd -Usa -Slocalhost,1401 -Q'USE WideWorldImporters;SELECT * FROM
[Application].[People];'
```

If all goes well, your screen should scroll across rows from the People table.

Now let's say you want to update SQL Server to the latest cumulative update. In the case of the container, you don't use tools like apt-get, but that is OK because as I've said earlier in this chapter, there is a better way to update SQL Server.

Let's run a new Docker container called sql2 but this time with the latest cumulative update. I also want to point this container to the same sqlvolume to access all the databases that were saved with the sql1 container. In order to minimize downtime, I'm going to pull down the latest SQL Server image manually instead of it being pulled when using docker run. Run the following command from the bash shell:

```
sudo docker pull microsoft/mssql-server-linux:2017-latest
```

Now let's stop the sql1 container with the following command from the bash shell

```
sudo docker stop sql1
```

This will execute a clean shutdown of SQL Server. Now let's start a new container called sql2 with the exact same parameters as before, including the same port mapping and volume name. Run the following command from the bash shell as found in the example script **dockerrunlatest.sh**:

```
sudo docker run -e 'ACCEPT_EULA=Y' -e 'MSSQL_SA_PASSWORD=Sql2017isfast'
-p 1401:1433 -v sqlvolume:/var/opt/mssql --name sql2 -d microsoft/mssql-
server-linux:2017-latest
```

Since I used the same port number as the sql1 container, I can run the exact same command as earlier to run a query against the WideWorldImporters database, as found in **dockerquery.sh**:

```
sqlcmd -Usa -Slocalhost,1401 -Q'USE WideWorldImporters;SELECT * FROM
[Application].[People];'
```

Now that is pretty cool. I was able to *switch* to a container running the latest cumulative update, minimizing downtime instead of patching the existing SQL Server. Now here is what you are going to really love. Since I did not remove the sql1 container, if I run into some issue with the latest CU build and my application, I can simply stop the sql2 container and start the sql1 container. Boom! I'm now running against the previous CU.

This is a great scenario to show updates to SQL Server and database persistence even if the container is removed. In the next section, I'm going to show you how to build your own Docker image to include SQL Server and a predefined database. To prove I can run two containers with SQL Server at once (not against the same volume), let's stop the sql1 container if you had sql1 running but leave the sql2 container running with the following commands:

```
sudo docker stop sql1
```

Build Your Own Container with a Dockerfile

What I've shown you so far is how to interact with and add data to a Docker container from the SQL Server image on the Docker Hub site. Docker containers with SQL Server could also help you with another interesting scenario. Let's say you have several developers working on an application with SQL Server. You typically set up a development server and let the developers access the server. One issue with this configuration is setting up an environment so developers have a consistent database with a consistent version of SQL Server for all of the developers.

Containers bring a new strategy to this scenario. You could build a Docker image based on the SQL Server image and include in the image a backup of the standard database you want all developers to use. Then any developer can pull the Docker image and run a container (like having their own sandbox). In addition, one of the great features of Docker images is reusability. You can *layer* images by creating images based on other images.

Let's use the exact steps from the self-paced labs at https://github.com/Microsoft/sqllinuxlabs/tree/master/containers to show an example of this. (I assume you have run the commands previous in the chapter to clone the GitHub repo for the labs.)

1. Change directory to the **mssql-custom-image-example** folder on your Linux server by running the following command from the bash shell:

   ```
   cd sqllinuxlabs/containers/mssql-custom-image-example
   ```

2. Create a Dockerfile that has the following contents (I have provided in the examples for the book the file **Dockerfile** for you to compare) by typing in the following commands from the bash shell (Note: when you run the cat command you will get a > prompt to type in the rest):

   ```
   cat <<EOF>> Dockerfile
   > FROM microsoft/mssql-server-linux:latest
   > COPY ./SampleDB.bak /var/opt/mssql/data/SampleDB.bak
   > CMD ["/opt/mssql/bin/sqlservr"]
   > EOF
   ```

When you build the Docker image using the **docker build** command, Docker will by default look for a file called Dockerfile. Let's unpack what these commands say in the file:

FROM microsoft/mssql-server-linux:latest: This command says to pull down the latest SQL Server Docker image as a base image (which is based on the Ubuntu base image) for our new image to be created. It is possible you want all developers testing and developing on a known build, so you could pick a specific CU, which I've shown you how to pull in the previous section. Note that for SQL Server 2017, microsoft/ mssql-server-linux:latest and Microsoft/mssql-server-linux:2017-latest are the same but we produce two different images for each name.

COPY ./SampleDB.bak /var/opt/mssql/data/SampleDB.bak: This command says to copy the SampleDB.bak file in the current directory into the Docker container image.

CMD ["/opt/mssql/bin/sqlservr"]: This command says to run the sqlservr program from the /opt/mssql/bin directory. This is how SQL Server runs in a container.

3. Now run the following command from the bash shell to build the new Docker image:

```
sudo docker build . -t mssql-with-backup-example
```

The "." is the PATH for the docker build command, which in this case is all the files in the current directory. The -t parameter is used to *tag* the new image with the name mssql-with-backup-example. This tag name can be referenced when you run a container from this image. On my Linux server, the results looked like the following:

```
Sending build context to Docker daemon  3.263MB
Step 1/3 : FROM microsoft/mssql-server-linux:latest
latest: Pulling from microsoft/mssql-server-linux
f6fa9a861b90: Already exists
da7318603015: Already exists
6a8bd10c9278: Already exists
d5a40291440f: Already exists
bbdd8a83c0f1: Already exists
3a52205d40a6: Already exists
```

```
6192691706e8: Already exists
1a658a9035fb: Already exists
344203922c4b: Already exists
5975df51ff07: Already exists
Digest: sha256:4f769a0b6603f9de2496e3ee455ce6b8b44db642714b5
0ed89b033e03e6e1e91
Status: Downloaded newer image for microsoft/mssql-server-
linux:latest
 ---> 812f44c37fc8
Step 2/3 : COPY ./SampleDB.bak /var/opt/mssql/data/SampleDB.bak
 ---> a85e222cc553
Step 3/3 : CMD ["/opt/mssql/bin/sqlservr"]
 ---> Running in 91b10bc07736
Removing intermediate container 91b10bc07736
 ---> 973ca0ed39a0
Successfully built 973ca0ed39a0
Successfully tagged mssql-with-backup-example:latest
```

4. Let's confirm our image was created, by running the following
   command from the bash shell:

```
sudo docker images
```

Your image should appear in the results like the following:

```
REPOSITORY                        TAG            IMAGE ID
CREATED         SIZE
mssql-with-backup-example         latest         973ca0ed39a0
2 minutes ago    1.44GB
microsoft/mssql-server-linux      2017-latest    c90c3ab55158
2 weeks ago      1.44GB
microsoft/mssql-server-linux      latest         812f44c37fc8
2 weeks ago      1.44GB
microsoft/mssql-server-linux      2017-CU8       229d30f7b467
2 months ago     1.43GB
```

5. Now let's run a container using the new image we built by running
    the following command from a bash shell (to put in your sa
    password: copy this into an editor, change the password, and
    then paste it back into the shell). Note: I used sql3 in this example
    because I already have a container running called sql2.

```
sudo docker run -e 'ACCEPT_EULA=Y' -e 'SA_PASSWORD=Sql2017isfast' \
    -p 1500:1433 --name sql3 \
    -d mssql-with-backup-example
```

6. Now see what containers are running by executing the following
    command from the bash shell:

```
sudo docker ps
```

You results should look like the following:

```
CONTAINER ID        IMAGE
COMMAND                     CREATED             STATUS
PORTS                       NAMES
c4740bfdafa9        mssql-with-backup-example
"/opt/mssql/bin/sqls…"    3 seconds ago       Up 2 seconds
0.0.0.0:1500->1433/tcp    sql3
38850dc61aa6        microsoft/mssql-server-linux:2017-latest
"/opt/mssql/bin/sqls…"    6 hours ago         Up 6 hours
0.0.0.0:1401->1433/tcp    sql2
```

This is a good example of two SQL Server instances running on the
same Linux host server by using containers (since SQL Server on Linux
does not support named instances).

7. Now let's restore the database in the container image by running
    the following command from the bash shell (put in your sa
    password). This one is long, so I included an example script called
    dockerrunmyimage.sh.

```
sudo docker exec -it sql3 /opt/mssql-tools/bin/sqlcmd \
    -S localhost -U SA -P Sql2017isfast \
    -Q 'RESTORE DATABASE ProductCatalog FROM DISK = "/var/opt/
mssql/data/SampleDB.bak" WITH MOVE "ProductCatalog" TO "/var/opt/
mssql/data/ProductCatalog.mdf", MOVE "ProductCatalog_log" TO "/
var/opt/mssql/data/ProductCatalog.ldf"'
```

8. Now I'll use sqlcmd on the Linux host server to connect to the new container and run a query against the database included in the image. Run the following command from the bash shell:

```
sqlcmd -Slocalhost,1500 -Usa
```

9. Now from the sqlcmd prompt, run the following T-SQL statement:

```
SELECT COUNT(*) FROM ProductCatalog.dbo.Product
GO
```

You should get a count of 14 rows.

Let's stop both the sql2 and sql3 containers by running the following command from the bash shell (yes, you can control more than one container at a time) and changing back to your home directory:

```
sudo docker stop sql2 sql3
cd ~
```

In the next section, I'll show you how to build a multicontainer application that includes SQL Server, using a concept called *compose*.

Compose a Multicontainer Application

Building a Docker container image using a Dockerfile is a great concept to build a single container. However, in many situations an application will use multiple containers with a dependency between them such as a web application and a database. Therefore, Docker provides a capability called *compose* that allows you to build and run a set of containers including references to Dockerfiles and dependencies. You can read the complete reference on docker compose at `https://docs.docker.com/compose/overview`.

Again, let's use the example from `https://github.com/Microsoft/sqllinuxlabs/tree/master/containers` lab to show you an example (Note: this example is similar to an example in the Docker documentation you can read at `https://docs.docker.com/compose/aspnet-mssql-compose`). For this example, I have two containers I need for my application:

- An SQL Server container that includes a database called ProductCatalog. In this case, I have a T-SQL script I'd like to run that creates the databases, logins, users, objects, and populates data.

- A container that contains an ASP.NET application based on .NET Core that will access the ProductCatalog database connecting and running queries against the SQL Server container. You will see that using the compose process with Docker will allow the application to connect to a logical name that maps to the SQL Server container.

Let's go through the process of composing the application using Docker and then I'll explain a few details on how these containers work:

1. First, we need to install the docker-compose package using the following commands from the bash shell:

```
sudo curl -L https://github.com/docker/compose/releases/
download/1.21.2/docker-compose-$(uname -s)-$(uname -m) -o /usr/
local/bin/docker-compose
sudo chmod +x /usr/local/bin/docker-compose
sudo ln -s /usr/local/bin/docker-compose /usr/bin/docker-compose
```

2. Change directory to the directory where all the files are located, running the following command from the bash shell:

```
cd sqllinuxlabs/containers/mssql-aspcore-example
```

3. Edit the **docker-compose.yml** file and put in your sa password in place of the value of the environment variable SA_PASSWORD (I use the nano editor). A docker-compose.yml file is a YAML file (YAML stands for YAML Ain't Markup Language), which is used to define container images, services, and dependencies. I'll describe below more about how this file works. Think of this file as the launching point to build the Docker images and run the containers.

4. Edit the file **./mssql-aspcore-example-db/db-init.sh** and put in the sa password for the -P parameter that is used for sqlcmd.

5. Run the following command from the bash shell to compose the Docker application, which will build the Docker images and run the containers:

```
sudo docker-compose up
```

A lot of information is going to scroll by as this executes. Figure 11-2 shows the docker compose in progress in my Linux ssh session.

```
[thewandog@bwdocker mssql-aspcore-example]$ sudo docker-compose up
[sudo] password for thewandog:
Creating network "mssql-aspcore-example_default" with the default driver
Building db
Step 1/4 : FROM microsoft/mssql-server-linux:latest
 ---> 812f44c37fc8
Step 2/4 : COPY . /
 ---> f86b4d353307
Step 3/4 : RUN chmod +x /db-init.sh
 ---> Running in 8978b5898e9f
Removing intermediate container 8978b5898e9f
 ---> 5dae0dca13c7
Step 4/4 : CMD /bin/bash ./entrypoint.sh
 ---> Running in fc46cebc9e56
Removing intermediate container fc46cebc9e56
 ---> d13e06a0f903
Successfully built d13e06a0f903
Successfully tagged mssql-aspcore-example_db:latest
WARNING: Image for service db was built because it did not already exist. To rebuild this image you must use
`docker-compose build` or `docker-compose up --build`.
Building web
Step 1/12 : FROM microsoft/dotnet:2.0-sdk AS build
2.0-sdk: Pulling from microsoft/dotnet
55cbf04beb70: Pull complete
1607093a898c: Pull complete
9a8ea045c926: Pull complete
d4eee24d4dac: Pull complete
d3c1dfaf9907: Pull complete
d3ae435cb72d: Extracting [==================================================>]  175.6MB/175.6MB
fe5e514ae93b: Download complete
```

Figure 11-2. Docker compose in progress

The containers are not run in the background, so when the compose is finished your screen may look like Figure 11-3.

```
------ -----------
db_1  |            17 BB Ball Bearing                           Magenta       62          3
7.9900          90              2018-08-24 02:39:41                9999-12-31 23:59:59
db_1  |            17 BB Ball Bearing                           Magenta       62          2
8.9900          80              2016-02-11 21:27:32                2018-08-24 02:39:41
db_1  |            17 BB Ball Bearing                           Magenta       62          3
7.9900          90              2015-11-07 03:40:09                2016-02-07 03:40:15
db_1  |            17 BB Ball Bearing                           Magenta       62          2
5.1900          65              2015-08-07 03:40:01                2015-11-07 03:40:09
db_1  |            17 BB Ball Bearing                           NULL          NULL        7
5.0000          20              2015-05-07 03:39:52                2015-08-07 03:40:01
db_1  |
db_1  | (5 rows affected)
db_1  | DateModified                     ProductID   Name
   PrevPrice           Price            NextPrice
db_1  | -----------------------------    ---------   -----------------------------
- -----------------------    ------------------------    ---------------------
db_1  |              2016-02-11 21:24:12            15 Adjustable Race
        100.0000            120.0000           100.0000
db_1  |              2015-11-07 03:40:09            16 Bearing Ball
         15.9900             .0000              15.9900
db_1  |              2016-02-11 21:27:32            17 BB Ball Bearing
         37.9900            28.9900             37.9900
db_1  |
db_1  | (3 rows affected)
db_1  | 2018-08-24 02:44:36.09 spid51      Using 'dbghelp.dll' version '4.0.5'
2018-08-24 02:44:39.17 spid51      Attempting to load library 'xplog70.dll' into memory. This is an informati
onal message only. No user action is required.
2018-08-24 02:44:39.26 spid51      Using 'xplog70.dll' version '2017.140.3035' to execute extended stored pro
cedure 'xp_msver'. This is an informational message only; no user action is required.
```

Figure 11-3. *Status in ssh after docker compose starts containers*

6. To run the application I need to open up a port for my Azure Virtual machine. The ASP.NET application is listening on port 5000. See the instructions at https://github.com/Microsoft/ sqllinuxlabs/tree/master/open_azure_vm_port to open up port 5000.

7. Now from your browser go to the following URL:

    http:<public IP address>:5000

You should see a page like Figure 11-4 when the webpage for the application renders.

Figure 11-4. *The initial ASP.Net container application screen*

Click on Product Catalog Demo at the top left of the page and your screen should now look like Figure 11-5.

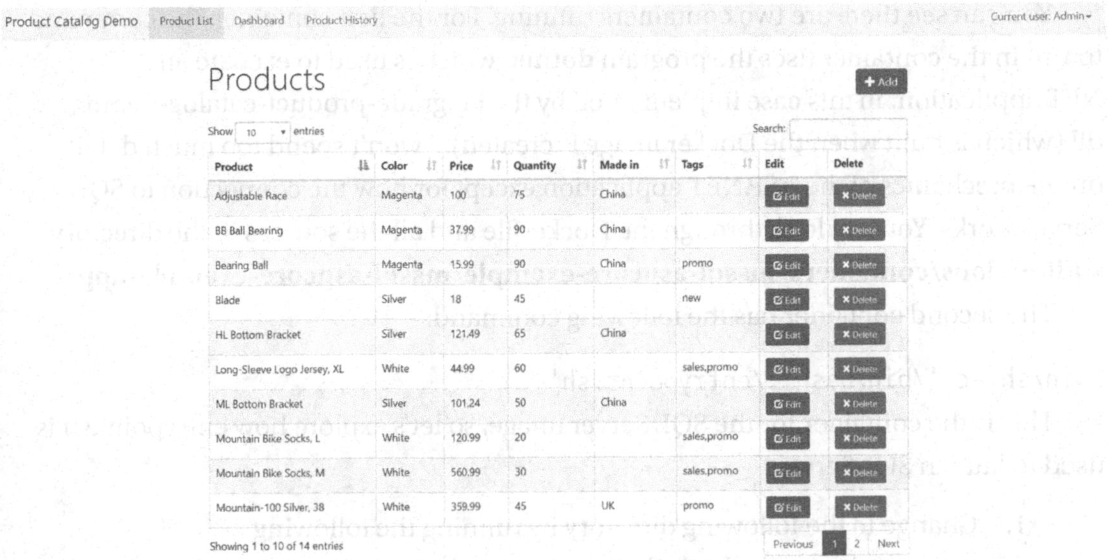
Product Catalog Demo
Product List
Dashboard
Product History
Current user: Admin
Products
+ Add
Show 10 entries
Search:
Product Color Price Quantity Made in Tags Edit Delete
Adjustable Race Magenta 100 75 China Edit Delete
BB Ball Bearing Magenta 37.99 90 China Edit Delete
Bearing Ball Magenta 15.99 90 China promo Edit Delete
Blade Silver 18 45 new Edit Delete
HL Bottom Bracket Silver 121.49 65 China Edit Delete
Long-Sleeve Logo Jersey, XL White 44.99 60 sales,promo Edit Delete
ML Bottom Bracket Silver 101.24 50 China Edit Delete
Mountain Bike Socks, L White 120.99 20 sales,promo Edit Delete
Mountain Bike Socks, M White 560.99 30 sales,promo Edit Delete
Mountain-100 Silver, 38 White 359.99 45 UK promo Edit Delete
Showing 1 to 10 of 14 entries
Previous 1 2 Next

***Figure 11-5.** The Product Catalog data from the ASP.Net docker container application*

Let's poke behind the scenes on how docker compose and these containers work.

From a separate ssh session (you can't use the current ssh session because these containers are not running in the background. If you type in <ctrl>+<c> you will end the containers), run the following command from the bash shell to see what containers are running. You can also force the containers to the background with <ctrl>+<z>:

```
sudo docker ps --no-trunc
```

You should see results like the following:

```
CONTAINER ID
IMAGE                                    COMMAND
CREATED               STATUS                PORTS                             NAMES
22b900fd8f3ea03ca7a9d923441291a507dc4b3eb07fb3189fea6b3c8a6e0935
mssql-aspcore-example_web    "dotnet belgrade-product-catalog-demo.dll"
16 minutes ago      Up 16 minutes        0.0.0.0:5000->5000/tcp
mssql-aspcore-example_web_1
549d476ec793d96049a0193aeec78c6f32dc1661d79370c8855d7e50cc9797aa
mssql-aspcore-example_db     "/bin/sh -c '/bin/bash ./entrypoint.sh'"
16 minutes ago      Up 16 minutes        0.0.0.0:1500->1433/tcp
mssql-aspcore-example_db_1
```

You can see there are two containers running. For the first container, the command to run in the container uses the program **dotnet**, which is used to execute an ASP. NET application, in this case implemented by the belgrade-product-catalog-demo. dll (which is built when the Docker image is created). I won't spend too much detail on the mechanics of the ASP.NET application except for how the connection to SQL Server works. You can look through the Dockerfile and all the sources in the directory **sqllinuxlabs/containers/mssql-aspcore-example/mssql-aspcore-example-app**.

The second container has the following command:

```
/bin/sh -c '/bin/bash ./entrypoint.sh'
```

This is the container for the SQL Server image, so let's explore how entrypoint.sh is used to launch SQL Server.

1. Change to the following directory by running the following command from the bash shell:

   ```
   cd ~/sqllinuxlabs/containers/mssql-aspcore-example/mssql-aspcore-example-db
   ```

2. First, let's look at the file called Dockerfile by executing `cat Dockerfile`. The results should look like the following:

   ```
   FROM microsoft/mssql-server-linux:latest

   COPY . /

   RUN chmod +x /db-init.sh
   CMD /bin/bash ./entrypoint.sh
   ```

So we know the Docker image in this directory will be built from the SQL Server latest image, all files in the current directory will be copied into the container, and then the db-init.sh script will be changed so it can be executed. Finally, the command to launch the container is the script entrypoint.sh.

3. We know entrypoint.sh is used to run the container, so let's look at this file by executing `cat entrypoint.sh`. The results should look like the following (I took out the comments from the output):

   ```
   /db-init.sh & /opt/mssql/bin/sqlservr
   ```

This command will execute db-init.sh in the background and then launch sqlservr in the foreground.

4. Now let's look at db-init.sh by executing `cat db-init.sh`. Your results should look like the following:

```
#wait for the SQL Server to come up
sleep 15s
#run the setup script to create the DB and the schema in the DB
/opt/mssql-tools/bin/sqlcmd -S localhost -U sa -P Sql2017isfast -d
master -i db-init.sql
```

Here is a little of where the magic lies. This script will wait for 15 seconds to let SQL Server start up and then execute the db-init.sql script using sqlcmd in the container. I'll let you look at db-init.sql further. but it basically creates the ProductCatalog database, creates logins and objects, and populates some data into the database.

5. Now you see the mechanics of how you can start an SQL Server container and launch a T-SQL script to create your database, objects, and data.

Let's look at the **docker-compose.yml file** to see how docker compose knows how to build each container.

1. Change to the original directory where the docker-compose.yml exists by executing the following command in the bash shell:

```
cd ~/sqllinuxlabs/containers/mssql-aspcore-example/
```

2. Now dump out the contents of the **docker-compose.yml** file by executing `cat docker-compose.yml`. Your results should look like the following:

```
version: "3"
services:
    web:
        build: ./mssql-aspcore-example-app
        ports:
            - "5000:5000"
        depends_on:
            - db
```

```
    db:
        build: ./mssql-aspcore-example-db
        environment:
            SA_PASSWORD: "Sql2017isfast"
            ACCEPT_EULA: "Y"
        ports:
            - "1500:1433"
```

The services: tag allows you to define specific containers that will be run as part of the application. For each service, you can define the location of the Dockerfile to build the image, the ports to use when running the container including the mapped port, and if one of the services depends on the other. In this case, the **web** service depends on the **db** service. This means the container for the db service will be created and started before the container for the web service.

You can also specify any environment variables needed for the container, which in this case are the EULA agreement and sa password for the SQL Server container. And for the container for the db service, port 1500 is mapped for SQL Server port 1433.

So in summary, when docker-compose up is executed, docker will use the docker-compose.yml file to build the container for the db service first by using the Dockerfile in the ./mssql-aspcore-example-db directory. It will then run the container based on this image using the environment variables specified, and the SQL Service is available on the host's port 1500.

Then it will run the container for the web service that is to create the Docker image from the Dockerfile in the ./mssql-aspcore-example-app directory and run a container based on that image using port 5000.

One last important observation: When I first looked at these containers I couldn't figure out how the ASP.NET application knows how to connect to port 1500 for the SQL Server container. The service definition in the docker-compose.yml file is the key. The service named **db** is effectively mapped to localhost,1500. So the ASP.NET application can use a servername of **db** in the connection string to connect to SQL Server in the container associated with the db service.

I know this feels a bit complex but only because I dove into the details behind the scenes to describe how composing a multicontainer application works. Now for some fun. Move on to the next section to see me take the SQL Mac challenge!

The SQL Mac Challenge

In February of 2018 I was speaking at one of my favorite events, SQLBits in London. One of my presentations was on SQL Server on Linux. I was using my trusty HP Zbook Studio laptop running Windows 10 to do the presentation and demos. Someone from the audience raised their hand and said "Bob, I love that Microsoft has adopted Linux, but I'm a MacBook user. You are using a PC here in these demos. But I don't see the commitment from Microsoft for the MacBook community."

Even though I had not researched the topic, I was confident in this reply. "We now have the software and tools where you can run and interact with SQL Server with no virtualization and no Windows tools on your MacBook. And I believe you can get this installed and up and running in 5 minutes." I called it "Take the SQL Mac challenge." The person in the audience said they would take me up on this challenge (you can see the result of this challenge on his tweet at `https://twitter.com/thofle/status/967437807697448965`).

I actually really didn't know if what I said was 100% accurate (especially the no virtualization and the five-minute part) but I knew two things to make this bold statement: (1) I knew our docker container image was portable and would run easily on a MacBook, since I knew Docker exists for macOS; and (2) our SQL Operations Studio tool is cross-platform so natively runs on macOS.

When I got back to Texas, I did something I thought I would never do as an employee at Microsoft. I asked my manager, Asad Khan, if I could buy a MacBook. He said with all the work I'm doing on Linux and containers that this made perfect sense. Once I got the MacBook, I decided myself to take the SQL Mac challenge (you know, put your money where your mouth is). And I'm here to say I was wrong. I was wrong in the sense that it took me four minutes, not five minutes, to get this software installed.

Let me walk you through the experience so all of you who are reading this book who are MacBook users can try this yourself.

1. The first thing I did was install and download Docker for Mac (Community Edition), as described at `https://store.docker.com/editions/community/docker-ce-desktop-mac`. (I used the Stable channel). Figure 11-6 shows this experience after the download.

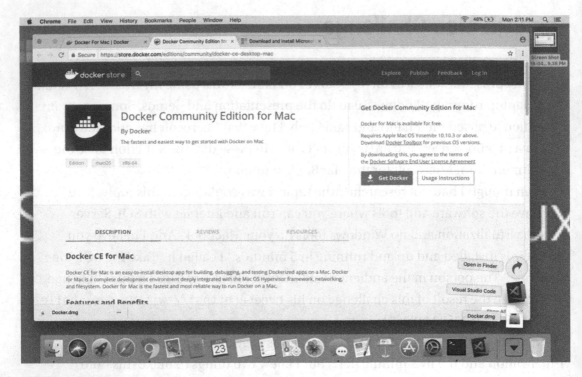

Figure 11-6. *Downloading Docker for Mac*

Note   In all transparency, there is some virtualization for macOS for Docker, but it is far better than before. Docker for Mac used to require VirtualBox, but now macOS has a built-in light hypervisor framework, so it is more accurate to say Docker for Mac does not require a separate heavy virtualization environment. You can read more about the Docker for Mac environment at `https://docs.` `docker.com/docker-for-mac/docker-toolbox/#the-docker-for-mac-` `environment`.

---

2. After the download for Docker for Mac is extracted, a new window pops up for you to install Docker as a Mac application by a simple drag and drop, as seen in Figure 11-7.

Figure 11-7. *Installing Docker for Mac*

3. Now that Docker is installed as an application, I launched it from the Launchpad application on my MacBook. Now at the top of my screen I get an icon for Docker and I can see it is starting, as seen in Figure 11-8.

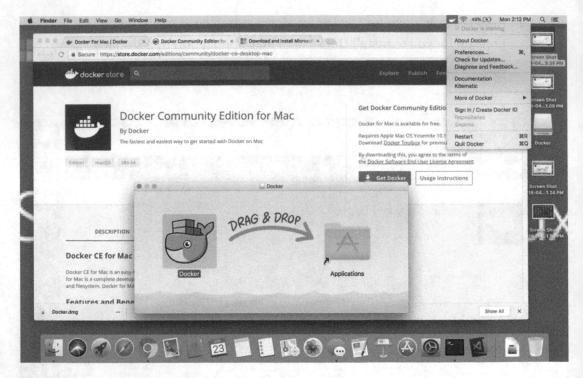

Figure 11-8. *Docker for Mac starting up*

4. Now I wanted to multitask, so while Docker was starting up I downloaded SQL Operations Studio for MacOS from `https://docs.microsoft.com/sql/sql-operations-studio/download`.

5. While this was downloading, Docker had started up. So I pulled down the SQL Server image using docker from the macOS Terminal, which is effectively a bash shell. I ran a command like the following:

```
docker pull microsoft/mssql-server-linux:2017-latest
```

6. While the pull was running, I then extracted the download from SQL Operations Studio. This extraction should look like Figure 11-9.

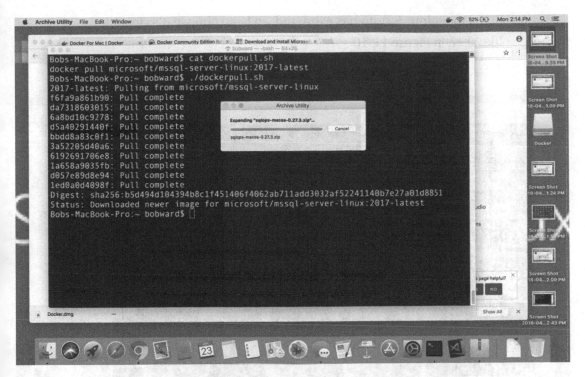

Figure 11-9. *Extracting SQL Operations Studio for macOS*

7. While this was extracting, the docker pull had completed for me,
so now I can run my container with the following command from
the MacOS terminal:

```
docker run -e 'ACCEPT_EULA=Y' -e 'MSSQL_SA_PASSWORD=Sql2017isfast'
-p 1401:1433 --name sql1 -d microsoft/mssql-server-linux:2017-
latest
```

8. SQL Operations Studio has extracted, so I can choose it to install like seen in Figure 11-10.

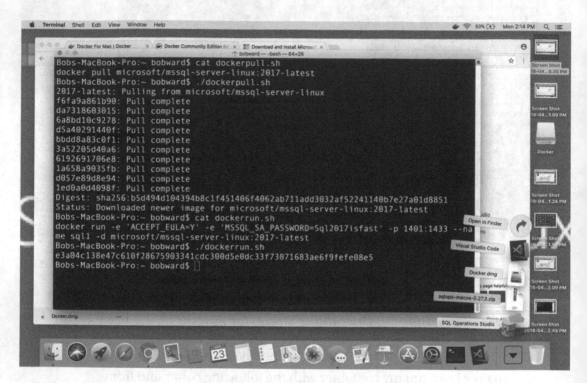

Figure 11-10. *Installing SQL Operations Studio for macOS*

9. I can now launch SQL Operations Studio from Launchpad, connect to localhost, 1401, and run queries against the container with SQL Server, as seen in Figure 11-11.

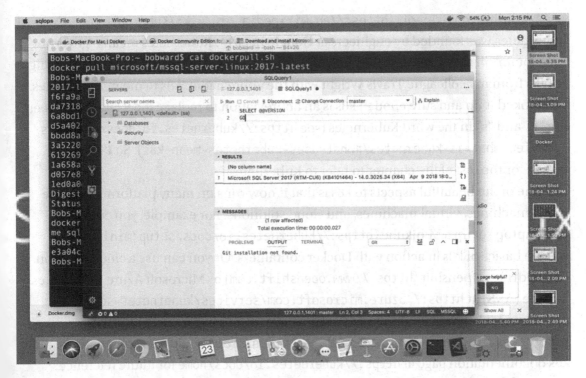

Figure 11-11. Running queries against an SQL Server container in macOS

There it is. If you just follow the steps without all of my commentary and you have a reasonable Internet connection, you can do all of this in less than five minutes. And you will have officially taken the SQL Mac challenge. Let's conclude the chapter by looking at a unique way to run containers with SQL Server in production using an environment called Kubernetes.

SQL Server and Kubernetes

Kubernetes as defined on their website at `https://kubernetes.io` is "an open-source system for automating deployment, scaling, and management of containerized applications"—also referred to as a *container orchestrator*. In a nutshell, Kubernetes is a system for deploying and managing a production set of containers. It is one thing to run a multicontainer application on your Linux server, but what if you want to deploy hundreds of containers. How do you deploy and manage these in an efficient manner? Furthermore, how can you set up an HADR system for your SQL Server containers? Kubernetes provides all of that.

According to Wikipedia (`https://en.wikipedia.org/wiki/Kubernetes`), Kubernetes was founded by engineers at Google in 2014. Kubernetes means "governor" or "captain" in Greek. When I first started working with Kubernetes, I remember seeing emails from my colleague Travis Wright with the abbreviation k8s to mean Kubernetes. So I looked it up and sure enough k8s is an abbreviation to replace the 8 letters between the "k" and "s" in the word Kubernetes (see `https://kubernetes.io/docs/concepts/overview/what-is-kubernetes/#what-does-kubernetes-mean-k8s`). So I'll use k8s myself for the rest of the chapter to refer to Kubernetes.

One of the beautiful aspects to k8s is that it now runs on many platforms: on bare metal machines, virtual machines, and cloud solutions. For example, you could on your laptop set up a Minikube (`https://kubernetes.io/docs/setup/minikube`) to see the basics of k8s in action with Docker containers. Or you can use a cloud solution like RedHat's Openshift (`https://www.openshift.com`) or Microsoft Azure Kubernetes Service (AKS) at `https://azure.microsoft.com/services/kubernetes-service/`.

Take a look through the complete set of known solutions for k8s at `https://kubernetes.io/docs/setup/pick-right-solution/`. You should also bookmark the main k8s documentation page at `https://kubernetes.io/docs/home` for future reference.

The Basics

There are many aspects of k8s you can learn to develop container applications or operate the entire k8s system. For the purposes of SQL Server with k8s, I think it is important you know these following terms:

- Cluster

  A k8s cluster is a deployment of containers through a set of nodes and pods, which I define next.

- Pod

  A pod in k8s is a group of one or more containers that can share storage, networking, and a specification on how to run the containers.

- Node

  I love the definition of a node from the k8s docs (at `https://kubernetes.io/docs/concepts/architecture/nodes/`). "A node is a worker machine in Kubernetes, previously known as minion.

A node may be a VM or physical machine." Effectively, think of nodes as a host for a set of one or more pods.

- Replica set

  A replica set defines how many instances of a specific pod should be running at any point time and helps define the high availability of pods. Replica sets are important to allow Kubernetes to automatically start new pods should a pod fail.

- Deployment

  A deployment is a declarative method to define pods and replica sets. It is recommended to use deployments to define the configuration of pods and replica sets for high availability. This is the method we will use to show how to define and configure HADR for SQL Server with k8s.

- Persistent volume claim

  K8s supports the concept of storage that can be used by pods through a PersistentVolume. This storage can be shared across pods (which lines up very well for a shared storage HADR solution for SQL Server). A Persistent volume claim is a request by a user for a PersistentVolume storage.

- Service

  A service is a logical set of pods that can be abstracted. One type of service is a load balancer for connectivity. You can specify an IP address for the load balancer service. Each pod has a unique IP address, but a load balancer is a known IP address. Think of this like the virtual IP address concept used by Failover Cluster Instance or the listener for Availability Groups. It will provide SQL Server with an abstracted IP address even when a k8s "failover" is executed.

You can read a more complete description of k8s components and architecture at `https://kubernetes.io/docs/concepts/`. With the knowledge of these terms, let's see them all in action by deploying an SQL Server container in k8s using AKS.

SQL Server HADR and Kubernetes

As I've described the fundamentals of k8s, perhaps you can see that k8s provides a platform that supports HADR for containers. SQL Server can take advantage of this built-in HADR capability, provided you structure your deployment and service in the correct way. In this section, I'll first describe how HADR works with k8s and then talk about a very nice tutorial you can use to walk through the process of deploying SQL Server with k8s.

How HADR Works with k8s

I've described the fundamental terms of nodes, pods, and services. Let me use some visualization to show how HADR work with pods, these concepts nodes, and services. Configuring SQL Server with pods and persistent volume claims is a shared storage HADR solution and provides similar functionality to an Always On Failover Cluster Instance.

First, if k8s detects a pod has an issue or fails, k8s will automatically create a new pod on the same node the pod currently runs on, which will start up any containers in that pod. Furthermore, if the pod is using a persistent volume claim, the container in the new pod will be able to access the same data stored in that persistent volume. Also, if you set up a load balancer service associated with the pod (which has a unique IP address), users can connect to the load balancer service, which has a fixed IP address, to avoid having to know the details of the pod IP address. Figures 11-12 shows the concept of a Pod failure.

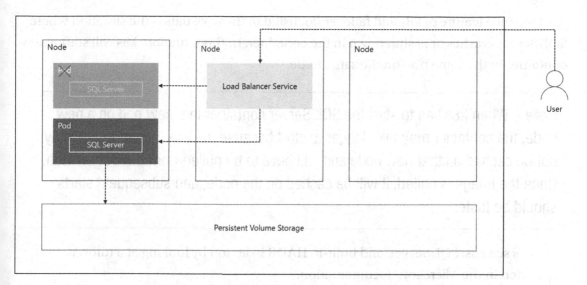

Figure 11-12. k8s HADR for a POD failure

K8s also supports failover if a node fails for any reason. A new pod on a new node
will be started and the load balancer service will be redirected to the new pod on the
new node. Because k8s supports node failures, any production k8s cluster for SQL Server
should have at least three nodes to support failover, not only for the SQL Server but also
for the load balancer service. Figure 11-13 shows this scenario.

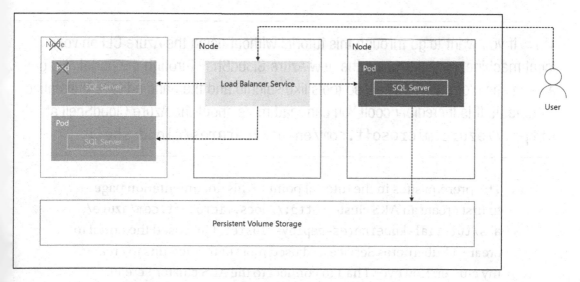

Figure 11-13. k8s HADR for a node failure

One nice feature of k8s and failover not listed in these visuals is the situation where SQL Server crashes or is shut down in the container. In this situation, k8s will start a new container in the same pod on the same node.

Note   When k8s has to start the SQL Server container in a new pod on a new node, the container may take longer to start because the SQL Server image may not be cached on that new node and will have to be pulled from the Docker Hub. Once the image is pulled, it will be cached on the node, and subsequent starts should be faster.

Let's see k8s, SQL Server, and built-in HADR in action by looking at a tutorial supported in the Microsoft documentation.

Using SQL Server with Azure Kubernetes Service

One of my colleagues, the very talented Mihaela Blendea, took time to build out a very nice tutorial on how to setup SQL Server with k8s using AKS. I'll let you use your Azure subscription to walk through this tutorial at `https://docs.microsoft.com/sql/linux/ tutorial-sql-server-containers-kubernetes`. I've been through this tutorial, so let me add a few observations:

Tip   If you want to go through this tutorial without using the Azure CLI on your local machine, consider using the new Azure CloudShell through the portal. You get a bash shell (or a PowerShell) so tools like sqlcmd and the nano editor are installed by default. It is incredibly cool! You can read more about the Azure CloudShell at `https://azure.microsoft.com/en-us/features/cloud-shell/`.

- The prerequisites in the tutorial point to this documentation page to first create an AKS cluster: `http://docs.microsoft.com/azure/ aks/tutorial-kubernetes-deploy-cluster`. I just used the portal to create a Kubernetes Service and used most of the defaults to create my cluster. However, I had to connect to the AKS cluster I created first, using the following steps in this part of the documentation: `https://docs.microsoft.com/azure/aks/tutorial-kubernetes-`

deploy-cluster#connect-to-cluster-using-kubectl. My
Kubernetes service (aka my k8s cluster) is called **bwsqlk8s** in the
resource group **bwk8s**. So I used the following command from the
Azure CloudShell to connect to my AKS service:

```
az aks get-credentials --resource-group bwk8s --name bwsqlk8s
```

Then, to verify my nodes, I ran the following command from the Azure Cloud Shell:

```
kubectl get nodes
```

I built a three-node cluster, so my results looked like

```
NAME                        STATUS    ROLES    AGE      VERSION
aks-agentpool-38442334-0    Ready     agent    21m      v1.11.2
aks-agentpool-38442334-1    Ready     agent    21m      v1.11.2
aks-agentpool-38442334-2    Ready     agent    21m      v1.11.2
```

Once this was completed, I could move forward with the tutorial.

- Use the following command to ensure your pod with the SQL Server
  container is running:

  ```
  kubectl get pods
  ```

It took about five minutes for my pod to show a status of Running. Your out should
look something like

```
NAME                                   READY    STATUS     RESTARTS    AGE
mssql-deployment-3813464711-h312s      1/1      Running    0           17m
```

- sqlcmd (Yes!) is built into the Azure CloudShell, so I was able to
  connect to my new SQL Server deployment by using the external IP
  address of the Load Balancer service.

- If you go through the exercise of deleting a pod to see how HADR
  works, it could take up to four minutes or so for the new pod to start
  up. This is unfortunately one of the weaknesses of using SQL Server
  with k8s. Four minutes can be a long time for SQL Server to be down.
  We are working in to bring other innovations the future to SQL Server
  and k8s to make this faster and better.

- Use the following command with kubectl to see which node your pod is running on:

  ```
  kubectl get pods -o wide
  ```

- K8s even supports restarting the container running SQL Server should it crash, or if SQL Server is shutdown. Try it yourself. Connect to the SQL Server container via the external IP address of the load balancer and execute the T-SQL SHUTDOWN command. If you then execute `kubectl get pods`, you will briefly see the STATUS of **Error** and **CrashLoopBackOff**, but then within the same pod it will be back to Running.

- Here is an advanced test. Try *draining* the node where the pod is running with the SQL Server container. Draining a node is a way to simulate a node failure. The `kubectl get pods -o wide` command shows the name of the node for the running pod. Using that name, execute the following command:

  ```
  kubectl drain <node name> --ignore-daemonsets
  ```

Now use `kubectl get pods -o wide` to see the SQL Server container get started with a new pod on a new node. To allow the node you drained to be used again, run the following command:

```
kubectl uncordon <node name>
```

You can see the power of built-in HADR with k8s. No failover cluster instance software is required, and SQL Server is quite frankly unaware it is running in this HADR environment. As with any SQL Server production environment, always include a solid backup strategy.

I have to admit this was one of the more fun chapters to write, as I believe containers and k8s are amazing new technologies that will become more and more popular for hosting application and database systems like SQL Server. In this chapter, I introduced you to the basics of containers, showed you how to deploy and use containers with SQL Server, and even challenged MacBook users to use SQL Server "Windows free." Then I concluded the chapter with a look at the new way to host SQL Server and containers called Kubernetes (k8s).

Summary

And with this chapter I have concluded the book, one of the most enjoyable yet difficult things I've done in my 25-year career at Microsoft. I have taken you on a journey starting with the history behind SQL Server on Linux and the deployment process and details. I then showed you how to build your own database and application. I then detailed out all the amazing tools and built-in features SQL Server provides for all of your needs. Then you were able to see how robust SQL Server truly is by seeing the capabilities of performance, security, and HADR. I then gave you insight into powerful management and monitoring features for SQL Server on Linux. In Chapter 10 I showed you migration techniques including a comparison of SQL Server with PostgreSQL. And then you just completed reading the chapter on the technology of containers bringing a new set of scenarios to deploy and run SQL Server. I hope you have enjoyed reading through the book and will be able to use it for your reference in the future for your journey with SQL Server on Linux and containers.

CHAPTER 12

Epilogue

The SQL Server Engineering team moves at the *speed of the cloud*. That is my observation since joining the team over two years ago. My good friend and architect of the SQL Server product, Conor Cunningham, once told me that if we wanted to, Microsoft could ship a quality release of SQL Server every month these days. That is a far cry from the days of Yukon (SQL Server 2005) when it took several years to ship a release. Of course we need value and new features to make a new release viable for the industry, so once a month is probably not the right cadence. SQL Server 2017 came right off the heels of SQL Server 2016, and a big part of that release was bringing SQL Server on Linux to market. So what is next for SQL Server, especially for SQL Server on Linux and containers?

As SQL Server 2017 was announced in October of 2017, our team was already working on the next release of SQL Server including improvements specifically targeted for SQL Server on Linux and containers. By the time this book releases, it is very likely we will have made announcements regarding how we are improving SQL Server on Linux and containers. These enhancements include but are not limited to:

- SQL Server Replication

- Machine Learning Services including R, Python, and maybe even other languages

- Distributed Transactions (DTC) support

- Active Directory integration for Replication and Linked Servers

- Polybase for SQL Server on Linux

© Bob Ward 2018
B. Ward, *Pro SQL Server on Linux*, https://doi.org/10.1007/978-1-4842-4128-8_12

We also want to continue to make containers a great experience, so we have plans for these improvements:

- Containers images for RHEL

- Moving containers to be registered in the Microsoft Container Registry (MCR; you can still find them on Docker Hub, but they will be linked to MCR). You can read more about MCR at `https://azure.microsoft.com/blog/microsoft-syndicates-container-catalog`.

- Kubernetes support for Always On Availability Groups. This one is exciting because it provides a far better RTO story for k8s with SQL Server than shared storage. Travis Wright has built a video already to preview the experience at `https://youtu.be/Xa1ec4z6XIk?list=PL-_k_UrAvrYsSydSyVeXIXy-vInFEruxr`.

You will also see that Microsoft has in store other new features and enhancements with the next release of SQL Server for both Windows and Linux. In addition, we are looking at new innovations for integration with Big Data systems and the General Availability of SQL Operations Studio (I wouldn't be surprised if there is a new name for this tool).

The future for SQL Server is bright. Shipping SQL Server on Linux has opened up new markets, new customers, and new opportunities for Microsoft. At the same time, we still strongly believe in SQL Server on Windows Server as a great combination. It is all about choice with compatibility: your choice. Doubling down on new technologies like containers and Kubernetes positions SQL Server as a data platform for all developers, applications, and private and public cloud environments. I look forward to continuing to help Microsoft make SQL Server the preferred modern data platform for years to come.

Index

© Bob Ward 2018
B. Ward, *Pro SQL Server on Linux*, https://doi.org/10.1007/978-1-4842-4128-8

Printed in the United States
By Bookmasters

Printed in the United States
By Bookmasters